THE MUST WORDS

THE MUST WORDS

THE 6000 MOST IMPORTANT WORDS FOR A SUCCESSFUL AND PROFITABLE VOCABULARY

by **Craig** and **Peter Norback**
WITH SACHEM PUBLISHING ASSOCIATES

McGRAW-HILL BOOK COMPANY

New York   St. Louis   San Francisco   Düsseldorf
London   Mexico   Sydney   Toronto

Printed in the United States of America

No part of this publication may be reproduced, stored in a retrieval system, or transmitted, in any form or by any means, electronic, mechanical, photocopying, recording, or otherwise, without the prior written permission of the publisher.

1 2 3 4 5 6 7 8 9   MUMU   7 8 3 2 1 0 9

LIBRARY OF CONGRESS CATALOGING IN PUBLICATION DATA
Norback, Craig T
  The must words.
   1. Vocabulary.   I.   Norback, Peter G., joint author.
II. Title.
PE1449.N59   428'.1   79-13424
ISBN 0-07-047136-3

Book design by Marsha Picker.

INTRODUCTION

The Must Words are those words you *need to know* in order to understand and communicate, no matter what type of work you do or what kind of life-style you have. It contains the most up-to-date list of words useful in a thinking person's vocabulary.

Keep *The Must Words* handy when you are watching TV, reading your favorite newspaper, magazine, or book, or talking with friends or business associates. If you do not understand the meaning or usage or a word you have heard or read many times, look in *The Must Words* for help.

One key objective of *The Must Words* is to define and use those words that a significant number of people do not know and that all *should* know. Many of these are words that people think they understand yet consistently use incorrectly.

To provide a sound basis for *The Must Words* the editors sought guidance from the Educational Testing Service (E.T.S.) of Princeton, New Jersey. E.T.S., the administator of the College Board examinations taken by almost all college-bound students, charts the status of college vocabularies. The core of *The Must Words* was the E.T.S. list of useful words missed by more than 40 percent of college freshmen at a large university.

The base list of words missed by 40 percent of college freshmen was modified and then augmented. Other vocabulary-building sources were searched, including word books, topical lists in specialized areas, and those contemporary areas of communication that influence every intelligent adult's working language—newspapers, radio, and television.

In addition to academic sources, word books, and the media, contemporary fiction and nonfiction works were screened for word-frequency usage, and the vocabulary of radio and television programs was studied. From these varied fields a large corpus of words evolved; from this corpus the editors chose *The Must Words,* those that seemed most important and were used most frequently. "Easy"

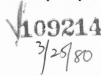

words, such as "happiness" and "dragon," with which educated people are familiar, were omitted. Obscure words with limited applications, such as "systolic" and "feuilleton," were also omitted.

One way to think about vocabulary is to divide it into three zones. The innermost zone contains only those few thousand words necessary for survival, not much more. That small vocabulary enables a person to function—to understand and be understood—on the simplest level.

The second zone is the one that enables a person to understand more fully and to communicate with clarity, precision, and effectiveness. Command of this zone is an invaluable asset in personal and social relationships, in occupational success, and in intellectual satisfaction.

The third, outermost zone of vocabulary has no known bounds; it involves dimensions that can only be compared to the limitless starry skies. Consider a few facts: The largest dictionary of English ever published contained about 650,000 words, only part of our vocabulary. In organic chemistry, almost 500,000 compounds have been characterized. About 1,000,000 species of insects have already been identified, but the actual number of living species may well total as much as 5,000,000. If the names of geographic places are included in "vocabulary"—and they should be—then "vocabulary" can be expanded by the estimated 3,500,000,000 place names in the world.

The third zone is not an essential ingredient in developing a solid, precise vocabulary. Important as a large part of it may be, it is a vocabulary that is generally acquired as a result of extensive reading, interest in special fields of knowledge, and the requirements of particular occupations. Nor need we concern ourselves too much with the first zone, since it is probably already within the vocabulary of most people who will be drawn to this book.

It is the second zone that is vital. In it are the words that express many essential ideas, words that convey shades of meaning with effectiveness, words that enable the speaker or writer to communicate with lucidity, with persuasiveness, with impact. "The difference between the *almost right* word and the *right* word," Mark Twain once said, "is really a large matter—'tis the difference between the lightning bug and the lightning." It is the zone of these exactly right words—the "must" words—with which this book is concerned.

The Must Words, therefore, contains a comprehensive list of words you hear and read every day. These words are the core of our language. If you want to understand better what is being said or written, study these words, memorize these words, and be mentally well equipped.

We have defined each word, we have given the proper pronunciation, and we have also provided sample sentences so you can understand quickly how a particular word is used. Many words have more than one meaning. Each meaning is defined, and each has a sample sentence.

Your success with *The Must Words* depends on your *using* the book. People often encounter words they do not really understand while reading a magazine or newspaper or listening to the news. Learning these words can make understanding more complete and enjoyable. For example a newspaper or radio report may call a state political convention a *donnybrook*. With *The Must Words* you can find what a *donnybrook* is and get a better idea of what happened at the convention.

By keeping it handy you can look up unfamiliar words as you encounter them. Learn the correct pronunciation of a word by speaking it aloud. This exercise will also reinforce the learning process. Make up a sentence or two with the word—using your own language.

Browse to learn, but also set up a systemic study of the book. Make it a habit to learn some new words each day. Don't try to do too much in each session, however. If you do, you may be like tourists who visit so many cities that they can't remember which museums are in which city. Limit each session to learning three or four new words. You'll soon be the master of *The Must Words*.

ACKNOWLEDGMENTS

Pronunciations for *The Must Words* from: *The Random House Dictionary of the English Language*, The Unabridged Edition, edited by Jess Stein & Laurence Urdang, copyright © 1971, 1970, 1969, 1967, 1966, by Random House, Inc. Reprinted by permission of Random House,, Inc.

We would like to thank Nat Hartshorne, a Director of Program Publications at Educational Testing Service, for his help and advice in creating this book.

PRONUNCIATION KEY

a	act	n	now	v	voice
ā	aid	n͡g	sing	w	west
â(r)	air	N	as in French bon	y	yes
ä	alms	o	ox	z	zeal
b	back	ō	over	zh	vision
ch	chief	ô	ought	ə	indicates sound of a in alone / e in system / i in easily / o in gallop / u in circus
d	do	oi	oil		
e	ebb	o͝o	book		
ē	equal	o͞o	ooze		
f	fit	ou	out	ə	to show syllabic qualities, as in cradle (krād′əl) and to show diphthongal quality, as in fire (fīər)
g	give	p	pot		
h	hit	r	read		
hw	white	s	see		
i	if	sh	shoe		
ī	ice	t	ten	′	to mark primary stress
j	just	th	thin		
k	kept	th	that	′	to mark secondary stress
l	low	u	up		
m	my	û(r)	urge		

Aa

abandon (ə ban′dən) v.t., to leave forever; forsake; desert. *The crew abandoned the sinking ship.*

abasement (ə bās′mənt) n., lowering of rank or esteem; degradation; humiliation. *Her abasement was manifested by her removal to the dingy back office.*

abash (ə bash′) v.t., to destroy one's self-confidence or composure; embarrass or shame. *He found it necessary to abash the pompous but promising student.*

abate (ə bāt′) v.i., to lessen in strength, amount, intensity; subside; diminish. *They waited for the storm to abate.*

abbey (ab′ē) n., 1. buildings of a monastery or convent. 2. church now or formerly attached to a monastery or convent. *Many famous people are buried at Westminster Abbey.*

abbreviate (ə brē′vē āt′) v.t., to shorten by omission, contraction, or substitution; make briefer; condense. *The staff abbreviated the second version of the annual report.*

abdicate (ab′də kāt′) v.t., to relinquish or renounce in a formal manner; to give up. *The queen abdicated her throne for the commoner she loved.*

abdomen (ab′də mən, ab dō′-) n., 1. in mammals, the part of the body between the thorax and pelvis. *He was hit in the abdomen.* 2. in certain invertebrates (as insects), the hind part of the body. *The ant had an elongated abdomen.*

abduct (ab dukt′) v.t., to carry off illegally, esp. by force; to kidnap. *Terrorists attempted to abduct the prime minister.*

aberrant (ə ber′ənt, ab′ər-) adj., straying or deviating from the correct, normal, or usual course. *The hermit led an aberrant existence.*

aberration (ab′ə rā′shən) n., deviation or departure from what is right, normal, or usual. *The hermit's aberrations were tolerated by the townspeople.*

abet (ə bet′) v.t., to encourage, assist, or sanction (esp. in wrongdoing). *She abetted the fugitive by giving him a map.*

abeyance (ə bā′əns) n., the state of temporary inaction or suspension; deferral; postponement. *Title to the property was held in abeyance until the judge gave his decision.*

abhor (ab hôr′) v.t., to regard with repugnance or intense distaste; to detest, loathe. *She abhors cruelty to animals.*

abide (ə bīd) v.i., to stay. *Abide with me for the rest of my life.* v.t., 1. to put up with; endure; tolerate. *He could not abide such treasonous talk.* 2. to be faithful; adhere to the rules. *The student was told he must abide by the rules of the school.*

abiding (ə bī′diñg) adj., continuing without change; steadfast. *They have an abiding faith in their leader.*

ability (ə bil′i tē) n., the skill, means, power, or capacity to do or act. *He had the ability to motivate people.*

abiogenesis (ā′bī ō jen′i sis, ab′ē ō-) n., origination of living organisms from lifeless matter; spontaneous generation. *Science has refuted the belief in abiogenesis.*

abject (ab′jekt, ab jekt′) adj., utterly humiliating or depressing; wretchedly degrading. *For generations they lived in abject poverty.*

abjure (ab jo͞or′) v.t., to renounce or forswear, often solemnly. *He abjured his errors and asked for forgiveness.*

able (ā′bəl) adj., having the skill, means, power, or capacity to do or act. *The wolf is able to run great distances.*

1

ablution (ab lōō′shən, ə blōō′-) n., act of washing, esp. as a ritual of purification. *Islamic law requires ablution before prayers.*

abnegate (ab′nə gāt′) v.t., 1. to relinquish or give up. *The shah was forced to abnegate all his powers.* 2. to refuse or deny oneself. *She had to abnegate sleep in order to study.*

abnormal (ab nôr′məl) adj., not normal, typical, or usual; unusual; irregular. *He has an abnormal fear of insects.*

abode (ə bōd′) n., a dwelling place; home; residence. *Their abode was a humble cottage in the woods.*

abolish (ə bol′ish) v.t., to put an end to; do away with. *Lincoln worked hard to abolish slavery.*

abolition (ab′ə lish′ən) n., abolishing or being abolished; end; termination. *The abolition of slavery brought about great social changes.*

abominable (ə bom′ə nə bəl) adj., utterly detestable, repugnant, or offensive. *His table manners were abominable.*

abomination (ə bom′ə nā′shən) n., something utterly loathed or detested. *Their treatment of prisoners was an abomination.*

aboriginal (ab′ə rij′ə nəl) adj., earliest; native; indigenous. *Aboriginal people are the first known inhabitants of a region.*

aborigine (ab′ ō rij′ə nē′, -ô rij′-) n., earliest inhabitant of a region. *The aborigines greeted the first settlers with hospitality.*

abort (ə bôrt′) v.i., 1. to give birth before the fetus is viable; miscarry. *Women who suffer severe trauma during pregnancy may abort.* 2. to halt at an earlier stage than planned. *The mission to the moon was aborted because of an engine failure.*

abortion (ə bôr′shən) n., the expulsion of a fetus from the womb before it is viable. *The doctors decided that an abortion was necessary.*

abortive (ə bôr′tiv) adj., without the planned or desired result; unsuccessful. *He made an abortive attempt to bring the two factions together.*

aboveboard (ə buv′bôrd′, -bôrd′) adj., adv., without deception or trickery; honest; straightforward. *Everyone knows her style is open and aboveboard. She deals aboveboard.*

abrade (ə brād′) v.t., 1. to rub or wear away; erode. *The waves have long abraded the cliff.* 2. to wear someone down. *Constant criticism will ′ surely abrade her self-confidence.*

abrasion (ə brā′zhən) n., an area worn away, scraped, or rubbed off by friction. *She suffered a small abrasion on her arm.*

abrasive (ə brā′ siv, -ziv) n., any substance that scrapes, wears away, or grinds. *He used steel wool as an abrasive to give the wood a smooth surface.* adj., tending to wear away, scrape, or rub off. *He cleaned the chrome with an abrasive cloth.*

abreast (ə brest′) adj., adv., 1. side by side; alongside. *They marched six abreast.* 2. fully informed or up to date. *The editor kept abreast of the news.*

abridge (ə brij′) v.t., to shorten or condense without omitting important parts. *They abridged the Bible for the young students.*

abroad (ə brôd′) adv., adj., 1. broadly; widely. *Rumor is abroad in the land.* 2. overseas. *She is vacationing abroad.* 3. astray. *The rockets went abroad of the ship.*

abrogate (ab′rə gāt′) v.t., to annul by an authoritative act; repeal; abolish. *They were forced to abrogate the unpopular law.*

abrupt (ə brupt′) adj., marked by sudden or unexpected change or termination. *His speech came to an abrupt end.*

abscess (ab′ses) n., inflamed pustular infection. *It was a painful gum abscess.*

abscond (ab skond′) v.i., to leave abruptly and secretly, and to continue to avoid detection. *They absconded with the stolen bonds.*

absence (ab′səns) n., 1. condition of being not present or of lacking. *The teacher recorded her absence.* 2. lack of attention. *Her absence of mind was getting worse.*

absentee (ab'sən tē') n., one who is absent. *The absentee made them one short of a quorum.* adj., pertaining to one who is absent. *He voted from Spain by absentee ballot.*

absolute (ab'sə lōōt') adj., 1. entire; perfect; complete. *She couldn't guarantee the absolute purity of the water.* 2. fixed; irrevocable; unconditional. *They had no choice but to obey his absolute decree.*

absolutely (ab' sə lōōt'lē, ab' sə lōōt'-) adv., without restriction or condition; completely. *She absolutely refused to join them.*

absolution (ab'sə lōō'shən) n., act of absolving, or state of being absolved; release from consequences, penalties, punishment; specifically, release from consequences of sin. *The priest granted him absolution.*

absolve (ab zolv', -solv') v.t., to release from obligation, penalty, or punishment; pardon. *The new evidence appeared to absolve the suspect.*

absorb (ab sôrb', -zôrb') v.t., 1. to take in, comprehend. *The filter began to absorb the fumes.* 2. to engross; involve completely. *Her ability to absorb herself in the project gave the group a good start.* 3. to assume responsibility for. *Her brother volunteered to absorb her debts when she became ill.*

absorbent (ab sôr' bənt, -zôr'-) adj., capable of absorbing or taking in; imbibing. *These paper towels are very absorbent.*

absorption (ab sôrp' shən, -zôrp'-) n., the act of absorbing or taking in; imbibing. *Plants have a unique system of absorption.*

abstain (ab stān') v.i., to refrain voluntarily; forbear, especially from a temptation. *The diabetic had to abstain from sweets.*

abstemious (ab stē'mē əs) adj., moderate in eating and drinking. *He attributed his longevity to his abstemious diet.*

abstinence (ab'stə nəns) n., voluntary restraint; forbearance; self-denial. *Total abstinence from drinking improved his health immediately.*

abstract (adj. ab'strakt, ab strakt'; n. ab'strakt; v. ab strakt', ab'strakt) n., summary. *He prepared an abstract of the proceedings.* adj., theoretical or ideal. *The abstract reasoning was hard to follow.* v.t., to take out; remove. *She abstracted portions of the senator's speech.*

abstraction (ab strak' shən) n., that mental concept which is ideal or theoretical only; an idea, term, or other mental construct. *It was hard to reconcile the abstraction with the reality.*

abstruse (ab strōōs') adj., difficult to understand, esoteric. *The students had trouble with the abstruse concepts.*

absurd (ab sûrd', -zûrd') adj., nonsensical; ridiculous; contrary to common sense. *None of them believed the absurd story.*

abundance (ə bun'dəns) n., a plentiful supply or quantity. *The field yielded an abundance of corn.*

abuse (n. ə byōōs'; v. ə byōōz') n., wrong or improper use; corrupt practice or violation. *He spoke about teenage drug abuse.* v.t., to misuse or misapply; maltreat, injure, violate, or defile. *He began to abuse his parents' trust.*

abusive (ə byōō'siv) adj., practicing abuse; pertaining to mistreatment or violation. *She immediately regretted her abusive words.*

abut (ə but') v.i., to join at a border or boundary; rest on or against. *He divided his property so the lot would abut upon the road.*

abutment (ə but'mənt) n., that which abuts or borders on something else; in engineering, steel or concrete supports at each end of a bridge. *The speeding car crashed into the bridge abutment.*

abysmal (ə biz'məl) adj., without boundary or end; having immeasurable depth. *She felt an abysmal despair when he left.*

abyss (ə bis') n., a bottomless gulf; any deep, immeasurable space. *He dreamed he fell into an abyss.*

academic (ak'ə dem'ik) adj., 1. of or pertaining to an advanced institution of learning. *He is a member of the aca-*

demic community. 2. theoretical, having no practical or further significance. *When he died his claim to the throne became academic.*

accede (ak sēd′) v.i., 1. to yield or comply. *They had to accede to the judge's decision.* 2. to take office or position. *The young executive acceded to the directorship.*

accelerate (ak sel′ə rāt′) v., 1. to cause to or to move faster. *The cyclist tried to accelerate his speed.* 2. to hasten the progress or development of. *This strain of wheat will accelerate the normal growing time.* 3. to bring about at an earlier time. *The prisoner's good behavior should accelerate his parole date.*

accent (*n.* ak′sent; *v.* ak′sent, ak sent′) n., 1. distinctive pronunciation. *The Texan had a heavy southern accent.* 2. emphasis on one syllable or musical phrase. *The accent fell on the last syllable.* 3. distinguishing mark placed over, through, or under a letter or number. *For the sake of meter she added the grave accent.* 4. emphasis. *The accent on the menu was Hungarian cooking.* v.t., 1. to stress or emphasize. *The costume managed to accent her gypsy heritage.* 2. to use distinguishing marks, or accents. *She forgot to accent the French word.*

accentuate (ak sen′choo āt′) v.t., to accent; stress; emphasize. *The tights accentuate his thin legs.*

acceptable (ak sep′tə bəl) adj., capable or worthy of being accepted or received with favor; welcome. *Margarine is usually an acceptable substitute for butter.*

acceptance (ak sep′təns) n., act of receiving or being received with approval. *Her acceptance by the medical school elated her.*

access (ak′ses) n., 1. entrance or passageway. *Access is through a series of corridors.* 2. ability to approach and speak with someone, esp. someone of high station. *He has easy access to the prince.* 3. ability to enter or to use. *He has access to classified information.*

accession (ak sesh′ən) n., coming, as into the possession of a right or station; attainment; entrance; induction. *The accession of the new chairman brought cheers from the board members.*

accessory (ak ses′ə rē) n., 1. something of secondary importance. *The scarf was a colorful accessory to the coat.* 2. one who aids or abets in commission of a crime, or who conceals knowledge of a crime. *She was held as an accessory to the embezzlement.*

acclaim (ə klām′) n., applause; verbal, enthusiastic commendation. *The townspeople's acclaim gratified the mayor.* v.t., to applaud; praise. *The students began to acclaim the spectacular touchdown.*

acclamation (ak′lə mā′shən) n., shouts of joy, applause, or other clamorous demonstrations of approval, affection, or support. *The president received a hearty acclamation when he stepped onto the stage.*

acclimate (ə klī′mit, ak′la māt′) v.t., to adapt, get used to, esp. to a new climate. *They had to acclimate themselves to Wisconsin winters.*

accolade (ak′ə lād′, ak′ə lād′) n., 1. ceremonial greeting or embrace. *The ambassador was greeted with a warm accolade.* 2. award, honor or prize. *The Nobel Prize is one of the world's most prestigious accolades.*

accommodate (ə kom′ə dāt′) v.t., to oblige; do a kindness or favor for. *He was glad to accommodate his friends.* 2. to adapt or adjust, esp. to encompass or contain differences. *The lease was loose enough to accommodate landlord and tenant.* 3. to house. *She couldn't accommodate everyone in her small apartment.*

accommodation (ə kom′ə dā′shən) n., 1. something provided for convenience, esp. lodging, transportation, and other services supplied for travelers. *She reserved a luxury accommodation in Paris.* 2. act of accommodating or state of being accommodated. *We thanked him for his thoughtful accommodation of our mother.*

accompaniment (ə kum′pə ni mənt, ə kump′ni-) n., 1. complementary or supportive instrument or voice. *The country singer's accompaniment was a banjo.* 2. complementary addition. *They served fried breads as accompaniment to the meal.*

accompany (ə kum′pə nē) v.t., 1. to go along or in company with. *His partner offered to accompany him on the trip.* 2. to play or sing an accompaniment. *She agreed to accompany her friend on the piano.*

accomplice (ə kom′plis) n., associate or partner, esp. in crime. *His girlfriend was an accomplice in the theft.*

accomplish (ə kom′plish) v.t., 1. to succeed in carrying out; fulfill; realize; attain. *He finally accomplished his goal.* 2. to finish; complete. *He managed to accomplish all his set tasks.*

accomplished (ə kom′plisht) adj., having attained skills and experience; perfected skills. *Leonard Bernstein is an accomplished composer and conductor.*

accord (ə kôrd′) n., agreement; harmony. *The workers were in accord with the union leadership.* v.t., to grant, give, or concede. *He wanted to accord her the honor himself.*

accost (ə kôst′, ə kost′) v.t., 1. to speak first; address. *He was eager to accost the famous writer.* 2. to meet in a bold manner. *The mugger accosted the elderly man on the deserted street.*

account (ə kount′) n., 1. financial record. *She opened an account at the new bank.* 2. explanatory or descriptive statement. *No satisfactory account of the mystery has surfaced.* 3. recital of facts or incidents. *They listened to the account of the kidnapping.* 4. self-justifying statement. *He gave a proud account of his stewardship.* 5. behalf; sake. *Look at the trouble I have gotten into on your account.* 6. importance; distinction. *What he says is of no account.*

accouterment (ə kōō′tər mənt) n., 1. equipment; accessories. *The officer's aide cared for all his accouterments.* 2. any outward identifying characteristic. *Slide rules and calculators are the accouterments of engineers.*

accredit (ə kred′it) v.t., to confer credit or authority on; to grant credentials. *The board voted to accredit the college.*

accreditation (ə kred′ə ta′shən) n., act of accrediting or the state of being accredited. *The school was given accreditation by the review board.*

accretion (ə krē′shən) n., process of growth or enlargement. *Draining the adjoining marsh contributed to the farm's accretion.*

accrue (ə krōō′) v.t., 1. to grow; accumulate. *Interest on savings accrued at an annual rate of six percent.* 2. to come into being legally. *She would accrue as full heir at the age of twenty-one.*

accumulate (ə kyōō′myə lāt′) v.t., to pile up; collect; bring together. *He began to accumulate a great fortune.* v.i., to grow in size, number, or quantity. *Public evils seemed to accumulate.*

accuracy (ak′yər ə sē) n., condition or quality of being accurate; extreme precision or exactness. *They applauded the marksman's accuracy.*

accurate (ak′yər it) adj., characterized by extreme care; free from error; exact. *The thermometer was entirely accurate.*

accusation (ak′yōō zā′shən) n., charge of wrongdoing. *He denied the sheriff's accusation.*

accustom (ə kus′təm) v.t., to make familiar through use. *She had to accustom herself to the stickshift.*

acerbity (ə sûr′bi tē) n., acidity or sourness of taste or disposition. *Her acerbity irritated her date.*

Achilles heel (ə kil′ēs hēl′), weak or vulnerable spot. *The ineffectual president was the company's Achilles heel.*

acidity (ə sid′i tē) n., quality of being acid or sour; sourness; tartness. *He tested the soil for acidity.*

acidulous (ə sij′ə ləs, ə sid′yə-) adj., acidy; sour; tart. *Acidulous apples make good pies.*

acknowledge (ak nol′ij) v.t., to admit or profess knowledge of; recognize. *He had to acknowledge her as his wife.* 2. to give evidence of recognizing. *He* wanted to acknowledge his father's generosity with a gift. 3. to certify the receipt or arrival of. *The letter would acknowledge the arrival of the package.*

acme (ak′mē) n., top or highest point; summit. *The performance marked the acme of his career.*

acolyte (ak′ə līt′) n., 1. altar boy. *The acolyte assisted during Communion.* 2. follower or assistant. *She was a devoted acolyte of the controversial biochemist.*

acoustics (ə kōō′stiks *or, esp. Brit.,* ə kou′-) n., science of sound. *The stereo salesman took a short course in acoustics.* 2. sound characteristics of a room, hall, auditorium, stadium, etc. *The excellent acoustics enhanced their enjoyment of the concert.*

acquaint (ə kwānt) v.t., 1. to make known to; familiarize with; introduce to. *He wanted to acquaint himself with his new ship.* 2. to furnish with knowledge or information. *He began to acquaint his lawyer with the details.*

acquaintance (ə kwān′t³ns) n., 1. state of being acquainted or conversant with. *He had a slight acquaintance with first aid.* 2. person known, though not intimately. *Her neighbor was only an acquaintance.*

acquiesce (ak′wē es′) v.i., to agree or submit passively. *He decided to acquiesce to their demand.*

acquiescence (ak′wē es′əns) n., act of acquiescing or giving tacit assent. *She marveled at the unruly child's acquiescence.*

acquire (ə kwī³r′) v.t., to come to have something through unspecified means or through sustained effort. *After months of practice he managed to acquire the correct accent.*

acquisition (ak′wi zi**sh**′ən) n., 1. act of acquiring. *Her acquisition of the property made headlines.* 2. that which is acquired. *The collector was delighted with his new acquisition.*

acquisitive (ə kwiz′i tiv) adj., desirous of acquiring things; covetous. *Poverty prevented him from satisfying his acquisitive nature.*

acquit (ə kwit′) v.t., 1. to release or discharge from an accusation, obligation, guilt, or suspicion. *The jury voted to acquit the defendant.* 2. to bear or conduct oneself. *The young actor managed to acquit himself like a professional.*

acquittal (ə kwit′³l) n., act of acquitting or state of being acquitted. *The defense attorney asked for an acquittal.*

acrid (ak′rid) adj., 1. sharp, unpleasant taste or smell. *The smokestack emitted acrid fumes.* 2. bitter and irritating. *He felt the bite of her acrid words.*

acrimonious (ak′rə mō′nē əs) adj., bitter; virulent; caustic; stinging. *Their acrimonious quarrel could be heard in the hall.*

acrimony (ak′rə mō′nē) n., bitterness; acerbity. *The counselor tried to assuage the acrimony between them.*

acronym (ak′rə nim) n., word formed by first or key letters in compound name. *The acronym for overdose is OD.*

acrophobia (ak′rə fō′bē ə) n., fear of heights. *He couldn't go by plane because of his acrophobia.*

activate (ak′tə vāt′) v.t., 1. to make active or intensify activity. *He activated the machine by pushing the button.* 2. to call into action. *The governor activated the National Guard.*

activism (ak′tə viz′əm) n., vigorous action intended to achieve a political or social goal. *The candidate hoped to exploit some of the student activism.*

actualize (ak′chōō ə līz′) v.t., to make real, actual. *To actualize your goal you must be self-disciplined.*

actuarial (ak′chōō âr′ē əl) adj., pertaining to an actuary. *He used an actuarial table to calculate her premium.*

actuary (ak′chōō er′ē) n., one who uses statistics to calculate premium rates, risks, dividends, life expectancy tables, etc. *The actuary retired from the insurance company.*

actuate (ak′chōō āt′) v.t., put into action; move or incite to action. *Revenge actuated his course for the remainder of his life.*

acumen (ə kyōō′mən, ak′yə-) n., quickness of perception; faculty of keen discrimination; mental acuteness or penetration. *Her business acumen garnered her the promotion.*

acute (ə kyo͞ot′) adj., 1. sharply pointed or angled. *An acute angle measures less than 90°.* 2. keen; sharp, critical. *She was acute enough to see the lie.* 3. sudden and intense. *She had an acute case of puppy love.*

adage (ad′ij) n., familiar saying metaphorically extolling common sense. *She embroidered the adage on the sampler.*

adagio (ə dä′jō, -zhē ō′; *It.* ä dä′ jô) n., 1. leisurely, graceful musical composition or movement. *The brisk opening movement contrasts with the following adagio.* 2. ballet duet or trio using difficult lifts, spins, and balancing movements. *They performed a breathtaking adagio.* adj. (or adv.), slowly, leisurely, and with grace. *The adagio solo is the most difficult part.*

adamant (ad′ə mənt, -mant′) adj., unyielding; definite; stubborn. *She could not alter his adamant opposition.*

adapt (ə dapt′) v.t., to make fit or suitable, often by changing. *He tried to adapt the novel for the screen.*

adaptation (ad′əp tā′shən) n., 1. the act of adapting. *She found adaptation to dormitory life difficult.* 2. that which has been adapted. *The movie was an adaptation of the short story.*

addendum (ə den′dəm) n., addition to something, particularly to a book. *The contract included a last minute addendum.*

addict (*n.* ad′ikt; *v.* ə dikt′) n., one who is addicted. *He was an addict to late night movies.* v.t., to surrender to compulsive need or craving. *He feared to addict his patient to the painkiller.*

addiction (ə dik′shən) n., state of being addicted, esp. to drugs. *They laughed at his addiction to poker.*

additive (ad′i tiv) n., that which is added. *Certain food additives are considered unhealthy.*

addle (ad′əl) v.t., v.i., 1. to make or become confused. *The contradictory directions addled the weary traveler.* 2.

to spoil or rot. *If you don't refrigerate the eggs they will addle.*

adduce (ə do͞os′, ə dyo͞os′) v.t., to cite in explanation or as proof. *Her colleague's respect should adduce her competence.*

adept (ə dept′) adj., proficient; competent; skilled. *He is adept at splitting wood.*

adequate (ad′ə kwit) adj., equal to the requirement or occasion. *He lacked adequate money for the trip.*

adhere (ad hēr′) v.i., 1. to stick fast; cleave. *The stamp would not adhere to the envelope.* 2. be devoted to or attached as a follower or upholder. *He adhered steadfastly to his opinion.*

adherence (ad hēr′əns) n., act or state of adhering. *The glue promised remarkable adherence.* 2. fidelity; steady attachment. *The calamity tested his adherence to his faith.*

adhesion (ad hē′zhən) n., strong attachment. *She was rewarded for her adhesion to the party.*

adhesive (ad hē′siv) n., that which holds things together; sticky substance. *Waterproof adhesive held the oar together.* adj., sticky; tenacious. *Adhesive tape will hold it together.*

ad hoc (ad hok′; *Lat.* äd hōk) Latin. To this; for this specific purpose. *An ad hoc committee chose the building site.*

adieu (ə do͞o′, ə dyo͞o′; *Fr.* A dy œ′) French. Parting salutation; farewell. *He bid adieu to his home town.*

ad infinitum (ad in′fə nī′t²m) Latin. To infinity; endlessly. *The lecturer seemed to drone on ad infinitum.*

adipose (ad′ə pōs′) adj., fatty. *The surgeon cut through the adipose tissue.*

adjacent (ə jā′sənt) adj., near, close, or contiguous. *The field was adjacent to the highway.*

adjoining (ə joi′nin͠g) adj., joining on; contiguous with. *The cows wandered into the adjoining corn field.*

adjourn (ə jûrn′) v.i., to suspend for specified or indefinite period. *The committee voted to adjourn for the holiday.*

adjournment (ə jûrn′mənt) n., suspension of a meeting to another time or place. *They called an adjournment pending the committee's report.*

adjudge (ə juj′) v.i., to judge; determine; deem. *He adjudged the racehorse a good risk.*

adjudicate (ə jōō′ də kāt′) v.t., to judge; award judicially. *They trusted her to adjudicate the case fairly.*

adjunct (aj′uŋgkt) n., something added in subordinate role. *The crafts business started as an adjunct to the school.*

adjure (ə jōōr′) v.t., 1. to command or enjoin solemnly. *He adjures complete loyalty from his officers.* 2. to beg or entreat earnestly. *The prisoner began to adjure the judge for mercy.*

adjust (ə just′) v.t., to alter to fit; adapt; make conformable. *He adjusted the wrench to fit the nut.*

adjustment (ə just′mənt) n., act of adjusting; state of being adjusted. *His watch needs adjustment.*

adjutant (aj′ə tənt) n., officer appointed to assist the commanding officer of a regiment; aide or assistant. *The general's adjutant met the dignitaries at the airport.*

ad lib (ad lib′, ad′-) n., extemporaneous or improvised words or actions. *The ad lib saved the comedian's act.* v.t., to deliver extemporaneously. *She tried to ad lib a believable explanation.* v.i., to improvise. *The comedian was confident in his ability to ad lib.*

administer (ad min′i stər) v.t., 1. to superintend the management or execution of. *He was hired to administer the program.* 2. to dispense or bring into operation. *She began to administer first aid.*

administration (ad min′i strā′shən) n., 1. act of administering; management. *The administration of government requires a great deal of paperwork.* 2. body of individuals entrusted with executive or administrative powers. *The city administration issued the school bond.*

admirable (ad′mər ə bəl) adj., worthy of esteem, admiration. *She had the admirable ability to get the best out of her employees.*

admiration (ad′mə rā′shən) n., act or feeling of approbation and esteem. *His batting skill earned him the team's admiration.*

admissible (ad mis′ə bəl) adj., capable or worthy of being admitted; allowable. *The evidence was not admissible in court.*

admission (ad mish′ən) n., 1. act of admitting; state of being admitted. *He sought admission to the meeting.* 2. price paid for admission; admittance. *The admission was one dollar.* 3. concession; allowance. *This admission lost him the argument.*

admonish (ad mon′ish) v.t., to counsel against something; caution or advise; warn; exhort. *His father admonished him not to drive recklessly.*

adobe (ə dō′ bē) n., 1. sun-dried brick, used as a building material. *The hut was made of adobe.* 2. building made of adobe bricks. *The adobe sheltered the small family.*

adolescent (ad′ə les′ənt) n., one who has entered puberty but not yet reached age of majority. *The adolescent worked after school at the store.* adj., pertaining to adolescence; immature. *She outgrew her adolescent clumsiness.*

Adonis (ə don′is, ə dō′nis) n., in Greek mythology, handsome youth loved by Aphrodite, hence any handsome young man. *The lifeguard was a teenage Adonis.*

adopt (ə dopt′) v.t., 1. to formally choose and raise a child as one's own. *The childless couple wanted to adopt the boy.* 2. to choose and take on voluntarily. *She wanted to adopt her husband's nationality.* 3. to select a text for required study. *The instructor would not adopt the cut version.*

adoration (ad′ə rā′shən) n., act or condition of adoring. *His intense adoration flattered her.*

adorn (ə dôrn′) v.t., to beautify or decorate; to embellish with ornaments. *She wanted to adorn the dress with pearls.*

adrenaline (ə dren′ə lin, -ə lēn′) n., adrenal hormone used as a heart stimulant, muscle relaxant, and a blood vessel constrictor. *Adrenaline is often administered for shock.*

adrift (ə drift′) adj., adv., 1. floating at random; not fastened by any kind of mooring. *The small boat went adrift during the night.* 2. purposeless; irresolute. *He felt adrift for weeks following graduation.*

adroit (ə droit′) adj., 1. skillful in the use of the hands; nimble. *The adroit artist finished the portrait quickly.* 2. mentally quick and resourceful; clever. *His adroit solution impressed the committee chairman.*

adulation (aj′ə lā′shən) n., excessive praise; unmerited compliments proceeding either from blind worship or the hope of advantage. *He smiled at the youngster's adulation.*

adulterate (ə dul′tə rāt′) v.t., to debase or change for the worse by adding foreign or inferior ingredients. *Unscrupulous vintners adulterate wine with water.*

adultery (ə dul′ tə rē) n., sexual intercourse by a married person with someone other than his or her spouse. *His wife accused him of adultery.*

adumbration (ad′um brā′shən) n., 1. vague foreshadowing; intimation. *The heavy stillness was an adumbration of the coming thunderstorm.* 2. partial, sketchy disclosure. *The letter contained only a brief adumbration of his deepseated prejudice.* 3. partial concealment; overshadowing. *His overprotective friends cast an adumbration on his true character.*

advance (ad vans′, -väns′) n., 1. forward movement; progress. *Cosmetics cannot stop the advance of age.* 2. offer. *They considered the attorney's advance.* 3. payment made before expected return, on credit. *She asked for a week's advance on her salary.* v.t., 1. to move or go forward; proceed. *They began to advance to the edge of the enemy camp.* 2. to put or set forth. *The philosopher advanced a new concept.* 3. to move forward in time; accelerate; progress; further. *Medical research will advance the fight against cancer.* 4. to supply beforehand; furnish on credit or before work is done. *She agreed to advance her friend the money.* 5. to promote. *He began to advance his son's interest in music.*

advantage (ad van′tij, -vän′-) n., state, condition, circumstance, opportunity, or means especially favorable to success, or any desired end; anything that aids, assists, or is of service. *He had the advantage of a strong constitution.*

advantageous (ad′vən tā′jəs) adj., of advantage, benefit, or profit. *It was advantageous to dress conservatively for the stockholders' meeting.*

advent (ad′vent) n., coming into place or being; arrival; accession. *The advent of the automobile changed the social structure of America.*

adverb (ad′vûrb) n., part of speech used to qualify—usually by expressing manner, time, degree, place, quality, number, cause, affirmation, or denial—a verb, adjective, or other adverb. *"Quickly" is an adverb.*

adversary (ad′vər ser′ē) n., opponent; contestant; enemy. *He defeated his adversary.* adj., opposed; opposite to; adverse. *The adversary forces met on the football field.*

adverse (ad vûrs′, ad′vûrs) adj., opposed; in a contrary direction; antagonistic. *He won the race despite adverse weather conditions.*

adversity (ad vûr′si tē) n., condition marked by misfortune, calamity, distress, or unhappiness. *The new widow could see only adversity ahead.*

advice (ad vīs′) n., opinion recommended or offered as worthy to be followed or heeded; counsel. *His doctor's advice was to quit smoking.*

advisable (ad vī′zə bəl) adj., prudent; expedient; proper. *It is not advisable to take a boat out in bad weather.*

advocacy (ad′və kə sē) n., act of supporting, pleading for, or recommending. *The senator's advocacy of the bill speeded its passage.*

advocate (*n.* ad′və kit, -kāt′; *v.* ad′ və kāt′)

n., one who pleads the cause of another in a court of law, as a lawyer, or one who espouses a cause by argument. *He was an advocate of free enterprise.* v.t., to plead in favor of; defend; support; recommend. *The parents advocated a new grading system.*

aegis (ē′jis) n., protective power or influence; sponsorship. *The bazaar was under the aegis of the Catholic Church.*

aerial (âr′ē əl) n., radio or television antenna. *He climbed the roof to adjust the aerial.* adj., of or pertaining to the air or atmosphere; existing or happening in the air; produced by or in the air. *The town was fortified against aerial attack.*

aeronautics (âr′ə nô′tiks, -not′iks) n., science of designing, constructing, navigating, and flying aircraft. *The student pilot studied the principles of aeronautics.*

aerosol (âr′ə sōl′, -sôl′, -sol′) n., suspension of liquid or fine solid particles in a gas, often used in a packaged product under pressure. *He prefers an aerosol to shaving soap.*

aerospace (âr′ə spās′) n., atmosphere above and beyond the earth and extending indefinitely into the cosmos. *An extensive satellite network operates in aerospace.*

aesthete (es′thēt *or, esp. Brit.,* ēs′-) n., person having or affecting sensitivity to the beauties of art or nature. *The art historian is both an aesthete and a scholar.*

aesthetic (es thet′ik *or, esp. Brit.,* ēs-) adj., pertaining to beauty in any of its manifestations; keenly appreciative of beauty; artistic. *The junkyard offended her aesthetic sensibilities.*

affable (af′ə bəl) adj., gracious; friendly; pleasant. *Their affable host put them at ease.*

affect (ə fekt′) v.t., 1. to influence; move or touch; produce a change upon. *Her illness began to affect her looks.* 2. to make a show of; pretend. *He tried to affect the speech of the upper class.*

affectation (af′ek tā′shən) n., artificiality of manner or conduct; pretense. *His*

English accent was clearly an affectation.*

affected (ə fek′tid) adj., 1. acted upon; influenced; impaired. *Her temper began to be affected by the hot weather.* 2. assumed artificially. *She found his affected manner repulsive.*

affectionate (ə fek′shə nit) adj., loving; tender; warm-hearted. *His affectionate aunt hugged him tightly.*

affidavit (af′i dā′vit) n., written statement signed and sworn to under oath before a notary public or other authorized person. *The affidavit was accepted as evidence by the court.*

affiliate (*v.* ə fil′ē āt′; *n.* ə fil′ē it, -āt′) v., to associate, unite, or ally with. *He tried to affiliate himself with the influential senator.* n., organization or individual closely associated with but subordinate to another. *The firm is an affiliate of a national corporation.*

affiliation (ə fil′ē ā′shən) n., association; alliance; connection. *His affiliation with the university began ten years ago.*

affinity (ə fin′i tē) n., 1. natural liking for or inclination to; inherent mutual attraction. *He felt an affinity for the Indian music.* 2. inherent likeness between things; conformity or resemblance. *There are many affinities between apes and men.*

affirm (ə fûrm′) v.t., 1. to assert positively. *He had to affirm the startling news.* 2. to confirm or ratify. *The appellate court affirmed the judgment.*

affirmation (af′ər mā′shən) n., 1. that which is affirmed; assertion that something is, or is true. *His affirmation of faith pleased the congregation.* 2. confirmation or ratification. *The certificate was an affirmation of the marriage.*

affix (ə fiks′) v.t., to fasten, attach, or join to. *He affixed the sticker to his front bumper.*

afflict (ə flikt′) v.t., to distress with mental or bodily pain; trouble greatly; harass or torment. *The illness began to afflict his spirits.*

affliction (ə flik′shən) n., state of being afflicted; mental or physical pain; misery; torment; grief. *The tormented man hardly felt the new affliction.*

affluence (af′loo əns) n., abundant supply; profusion, esp. of material goods; wealth. *The sweepstakes brought them instant affluence.*

affluent (af′loo ənt) adj., rich; prosperous; wealthy. *The affluent man contributed handsomely.*

afford (ə fōrd′, ə fôrd′) v.t., 1. to be able to meet or bear the expense of. *We can afford to buy the house.* 2. to yield, furnish, or supply as an effect or result. *The recess will afford us extra time.*

affray (ə frā′) n., brawl; fray. *The playground affray ended with two bloody noses.*

affront (ə frunt′) n., insult; indignity; impertinence; offense; rudeness. *She took his criticism as a personal affront.* v.t., to offend publicly or openly; insult. *The remark was intended to affront him before the court.*

aficionado (ə fish′ yə nä′dō; *Sp.* ä fē′ thyô nä′thô) n., fan; devotee. *The opera aficionado has a lifetime subscription.*

afield (ə fēld′) adv., 1. away from home; abroad. *He traveled far afield last summer.* 2. out of the way, off the beaten path; astray. *Research for her biography led her afield.*

afloat (ə flōt′) adv., borne on the water; floating. *The capsized canoe nevertheless stayed afloat.*

afoul (ə foul′) adv., in collision, entanglement, or conflict with. *The truant ran afoul of school regulations.*

aft (aft, äft) adv., behind; in the rear; in, near, or toward the stern of a ship. *The captain ordered everyone aft while the crew examined the damage.*

aftermath (af′tər math′, äf′-) n., consequences, esp. following a violent or calamitous event. *The aftermath of the flood left them homeless.*

agape (*n.* ä gä′pä, ä′gə pä′, ag′ə-; *adj.* ə gāp′, ə gap′) n., unselfish love, of God for man, man for God, or for fellowman. *The minister urged them toward fulfillment in agape.* adj., with the mouth wide open; in an attitude of wonder or eager attention. *The children were agape at the daredevil's ride.*

agar (ä′gär, ag′ər) n., gelatinlike extract of red algae used as a base for culture media and as a solidifying agent in foods and adhesives. *She added the agar to the petri dish.*

agency (ā′jən sē) n., 1. agent's place of business. *The models protested the agency's policy.* 2. department of government. *They didn't know which agency was responsible.* 3. means or instrument for producing effects. *The strike was settled through the agency of impartial judges.*

agenda (ə jen′də) n., list or program of things to be done; items of business to be brought before a committee, council, board, etc. *The first item on the agenda is the new budget.*

agent (ā′jənt) n., 1. active or effective cause. *He was the agent of his own downfall.* 2. person acting on behalf of someone else. *His agent got him a part in the movie.* 3. official. *She is an agent of the F.B.I.* 4. spy. *He is a secret agent.*

agglomerate (*n., adj.* ə glom′ ər it,-ə rāt′; *v.* ə glom′ə rāt′) n., jumbled mass. *The drawer was an agglomerate of unmatched mittens, gloves, hats, and scarfs.* v.t., to gather into a ball or cluster. *He thought to agglomerate the largest collection of string on record.* adj., gathered in a ball or clustered. *He designed several agglomerate but independent resorts.*

agglomeration (ə glom′ə rā′shən) n., state of gathering or being gathered into a mass; heap or collection formed by random juxtaposition. *A mere agglomeration of facts confuses the reader.*

agglutination (ə gloot′ənā′shən) n., 1. joining together of distinct parts. *The poet experimented with agglutination of nonsense syllables.* 2. whole formed by the joining together of distinct parts. *The painting was an agglutination of tempera and watercolor.*

aggrandize (ə gran′dīz, ag′rən dīz′) v.t., 1. to make greater; enlarge or increase.

The marriage will aggrandize his political influence. 2. to cause to appear greater; overpraise. *She tried to aggrandize her importance to the firm.* 3. to enhance. *The award will certainly aggrandize his reputation.*

aggravate (ag′rə vāt′) v.t., 1. to make worse; intensify; increase the weight or pressure of. *He aggravated the sprain by walking on it.* 2. to provoke; irritate. *His persistence began to aggravate her.*

aggregate (*n., adj.,* ag′rə git, -gāt′; *v.* ag′rə gāt′) n., sum, mass or assemblage of particulars; any combined whole considered with reference to its constituent parts. *The aggregate of the family's possessions showed great wealth.* adj., total. *The family's aggregate wealth is overwhelming.* v.i., to amass or collect into one sum. *The collected pennies will aggregate a substantial amount.*

aggression (ə gresh′ən) n., hostile or offensive act; encroachment; assault; inroad. *The U.N. guarded the area against acts of aggression.*

aggressive (ə gres′iv) adj., 1. characterized by aggression; offensive. *They favored an aggressive foreign policy.* 2. inclined to take the initiative; forceful; self-assertive. *The aggressive salesman boosted their sales record.*

aghast (ə gast′, ə gäst′) adj., filled with sudden fright or horror. *She was aghast at the sudden attack.*

agile (aj′əl *or, esp. Brit.,* aj′īl) adj., having the faculty of quick motion; nimble. *Her agile mind quickly found a solution.*

agility (ə jil′ i tē) n., state or quality of being agile; nimbleness. *Acrobatics needs agility.*

agitate (aj′i tāt′) v.t., to rouse; disturb; shake. *She tried to agitate the machine into action.* v.i., to incite; stir up. *The students decided to agitate for lower tuition.*

agnostic (ag nos′tik) n., one who believes the existence of God is unknowable. *The agnostic listened without conviction to the sermon.* adj., pertaining to religious noncommittal or doubt. *She resigned herself to an agnostic point of view.*

agonize (ag′ə nīz′) v.i., to suffer extreme and often prolonged bodily or mental pain; experience violent anguish. *The general agonized over the life-or-death decision.*

agoraphobia (ag′ər ə fō′bē ə) n., abnormal fear of being in open places. *Agoraphobia made him uncomfortable in the wide Place de la Concorde.*

agrarian (ə grâr′ē ən) adj., pertaining to land, especially farm lands, and to ownership and cultivation. *Colonial America was mostly agrarian.*

agreeable (ə grē′ə bəl) adj., 1. pleasing to the mind or to the senses. *The coffee had an agreeable aroma.* 2. willing, or ready to agree; concurring. *They were agreeable to her proposal.*

aground (ə ground′) adv., on the ground; nautical term signifying that the bottom of the ship has come to rest on the ground because of shallow water. *They ran aground at low tide.*

aileron (ā′lə ron′) n., movable part of an airplane wing. *The ailerons on biplanes move simultaneously.*

ailurophobia (ī loor′ə fō′bē ə) n., abnormal fear of cats. *Ailurophobia prevented her from touching the cat.*

akimbo (ə kim′bō) adj., adv., with the hand on the hip and the elbow turned outward. *She intentionally blocked the door with her arms akimbo.*

à la carte (ä′lə kärt′, al′ə-; *Fr.* A LA KART′) adv., requiring that each menu item be ordered separately. *Ordering à la carte can be more expensive.*

alacrity (ə lak′ri tē) n., cheerful readiness or briskness. *He did his work with alacrity.*

alarmist (ə lär′mist) n., one who excites or alarms by exaggerating bad news or prophesying calamities and disasters. *He was disregarded as an alarmist.*

albatross (al′bə trôs′, -tros′) n., 1. webfooted seabird of the petrel family. *The albatross inhabits the South Pacific.* 2. perennial burden. *The I.R.S. was an albatross around his neck.*

albeit (ôl bē′it) conj., although; notwithstanding that. *Hitler was a genius, albeit an evil one.*

albino (al bī'nō *or, esp. Brit.,* -bē'-) n., person or animal with milky skin, light or white hair, and pink eyes, caused by a congenital lack of pigmentation. *Albinos occur among all races of men.*

alchemy (al'kə mē) n., medieval chemistry; esp. refers to the search for a process by which base metals could be turned into gold. *Love's alchemy changed her into a beauty.*

alcoholic (al'kə hô'lik, -hol'ik) n., one who indulges excessively in alcoholic beverages; drunkard. *The alcoholic went to the doctor for help.* adj., pertaining to the nature of alcohol; containing or using alcohol. *No alcoholic beverages were served at the party.*

alcoholism (al'kə hô liz'əm, -ho-) n., continued excessive or compulsive use of alcoholic beverages. *She sought treatment for her alcoholism.*

alderman (ôl'dər mən) n., member of a city legislature. *The newly-elected alderman was a woman.*

al fresco (al fres'kō) adj., adv., in the open air. *We enjoy dining al fresco on the terrace.*

alias (ā'lē əs) n., assumed name. *He registered under the alias of John Kenton.*

alibi (al'ə bī') n., 1. fact or claim of having been elsewhere when something happened. *The suspect had an air-tight alibi.* 2. credible excuse; apology. *He accepted the alibi for her absence.*

alien (āl'yən, ā'lē ən) n., one born in or belonging to another country who has not acquired citizenship by naturalization; foreigner. *The alien applied for a work visa.* adj., foreign. *The new apartment seemed alien at first.*

alienate (āl'yə nāt') v.t., to repel or cause to turn away from; make hostile, indifferent, or averse; estrange. *His heavy drinking began to alienate his family.*

align (ə līn') v.t., 1. to put in a straight line; make equal or even. *We began to align chairs for the ceremony.* 2. to side with; ally or unite with. *He aligned himself with the dissenters.*

alignment (ə līn'mənt) n., act of aligning, laying out, or regulation; adjusting various parts of a mechanism. *His front-wheel alignment needed adjustment.*

alimentary (al'ə men'tə rē) adj., concerned with nutrition. *She studied alimentary science in health class.*

alimony (al'ə mō'nē) n., maintenance allowance that one is required by a court to pay his or her spouse during a legal separation or after a divorce. *The judge awarded the requested alimony.*

alkali (al'kə lī') n., 1. soluble salt, primarily potassium or sodium carbonate, obtained from the ashes of plants. *They added pine needles to counteract the soil's excess alkali.* 2. base that neutralizes acids to form salts. *An alkali turns red litmus paper blue.*

allay (ə lā') v.t., to calm, relieve; soothe. *He tried to allay his patient's fear of surgery.*

allegation (al'ə gā'shən) n., 1. act of alleging or asserting without proof. *She made several erroneous allegations.* 2. legal plea, excuse, or justification. *The prosecution attacked the defendant's allegation of temporary insanity.* 3. legal statement of that which a party to a proceeding tries to prove. *The plaintiff's allegation was difficult to prove.*

allege (ə lej') v.t., 1. to declare, assert, or affirm without proof. *She could only allege the fact.* 2. in law, to produce as an argument, plea, or excuse. *The defendant tried to allege his innocence.* 3. in law, to state a case. *He alleged the defendant embezzled the money.*

allegiance (ə lē'jəns) n., obligation and/or fidelity, esp. of a citizen or subject to his or her government or leadership. *He swore allegiance to the young monarch.*

allegory (al'ə gōr'ē, -gôr'ē) n., symbolic representation of ideas, persons, or events. *The ballet was an allegory about filial duty.*

allergy (al'ər jē) n., hypersensitivity to specific substances or situations, resulting in extreme or unusual bodily reaction such as respiratory difficulties or skin rashes. *She treated his allergy with antihistamines.*

alleviate (ə lē'vē āt') v.t., to moderate;

palliate; relieve. *The medicine began to alleviate the pain.*

alliance (ə lī′əns) n., 1. formal or acknowledged state or act of unity, esp. between nations or other political entities. *The Third World alliance met to discuss the food shortage.* 2. any acknowledged affinity or close relationship. *Their marriage created an alliance between their families.*

allied (ə līd′, al′īd) adj., connected; closely associated; united. *Swimming and water polo are allied sports.*

alliteration (ə lit′ə rā′s̲h̲ən) n., repetition of consonant sounds in two or more successive words or syllables. *The familiar "Peter Piper" verse is an example of alliteration.*

allocate (al′ə kāt′) v.t., to set apart for a particular purpose; assign; allot. *The town voted to allocate money for a new school.*

allotment (ə lot′mənt) n., act of allotting or that which is allotted. *The needy family received a generous allotment of food and clothing.*

allowance (ə lou′əns) n., 1. specific sum or grant set aside or distributed. *His weekly allowance was raised on his birthday.* 2. act of considering mitigating circumstances; concession. *The judge's sentence made allowance for her extreme youth.*

alloy (n. al′oi, ə loi′; v. ə loi′) n., 1. compound created between metals, usually through fusion. *Copper and tin form the alloy of bronze.* v.t., to debase by mixing with inferior substance. *Her father's bitterness failed to alloy the bride's joy.*

allude (ə lōōd′) v.i., to refer to casually or indirectly. *He meant to allude to his opponent's past indiscretion.*

allure (ə lōōr′) n., attractiveness; appeal; charm. *Her allure was irresistible.* v.t., to tempt; entice; attract. *The sirens' song began to allure Ulysses' sailors.*

allusion (ə lōō′z̲h̲ən) n., casual or implied reference; hint. *She didn't catch his pointed allusion.*

alluvium (ə lōō′vē əm) n., deposit of clay,

silt, or sand left by running water. *The flood left behind a rich alluvium.*

almanac (ôl′mə nak′) n., publication giving meteorological and astronomical information in calendar format, and often including other miscellaneous information. *The farmer swears by the almanac's weather forecasts.*

aloft (ə lôft′, ə loft′) adv., in the air. *The eagle soared aloft.*

aloof (ə lōōf′) adv., at a distance; intentionally uninvolved. *He remained aloof from their quarrel.* adj., reserved; indifferent. *They thought him a rather cold, aloof father.*

altar (ôl′tər) n., elevated structure or table used for sacrifice, burning of incense, or as ritual center of worship. *The priest consecrated the wine at the altar.*

alter (ôl′tər) v.t., 1. to change or vary. *He asked them to alter the suit to fit his brother.* 2. to spay or neuter. *She asked the vet to alter the stray cat.*

altercation (ôl′tər kā′shən, al′-) n., noisy argument. *The altercation woke the neighbors.*

alternate (n., adj. ôl′tər nit, al′-; v. ôl′tər nāt′, al′-) n., one who substitutes for or alternates with another. *She was chosen as the first alternate.* v.i., 1. to follow one another in time or place. *Flood and ebb tides alternate with each other.* 2. to pass from one state to a second, then back to a first, and so on indefinitely. *He seemed to alternate between hope and despair.* adj., every other; every second; recurringly. *He was torn by alternate waves of fear and desire.*

alternative (ôl tûr′nə tiv, al-) n., choice between two dissimilar things. *The only alternative to waiting for the firemen was to jump from the burning building.* adj., offering or suggesting a choice. *They suggested an alternative route.*

altitude (al′ti tōōd′, -tyōōd′) n., vertical elevation above the horizon or above sea level; height. *The plane's cruising altitude was 35,000 feet.*

alto (al′tō) n., 1. lowest singing range for

the female voice. *The alto performed a solo as part of the program.* 2. instrument with second highest range among instruments of its kind. *He played the viola, the alto in the violin family.*

altruism (al'troo iz'əm) n., devotion to or concern for the welfare of others. *Altruism prompted him to give the old woman his seat.*

alumnus (ə lum'nəs) n., graduate of a particular school, college, or university. *The alumnus planned to attend the reunion.*

amalgamate (ə mal'gə māt') v., to combine; unite; blend. *The two companies agreed to amalgamate.*

amass (ə mas') v.t., to collect or bring together a great amount of quantity. *He would later amass a fortune from the small investment.*

amateur (am'ə choor', -tyoor', am'ə tûr') n., 1. one who pursues an interest for pleasure rather than profit. *The amateur competed in the Olympic trials.* 2. one who lacks expertise in some particular endeavor. *She was still an amateur.* adj., nonprofessional; inexpert. *He retained his amateur status for the competition.*

amatory (am'ə tōr'ē, -tôr'ē) adj., expressing or pertaining to sexual love. *She cast an amatory glance at the handsome young man.*

Amazon (am'ə zon', -zən) n., in Greek legend, one of a race of warlike women who lived on the Black Sea coast and in the Caucasus mountains; now sometimes applied to a woman with strong, aggressive, dominating, or quarrelsome characteristics. *The ferocious Amazon guarded the child closely.*

ambassador (am bas'ə dər) n., 1. high-ranking resident diplomatic representative. *The new ambassador presided over the embassy tea.* 2. authorized or unofficial envoy. *The company sent their ambassador to open negotiations.*

ambidextrous (am'bi dek'strəs) adj., ability to use either hand with equal dex-

terity. *The broken wrist didn't affect the ambidextrous girl's schoolwork.*

ambiguity (am'bə gyoo'i tē) n., unclearness or uncertainty in meaning. *Ambiguity resulted from the extreme brevity of the message.*

ambiguous (am big'yoo əs) adj., equivocal; unclear; open to various interpretations. *His ambiguous directions didn't help much.*

ambition (am bish'ən) n., 1. desire for specific goal or reward. *It was her ambition to dance professionally.* 2. desire for power, wealth, or rank. *Ambition made him ruthless.*

ambitious (am bish'əs) adj., possessed of ambition; desirous of obtaining power, superiority, or other mark of distinction. *The company encouraged ambitious salesmen.*

ambivalence (am biv'ə ləns) n., conflicting feelings toward a person or thing. *The atrocity shook him out of his ambivalence.*

ambivert (am'bə vûrt') n., someone whose personality is between that of an introvert and an extrovert. *The ambivert is comfortable alone and in a group.*

amble (am'bəl) v.i., to walk or move at a leisurely pace; saunter. *We began to amble through the fascinating exhibit.*

ambrosia (am brō'zhə) n., 1. food, drink, or perfume of the classical gods. *Zeus dined on ambrosia.* 2. anything extremely pleasing to the sense of taste or smell. *In the open, clear air the simple fare tasted like ambrosia.*

ambulatory (am'byə lə tōr'ē, tôr'ē) adj., 1. pertaining to walking. *She rejected the car in favor of ambulatory pleasures.* 2. able to walk. *The recuperating patient was now ambulatory.* 3. moving from place to place. *Nomads are ambulatory.* 4. capable of being changed; alterable. *He reminded his heirs that his will was ambulatory.*

ameliorate (ə mēl'yə rāt') v.t., to make better or more tolerable; improve. *The new warden hoped to ameliorate conditions in the prison.*

amenable 16

amenable (ə mē'nə bəl, ə men'ə-) adj., disposed to yield, agree, submit, as to advice or influence; submissive. *The professor was amenable to her unusual interpretation.*

amend (ə mend') v.t., 1. to change for the better; improve. *He tried to amend his thoughtless remark.* 2. to change, esp. in wording. *She was told to amend the terms of the contract.*

amendment (ə mend'mənt) n., 1. act of amending. *He resented the amendment of his plans.* 2. constitutional or parliamentary change or process of changing. *The amendment passed overwhelmingly in the House.*

amenity (ə men'i tē, ə mē'ni-) n., 1. quality of being pleasant or agreeable. *Her amenity made her visit very enjoyable.* 2. something that contributes to comfort or pleasure. *The kitchen lacks the amenity of a dishwasher.* 3. social act or custom. *We enjoyed the amenity of high tea.*

amiable (ā'mē ə bəl) adj., friendly; amicable; agreeable. *They took advantage of his amiable nature.*

amicable (am'ə kə bəl) adj., friendly; peaceable; harmonious. *They became good friends after the amicable discussion.*

amino acid (ə mē'nō, am'ə nō') organic acid containing the amino group NH₃, esp. those that are the chief component of proteins. *Eight amino acids are essential in the human diet.*

amiss (ə mis') adj., improper; wrong; faulty. *That something was amiss showed in their faces.* adv., improperly; wrongly; faultily. *She took the remark amiss.*

ammeter (am'mē'tər) n., instrument for measuring electric current in amperes. *A defective ammeter invalidated the electrical engineer's experiment.*

amnesia (am nē'zhə) n., loss of memory. *He suffered amnesia after the fall.*

amnesty (am'ni stē) n., general pardon or conditional offer of pardon of offenses or of a class of offenses against a gov-

ernment. *The deserters were granted amnesty by the President.*

amok (**amuck**) (ə muk', ə mok') adv., in a state of murderous frenzy. *Having scaled the garrison walls, the invaders ran amok.* adj., carried away by mindless frenzy. *The mob seemed amok.*

amoral (ā môr'əl, a môr'-, ā mor'-, a mor'-) adj., without a sense of right and wrong; outside moral considerations. *She was disturbed by the amoral point of view.*

amorous (am'ər əs) adj., inclined to love; conveying love; loving; sexually attracted. *The amorous suitor defied her parents' opposition.*

amorphous (ə môr'fəs) adj., having no definite shape; formless. *They tried to identify the amorphous creature.*

amortization (am'ər ti zā'shən), ə môr'-) n., act of writing off or terminating a debt, a loss, or cost over an extended period of time. *He recommended a 5-year amortization of the loss.*

amortize (am'ər tīz', ə môr'tīz) v.t., 1. to set aside money over a period of time for gradual payment of a debt. *They were able to amortize several thousand dollars.* 2. in accounting, to prorate over a fixed period in order to write off, as expenditures. *The firm decided to amortize its debt over the next five years.*

ampere (am'pēr, am pēr') n., unit of electrical current equal to the current produced by one volt acting through a resistance of one ohm. *One ampere is equal to one coulomb per second.*

amphetamine (am fet'ə mēn', -min) n., drug, used to relieve respiratory distress or, taken internally, to stimulate the central nervous system, to depress the appetite for food, or to relieve fatigue or depression. *The amphetamine helped him curb his appetite.*

amphibian (am fib'ē ən) n., 1. one of a class of vertebrate animals, including the frogs, toads, and salamanders, that live on both land and in the water. *Many amphibians lay their eggs in water.* 2. anything able to live or operate on both land and water. *The amphibian landed smoothly on the lake.*

amphitheater (am'fə thē'ə tər, -thēə'tər) n., 1. outdoor, partially open, or very large theater including tiered seats in round or oval formation. *They used the old amphitheater for the summer concert.* 2. medical or surgical observation gallery. *They watched the operation from the amphitheater.*

ample (am'pəl) adj., 1. of great size, extent, capacity, or bulk; spacious; copious. *The large family needed ample living quarters.* 2. sufficient. *They bought ample camping provisions.*

amplification (am'plə fə kā'shən) n., 1. act of amplifying; enlarging. *The article criticized the continual amplification of federal control over state government.* 2. expansion of argument, description, narration, etc., by elaboration or addition of material. *The brief proposal needed amplification.*

amplify (am'plə fī') v.t., 1. to make larger in volume, extent, capacity, amount; enlarge; expand. *The microphone amplified the singer's voice.* 2. to expand an argument, story, narration, etc., by the addition or elaboration of material. *He was asked to amplify his remarks.*

amplitude (am'pli tōōd', -tyōōd') n., state or quality of being ample in size, extent, amount; extension in space, esp. breadth or width; fullness; largeness. *The amplitude of the buffet delighted the hungry guests.*

amputate (am'pyōō tāt') v.t., to cut off, as a limb or other part of the body. *The doctor had to amputate the gangrenous leg.*

amuck (amok) (ə muk', ə mok') adv., in a murderous, violently uncontrollable frenzy. *The infection ran amuck in the nursery, claiming three victims.*

amulet (am'yə lit) n., object worn as protection against bad luck, sickness, or evil; charm; fetish. *He wore the ancient amulet for good fortune.*

anabolism (ə nab'ə liz'əm) n., synthesis in living organisms of more complex substances from simpler ones; constructive metabolism. *The transformation of food into living tissue is an example of anabolism.*

anachronism (ə nak'rə niz'əm) n., error with respect to time; anything out of keeping with a specified time. *The Model-T was an anachronism at the new car show.*

anagram (an'ə gram') n., transposition of letters of a word or sentence to form a new word or sentence. *"Ulatf" is an anagram for "fault."* v.t., to rearrange letters or words to reveal concealed message. *He began to anagram the urgent missive.*

analgesic (an'əl jē'zik, -sik) n., that which alleviates pain. *Aspirin is an analgesic.*

analogous (ə nal'ə gəs) adj., partially similar; being an analogue to something. *A bird's wing is analogous to a plane's wing.*

analogy (ə nal'ə jē) n., partial agreement, likeness, or similarity, esp. between the relations of things to one another. *They discussed his analogy between learning and light.*

analytic (an'əlit'ik) adj., of or pertaining to analysis. *She is a keenly analytic mathematician.*

analyze (an'əlīz') v.t., 1. to separate into component parts; ascertain constituents or causes of. *The laboratory analyzed the rock samples.* 2. to examine critically so as to bring out the essential elements or give the essence of. *The teacher analyzed the poem.*

anarchy (an'ər kē) n., 1. absence of government. *The student espoused the concept of anarchy.* 2. state of disorder, upheaval, and lawlessness due to lack of effective government. *Anarchy reigned in the streets after the coup.*

anathema (ə nath'ə mə) n., 1. someone or something cursed or denounced by ecclesiastical authority. *The idea of abortion was anathema to the priest.* 2. ecclesiastical denunciation; excommunication. *The church pronounced anathema against the willful heretic.* 3. any curse; execration. *Uttering a thousand anathemas, he strode to the scene of combat.*

anatomy (ə nat′ə mē) n., 1. study of body structure. *The premed student registered for the course in anatomy.* 2. dissection. *The coroner performed a partial anatomy on the corpse.* 3. human body. *The infection spread over much of her anatomy.*

anemia (ə nē′mē ə) n., deficiency of red blood cells, hemoglobin, or volume in blood. *She took iron pills for the anemia.*

anemometer (an′ə mom′i tər) n., instrument for measuring the speed or force of the wind. *The anemometer showed the gathering force of the gale.*

aneroid (an′ə roid′) adj., using no liquid. *An aneroid barometer has a partial vacuum chamber instead of a mercury chamber.*

anesthesia (an′is thē′ zhə) n., state of insensibility to pain. *The anesthesia wore off two hours after the operation.*

anesthetic (an′is thet′ik) n., substance capable of producing anesthesia. *Ether is an anesthetic.* adj., producing temporary loss or impairment of sensation or feeling; producing anesthesia. *The dull play had an anesthetic effect on the audience.*

aneurysm (**aneurism**) (an′yə riz′əm) n., localized dilation of an artery due to the pressure of the blood acting on a part weakened by accident or disease. *The surgeon repaired the aneurysm in his leg.*

anguish (ang′gwish) n., excruciating or agonizing pain of either body or mind; acute suffering; agony; grief. *They waited in anguish for news of their missing son.*

angular (ang′gyə lər) adj., 1. having an angle or angles; having corners pointed. *The angular new building was striking.* 2. having or exhibiting protuberances of joint or limb; acting or moving awkwardly as if in angles. *The angular center sprang to the net for a clean basket.*

animate (*v.* an′ə māt′; *adj.* an′ə mit) v.t., 1. to give life to; quicken; make alive. *The soul animates the body.* 2. to affect with an appearance of life; actuate as if with life. *The puppeteer began to animate his puppets.* adj., 1. possessing animal life. *He preferred to study animate creatures rather than fossils.* 2. having lifelike appearance. *The puppets seemed animate.*

animated (an′ə mā′tid) adj., 1. lively. *After a slow start, the party became quite animated.* 2. made to look alive. *The child laughed at the animated cartoon.*

animation (an′ə mā′shən) n., 1. act of animating or the state of being animated; liveliness; briskness. *He read the story with animation.* 2. process by which film cartoons are prepared. *The Disney studio has mastered the art of animation.*

animosity (an′ə mos′i tē) n., active enmity; hatred or ill-will manifested in active opposition; malice; hostility. *There was personal animosity between the two prizefighters.*

animus (an′ə məs) n., 1. basic disposition or attitude. *His gloomy animus damped the meeting.* 2. hostility; animosity. *His animus made him refuse the attempt at reconciliation.*

annals (an′əlz) n., yearly recording of events; historical records. *The novelist researched the annals of the period.*

anneal (ə nēl′) v.t., to strengthen or toughen, usually by heating then cooling. *They prepared to anneal the order of steel.*

annihilate (ə nī′ə lāt′) v.t., to reduce to nothing; destroy. *The fire annihilated the forest.*

annotate (an′ō tāt′) v.t., to comment or remark upon, esp. in notes. *The editor began to annotate the manuscript.*

annoy (ə noi′) v.t., to be hateful, troublesome, or vexatious; disturb; harass. *His persistence began to annoy her.*

annual (an′yoo əl) n., 1. a publication issued yearly, such as a sports annual. 2. a plant or animal whose natural term of life is one year or one season. *The* *marigold is an annual.* adj., pertaining to a year; yearly. *The company issued its annual report.*

annuity (ə nōō'i tē, ə nyōō'-) n., periodical payment of money, amounting to a yearly fixed sum. *Her father left her a small annuity.*

annul (ə nul') v.t., to void; annihilate; nullify. *They sought to annul the impromptu marriage.*

anoint (ə noint') v.t., to consecrate, esp. a king, priest, or prophet, with oil or any unctuous substance. *They began to anoint her queen.*

anomaly (ə nom'ə lē) n., anything that deviates from the norm; irregularity. *She didn't understand the anomaly in the cycle.*

anonymous (ə non'ə məs) adj., 1. withholding of a name. *The author preferred to remain anonymous.* 2. lacking distinction or character. *She wore an anonymous brown raincoat.*

antagonist (an tag'ə nist) n., one who engages another in combat or argument; opponent; adversary. *His antagonist wouldn't concede the point.*

antagonize (an tag'ə nīz') v.t., 1. to act against. *She didn't mean to antagonize his tribal feeling.* 2. to incur anger of; provoke. *She began to antagonize the other players with her arrogance.*

ante (an'tē) n., 1. in poker, the stake or bet deposited in the pool by each player before drawing new cards. *The ante was one dollar.* 2. prefix meaning before, either in place or time, as in *antechamber, antedate, antebellum.*

antecedent (an'ti sēd'ənt) n., 1. person or thing that precedes, esp. as influential or causative factor. *The conversation was the antecedent to their merger.* 2. word or word group replaced or referred to by another. *The antecedent of her allusion was unclear.* adj., coming before in time, place, rank, or logical order; preceding. *He held the antecedent claim to the estate.*

antediluvian (an'tē di lōō' vē ən) n., one who lived before the Flood. *The chairman is antediluvian!* adj., 1. before

the biblical Flood. *Noah was an antediluvian patriarch.* 2. belonging to very ancient times; antiquated, primitive. *She harbored several antediluvian ideas.*

antenna (an ten'ə) n., 1. one of two sensitive appendages projecting from the head of arthropods. *The ant sensed the terrain through its antennae.* 2. apparatus for sending and receiving radio and television signals. *The storm blew down the antenna.*

anterior (an tēr'ē ər) adj., 1. situated in front or forward. *The first class seats were in the plane's anterior section.* 2. going before; preceding; antecedent. *Her anterior beau tried to prevent her marriage.*

anteroom (an'tē rōōm', -rŏŏm') n., small room serving as waiting area or entrance to another larger room. *The messenger cooled his heels in the anteroom.*

anthem (an'thəm) n., celebratory or laudatory song or hymn. *The band played the national anthem.*

anthology (an thol'ə jē) n., collection of selected literary works. *He bought an anthology of modern poetry.*

anthropomorphic (an'thrə pə môr'fik, -pō-) adj., pertaining to anthropomorphism. *The man had an anthropomorphic view of his dog.*

anthropomorphism (an'thrə pə môr'fiz əm, -pō-) n., ascription of human attributes to nonhuman objects or concepts. *Anthropomorphism gave mythological gods human form.*

antibiotic (an'ti bī ot'ik, -bē-, an'tē-, -tī-) n., substance produced by fungi or bacteria that inhibits or kills other microorganisms. *Penicillin is an antibiotic.*

antibody (an'ti bod'ē, an'tē-) n., protein produced in the body to combat and provide immunity to a specific antigen. *The body generates antibodies to combat harmful microorganisms.*

antic (an'tik) n., outrageous caper. *The antic got him suspended from school.* adj., extremely funny, gay, frolicsome. *Her antic performance delighted the audience.*

anticipate (an tis′ə pāt′) v.t., 1. to realize beforehand; foresee; expect. *He anticipated that point in his opponent's argument.* 2. to look forward to. *We anticipated good weather for the trip.*

anticlimax (an′ti klī′maks) n., 1. in literature or drama, abrupt transition to less serious or more trivial tone or event. *Their reunion was an anticlimax to the tragedy.* 2. closing event that is notably less important than events preceding. *Her remarks provided an anticlimax to the President's bombshell.*

antidote (an′ti dōt′) n., something that counteracts injurious effects or influences. *The child was given an antidote for the snake bite.*

antihistamine (an′ti his′tə mēn′, -min) n., any of several compounds used to relieve cold and allergy symptoms. *An antihistamine will relieve the discomfort of hay fever.*

antipasto (an′ti pä′stō, -pas′tō; *It.* än′tē päs′tô) n., appetizer consisting of assorted meats, vegetables, and cheese. *The antipasto was a meal in itself.*

antipathy (an tip′ə thē) n., aversion; distaste; repugnance. *They looked with antipathy on his foul scheme.*

antipodes (an tip′ə dēz′) n., two places on the surface of the globe diametrically opposite to each other; region on the opposite side of the globe. *The North Pole and the South Pole are antipodes.*

antiquated (an′tə kwā′tid) adj., grown old; obsolete or obsolescent; old-fashioned. *They tried to repeal the antiquated law.*

antique (an tēk′) n., 1. any relic or object from considerably earlier period. *She collects colonial antiques.* 2. by U.S. customs law, artwork, furniture, etc., predating 1830. *The antique came from George Washington's study.* adj., pertaining to an antique. *It was an antique antimacassar.*

antiquity (an tik′wi tē) n., 1. ancient times. *The custom originated in antiquity.* 2. character of being ancient. *Her family tree describes great antiquity.*

antiseptic (an′ti sep′tik) n., something

that destroys or inhibits the microorganisms of disease; disinfectant. *He bathed the wound with an antiseptic.* adj., 1. pertaining to an antiseptic. *She applied an antiseptic dressing on the cut.* 2. scrupulously clean. *She keeps the bathroom antiseptic.* 3. sterile; impersonal. *He considered the all-white living room too antiseptic.*

antisocial (an′tē sō′shəl, an′tī-) adj., 1. adverse to social intercourse or sociality. *The antisocial man avoids parties.* 2. opposed to social order, or the principles upon which society is ordered. *Their program seems to include some antisocial principles.*

antithesis (an tith′i sis) n., 1. rhetorical juxtaposition of opposites. *He discussed the antithesis of love and hate.* 2. second element in such a juxtaposition. *Hate is the antithesis of love.*

antonym (an′tə nim) n., word carrying an opposite meaning. *"Life" is the antonym of "death."*

anxiety (aṅg zī′i tē) n., apprehension; disturbance; uneasiness. *His anxiety grew as the exam date approached.*

anxious (aṅgk′shəs, aṅg′-) adj., full of anxiety; greatly troubled; worried. *He was anxious about the doctor's diagnosis.*

apace (ə pās′) adv., quickly; at a quick pace; speedily. *The weeds grew apace despite heavy mulching.*

apathetic (ap′ə thet′ik) adj., characterized by apathy; having or exhibiting little or no emotion. *The voters remained apathetic despite the lively campaign.*

apathy (ap′ə thē) n., lack of feeling or excitement; indifference. *Voter apathy was manifested by the small turnout.*

apéritif (ä per′i tēf′, ə per′-; *Fr.* A pā Rē tēf′) n., alcoholic beverage taken before a meal to stimulate the appetite. *She finished her apéritif and began her salad.*

aperture (ap′ər chər) n., hole, gap, or chasm; passage or perforation. *The lens aperture needed adjustment.*

apex (ā′peks) n., tip, point, or summit of

anything; highest point. *The pitcher was at the apex of his career.*

aphorism (af'ə riz'əm) n., definition or concise statement of a principle; axiom; maxim; saying. *She embroidered the aphorism on a sampler.*

aphrodisiac (af'rə diz'ē ak') n., something that excites sexual desire. *Champagne acts as an aphrodisiac.* adj., pertaining to aphrodisiacal effect. *They sought the aphrodisiac drug from the witch.*

apiary (ā'pē er' ē) n., place where bees are kept; bee house containing a number of bee hives. *He gathered honey from his apiary.*

aplomb (ə plom', ə plum') n., self-assurance; poise. *She accepted their applause with great aplomb.*

apocalypse (ə pok'ə lips) n., 1. (cap.) Judeo-Christian prophecy of cataclysm in which God will destroy evil forever and raise the righteous to a messianic kingdom. *The Apocalypse is the subject of the Book of Revelation.* 2. any cataclysm. *He survived the apocalypse of the fire bombing.*

apocryphal (ə pok'rə fəl) adj., of doubtful authorship or authenticity; non-canonical. *Many tales of the old West are apocryphal.*

apoplexy (ap'ə plek'sē) n., sudden loss or impairment of consciousness and voluntary motion, caused by rupture of a blood vessel in the brain; stroke. *He died of apoplexy.*

apostate (ə pos'tāt, -tit) n., one who abandons his or her religion or other loyalty. *He became an apostate when he left the Church.*

apostle (ə pos'əl) n., one who is sent on foreign missions, esp. to preach religious doctrine; missionary; disciple. *John Eliot was an apostle to the Indians.*

apothecary (ə poth'ə ker'ē) n., one who prepares and sells medicines; pharmacist. *The apothecary filled the doctor's prescription.*

apothegm (ap'ə them') n., short, pithy, instructive saying; maxim. *We groaned at the familiar apothegm.*

appall (ə pôl') v.t., to terrify; dismay. *The governor's committee was appalled at prison conditions.*

apparatus (ap'ə rat'əs, -rā'təs) n., collection of equipment or tools necessary for a particular purpose. *The apparatus was designed to purify water.*

apparel (ə par'əl) n., clothing. *The apparel oft proclaims the man.*

apparent (ə par'ənt, ə pâr'-) adj., 1. visible. *The planet became apparent at dusk.* 2. clearly understood; plain; evident. *Her distress was readily apparent.* 3. seeming, as distinct from what is true or real. *He calculated the apparent motion of the sun.*

appeal (ə pēl') n., 1. call for sympathy, mercy, aid or the like. *We must make an appeal for help.* 2. legal proceeding taken to reverse or amend a decision by a lower authority. *His appeal was denied by the higher court.* v.t., to petition a higher court. *We will appeal this case.* v.i., 1. to take to a higher court. *Our client wants us to appeal.* 2. to request corroboration, vindication, help, or sympathy from another; entreat. *She had to appeal to her father for the loan.* 3. to attract; please. *The idea appeals to me.*

appease (ə pēz') v.t., to pacify; soothe; conciliate. *The ministers tried to appease their angry monarch.*

appeasement (ə pēz'mənt) n., act of appeasing, or the state of being appeased; pacification. *The diplomats worked for appeasement of hostilities.*

appellate (ə pel'it) adj., pertaining to appeals; having the authority to review the decision or judgment of another court. *The appellate court overturned the lower court's ruling.*

append (ə pend') v.t., to attach or add as an accessory; annex; affix. *He wanted to append a note with the gift.*

appendage (ə pen'dij) n., 1. subordinate attached part of anything. *A finger is an appendage.* 2. something added to a principal or greater thing; addition. *The porch is the newest appendage to the house.*

appendectomy (ap'ən dek' tə mē) n., surgical excision of the vermiform appendix. *They performed an emergency appendectomy on him.*

appendix (ə pen'diks) n., 1. in anatomy, a process, prolongation, or projection such as the vermiform appendix. *His appendix was severely inflamed.* 2. addition to a document or book. *The appendix includes substantial data.*

appetizer (ap'i tī'zər) n., morsel of food or short drink served before a meal to whet the appetite. *She served oysters as an appetizer.*

appetizing (ap'i tī'ziñg) adj., exciting the appetite; giving a relish for food. *The aroma was extremely appetizing.*

applaud (ə plôd') v.t., to praise or show approval of by clapping the hands. *The audience began to applaud.* v.i., to praise in any way, as by words or actions; commend; approve. *I applaud your integrity.*

appliance (ə plī'əns) n., device or tool, esp. one run by electricity and used in the home. *He uses the appliance to chop vegetables.*

applicable (ap'lə kə bəl, ə plik'ə-) adj., capable of being applied; having relevance; pertinent. *The warranty is applicable to parts only.*

appoint (ə point') v.t., 1. to assign to a post or office. *The president will appoint a new cabinet.* 2. to fix, name, or determine by authority or upon agreement. *They will appoint a new time for the meeting.* 3. to provide with what is requisite or needed; furnish. *We will appoint the lobby with plants.*

appointee (ə poin tē', ap'oin tē') n., one who is appointed to an office or post. *The new appointee was sworn in.*

apportion (ə pōr'shən, ə pôr'-) v.t., to divide and assign according to some rule; distribute proportionally; allot. *He wanted to apportion his estate equally among his children.*

appraisal (ə prā'zəl) n., act of appraising; estimation of value or worth. *She submitted her appraisal of the house.*

appraise (ə prāz') v.t., 1. to set an official price upon; estimate the value of. *We asked him to appraise the antique.* 2. to estimate generally, in regard to quality, service, size, weight, etc. *We appraise each teacher monthly.*

apprehend (ap'ri hend') v.t., 1. to take into custody; make prisoner; arrest by legal warrant or authority. *The police will apprehend the thief.* 2. to perceive; grasp the meaning of; understand. *She tried to apprehend the cryptic warning.*

apprehensive (ap'ri hen'siv) adj., in a state of apprehension or fear; feeling alarm; fearful; anxious. *She was apprehensive about moving.*

apprentice (ə pren'tis) n., one who is formally or informally beginning instruction in a trade or skill; novice. *The mason showed his apprentice how to mix the mortar.*

apprise (ə prīz') v.t., to give verbal or written notice to; inform; advise. *He apprised his father of his plans.*

approbation (ap'rə bā'shən) n., act of approving or commending; assenting to something as proper or praiseworthy. *He sought the approbation of his peers.*

appropriate (*adj.* ə prō'prē it; *v.* ə prō'prē āt') adj., suitable; fit; proper; apt. *The film was not appropriate for a child.* v.t., 1. to set apart for or assign to a particular purpose or use. *The company will appropriate money for a party.* 2. to take for any use; confiscate; take. *The bank will appropriate the property.*

approve (ə prōōv') v.t., 1. to pronounce good; think or judge well of; admit the propriety or excellence of; commend. *I approve your choice.* 2. to sanction officially; ratify authoritatively; pass. *Congress will narrowly approve the bill.*

approximate (*adj.* ə prok'sə mit; *v.* ə prok'sə māt') adj., almost exact, accurate, or complete. *The approximate weight of this ship is 42 tons.* v.t., to compute the value, quantity, or degree of. *He tried to approximate the amount of water remaining.*

appurtenance (ə pûr'tᵊnəns) n., that

which appertains or belongs to something else; appendage; accessory. *He sold the shop and its appurtenances.*

a priori (ä′prī ōr′ī, -ôr′ī, ä prē ōr′ē, -ôr′ē, ä′prē ōr′ē, -ôr′ē) adj., from the former; from that which precedes; hence, from antecedent to consequence, or from cause to effect. *His entire proposal was based upon a priori reasoning.*

apt (apt) adj., 1. possessing the qualities necessary or proper for a certain purpose or end; fit; suited. *It was an apt title.* 2. inclined; predisposed; disposed; prone. *He is apt to lose his temper.* 3. prompt; quick; unusually intelligent. *The apt pupil caught on quickly.*

aptitude (ap′ti tōod′, -tyōod′) n., readiness in learning; talent; quickness to understand. *She has an aptitude for math.*

aquarium (ə kwâr′ē əm) n., glass tank, or series of glass tanks, containing water in which aquatic animals and plants are kept. *The aquarium houses 567 species of fish.*

aquatic (ə kwat′ik, ə kwot′-) adj., pertaining to water; living in or frequenting the water. *The aquarium has many species of aquatic animals.*

arable (ar′ə bəl) adj., fit for plowing or tillage. *Arizona has relatively little arable land.*

arbiter (är′bi tər) n., someone chosen by the interested parties in a controversy to decide their differences; one who decides points at issue; arbitrator; referee; umpire. *Labor and management ageed upon an arbiter.*

arbitrary (är′bi trer′ē) adj., 1. not regulated by rule or law; determinable as occasion arises; subject to individual will or judgment; discretionary. *I resent your arbitrary decision that we leave the party early.* 2. uncontrolled by law; using or abusing unlimited power; despotic; tyrannical. *He wielded unconstitutional arbitrary power.*

arbitrate (är′bi trāt′) v.t., to submit to or settle by arbitration. *They agreed to*

arbitrate the contract dispute. v.i., to act as arbiter. *He was asked to arbitrate in the dispute.*

arbitration (är′bi trā′shən) n., hearing and determination of a case between disputing parties by an arbiter. *The strike was settled by arbitration.*

arcade (är kād′) n., long arched passageway; covered avenue, esp. one lined with shops. *We window-shopped in the arcade.*

archaeology (archeology) (är′kē ol′ə jē) n., scientific study of the remains of past civilizations. *After the dig she decided to major in archaeology.*

archaic (är kā′ik) adj., old or old-fashioned; antiquated; obsolete. *Shakespeare's work is full of archaic words.*

archetype (är′ki tīp′) n., original pattern after which a thing is made; prototype; model. *The archetype of this engine is in the museum.*

architect (är′ki tekt′) n., one who designs and supervises construction of buildings. *A prominent architect designed their home.*

archives (är′kīvz) n., public documents and records; also place where such material is stored. *The old treaty is preserved in the town's archives.*

arctic (ärk′tik, är′tik) adj., pertaining to the North Pole or the northern polar regions. *She was dressed for frigid arctic temperatures.*

ardent (är′dənt) adj., passionate; affectionate; zealous; intense; fervent. *Romeo was an ardent lover.*

ardor (är′dər) n., warmth or heat, as of the passions and affections; eagerness; intensity. *Her coldness did not allay his ardor.*

arduous (är′jōo əs or, esp. Brit., är′dyōo-) adj., difficult; laborious. *Unloading the truck was an arduous task.*

argue (är′gyōo) v.t., to state the pros and cons. *The debaters argued the question for two hours.* v.i., 1. reason for or against something. *The president will argue for passage of the bill.* 2. to dispute; quarrel. *They began to argue heatedly.*

argument (är'gyə mənt) n., 1. reasoned statement of a position. *It is her argument that a merger is inappropriate at this time.* 2. act of arguing. *He apologized for starting the argument.*

aria (är'ē ə, âr'ē ə) n., in opera or oratorio, a solo melody or song. *The first act ends with a soprano aria.*

arid (ar'id) adj., 1. dry; parched. *They irrigated the arid field.* 2. lifeless; dull; listless. *He tired of the arid conversation.*

aristocracy (ar'i stok'rə sē) n., governing body or select class of hereditary nobles. *The queen chose her attendants from the aristocracy.*

aristocrat (ə ris'tə krat', ar'i stə-) n., member of the aristocracy; noble. *The aristocrat considered trade beneath him.*

armada (är mä'də, -mā'-) n., fleet of warships. *The English repulsed the Spanish Armada in 1588.*

armistice (är'mi stis) n., temporary suspension of hostilities by mutual agreement; truce. *The Christmas armistice ends tomorrow.*

armor (är'mər) n., 1. any covering worn for protection against offensive weapons. *The old armor weighs 100 pounds.* 2. protective metal plate or sheathing. *The artillery shell did not pierce the tank's armor.*

aroma (ə rō'mə) n., agreeable odor; pleasant fragrance. *We smelled the delicious aroma of baking bread.*

aromatic (ar'ə mat'ik) adj., giving out an aroma; fragrant; sweet-scented. *The gardenia is very aromatic.*

arouse (ə rouz') v.t., to excite into action or motion; awaken. *Don't arouse her suspicion.*

arraign (ə rān') v.t., 1. to call a prisoner before a court to answer an accusation. *He arraigned her at the district court house.* 2. to call into question for faults, before any tribunal; accuse or charge in general. *The tribunal will arraign the finance minister.*

arrangement (ə rānj'mənt) n., 1. style or way in which things are put in order. *The flower arrangement was lovely.* 2. preparation. *We have made arrangement for your trip.* 3. scoring of a musical piece for voices or orchestra. *The chorus sang a new arrangement of "Summertime."*

arrant (ar'ənt) adj., 1. notorious. *We were warned about the arrant latecomer.* 2. unmitigated; confirmed. *He is an arrant coward.*

array (ə rā') v.t., 1. to place or put in order. *They tried to array all his awards on the wall.* 2. to deck or dress. *She arrayed the child in black velvet.* n., 1. orderly collection or assemblage, esp. a body of soldiers. *The troops were in full battle array.* 2. imposing display. *They mounted a dazzling array of antique clocks.* 3. dress; apparel. *She appeared in shabby array.*

arrears (ə rērz') n., that which is behind in payment; outstanding. *His rent is six months in arrears.*

arrest (ə rest') n., seizure or capture, esp. legal. *His arrest took place without struggle.* v.t., 1. to stop; slow; inactivate. *They tried to arrest the progress of the disease.* 2. to seize, esp. by legal authorities. *They can't arrest the foreign diplomat.*

arrogant (ar'ə gənt) adj., exaggerated in opinion of one's own worth or importance; overbearingly proud; haughty. *The arrogant man looked contemptuously at us.*

artery (är'tə rē) n., 1. one of a system of membranous, elastic vessels or tubes that carry blood from the heart to all parts of the body. *The pulmonary artery carries blood to the lungs.* 2. main channel or route in any system. *The freeway is the city's main traffic artery.*

articulate (v. är tik'yə lāt'; adj. är tik'yə lit) v.i., 1. to utter clearly distinct syllables or words. *Please articulate distinctly.* 2. to pronounce; enunciate. *He tried to articulate his feeling.* adj., 1. clear; distinct; able to express oneself clearly and aptly. *The debater is very* *articulate.* 2. jointed. *The leg is an articulate limb.*

artifact (är′tə fakt′) n., anything made or modified by human workmanship. *Archaeologists discovered the intriguing artifact.*

artifice (är′tə fis) n., 1. cunning deception; trick; crafty ruse; artful contrivancy. *The con man's artifice relies on human greed.* 2. inventiveness. *The poem uses artifice delightfully.*

artificial (är′tə fish′əl) adj., 1. man-made; synthetic. *Dacron is an artificial fiber.* 2. made to imitate or substitute for that which is real or natural. *Artificial flowers filled the lobby.*

artifi′cial insemina′tion, introduction of sperm into the uterus through artificial means. *Many farm animals are bred by artificial insemination.*

artillery (är til′ə rē) n., 1. large-caliber guns designed to fire heavy shells or rockets; cannons. *The artillery was brought to the front.* 2. science of gunnery. *The cadets studied artillery.* 3. section of the army specializing in the use of such guns. *He served in the artillery.*

artisan (är′ti zən) n., one skilled in an art or trade; craftsman. *The artisan gave a demonstration of his craft.*

artistic (är tis′tik) adj., pertaining to art; characterized by or in conformity with art or with an art. *She admired the artistic flower arrangement.*

artless (ärt′lis) adj., 1. free from guile, craft, or stratagem; ingenuous. *He knew the artless child spoke the truth.* 2. unskillful. *The artless sampler showed little promise.*

ascend (ə send′) v.t., 1. to move upward; climb; rise. *They will ascend the mountain today.* 2. to rise or proceed from inferior to superior, from mean to noble, etc. *Bolingbroke will ascend the throne.* 3. to slope upward. *The road ascends the mountain from east to west.*

ascertain (as′ər tān′) v.t., to make sure of; determine, esp. by trial, examination, or experiment. *The x-ray will ascertain the extent of the injury.*

ascetic (ə set′ik) n., one who lives an ascetic life, esp. one who retires from worldly occupations to engage in pious exercises; hermit; recluse. *The ascetic lived in a bare cell.* adj., practicing special acts of self-denial as a religious exercise; severe; austere. *The ascetic fare left her still hungry.*

ascribe (ə skrīb′) v.t., to attribute; impute; assign, as to a cause or source. *He ascribed his success to hard work.*

aseptic (ə sep′tik, ā sep′-) adj., free from the germs of disease, fermentation, or putrefaction; uncontaminated. *Surgery requires aseptic conditions.*

asexual (ā sek′shoo əl) adj., 1. having no sex or sexual organs; neuter. *Her asexual garb allowed her to pass as a boy.* 2. produced by other than sexual processes, as in cell-division, budding, etc. *Some plants propagate by asexual reproduction.*

ashen (ash′ən) adj., consisting of or resembling ashes; ash-colored. *The corpse was ashen.*

asinine (as′ə nīn′) adj., 1. pertaining to an ass. *He had an asinine voice.* 2. stupid; obstinate. *Her asinine remark embarrassed us.*

askance (ə skans′) adv., 1. sidewise, esp. out of the corner of the eye; obliquely. *She looked at him askance.* 2. to regard with disapproval, distrust, or scorn. *The old woman looked askance at their short skirts.*

askew (ə skyoo′) adv., in an oblique position; awry; out of the proper position or arrangement; crooked. *The jostling of the crowd knocked his hat askew.*

aspect (as′pekt) n., 1. countenance; look or particular appearance; air. *The city has an entirely different aspect at night.* 2. point or consideration. *The senator forgot that aspect of the bill.*

asperity (ə sper′i tē) n., roughness or ruggedness of temper; bitterness; harshness. *He chided the girl with asperity.*

aspersion (ə spûr′zhən, -shən) n., defamation. *They tried to cast aspersions on her integrity.*

asphyxiate (as fik′sē āt′) v.t., to make

unconscious or kill by depriving of necessary oxygen. *The smoke began to asphyxiate the firemen.*

aspirant (ə spī³r′ənt, as′pər ənt) n., one who aspires; one who seeks advancement, elevation, or preference. *The senatorial aspirant waited for the returns.*

aspiration (as′pə rā′shən) n., 1. act of aspiring or desiring to achieve; ambition. *It was her aspiration to finish medical school.* 2. act of breathing. *The aspiration of frigid air left her throat sore.*

aspire (ə spī³r′) v.i., to have a goal, ardent wish, or desire; be ambitious. *She aspires to a career in the theater.*

assail (ə sāl′) v.i., to assault; attack violently. *The gang assailed the old shopkeeper.*

assassinate (ə sas′ə nāt′) v.t., to kill or attempt to kill by surprise or secret assault. *The group plotted to assassinate the minister.*

assault (ə sôlt′) n., 1. violent attack. *They mounted an assault upon the fortress.* 2. in law, an unlawful attack or an attempt or threat of such an attack. *She was charged with assault.* 3. rape. *She was afraid to report the assault.*

assay (n. ə sā′, as′ā; v. ə sā′) n., 1. sample assayed. *The assay contains 80% mica.* 2. results or data obtained from assaying. *The assay was incomplete.* v.t., to analyze an ore or metallic compound to determine its metallic components or other characteristics. *The miner hired a chemist to assay the ore.*

assemblage (ə sem′blij) n., collection of individuals or particular things. *It was an assemblage of great minds.*

assemble (ə sem′bəl) v.t., 1. to collect in one place or body; bring or call together; convene. *The guide assembled the climbers for a briefing.* 2. to fit together. *The child tried to assemble a model airplane.* v.i., to meet or come together; congregate. *The students will assemble in the auditorium.*

assent (ə sent′) n., consent; concurrence; acquiescence; approval. *The board sought our unanimous assent.* v.i., to agree; acquiesce; concur. *The board must assent to our proposal.*

assert (ə sûrt′) v.t., to maintain or defend by words or actions; state as true; affirm; declare; aver. *The prisoner continues to assert his innocence.*

assertion (ə sûr′shən) n., 1. act of stating something as true. *The prosecutor challenged the defendant's assertion.* 2. unsupported statement or affirmation. *His assertion proved to be false.*

assertive (ə sûr′tiv) adj., tending to confident asserting; aggressive. *The assertive salesman convinced us to buy.*

assess (ə ses′) v.t., 1. to estimate the value or amount of as a basis for taxation. *He assessed our estate at a million dollars.* 2. to set, fix, charge, or levy a certain sum upon, by way of tax. *The club will assess each member ten dollars.* 3. to determine; evaluate; judge. *The captain will assess the damage.*

assessment (ə ses′mənt) n., tax levied upon a person or property. *He paid the assessment on his property.* 2. official valuation of property, profits, or income for purposes of taxation. *He appealed his property assessment.* 3. judgment; evaluation. *His assessment of the enemy's firepower proved accurate.*

asset (as′et) n., 1. valuable thing or quality. *Charm was her best asset.* 2. property, goods, or right of action applicable to the payment of one's debts; wealth. *The house was his biggest asset.*

assiduous (ə sij′ōō əs) adj., diligent; unremitting; persevering. *The assiduous worker finished first.*

assign (ə sīn′) v.t., 1. to apportion; distribute; allot. *We will assign you a new locker.* 2. to select for a duty or office. *I will assign him to the midnight watch.* 3. to attribute. *They assigned the cause of the fire to faulty wiring.*

assimilate (ə sim′ə lāt′) v.t., to incorporate; take in; digest; absorb. *The cloth did not assimilate the dye evenly.*

assistance (ə sis′təns) n., help; aid; succor. *She offered her niece financial assistance.*

associate (n., adj. ə sō′shē it, -āt′, -sē-;

v. ǝ sō′ shē āt′, -sē-) n., 1. partner or comrade. *My associate will join us later.* v.t., 1. to keep company with; accompany; join. *She plans to associate with them no longer.* 2. to connect one thing with another. *He began to associate money with worth.* adj., not of the highest rank; secondary or subordinate. *She is an associate professor at Cornell.*

association (ǝ sō′sē ā′shǝn, -shē-) n., 1. act of associating. *We dislike her association with the youth.* 2. state of being associated. *His association with the firm ended yesterday.* 3. group organized for a common purpose. *They belong to an association that helps the elderly.* 4. process of mentally or intuitively connecting ideas or sensations. *I still associate fall with going back to school.*

assonance (as′ǝ nǝns) n., repetition of vowel sounds. *The poet made an effective use of assonance.*

assorted (ǝ sôr′tid) adj., consisting of selected kinds. *The assorted cargo included spices and building materials.*

assortment (ǝ sôrt′mǝnt) n., collection of assorted things. *The table held an assortment of dishes.*

assuage (ǝ swāj′) v.t., to soften or lessen; allay; ease. *He tried to assuage her grief.*

assume (ǝ soōm′) v.t., 1. to take for granted or without proof. *We must assume his integrity.* 2. to take upon one's self; undertake. *She will assume responsibility for her work.*

assumption (ǝ sump′shǝn) n., 1. act of taking for granted, or supposing without proof; supposition. *His assumption proved to be unjustified.* 2. a taking upon one's self; undertaking. *His unlawful assumption of power caused a week of rioting.*

assurance (ǝ shoōr′ǝns) n., 1. positive declaration intended to give confidence; pledge. *He offered his assurance of my quick recovery.* 2. freedom from timidity; confidence; self-reliance. *She played with assurance and dignity.*

asterisk (as′tǝ risk) n., symbol (*) used arbitrarily, as a mark of classification, to refer to a pertinent note, or to indicate an omission. *An asterisk referred the reader to the marginal note.*

asteroid (as′tǝ roid′) n., any of the thousands of small objects lying between the orbits of Mars and Jupiter; also called planetoids. *The astronomers studied the asteroid.* adj., starlike. *The ornament was asteroid in shape.*

astigmatism (ǝ stig′mǝ tiz′ǝm) n., blurred vision caused by an abnormal curvature of the refracting surface of the eye. *Glasses will correct his astigmatism.*

astonish (ǝ ston′ish) v.t., to strike or impress with sudden fear, wonder, surprise, or admiration. *His talent will astonish you.*

astound (ǝ stound′) v.t., to astonish; strike dumb with amazement. *The news astounded him.*

astray (ǝ strā′) adv., out of the right way or proper place. *Poor directions caused them to go astray.*

astride (ǝ strīd′) adv., with one leg on each side, esp. with the legs wide apart. *He sat astride a big chestnut mare.*

astringent (ǝ strin′jǝnt) n., something with an astringent effect. *A styptic pencil is an astringent.* adj., 1. causing constriction or puckering. *The astringent lotion is a skin toner.* 2. austere. *The astringent atmosphere of the dining hall matched the tasteless food.*

astronaut (as′trǝ nôt′) n., one who participates in space travel. *The astronaut prepared for her first flight.*

astronomer (ǝ stron′ǝ mǝr) n., one who is versed in astronomy. *The astronomer lectures at the planetarium.*

astronomical (as′trǝ nom′i kǝl) adj., 1. pertaining to astronomy. *The astronaut studied the astronomical data.* 2. extremely large. *The singer attracted an astronomical following.*

astronomy (ǝ stron′ǝ mē) n., science of the heavenly bodies. *Space research contributes largely to the study of astronomy.*

astute (ǝ stoōt′, ǝ styoōt′) adj., of keen perception or discernment; cunning;

sagacious. *The astute lawyer discovered the precedent.*

asunder (ə sun′dər) adv. (or adj.), in or into a divided state; into separate parts; in pieces; split apart. *The expanding ice split the rock asunder.*

asylum (ə sī′ləm) n., 1. institution that cares for physically or mentally afflicted patients, orphans, etc. *She lives at an asylum for the blind.* 2. inviolable shelter; protection from pursuit or arrest; sanctuary. *The fugitive found asylum in the church.*

asymmetrical (ā′sə met′ri kəl) adj., not symmetrical; unsymmetrical. *The artist experimented with asymmetrical composition.*

atheism (ā′thē iz′əm) n., doctrine that there is no God; denial of the existence of God. *Atheism is a disbelief in the existence of God.*

atlas (at′ləs) n., bound map collection. *We traced our route on the atlas.*

atmosphere (at′məs fēr′) n., 1. gaseous envelope surrounding the earth; air. *The meteor burned when it entered the earth's atmosphere.* 2. moral, emotional, or intellectual environment. *The atmosphere was very solemn.*

atom (at′əm) n., 1. smallest particle of matter. *Atoms of hydrogen and oxygen combine to make water.* 2. anything extremely small; minute quantity. *He doesn't have an atom of sense.*

atomic (ə tom′ik) adj., pertaining to atoms or to atomic energy. *The United States developed the first atomic power plant.*

atonement (ə tōn′mənt) n., satisfaction or reparation given for wrong or injury. *Money could not supply atonement for the injury.*

atrocious (ə trō′shəs) adj., 1. extremely heinous, criminal, or cruel; monstrous; enormously or outrageously wicked. *The atrocious crime shocked the town.* 2. very bad; execrable. *We groaned at her atrocious pun.*

atrocity (ə tros′i tē) n., specific act of extreme heinousness or cruelty. *They were executed for their part in the atrocity.*

atrophy (a′trə fē) n., wasting away of the body, or part of it, owing to malnutrition, disease, or lack of exercise. *He suffered progressive muscular atrophy.* v.i., to waste away. *The tail gradually shrinks and atrophies.*

attaché (at′ə shā′ or, esp. Brit., ə tash′ā; Fr. A TA shā′) n., one attached to an embassy in a country other than one's own. *We met with the British attaché in Washington.*

attain (ə tān′) v.t., to reach, achieve, or accomplish; acquire; gain. *She deserves to attain her goals.*

attempt (ə tempt′) n., 1. effort; endeavor. *His attempt to set a new speed record failed.* 2. attack or assault. *She was arrested for the attempt on his life.* v.t., to endeavor to perform; try. *He will attempt to set a new speed record.*

attendant (ə ten′dənt) n., one who attends or waits on another; servant. *We tipped the parking lot attendant.* adj., concomitant; accompanying. *He accepted her with her attendant financial woes.*

attentive (ə ten′tiv) adj., 1. alert; intent; heedful. *She is an attentive listener.* 2. assiduous in ministering to the comfort of others; polite; courteous. *He was attentive to the ladies.*

attenuate (ə ten′yōō āt′) v.t., 1. to make thin or slender; reduce in thickness. *The wasting illness attenuated his arm.* 2. to lessen in complexity or intensity; weaken; rarify. *Pasteur discovered how to attenuate the rabies virus.*

attest (ə test′) v.t., 1. to affirm or authenticate, esp. by signing. *Two witnesses must attest your marriage.* 2. to manifest. *He attested his hatred in the attack.* v.i., to bear witness; testify. *We will attest at his trial.*

attire (ə tīʳr′) v.t., to dress; clothe; array, esp. in richness. *They will attire her in designer originals.* n., clothes; apparel. *Formal attire was required.*

attitude (at′i tōōd′, -tyōōd′) n., 1. meaningful posture or position of the body. *The guard dog was frozen in an attitude of watchfulness.* 2. disposition; point of view; way of regarding something. *He has a defeatist attitude.*

attorney (ə tûr′nē) n., one legally empowered to act on behalf of another; lawyer. *His attorney began his summation of the case.*

attribute (*n.* a′trə byōot′; *v.* ə trib′yōot) n., characteristic or distinguishing trait. *Power is an attribute he intends to acquire.* v.t., to ascribe; impute; consider as belonging or as due; assign. *She can attribute her success to hard work.*

attrition (ə trish′ən) n., 1. act of wearing away by rubbing; friction. *The stones had been worn smooth by attrition.* 2. any gradual wearing down or weakening, esp. through exhaustion of supplies and loss of personnel. *Disease and famine made it a war of attrition.* 3. decline in the number of members in an organization owing to resignations, deaths, retirements. *Attrition reduced the department from ten to seven workers.*

attune (ə tōon′, ə tyōon′) v.t., to tune; make accordant. *Her eyes began to attune themselves to the dim light.*

atypical (ā tip′i kəl) adj., not typical; uncharacteristic; unusual. *The atypical cloud formation worried us.*

audacity (ô das′i tē) n., 1. boldness; daring. *His audacity in the battle won him a medal of honor.* 2. effrontery; presumptuous impudence. *He had the audacity to come uninvited.*

audible (ô′də bəl) adj., capable of being heard; perceivable by the ear. *The audible drip kept me awake.*

audit (ô′dit) v.t., 1. to examine methodically an account or accounts. *The I.R.S. will audit your tax return.* 2. to attend a course without receiving or expecting to receive academic credit for it. *I will audit a course in economics.*

audition (ô dish′ən) n., trial performance intended to evaluate the performer's skill or suitability for a particular job. *More than seventy actors performed at the audition.* v.i., to perform on a test basis for a particular role or job; try out. *We will audition for the comedy spot.*

auditorium (ô′di tōr′ē əm, -tôr′-) n., large hall or theater designed to hold an audience. *The film was shown in the auditorium.*

auditory (ô′di tōr′ē, -tôr′ē) adj., pertaining to hearing or to the sense or organs of hearing. *The explosion damaged her auditory nerve.*

augment (ôg ment′) v.t., to increase; enlarge in size or extent; add to. *He will augment his income by tending bar at night.*

augur (ô′gər) v.i., to betoken; portend; presage; foreshadow. *The mishap augured ill for their undertaking.*

august (ô gust′) adj., inspiring reverence and admiration; majestic; magnificent; imposing. *They knelt before the august figure of their king.*

au revoir (*Fr.* ō Rə VWAR′; *Eng.* ō′rə vwär′) parting phrase meaning "until we meet again"; good-bye. *They bid each other au revoir.*

auspices (ô′spi siz) n., sponsorship; endorsing agency or institution; patronage. *The plant sale was under the auspices of the garden club.*

auspicious (ô spish′əs) adj., betokening success; favorable; promising. *The critics raved over her auspicious debut.*

austere (ô stēr′) adj., 1. stern; severe; harsh. *We trembled under his austere look.* 2. severely simple; unadorned. *Her austere apparel enhanced her natural beauty.*

authentic (ô then′tik) adj., real, genuine. *You cannot contest the authentic will.*

authenticate (ô then′tə kāt′) v.t., to prove or establish as genuine. *The curator will authenticate the painting.*

authoritative (ə thôr′i tā′tiv, ə thor′-) adj., 1. having authority; entitled to credence or obedience. *He published an authoritative economic theory.* 2. having an air of authority; peremptory; dictatorial. *They resented his dogmatic and authoritative manner.*

authority (ə thôr′i tē, ə thor′-) n., 1. power or right to command or act. *No one questioned the king's authority.* 2. person or persons exercising power or command. *They appealed to the chief authority of the school.* 3. something or someone deferred to or cited for support, defense, or expertise. *He found scriptural authority for his view.*

authorize (ô'thə rīz') v.t., to give authority, warrant, or legal power to someone or for something. *The governor authorized the emergency fund.*

autobiography (ô'tə bī og'rə fē, -bē-) n., self-written biography or memoir. *The president began his autobiography.*

autocracy (ô tok'rə sē) n., unlimited authority over others, invested in one person; government of an absolute monarch. *Government under the czars was an autocracy.*

autocrat (ô'tə krat') n., 1. one who rules as by inherent right, unrestricted; absolute sovereign. *The emperor called himself "the autocrat of all the Russias."* 2. one who is invested with or assumes unlimited authority in any relation. *His daughter called him an unreasonable autocrat.*

autograph (ô'tə graf', -gräf') n., something handwritten, esp. a manuscript or a signature. *The autograph sold for $500.* v.t., to handwrite or sign. *She will autograph her book for you.*

automatic (ô'tə mat'ik) n., machine or device that operates automatically, esp. a revolver. *He fired his automatic at the retreating thief.* adj., 1. more-or-less involuntary; reflex. *His automatic response was "thank you."* 2. unconscious; mechanical. *Criticism often triggers an automatic defensiveness.* 3. having self-regulating or self-operating ability. *The automatic change machine was out of quarters.*

automaton (ô tom'ə ton', -tən) n., 1. self-operated machine, or one actuated so that it can carry on for a time with the aid of an external impulse. *A mechanical rocking horse is an automaton.* 2. one whose actions are purely involuntary or mechanical. *The monotony of his work has made him an automaton.*

autonomous (ô ton'ə məs) adj., inde-

pendent in government; self-governing. *The former colony is now autonomous.*

autonomy (ô ton'ə mē) n., right or power of self-government, whether by a community or an individual. *The manager wanted greater autonomy for his department.*

autopsy (ô'top sē, ô'təp-) n., dissection and inspection of a dead body to discover the cause of death. *The autopsy revealed death by poisoning.*

auxiliary (ôg zil'yə rē, -zil'ə-) n., person or thing that helps or aids. *The auxiliary visited the elderly patients.* adj., 1. helping; supporting. *We thanked her for her auxiliary work.* 2. secondary; subordinate. *The auxiliary power is on.*

avail (ə vāl') n., advantage; profit; benefit. *His pleas were to no avail.* v.t., to be of value, use, or profit. *We availed ourselves of all the hotel's services.*

available (ə vā'lə bəl) adj., ready; at hand. *The new product is now available.*

avalanche (av'ə lanch', -länch') n., 1. fall or sliding down of a mass of snow, rock, or ice from a mountain slope. *The avalanche buried the campsite.* 2. sudden large amount. *The avalanche of paperwork caused her late hours at the office.*

avant garde (ə vänt'gärd', ə vant'-; *Fr.* A vän gÄRd') n., innovators, esp. in the creative fields, whose collective work is seen as a new movement; vanguard. *The avant garde often provokes controversy.*

avarice (av'ər is) n., inordinate desire for wealth; greediness. *Avarice motivated the gambler.*

avenge (ə venj') v.t., to take revenge on; deal with revengefully. *He vowed to avenge his father's murder.*

averse (ə vûrs') adj., reluctant; disinclined; loath. *He was averse to the prospect of moving.*

aversion (ə vûr'zhən, -shən) n., dislike; antipathy. *He had an aversion to hard work.*

avert (ə vûrt') v.t., 1. to turn away. *Avert your eyes from the eclipse.* 2. to ward off; prevent from happening. *The negotiations must avert the strike.*

aviary (ā′vē er′ē) n., large cagelike building or enclosure in which birds are kept. *The buzzard perched just under the top of the aviary.*

avid (av′id) adj., eager; enthusiastic; zealous. *She was an avid hockey fan.*

avocation (av′ə kā′shən) n., subordinate or occasional occupation; hobby. *His avocation evolved into a business.*

avoirdupois (av′ər də poiz′) n., system of weight in which one pound contains sixteen ounces. *Avoirdupois is used to determine the weights of all commodities except gems and precious metals.*

avow (ə vou′) v.t., to declare openly; admit; confess; acknowledge. *Let me avow my admiration for your work.*

await (ə wāt′) v.t., to wait for; look for or expect. *We will await our guests upstairs.*

awe (ô) n., fear mingled with admiration, reverence, or exaltation. *They stood in awe of his regard.* v.t., to strike with reverential fear, respect, or profound admiration. *The majestic beauty of the Alps will awe you.*

awesome (ô′səm) adj., inspiring awe. *The avalanche was an awesome sight.*

awkward (ôk′wərd) adj., 1. ungraceful; ungainly; clumsy. *The awkward girl bumped into the table.* 2. unwieldy. *They tried to move the awkward piano.* 3. difficult to deal with; trying. *She tried to get out of the awkward situation.*

awry (ə rī′) adj., turned or twisted toward one side; not in a straight or true direction or position. *The fall knocked his hat awry.* adv., amiss. *Things often go awry when you're in a hurry.*

axiom (ak′sē əm) n., principle or proposition universally accepted as being true; self-evident truth; maxim. *She recalled the old axiom that birds of a feather flock together.*

axis (ak′sis) n., imaginary line about which a rotating body, such as the earth, turns. *The earth turns around its axis once in a twenty-four-hour period.*

azure (azh′ər, ā′zhər) n., sky. *He longed to soar through the azure.* adj., resembling the clear blue color of the sky. *He looked deep into her azure eyes.*

Bb

babble (bab′əl) n., foolish, meaningless, and/or excessive utterance. *The babble of their guests filled the room.* v.i., to chatter incoherently or to excess. *The child began to babble excitedly.* v.t., to thoughtlessly reveal information. *She had babbled the news before she realized it.*

bacchanal (bä′kə näl′, bak′ə nal′, bak′ə nəl) n., drunken revelry; orgy. *The fraternity was suspended for sponsoring the bacchanal.*

bacillus (bə sil′əs) pl. -cilli, n., one of several rod-shaped bacteria. *Many bacilli are parasites.*

backward (bak′wərd) adj., lacking in development or refinement. *The backward man was confused by the fingerbowl.* adv., toward the back, or in reverse order. *Her sweater was on backward.*

bacteria (bak tēr′ē ə) n., any of the microorganisms of the class Schizomycetes. *Intestinal bacteria are essential to digestion.*

bacteriology (bak tēr′ē ol′ə jē) n., science that studies bacteria. *Bacteriology has applications in medicine, agriculture, and industry.*

badger (baj′ər) n., any of several burrowing mammals common in the Northern Hemisphere. v.t., to harass; annoy. *The boys badgered him for the candy.*

badinage (bad′ə näzh′, bad′ə nij) n., banter. *The coffee break was spent in harmless badinage.*

baffle (baf′əl) n., plate, screen, or other device used to obstruct or regulate flow. *The baffle snapped and the water roared through the pipe.* v.t., 1. to obstruct or control flow. *They tried to baffle the enemy supply line.* 2. to frustrate or thwart; confuse. *The question baffled him.*

bagatelle (bag′ə tel′) n., something of little value; trifle. *She kept the bagatelle as a souvenir.*

bail (bāl) n., security used to release accused person pending final legal decision. *Her bail was set at $2,500.* v.t., 1. to obtain one's release by giving bail. *The lawyer bailed out his client.* 2. to help out of trouble. *His father bailed him out with a small loan.* 3. to clear water from a boat. *He had to bail to keep from sinking.*

bailiff (bā′lif) n., 1. British legal official who serves writs and makes arrests; officer of some U.S. courts. *The bailiff escorted the prisoner.* 2. estate or farm manager. *The bailiff kept detailed account books.*

bailiwick (bā′lə wik) n., 1. jurisdiction of a bailiff. *His bailiwick was more peaceful than his colleague's.* 2. one's area of expertise. *Her bailiwick was Russian ballet.*

baker's dozen (bā′kərz duz′ən) n., thirteen; derives from tradition of adding one extra count to a dozen baked goods. *The spaniel delivered a baker's dozen of pups.*

balance (bal′əns) n., 1. device used for determining weight. *The balance settled at exactly five pounds.* 2. equilibrium; stasis. *The gymnast lost her balance and fell.* 3. portion left over; remainder. *The balance was due in two weeks.* v.t., to bring equilibrium; to settle or equalize. *Their assets and debits finally balanced.*

balderdash (bôl′dər dash′) n., nonsense. *The slogan was pure balderdash.*

baleful (bāl′fəl) adj., ominous, sinister. *The doctor's face was baleful.*

balk (bôk) n., the failure of a competitor, after making an approach, to complete a play. *The umpire called it a balk.* v.i., to refuse or shy away from. *The horse balked at the jump.* v.t., to obstruct or thwart. *The detour sign balked their progress.*

ballad (bal′əd) n., short narrative poem suitable for singing; popular song. *It was a lively rendition of the old ballad.*

ballistics (bə lis′tiks) n., science of projectiles in motion, esp. firearms. *The study of ballistics is critical in police work.*

balloon (bə lo͞on′) n., nonporous flexible receptacle made buoyant by filling with gas. *The balloon floated over the trees.* v.i., to inflate or swell up. *The gust of wind made her skirt balloon around her.*

ballot (bal′ət) n., slip of paper or other device used for casting a vote. *He pushed his ballot into the full box.* v.i., to vote. *"I must ballot before I go home,"* she remembered.

ballyhoo (bal′ē ho͞o′) n., 1. noisy demonstration or speech. *The candidate tried to speak above the ballyhoo.* 2. propaganda or promotion. *A lot of ballyhoo preceded the circus into town.*

balm (bäm) n., aromatic ointment, particularly derived from tropical evergreen trees; restorative agent. *The nurse spread balm on his wounds.*

balmy (bä′mē) adj., 1. having qualities of balm; soothing. *They breathed the balmy night air.* 2. mentally unstable. *They thought the sailor was balmy.*

bamboozle (bam bo͞o′zəl) v.t., to deceive or hoodwink. *The salesman bamboozled them into buying the car.*

banal (bān′əl, bə nal′, -näl′, ba′n^əl) adj., common; ordinary; trite. *His banal jokes got no laughs.*

bandanna (bandana) (ban dan′ə) n., large kerchief, usually brightly colored. *A bandanna covered her hair.*

bandy (ban′dē) v.t., 1. to throw to and fro, or from side to side; to exchange. *They bandy the basketball with skill.* 2. to use off-handedly, casually. *The friends bandied insults at each other.* adj., bowlegged. *He was bandy-legged after his ride.*

bane (bān) n., source of mischief or harm. *Fleas are the bane of a dog's life.*

baneful (bān′fəl) adj., causing woe or injury; pernicious. *The prison spread a baneful shadow over the town.*

banish (ban′ish) v.t., to expel from country, home, or residence, for any set length of time. *The king banished the nobleman for three years.*

banister (ban′i stər) n., handrail and supports along a staircase. *The old woman gripped the banister to keep from falling.*

bankrupt (bang̃k′rupt, -rəpt) n., one who is insolvent; one whose estate is legally administered by his creditors. *The bankrupt expected the foreclosure.* v.t., to reduce to insolvency. *His partner cheated and finally bankrupted him.*

banner (ban′ər) n., 1. piece of cloth attached to upper part of pole or staff, serving as a standard or flag for a sovereign, a country, or other unit. *The banner waved above the battle.* 2. headline in newspaper. *The banner declared war was over.* adj., outstanding, successful. *It was a banner day for the class.*

banquet (bang̃′kwit) n., festive, often ceremonious dinner; feast. *A banquet was held for the winning team.* v.i., to participate in a feast. *They banqueted on fried trout.*

banshee (ban′shē, ban shē′) n., in Gaelic folklore, female spirit whose cry warns of impending death of a family member. *The child began to wail like a banshee.*

banter (ban′tər) n., good-humored teasing. *The boy laughed at his sister's banter.* v.i., to speak playfully. *He bantered with her about her passport photo.*

baptism (bap′tiz əm) n. 1. sacramental water ritual that admits recipient into Christian community. *Her baptism was held on her first birthday.* 2. experience or ordeal that purifies, sanctifies, initiates, or names. *The role provided his baptism into repertory theater.*

baptize (bap tīz′, bap′tīz) v.t., to administer the rite of baptism. *They vowed to baptize their grandchild.*

bar (bär) n., 1. straight piece of rigid material that is longer than it is wide, used to support, or fasten, or obstruct, etc. *He used the bar to pry open the window.* 2. impediment or obstruction. *Her weakness in chemistry was a bar to her progress in medical school.* 3. submerged bank along a shore that hinders navigation. *The ship ran aground on the bar.* 4. railing in a courtroom that encloses the judge's area or that signifies where particular legal business is transacted. *The judge asked the attorneys to approach the bar.* 5. place where alcoholic drinks are sold; pub. *They stopped at the bar for a beer.* v.t., to obstruct or impede; to exclude. *We will bar him from this meeting.* prep., except for. *This is the best brand, bar none.*

barb (bärb) n., 1. sharp point projecting backward from the penetrating extremity, as in an arrow or fishhook. *He could not pull the barb out of his heel.* 2. pointed or critical remark. *She ignored his barb about punctuality.* v.t., to supply a barb. *He barbed the wire to prevent its breaking again.*

barbarian (bär bâr′ē ən) n., uncivilized person; savage. *The barbarian wiped his greasy fingers on his chest.* adj., lacking refinement; crude; rough. *His barbarian appearance appalled her parents.*

barbaric (bär bar′ik) adj., characteristic of barbarians; crude, uncivilized; unrestrained. *They uttered barbaric cries of anger.*

barbarous (bär′bər əs) adj., 1. uncivilized; crude; rude; ignorant. *His barbarous handwriting dismayed his teacher.* 2. cruel, harsh. *She deplored his barbarous treatment of the horse.*

barbiturate (bär bich′ə rāt′, -ər it; bär′bə tyo͞or′-āt, -it) n., any of several derivatives of barbituric acid, used as a sedative or hypnotic. *The doctor cautioned her about using the barbiturate.*

barely (bâr′lē) adv., only just; no more than; with nothing to spare. *They just barely made the train.*

bargain (bär′gin) n., 1. agreement between parties that settles terms of their interaction or transaction. *The bargain satisfied them both.* 2. something obtained through the process of bargaining, esp. an advantageous acquisition. *She was pleased with the bargain she found at the sale.* v.i., to negotiate terms of purchase or agreement; to haggle. *They tried to bargain with the salesman.*

baritone (bar′i tōn′) n., male singing voice falling between bass and tenor; one with such a voice. *He sang baritone in the chorus.*

barometer (bə rom′i tər) n., 1. instrument for measuring atmospheric pressure, used in weather forecasting. *The barometer registered an alarming drop in pressure.* 2. Anything that registers changes. *Her blushes provide a barometer of her feelings.*

baroque (bə rōk′; *Fr.* bA RÔk′) adj., refers to highly elaborate ornamentation and ingenious, even bizarre, art expressions prevalent during the 17th century. *The gargoyles peered down from the baroque cathedral.*

barrage (bə räzh′; *esp. Brit.* bar′äzh, bär′ij) n., 1. dam used to regulate water levels for navigation or irrigation. *The barrage was important for flood control.* 2. heavy artillery fire used to protect front-line troops. *A momentary respite was gained during the barrage.* 3. concentrated supply of writing or speech. *The nurses were given a barrage of instructions as wounded poured in.*

barren (bar′ən) n., piece of infertile land. *The barren was next to the old farmhouse.* adj., 1. producing little or no vegetation or offspring; fruitless; sterile. *The desert is not so barren as it appears.* 2. mentally unproductive; dull. *His work was barren of results or pleasure.*

barricade (bar′ə kād′, bar′ə kād′) n., fortification or obstruction impeding approach by outsiders. *The firemen set up a barricade to protect the bystanders.* v.t., to block off or obstruct with a barricade. *The students will barricade the administrators' offices.*

barrier (bar′ē ər) n., any obstruction,

material or immaterial, causing separation or hindering progress; obstacle. *The gorge formed a barrier between them.*

barrister (bar′i stər) n., in Great Britain, a lawyer who represents clients in superior court. *She engaged the leading barrister for her son.*

barter (bär′tər) n., 1. act of trading by exchanging goods. *They were forced to barter for the gas.* 2. commodity used in bartering. *She was forced to use her watch as barter.* v.t., to exchange one commodity for another as a method of trade. *She was able to barter her book for his flashlight.*

base (bās) n., 1. bottom or foundation, providing support. *It was about thirty feet from the base to the top.* 2. essential ingredient. *The soup's base was fish broth.* 3. site of headquarters of any civil, or scientific unit. *The astronauts hope to establish a moon base.* 4. in mathematics, root number, from which a mathematical table is constructed. *He used the number 4 as his base.* 5. starting place or goal in several games. *His hit brought in the runner from third base.* 6. any water-soluble compound that reacts with an acid to form a salt. v.t., to serve as a base for; establish. *He based his case on circumstantial evidence.* adj., 1. lowborn, lowly. *She was a base scullery maid.* 2. of relatively little value; inferior. *The base metal gave strength to the gold chain.*

baseless (bās′lis) adj., without any base or support. *He was angered by the baseless accusation.*

bash (bash) n., 1. festive occasion; party. *They had a big anniversary bash.* 2. blow or punch. *She got quite a bash on her head.* v.t., to hit or smash. *They had to bash in the door to get in.*

bashful (bash′fəl) adj., inclined to be shy or diffident. *He was too bashful to go in alone.*

basilica (bə sil′i kə) n., 1. building used in ancient Rome for public meetings and as a court of justice. *A loud voice was heard in the basilica.* 2. early Christian church including nave and aisles, and transept with projecting apse. 3. Roman Catholic church with ceremonial privileges. *They held the ordination in the basilica.*

basin (bā′sən) n., 1. dish or vessel with curved sides used for washing. *The basin was filled with soaking sweaters.* 2. water area that is at least partly enclosed. *They tied up at the dock in the basin.* 3. concave land surface drained by a river or the depression filled by a sea. *Standing on a hill they surveyed the gently sloping basin.*

basis (bā′sis) n., essential core or foundation; supporting principle. *The basis of religious belief is faith.*

bask (bask, bäsk) v.i., to lie in or be exposed to a pleasant warmth or other gratifying sensation. *The cat basked in the sunny windowsill.*

bas-relief (bä′ri lēf′, bas′-; bä′ri lēf′, bas′-) n., sculpture in which the figure is only slightly and partially raised from the surface. *The bas-relief depicts the serpent's tempting of Eve.*

bassinet (bas′ə net′, bas′ə net′) n., cradle or perambulator, often higher at one end. *The baby slept in the wicker bassinet.*

basso (bas′ō, bä′sō; *It.* bäs′sô) n., one who sings bass. *The low tones of the basso filled the theater.*

bastard (bas′tərd) n., 1. illegitimate child. *The king's only heir was a bastard.* 2. something of spurious origin. *The tract was a bastard for which no one would take credit.* adj., 1. illegitimate. *It was rumored she was his bastard daughter.* 2. spurious; false, or adulterated. *It was a bastard version of the famous painting.*

bastion (bas′chən, -tē ən) n., 1. fortress or rampart; fortified position or area. *The bastion withheld the enemy's attack for three weeks.* 2. stronghold, or well-fortified position. *The courts are the bastions of justice.*

batch (bach) n., quantity produced at one time. *Each batch of cookies came out different.* v.t., to make by the batch. *He* had to batch his output in order to keep track of it.

bate (bāt) v.t., lessen the force or intensity of; moderate. *The diminishing winds helped to bate the storm.*

bathos (bā′thos) n., 1. sudden banality in an otherwise elevated style or production; letdown. *The critic derided the bathos in the third act.* 2. insincere or ingenuous sentimentality. *The class snickered at the bathos in the poem.*

baton (ba ton′, bə-, bat′ən) n., 1. stick with which a leader directs a musical group. *The orchestra watched his baton.* 2. ceremonial or honorific staff. *He carried the baton with a humble dignity.* 3. hollow metal rod with rubber ends used by a drum major. *The baton flashed in her hands.* 4. object passed from one team member to another during a relay race. *She lost precious seconds retrieving the fallen baton.*

batten (bat′ən) n., thin narrow strip of wood used to seal or reinforce a joint. *The batten was replaced to keep the boat watertight.* v.t., 1. to fasten or seal with battens. *The carpenter began to batten the attic vents.* 2. to fatten. *The milk will batten the calf.* v.i., to grow fat; prosper. *Their stock portfolio began to batten.*

batter (bat′ər) n., 1. in cooking, mixture of wet and dry ingredients that is thin enough to pour or spread. *The batter was whipped until it was smooth.* 2. one who bats, esp. in baseball. *The batter stepped up to the plate.* v.t., to strike repeatedly or subject to hard use, causing damage or wear. *He had to batter down the door to rescue the children.*

bauble (bô′bəl) n., small, showy, but comparatively worthless item; trinket. *The child pocketed the cherished bauble.*

bawdy (bô′dē) adj., obscene or lewd. *The bawdy photos embarrassed the schoolboys.*

bazaar (bə zär′) n., 1. marketplace containing assorted stalls and shops. *The Turkish bazaar lived up to its reputation.* 2. temporary market dedicated to fund raising for a particular cause or institution. *The church bazaar was a huge success.*

beacon (bē′kən) n., guiding or warning signal established at a fixed point, as a lighthouse; signals of a radio transmitter used in air navigation. *The pilot recognized the beacon and circled.* v.i., to emit a signal. *She beaconed with the lantern.*

bearing (bâr′ing) n., 1. one's carriage or deportment; mien. *The heiress had an elegant bearing.* 2. act of producing offspring or fruit; product of that bringing forth. *They sampled the year's raspberry bearing.* 3. connection. *It has no bearing on the subject.* 4. parts of a machine that bear the friction. *The bearing was worn out.* 5. relative position of one point to another or to the compass. *She consulted the map to find her bearings.*

beatific (bē′ə tif′ik) adj., having an extremely happy appearance or expression; bestowing bliss. *The new father had a beatific smile.*

beatify (bē at′ə fī′) v.t., 1. to make very happy. *The child's achievement beatified her proud mother.* 2. to recognize a deceased person as worthy of special respect for having attained a "blessed" state in heaven. *The parishioners began to beatify their deceased priest.*

beatitude (bē at′ə tōōd′, -tyōōd′) n., 1. condition of extreme bliss. *The priest approached beatitude in his prayer.* 2. any of the statements beginning "Blessed are" in the Sermon on the Mount (Matt. 5:3–11). *He intoned the first beatitude.*

beau (bō) n., suitor; boyfriend. *Her beau had the first dance.*

beaux-arts (bō zär′; *Fr.* bō ZAR′) n., fine arts. *She has a master's degree in the beaux-arts.*

beckon (bek′ən) v.i., to signal or gesture for a particular reason. *The doorman beckoned to the cabdriver.* v.t., to attract without overt gesture. *The song beckons unwanted memories.*

bedazzle (bi daz′əl) v.t., to dazzle or enchant. *He danced to bedazzle the audience.*

bedizen (bi dī′zən, -diz′ən) v.t., to adorn with gaudy or vulgar finery. *The child wanted to bedizen herself in the violet scarf and rhinestone choker.*

bedlam (bed′ləm) n., place of disruption and confusion, deriving from popular name of a London insane asylum. *There was bedlam when the police entered.*

bedraggle (bi drag′əl) v.t., to soak thoroughly; drench. *The rain bedraggled the children.*

befall (bi fôl′) v.i., to happen to or to occur. *Illness can befall anyone.*

befitting (bi fit′ing) adj., appropriate; suitable. *It was a befitting occasion for a toast.*

beforehand (bi fôr′hand′, -fôr′-) adv., in advance; early; prior to. *They prepared the ingredients beforehand.*

befriend (bi frend′) v.t., to make a friend of; help or assist. *She tried to befriend the hostile child.*

befuddle (bi fud′əl) v.t., 1. to confuse or perplex. *The teacher didn't intend to befuddle his students.* 2. to stupify with intoxicants. *The wine began to befuddle her.*

beget (bi get′) v.t., 1. to procreate, usually used for fathering only. *He wanted to beget a daughter.* 2. to cause. *Her trip could beget a host of problems at home.*

begrudge (bi gruj′) v.t., to give or view without pleasure, reluctantly; to envy another's pleasure or possession. *He was said to begrudge his brother's success.*

beguile (bi gīl′) v.t., 1. to delude; deceive. *He beguiled her into a false sense of security.* 2. to convince or please by the use of charm. *They could beguile anything from the doting grandmother.*

behavior (bi hāv′yər) n., 1. manner of conducting oneself. *His behavior improved under the school's strict discipline.* 2. response to one's environment. *The experiment tested the effects of crowding on rats' behavior.*

behead (bi hed′) v.t., to cut off the head of; decapitate. *In the end they decided to behead Charles I.*

behemoth (bi hē′məth, bē′ə-) n., 1. enormous animal. *The whale has been called*

the behemoth of the sea. 2. anything especially large. *The governor's car is a shiny black behemoth.*

behest (bi hest′) n., command or order; urgent request. *They were punished at the captain's behest.*

behold (bi hōld′) v.t., to observe; gaze at. *He was forced to behold the execution.*

beholden (bi hōl′dən) adj., indebted; obliged by a favor. *He was beholden to his father.*

behoove (bi hōōv′) v.t., to be advantageous, necessary, or suitable for. *It would behoove you to study for this exam.*

belabor (bi lā′bər) v.t., to work at or on far beyond necessity. *He chose not to belabor the argument.*

belated (bi lā′tid) adj., late; delayed past appointed or usual time. *She received a belated birthday card.*

beleaguer (bi lē′gər) v.t., to besiege; surround; harass. *The beleaguered battalion surrendered.*

belfry (bel′frē) n., 1. room, tower or other enclosure containing a suspended bell. *The noise in the belfry was ear-splitting.* 2. (slang) mental faculties; head. *She had bats in her belfry.*

belie (bi lī′) v.t., to misrepresent or conceal true nature of. *Her behavior belied her story.*

belittle (bi lit′əl) v.t., to undercut, deprecate, or disparage. *She tried to belittle her boss.*

belles-lettres (bel le′tRə) French n., literature for its own sake, without practical or informative use. *He composed the belles-lettres purely for his own pleasure.*

bellicose (bel′ə kōs′) adj., belligerent; quarrelsome. *Drinking makes him bellicose.*

belligerent (bə lij′ər ənt) n., one who is engaged in recognized war. *The northern belligerent retreated.* adj., 1. quarrelsome; inflammatory; combative. *His belligerent attitude got him into trouble.* 2. waging war. *The belligerent armies met at dusk.*

bellow (bel′ō) n., loud outcry. *They heard*

an angry bellow. v.i., to yell loudly. *They had to bellow to be heard.*

bellwether (bel'weŧh'ər) n., one who takes the lead. *She became the bellwether of the movement.*

bemoan (bi mōn') v.t., to express grief, disappointment, or regret. *She could only bemoan her lost opportunity.*

bemuse (bi myōoz') v.t., to perplex or make thoughtful. *Her maneuvers bemused the traffic cop.*

benediction (ben'i dik'shən) n., invocation of blessing that closes church services, or is used for occasions such as marriage, christening, etc. *The priest offered the benediction.*

benefactor (ben'ə fak'tər, ben'ə fak'-) n., one who helps or supports; patron. *The benefactor was generous to the school.*

beneficence (bə nef'i səns) n., quality or state of doing or producing good. *The survivors needed the church's beneficence.*

beneficent (bə nef'i sənt) adj., performing acts of goodness. *The beneficent woman opened her home to the rescue workers.*

beneficial (ben'ə fish'əl) adj., advantageous; helpful; profitable. *She thanked him for the beneficial information.*

beneficiary (ben'ə fish'ē er'ē, -fish'ə rē) n., one who receives income, profit, or advantage. *She was sole beneficiary of the estate.*

benefit (ben'ə fit) n., 1. fund-raising event. *Proceeds of the benefit go to the orphanage.* 2. one's advantage or well-being. *The hard work was to his benefit.* v.t., to assist or bring advantage to. *The money was intended to benefit the children.* v.i., to gain; receive advantage. *They hoped she would benefit from the experience.*

benevolence (bə nev'ə ləns) n., 1. kindly disposition; desire to promote welfare of others. *The nurse's benevolence soothed the child.* 2. charitable gift or act of kindness. *Her benevolence enabled the camp to reopen.*

benevolent (bə nev'ə lənt) adj., characterized by benevolence, good will. *His benevolent manner endeared him to his pupils.*

benighted (bi nī'tid) adj., 1. overtaken by night or darkness. *We were benighted before we reached the inn.* 2. in moral or intellectual darkness; unenlightened. *The missionary sought to convert the benighted natives.*

benign (bi nīn') adj., of a gentle, kind disposition or aspect. *The red evening sky was a benign omen.*

bequeath (bi kwēŧh', -kwēŧh') v.t., to leave by will, to hand down. *He wanted to bequeath everything to his son.*

bequest (bi kwest') n., act of bequeathing; that which is bequeathed; legacy. *The generous bequest paid for her education.*

berate (bi rāt') v.t., to scold or chide vehemently. *He began to berate the truants.*

bereave (bi rēv') v.t., to take away from or dispossess, esp. by death. *Illness bereaved the family of their father.*

bereft (bi reft') adj., 1. left desolate by someone's death. *The bereft mother broke down at the funeral.* 2. deprived of the possession or use of something. *Divorce left him bereft of family or home.*

beriberi (ber'ē ber'ē) n., disease caused by thiamine deficiency, resulting in anemia, emaciation, and partial paralysis of the extremities. *She developed beriberi from lack of vitamin B_1.*

berserk (bər sûrk', -zûrk') adj., insane, wild; out of control. *He went berserk when he heard the news.*

beseech (bi sēch') v.t., to beg or importune. *He beseeched forgiveness for his folly.*

beset (bi set') v.t., 1. to set or place upon or within. *The orchard was beset with exotic trees.* 2. to harass or assail; surround. *The garrison was beset by the enemy.*

besiege (bi sēj') v.t., 1. to surround; lay siege to. *The marauders besieged the village.* 2. to beset or harass. *The parents began to besiege him with their demands.*

besmirch (bi smûrch') v.t., to soil; sully; defile. *The rejected suitor sought to besmirch her reputation.*

besom (bē'zəm) n., broom made of twigs. *The peasant woman shoved the cat away with her besom.*

bestial (bes'chəl, best'yəl) adj., of or like beasts; debased; inhuman. *The inmates lived in bestial surroundings.*

bestow (bi stō') v.t., to give, deposit, or confer. *The school intended to bestow the award.*

bestride (bi strīd') v.t., 1. to straddle. *The wrestler bestrode his opponent.* 2. to tower over; dominate. *The Twin Towers bestride lower Manhattan.*

bête noire (bet nwAR'; *Eng.* bāt'nwär') *French.* someone or something strongly disliked or avoided. *The tax collector was the village bête noire.*

betray (bi trā') v.t., 1. to place in the power of an enemy by disloyalty or deceit; to violate a trust. *He set out to betray the candidate.* 2. to reveal inadvertently. *Her voice betrayed her fear.*

betroth (bi trōth', -trôth') v.t., to vow to marry; affiance. *The couple was betrothed and planned to marry during the summer.*

bevy (bev'ē) n., group of animals, esp. quail; any large group. *A bevy of admiring fans surrounded him.*

beware (bi wâr') v.i., to be alert or wary; take heed. *The rescue unit had to beware of the fallen wire.*

bewilder (bi wil'dər) v.t., to perplex or confuse. *They tried not to bewilder the frightened dog.*

bewitch (bi wich') v.t., to charm; cast a spell over. *She could bewitch with her smile.*

biannual (bī an'yōō əl) adj., half-yearly, or twice a year. *The biannual meetings were well attended.*

bias (bī'əs) n., 1. prejudice or tendency. *Her bias forced her to disqualify herself.* 2. diagonal of fabric grain. *The skirt was cut on the bias.* v.t., to give prejudice to. *They tried to bias the judge in their favor.* adj., diagonal; slanting. *The bias cut fit gracefully.* adv. diagonally. *She bias-cut the knit.*

bibliography (bib'lē og'rə fē) n., description, identification, or source of writings; list containing this information. *The bibliography was valuable in her research.*

bibliophile (bib'lē ə fīl', -fil) n., lover of books or book collector. *The bibliophile enjoys browsing in the bookstore.*

bicameral (bī kam'ər əl) adj., having or pertaining to two-chambered legislature. *We have a bicameral Congress.*

bicentennial (bī'sen ten'ē əl) n., pertaining to a 200th anniversary. *The United States celebrated its bicentennial in 1976.*

biceps (bī'seps) n., 1. two-headed muscle, as of front upper arm. *He used weights to develop his biceps.*

bicker (bik'ər) v.i., to quarrel. *The sisters started to bicker.*

bicuspid (bī kus'pid) n., human premolar tooth. *The child's bicuspid was coming in.* adj., having two points. *The bicuspid valve worked well.*

bid (bid) n., 1. offer of a price. *The man's bid for the lamp was $5.* 2. announcement of intent by a card player. *She did not understand her partner's bid.* 3. effort to win or achieve something. *His bid for her hand failed.* v.i., to proffer a price or intention. *He bid too low.* v.t., to command or direct. *He bid her enter.*

bide (bīd) v.t., to continue in established manner. *He determined to bide his time until he saw the right car.* v.i., to wait. *He told her to bide in the church until 2 PM.*

biennial (bī en'ē əl) adj., every two years, or lasting for two years. *The biennial pansy flowered in the second year.*

bifocal (bī fō'kəl, bī'fō-) n., lens with two lengths of focus. *The bifocal was helpful with the work.* adj., having two focal lengths. *He peered through the bifocal lenses.*

bigamist (big'ə mist) n., one who has two spouses. *His wives accused the bigamist.*

bigamy (big'ə mē) n., illegal act of knowingly marrying one person while being already married to another. *His weakness led to bigamy.*

bigot (big'ət) n., one who is intolerant of

other beliefs or positions. *The bigot fought to exclude them from the club.*

bigoted (big′ə tid) adj., pertaining to a bigot; obstinately intolerant. *The bigoted woman snubbed the new family.*

bigotry (big′ə trē) n., condition of belligerent intolerance. *The real problem in the school was bigotry.*

bilateral (bī lat′ər əl) adj., 1. having two sides; affecting both sides. *The bilateral treaty was a relief.* 2. with symmetrical sides. *There was one flower on each side of the bilateral stalk.*

bile (bīl) n., 1. digestive fluid secreted by the liver. *They removed some bile through a catheter.* 2. susceptibility to anger; spleen. *His bile rose when he looked at the excavation.*

bilingual (bī liñg′gwəl) adj., having fluency in two languages. *The bilingual teacher helped the student.*

bilious (bil′yəs) adj., 1. pertaining to indigestion resulting from liver dysfunction. *His bilious condition kept him home.* 2. bad-natured, choleric. *The bilious sailor caused the fight.*

bilk (bilk) n., one who cheats or deceives. *The bilk was arrested for fraud.* v.t., to cheat or defraud. *The gang tried to bilk the old lady.*

bill (bil) n., 1. mouthpiece of birds or that resembling a beak in other animals, e.g. turtles. *The robin had a worm in her bill.* 2. written invoice or statement of accounts. *She was aghast at the large florist's bill.* 3. legislative enactment. *The House finally passed the bill.* 4. written advertisement of an event; entertainment scheduled. *The bill promised an interesting evening.* 5. paper money; currency. *One rarely sees a $500 bill.* v.t., 1. to prepare and present an invoice. *He promised to bill her for the lessons.* 2. to advertise or arrange for presentation of. *He wanted to bill her as a comedienne.*

billet-doux (bil′ē dōō′, bil′ā-; *Fr.* bē yä dōō′) n., love letter. *She tucked his billet-doux under her pillow.*

billiards (bil′yərdz) n., any of several table games played with a driving stick,

or cue, and small balls; pool. *Her grandfather taught her billiards.*

billow (bil′ō) n., great surge of water or other mass with appearance of big wave. *A billow of smoke came from the kitchen.* v.i., to rise or bulge in wavelike motion. *The sail began to billow in the wind.*

bimonthly (bī munth′lē) n., publication issued twice a month, or every other month. adj. occurring twice monthly, or every two months. *The bimonthly visit was a special treat.*

bind (bīnd) n., something that holds tight; place where binding occurs. *They were in a bind over the sublet.* v.t., 1. to hold fast, restrain, or confine by tying. *He had to bind the wound.* 2. to secure or obligate; legally settle. *They tried to bind the landlord to his word.* 3. to constipate. *Cheese helps to bind the intestinal tract.* 4. to put cover on and secure pages of a book. *They decided to bind it with staples.*

binge (binj) n., unrestrained indulgence or spree; wild party. *She later regretted the shopping binge.*

binocular (bə nok′yə lər, bī-) adj., pertaining to use of both eyes. *He used a binocular microscope.*

binoculars (bə nok′yə lərz, bī-) n., optical device with two eyepieces; fieldglasses. *He used the binoculars for bird watching.*

biochemistry (bī′ō kem′i strē) n., study of the chemistry of biological processes. *Biochemistry explores such processes as photosynthesis and metabolism.*

biofeedback (bi′ō fēd′bak′) n., technique of using the brain to control involuntary responses such as heartbeat by means of feedback from monitoring devices. *Biofeedback helped relieve his hypertension.*

biogenesis (bī′ō jen′i sis) n., 1. creation of life from living organisms. *Researchers study the process of biogenesis.* 2. supposition that species evolutionary history recurs during the embryonic development of an individual; recapitulation theory. *Biogenesis offers an* *explanation for the gill-like formations in the human embryo.*

biographical (bi'ə graf'i kəl) adj., pertaining to a biography. *Her birthday was listed in the biographical dictionary.*

biography (bī og'rə fē, bē-) n., history, usually written, of another person. *The letters were important in the biography.*

biology (bī ol'ə jē) n., science of life. *His interest in biology dated from that field trip.*

biome (bī'ōm) n., animal and plant community whose constitution is determined by climatic and soil conditions. *The scientist studied the tropical biome for three years.*

biopsy (bī'op sē) n., examination of fluids, tissues, or cells removed from living organism. *The biopsy proved the tumor benign.*

biped (bī ped) n., two-legged animal. *Man is a featherless biped.*

biplane (bī'plān') n., airplane with two wings, one above the other. *The biplane is an antique.*

birth (bûrth) n., 1. emergence of offspring from parent body. *He was present at his daughter's birth.* 2. lineage or extraction. *The child was of noble birth.* v.t., to bring forth offspring; to mother. *She wanted to birth a large family.*

birthright (bûrth'rīt') n., right granted by birth; heritage. *Freedom of speech is a birthright of Americans.*

biscuit (bis'kit) n., 1. soft, raised bread product, usually baked in small flats or rounds. *She spread butter and jam on her biscuit.* 2. in pottery, product after first firing and before glazing; bisque. *The biscuit was set aside for painting.*

bisect (bī sekt', bī'sekt) v.t., to divide into two parts; intersect. *They plan to bisect the field with trees.*

bison (bī'sən, -zən) n., more commonly called buffalo; large, shaggy grazing mammal with horns and fleshy hump over heavy forequarters.

bisque (bisk) n., 1. thick, often creamed, soup. *The lobster bisque was delicious.* 2. unglazed, hard-fired ceramic ware. *The bisque held up to hard use.*

bitch (bich) n., 1. female carnivore, esp. dog. *The bitch was a champion hunter.* 2. derogatory epithet, referring to unpleasant, lewd, or malicious woman. *He slapped her and called her a bitch.* v.i., (slang) to complain or nag. *He bitched about the extra work.* v.t., (slang) to botch or ruin. *She didn't mean to bitch up the tiles.*

bite (bīt) n., 1. act of biting, holding grip. *He finally got a bite on the rope.* 2. morsel of food. *She savored every bite of cake.* 3. wound caused by biting. *He scratched the insect bite.* v.t., 1. to grip, enter, or wound with teeth or similar device. *She tried to bite her assailant.* 2. to corrode, cut, or pierce. *His words managed to bite into her pride.* 3. to take the bait. *He asked if the fish were biting.*

bitheism (bī'thē'iz əm) n., belief in two gods. *Bitheism is an uncommon form of religious belief.*

biting (bī'tiñg) adj., causing sharp discomfort. *The biting frost killed the lemon trees.*

bitter (bit'ər) adj., 1. acrid or otherwise disagreeable taste. *The cider was too bitter to drink.* 2. grievous; painful; galling; resentful. *It was a bitter court battle.*

bivalve (bī'valv') n., mollusk with a two-part shell. *The clam is a common bivalve.*

bivouac (biv'ōō ak', biv'wak) n., temporary shelter; camp. *They decided to set up bivouac in the field.*

bizarre (bi zär') adj., extremely odd or unusual; weird. *The bizarre tale delighted the child.*

blackball (blak'bôl') n., small dark ball used as negative ballot. *He was sorry to see the blackball.* v.t., to reject or exclude by using blackball or similar device. *He decided to blackball the informant.*

blacken (blak'ən) v.t., 1. to make black. *They were told to blacken their faces.* 2. to besmirch; sully. *They tried to blacken her reputation.*

blackguard (blag'ärd, -ərd) n., scoundrel.

The blackguard ruined the party with his underhanded remarks.

blacklist (blak′list′) n., list of persons who are to be punished, boycotted, or otherwise shunned. *The producer was on the Hollywood blacklist.* v.t., to put a person on a blacklist, figuratively or otherwise. *He determined to blacklist the manufacturer.*

blackmail (blak′māl′) n., 1. demand for something in return for keeping a damaging secret; extortion. *The nurse resorted to blackmail.* 2. extortion payment. *The blackmail was left under a tree.* v.t., to extort something by means of intimidation or threats. *She determined to blackmail her employer.*

blade (blād) n., broad, flat part of knife, fan, propeller, etc.; leaf. *The skate blade needs sharpening.*

blame (blām) n., culpability; responsibility for wrongdoing. *He accepted the blame for the fire.* v.t., to censure or accuse of wrongdoing. *He had to blame himself for the accident.*

blanch (blanch, blänch) v.t., 1. to take the color out of; bleach. *The sun began to blanch the curtains.* 2. to scald or parboil. *She will blanch the peas prior to freezing them.* v.i., to make ashen or pale. *The sudden turbulence caused him to blanch with fear.*

bland (bland) adj., unremarkable; smooth; mild; almost tasteless. *She was bored by the bland novel.*

blandish (blan′dish) v.t., to cajole or flatter. *He intended to blandish her with gifts.*

blanket (blañg′kit) n., warming cover, usually a soft fabric. *The blanket was too small for the bed.* v.t., to cover with a blanket; cover in order to suppress or inhibit. *They tried to blanket the news media.* adj., uniform covering; universally applicable. *Her blanket statement angered the group.*

blare (blâr) n., loud roar. *She couldn't stand the blare of the radio.* v.t., to make a loud noise. *He wanted to blare it from the rooftops.*

blarney (blär′nē) n., smooth flattery. *He wasn't taken in by her blarney.*

blasé (blä zā′, blä′zā; Fr. blʌ zā′) adj., jaded, excessively bored or apathetic. *The stewardess was blasé about air travel.*

blaspheme (blas fēm′, blas′fēm) v.t., to treat irreverently; to revile. *He didn't want to blaspheme the priest.*

blasphemy (blas′fə mē) n., impious or profane behavior or words; irreverence. *The deranged man yelled words of blasphemy at the priest.*

blatant (blāt′ᵊnt) adj., 1. conspicuous; obtrusive. *The blatant error stood out in the column of figures.*

blaze (blāz) n., 1. intense fire or bright display. *The sky was a blaze of color.* 2. sudden outburst. *His blaze of anger surprised them.* 3. white mark on horse's or ox's face; trail marker on a tree or post. *He inherited the blaze on his forehead from his father.* v.t., 1. to publicize or make obvious, proclaim. *He promised to blaze her name on the marquee.* 2. to mark, particularly a trail. *They used blue paint to blaze the trail.* v.i., to flare up; burn brightly. *The campfire began to blaze in the darkness.*

bleak (blēk) adj., bare; desolate; lacking in comfort or warmth. *The casualty report was bleak.*

bleary (blēr′ē) adj., dim or weary; esp. of eyesight. *Her eyes were bleary after the exam.*

blemish (blem′ish) n., imperfection of appearance, not affecting function. *She got the pot cheaply because of its blemish.* v.t., to impair superficially; make imperfect. *The incident blemished their vacation.*

blight (blīt) n., 1. in plants, disease or injury that causes withering and death without rotting. *The blight ruined his potato crop.* 2. something that thwarts one's hopes or plans; something that impairs or ruins. *Her death was a blight on his life.* v.t., to ruin or to cause to suffer from blight. *He didn't mean to blight his son's chances.*

blighted (blī′tid) adj., deteriorated; impaired. *The blighted neighborhood seemed beyond rehabilitation.*

blind (blīnd) n., 1. something to conceal or darken, as a windowshade. *She peered through the blind.* 2. hiding place or ambush; subterfuge. *The bingo tables were merely a blind.* v.t., to render sightless. *The acid blinded him temporarily.* adj., 1. sightless. *The dog guided the blind man.* 2. prejudiced or unreasonable; using faulty reasoning or incomplete information. *He was blind to his friend's faults.* 3. having no exit. *They chased him into a blind alley.*

blindfold (blīnd'fōld') n., something that covers the eyes, obscuring vision. *The child felt the blindfold slip.* v.t., to wrap the eyes with covering material to prevent vision; obscure understanding. *Her wealth blindfolded her to his embarrassment.*

bliss (blis) n., ecstasy; great happiness. *They found bliss together.*

blithe (blīŧh, blīth) adj., easygoing; lighthearted; gay. *Her blithe disposition was endearing.*

bloat (blōt) n., one who or that which is swollen; flatulent digestive upset of some animals. *Some of his cows had the bloat.* v.t., to fill to a swelling point; inflate. *He began to bloat on the beer.*

bloc (blok) n., group of individuals, factions, parties, nations, etc. formed temporarily for a specific purpose. *Delegates from the Eastern Bloc walked out.*

blockade (blo kād') n., restrictive measure associated with war that impedes commerce and communications of hostile forces. *They had to break the enemy's blockade.* v.t., to institute an obstacle impeding commerce or communication by unfriendly force. *She tried to blockade the proposed change.*

bloomers (blōo'mərz) n., baggy short pants. *Bathing apparel has come a long way from bloomers to bikinis.*

blossom (blos'əm) n., 1. flower; bloom. *The orange blossom brightened the bouquet.* 2. stage of development analogous to flowering. *The school was the blossom of her career.* v.i., to flower; unfold; prosper. *The dancer began to blossom under his training.*

blot (blot) n., stain or blemish; disgrace. *The argument was a blot in their relationship.* v.t., 1. to stain or spot. *The leak began to blot the countertop.* 2. to soak up excess liquid. *He stopped to blot the ink.* 3. to make obscure. *He tried to blot out the memory.*

blotch (bloch) n., imperfection; stain. *She couldn't remove the blotch.*

bludgeon (bluj'ən) n., club or blunt instrument used as a weapon. *It was a dangerous looking bludgeon.* v.t., to beat with a blunt instrument. *He had to bludgeon the snake.*

blue chip (blōo' chip') n., blue poker chip assigned high value; valuable stock issue. *Her portfolio contained two blue chips.*

blue laws (blōo' lôz') n., statutes regulating commerce and recreation on Sundays; any of several religious laws in effect in colonial New England. *The blue laws were revoked.*

bluff (bluf) n., steep cliff. *The house overlooked the bluff.* v.t., to feign a better hand in cards than one is really holding. *He tried to bluff them by raising the ante.* v.i., to deter or intimidate by false display of strength. *He tried to bluff his way out of the predicament.* adj., brusque; gruff; blunt. *His bluff exterior hid a kind heart.*

blunder (blun'dər) n., awkward mistake. *His blunder cost him a friend.* v.i., 1. to commit a stupid error. *He blundered when he bought the car.* 2. to break in awkwardly; to act stupidly. *He started to blunder into the meeting.*

blunderbuss (blun'dər bus') n., 1. blunderer. *The blunderbuss embarrassed his wife.* 2. obsolete firearm. *The old man grabbed his blunderbuss.*

blunt (blunt) v.t., to make or become bluff or dull. *The hedge blunted the impact of her fall.* adj., 1. untactful; straightforward. *She was blunt to the point of rudeness.* 2. having an unsharp edge; flat; dull. *He hit it with the blunt edge of the ax.*

blur (blûr) n., something seen unclearly, as in a haze. *The view became a blur as they gained speed.* v., to obscure or make indistinct by smearing; to become confused or indistinct. *Her face began to blur in his memory.*

blurt (blûrt) v.t., to utter suddenly and spontaneously. *The girl blurted out the answer.*

bluster (blus′tər) n., 1. violent wind or commotion. *The bluster shook the trees.* 2. pompous speech. *He was full of bluster with little sense.* v.i., 1. to blow violently, as a wind. *It began to bluster and rain.* 2. to speak or behave ostentatiously and noisily. *He started to bluster through a long speech.*

boa constrictor (bō′ə kən strik′tər) n., large light brown tropical American snake, often growing to 10 feet or longer.

board (bōrd, bôrd) n., 1. piece of milled lumber. *The walnut board made a fine shelf.* 2. table filled with food; daily meals. *They received room and board for their work.* 3. group with definite responsibilities and powers. *The school board presented the budget.* v.t., 1. to come aboard. *The passengers waited to board the plane.* 2. to provide regular meals and accommodation for. *They decided to board the dog.* 3. to cover with boards. *It was time to board up the windows.*

bode (bōd) v.t., to portend or presage. *The dark sky did not bode well for the picnic.*

bodkin (bod′kin) n., 1. small dagger or stiletto. *The child tucked the bodkin into his sash.* 2. small pointed instrument for puncturing cloth; ornamental hairpin. *He pierced the belt with his bodkin.*

bog (bog, bôg) n., wet, spongy ground; quagmire or swamp. *The bog was alive with mosquitos.* v., to mire or sink into. *He started to bog down under the pressure.*

boggle (bog′əl) v.i., 1. to amaze or astonish. *They boggle the crowd with their trapeze act.* 2. to hesitate or falter. *She began to boggle in her intention.*

bogus (bō′gəs) adj., false; fake. *The bogus mustache fooled no one.*

Bohemian (bō hē′ mē ən, -hēm′ yən) n., 1. native or resident of Bohemia; language of Bohemia. 2. (l.c.) unconventional, often artistic, person or place. *The bohemian kept very irregular hours.* 3. pertaining to native of Bohemia or to unconventional character or place. *The Bohemian district attracted tourists.*

boisterous (boi′stər əs, -strəs) adj., rowdy; tumultuous; exuberant. *It was a boisterous celebration.*

Bolshevism (bōl′shə viz′əm, bol′-) n., political doctrine originated by radical Russians (1903–17), advocating seizure by force of governmental power by the proletariat. *Bolshevism is now synonymous with Soviet Communism.*

bolster (bōl′stər) n., large pillow or back cushion. *She decided to recover the bolster.* v.t., to support or reinforce. *Her story helped to bolster his intention.*

bolt (bōlt) n., 1. lightning or electrical stroke. *The bolt of electricity shocked him.* 2. bar used to lock or secure. *She checked the bolt before going to bed.* 3. roll of cloth or paper. *She carried the bolt to the salesman.* 4. to flee or dash off. *The prisoner decided to bolt from the yard.* v.t., to eat hastily. *Her hunger made her bolt her food.*

bombard (bom bärd′) v.t., 1. to attack with bombs or gunfire. *The plane began to bombard the enemy arsenal.* 2. to assail or barrage vigorously. *She began to bombard him with questions.*

bombast (bom′bast) n., pompous or pretentious speech or writing. *He delivered his warning with great bombast.*

bona fide (bō′nə fīd′, bon′ə-; bō′nə fī′dē) Latin adj., genuine; authentic. *It was a bona fide Tiffany lamp.* 2. sincere or earnest. *She made a bona fide effort to please them.*

bonanza (bə nan′zə, bō-) n., outstanding lode of gold or silver; an exceptional profit. *The dividend was an unexpected bonanza.*

bonbon (bon′bon′; Fr. bôɴ bôɴ′) n.,

chocolate or fondant candy. *She proffered a large box of bonbons.*

bondage (bon′dij) n., servitude; slavery. *His bondage was to last seven years.*

bonnet (bon′it) n., 1. hat. *Her Easter bonnet was lovely.* 2. British term for hood of car. *He lifted the bonnet to check the oil.*

bon vivant (bôN vē väN′). *French.* n., one who enjoys an epicurean lifestyle. *The restaurateur was a true bon vivant.*

booby hatch (boo′bē hach′) n., (slang) insane asylum. *His wife committed him to the booby hatch.*

bookkeeper (book′kē′pər) n., one who keeps accounts. *Her bookkeeper kept orderly accounts.*

boomerang (boo′mə rang′) n., 1. curved throwing stick that returns after being thrown. *The boomerang made a whipping sound.* 2. remark or act that has damaging repercussions. *To his dismay, the accusation was beginning to become a boomerang.*

boor (boor) n., crude or insensitive person. *The boor insulted my guests.*

boorish (boor′ish) adj., rude and insensitive. *His boorish manners irritated them.*

boost (boost) n., 1. upward push. *She gave her a boost over the wall.* 2. an increase. *The contribution was a boost to the campaign.* 3. encouraging or helpful act. *The compliment was a boost to her spirits.* v.t., 1. to push upward. *He tried to boost her over the wall.* 2. to increase or accelerate. *He tried to boost the engine's power.* 3. to support actively. *He wanted to boost the product on TV.*

bootleg (boot′leg′) n., 1. upper part of boot. *He grabbed his bootleg and pulled.* 2. contraband liquor or other goods. *They were caught with a truckload of bootleg.* v.t., to make, sell, or handle contraband items. *The gang bootlegged enormous quantities of cigarettes.*

booty (boo′tē) n., spoils of war or piracy; rich gain. *They lived for a year on the booty.*

bore (bōr, bôr) n., 1. hole. *The carpenter ants dug a small bore in the board.* 2. interior cylindrical cavity. *He was looking down the bore of her gun.* 3. measurement of a hole; gauge. *It had a 3″ bore.* 4. one who causes boredom or tedium. *The bore made us restless.* v.t., 1. to drill or dig with rotary device. *They bore deep into the earth.* 2. to cause irritating tedium. *He didn't want to bore his audience.*

boredom (bōr′dəm, bôr′-) n., condition of weariness or tedium. *Racing helped alleviate his boredom.*

borough (bûr′ō, bur′ō) n., municipal corporation. *New York City comprises five boroughs.*

botany (bot′ᵊnē) n., science of plant biology. *The nursery owner used to teach botany.*

botch (boch) n., mess or patchwork. *He made a botch of the breakfast.* v.t., to repair badly. *He tried not to botch the painting.*

bothersome (both′ər səm) adj., irritating; troublesome. *The bothersome noise kept them awake.*

bough (bou) n., tree limb. *The swing hung from the bough.*

bouillabaise (bool′yə bäs′, bool′yə bäs′; *Fr.* boo yA bes′) n., fish stew. *She chose flounder and perch for the bouillabaise.*

bouillon (bool′yon, -yən; *Fr.* bool yôN′) n., clear seasoned broth. *The invalid asked for some bouillon.*

bound (bound) n., jump or bounce. *He was over the wall in one bound.* v.t., to circumscribe or limit. *She tended to bound her children too closely.* v.i., to leap or bounce. *She bounded over the fence.* adj., 1. confined or enclosed. *The yard was bound by the fence.* 2. obliged or constrained. *She was bound to pay off the loan.* 3. determined. *They are bound to reach Boston today.* 4. constipated. *The child was bound up for a week.* 5. destined. *The singer is bound for greatness.*

boundary (boun′də rē, -drē) n., outside perimeter or limit of. *The boundary was a river.*

boundless (bound′lis) adj., without boundaries or limits. *The sky was a boundless blue.*

bountiful (boun′tə fəl) adj., abundant; generous. *It was a bountiful harvest.*

bounty (boun′tē) n., 1. generosity or munificence. *His bounty included a large turkey.* 2. yield or produce. *The bounty of the orchard surprised them.* 3. reward or prize. *The bounty was raised to $10,000.*

bouquet (bō kā′, bōō-) n., 1. bunch of flowers. *They brought a bouquet of roses to the hospital.* 2. aroma or fragrance. *The wine had a delicate bouquet.*

bourgeois (bōōr zhwä′, bōōr′zhwä; *Fr.* bōōR zhwA′) adj., 1. pertaining to the middle class. *It was a mostly bourgeois neighborhood.* 2. having tendencies toward mediocre respectability. *She could not tolerate her complacent, bourgeois neighbor.*

bourgeoisie (bōōr′ zhwä zē′; *Fr.* bōōR zhwA zē′) n., social group composed of the middle class. *The ambassador's roots are in the bourgeoisie.*

bourn (bōrn, bôrn, bōōrn) n., 1. boundary; limit. *The hiker reached the bourn of the marked trail.* 2. goal; destination. *His bourn was the top of the mountain.*

Bourse (bōōrs) n., stock exchange in Europe. *The American broker visited the Paris Bourse.*

bout (bout) n., 1. active period; attack. *She suffered another bout of poison ivy.* 2. contest or session. *The championship bout was a sellout.*

bovine (bō′vīn, -vin, -vēn) n., cow or other animal of the ox family. *Hindus consider the bovine sacred.* adj., 1. of or relating to a member of the ox family. *The bovine animals drew near.* 2. cowlike. *The heavy girl has a bovine appearance.*

bow (bou *n.* 1, 2; *v.;* bō *n.* 3, 4, 5) n., 1. inclination of the head or body betokening greeting or submission. *He gave her an elaborate bow.* 2. front of a boat or ship. *The waves crashed over the bow.* 3. knot with loops. *The present*

had a big red bow on it. 4. device for discharging arrows. *The arrow flew from the bow.* 5. rod used to play a stringed instrument. *He held the bow poised over the violin.* v.i., 1. to bend the head or body in meaningful manner. *He bowed in courtly greeting.* 2. to submit. *He was forced to bow to her orders.* v.t., to crush or overwhelm with weight. *The news bowed him with grief.*

bowdlerize (bōd′lə rīz′, boud′-) v., to expurgate by altering or omitting parts considered to be vulgar or immoral. *The Victorian edition bowdlerized Romeo and Juliet.*

boycott (boi′kot) n., act or condition of boycotting. *The boycott achieved lower prices.* v.t., to refuse to deal with, usually by a group, as a means of influencing or pressuring. *They decided to boycott the parking garage.*

bracket (brak′it) n., 1. projection from wall designed to support or strengthen. *They hung the plant from the bracket.* 2. symbol used to enclose parenthetical material. *The translation appeared in brackets.* 3. classification or niche. *They were in a high tax bracket.* v.t., 1. to enclose in brackets. *She decided to bracket the information.* 2. to classify or distinguish. *He bracketed him right away as a liberal.*

braggadocio (brag′ə dō′shē ō′) n., 1. one who brags. *The braggadocio embarrassed his son.* 2. pompous, conceited, or boastful manner or speech; bombast. *The prizefighter was full of braggadocio.*

braggart (brag′ərt) n., one who brags or boasts. *The braggart annoyed everyone.*

branch (branch, bränch) n., natural offshoot of a plant stem, body of water, or other main axis. *He worked at the Chicago branch.* v.i., to grow out of or divide up central body. *She wanted to branch into sales.*

brandish (bran′dish) v.t., to shake or otherwise exhibit aggressively. *The cook brandished his spoon at the impatient waiter.*

brash (brash) adj., impetuous; unrestrained; self-assertive; uncomfortably sharp. *The teacher sought to control the brash boy.*

brassy (bras′ē, brä′sē) adj., 1. pertaining to brass. *Her hair had a brassy tint.* 2. flashy or impudent. *Her brassy manner offended them.*

bravado (brə vä′dō) n., swaggering, pretentious bravery. *He tried to hide his fear with bravado.*

brawl (brôl) n., loud fight or uproar. *He cut his lip in the brawl.* v.i., to engage in a noisy fight or quarrel. *They began to brawl over the tickets.*

brawn (brôn) n., muscular strength. *He was all brawn and no brain.*

brazen (brā′zən) adj., 1. having characteristics of brass. *The brazen vase glowed in the light.* 2. defiant; immodest. *The brazen girl spat at him.* v.t., to face defiantly. *She had to brazen their disapproval.*

brazier (brā′zhər) n., 1. worker in brass. *The brazier will exhibit his brass lamps.* 2. pan for holding burning coals. *She filled the brazier with coals from the kitchen fire.* 3. wire-grill utensil for holding food over an open fire. *The scouts grilled hot dogs in a brazier.*

breach (brēch) n., opening, gap, or break; legal, moral, or social violation. *It was a breach in etiquette.* v.t., 1. to cause an opening or break. *They managed to breach the fortress.* 2. to violate. *He was afraid to breach the contract.* v.i., whale's leap from the water. *The sperm whale began to breach.*

breadth (bredth, bretth) n., width or scope. *He searched the breadth of the inlet.*

break (brāk) n., 1. result of breaking. *The break could be repaired.* 2. sudden or noteworthy interruption, as a break of subject or from work. *The carpenters took a coffee break.* 3. place where word division occurs. *He decided to make the break in the word before the last syllable.* 4. opening shot in billiards. *She made a good break.* 5. sudden or unexpected good luck. *The meeting was a lucky break.* v.t., 1. to rupture, tear, or otherwise separate suddenly. *Don't break the glass.* 2. to violate or renege. *She hated to break her word.* 3. to change or interrupt. *The runner had to break her pace.* 4. to disrupt or destroy. *They had to break up the rebellion.* 5. to discover or decode; to solve. *They had to break the code.* 6. to classify, divide, or separate. *They broke up into three teams.*

breakdown (brāk′doun) n., 1. failure or falling apart; collapse. *The breakdown cost them half a day.* 2. itemization. *They received a clear breakdown of the cost.*

breathless (breth′lis) adj., 1. without breath; dead. *The nurse tried to rouse the breathless woman.* 2. gasping for breath; out of breath. *The breathless runner collapsed at the finish line.* 3. still; airless; stale. *It was a breathless summer day.* 4. excited; eager. *They listened in breathless wonder.*

breathtaking (breth′tā king) adj., exciting; stunning. *It was a breathtaking likeness.*

breed (brēd) n., group of plants or animals apparently related by ancestors and similarities. *She belonged to a rare breed of hawks.* v., to beget, to parent; to mate with. *They decided to breed her to the spaniel.*

brevity (brev′i tē) n., shortness; conciseness. *He admired the brevity of her report.*

bribe (brīb) n., surreptitious promise or payment for service or consideration. *The generous bribe got him what he wanted.* v.t., to make an illegal or immoral payment or promise in return for a service or consideration. *He tried to bribe the traffic officer.*

bric-a-brac (brik′ə brak′) n., curios; odd assorted items such as china or ornaments. *The bric-a-brac crowded the mantel.*

bridle (brīd′əl) n., 1. horse's leather and metal headgear, including reins, bit, and headpiece. *The horse shied at the bridle.* 2. restraint or control. *The trustee was* *a bridle to her impetuosity.* v.t., to restrain. *She tried to bridle her curiosity.* v.i., to react with hostility or contrariness. *She bridled at his insinuation.*

brief (brēf) n., 1. summary or outline; short report or document. *The lawyer presented his brief.* 2. short, close-fitting underpants. *He bought the new style of brief.* adj., short; concise. *They only had time for a brief chat.*

brigade (bri gād′) n., large military unit; group organized for particular purpose. *It was the hot dog brigade at last!*

brigand (brig′ənd) n., bandit; outlaw. *The brigand demanded her jewels.*

brighten (brīt′ᵊn) v., to make or become lighter, more lustrous, or happier. *The music helped to brighten their mood.*

brilliant (bril′yənt) n., diamond or other jewel with reflective facets. *The brilliant glinted in the sun.* adj., 1. sparkling; bright. *It was a brilliant sunny day.* 2. exceptionally intelligent or clever. *He was a brilliant speaker.*

brine (brīn) n., very salty water. *They preserved the fish in brine.*

brink (bringk) n., edge, margin, or border; precipice or bank. *They were on the brink of divorce.*

brisk (brisk) adj., lively, invigorating; sharp in manner. *Her tone was brisk and to the point.*

bristle (bris′əl) n., short, coarse hair or filament. *The bristles fell out of the brush.* v.i., to stand erect suddenly in fear, anger, or hostility. *He bristled at her offensive suggestion.*

bristly (brist′lē) adj., 1. consisting of or resembling bristles. *His bristly crewcut was out of fashion.* 2. easily ruffled; belligerent. *She tried to avoid arguing with the bristly clerk.*

brittle (brit′ᵊl) adj., fragile; easily crumbled or broken. *The brittle pages crumbled in her hands.*

broach (brōch) n., woman's decorative pin; brooch. *It had been her mother's broach.* v.t., 1. to open or tap into. *They finally managed to broach the keg.* 2. to make known or to discuss for first time. *She decided to broach the subject.*

broaden (brôd′ᵊn) v.t., to make wider, increase in comprehension. *The trip managed to broaden his interest.*

broad-minded (brôd′mīn′did) adj., tolerant; open to varying ideas. *She appreciated his broad-minded views.*

broadside (brôd′sīd′) n., 1. printed sheet of paper. *The broadside announced a sale.* 2. side of a ship from bow to waterline. *They tied up along the broadside.* 3. abusive attack. *The broadside alarmed the candidate.* adv., alongside; widely or at random. *The missiles fell broadside in the water.*

brocade (brō kād′) n., rich, heavy embossed silken fabric. *The brocade wallpaper matches the chair.*

brochure (brō shoor′) n., pamphlet or booklet. *The brochure described the game.*

broker (brō′kər) n., middleman or agent who negotiates purchases, sales, and other transactions. *The stock broker advised her to sell.*

bromidic (brō mid′ik) adj., dull; trite; boring. *His bromidic observations took the life out of the conversation.*

bronchial (brong′kē əl) adj., of or relating to the windpipe and its extensions (bronchi) into the lungs. *Bronchial asthma followed her allergy attack.*

brooch (brōch, brōōch) n., piece of women's jewelry; ornamental pin. *She wore the old brooch.*

brood (brōōd) n., animal young; group with similar interests or background. *They took their brood to the fair.* v.t., to incubate eggs. *The hen began to brood.* v.i., to ponder or dwell upon at length. *They didn't want him to brood over his loss.* adj., pertaining to incubation. *The brood hen only left the nest to eat.*

brothel (broth′əl, broth′-, brô′thəl, -thəl) n., house of prostitution. *The police closed the brothel.*

browbeat (brou′bēt′) v.t., to harass or oppress; bully. *She deplored the way he browbeat the child.*

browse (brouz) n., act of browsing. *The shoppers had a useful browse.* v.i., to graze or skim. *They let the cows browse in the field.*

bruise (brōoz) n., contusion or discolored wound that does not break the skin but involves small ruptured blood vessels. *She got a bruise when she fell.* v.t., to cause or receive a contusion. *She didn't always bruise so easily.*

bruit (brōot) v.t., to sound abroad or widely. *He wanted to bruit the news all over town.*

brunt (brunt) n., impact or force of attack. *He took the brunt of her accusations.*

brusque (brusk; *esp. Brit.* brōosk) adj., abrupt or harsh. *She is often brusque when interrupted.*

brutal (brōot'əl) adj., cruel; rough; brutish. *Her brutal words shocked him.*

buccaneer (buk'ə nēr') n., pirate or unscrupulous adventurer. *The buccaneer captured the Spanish ship.*

buckle (buk'əl) n., 1. metallic clasp. *His belt buckle broke.* 2. result of buckling. *They bumped over the buckle in the road.* v.t., to fasten or clasp. *They were told to buckle their seat belts.* v.i., to bend or collapse. *The bridge began to buckle.*

bucolic (byōo kol'ik) adj., rustic; rural; pastoral. *He sketched the bucolic harvest scene.*

budding (bud'ing) adj., in an early, but promising, stage of development. *The fourteen-year-old had a budding tennis career.*

budge (buj) v., to start to move. *The piano wouldn't budge.*

buff (buf) n., 1. flat yellow beige color. *The chamois was buff.* 2. nudity; bare skin. *They swam in the buff.* 3. dust cloth. *The maid carried the furniture buff.* 4. fan or booster. *She was an old-movie buff.* v.t., to polish or rub with soft material. *He liked to buff his new car.*

buffer (buf'ər) n., 1. cushion or insulator. *His jacket was a buffer against the cold.* 2. neutralizing solution. *The buffer quieted the mixture.* v.t., to insulate or protect. *The pension could not buffer her against inflation.* adj., pertaining to a buffer. *They crossed the buffer zone safely.*

buffet (*n.* 1, *v.* buf'it; *n.* 2 bə fā', bōo-; *Brit.* buf'it; *Fr.* bʏ fe') n., 1. blow by the hand. *He gave the boy a playful buffet.* 2. smorgasbord, or self-service meal; table on which food is served. *The diners lined up for the buffet.* v.t., to hit or bump into repeatedly. *The wind began to buffet the boat.*

buffoon (bə fōon') n., clown. *The drunkard acted like a buffoon.*

buffoonery (bə fōo'nə rē) n., coarse, undignified attempt at being amusing. *His buffoonery brought stares from the other diners.*

bugaboo (bug'ə bōo') n., source of fear or anxiety. *Spiders were her bugaboo.*

bugbear (bug'bâr') n., dreadful object of anxiety; goblin or specter. *The old nurse invented the bugbear.*

bull (bōol) n., 1. male bovine, esp. with sexual organs intact. *The bull was a prized breeder.* 2. in business or the stock market, one who sees or foresees favorable economic conditions. *The bull bought heavily, expecting prices to rise.* 3. papal document or decree. *The bull caused some controversy in the Church.*

bullion (bōol'yən) n., gold or silver bars or ingots; uncoined gold or silver. *Bullion is stored at Fort Knox.*

bully (bōol'ē) n., one who harasses or takes advantage of others. *The children feared the bully.* v.t., to harass or browbeat another. *He began to bully the smaller man.* adj., fine; excellent. *It was a bully evening.*

bulwark (bōol'wərk) n., fortification or support. *He was a bulwark during the crisis.* v.t., to protect with a bulwark. *He prepared to bulwark against the storm.*

bumptious (bump'shəs) adj., self-satisfied; conceited; smug and overbearing. *The bumptious peacock strutted around.*

bungle (bung'gəl) v.t., to mess up or ruin, often through clumsiness or ineptness.

He was sure to bungle the delicate repair.

bunk (bŭngk) n., 1. nonsense; humbug. *She found his claim to be nothing but bunk.* 2. a bed built on a platform. *His bunk on the ship was not as comfortable as his bed at home.*

buoyancy (boi′ən sē, bōō′yən sē) n., 1. ability to float. *It lost its buoyancy and sank.* 2. liveliness; resiliency. *Her buoyancy gave the survivors hope.*

burdensome (bûr′dᵊn səm) adj., heavy or hard to bear; oppressive. *The rules were burdensome to him.*

bureau (byōōr′ō) n., 1. chest of drawers. *The bureau was full of sweaters.* 2. administrative department. *The bureau issued her a new desk.* 3. business set up as a liaison agency. *The bureau matched up the roommates.*

bureaucracy (byōō rok′rə sē) n., system of administrative departments staffed by civil servants. *The bureaucracy was slow to respond.*

burgeon (bûr′jən) v.i., to expand or blossom. *The story began to burgeon into a novel.*

burlesque (bər lesk′) n., 1. slapstick or striptease entertainment. *The comedian got started in burlesque.* 2. caricature or imitation. *He was a burlesque of his former self.* v.t., to imitate or mock. *He tried to burlesque her walk.* adj., pertaining to burlesque. *It was a burlesque act.*

burly (bûr′lē) adj., husky; hearty. *The burly man clapped him on the back.*

burnish (bûr′nish) n., luster. *The pewter had a soft burnish.* v.t., to apply a lustrous finish. *She began to burnish her nails.*

burro (bûr′ō, bōōr′ō, bur′ō) n., a small donkey used as a pack animal.

butte (byōōt) n., sharply inclined, lone hill or small mountain. *The eagle nested on the butte.*

buttress (bu′tris) n., projecting support of a wall or building. *The flag hung from the buttress.* v.t., to support or fortify. *He had to buttress the leaning wood pile.*

buxom (buk′səm) adj., full-bosomed. *The buxom wench served ale.*

byline (bī′līn′) n., written credit for an author or reporter. *His byline appeared on the first page.*

Cc

cabal (kə bal′) n., small secret group dedicated to overthrow, esp. in politics; plotters. *The military cabal initiated the coup.* 2. secret plot, esp. for overthrow. *The king managed to discredit their cabal.*

cabala (cabbala, or cabbalah) (kab′ə lə, kə bä′-) n., 1. system of Jewish mysticism and theosophy. *The cabala advocates using a cipher to interpret Scripture.* 2. secret or esoteric doctrine. *The community looked with fear and suspicion on the mysterious cabala.*

cabinet (kab′ə nit) n., 1. advisory council to a political head, often with executive power; also, this body's advice and actions. *The Senate approved the nominee to the president's cabinet.* 2. cupboard with doors and shelves, used for storage. *The cabinet holds his stamp collection.* 3. console or case. *She refinished the TV cabinet.*

cache (kash) n., provisions or other things stored or concealed for present convenience or future use. *The trapper retrieved the cache of furs from the cave.* v.t., to put into a cache; store; secrete. *We decided to cache our valuables.*

cacophony (kə kof′ə nē) n., unpleasant, discordant sounds. *He listened to the cacophony of protest.*

cadaver (kə dav′ər, -dä′vər) n., dead body; corpse, esp. one used for dissection. *She exposed the muscles in the cadaver's right arm.*

cadaverous (kə dav′ər əs) adj., pertaining to a corpse; having the appearance of a dead body; pale; wan; ghastly. *His cadaverous face frightened the children.*

cadence (kād′ᵊns) n., measure or beat in speaking, dancing, marching, or in rhythmical movement of any kind. *The drill instructor kept the marchers in cadence.*

cadenza (kə den′zə) n., elaborate solo passage added toward the end of a concerto, or parenthetical embellishment toward the close of an aria. *The aria's final cadence seemed anticlimactic after the exciting cadenza.*

cadre (kä′drə; *Mil. usually* kad′rē) n., key group trained to assume leadership. *He selected his successor from his own trained cadre.*

caduceus (kə doo′sē əs, -dyoo′-) n., medical professional emblem consisting of a winged staff intertwined with two serpents. *The new doctor proudly fixed the caduceus to his bumper.*

caesura (si zhoor′ə, -zoor′ə, siz yoor′ə) n., pause; in poetry, pause within a line for sense or prosodic effect; in music, rhythmic dividing point. *A medial caesura is common in Old English poetry.*

cairn (kârn) n., heap of stones piled up as a memorial or landmark. *The cairn marks a Viking burial site.*

caitiff (kā′tif) adj., base; despicable; cowardly. *The caitiff informer destroyed their chance of escape.*

cajole (kə jōl′) v.t., to induce compliance through flattery, false promises, and the like; wheedle; coax. *Exeter did cajole Elizabeth with high compliments.*

calamity (kə lam′i tē) n., disaster; catastrophe, great misfortune. *The flood was a calamity for the villagers.*

calcify (kal′sə fī′) v.i., to turn into bone or bony material by the secretion or deposition of lime salts. *Some tissue began to calcify and had to be removed.*

calculate (kal′kyə lāt′) v.t., 1. to compute; reckon; count. *He began to calculate* the losses from the fire. 2. to preplan. *The effect on the customer was calculated well by the package designer.*

caliber (kal′ə bər) n., 1. diameter of the hollow inside of a cylinder, esp. the bore of a firearm. *He bought a .32 caliber gun.* 2. level or quality. *Men of his caliber do not usually make such errors.*

caliph (calif) (kā′lif, kal′if) n., title for civil and religious leader recognized as a successor to Mohammed. *The caliph accepted the gift of the costly Koran.*

calligrapher (kə lig′rə fər) n., one skilled in calligraphy. *The calligrapher inscribed the names on the diplomas.*

calligraphy (kə lig′rə fē) n., art of elegant penmanship; beautiful writing; by extension, handwriting in general. *The calligraphy enhanced the manuscript.*

calling (kô′lĭng) n., occupation; trade; vocation; profession. *He was a mason by calling.*

calliope (kə lī′ə pē, kal′ē ōp′) n., musical instrument consisting of steam whistles tuned to produce different tones. *The merry-go-round revolved to the music of a calliope.*

callous (kal′əs) adj., hard; hardened, esp. in mind or feelings; insensitive, unfeeling. *The callous man was unmoved by her tears.*

callow (kal′ō) n., unfledged; immature; juvenile. *They dismissed him as a callow prankster.*

caloric (kə lôr′ik, -lor′-) adj., 1. of or relating to heat. *The solar heat researcher checked the caloric absorption of the material.* 2. of or relating to calories. *Gelatine dessert has a low caloric content.*

calumniate (kə lum′nē āt′) v.t., to accuse falsely or misrepresent in order to defame; to slander. *Fear drove him to calumniate his opponent.*

calumny (kal′əm nē) n., knowingly or maliciously false accusation of crime, misconduct, or defect. *He sought to prevent the calumny of his bitter rival.*

camaraderie (kä′mə rä′də rē) n., good-fellowship; hearty or intimate companionship. *He enjoyed the camaraderie of army life.*

cameo (kam′ē ō) n., engravings in relief upon a gem or other material. *She wore a cameo on her index finger.* adj., small but spotlighted role or appearance. *The English actor had a cameo role in the film.*

camouflage (kam′ə fläzh′) n., concealment by deceit or disguise. *The fawn's coloring and spots provide good forest camouflage.* v.t., to conceal by deceit or disguise. *They managed to camouflage their fear with bravado.*

canaille (kə näl′; *Fr.* kA nä′yə) n., rabble; riffraff. *The demagogue played upon the baser instincts of the canaille.*

canard (kə närd′; *Fr.* kA nAR′) n., false story; hoax. *The incredible canard made the front page.*

candid (kan′did) adj., honest and frank; open and sincere; outspoken. *The child's candid refusal was disconcerting.*

candor (kan′dər) n., frankness; sincerity; openness; honesty. *His candor sometimes makes him unpopular.*

canine (kā′nīn, kə nīn′) n., 1. dog. *The canine chewed on the bone.* 2. sharp pointed tooth. *The dentist capped the chipped canine.* adj., pertaining to a dog, or to the family *Canidae,* including dogs, jackals, foxes, and wolves. *The inoculation protected the dog from canine rabies.*

canker (kaṅg′kər) n., ulcerous, cancerous, or gangrenous sore in animals or plants. *The canker marked a weak point in the tree.*

canny (kan′ē) adj., clever, cautious, and shrewd. *His canny investments reaped high profits.*

canon (kan′ən) n., 1. rule or law; standard; criterion. *She described the school canon of dress.* 2. Roman Catholic Church rule of doctrine or discipline decreed by a council or other competent authority. *The canon was observed by the Vatican.*

canonization (kan′ən ī zā′shən) n., formal act or process of declaring sainthood. *She observed the anniversary of St. Theresa's canonization.*

cant (kant) n., 1. ostentatious or insincere use of solemn or religious phraseology; insincere enthusiasm for high thoughts or aims. *Their elaborate piety is mere cant.* 2. jargon of a class, sect, or profession: used in an unfavorable sense. *The sociologists' cant obscured the simple concept.*

cantankerous (kan tang'kər əs) adj., cross; ill-tempered; waspish; contentious. *The cantankerous old man refused to sit down.*

cantata (kən tä'tə) n., lyric drama or story adapted to music and sung by a chorus accompanied by organ, piano, or orchestra. *They heard Bach's cantata Gottes Zeit.*

canter (kan'tər) n., moderate running pace of a horse; moderate or easy gallop. *He spurred his horse into an easy canter.* v.i., to gallop easily. *The horse began to canter as the trail widened.*

cantilever (kan'tªlev'ər, -tªlē'vər) n., one of two long brackets or arms projecting toward each other from opposite banks or piers, serving to form a bridge when joined together. adj., formed on the principle of the cantilever. *The harbor is spanned by a cantilever bridge.*

canto (kan'tō) n., major division of a long poem. *One canto was quoted more often than the rest of the poem.*

canvas (kan'vəs) n., dense, heavy cloth of hemp or flax notable for its strength and durability. *They packed their gear in canvas knapsacks.*

canvass (**canvas**) (kan'vəs) v.t., to investigate by inquiry to ascertain a probable result, as of an election; to survey opinion or intention. *He began to canvass the delegations to determine his candidate's strength.*

capability (kā'pə bil'i tē) n., present or potential ability. *The enemy's missile-launching capability concerned the senators.*

capacious (kə pā'shəs) adj., very large; spacious. *The capacious limousine held nine.*

caparison (kə par'i sən) n., rich and decorative clothing or equipment, usually for a horse. *The horse was decked in silver and crimson caparison.*

capillary (kap'ə ler'ē) n., tube with very small diameter, esp. one of the minute blood vessels forming a network between the arteries and veins. *A close examination revealed the ruptured capillary.* adj., pertaining to capillaries. *The teacher explained the phenomenon of capillary attraction.*

capital (kap'i tªl) n., 1. city serving as official seat of government. *The governor lives in the capital.* 2. wealth specifically represented by accumulated goods or devoted to production of goods. *The entrepreneur searched for a source of capital.* 3. upper-case letter. *The calligrapher embellished the capital.*

capitalism (kap'i tªliz'əm; Brit. also kə pit'ªliz'əm) n., economic system characterized by private or corporate ownership and a free market. *Laissez-faire is one tenet of capitalism.*

capitation (kap'i tā'shən) n., uniform tax or fee imposed per capita. *The club's capitation was waived for members' guests.*

capitol (kap'i tªl) n., building occupied by U.S. Congress in Washington, or in which a state legislature meets. *Congress meets in the Capitol.*

capitulate (kə pich'ə lāt') v.i., surrender to an enemy on stipulated terms. *At the end of three days the enemy capitulated.*

caprice (kə prēs') n., sudden and unexpected change of humor or opinion without apparent or adequate motive; whim. *She later regretted her caprice.*

capricious (kə prish'əs) adj., whimsical; impulsive; unpredictable. *The capricious man seemed ill-suited to the sober life of a banker.*

captain (kap'tən, -tin) v.t., to act as captain; command. *He captained the championship team.* n., 1. military rank between 1st lieutenant and major. *He was promoted to captain.* 2. leader. *He was the captain of the football team.*

caption (kap′shən) n., 1. heading in a book, magazine, or newspaper. *The caption attracted his notice.* 2. explanatory text appearing with photographs and illustrations. *The caption indicated the photo was taken in 1914.*

captious (kap′shəs) adj., 1. purposefully confusing in order to entrap. *The interviewer's captious questions annoyed the author.* 2. hypercritical; difficult to please. *The captious chef abhored the student's cooking.*

captivate (kap′tə vāt′) v.t., to hold; enchant by the power of one's beauty or charm; bewitch. *She captivated the young man.*

captivating (kap′tə vā′ting) adj., enchanting; bewitching. *He found her a captivating woman.*

carafe (kə raf′, -räf′) n., glass water-bottle or decanter. *They ordered a carafe of wine.*

carat (kar′ət) n., unit of weight for gems and pearls equal to 200 milligrams. *Her engagement diamond is one carat.*

carcinogenic (kär′sə nō jen′ik) adj., cancer-causing. *Certain herbicides are thought to be carcinogenic.*

carcinoma (kär′sə nō′mə) n., tumor, esp. a cancerous one. *He had the carcinoma removed.*

cardiac (kär′dē ak′) adj., of or pertaining to the heart. *The victim suffered a cardiac arrest.*

careen (kə rēn′) v.i., to lean to one side. *As it came about, the boat careened sharply.*

cargo (kär′gō) n., goods transported in a ship, airplane, or truck; freight. *The cargo was unloaded quickly.*

caricature (kar′ə kə chər, -choor′) n., satirical drawing or literary work. *The amusing caricature appeared on the editorial page.*

carnage (kär′nij) n., great destruction of men or animals by bloody violence; massacre; slaughter. *He deplored the carnage of the battle.*

carnal (kär′nəl) adj., pertaining to the flesh of the body, its passions and appetites; sensual; lustful; fleshly. *They enjoyed a carnal love affair.*

carnivore (kär′nə vōr′, -vôr′) n., carnivorous animal. *A dog is a carnivore.*

carnivorous (kär niv′ər əs) adj., flesh-eating. *The venus flytrap is a carnivorous plant.*

carouse (kə rouz′) v.i., to drink freely and noisily; revel. *They caroused until early in the morning.*

carp (kärp) v.i., to find fault with, particularly without reason; to censure. *His son began to carp at his allowance.*

carrion (kar′ē ən) n., dead body, esp. in state of putrefaction; flesh so corrupted as to be unfit for food. *The jackals fed upon the carrion.*

carrousel (kar′ə sel′, -zel′; kar′ə sel′, -zel′) n., merry-go-round. *The child loved to ride on the carrousel.*

cartographer (kär tog′rə fər) n., one who makes maps or charts. *The cartographer was hired by the atlas publisher.*

cartography (kär tog′rə fē) n., art or science of making maps or charts. *He was a master of cartography.*

castigate (kas′tə gāt′) v.t., to chastize, correct, or punish. *The wife castigated her husband for his carousing.*

caulk (kôk) v.t., to press puttylike material into seams of a vessel, or into open joints of any kind. *He caulked the windows to keep out rainwater.*

cenotaph (sen′ə taf′, -täf′) n., tomblike monument erected to someone whose remains are elsewhere. *A cenotaph was erected for those lost at sea.*

censer (sen′sər) n., vessel or cup in which incense is burned before an altar. *The priest gently swung the smoking censer.*

censor (sen′sər) n., official authorized to examine and to prevent publication of printed, published, or recorded materials that violate an established religious, moral, or political code. *The publisher protested the censor's decision.* v.t., to edit or prohibit publication of material judged offensive. *They decided to censor portions of the movie.*

censure (sen′shər) n., expression of blame or disapprobation; criticism; condemnation. *He thought the censure unjustified.* v.t., to criticize adversely, disapprove; find fault with; condemn. *We will have to censure her poor judgment.*

census (sen′səs) n., official counting of a population. *The census revealed a declining birth rate.*

centaur (sen′tôr) n., mythological creature with human head, torso, and arms but with the rest of the body that of a horse. *Some centaurs are also depicted with wings.*

centenarian (sen′tᵊnâr′ē ən) n., one who is at least one hundred years old. *They celebrated the centenarian's birthday with a party.* adj., of or pertaining to one who is at least one hundred years old. *The centenarian sailor had a treasure of sea tales.*

centennial (sen ten′ē əl) n., one-hundredth anniversary celebration. *The U.S. centennial was celebrated in 1876.* adj., 1. consisting of or lasting a hundred years. 2. occurring every hundred years. *The centennial celebration drew enormous response.*

centigrade (sen′tə grād′) adj., pertaining to the temperature scale by which the difference between the freezing and boiling points of water is divided into one hundred units (degrees). Abbr. *C. Most people find 22° centigrade a comfortable room temperature.*

centipede (sen′tə pēd′) n., any of a class of arthropods noted for the many legs (not necessarily one hundred) arranged in pairs, one pair to each segment of the body. *Tropical centipedes can be very poisonous.*

centrifugal (sen trif′yə gəl, -ə gəl) adj., flying off or proceeding from a center; radiating or moving outward from a focus or central point. *The washing machine uses centrifugal force to extract water from the clothes.*

centrifuge (sen′trə fyōōj′) n., a machine for separating matter of different densities by means of centrifugal force. *The spinning centrifuge soon separated the white blood cells from the red.*

centurion (sen tŏŏr′ē ən, -tyŏŏr′-) n., in ancient Rome, an officer commanding a century, or company of one hundred infantry; equivalent to the modern rank

of captain. *Gaius Claudius, the centurion, ordered his men to break camp at dawn.*

ceraunophobia (se rô′nə fo′bē ə) n., irrational fear of thunder and lightning. *At the first flash his ceraunophobia overcame him.*

cerebellum (ser′ə bel′əm) n., portion of the brain in back of and below the cerebrum that coordinates voluntary movements and balance. *The damaged cerebellum caused temporary vertigo.*

cerebral (ser′ə brəl, sə rē′-) adj., 1. pertaining to the brain or cerebrum. *He suffered a cerebral hemorrhage.* 2. appealing to the intellect. *The child was excluded from their cerebral discussion.*

cerebration (ser′ə brā′shən) n., thinking. *This problem requires serious cerebration.*

cerebrum (ser′ə brəm, sə rē′-) n., top and largest part of the brain. *Conscious mental processes are centered in the cerebrum.*

cervical (sûr′vi kəl) adj., pertaining to the neck, or to the cervix of the uterus. *She was checked for cervical cancer.*

cessation (se sā′shən) n., stop, rest, ceasing, or discontinuance of motion or action. *The United Nations called for an immediate cessation of hostilities.*

cession (sesh′ən) n., act or product of yielding to another; concession. *She made a graceful cession to her mother's request.*

chafe (chāf) v.t., 1. to heat or warm by friction. *They chafed his hands until the color returned.* 2. to abrade or wear away by friction; make sore by rubbing. *The tight shirt chafes my neck.* 3. to irritate; annoy; make angry. *His attitude would chafe a saint.* v.i., 1. to be abraded or worn by rubbing. *The rope chafed against the rock.* 2. to be irritated or annoyed. *They chafe at the delay.*

chaff (chaf, chäf) n., 1. husk separated during the threshing of grain. *They swept the chaff from the floor.* 2. anything worthless. *She discarded the chaff of last night's party.* 3. good-natured teasing; banter. *He missed the chaff of his friends in the car pool.* v., to tease good-naturedly. *Her friend began to chaff her about her new beau.*

chagrin (s̲h̲ə grin′) n., embarrassment due to failure, mistake, or humbling; mortification; vexation. *His chagrin at his failure was great.* v.t., to vex, mortify, disappoint through failure or mistake. *Her clumsiness began to chagrin the dancer.*

chalice (c̲h̲al′is) n., drinking cup or goblet, esp. that used in the celebration of the eucharist. *The priest raised the chalice and blessed the wine.*

challis (s̲h̲al′ē) n., lightweight wool, or wool and cotton fabric. *She wore a blouse of soft challis to the picnic.*

chamberlain (c̲h̲ām′bər lin) n., 1. one of the high officers of a European court, originally a steward of the nobleman's household. *The lord chamberlain managed the servants.* 2. treasurer; keeper of public funds. *The city chamberlain receives and disburses all monies.*

chameleon (kə mē′lē ən) n., lizardlike reptile noted for its ability to change color according to its moods or surroundings. *We almost missed seeing the chameleon on the rock.* adj., changeable; rapidly changing. *His chameleon spirits were perplexing.*

champ (c̲h̲amp) v.i., to bite repeatedly and impatiently with force. *Our horses champed at their bits.* n., short for champion.

champagne (s̲h̲am pān′) n., sparkling dry white table wine. *They celebrated with a bottle of champagne.*

chandler (c̲h̲and′lər, c̲h̲änd′-) n., 1. maker and/or seller of candles. *The chandler used beeswax for his finest candles.* 2. seller of specialized provisions and supplies. *The chandler outfitted some of this century's major safaris.*

changeling (c̲h̲ānj′liñg) n., one that is left or taken in the place of another; anything exchanged, esp. secretly, for another. *Even the mother couldn't tell the changeling from her child.*

chaotic (kā ot′ik) adj., totally confused; in turmoil; without order. *The campaign rally was chaotic.*

chapeau (s̲h̲a pō′; *Fr.* s̲h̲A pō′) n., hat. *She was complimented on her chapeau.*

chaperon(e) (s̲h̲ap′ə rōn′) n., one, usually older or married, who escorts a young, unmarried person or group in public or at social functions. *The girl resented her chaperon's omnipresence.* v.t., to act as escort. *They had agreed to chaperon the party.*

character (kar′ik tər) n., 1. features and traits that distinguish something or someone. *The Francophile extolled the unique character of Frenchmen.* 2. reputation. *Her known character resisted his attempted calumny.* 3. integrity; strength of personality. *It takes character to defend an unpopular but worthy cause.* 4. odd or eccentric person. *The short story described the outrageous character.*

charisma (kə riz′mə) n., extraordinary personal attractiveness, esp. as manifested by public figures. *He won the election largely on the basis of his charisma.*

charlatan (s̲h̲är′lə tᵊn) n., one who pretends to knowledge, skill, importance, etc.; quack; mountebank; fraud. *That charlatan tried to convince me he was a doctor.*

charnel (c̲h̲är′nᵊl) n., repository for dead bodies. *The ancient charnel was filled with bones.*

charter (c̲h̲är′tər) n., grant of rights or privileges. *The city's charter is five hundred years old.* v.t., to establish, grant, or transport by charter. *The state legislature has agreed to charter the new college.*

chary (c̲h̲âr′ē) adj., cautious; wary. *She was chary of permissive education.*

chasm (kaz′əm) n., wide gap in the earth; gulf; cleft; fissure. *He tried to leap over the chasm.*

chassé (s̲h̲a sā′; *or, esp. in square dancing,* sa s̲h̲ä′) n., type of gliding dance movement. *She added the chassé as a preparation for the jump.* v.i., to perform a chassé dance movement. *The dancers began to chassé in two rows.*

chassis (s̲h̲as′ē, -is, c̲h̲as′ē) n., frame or framework, esp. of an automobile or other vehicle. *The chassis was damaged in the accident.*

chaste (c̲h̲āst) adj., sexually pure; virtuous; innocent; modest. *The chaste young girl was embarrassed by the picture.*

chastise (c̲h̲as tīz′) v.t., to punish; discipline physically or severely. *They will chastise him for his crime.*

chastisement (c̲h̲as tīz′mənt) n., punishment, esp. corporal. *His chastisement was an example to the others.*

château (s̲h̲a tō′; *Fr.* s̲h̲ä tō′) n., large country residence; castle; manor house. *They hoped to tour the gracious château.*

chattel (c̲h̲at′əl) n., personal property; assets other than real estate, including slaves or bonded servants. *She objected to being treated as chattel.*

chauvinism (s̲h̲ō′və niz′əm) n., excessive devotion to one's country, group, or cause. *The militant feminist unconsciously exhibited the chauvinism she decried.*

chauvinist (s̲h̲ō′və nist) n., one who expresses an exaggerated, enthusiastic, unreasonable devotion to a cause or idea. *She accused him of being a male chauvinist.*

checkered (c̲h̲ek′ərd) adj., 1. varied. *Her checkered career taught her many different skills.* 2. marked off in squares. *He bought a black and white checkered suit.*

cheep (c̲h̲ēp) n., high-pitched chirping or peeping sound; squeak. *They heard the cheep of a nearby bird.* v., to utter a chirping or peeping sound; to squeak. *A cricket cheeped on the hearth.*

chef d'oeuvre (s̲h̲e d œ′vrə) *French.* n., masterpiece. *The critic calls* The Great Gatsby *Fitzgerald's chef d'oeuvre.*

chemise (s̲h̲ə mēz′) n., woman's shirtlike shift or undergarment. *She wore a loose-fitting cotton chemise.*

chemistry (kem′i strē) n., science dealing with the composition, structure, and properties of and changes in basic substances. *The most important contribution to the development of chemistry was John Dalton's atomic theory.*

chesterfield (c̲h̲es′tər fēld′) n., 1. man's dress coat with a velvet collar. *He wore his chesterfield to the opera.* 2. large, heavily upholstered, full-armed sofa. *The heirloom chesterfield was perfect in the Victorian house.*

chic (s̲h̲ēk, s̲h̲ik) n., style; easy elegance; sophistication. *Her costume expressed the height of chic.* adj., stylish; elegant; smart. *Chic fashion need not be expensive.*

chicanery (s̲h̲i kā′nə rē) n., trickery; deceit; duplicity, esp. when accomplished legally. *Their chicanery was later discovered.*

chide (c̲h̲īd) v., to reprove; rebuke; reprimand. *She began to chide her son for forgetting.*

chihuahua (c̲h̲i wä′wä, -wə) n., very small dog, native to Mexico and the southwest U.S. *She carried her chihuahua in a little basket.*

chimerical (ki mer′i kəl, -mēr′-, kī-) adj., wildly unreal; fantastical. *His chimerical imagination served the science-fiction writer well.*

chirography (kī rog′rə fē) n., art of handwriting. *A master of chirography inscribed their invitations.*

chiropodist (kī rop′ə dist′, ki-) n., one who treats minor ailments of the feet. *The chiropodist treated the painful ingrown toenail.*

chiropractic (kī′rə prak′tik) n., art of manipulating the joints, esp. the spine, as treatment for disease. *Chiropractic relieved his lower back pain.*

chivalrous (s̲h̲iv′əl rəs) adj., having traditional qualities of medieval knights, particularly gallantry, courtesy, and courage. *She appreciated his chivalrous manner.*

choleric (kol′ər ik, kə ler′ik) adj., inclined to, or expressing, anger easily; irritated; irascible; angry. *His choleric speech won him no friends.*

cholesterol (kə les′ tə rōl′) n., a fatty alcohol found in animal fats, yolk, blood, etc. *We must reduce our blood cholesterol.*

choreographer (kōr′ē og′rə fər, kôr′-) n., one who composes and arranges a dance performance. *The choreographer rehearsed the dancers.*

choreography (kōr′ē og′rə fē, kôr′-) n., art of creating and co-ordinating the movements of a dance. *Modern ballet choreography draws from a long tradition.*

chromatic (krō mat′ik, krə-) adj., 1. pertaining to color. *They admired the painting's chromatic composition.* 2. in music, involving tones normally not found in a key or scale, e.g., sharp and flat notes. *He prefers pieces composed in chromatic keys.*

chromosome (krō′mə sōm′) n., any of the rod-shaped bodies within a cell nucleus carrying the genes that determine heredity. *The X and Y chromosomes determine the sex of the individual.*

chronic (kron′ik) adj., continuing a long time; continuous; constant. *Arizona's climate improved his chronic asthma.*

chronological (kron′əloj′i kəl) adj., relating to chronology; in sequential order. *The chronological retrospective concerned the history of watercolors.*

chronology (krə nol′ə jē) n., 1. study of time; its division into regular intervals, and the order in which events occur. *Scientists working in chronology use light waves to increase the accuracy of their measurements.* 2. chart, list, or table of events in order of their occurrence. *They published a chronology of events leading to World War II.*

chrysanthemum (kri san′thə məm) n., a plant of the aster family, noted for its many-petaled flowers; also, the flower itself. *She planted a yellow chrysanthemum.*

churlish (chûr′lish) adj., 1. vulgar; illbred. *The churlish man offended his genteel secretary.* 2. difficult to deal with; surly; obstinate. *The churlish clerk deliberately antagonized the customer.*

cinnabar (sin′ə bär′) n., mercury sulfide (HgS), used as a pigment because of its brilliant red color; vermilion. *The artist used cinnabar in her sunsets.*

cipher (sī′fər) n., 1. character "0" de-

noting null quantity; naught; zero; also, any Arabic numeral. *A million is one followed by six ciphers.* 2. secret writing; code or cryptogram; also, the key to reading the code. *The message was written in a 5-digit cipher.* v.t., to use figures; compute mathematically. *We can cipher this problem without a calculator.*

circumference (sər kum′fər əns) n., boundary line, esp. of a circle. *The belt highway was built on the circumference of the city.*

circumlocution (sûr′kəm lō kyoo′shən) n., intentionally indirect or evasive use of language in speech or writing. *His circumlocution failed to obscure the truth.*

circumscribe (sûr′kəm skrīb′, sûr′kəm skrīb′) v.t., to mark out limits for; bound; confine; restrain. *It was necessary to circumscribe the toddler's play area.*

circumspect (sûr′kəm spekt′) adj., heedful of all circumstances affecting a situation; watchful; cautious; wary. *She was circumspect in her dealings with the foreign firm.*

circumstance (sûr′kəm stans′ or, esp. Brit., -stəns) n., a fact or condition modifying or accompanying another fact or event; something attending, relative or incidental. *The circumstances of his youth could not exonerate the thief.*

circumvent (sûr′kəm vent′, sûr′kəm vent′) v.t., to gain advantage over by stratagem or deception; get the better of by cunning; get around. *They tried to circumvent the official red tape.*

cirrhosis (si rō′sis) n., chronic inflammation of connective tissue, esp. of the liver. *Alcoholics often suffer from cirrhosis of the liver.*

cirrus (sir′əs) n., light, fleecy type of cloud usually formed of ice crystals at altitudes between 20,000 and 40,000 ft. *The autumn sky was laced with cirrus clouds.*

citadel (sit′ə dəl, -ə del′) n., fortress or castle designed to subject or defend a city; fortress. *The massive citadel loomed over the town.*

cite (sīt) v.t., 1. to call upon officially to appear, esp. before a court or tribunal. *The prosecutor vowed to cite every conspirator.* 2. to quote, or refer to for support, proof, or confirmation. *She could cite several precedents to strengthen her case.*

civil (siv′əl) adj., 1. pertaining to the state, to organized society, to the citizen in relation to other citizens and the state. *She took her case to a civil court.* 2. courteous; obliging; well bred; often merely or formally polite. *He managed to remain civil despite her rudeness.*

civility (si vil′i tē) n., politeness; courtesy; good breeding; act of courtesy or politeness. *The team captains exchanged civilities before the kickoff.*

clairvoyance (klâr voi′əns) n., power of understanding or perceiving data or events not explainable by perception or memory. *She attributed her premonition to clairvoyance.*

clairvoyant (klâr voi′ənt) n., one said to possess the power of clairvoyance. *The clairvoyant told his fortune.* adj., of or having clairvoyance. *Her premonition appeared to be clairvoyant.*

clamor (klam′ər) n., loud and prolonged outcry or noise. *The clamor awakened the whole neighborhood.* v.t., to utter loud cries; shout. *The audience clamored for more.*

clandestine (klan des′tin) adj., secret; hidden; furtive. *The police broke up the terrorists' clandestine meeting.*

claret (klar′it) n., any red Bordeaux or other dry red table wine. *Our host served a California claret with the roast.* adj., having the color of claret; purple-red. *Her coat was claret with silver buttons.*

clarion (klar′ē ən) n., 1. small high-pitched trumpet. *The herald sounded his clarion.* 2. sound as of a clarion. *The cock's clarion greeted the sunrise.* adj., clear, loud. *The clarion call-to-arms echoed through the valley.*

classify (klas′ə fī′) v.t., to arrange or group according to common characteristics. *Scientists classify humans with the other primates.*

claustrophobia (klô′strə fō′bē ə) n., irrational fear of confined spaces, closed rooms, narrow areas. *Her claustrophobia prevented her from entering the elevator.*

clavicle (klav′ə kəl) n., collarbone; part of the pectoral arch in vertebrates. *One of the accident victims had a broken clavicle.*

clavier (klə vēr′, klav′ē ər, klā′vē-) n., keyboard of a musical instrument, or the instrument itself, as a clavichord, pianoforte, or harpsichord. *The clavier was the forerunner of the modern piano.*

cleavage (klē′vij) n., act of cleaving or splitting; state of being split or cloven; division. *The cleavage of their political ideas strained their friendship.*

cleave (klēv) v.t., 1. to part or divide by force; rend apart; split; cut. *We watched the lightning cleave the tree to its roots.* 2. to come apart; slit; divide. *The machinery cleaved the trees to make a new road.* v.i., to stick; adhere; be attached; cling. *Iron filings will cleave to a magnet.*

cleft (kleft) n., space or opening made by cleavage; crevice; fissure; furrow. *The mountaineers camped in a cleft near the summit.*

clemency (klem′ən sē) n., 1. disposition to spare or forgive; mercy; leniency; forbearance. *He inclined to clemency for first offenders.* 2. act of mercy or forgiveness. *Her clemency saved the wounded animal.* 3. softness or mildness, as of the weather. *The skier cursed the winter's clemency.*

cliché (klē shā′, kli-; *Fr.* klē shā′) n., trite expression. *We groaned at the tired cliché.*

clientele (klī′ən tel′) n., clients collectively; body of clients. *This shop appeals to a very select clientele.*

climactic (klī mak′tik) adj., pertaining to a critical period, crisis, or climax. *She had reached the climactic point of her story.*

climax (klī'maks) n., highest point; culmination; acme. *The knockout was the climax of the exciting fight.* v.t., to bring to the highest point. *She decided to climax the party with champagne.* v.i., to reach the apex; culminate. *The excitement climaxed with the appearance of the guest of honor.*

clime (klīm) n., tract or region, esp. its climate; climate. *She dreamed of the tropical clime of Trinidad.*

clinical (klin'i kəl) adj., 1. pertaining to the direct observation of disease in patients. *He applied for a clinical research grant.* 2. dispassionate; analytical. *She requested his clinical appraisal of her painting.*

clique (klēk, klik) n., exclusive group of people; coterie. *The newcomer was accepted into the cheerleaders' clique.*

cloister (kloi'stər) n., 1. monastery, convent, or other place of religious seclusion. *After he joined the order he never left the cloister.* 2. any arcade or colonnade around an open court. *We sought the shade of the cloister.* v.t., to confine as in a cloister; shut away. *They tried to cloister him at the military school.*

closure (klō'zhər) n., 1. act of shutting or state of being closed. *The theater's closure surprised us all.* 2. in legislation, the closing off or stopping of debate; cloture. *The legislature will vote tomorrow on closure.* v.t., to end by closure. *The senator tried to closure the filibuster yesterday.*

coagulate (kō ag'yə lāt') v.t., to change from a fluid to a thickened mass; curdle; clot; congeal. *The substance began to coagulate the milk.* v.i., to become coagulated. *The blood began to coagulate.*

coalesce (kō'ə les') v.t., to grow, combine, or collect together into one body. *The issue seemed to coalesce the neighborhood.* v.i., to become joined; fuse. *At last their goals began to coalesce.*

coalition (kō'ə lish'ən) n., act or state of union; temporary alliance. *The coalition broke up soon after their goal was reached.*

coax (kōks) v.t., to persuade by pleading or flattery; wheedle. *We had to coax the old mare up the ramp.*

cochineal (koch'ə nēl', koch'ə nēl') n., red dye made from the bodies of female cochineal insects. *Cochineal is used as a coloring.*

cocky (kok'ē) adj., pert; self-confident; arrogant. *He's pretty cocky considering the trouble he is in.*

codify (kod'ə fī', kō'də-) v.t., to reduce to a code or digest; arrange or systematize. *She will codify the works of Dickens.*

coerce (kō ûrs') v.t., to restrain or compel, esp. by force. *He was warned not to coerce the witness.*

coffer (kô'fər, kof'ər) n., box, casket, or large chest used for keeping valuables; hence, a treasury. *She kept the documents in a fireproof coffer.*

cog (kog, kôg) n., 1. tooth projecting from a gear or wheel. *The clockmaker repaired the worn cog.* 2. person or thing in subordinate role. *The bureaucrat was a little cog in the party machine.*

cogent (kō'jənt) adj., not easily denied or refuted; convincing. *He approved her cogent plan for reconstruction.*

cogitate (koj'i tāt') v.t., to think over; reflect on. *He began to cogitate the proposal.* v.i., to ponder; meditate. *Her answer gave him a lot to cogitate.*

cogitation (koj'i tā'shən) n., act of thinking; reflection; meditation; contemplation. *He didn't wish to disturb her cogitation.*

cognate (kog'nāt) n., 1. one related to another by birth. *My sister and I are cognates.* 2. anything related to another by origin or derivation. *English and French cognates derive from Latin.* adj., related in origin; allied in nature, quality, or form. *Cognate words can be traced to the same root.*

cognition (kog nish'ən) n., knowledge, as from personal experience; perception; cognizance. *His cognition of the situation was hampered by the loud noise.*

cognizance (kog'ni zəns, kon'i-) n.,

knowledge or notice; perception; observation. *We must take cognizance of all the facts in this case.*

cognizant (kog′ni zənt, kon′i-) adj., having cognizance or knowledge of. *They were cognizant of her presence.*

coherent (kō hēr′ənt) adj., 1. sticking, or sticking together; cleaving; adhesive. *The cake began as twelve coherent balls of dough.* 2. consistent; logical; having agreement of parts. *His lecture was coherent and well reasoned.*

cohesion (kō hē′zhən) n., act or state of cohering, uniting, or sticking together. *The campaign lent cohesion to the disparate students.*

cohort (kō′hôrt) n., comrade or follower; also group of comrades. *He and his cohort celebrated their victory.*

coiffure (kwä fyo͞or′; *Fr.* kwa fyʀ′) n., hairstyle. *The marquise appeared in an elaborate coiffure.* v.t., to arrange or style the hair into a coiffure. *She tried to coiffure the unruly hair.*

coincide (kō′in sīd′) v.i., to occupy the same point in space or time. *Zero centigrade and 32° Fahrenheit coincide.* 2. to concur; agree; correspond exactly. *His opinions did not coincide with mine.*

coincidence (kō in′si dᵊns) n., 1. correspondence in position or time; concurrence; contemporaneousness. *Coincidence exists between fire and heat.* 2. noteworthy, apparently accidental, concurrence of two or more events or circumstances. *Our meeting was a fortunate coincidence.*

coincident (kō in′si dᵊnt) adj., occupying the same point in space or time; concurrent. *Her birthday was coincident with the meteor shower.*

colic (kol′ik) n., severe spasms of abdominal pain caused by distension or obstruction of visceral passages. *The baby suffered an attack of colic.*

collaborate (kə lab′ə rāt′) v.i., 1. to work with another or others; cooperate with; act jointly. *If we collaborate on this we will finish more quickly.* 2. to assist willingly, cooperate with, or aid enemy

forces in time of war. *She was accused of collaborating for personal gain.*

collaborator (kə lab′ə rā′tər) n., 1. associate; one who cooperates or works with another or others. *Our collaborator on this book is also here tonight.* 2. One who actively aids the enemy in time of war. *Every collaborator was rounded up after the enemy's defeat.*

collate (ko lāt′, kə-, kol′āt, kō′ lāt) v.t., 1. to bring together and compare points of agreement and disagreement. *He tried to collate the various Christian doctrines.* 2. to bring together in proper order; verify the arrangement of. *Please collate these pages into booklets.*

collateral (kə lat′ər əl) n., security given for payment of a loan. *Their house was collateral for the loan.* adj., 1. occupying a secondary or subordinate position; concomitant. *The collateral heat from the wood stove kept our heating bills down.* 2. accompanying; attendant. *Travel was a collateral bonus to the promotion.* 3. secured by collateral. *They obtained a collateral loan.*

colleague (kol′ēg) n., professional associate. *The doctor asked his colleague's opinion.*

collectivism (kə lek′tə viz′əm) n., system or theory of centralization of the means of production in the state. *Collectivism has in practice been incompatible with individual freedom.*

colloquial (kə lō′kwē əl) adj., peculiar or appropriate to common or familiar conversation; belonging to ordinary everyday speech, as opposed to formal usage. *He couldn't find the colloquial usage in his French text.*

colloquialism (kə lō′kwē ə liz′əm) n., word, phrase, or usage peculiar to common or familiar conversation. *"You all" is a colloquialism that is no longer confined to the South.*

colloquy (kol′ə kwē) n., conversation, esp. in form of a discussion or conference. *The mayors met for a colloquy on urban problems.*

collusion (kə lo͞o′zhən) n., secret agreement for fraudulent or harmful purposes; conspiracy. *The companies were accused of collusion when they raised their prices.*

colonel (kûr′nəl) n., a field grade officer one rank below general. *The colonel directed operations in the field.*

colonialism (kə lō′nē ə liz′əm) n., government policy that seeks to retain or extend its authority over other territories. *The independence of India in 1950 marked the beginning of the end of British colonialism.*

colossal (kə los′əl) adj., of extraordinary size; huge; gigantic. *They were astonished at the colossal monument.*

columnar (kə lum′nər) adj., having the form of a column; formed in columns. *The bookkeeper made an entry in the columnar sheet.*

coma (kō′mə) n., state of prolonged unconsciousness, resembling sleep, caused by disease, accident, etc., and from which it is difficult or impossible to rouse the patient; stupor. *Shortly after the crash the victim fell into a coma.*

comatose (kom′ə tos′, kō′mə-) adj., pertaining to or resembling coma; affected with coma; dull; lethargic. *The comatose patient required constant care.*

combative (kəm bat′iv, kom′bə tiv, kum′-) adj., disposed to combat; pugnacious; showing a disposition to fight. *He became very combative when opposed.*

combine (n. kom′bīn; v. kəm bīn′) n., 1. combination, usually of persons or groups, to further special interest. *The DeBeers mining combine dominates the world diamond market.* 2. mechanical grain harvester. *The combine moved slowly through the wheatfield.* v.i., to associate, join; unite; coalesce. *Oil and water do not readily combine.*

combustible (kəm bus′tə bəl) n., flammable substance. *The lumber yard was full of combustibles.* adj., capable of taking fire and burning; flammable. *The cloth had been soaked in a combustible liquid.*

comely (kum′lē) adj., handsome; graceful; pleasing in appearance. *The comely garden was a source of pride.*

comity (kom′i tē) n., mutual civility; courtesy. *Comity helped them overcome the misunderstanding.*

commandeer (kom′ən dēr′) v.t., 1. to seize a person or property for military or other public service. *He was ordered to commandeer every able-bodied man in the village.* 2. to seize arbitrarily. *The hijackers intend to commandeer the plane.*

commando (kə man′dō, -män′-) n., any military unit, or member of such unit, specially trained to conduct surprise, hit-and-run, or other specific detailed operations. *A German antiterrorist commando staged the raid.* adj., pertaining to the tactics or operations of a commando. *The radar station was destroyed in a commando raid.*

commence (kə mens′) v.t., to initiate; open. *They wanted to commence the dinner with a toast.* v.i., to start; begin. *The parade will commence at noon.*

commend (kə mend′) v.t., 1. to praise; mention with approbation. *We commend your presence of mind during the emergency.* 2. to commit; deliver with confidence; entrust. *You must commend her to the doctor's care.*

commendable (kə men′də bəl) adj., capable of being commended; worthy of commendation; praiseworthy. *Her quick thinking was commendable.*

commendation (kom′ən dā′shən) n., 1. act of commending; praise; approbation. *His heroism deserves commendation.* 2. that which commends. *She received a commendation for her work.*

commensurate (kə men′sər it, -shər-) adj., reducible to a common measure; of equal size; corresponding in amount, degree, or magnitude. *Salary is commensurate with experience.*

commentary (kom′ən ter′ē) n., 1. series or collection of comments, annotations, or explanations. *The commentary clarified the more obscure passages.* 2.

anything that serves to explain or illustrate. *Her running commentary was for those of us who could not see the race.*

commingle (kə miṅg'gəl) v., to mix together; mingle; blend. *The soup's flavors commingle well.*

commiserate (kə miz'ə rāt') v., to feel sorrow, regret or compassion for; sympathize; pity. *We commiserate with you on your loss.*

commiseration (kə miz'ə rā'shən) n., act of commiserating; pity; compassion. *There was universal commiseration upon her death.*

commissary (kom'i ser'ē) n., dining hall or food supply store, esp. an institutional one. *We lunched at the TV studio commissary.*

commode (kə mōd') n., 1. low piece of furniture containing drawers and shelves. *He dropped his hat and gloves on the commode.* 2. small piece of furniture containing a chamber pot and drawer and shelf combination; toilet. *The flower planter was an antique commode.*

commodious (kə mō'dē əs) adj., affording good accommodations; convenient and roomy; suitable and spacious. *The commodious harbor can handle ten ships a day.*

communiqué (kə myoō'nə kā', kə myoō'nə kā') n., official communication; bulletin. *The government issued a communiqué about the riots.*

communism (kom'yə niz'əm) n., economic theory or system advocating total or partial abolition of the right of private property, actual ownership being ascribed to the community as a whole or to the state. *Many religious orders practice a form of communism.*

commutation (kom'yə tā'shən) n., 1. act of substituting one thing for another; substitution; alteration; exchange. *The convict hoped for a commutation of his sentence.* 2. regular travel between residence and work. *The daily commutation took its toll on his nerves.*

commute (kə myoōt') v.t., to exchange;

put in place of; substitute another for. *The judge commuted his sentence from twenty years to ten.* v.i., to travel regularly between residence and work. *We commute 30 miles a day.*

compact (*n.* kom'pakt; *v., adj.* kəm pakt') n., 1. agreement; contract. *Their compact called for completion in 90 days.* 2. small, hand-held, make-up kit. *She always carried a compact in her purse.* 3. small automobile. *Their new compact gets 40 miles per gallon.* v.t., to drive, pack, or press closely together; consolidate; condense. *You must compact the clay before molding it.* adj., 1. closely and firmly united; pressed or packed together; solid; dense. *A compact mass of people crowded into the theater.* 2. small; arranged in a small space. *Compact cars are relatively lightweight.* 3. concise; pithy; terse. *She gave a compact discourse on world affairs.*

companion (kəm pan'yən) n., person or thing which associates with or accompanies another or others. *My brother and his companion left yesterday.*

comparable (kom'pər ə bəl) adj., 1. capable of being compared. *The U.S. and British legal systems are comparable.* 2. worthy of comparison. *The prices of these two items are comparable.*

compassion (kəm pash'ən) n., feeling of sorrow for the misfortunes of another; sympathy; commiseration; pity. *He was full of compassion for their distress.*

compassionate (kəm pash'ə nit) adj., full of compassion or pity; easily moved to sympathy. *The compassionate woman tried to help.*

compatible (kəm pat'ə bəl) adj., 1. capable of existing together in harmony; suitable; agreeable; congenial. *The flavors of chocolate and mint are compatible.* 2. consistent; reconcilable; congruous. *His story is not compatible with the facts.*

compelling (kəm pel'iṅg) adj., 1. tending to compel; forcing; obliging. *He had compelling reasons for refusing.* 2. requiring respect, admiration, or attention. *It was a powerful and compelling story.*

compendium (kəm pen'dē əm) n., brief account of the leading points of a subject; abridgement; summary; epitome. *They wrote a compendium of 20th-century physics.*

compensatory (kəm pen'sə tōr'ē, -tôr'ē) adj., serving to compensate or as compensation. *The court awarded him compensatory damages.*

competent (kom'pi tᵊnt) adj., properly qualified; having ability or capacity; suitable; fit; sufficient or adequate. *She is competent to decide herself.*

compilation (kom'pə lā'shən) n., 1. act of bringing together; compiling. *The compilation of all the data took hours.* 2. that which is compiled. *This compilation of tales is very interesting.*

complacency (kəm plā'sən sē) n., feeling of quiet pleasure; self-satisfaction; smugness. *She tried to jar him out of his complacency.*

complacent (kəm plā'sənt) adj., pleased, esp. with oneself; self-satisfied; smug. *The lack of challenge made him complacent.*

complaisant (kəm plā'sənt, -zənt, kom'plə zant') adj., disposed to please; compliant; affable; obliging; gracious or agreeable. *The complaisant guide agreed to the change of route.*

complement (kom'plə mənt) n., that which completes or perfects; addition that makes whole or full; part. *The dessert was a perfect complement to our meal.* v.t., to make whole; to complete. *Her new boots complemented the outfit.*

complex (*n.* kom'pleks; *adj.* kəm pleks', kom'pleks) n., complicated, intricate union of interconnected parts. *The shopping complex took three years to build.* adj., involved; intricate; complicated; perplexing. *This complex problem will take time to solve.*

compliant (kəm plī'ənt) adj., yielding; accommodating; consenting; obliging. *The compliant porter agreed to get the tickets for them.*

complicity (kəm plis'i tē) n., state of being an accomplice; partnership in wrongdoing. *She was innocent of complicity in the theft.*

compliment (*n.* kom'plə mənt; *v.* kom'plə ment') n., 1. expression of praise, commendation, or admiration. *She smiled at his hearty compliment.* 2. pl., formal act or expression of civility or respect; regards. *Our compliments on the birth of your new baby!* v.t., to give praise or congratulations. *We want to compliment you on your fine children.*

component (kəm pō'nənt) n., constituent part. *She bought a new component for her stereo system.* adj., composing; constituent; a part of. *The component parts covered the table.*

compose (kəm pōz') v.t., 1. to make or form by combining, framing, fashioning, or arranging things. *He tried to compose a new song for the play.* 2. to be an element or part of. *A fence marks off the buildings that compose the campus.* 3. to settle; adjust; reconcile. *They must learn to compose their differences.* v.i., to practice composition. *The pianist wanted to learn to compose.*

composition (kom'pə zish'ən) n., 1. act of composing. *He studied composition at Juilliard.* 2. musical or literary work. *Her composition included elements of farce and fantasy.* 3. general constitution or make-up; structure. *The composition of this painting is very unusual.*

compound (*n.* kom'pound; *v.* kəm pound'; *adj.* kom'pound, kom pound') n., 1. something produced by combining two or more ingredients. *The alloy was a compound of iron and chromium.* 2. enclosure, esp. one containing buildings used as residences, offices, etc. *The prisoners were all kept in one compound.* v.t., 1. to put together or mix; join or couple; form by uniting; make; constitute; form. *The pharmacist uses a mortar and pestle to compound drugs.* 2. to settle or adjust by agreement, esp. to lessen. *His creditors agreed to compound his debts.* 3. to agree, for a consideration, not to prosecute or punish a wrongdoer. *He was charged with attempting to compound a felony.* 4. to pay (interest) on accumulated interest as well as the principal. *The bank will compound interest monthly.* 5. to increase or add to. *Ill-health compounds his other problems.* adj., composed of two or more elements, parts, or ingredients. *The skier suffered a compound fracture.*

comprehend (kom′pri hend′) v.t., 1. to understand; grasp the nature or character of. *I cannot comprehend calculus.* 2. to take in; include; embrace. *The charge comprehends a multitude of offenses.*

comprehensible (kom′pri hen′sə bəl) adj., capable of being understood; conceivable by the mind; intelligible. *The code was surprisingly comprehensible.*

comprehensive (kom′pri hen′siv) adj., of large scope; capacious; inclusive. *They issued a comprehensive report on urban crime.*

compromise (kom′prə mīz′) n., 1. settlement of differences by mutual concessions; also, result of such a settlement or agreement. *They reached a compromise just before the strike deadline.* 2. thing intermediate in qualities between other things. *The color was a compromise between red and yellow.* v.t., to expose to risk, hazard, or scandal. *By revealing his source the reporter compromised his credibility.* v.i., to come to terms; make a compromise. *He refused to compromise over salary.*

compulsion (kəm pul′shən) n., act of compelling; also, state of being compelled. *He used compulsion to get his way.* 2. impulse, usually irresistible, to perform an act contrary to one's will. *He felt a compulsion to climb to the very top.*

compulsive (kəm pul′siv) adj., compelling; pertaining to or involving compulsion; compulsory. *He was a compulsive drinker.*

compulsory (kəm pul′sə rē) adj., 1. exercising compulsion; tending to compel; compelling; constraining. *A compulsory*

curfew prevented further trouble. 2. obligatory; mandatory; enforced without exception. *The course was compulsory for French majors.*

compunction (kəm puṅgk′shən) n., uneasiness of the conscience as a result of wrongdoing; feelings of unease; contrition; remorse. *He felt no compunction about saying no.*

compute (kəm pyoot′) v.t., to determine by calculation; count; reckon; calculate. *He wanted to compute the answer himself.*

concave (n. kon′kāv; adj. kon kāv′) n., inwardly curved surface, plane, etc. *The concave of the amphitheater provided excellent acoustics.* adj., curved or rounded, as the inside surface of a sphere; incurved. *The concave lens distorted the light passing through it.*

concede (kən sēd′) v.t., 1. to admit as true, just, or proper; acquiesce in. *She refused to concede defeat.* 2. to make a concession of; yield up; allow. *Management decided to concede the issue of overtime.* v.i., to make a concession; yield; admit. *Despite setbacks we will not concede.*

concentric (kən sen′trik) adj., having a common center, as circles, spheres, etc. *The pebble created dozens of concentric ripples in the pond.*

conception (kən sep′shən) n., 1. act or power of forming a concept, notion, or idea. *She was responsible for the conception of new ideas.* 2. that which is conceived; notion; idea; plan. *This whole project was his conception.* 3. inception of pregnancy; fertilization. *Conception occurs when a sperm unites with an egg.*

conceptual (kən sep′choo əl) adj., pertaining to conception or the formation of concepts. *His conceptual abilities were well developed.*

concerto (kən cher′tō; *It.* kôn cheR′tô) n., musical composition, usually in symphonic form, written for one or more solo instruments with orchestral accompaniment. *The program featured a piano concerto.*

conciliate (kən sil′ē āt′) v.t., to overcome the distrust or hostility of; pacify; placate; soothe; win over. *We made one more attempt to conciliate her parents.*

concise (kən sīs′) adj., expressing much in few words; brief but comprehensive; terse; succinct. *His concise summary helped save time.*

conclave (kon′klāv, kong′-) n., 1. any private meeting; closed assembly. *The authors of the Constitution met in conclave at Philadelphia.* 2. place in which the College of Cardinals of the Roman Catholic Church meets privately to elect a pope. *The doors of the conclave are walled up to maintain secrecy.* 3. assembly of the cardinals for the election of a pope. *The conclave reached a decision after three ballots.*

conclusive (kən kloo′siv) adj., 1. serving to decide an argument or question; decisive; convincing. *The evidence was not conclusive.* 2. tending to bring to an end; concluding. *The conclusive lecture summarized the conference.*

concoct (kon kokt′, kən-) v.t., 1. to combine and prepare the materials of, as in cookery. *She began to concoct his birthday cake.* 2. to devise; plan; contrive; plot. *They tried to concoct a believable excuse.*

concomitant (kon kom′i tənt, kən-) n., thing conjoined or concurrent with another; accompaniment; accessory. *The lightning and its thunderous concomitant filled the sky.* adj., accompanying; conjoined with; concurrent; attending. *He desired wealth and its concomitant power.*

concordat (kon kôr′dat) n., agreement; compact; convention, esp. between the Vatican and a state. *The concordat specified their rights and obligations.*

concourse (kon′kōrs, -kôrs, kong′-) n., 1. assembly; throng; crowd. *The great concourse began to push forward.* 2. open gathering place; promenade; boulevard. *The concourse was filled with Sunday strollers.*

concur (kən kûr′) v.i., 1. to agree; be in accord. *We concur with your opinion.* 2. to unite; combine; be associated. *He will concur with us on this matter.*

concurrent (kən kûr′ənt, -kur′-) n., that which concurs; joint or contributory thing. *Ink manufacturing is a concurrent of the printing industry.* adj., 1. in agreement; in accord. *Their plans are concurrent with ours.* 2. united; associated; combined. *Our concurrent efforts will carry the day.*

condensation (kon′den sā′shən, -dən-) n., 1. act of making, or the state of being made, dense or compact; reduction of volume; concentration; abridgment. *The booklet was a condensation of the original report.* 2. act or process of reducing a gas or vapor to a liquid or solid form. *Cold weather caused condensation on the windows.*

condescend (kon′di send′) v.i., to voluntarily waive dignity or superiority and assume equality with an inferior; stoop; deign. *He would not condescend to speak with them.*

condescension (kon′di sen′shən) n., act of condescending; voluntary stooping or inclining to an equality with an inferior; patronizing behavior. *His constant condescension at last turned friends away.*

condiment (kon′də mənt) n., something used to give extra flavor to foods; relish; seasoning; spices. *She filled the dish with homemade condiments.*

condolence (kən dō′ləns) n., expression of sympathy addressed to a person in distress, misfortune, or bereavement. *We offered our condolences to the young widow.*

condominium (kon′də min′ē əm) n., joint or concurrent dominion, particularly with regard to individually owned dwelling units in a single complex or building where each owner receives a deed and may sell, mortgage, etc., his unit independently of the other owners; the individual unit in such a complex or building. *We just bought a condominium.*

condone (kən dōn′) v.t., to forgive or pardon, esp. by implication, a wrong or offense; overlook an act or fault. *We should not condone his arrogance.*

conducive (kən dōo′siv, -dyōo′-) adj., conducing; furthering; advancing; helpful. *Peace and quiet are conducive to studying.*

conduit (kon′dwit, -dōo it, -dyōo it, -dit) n., 1. pipe, tube, or other channel for the conveyance of water or other fluids. *The blocked conduit backed up the stream.* 2. medium or means of conveying; anything serving as a channel for passage or transmission. *He was the conduit for the stolen goods.*

confederate (*n., adj.* kən fed′ər it, -fed′rit; *v.* kən fed′ə rāt′) n., one who is united with another or others in a compact or league; ally; associate; accomplice. *Her confederate is responsible for her trouble.* v.i., to unite in a league or alliance. *They chose to confederate for their mutual protection.* adj., united in a league; allied by compact or treaty. *The confederate powers were confident of victory.*

confer (kən fûr′) v.t., to bestow as a gift or honor. *We wish to confer this medal upon you.* v.i., to consult together; compare opinions; carry on a discussion or deliberation. *We must confer before making any decisions.*

confidant (kon′fi dant′, -dänt′, kon′fi dant′, -dänt′) n., person entrusted with the confidence of another; one to whom secrets are confided. *Her sister was her trusted confidant.*

confidential (kon′fi den′shəl) adj., 1. intended to be treated as private, or kept in confidence; spoken or written in confidence; secret. *He refused to allow publication of the confidential letters.* 2. enjoying the confidence of another; entrusted with secrets or private affairs. *His confidential clerk noted the appointment.*

configuration (kən fig′yə rā′shən) n., external form, figure, or shape resulting from the disposition and relation of the parts. *The configuration of the new model hasn't changed much.*

confiscate (kon′fi skāt′, kən fis′kāt) v.t.,

1. to adjudge to be forfeited to the public treasury, by way of penalty; to appropriate to public use. *The court ruled to confiscate the rebel's property.* 2. to take away from another as if by authority; appropriate summarily; seize as forfeited for any reason. *They tried to confiscate her personal papers.* adj., seized; forfeited; appropriated to public use. *In the end, all their lands were confiscate.*

conflagration (kon′flə grā′shən) n., fire, esp. a very large, extensive one. *The conflagration engulfed the entire area.*

conformity (kən fôr′mi tē) n., 1. correspondence in form or manner; resemblance; agreement; congruity; likeness. *The junkyard was not in conformity to the residential neighborhood.* 2. compliance; accordance; acquiescence. *They required conformity to the dress code.*

confound (kon found′, kən-) v.t., 1. to throw into confusion; perplex; amaze; bewilder. *A good magician can confound most audiences.* 2. to contradict or refute. *She tried to confound their arguments.* 3. to treat or regard erroneously as identical; mix or associate by mistake. *He would often confound politics and diplomacy.*

confront (kən frunt′) v.t., 1. to stand facing; be in front of; face. *The warehouses confront the harbor.* 2. to stand in direct opposition to; meet in hostility; oppose; challenge. *The two will confront each other at dawn.* 3. to be in one's way. *There are still questions that confront us.* 4. to set face to face; bring into the presence of, as for proof or verification. *They had to confront him with his folly.*

congeal (kən jēl′) v.i., 1. to change from a fluid to a solid state; harden; stiffen; thicken; freeze. *As the temperature dropped, the various liquids began to congeal.* 2. to fix or become fixed, as ideas, etc. *His opinion began to congeal into doctrine.*

congenial (kən jēn′yəl) adj., 1. suited or adapted in character or feeling; agree-

congenital

68

able; sympathetic; companionable. *They were well liked because of their congenial natures.* 2. naturally suited or adapted; agreeable; pleasing. *He found the outdoor work very congenial.*

congenital (kən jen′i təl) adj., existing at birth; innate; inborn. *He suffers from a congenital heart murmur.*

conglomerate (*n., adj.* kən glom′ər it; *v.* kən glom′ə rāt′) n., 1. anything composed of heterogeneous or incongruous materials. *The building was a conglomerate of different styles.* 2. large corporation made up of several, often unrelated, subsidiaries. *The conglomerate began to gobble up the small farmers.* v.t., to collect together into a mass. *She conglomerated the different cheeses into a ball.* adj., collected or clustered together. *The conglomerate atoms formed into molecules.*

conglomeration (kən glom′ə rā′shən) n., 1. act of gathering into a mass; state of being gathered; collection; accumulation. *The conglomeration of noises began to sound like music.* 2. that which is collected into a mass; mixed or incongruous mass; heterogeneous mixture. *The room was a conglomeration of children and pets.*

congratulate (kən grach′ə lāt′) v.t., to express sympathetic pleasure at another's joy, good fortune, etc. *We congratulate you on the birth of your child.*

congregation (kong′grə gā′shən) n., 1. act of congregating; state of bringing together or assembling. *The congregation of the puzzle pieces may take days.* 2. collection or assembly of things or persons. *The congregation rose to sing.*

congruence (kong′grōō əns) n., agreement; consistency; correspondence. *A congruence of goals brought us together.*

congruent (kong′grōō ənt) adj., agreeing; corresponding; appropriate; joined or related. *The congruent piece of the puzzle was missing.*

congruous (kong′grōō əs) adj., harmonious; well adapted; appropriate; consist-

ent. *His opinions are often congruous with mine.*

conical (kon′ə kəl) adj., having the form of a cone. *The volcano created a conical mountain.*

conifer (kō′nə fər, kon′ə-) n., plant that produces seeds or pollen in cones, as the evergreen trees and shrubs including the pine, fir, spruce, etc. *Conifers served as a windbreak against the house.*

conjecture (kən jek′chər) n., act of forming an opinion without definite proof; opinion formed on insufficient evidence; surmise; guess. *The conjecture later proved false.* v.t., to draw conclusions or make opinions from insufficient evidence. *They may conjecture the wrong answer from the incomplete data.* v.i., to form conjectures; surmise; guess. *Without further proof, he can only conjecture.*

conjoin (kən join′) v., to join together; associate; connect; unite. *He will conjoin them in matrimony.*

conjugal (kon′jə gəl) adj., pertaining to marriage or to the relation of husband and wife. *They reiterated their conjugal vows.*

conjunction (kən jungk′shən) n., joining or meeting of individuals or distinct things; union; connection; combination; association. *They liked working in conjunction with him.*

conjure (kon′jər or, esp. Brit., kun′-) v.t., 1. to call on or summon by invocation or spell. *He tried to conjure her image.* 2. to produce or influence as if by magic; create magically. *She conjured up pen and paper.* 3. to bring to mind; recall. *He tried to conjure their previous conversation.* v.i., to practice the arts of a conjurer; engage in magic. *The sorcerer began to conjure as a crowd gathered.*

connivance (kə nī′vəns) n., act of conniving, esp. as tacit or implied encouragement to wrongdoing. *He committed the plagiarism with his editor's connivance.*

connive (kə nīv′) v.i., 1. to refrain from noticing a wrongdoing; aid or encourage by silence or forbearance; conceal knowledge of a fault or wrong. *The police agreed to connive at the mayor's misdemeanor.* 2. to conspire; have a clandestine understanding. *They connive in all sorts of pranks.*

connoisseur (kon'ə sûr', -sŏor') n., knowledgeable critic or judge of any art or field. *She is a connoisseur of fine wines.*

connubial (kə nōō'bē əl, -nyōō'-) adj., proper to the state of marriage; pertaining to marriage; matrimonial; conjugal. *They agreed to discuss their connubial duties.*

conquistador (kon kwis'tə dôr'; *Sp.* kôn̄g kēs'tä-t̂hôʀ') n., one of the 16th-century conquerors of Central and South America; conqueror. *The conquistador's statue loomed over the plaza.*

consanguinity (kon'sang gwin'i tē) n., relationship by blood; relationship by descent from a common ancestor. *The brothers' consanguinity was evident.*

conscientious (kon'shē en'shəs, kon'sē-) adj., controlled or governed by conscience; according to the dictates of conscience. *The conscientious worker never left early.*

conscript (*n., adj.* kon'skript; *v.* kən skript') n., one who is compulsorily enrolled in military service; draftee. *The conscript was a reluctant soldier.* v.t., to enroll compulsorily for military service; draft. *The government plans to conscript a million men.* adj., drafted; registered; enrolled. *Conscript soldiers were released from duty after the war.*

conscription (kən skrip'shən) n., compulsory enrollment of men for military service; draft. *Congress may decide to reinstate conscription.*

consecrate (kon'sə krāt') v.t., 1. to make or declare sacred; appropriate or dedicate to sacred uses. *We shall consecrate the new church next week.* 2. to devote or dedicate to a purpose. *She consecrated her life to teaching.* 3. to make inviolate or hallow. *The cloth was consecrated as a relic.*

consecutive (kən sek'yə tiv) adj., uninterrupted in course or succession; successive. *It was his sixth consecutive strike-out.*

consensus (kən sen'səs) n., general agreement or concord. *We finally reached a consensus on the subject.*

consequence (kon'sə kwens', -kwəns) n., 1. that which follows from or grows out of any act, cause, proceeding, or series of actions. *Be prepared to accept the consequences of your actions.* 2. importance; moment; influence; significance of a thing, or distinction of a person. *She was a historian of great consequence.*

conservation (kon'sər vā'shən) n., act of conserving; preservation; keeping in a safe or entire state. *She lobbied for conservation of endangered species.*

conservative (kən sûr'və tiv) n., one who is disposed toward preservation of established institutions, conditions, conventions; traditionalist, esp. one who is cautious and opposed to abrupt change. *The conservative opposed the radical concept.* adj., pertaining to a conservative. *The conservative position appealed to him.*

consign (kən sīn') v.t., 1. to deliver or transfer formally, as a charge or trust; commit; entrust. *He wanted to consign his paintings with the store.* 2. to address for shipment, or ship, as by common carrier for sale or custody. *We intend to consign all new models to the Boston office.*

consignment (kən sīn'mənt) n., act of consigning; that which is consigned. *There is a large consignment due you tomorrow.*

consistent (kən sis'tənt) adj., standing together or in agreement; compatible; congruous; uniform; not contradictory or opposed. *The decision was consistent with her long-term goals.*

console (*n.* kon'sōl; *v.* kən sōl') n., 1. desklike structure of an organ, containing the keyboards, pedals, etc. *The audience fell silent as he sat at the great* *console.* 2. free-standing cabinet containing a radio, phonograph, or television. *The components were removed from the console for repair.* 3. unit of a computer containing the keyboard and monitoring devices. *This console shares time with three others.* 4. control unit of an electric or electronic switchboard or other system. *She manned the light console as the curtain came up.* v.t., to alleviate the grief, despondency, or distress of; comfort; cheer up; give solace; soothe. *She tried to console the weeping man.*

consolidate (kən sol′i dāt′) v., to unite; combine; form into a more compact mass. *If we consolidate our assets, we can expand.*

consonant (kon′sə nənt) n., alphabetic element or sound other than a vowel; letter representing such an element. *Consonants and vowels combine to form syllables.* adj., harmonious; agreeing; congruous; consistent. *The story is not consonant with the facts.*

consort (*n.* kon′sôrt; *v.* kən sôrt′) n., companion; partner; intimate associate, esp. a spouse. *She and her consort attended the party.* v.i., to associate; unite; join. *They began to consort with questionable characters.*

conspicuous (kən spik′yo͞o əs) adj., open to view; easily seen; obvious; clearly perceived; striking. *The hat made her conspicuous in the crowd.*

constant (kon′stənt) n., that which is not subject to change. *Gravity is a constant in physics.* adj., 1. not subject to variation; fixed; unchanging. *We must try to keep the temperature constant.* 2. continuing for a long time; lasting; incessant; ceaseless. *The constant, gentle motion lulled him to sleep.* 3. regularly recurring; continually renewed; persistent. *The constant wail of a foghorn helped us navigate.* 4. faithful; true; loyal; trusty. *Her dog was her constant companion.*

constellation (kon′stə lā′shən) n., 1. group of stars to which a definite name has been given. *Ursa Major—the Big*

Dipper—is a familiar constellation. 2. any assemblage of persons or things of a brilliant, distinguished, or exalted nature. *The program offers a constellation of noted performers.*

consternation (kon′stər nā′shən) n., extreme surprise, with confusion and panic; incapacitating amazement or dismay; astonishment. *The explosion caused great consternation.*

constituency (kən stich′o͞o ən sē) n., 1. body of constituents, esp. the residents of a district represented by an elected official. *The senator's constituency was predominantly rural.* 2. any body of supporters, customers, clientele. *They claimed all consumers as their constituency.*

constituent (kən stich′o͞o ənt) n., 1. that which constitutes a part of; formative element. *Flour is the primary constituent of bread.* 2. one who empowers another to transact business for him, esp., a voter in a district represented by an elected official. *The governor made time to talk to his constituents.* adj., forming or composing a necessary part; component. *The constituent parts of water are hydrogen and oxygen.*

constitution (kon′sti to͞o′shən, -tyo͞o′-) n., 1. composition, make-up, or natural condition of anything. *The data revealed a lot about the moon's constitution.* 2. general physical strength and health; physique. *His good constitution helped him recover rapidly.* 3. formal, usually written, system of fundamental principles, rules, or laws for the government of a political unit, corporation, or other collective. *The club's constitution explicitly prohibits racial discrimination.*

constrain (kən strān′) v.t., 1. to compel; necessitate; oblige; force. *You may not constrain him to stay.* 2. to confine or hold by force; restrain; repress. *We shall constrain him until the trial.*

constraint (kən strānt′) n., 1. irresistible force or its effect; compulsion; coercion; restraint. *The prisoner is subject to the court's constraint.* 2. repression of one's emotion or behavior. *He felt constraint against interfering.* 3. embarrassment. *Her constraint at his importuning was obvious.*

constrict (kən strikt') v.t., 1. to draw together; contract; cause shrinkage; compress. *Pinching the hose will constrict the flow of water.* 2. to slow or limit the development or course of. *His lack of education will constrict his future opportunities.*

construe (kən strōō' or, esp. Brit., kon'strōō) v.t., 1. to interpret; explain; show or understand the meaning of. *If I construe your meaning correctly, you accept.* 2. to deduce; infer. *He construed her condition from her outward symptoms.*

consul (kon'səl) n., agent appointed by one country to look after its citizens and commerce in a foreign country. *The American consul in Paris should be able to advise you.*

consultant (kən sul't²nt) n., one who gives expert or professional advice. *The consultant advised them to employ a computer service.*

consultation (kon'səl tā'shən) n., act of consulting; meeting of persons to consult together. *I wanted a consultation with another doctor before deciding.*

consummate (v. kon'sə māt'; adj. kən sum'it, kon'sə mit) v.t., 1. carry or bring to completion; complete; achieve; finish. *The new government will consummate the revolution.* 2. to complete (a marriage) by sexual intercourse. *It is customary to consummate one's marriage on the honeymoon.* adj., complete; perfect; superb. *We acclaimed the consummate actor.*

contagion (kən tā'jən) n., infectious communication of a disease, directly or indirectly; also the disease or the medium of communication. *They set up a quarantine to contain the contagion.*

contagious (kən tā'jəs) adj., 1. communicable by contagion; catching. *The common cold is very contagious.* 2. containing or generating contagion. *Stay away from him; he's contagious.* 3.

tending to spread from person to person. *Their laughter was contagious.*

contaminate (kən tam'ə nāt') v.t., to render impure by mixture or contact; defile; pollute; taint; corrupt. *The overflowing sewage began to contaminate the well.*

contemporary (kən tem'pə rer'ē) n., one belonging to the same time as another. *My grandfather was a contemporary of the Wright brothers.* adj., 1. living or occurring at the same time. *Mastodons were contemporary with the last Ice Age.* 2. of the present time; modern. *We prefer contemporary furniture to antiques.*

contempt (kən tempt') n., 1. act of despising; disdain. *She felt contempt for his cowardice.* 2. in law, disobedience to, or open disrespect of, the rules, orders, or process of a court or legislative body. *The judge ruled he was in contempt.*

contemptible (kən temp'tə bəl) adj., worthy of contempt; despicable; mean. *His ingratitude was contemptible.*

contemptuous (kən temp'chōō əs) adj., manifesting or expressing contempt or disdain. *He was openly contemptuous of our prospects.*

contention (kən ten'shən) n., 1. struggle; strife; physical contest, debate, or competition. *He tried to avoid contention with her mother.* 2. point put forth during debate or argument. *Her contention was eventually borne out by the facts.*

contentious (kən ten'shəs) adj., 1. apt to contend; quarrelsome. *The contentious man started the fight.* 2. characterized by contention or debate. *It was a lively, even contentious, meeting.*

context (kon'tekst) n., 1. that surrounding part of a written or oral statement influencing the meaning or effect of a particular word or phrase. *She complained that she was quoted out of context.* 2. circumstances or facts surrounding a particular event, situation, etc. *Your decision is justifiable in that context.*

contiguity (kon'tə gyōō'i tē) n., state of being in contact; proximity; continuous extent or mass. *The contiguity of the forest was unbroken.*

contiguous (kən tig′yo͞o əs) adj., touching; neighboring; bordering or adjoining; adjacent. *They shared contiguous apartments.*

continence (kon′tᵊ nəns) n., self-restraint with regard to desires and passions, esp. sexual. *His habitual continence did not extend to food.*

continent (kon′tᵊ nent) n., one of the largest land masses of the globe. *North America is the third-largest continent.* adj., restrained; moderate; temperate; esp. in sexual desires. *He was continent during his recuperation.*

contingent (kən tin′jənt) n., that portion which falls to one party in a division; quota, esp. of troops to be furnished. *The Prussian contingent arrived in the afternoon.* adj., dependent on something not yet certain; conditional. *The championship is contingent upon winning the semi-finals.*

contort (kən tôrt′) v.t., to twist, draw, bend, or wrench out of shape; distort. *Don't contort my words to agree with your assumptions.*

contortion (kən tôr′shən) n., act of twisting or wrenching; state of being twisted or wrenched; distortion. *The stress overload caused a serious contortion of the beam.*

contortionist (kən tôr′shə nist) n., 1. one who practices gymnastic feats involving contorted or unnatural postures. *The contortionist became a human pretzel.* 2. one who practices mental or verbal contortion. *The contortionist managed to deflect suspicion from himself.*

contraband (kon′trə band′) n., anything prohibited to be imported or exported by law; illegal or prohibited trade. *The Coast Guard confiscated a ship carrying contraband.* adj., prohibited or excluded by law, proclamation, or treaty. *The smuggler deals in contraband goods.*

contraception (kon′trə sep′shən) n., prevention of conception by various devices or techniques; birth control.

Contraception avoids unwanted pregnancies.

contraceptive (kon′trə sep′tiv) n., device, drug, etc. to prevent conception. *The diaphragm is a popular contraceptive.* adj., serving to prevent conception. *Contraceptive drugs help couples limit family size.*

contradict (kon′trə dikt′) v., to assert the contrary or opposite of; deny directly and categorically. *His mean actions contradict his fine words.*

contrary (kon′trer ē; *for adv. also* kən trâr′ē) n., something opposite or opposed in character, direction, or position. *The contrary of good is evil.* adj., opposite; opposed; at the opposite point or in an opposite direction. *He took a contrary position to her.* adv., in a contrary way; in opposition; oppositely. *All my plans have gone contrary.*

contravene (kon′trə vēn′) v.t., 1. to come or be in conflict with; oppose. *We must contravene his orders.* 2. to violate; transgress. *They have tried repeatedly to contravene the rule.*

contretemps (kon′trə tän′; *Fr.* kôN tRᵊ tän′) n., unexpected and untoward event; embarrassing accident. *The oversale of tickets caused a minor contretemps in the theater.*

contrite (kən trīt′, kon′trīt) adj., suffering a sense of guilt; conscience-stricken; humbled; penitent. *The contrite child apologized.*

contrition (kən trish′ən) n., deep sorrow for sin or guilt; sincere penitence. *Contrition forced him to make the confession.*

contrive (kən trīv′) v., to scheme or design; plot; invent. *She began to contrive her revenge.*

controversial (kon′trə vûr′shəl) adj., of or pertaining to controversy; characterized by or connected with disputation. *The controversial bill passed by a narrow vote.*

controversy (kon′trə vûr′sē) n., disputation; debate; argument; contention. *A controversy arose over his power to break the treaty.*

controvert (kon′trə vûrt′, kon′trə vûrt′) v.t., to dispute; oppose by argument; contend against. *We must controvert his suitability for the job.*

contumacy (kon′tŏŏ mə sē, -tyŏŏ-) n., willful and persistent resistance to authority, esp. to a court of law. *His contumacy prejudiced the jury against him.*

contumely (kon′tŏŏ mə lē, -tyŏŏ-; kən tŏŏ′mə lē, -tyŏŏ′-; kon′təm lē) n., insulting, offensive, or abusive speech; humiliating treatment. *She braved their contumely by appearing alone.*

contusion (kən tŏŏ′zhən, -tyŏŏ′-) n., injury that does not break the skin; bruise. *He received a minor contusion when he slipped on the ice.*

convene (kən vēn′) v.t., to cause to assemble; call together; convoke. *The chairman will convene the annual stockholders' meeting.* v.i., to come together; meet in the same place; assemble. *The legislature will convene in January.*

conventional (kən ven′shə nəl) adj., arising out of custom or usage; adhering to accepted standards. *The conventional toast generated little interest.*

converge (kən vûrj′) v., to tend to meet in a point or line; approach nearer together. *Our thoughts converge over this, then?*

conversant (kən vûr′sənt, kon′vər-) adj., 1. acquainted by familiar use or study; proficient. *I am conversant with my car's engine.* 2. familiar by companionship; intimately associating. *He was conversant with the greatest artists of his time.*

converse (*n.* kon′vûrs; *v.* kən vûrs′; *adj.* kən vûrs′, kon′vûrs) n., something opposite or contrary to another. *She said she was happy but her eyes said the converse.* v.i., to talk informally with another. *Two such old friends may converse for hours.* adj., turned around; opposite or contrary. *The converse proposition may also be valid.*

conversion (kən vûr′zhən, -shən) n., act or state of changing or being changed.

The factory will undergo conversion from oil to coal.

convertible (kən vûr′tə bəl) n., automobile or boat having a removable top. *We went for a ride in the new convertible.* adj., capable of being changed in form, substance, or condition. *The couch was a convertible bed.*

convex (*n.*kon′veks; *adj.* kon veks′, kən-) n., outwardly curved body or space. *The bulging wall formed a convex.* adj., having an outwardly curved surface. *A convex mirror distorts what it reflects.*

conveyance (kən vā′əns) n., 1. act of carrying; transmission; transport. *We chose the cheapest form of conveyance.* 2. means of transport; vehicle. *The stagecoach is an outmoded conveyance.*

convivial (kən viv′ē əl) adj., relating to or in the nature of a feast or merrymaking; festal; jovial; agreeable. *It was a convivial celebration.*

conviviality (kən viv′ē al′i tē) n., convivial spirit or disposition; good humor; good fellowship. *She enjoyed the conviviality of old friends.*

convocation (kon′və kā′shən) n., 1. act of calling together or assembling by summons. *His urgent convocation surprised them.* 2. assembly. *The convocation passed five resolutions.*

convoke (kən vōk′) v.t., to call together; assemble by summons. *They will convoke the representatives at noon.*

convolution (kon′və lŏŏ′shən) n., 1. act of rolling or winding, or the state of being rolled or wound together. *The little boat tossed in the convolution of the waves.* 2. turn or winding; fold; whorl. *A convolution in the road concealed the ambush.*

convoy (*n.* kon′voi; *v.* kon′voi, kən voi′) n., 1. armed escort force. *It's risky to go without a convoy.* 2. that which goes under protective escort. *The convoy sails at dawn.* 3. act of convoying. *His convoy saved the mission.* v.t., to accompany for protection; escort. *We must convoy all merchant ships for the war's duration.*

convulsion (kən vul′shən) n., 1. violent, involuntary muscular contraction. *The convulsion marked the onset of her illness.* 2. any violent, irregular motion; turmoil; tumult; commotion. *The ground heaved in violent convulsion during the earthquake.*

cope (kōp) v.i., to strive or contend on equal terms; oppose. *She can cope with these problems.*

copious (kō′pē əs) adj., abundant; plentiful; ample; large in quantity or number. *He took copious notes at every lecture.*

cordial (kôr′jəl *or, esp. Brit.,* -dē əl) n., sweet, aromatic liquor. *Our host served a cordial with dessert.* adj., courteous; warm; friendly. *We maintain cordial relations with our neighbors.*

cordovan (kôr′də vən) n., soft, colored leather, originally from Córdoba, Spain. *His jacket was made of cordovan.* adj., made of cordovan. *She carried cordovan accessories.*

cornucopia (kôr′nə kō′pē ə) n., in classical mythology, the Horn of Plenty, a conical horn containing an endless supply of food and drink; hence, an abundant, overflowing supply. *The meal was a cornucopia of gourmet dishes.*

corollary (kôr′ə ler′ē, kor′-; *esp. Brit.,* kə rol′ə rē) n., in math, a proposition incidentally proved in proving another; hence, any immediate or easily drawn inference; natural consequence. *Her respect was a corollary to her love.*

coronary (kôr′ə ner′ē, kor′-) n., coronary thrombosis; heart attack. adj., pertaining to the human heart or the crownlike structure of blood vessels that supply the heart. *Coronary disease is a major health problem.*

corporeal (kôr pōr′ē əl, -pôr′-) adj., relating to a material body or material things; of a physical nature. *The ascetic renounced interest in corporeal matters.*

corpulence (kôr′pyə ləns) n., bulkiness or largeness of body; fleshiness; portliness; fatness. *Corpulence puts a strain on the cardiovascular system.*

corpulent (kôr′pyə lənt) adj., fleshy; portly; stout; fat. *He eased his corpulent frame into the chair.*

corpuscle (kôr′pə səl, -pus əl) n., minute particle; small body; cell, esp. a blood cell. *Blood is composed of red and white corpuscles.*

correlate (kôr′ə lāt′, kor′-) n., either of two related things. *Freedom is sometimes considered a correlate of responsibility.* v.t., to place in reciprocal relation. *Now we must correlate all the data.* v.i., to be reciprocally related. *His results do not correlate with hers.* adj., reciprocally related in any way. *The correlate motions of the trains created an optical illusion.*

correlation (kôr′ə lā′shən, kor′-) n., reciprocal relation; interdependence; interconnection. *There is little correlation between her words and her deeds.*

corroborate (kə rob′ə rāt′) v.t., to confirm; make more certain. *The witnesses will corroborate his testimony.*

corroboration (kə rob′ə rā′shən) n., act of confirming; verification; that which confirms. *We need corroboration of your identity.*

corrosive (kə rō′siv) n., anything that eats or wears away. *This chemical is a potent corrosive.* adj., having power to corrode; vexing. *Her corrosive manner alienated us.*

cortege (kôr tezh′, -tāzh′) n., train or procession of attendants or followers. *The funeral cortege turned into the cemetery.*

cosmetology (koz′mi tol′ə jē) n., art or profession of applying cosmetics. *The hairdresser was also trained in cosmetology.*

cosmic (koz′mik) adj., 1. pertaining to or characteristic of the universe. *Astronomers study the cosmic order.* 2. inconceivably prolonged or protracted. *This decision may have cosmic repercussions.*

cosmopolitan (koz′mə pol′i tən) n., one who is free from provincial or national prejudices; citizen of the world. *The* *true cosmopolitan feels at home almost anywhere.* adj., 1. belonging to all parts of the world; universal. *Poverty and ignorance are cosmopolitan problems.* 2. free from local, provincial, or national prejudices. *He displayed a cosmopolitan tolerance of strange ways.*

cosmopolite (koz mop′ə līt′) n., citizen of the world; one who is cosmopolitan in ideas or life. *The cosmopolite abhorred xenophobia.*

cosmos (koz′məs, -mōs) n., 1. orderly, harmonic universe, opposite of chaos. *He created a perfect cosmos in the poem.* 2. any of the *Cosmos* genus of American herbs, esp. a tall annual with showy ray flowers. *She made up a bouquet of cosmos.*

coterie (kō′tə rē) n., closely associated group of people with common interest; clique. *The coterie included several well-known writers and artists.*

council (koun′səl) n., 1. any assembly of persons summoned or convened for consultation, deliberation, or advice. *We held a family council.* 2. any body or group of persons wielding political power. *The town council voted for new street lights.*

counsel (koun′səl) n., 1. advice or opinion, esp. after deliberation. *I thanked him for his thoughtful counsel.* 2. consultation; deliberation. *After lengthy counsel we arrived at a decision.* 3. one who gives counsel, esp. in matters of law. *Is counsel for the defense ready?* v.t., to advise; admonish; instruct. *She can counsel you about career planning.* v.i., to consult; take counsel; deliberate. *We don't have time to counsel tonight.*

counselor (koun′sə lər) n., 1. one who counsels; adviser. *The guidance counselor recommended several colleges.* 2. lawyer, esp. a trial lawyer. *My counselor has prepared an excellent defense.*

countenance (koun′tᵊnəns) n., 1. appearance or expression of the face; look; aspect; visage. *His weathered countenance belied his youth.* 2. appearance of favor or good will; approval; en-

couragement. *She gave her countenance to the plan.* v.t., to appear friendly to; favor; encourage; aid. *I cannot countenance such behavior.*

counterfeit (koun′tər fit) n., imitation or copy designed to pass as the original; forgery. *This is not an antique, but a counterfeit.* v., make or be a copy; forge; imitate. *He tried to counterfeit happiness but he didn't fool her.* adj., made in imitation of an original with fraudulent intent; forged; sham. *These counterfeit papers would not fool anyone.*

countermand (n. koun′tər mand′, -mänd′; v. koun′tər mand′, -mänd′) n., contrary order; revocation of a former order. *The countermand arrived just in time to stay the execution.* v.t., to revoke an order; cancel a previous order by a new one. *He decided to countermand his first order.*

counterpoint (koun′tər point′) n., 1. harmonic blend of two or more independent melodies; polyphony. *He achieved an interesting counterpoint in this movement.* 2. opposite. *Black is the counterpoint of white.* 3. artistic use of contrastic elements. *His somber palette was a counterpoint to the romantic subject.*

countervail (koun′tər vāl′) v.t., to act against with equal force; counteract; offset. *My promise should countervail her anger.*

coup (kōō) n., successful move, act, or stroke; clever act. *We must congratulate you on the coup.*

coup de grace (kōōdᵊ grÄs′) n., death blow; finishing or decisive stroke, esp. done mercifully. *It was the coup de grace for the weakened party.*

coup d'etat (kōō′dä tä′) n., sudden, decisive political action; forceful overthrow of a government. *The coup d'etat brought in military rule.*

couplet (kup′lit) n., in poetry, two successive rhyming lines of the same length. *He sought a rhyme to finish the couplet.*

courier (kûr′ē ər, kŏŏr′-) n., messenger sent in haste with letters or despatches. *I'll send it by courier the moment it arrives.*

court-martial (kôrt′mär′shəl, -mär′-, kôrt′-) n., 1. military court. *The court-martial tried them for meeting.* 2. trial or conviction by, or session of, such a court. *He faces court-martial for desertion.* v.t., to arraign and try by court-martial. *We will court-martial the deserter.*

couturier (kŏŏ tŏŏr′ē ā′, -ē ər, -tŏŏr′yā; *Fr.* kŏŏ ty RYä′) n., one who makes, designs, and sells fashionable clothes. *The Italian couturier is sought after by fashionable women.*

covenant (kuv′ə nənt) n., formal, binding, mutual agreement of two or more persons; contract; compact. *They entered into a covenant to protect their goods.*

covert (kuv′ərt, kō′vərt) adj., covered; hidden; private; secret; concealed; disguised. *She shot a covert look at the young man.*

covet (kuv′it) v.t., to desire inordinately or without due regard to the rights of others. *She covets world recognition.*

covetous (kuv′i təs) adj., inordinately desirous; excessively eager to obtain and possess. *Her covetous brother tried to undermine her rights.*

cower (kou′ər) v.i., to crouch or stoop in fear or shame. *The inmate cowers under the brutal lash.*

cowl (koul) n., attached hood or hoodlike part of a garment, or of a thing. *He pulled the cowl over his head.*

coy (koi) adj., 1. shy, or affecting shyness. *The child was coy around strangers.* 2. trying to avoid commitment. *Stop being coy and give me your answer.*

crabbed (krab′id) adj., 1. perverse; cross; peevish; morose. *Old, crabbed Mr. Wilson never smiles.* 2. obtuse; difficult to understand. *The crabbed article needs heavy editing.*

craftily (kraf′tə lē, kräf′-) adj., with cunning; artfully; slyly. *He craftily rearranged the whole plan.*

crag (krag) n., steep, rugged rock or projecting part of a rock. *Near the summit a crag overhung the trail.*

crass (kras) adj., gross; stupid; obtuse. *His crass insensitivity lost him a friend.*

crave (krāv) v.t., 1. to long for or desire eagerly. *I crave something sweet.* 2. to ask for earnestly; beg or entreat for. *The prisoners crave pardon.* v.t., to ask earnestly; beg; sue; plead. *We crave your attention.*

craven (krā′vən) n., coward. *The craven ran from the battlefield.* v.t., to make cowardly. *Fear cravens their spirits.* adj., cowardly; mean-spirited. *He was dishonored by his craven behavior.*

credence (krēd′əns) n., belief; credit. *I can give no credence to the outrageous story.*

credo (krē′dō, krā′-) n., formula of belief; creed. *Our credo is "one for all and all for one."*

credulous (krej′ə ləs) adj., characterized by gullibility; uncritical; easily deceived. *My credulous nature often embarrasses me.*

creed (krēd) n., organized system of belief; accepted doctrine, esp. religious doctrine. *We do not discriminate on the basis of race, creed, or nationality.*

cremate (krē′māt) v.t., to burn up or destroy by heat; consume (a dead body) by fire as a substitute for burial. *Her will specified that we should cremate her remains.*

crème de la crème (kRem′də lA kRem′) *French.* n., best of the best. *These recordings represent the crème de la crème of her work.*

crescendo (kri shen′dō, -sen′dō; *It.* kRe shen′dô) n., gradual increase in volume, loudness, or force. *There was a crescendo of activity just before the deadline.* v.i., to increase in loudness or force. *The violins crescendo in this passage.* adj., gradually increasing in volume, loudness, or force. *The crescendo rumblings reinforced our fears.*

crescent (kres′ənt) n., curved figure resembling a segment of a ring terminating in points at either end, as a quarter moon. *The silver crescent hung in the* *night sky.* adj., shaped like a crescent; curved; resembling a quarter moon. *Waves washed the crescent beach.*

crestfallen (krest'fô'lən) adj., dejected; bowed; chagrined; dispirited. *He was crestfallen at the defeat.*

crevice (krev'is) n., narrow opening; cleft; crack; fissure. *They found shelter in a crevice in the rock.*

criminology (krim'ə nol'ə jē) n., study of crime and criminal behavior. *The detective had a degree in criminology.*

crimp (krimp) n., 1. that which has been curled or waved. *This sheet of metal has a crimp in it.* 2. that which hinders or interferes. *The rain put a crimp in our picnic.* v.t., 1. to make wavy; curl; corrugate. *Next, crimp the edge of the pie.* 2. to check; hinder; arrest. *These new rules will crimp production.*

criterion (krī tēr'ē ən) n., standard of judgment or criticism. *In this case, the most important criterion is cost.*

critique (kri tēk') n., act of criticizing or assessing, esp. as an article or essay. *Here is a favorable critique of the comedy.*

croissant (*Fr.* kʀwä säɴ') n., crescent-shaped pastry roll. *She breakfasted on a croissant and coffee.*

crony (krō'nē) n., intimate companion; familiar friend; associate. *He and his crony were virtually inseparable.*

crosier (krō'zhər) n., bishop's or abbot's staff, curved at the end like a shepherd's crook. *The bishop, with his crosier, led the procession.*

cross-examination (krôs'ig zam'ə nā'shən, kros'-) n., courtroom examination of a witness by the opposing side. *Our witness held up under her intense cross-examination.*

crotchety (kroch'i tē) adj., given to odd fancies or notions; eccentric; grouchy. *The crotchety man wouldn't listen to reason.*

crouton (kroo'ton, kroo ton') n., small cube of fried or toasted bread used as a garnish in salads, soups, etc. *She sprinkled croutons on her salad.*

crucify (kroo'sə fī') v.t., 1. to put to death by nailing or otherwise affixing to a cross. *It was common for the Romans to crucify highway robbers.* 2. to persecute; treat with gross injustice. *They'll crucify him if he brings that up again.*

cruet (kroo'it) n., vial or small glass bottle, esp. one for holding vinegar or oil for table use. *I admired the cut-glass cruet.*

crusade (kroo sād') n., 1. (*often cap.*) military expedition for religious ends, specifically one of the medieval expeditions undertaken by European Christians to capture the Holy Lands from the Moslems. *Richard the Lion-hearted helped lead the third Crusade.* 2. any vigorous concerted action for the defense or advancement of an idea or cause. *They led a crusade against higher prices.* v.i., to engage in a crusade; support or oppose any cause with zeal. *She will crusade with us for better safety.*

crux (kruks) n., essence. *We haven't yet gotten to the crux of the problem.*

cryptic (krip'tik) adj., 1. hidden; secret; occult. *The cryptic writing could be read only through a filter.* 2. ambiguous; puzzling; mysterious. *I didn't understand her cryptic warning.* 3. involving the use of codes or ciphers. *The cryptic transmissions were indecipherable.*

cryptography (krip tog'rə fē) n., act, art, or system of secret writing, codes, ciphers. *Spies are often trained in cryptography.*

crystallize (kris'tə līz') v.t., to form into crystals; cause to assume crystalline form. *The scientist tried to crystallize the chemicals.* v.i., to assume a crystalline form. *These chemicals will crystallize if heated.*

cudgel (kuj'əl) n., short, thick stick used as a weapon; club. *He used the log as a cudgel.* v.t., to strike with a cudgel or club; beat. *He will cudgel them if they dare return.*

cuisine (kwi zēn') n., manner or style of cooking; cookery. *They are particularly fond of Chinese cuisine.*

culinary (kyōō′lə ner′ē, kul′ə-) adj., pertaining or relating to the kitchen or the art of cookery; used in kitchens or cookery. *The chef mastered the culinary arts.*

cull (kul) n., something picked out, set aside, or rejected, usually for inferior quality. *The culls were sent to be recycled.* v.t., to pick out; select or separate one or more from others. *Try to cull the large from the small oysters.*

culminate (kul′mə nāt′) v.t., to complete; climax; bring to a close. *One encore will culminate the show.* v.i., to end; conclude; terminate. *The celebrations will culminate in fireworks.*

culmination (kul′mə nā′shən) n., 1. act or state of culminating. *This program will not reach its culmination until midnight.* 2. that in which anything reaches its zenith; climax; peak; acme. *This work marks the culmination of her career.*

culpable (kul′pə bəl) adj., deserving censure; blameworthy. *By ignoring it you're just as culpable as he.*

culprit (kul′prit) n., person arraigned for, or convicted of, a crime or offense. *The culprit was sentenced to jail.*

cult (kult) n., system of religious belief and ritual; also, its worshipers. *The Eastern cult devised its own ceremony.*

cultivate (kul′tə vāt′) v.t., 1. to prepare and work (land) to produce crops; till. *In the spring we cultivate our garden.* 2. to raise or produce by tillage. *I can't cultivate anything but weeds.* 3. to direct special attention to; devote study, labor, or care to. *She wants to cultivate new friends.*

cultured (kul′chərd) adj., 1. having culture; refined; cultivated. *The cultured woman speaks five languages.* 2. artificially grown or nurtured. *This necklace is made of cultured pearls.*

cumbersome (kum′bər səm) adj., 1. burdensome; troublesome; vexatious. *He was afflicted by a cumbersome grief.* 2. inconvenient; awkward; unwieldy. *We struggled to move the cumbersome piano.*

cumulative (kyōō′myə lā′tiv, -lə tiv) adj., increasing by successive additions. *The cumulative impact of the drought was devastating.*

cumulus (kyōō′myə ləs) n., cloud formation resembling thick, snowy-white hills with darker horizontal base. *Cumulus rolled ominously across the sky.*

cuneiform (kyōō nē′ə fôrm′, kyōō′nē ə-) n., wedge-shaped writing developed by the Sumerians and used throughout the ancient Near East. *The archeologist set about deciphering the cuneiform.* adj., 1. pertaining to cuneiform. *They discovered several cuneiform tablets.* 2. wedge-shaped. *The dress was trimmed with a cuneiform embroidery.*

cupidity (kyōō pid′i tē) n., eager desire to possess something; inordinate desire; greed. *His cupidity will be his downfall.*

curate (kyōōr′it) chiefly Brit., n., clergyman employed as an assistant to a vicar or rector. *The curate will assume some of the pastoral duties.*

curator (kyōō rā′tər, kyōōr′ā-) n., one who is in charge of a museum, art collection, etc. *The curator gave us a preview of the exhibit.*

curfew (kûr′fyōō) n., 1. order specifying a time in the evening after which certain rules and regulations will take effect. *The townspeople obeyed the curfew.* 2. signal noting the beginning of a curfew. *The curfew sounded at sunset.* 3. time when a curfew begins. *Freshman curfew was 11 p.m.*

curmudgeon (kər muj′ən) n., irascible, churlish person. *The curmudgeon frightened the neighborhood children.*

currency (kûr′ən sē, kur′-) n., 1. that which is used as a medium of exchange; money. *She exchanged dollars for French currency.* 2. state or fact of being current. *The rumor gained wide currency.*

curry (kûr′ē, kur′ē) n., 1. pungent dish of spiced vegetables, meat, etc., served over rice. *We ordered curry at the Indian restaurant.* 2. any dish flavored with curry powder or other pungent spices. *They served lamb curry.* v.t., 1. to prepare (food) as a curry. *This dish will be more interesting if we curry it.* 2. to rub and clean (a horse) with a comb; groom. *Curry your mount after a day's ride.* 3. to seek advancement or gain through flattery. *Don't try to curry favor with me.*

cursorily (kûr′sə rə lē) adv., in a hasty manner; superficially; hastily. *The harried official glanced cursorily at her identification card.*

cursory (kûr′sə) adj., hasty; superficial; careless. *He gave only a cursory glance in the mirror.*

curtail (kər tāl′) v.t., to cut short; cut off the end or a part of; diminish; abridge. *She had to curtail her speech.*

custody (kus′tə dē) n., 1. keeping; guarding; care; watch. *The documents are all in her custody.* 2. confinement; imprisonment; incarceration. *The escapee was returned to custody.*

custom (kus′təm) n., 1. common use or practice; established manner or way. *It is our custom to say grace before dinner.* 2. legal toll, tax, or duty imposed on merchandise imported and exported. *These goods are subject to custom.* adj., made to order; done for individual customers. *He wears custom boots.*

cybernetics (sī′bər net′iks) n., study of electrical and mechanical systems designed to replace human control functions. *They were studying for degrees in cybernetics.*

cyclic (sī′klik, sik′lik) adj., pertaining to or moving in a cycle or circle; governed by a regular law of variation. *The economy undergoes many cyclic fluctuations.*

cynic (sin′ik) n., one who believes human actions are motivated only by self-interest. *A cynic doesn't believe in generosity.*

cynical (sin′i kəl) adj., like or characteristic of a cynic; sarcastic; captious. *He was cynical about her so-called benevolence.*

cytology (sī tol′ə jē) n., study of the structure, functions, and formation of cells. *She worked in the hospital's department of cytology.*

Dd

dactyl (dak′t²l, -til) n., in poetry, metric foot composed of one long and two short syllables. *The student tried to use the dactyl in his verse.*

daguerreotype (də ger′ə tīp′, -ē ə tīp′) n., early form of photograph, made with a silver or silver-covered copper plate. *He had a fine collection of old daguerreotypes.*

dais (dā′is, dī-′, dās) n., raised platform used for seating or prominent display. *All eyes were on the king's dais.*

dale (dāl) n., valley. *They looked down on the green dale.*

dalliance (dal′ē əns, dal′yəns) n., 1. idleness; loafing. *His boss reprimanded him for his dalliance.* 2. amorous play; flirtation. *Their affair grew out of a careless dalliance.*

dally (dal′ē) v.i., 1. to linger. *He began to dally around the music hall.* 2. to act playfully or casually. *He didn't want the man to dally with her affections.*

damask (dam′əsk) n., 1. cloth with a woven surface design. *The heavy draperies were silk damask.* 2. pink, as the hue of a Damask rose. *The damask matched the blush in her cheeks.* adj., rose-colored. *A damask glow heralded the sunrise.*

dank (daṅk) adj., unpleasantly damp. *They threw him into the dank cell.*

dappled (dap′əld) adj., spotted; speckled; mottled, often referring to an animal's coat of fur. *He jumped astride his dappled steed.*

dastard (das′t²rd) n., one who commits cowardly or treacherous acts. *The dastard betrayed his friends.*

daunt (dônt, dänt) v.t., to intimidate; dispirit; cow; discourage; inhibit. *Heavy storms did not daunt the sailors.*

dauntless (dônt′lis, dänt′-) adj., fearless;

undismayed. *They sailed the dauntless ship through the rocks.*

dauphin (dô′fin; *Fr.* dō faɴ′) n., title of oldest son of a king of France. *The dauphin was a child when he became king.*

davit (dav′it, dā′vit) n., one of a pair of upright supports of an apparatus used to raise or lower objects along the side of a ship. *The lifeboats were lowered from the davits.*

dawdle (dôd′²l) v.i, to waste time; idle or delay. *The woman told him not to dawdle on the way home.*

dazzle (daz′əl) v.t., 1. to shine brightly upon. *The lamp dazzled them.* 2. to impress or inspire with awe. *She wanted to dazzle her new beau.*

dearth (dûrth) n., extreme scarcity. *There was a dearth of jobs for the applicants.*

debacle (dā bä′kəl, -bak′əl, də-) n., tumultuous disruption; rout. *The police precipitated a debacle.*

debar (di bär′) v.t., to exclude or prevent. *The guard tried to debar the newsmen.*

debase (di bās′) v.t., to reduce in status, quality, or character. *She didn't want to debase the significance of his work.*

debauch (di bôch′) n., corrupt act or event; orgy. *He was shocked at the wanton debauch.* v.t., to seduce; corrupt into wantonness. *His attempt to debauch the young girl failed.*

debenture (di ben′chər) n., written acknowledgement of indebtedness; bond. *The insolvent bank could not honor its debentures.*

debilitate (di bil′i tāt′) v.t., to weaken. *The humid weather tended to debilitate them.*

debility (di bil′i tē) n., handicap; weakness. *Her debility was her illiteracy.*

debonair (deb′ə nâr′) adj., charming; urbane. *His debonair manners won them over.*

debris (də brē′, dä′brē *or, esp. Brit.,* deb′rē) n., scattered remains, ruins; untidy accumulation of rocks and/or other materials. *The flood washed debris all over their yard.*

debutante (deb′yo͞o tänt′, -tant′) n., young woman upon being formally introduced to society for the first time. *The debutante received her guests.*

decade (dek′ād) n., ten years' time. *The anniversary marked a decade in business.*

decadence (dek′ə dəns, di kād′᷉ns) n., deterioration; decay; degeneration, esp. in a moral sense. *The moralist decried the decadence of modern society.*

decadent (dek′ə dənt, di kād′᷉nt) n., one who is undergoing decline or decay. *The decadent ceased to care about his looks.* adj., pertaining to a condition of decline or decay. *The decadent art form finally went out of fashion.*

decamp (di kamp′) v.i., 1. to break camp; move an encampment. *The army prepared to decamp.* 2. leave abruptly; take off; abscond. *The burglar hastily decamped.*

decant (di kant′) v.t., to siphon off top layer of liquid only, without disturbing sediment. *They began carefully to decant the wine.*

decanter (di kan′tər) n., container for decanting or holding decanted liquids. *He poured the sherry into the glass decanter.*

decapitate (di kap′i tāt′) v.t., to behead. *The farmer had to decapitate the hen.*

deceit (di sēt′) n., act or intention of tricking or betraying. *She used deceit to get the job.*

decelerate (dē sel′ə rāt′) v., to slow down or cause to slow down. *The car began to decelerate.*

deciduous (di sij′o͞o əs) adj., having parts that fall off, esp. leaves. *Deciduous trees are bare in the winter.*

decimate (des′ə māt′) v.t., to destroy or eliminate a large part of; eliminate one

tenth of. *Smallpox began to decimate the population.*

declaim (di klām′) v., 1. to speak rhetorically; recite as a formal exercise. *He began to declaim in French.* 2. to harangue. *He began to declaim heatedly against the proposal.*

declamatory (di klam′ə tōr′ē, -tôr′ē) adj., pertaining to a rhetorical display. *Her declamatory style impressed the audience.*

declarative (di klar′ə tiv) adj., making a declaration. *Her declarative sentence left no room for doubt.*

declension (di klen′shən) n., class of nouns or adjectives that commonly undergo similar changes of form in different cases, genders, tenses, persons, moods, or voices. *The student was studying Latin declensions.*

declination (dek′lə nā′shən) n., 1. downward slope or bend; decline. *The novice gaped at the declination of the ski slope.* 2. deviation from a normal point or course; turning away. *The hermit chose declination from social contact.* 3. negative response; refusal. *It was a polite but firm declination.* 4. deterioration; decadence. *The red house was in a woeful state of declination.*

declivity (di kliv′i tē) n., downward slope, inclination, or incline. *The earthquake created a deep declivity on the mountainside.*

décolleté (dā′kol tā′, -kol ə-, dek′ə lə-; *Fr.* dā kôl tā′) adj., having a low-cut neckline; wearing a garment in such style. *Her décolleté gown was inappropriate for the afternoon tea.*

decompose (dē′kəm pōz′) v.i., to break down into component parts; rot. *The leaves were left to decompose.*

decorous (dek′ər əs, di kōr′əs, -kôr′-) adj., proper; in good taste; conventional. *Her decorous behavior pleased her grandmother.*

decorum (di kōr′əm, -kôr′-) n., propriety; good taste. *Her outlandish costume was a breach of decorum.*

decoy (*n.* di koi′, dē′koi; *v.* di koi′) n., device or person used as lure. *The* *policewoman was a decoy.* v.t., to lure or entice. *She tried to decoy him into her apartment.*

decrepit (di krep′it) adj., worn out and deteriorated; old or weak. *She was afraid to stand on the decrepit porch.*

decry (di krī′) v.t., to express disapproval of. *The candidate liked to decry his opponents' views.*

dedicate (ded′ə kāt′) v.t., 1. to set aside for specific purpose. *He dedicated one tenth of his salary to the church.* 2. to become devoted or committed to. *She decided to dedicate herself to nursing.* 3. to inscribe, or ceremoniously open to the public. *The town decided to dedicate the school to her.*

deduce (di dōōs′, -dyōōs′) v.t., to conclude from logical reasons; infer. *He was able to deduce her motive.*

deducible (di dōōs′ə bəl, -dyōōs′-) adj., permitting revelation through the reasoning process; deductible. *The experiment provided deducible proof of his theory.*

deduct (di dukt′) v.t., to take away from; subtract. *He can deduct his office expenses from his income tax.*

deduction (di duk′shən) n., 1. act of taking away, or subtracting. *After the deduction for taxes, there was little left.* 2. that which is taken away or subtracted. *It was a questionable deduction.* 3. an inference. *His deduction proved correct.*

deed (dēd) n., 1. an exploit or performance; something that is done. *It was too late; the deed was done.* 2. a legal document indicating ownership or other agreement. *The deed was contested in court.*

deem (dēm) v.t., to come to believe or think. *He began to deem it impossible to continue.*

deface (di fās′) v.t., to damage superficially. *They were caught trying to deface the mural.*

de facto (dē fak′tō) adj., actual; extant. *It was a case of de facto segregation.*

defalcate (di fal′kāt, -fôl′-) v.t., to steal portions of funds held in trust. *The treasurer tried to defalcate part of her inheritance.*

defalcation (dē′fal kā′shən, -fôl-) n., theft of funds held in trust. *His defalcation considerably reduced her annuity.*

defamation (def′ə mā′shən, dē′fə-) n., the act of injuring another's reputation. *She sued the newspaper for defamation of character.*

defamatory (di fam′ə tōr′ē, -tôr′ē) adj., pertaining to the act of attacking the reputation of another. *Her defamatory remarks were unjust.*

default (di fôlt′) n., legal or moral failure to do something; failure to appear as required. *They lost the game by default.* v.i., to fail to meet a legal, financial, or moral obligation. *She defaulted on her car loan.*

defeatist (di fē′tist) n., one who is resigned to defeat. *The defeatist depressed the others.* adj., pertaining to a negative, resigned attitude. *Her defeatist attitude made her give up too soon.*

defecate (def′ə kāt′) v.i., to discharge excrement; have a bowel movement. *He was forced to defecate in the woods.*

defect (*n.* dē′fekt, di fekt′; *v.* di fekt′) n., imperfection; incompleteness. *The table was on sale because of the defect.* v.i., to abandon a cause or country, often to join another. *He wanted to defect to Sweden.*

defection (di fek′shən) n., 1. desertion; betrayal of allegiance. *She was court-martialed for defection of duty.* 2. defect; flaw; imperfection; lack. *She tried to repair the defection in the dress.*

defective (di fek′tiv) n., one who is physically or mentally subnormal. *The defective spent two years in the hospital.* adj., pertaining to imperfection or abnormality. *He returned the defective radio to the store.*

defendant (di fen′dənt) n., the one against whom a charge is brought by a plaintiff in legal action. *The defendant conferred with her lawyer.*

defer (di fûr') v.t., to delay or postpone. *They decided to defer the vote for a week.* v.i., to yield to another's request or decision. *She had to defer to her sister's desire.*

deference (def'ər əns) n., honoring of another's wishes. *In deference to his father, he declined.*

deferential (def'ə ren'shəl) adj., pertaining to courteous, respectful, or ingratiating attitude. *His deferential manners pleased her.*

defiant (di fī'ənt) adj., antagonistic; insolent; challenging. *The defiant girl angered the teacher.*

deficient (di fish'ənt) adj., lacking; subnormal; incomplete. *Their diet was deficient in nutrients.*

deficit (def'i sit; *Brit. also* di fis'it) n., the state of having greater debts than assets. *The national deficit alarmed the senator.*

defile (di fīl') v.t., to contaminate, or make unclean or impure. *They attempted to defile the water supply.*

definitive (di fin'i tiv) adj., 1. authoritative and complete. *It was the definitive edition of Twain's works.* 2. final; conclusive. *It was the definitive battle of the war.*

deflate (di flāt') v., to remove air from; reduce in size or significance. *She didn't want to deflate his happy confidence.*

deflect (di flekt') v.t., to cause to turn aside; deviate. *He was able to deflect her attention.*

deflower (di flou'ər) v.t., to ravish, or deprive of innocence. *He deflowered her of her noble ideas.*

deforestation (dē fôr'ə stā'shən, -for'-) n., complete clearing or removal of trees from a forest area. *The deforestation caused serious soil erosion.*

defray (di frā') v.t., to pay costs for. *He promised to defray her moving expenses.*

deft (deft) adj., having qualities of skill and grace. *Her deft fingers opened the box quickly.*

defunct (di fungkt') adj., finished; ended.

The defunct business closed its doors.

degenerate (*n.* di jen'ər it; *v.* di jen'ə rāt') n., one who has undergone decline or debasement. *The degenerate could no longer support his child.* v.i., to deteriorate or decline. *The party began to degenerate into a brawl.*

degradation (deg'rə dā'shən) n., the condition of debasement or decline. *Alcohol was the chief cause of her degradation.*

degrade (di grād', dē grād') v.t., 1. to reduce in status or rank. *They had to degrade her to clerk.* 2. to pervert or corrupt. *She couldn't degrade him with her wiles.*

dehydrate (dē hī'drāt) v.t., to remove water from foods. *They decided to dehydrate the apple slices.* v.i., to lose body fluids. *She dehydrated during her illness.*

deify (dē'ə fī') v.t., to worship or glorify as god. *Some kings attempted to deify themselves.*

deign (dān) v.i., to condescend. *He would not deign to discuss it.*

déjà vu (dā zha voo') n., mental illusion that a current happening has been previously experienced. *His remark prompted an uncanny sensation of déjà vu.*

dejected (di jek'tid) adj., in low spirits; depressed. *They tried to cheer up the dejected boy.*

de jure (dē joor'ē; *Lat.* de yoo're) by the law; according to law; by right. *Citizen arrest is de jure in an emergency situation.*

delectable (di lek'tə bəl) adj., very pleasing; delicious. *The delectable blonde smiled at his compliment.*

delegate (*n.* del'ə gāt', -git; *v.* del'ə gāt') n., one who acts for or represents another. *The delegate outlined his party's position.* v.t., to assign or appoint. *The chairman began to delegate committee members.*

delete (di lēt') v.t., to leave out; omit. *The lawyer had to delete the clause from the contract.*

deleterious (del'i tēr'ē əs) adj., harmful;

pernicious. *The restriction had a deleterious effect on their efforts.*

delicate (del′ə kit) adj., 1. fragile; dainty; fine. *The delicate lace was very expensive.* 2. squeamish; sickly. *She was in delicate health.*

delineate (di lin′ē āt′) v.t., 1. to sketch; draw in outline. *The highway is clearly delineated on the map.* 2. to describe clearly; portray; depict. *Shakespeare excels in ability to delineate character.*

delineation (di lin′ē ā′shən) n., that produced by careful description. *Her delineation of the character was lifelike.*

delinquent (di liñg′kwənt) n., 1. one who is late in payment. *The bill collector called the delinquent.* 2. one who falls short of duty or requirement. *The delinquent sneered at the priest.* adj., 1. being late in making payment. *She was delinquent in her taxes.* 2. falling short in duty or obligation. *He was a casual, even delinquent, parent.*

delirium (di lēr′ē əm) n., frenzied mental state; feverish disturbance. *She said some strange things in her delirium.*

delta (del′tə) n., 1. fourth letter in Greek alphabet: Δ or δ. 2. alluvial deposit at river mouth. *The soil around the delta was mineral-rich.*

delude (di lōōd′) v.t., to mislead or deceive. *He managed to delude them about his plans.*

deluge (del′yōōj) n., overflow, as in heavy rain or flood. *The deluge threatened to destroy the crops.* v.t., to inundate; overflow. *The committee deluged the congressman with protests.*

delusion (di lōō′zhən) n., that which is falsely or misguidedly believed or seen. *It was a delusion of fame that drove him.*

delusive (di lōō′siv) adj., 1. misleading; false; deceptive. *The bird's delusive behavior was designed to protect its nest.* 2. as in a delusion; unreal; imaginary. *Mental illness was obvious from her delusive babbling.*

delve (delv) v.t., to investigate; to dig deeply into. *He began to delve into his mother's past.*

demagogue (dem′ə gôg′, -gog′) n., leader who appeals to prejudice and/or fear to gain power. *The demagogue jailed his chief opponents.*

demean (di mēn′) v.t., to debase or lower. *She would not demean herself for the promotion.*

demeanor (di mē′nər) n., outward manner; bearing. *Her gracious demeanor put them at ease.*

demerit (dē mer′it) n., mark of disapproval or disfavor. *The cadet received a demerit for the remark.*

demesne (di mān′, -mēn′) n., 1. lawful ownership of land. *A thorough title search guarantees the landholder's demesne.* 2. private estate, owned by its occupant. *The manor lord offered to rent part of his demesne.* 3. estate grounds. *The wealthy nobleman rode over his ancestral demesne.*

demise (di mīz′) n., death; cessation. *They all mourned his demise.*

demitasse (dem′i tas′, -täs′; *Fr.* də mē täs′) n., small cup, and/or the strong black coffee served in it. *They enjoyed the demitasse after dinner.*

democracy (di mok′rə sē) n., 1. government by the people through an open electoral system. *The U.S. is a representative democracy.* 2. society wherein social conditions are equal, and personal rights are guaranteed. *Democracy needs freedom of speech to prevail.*

demography (di mog′rə fē) n., the formal study of populations, including size, density, distribution, migration, and vital statistics. *Demography is helpful in determining future school needs.*

demolish (di mol′ish) v.t., to tear down; raze; destroy. *They had to demolish the old house.*

demolition (dem′ə lish′ən, dē′mə-) n., the act of razing or tearing down. *They protested the demolition of the landmark.*

demoniac (di mō′nē ak′, dē′ mə nī′ak) adj., pertaining to a demon; possessed by a demon. *Her demoniac laughter echoed in the hall.*

demur (di mûr′) n., objection or qualm.

They did not raise a demur about it.
v.i., to hesitate or object. *They had to demur this time.*

demure (di myŏŏr′) adj., shy, modest. *The demure young woman remained silent.*

demurrage (di mûr′ij) n., detention of a cargo ship or a land freight conveyance by shipper; also, charge levied for such a delay. *The delay in unloading cost him a heavy demurrage.*

denigrate (den′ə grāt′) v.t., to defame; sully. *They tried to denigrate the opposition party.*

denizen (den′i zən) n., one who dwells within; occupant; inhabitant. *The exotic bird is a denizen of the jungle.*

denomination (di nom′ə nā′shən) n., 1. value or size, as in money. *They could not cash the large denomination.* 2. religious administrative unit. *Several denominations met to discuss the problem.*

denotation (dē′nō tā′shən) n., 1. indication; mark; sign. *The packed theater was a denotation of the actor's popularity.* 2. meaning; designation. *A prefix changes a word's denotation.*

denote (di nōt′) v.t., to mean or indicate meaning. *The signal seemed to denote readiness.*

denouement (dā′nōō mäN′) n., 1. resolution or unravelling of a plot. *The novel makes no moral in its denouement.* 2. solution; outcome. *The congressional investigation reached its denouement after five long years.*

denounce (di nouns′) v.t., to accuse or proclaim as evil. *They prepared to denounce the traitor.*

density (den′si tē) n., 1. mass per unit volume, usually given in grams per cubic centimeter. *The student will measure the density of the gas.* 2. stupidity; lack of intelligence. *Please excuse my density; I didn't understand.*

dentifrice (den′tə fris) n., substance for cleaning teeth. *The dentist recommended a new dentifrice.*

denude (di nōōd′, -nyōōd′) v.t., to strip; lay bare. *The flood denuded the landscape.*

dependable (di pen′də bəl) adj., reliable; trustworthy. *The dependable worker was promoted.*

depersonalization (dē pûr′sə nᵊli zā′shən) n., process whereby individuality is removed. *They resented the depersonalization of their jobs.*

depict (di pikt′) v.t., to represent graphically or verbally. *The artist tried to depict the entire battle.*

depilate (dep′ə lāt′) v.t., remove hair from. *The fire depilated his eyebrows.*

deplete (di plēt′) v.t., to exhaust; empty. *The siege began to deplete their supplies.*

deplorable (di plōr′ə bəl, -plôr′-) adj., regrettable; very unfortunate. *The prisoners lived in deplorable conditions.*

deploy (di ploi′) v., to arrange or use machinery or manpower strategically. *The lieutenant began to deploy his scouts.*

deport (di pōrt′, -pôrt′) v.t., 1. to conduct; behave. *She couldn't deport herself in a seemly way.* 2. to expel; banish. *The court agreed to deport the felon.*

depose (di pōz′) v.t., to remove from high position, esp. from monarchy. *The rebels sought to depose the king.*

deposition (dep′ə zish′ən, dē′pə-) n., formal declaration or statement used in legal actions. *The officer took her deposition before she left.*

depository (di poz′i tōr′ē, -tôr′ē) n., place where something is left for safekeeping. *They returned their books to the library depository.*

deprave (di prāv′) v.t., to corrupt, malign, or debase. *They feared the home conditions would deprave the child.*

depravity (di prav′i tē) n., corruption; baseness. *His depravity was consummated by the theft.*

deprecate (dep′rə kāt′) v.t., to express disapproval of. *She had to deprecate her son's disobedience.*

depreciate (di prē′shē āt′) v.t., to disparage; belittle. *She didn't want to depreciate his work.* v.i., to lose value. *The car began to depreciate rapidly.*

depredation (dep′ri dā′shən) n., act or condition of ravaging, plundering. *They* *were horrified at the depredation of the town.*

depression (di presh′ən) n., 1. low area; hollow. *The prehistoric footprints left a fossilized depression in the rock strata.* 2. severe economic slow-down. *Unemployment was severe during the depression of the '30s.* 3. melancholia; dejection; despondency. *The defeated congressman suffered from depression.*

deprivation (dep′rə vā′shən) n., act or state of loss or removal. *The weeks of deprivation showed in their faces.*

deputize (dep′yə tīz′) v.t., to appoint as deputy. *The sheriff had to deputize five new people.*

deranged (di rānjd′) n., mentally unstable; insane. *The deranged woman clawed at her own face.*

derby (dûr′bē; *Brit.* där′bē) n., 1. (cap.) annual horse race at Epsom Downs, England; also at Churchill Downs, Ky. *The Derby is a social as well as a sporting event.* 2. any open-to-all contest. *The boys entered the soap box derby.* 3. narrow-brimmed, round, stiff felt hat; "bowler." *He touched his derby in greeting.*

derelict (der′ə likt) n., 1. something abandoned. *They could see the derelict off the coast.* 2. tramp or bum. *The derelict slept on the park bench.* adj., negligent. *She was derelict in her duty to the child.*

dereliction (der′ə lik′shən) n., intentional negligence or abandonment. *They were charged with dereliction of duty.*

deride (di rīd′) v.t., to belittle; ridicule. *They began to deride her guillibility.*

derision (di rizh′ən) n., act or state of ridicule; contempt. *She was humiliated by their derision.*

derisive (di rī′siv) adj., expressing or pertaining to act of deriding. *Their derisive remarks hurt him.*

derive (di rīv′) v.t., 1. to obtain or draw from. *They were able to derive salt from the sea.* 2. to infer or conclude. *She began to derive satisfaction from the work.* v.i., to stem from. *He derives from very good stock.*

dermatologist (dûr′mə tol′ə jist) n., physician specializing in skin diseases,

functions, and structure. *The dermatologist recommended a special soap.*

derogate (der′ə gāt′) v.t., to belittle or detract from. *She wanted to derogate her own role in order to amplify his.*

derogative (di rog′ə tiv) adj., disparaging; belittling. *Her derogative report found nothing right.*

derogatory (di rog′ə tōr′ē, -tôr′ē) adj., disparaging; negative. *Her derogatory remarks alienated them.*

derrick (der′ik) n., 1. apparatus used to lift heavy objects, often employing ropes, gears, pulleys, and cross-beams; hoist. *The derrick lifted the heavy steel beam.* 2. structure placed over an oil well to house drilling machinery. *The derrick was destroyed in the hurricane.*

derringer (der′in jər) n., small pistol with a short barrel, used effectively at close range. *President Lincoln was shot with a derringer.*

dervish (dûr′vish) n., one of a Muslim sect noted for its whirling dances. *The dervish spun himself into a trance.*

descant (*n.* des′kant; *v.* des kant′, dis-) n., the higher voices in part music or singing; a counterpoint soprano song or melody. *The descant rose above the hymn.* v.i., to sing, talk, or write at length. *She prepared to descant to the audience.*

descend (di send′) v.i., 1. to come down; swoop; drop; decline. *The eagle began to descend from her perch.* 2. to proceed from. *She descended from an ancient family.*

descendant (descendent) (di sen′dənt) n., one derived from another or another group. *She was a descendant of Anne Hutchinson.* adj., proceeding from; descending. *He was descendant from a long line of scientists.*

descry (di skrī′) v.t., 1. to detect; perceive; espy. *They did not descry land for three months.* 2. to proclaim; announce; tout. *The vendor began to descry her wares.*

desecrate (des′ə krāt′) v.t., to treat profanely or contemptuously. *They didn't want to desecrate the altar.*

desensitization (dē sen′si tī zā′shən) n.,

act of rendering less sensitive or non-reactive. *The desensitization process left him without emotions.*

deserter (di zûr′tər) n., one who abandons his post or leaves without permission. *The deserter fled behind enemy lines.*

desiccate (des′ə kāt′) v.t., to dehydrate; to dry up emotionally, creatively, or intellectually. *The hot Saharan wind began to desiccate them.*

design (di zīn′) n., 1. plan or outline; purpose; strategy. *It was his design to surprise them.* 2. underlying motif or pattern. *The geometric design repeated on the edges.* v.t., to plan or contrive. *She wanted to design her own wedding dress.*

desist (di zist′, -sist′) v.i., cease; stop. *They were told to desist in their demands.*

desolate (*adj.* des′ə lit; *v.* des′ə lāt) adj., bleak, barren; gloomy. *The desolate landscape chilled their hearts.* v.t., to make barren. *The locusts desolated the corn fields.*

despicable (des′pi kə bəl; *for emphasis* di spik′ə bəl) adj., hateful; mean; contemptible. *It was a despicable trick.*

despise (di spīz′) v.t., to hold in contempt; dislike. *She began to despise the meddling woman.*

despoil (di spoil′) v.t., to pillage; plunder, rob; lay waste. *The marauders despoiled the tiny village.*

despondent (di spon′dənt) adj., listless; unhappy; depressed. *The despondent patient worried him.*

despot (des′pət, -pot) n., 1. absolute ruler; autocrat. *The despot kept tight hold on the treasury.* 2. tyrant; one who abuses his or her power. *The despot closed down all the newspapers.*

despotism (des′pə tiz′əm) n., autocratic rule; system of absolutism. *His despotism was ruining the country.*

destitute (des′ti tōōt′, -tyōōt′) adj., totally lacking in necessary resources and support. *The destitute woman pleaded for help.*

destroy (di stroi′) v.t., to demolish or break apart; to cause annihilation. *The*

awful noise destroyed her peace of mind.*

desuetude (des′wi tōōd′, -tyōōd′) n., condition of disuse; obsolescence. *The custom of curtsying is in virtual desuetude.*

desultory (des′əl tōr′ē, -tôr′ē) adj., unconnected; random. *The maid's desultory cleaning exasperated him.*

détente (dā tänt′; *Fr.* dā tÄNt′) n., in politics, a policy of restraint. *Détente was preferable to outright hostilities.*

deter (di tûr′) v.t., to prevent or turn aside; to inhibit. *She tried to deter them from leaving.*

detergent (di tûr′jənt) n., any of various chemical cleansing agents, often referred to as synthetic detergents to differentiate them from common soap. *She bought a new dishwashing detergent.* adj., cleansing; purifying; purging. *The detergent antiseptic should prevent infection.*

deteriorate (di tēr′ē ə rāt′) v.i., to decompose; break down; degenerate. *The discussion began to deteriorate into a quarrel.*

determinate (di tûr′mə nit) adj., pertaining to established limits; definitive. *The determinate instructions left him no choice.*

deterrent (di tûr′ənt, -tur′-, -ter′-) n., that which stops or inhibits. *It was a deterrent to their progress.* adj., pertaining to inhibition or blockage. *The deterrent factor was their stubbornness.*

detestable (di tes′tə bəl) adj., hateful; abominable. *The detestable braces were finally removed.*

detonate (det′ənāt′) v., to explode or cause to explode. *He went in to detonate the bomb.*

detonation (det′ə nā′shən) n., 1. exploding or causing explosion. *The landmine was capable of detonation at the slightest contact.* 2. explosion, accompanied by noise and shock-waves. *The detonation of the bomb was felt for miles around.*

detoxify (dē tok′sə fī′) v.t., to remove poisons from. *They had to detoxify him quickly to save his life.*

detract (di trakt′) v.t., 1. to withdraw or

take away; back away from. *The paper had to detract the story because the facts could not be verified.* 2. to disparage. *The hat seemed to detract from her appearance.*

detraction (di trak′shən) n., that which causes lowering of reputation or status; disparagement. *The reprimand was a detraction from his good record.*

detriment (de′trə mənt) n., disadvantage or harm. *The loss was a detriment to morale.*

de trop (də trō′) French. adj., superfluous. *The de trop remark added nothing to his argument.*

devastate (dev′ə stāt′) v.t., to ruin; ravage. *They feared the frost would devastate the orchards.*

deviate (n., adj. dē′vē it; v. dē′vē āt′) n., one who is abnormal. *The deviate showed no understanding of the situation.* v.i., to vary or stray from normal or established way. *They decided to deviate from their routine.* adj., pertaining to abnormal behavior. *They hoped to rehabilitate the deviate girl.*

devious (dē′vē əs) adj., 1. tricky; crafty. *The devious bargain had him trapped.* 2. twisted; roundabout. *The devious path wound through the trees.*

devoid (di void′) adj., lacking; empty. *She was devoid of humor.*

devoir (də vwär′, dev′wär; *Fr.* də vwAR′) n., responsibility; obligation; respect. *It was his devoir to see her home at that late hour.*

devolve (di volv′) v.i., 1. to come about in time; come to pass. *Your ambition may devolve; be patient.* 2. to fall upon; be passed down; be relegated. *In case of disability, a president's duties devolve upon the vice president.*

devotee (dev′ə tē′) n., one who is devoted to or enthusiastic about something. *She was a devotee of the ballet.*

devout (di vout′) adj., pious; devoted to religion. *The devout woman knelt to pray.*

dew point (dōō′point′) temperature at which air becomes saturated when cooled without addition of moisture or change of pressure. *Fog and dew are formed when air temperature drops beneath the dew point.*

dexterity (dek ster′i tē) n., facility; adroitness. *He accomplished his tasks with surprising dexterity.*

dexterous (dek′strəs, -stər əs) adj., expert; skillful. *His dexterous planing smoothed the shelf.*

diabolic (dī′ə bol′ik) adj., devilish; fiendish. *Her diabolic plan almost got them.*

diabolical (dī′ə bol′ə kəl) adj., 1. of or pertaining to the devil; demonic. *The witch muttered a diabolical incantation.* 2. cruel; wicked; fiendish. *The diabolical director brought the actress to tears.*

diadem (dī′ə dem′) n., crown or band symbolic of royalty. *The sun shone like a diadem on his hair.*

diagnosis (dī′əg nō′sis) n., medical or professional conclusion or description. *The lab tests confirmed his diagnosis.*

diagnostic (dī′əg nos′tik) n., profession of diagnosis. *He was skilled in diagnostic.* adj., pertaining to diagnosis. *The disease was often a diagnostic puzzle.*

diagonal (dī ag′ə nəl) n., straight oblique line, plane, or direction. *She cut the material on the diagonal.* adj., pertaining to a line or plane that joins or passes through two nonadjacent edges of a rectangle or polyhedron. *He drew a diagonal line to form two triangles.*

diagram (dī′ə gram′) n., explanatory drawing or rendering. *He followed the instructions on the diagram.* v.t., to illustrate by rendering a diagram. *He tried to diagram the intricate mechanism.*

dialect (dī′ə lekt′) n., 1. regional version of language distinct from those of other regions but forming with them one basic language. *The peasant found his visiting relatives' dialect amusing.* 2. jargon used by members of an occupational or social group. *He found the scientific dialect difficult.*

dialectic (dī′ə lek′tik) n., 1. investigative, intellectual dialogue. *They met to review the Platonic dialectic.* 2. systematic reasoning juxtaposing conflicting ideas in an attempt to resolve them. *The play* *set up the dialectic between appearance and reality.*

dialogue (dī′ə lôg′, -log′) n., 1. verbal exchange; conversation or written representation of a conversation. *She enjoyed the play's witty dialogue.* 2. exchange of ideas. *They wanted to keep the dialogue open.* v.t., to converse or render a conversation. *She had to dialogue the scene.*

dialysis (dī al′i sis) n., separation of substances in a solution through a semipermeable membrane, made possible by varying molecular sizes. *The kidney patient undergoes dialysis twice a week.*

diapason (dī′ə pā′zən, -sən) n., 1. full harmonious instrumental or vocal outburst. *The choir's diapason filled the church.* 2. tuning fork, or other standard of pitch. *She sounded the diapason for the other instruments.* 3. one of two organ stops. *The organist finished with both diapasons open.*

diaphanous (dī af′ə nəs) adj., so fine or filmy as to be transparent. *Her diaphanous gown seemed part of the moonlight.*

diaphragm (dī′ə fram′) n., 1. membrane or muscular divider. *The doctor felt around the area of the diaphragm.* 2. disk that vibrates. *He replaced the diaphragm in the microphone.* 3. contraceptive device. *The gynecologist fitted her with a diaphragm.*

diathermy (dī′ə thûr′mē) n., production by electric current of heat in tissues, esp. for therapeutic purposes. *The doctor used diathermy to ease the muscle pain.*

diatom (dī′ə təm, -tom′) n., any of several one-celled fresh- or salt-water algae whose siliceous skeletons form diatomite. *He studied the diatoms under the microscope.*

diatomite (dī at′ə mīt′) n., also called diatomaceous earth, siliceous sediment formed from diatomaceous skeletons, often used for filtration and cosmetic purposes. *Diatomite is used as a nail abrasive.*

diatribe (dī′ə trīb′) n., bitter, denunciatory, or satirical speech or writing. *He*

let loose a diatribe against the regulation.

dichotomy (dī kot′ə mē) n., split or division between two opposites or contradictions. *He discussed the dichotomy between love and hate.*

Dictaphone (dik′tə fōn′) n., trademark of a dictating machine. *The Dictaphone sat on his desk.*

dictate (n. dik′tāt; v. dik′tāt, dik tāt′) n., ruling principle or command. *It defied the dictate of common sense.* v.t., 1. to command or order. *She began to dictate their responsibilities.* 2. to speak or read for transcription or recording. *She began to dictate the message.*

dictatorship (dik tā′tər ship′, dik′tā-) n., office or rule of absolute ruler. *His was a benign dictatorship.*

diction (dik′shən) n., speech, esp. as regards correct enunciation and pronunciation. *Her diction needed refinement.*

dictum (dik′təm) n., authoritative declaration, formal statement, or judicial decision. *His dictum was met with heavy opposition.*

didactic (dī dak′tik) adj., intended or suited to convey information or instruction, esp. moral; educational. *The didactic fable amused the child.*

dietetic (dī′i tet′ik) adj., pertaining to normal or special diets. *The dietetic instruction helped her plan their meals.*

dietetics (di′i tet′iks) n., study or science of nutritive meal-planning. *He studied dietetics in cooking school.*

differentiate (dif′ə ren′shē āt′) v.t., to distinguish between; express difference in. *The child slowly learned to differentiate colors.*

diffidence (dif′i dəns) n., qualities or condition of timidity or shy reserve. *Her diffidence put her at a disadvantage.*

diffident (dif′i dənt) adj., reserved; shy; unassuming. *He was very diffident with her parents.*

diffraction (di frak′shən) n., modification of light or sound waves as result of their passing through or being reflected by something. *The diamond is cut to maximize light diffraction.*

diffuse

diffuse (*n.* di fyo͞oz′; *adj.* di fyo͞os′) v.t., to spread out; break up and scatter. *The trees began to diffuse the sunlight.* adj., scattered; spread out; prolix. *Her diffuse remarks confused the students.*

digestion (di jes′chən, -jesh′-, dī-) n., process by which food passes through the alimentary canal and is absorbed by the body. *Enzymes are important in the process of digestion.*

dignified (dig′nə fīd′) adj., having or expressing dignity; distinguished. *She made a dignified acceptance speech.*

dignitary (dig′ni ter′ē) n., highly placed or regarded official. *The French dignitary attended the ceremony.*

digress (di gres′, dī-) v.i., to deviate from main point or direction, esp. in speech or writing. *The speaker began to digress with an amusing anecdote.*

digression (di gresh′ən, dī-) n., a turning aside in speech or writing. *It was the digression we enjoyed most.*

dilapidated (di lap′i dā′tid) adj., partially ruined or falling apart. *They began to tear apart the dilapidated porch.*

dilapidation (di lap′ə dā′shən) n., state of neglect; ruinous condition. *The vacant building fell into dilapidation.*

dilate (dī lāt′, di-) v.i., 1. to swell or expand. *Her pupils began to dilate.* 2. to speak at length. *He intended to dilate on the complex issue.* v.t., to enlarge or extend. *The drops began to dilate her pupils.*

dilatory (dil′ə tōr′ē, -tôr′ē) adj., causing lateness; slow; procrastinating. *Her dilatory packing exasperated him.*

dilemma (di lem′ə) n., problem requiring a choice between equally undesirable alternatives; predicament. *She was in a dilemma about the courses.*

dilettante (dil′i tan′tē, -tän′tā, -i tänt′, dil′i tänt) n., amateur; one who superficially or occasionally dabbles in art or other areas of endeavor. *The dilettante lacked the discipline to continue.*

diluent (dil′yo͞o ənt) n., thinning agent. *The turpentine was his diluent.* adj., causing to thin or dilute. *It was a diluent acid.*

dilute (di lo͞ot′, dī-) n., less-concentrated substance or mixture. *It was a dilute of turpentine.* v.t., to lower concentration of; thin; attenuate. *She began to dilute the turpentine.*

diluvial (di lo͞o′vē əl) adj., pertaining to a flood or deluge. *The diluvial waters overflowed the bridge.*

dimension (di men′shən) n., size in terms of space or perception; scope. *The child added a new dimension to their marriage.*

diminish (di min′ish) v., to reduce or decrease; belittle. *Their hopes began to diminish when he didn't come back.*

diminution (dim′ə no͞o′shən, -nyo͞o′-) n., decrease; lessening; falling off. *Antibiotics have achieved a marked diminution in the death rate from pneumonia.*

diminutive (di min′yə tiv) n., second word created from an original, usually by the addition of a suffix to indicate smaller size, insignificance, or endearment. *Duckling is the diminutive of duck.* adj., small; miniature. *She fingered the diminutive doll house furniture.*

dint (dint) n., 1. power; force; effort. *By dint of hard labor, the task was completed.* 2. mark; dent. *The contribution won't make a dint in her fortune.*

diocese (dī′ə sēs′, -sis) n., section of population under the care of a bishop; bishopric. *The bishop summoned all of the priests of his diocese.*

diphtheria (dif thēr′ē ə, dip-) n., contagious febrile disease, characterized by respiratory difficulties and sometimes affecting temporarily the nervous system and heart. *Children are now routinely immunized against diphtheria.*

diphthong (dif′thông, -thong, dip′-) n., 1. ligatures æ or œ. 2. flowing vowel combination, as in *boy*. *The poem used the diphthong effectively.*

dipsomania (dip′sə mā′nē ə) n., unrestrainable desire for alcoholic liquors. *She suffered from dipsomania.*

dipsomaniac (dip′sə mā′nē ak′) n., one who suffers from dipsomania. *They had to restrain the dipsomaniac.*

dire (dīr) adj., desperately urgent; terrifying; foreboding. *Her dire request could not be ignored.*

dirge (dûrj) n., solemn or funereal song. *They were moved by the sad dirge.*

dirk (dûrk) n., long, straight dagger. *Eighteenth-century Scottish highlanders carried dirks.*

disavow (dis'ə vou') v.t., to deny knowledge of or responsibility for. *He tried to disavow the statement.*

disavowal (dis'ə vou'əl) n., denial; negation; repudiation. *The witness's disavowal was damaging to his case.*

disbar (dis bär') v.t., to exclude from legal profession. *They voted to disbar him because of the crime.*

disburse (dis bûrs') v.t., to pay out; distribute money. *He forgot to disburse the necessary funds for their services.*

discern (di sûrn', -zûrn') v.t., to perceive; discriminate. *He began to discern the reason for her anxiety.*

discernible (di sûr'nə bəl, -zûr'-) adj., capability of being perceived. *There was little discernible difference between them.*

discernment (di sûrn'mənt, -zûrn'-) n., 1. perception; penetration; insight. *Her discernment led to unraveling of the mystery.* 2. differentiation; discrimination. *We complimented her on her discernment in home furnishings.*

disciple (di sī'pəl) n., follower; adherent; enthusiast. *She was a disciple of pop art.*

disclaim (dis klām') v.t., to deny or disavow; renounce. *She had to disclaim the inheritance.*

disclose (di sklōz') v.t., to reveal or open up. *He began to disclose the information.*

discomfit (dis kum'fit) v.t., 1. to defeat; beat; rout. *They hope to discomfit the rival team.* 2. to embarrass; disconcert. *The unexpected praise discomfited her.*

discomfort (dis kum'fərt) n., uneasiness. *The prisoners shared the same discomfort.* v.t., to make uncomfortable or uneasy. *He tried to discomfort the spy.*

disconcert (dis'kən sûrt') v.t., to make uncomfortable; embarrass. *Her suggestive manner began to disconcert him.*

disconsolate (dis kon'sə lit) adj., unconsolable; cheerless. *They tried to comfort the disconsolate widow.*

discontinue (dis'kən tin'yōō) v.t., to end; terminate. *They decided to discontinue the subscription.*

discordant (dis kôr'dənt) adj., jarring; out of tune; unpleasantly harsh. *Her discordant remarks precipitated a fight.*

discothèque (dis'kō tek') n., café or club offering dancing to recorded music. *They enjoyed the evening at the discothèque.*

discountenance (dis koun'tənəns) v.t., 1. to look with disfavor on. *The priest had to discountenance the violence.* 2. to disconcert. *She discountenanced her family with the unexpected announcement.*

discredit (dis kred'it) n., lack of credibility or credit. *It was to his discredit that she left.* v.t., to disbelieve. *He had to discredit the preposterous rumor.*

discreet (di skrēt') adj., capable of keeping a confidence; prudent; considerate, modest behavior. *The old count was discreet in his inquiries.*

discrete (di skrēt') adj., distinct; separate. *The book consists of three discrete parts.*

discretion (di skresh'ən) n., 1. circumspection. *Thanks to her discretion there was no scandal.* 2. ability or power to make choices or decisions. *It was in his discretion to hire or fire them.*

discrimination (di skrim'ə nā'shən) n., 1. act of discriminating or distinguishing. *Discrimination between the identical twins was difficult.* 2. showing favoritism, or the reverse; being unfair. *He saw discrimination behind every personal failure.* 3. ability to discern; make distinctions. *The magazine extolled her fashion discrimination.*

discursive (di skûr'siv) adj., tendency to stray from set point or goal; digressive. *She wrote a chatty, discursive letter.*

disdain (dis dān') n., contempt; scorn. *She looked with disdain upon his offer.* v.t., to scorn or despise; contemptuously refuse. *She would disdain to accept the humble lodging.*

disdainful (dis dān′fəl) adj., contemptuous; scornful; haughty. *Marie Antoinette was disdainful of the mob.*

disenfranchisement (dis′en fran′chiz mənt) n., deprivation of a person's or a citizen's rights, esp. the right to vote. *Conviction for a felony can result in disenfranchisement.*

disgruntle (dis grun′t^əl) v.t., to displease or dissatisfy; make grumpy. *She feared to disgruntle her uncle.*

disheveled (di shev′əld) adj., untidy; disordered. *She tried to comb her disheveled hair.*

disillusion (dis′i loo′zhən) n., disenchantment. *She was sorry to see the child's disillusion.* v.t., to remove illusion; disenchant. *She didn't want to disillusion him.*

disingenuous (dis′in jen′yoo əs) adj., insincere; devious. *We cannot trust the disingenuous woman.*

disinherit (dis′in her′it) v.t., to deprive of rights or privileges of inheritance. *He decided to disinherit his profligate son.*

disintegrate (dis in′tə grāt′) v.t., to destroy by causing to break up into component parts; to disunify. *The alcohol began to disintegrate his concentration.* v.i., to break into component parts; decompose. *The paint began to disintegrate.*

disinterested (dis in′tə res′tid, -tri stid) adj., unbiased; without prejudice; impartial. *They chose him as a disinterested judge.*

disjoin (dis join′) v.t., to detach; undo. *She had to disjoin the sleeve and start over.*

disjointed (dis join′tid) adj., unconnected; random; incoherent. *They couldn't follow his disjointed speech.*

dismal (diz′məl) adj., bleak; miserable. *She tried to brighten up the dismal room.*

dismantle (dis man′t^əl) v.t., to take apart. *He began to dismantle the display.*

dismay (dis mā′) n., unexpected disappointment or fear. *She tried to hide her dismay at his attire.* v.t., to deprive suddenly of confidence or resolution. *His unexpected criticism dismayed the child.*

dismember (dis mem′bər) v.t., to cut off or remove the parts or limbs of. *They had to dismember the mannequin to put on the new dress.*

disparage (di spar′ij) v.t., to degrade or belittle. *She began to disparage the paint job.*

disparaging (di spar′ə jing) adj., discrediting; depreciating; belittling. *Her disparaging attitude concealed a deep jealousy.*

disparagingly (di spar′ij ing lē′) adv., slightingly; with contempt; scornfully. *The politician spoke disparagingly of his opponent.*

disparate (dis′par it, di spar′-) adj., different; dissimilar. *The disparate textures complemented each other.*

disparity (di spar′i tē) n., dissimilarity. *The disparity of their backgrounds didn't matter.*

dispassionate (dis pash′ə nit) adj., calm; fair; orderly. *His dispassionate manner soothed them.*

dispatch (di spach′) n., 1. shipment; important news item or official message sent quickly. *The dispatch reached them the same morning.* 2. haste; speed. *They sent the message with all dispatch.* v.t., 1. to send with speed or promptness. *They hurried to dispatch the letter.* 2. to dispose of; put to death. *They dispatched him to a watery grave.*

dispel (di spel′) v.t., to scatter or dissipate. *They tried to dispel the rumor.*

dispense (di spens′) v.t., 1. to give out; administer. *They had to dispense first aid.* 2. to do without; give up. *He decided to dispense with formality.*

dispersion (di spûr′zhən, -shən) n., 1. dispersed solution or substance. *The chemist stored the dispersion.* 2. process or act of dispersing. *The troop dispersion took three hours.*

dispirited (di spir′i tid) adj., downcast; disheartened; discouraged; depressed. *Business failure caused the man to become dispirited.*

displace (dis plās′) v.t., to take out of usual place; supplant. *He began to displace the older man.*

disport (di spōrt′, -spôrt′) v.i., to amuse; entertain; frolic; play. *The costumed revelers will disport all night.*

dispose (di spōz′) v.t., 1. to incline or prepare. *He tried to dispose her toward the move.* 2. (dispose of), to get rid of; to arrange conclusively. *He hoped to dispose of the matter quickly.*

disproportion (dis′prə pōr′shən, -pôr′-) n., imbalance; lack of proportion. *Her anger was in disproportion to his mild criticism.*

disputation (dis′pyo͞o tā′shən) n., argument; controversy; debate; wrangling. *The disputation developed into a schoolyard fight.*

disputatious (dis′pyo͞o tā′shəs) adj., argumentative; quarrelsome; bellicose; contentious. *She has the reputation of being a disputatious troublemaker.*

dispute (di spyo͞ot′) n., argument; disagreement; wrangle. *He had to mediate the dispute.* v., 1. to argue or debate. *She didn't mean to dispute with the teacher.* 2. to contest. *They decided to dispute the will.*

disquiet (dis kwī′it) n., uneasiness; anxiety. *Disquiet lingered after the fight.*

disquisition (dis′kwi zish′ən) n., discourse; formal inquiry or study. *The disquisition concerned the theory of relativity.*

disregard (dis′ri gard′) n., state of deliberate neglect. *They held the old customs in disregard.* v.t., to ignore or neglect. *They chose to disregard the report.*

disreputable (dis rep′yə tə bəl) adj., having a bad reputation. *The disreputable salesman began to lose customers.*

disrupt (dis rupt′) v.t., to break up or rupture. *He waited for the bell to disrupt his class.*

dissect (di sekt′, dī-) v.t., to separate into component parts for analysis or investigation. *The police began to dissect her story.*

dissection (di sek′shən, dī-) n., 1. process of dissecting. *The dissection revealed the nervous system.* 2. that which is dissected; the specimen. *The dissection was stored for future work.*

dissemble (di sem′bəl) v.i., to conceal information or feelings by false manner or demeanor. *The child learned to dissemble to avoid punishment.*

disseminate (di sem′ə nāt′) v.t., to spread or scatter widely. *They began to disseminate the news.*

dissension (di sen′shən) n., discord; disunity. *There was dissension over the new law.*

dissent (di sent′) n., disagreement; nonconcurrence. *His dissent prevented a unanimous vote.* v.i., to disagree or withhold agreement. *She had to dissent from the plan.*

dissenter (di sen′tər) n., 1. one who dissents. *The dissenter refused to accept the vote.* 2. nonconformist. *The dissenter could no longer remain in the community.*

dissertation (dis′ər tā′shən) n., lengthy, usually written, treatise. *The dissertation represented five years of work.*

disservice (dis sûr′vis) n., injury. *His temper did him a disservice.*

dissident (dis′i dənt) adj., separated because of disagreement; disaffected. *The dissident delegation left the hall.* n., one who dissents. *The dissidents were ejected from the meeting.*

dissimilitude (dis′si mil′i to͞od′, -tyo͞od′) n., lack of similarity or resemblance. *The brothers' dissimilitude was surprising.*

dissimulate (di sim′yə lāt′) v., to hide one's true feelings or thoughts; engage in dissembling. *She discovered he had dissimulated his true concern until he was alone.*

dissimulation (di sim′yə lā′shən) n., hypocrisy; deceit; pretense; misrepresentation. *Law prohibits dissimulation in advertising.*

dissipate (dis′ə pāt′) v.t., to break up and thin out. *The police tried to dissipate the crowd.* v.i., to dwindle almost to nothingness. *He allowed his fortune to dissipate.*

dissolute (dis′ə lo͞ot′) adj., unrestrained, lacking moral strength. *He had to bail out the dissolute young man.*

dissonance (dis′ə nəns) n., discord, esp. of sounds. *The composer experimented with dissonance.*

dissonant (dis′ə nənt) adj., discordant; lacking harmony. *He couldn't get used to the dissonant music.*

dissuade (di swād′) v.t., to advise or persuade against. *They tried to dissuade him from joining.*

dissuasion (di swā′zhən) n., act of dissuading; counsel against. *His dissuasion convinced her not to buy the stock.*

distemper (dis tem′pər) n., 1. ill-humor. *The child was in a distemper.* 2. viral disease of animals such as dogs and cats characterized by fever, respiratory and/or nervous symptoms. *The puppy was inoculated against distemper.* 3. painting process or mixture using an emulsion of egg yolk or white. *They used a distemper for the scenery in Act 1.*

distend (di stend′) v.i., to swell out. *The ankle began to distend.*

distichous (dis′tə kəs) adj., divided into two vertical rows or sections. *They identified the plant by its distichous leaves.*

distill (di stil′) v.t., to extract or concentrate, esp. by condensation or precipitation. *They began to distill the mixture.*

distillate (dis′tᵊlit, -tᵊlāt′, di stil′it) n., liquid condensed during distillation. *They removed the distillate for refining.*

distillation (dis′tᵊlā′shən) n., 1. process of vaporizing then condensing gas or vapor from a substance, in order to purify or modify the substance or to obtain a new substance. *Distillation is involved in perfume manufacture.* 2. extraction; abstraction; condensation. *His book includes a fine distillation of modern poetry.*

distort (di stôrt′) v.t., to twist or render abnormal or untrue. *He tended to distort the importance of the find.*

distortion (di stôr′shən) n., act or product of distorting; false image or report. *She laughed at the distortion in the trick mirror.*

distract (di strakt′) v.t., 1. to draw away from; divert. *The music began to distract him from the book.* 2. to confuse or harass. *The noise and the crowd began to distract the puppy.*

distraction (di strak′shən) n., 1. the act of distracting. *The distraction helped him to forget the problem momentarily.* 2. confusion or harassment. *The noise drove him to distraction.* 3. amusing diversion. *The movie was a good distraction.*

distrait (di strā′; *Fr.* dēs tRe′) adj., 1. distracted; absent-minded; bewildered. *The distrait woman was incoherent.* 2. perplexed; troubled; bewildered; distraught. *Distrait at his hopeless indebtedness, the man declared bankruptcy.*

distraught (di strôt′) adj., anxious; agitated. *They tried to calm the distraught child.*

dithyramb (dith′ə ram′, -ramb′) n., short, wild, or inspired poem, chant, or other composition. *They laughed at his gay dithyramb.*

diurnal (di ûr′nᵊl) adj., pertaining to a daily cycle or occurrence. *He took care of the diurnal feedings.*

diva (dē′vä) n., female classical soloist; prima donna. *The renowned diva sang with gusto and brilliance.*

diverge (di vûrj′, dī-) v.i., to draw apart or deviate. *Their interests began to diverge.*

divergent (di vûr′jənt, dī-) adj., differing; deviant. *They seldom met during their divergent travels.*

divers (dī′vərz) adj., various. *They were offered divers roles in the play.*

diverse (di vûrs′, dī-, dī′vûrs) adj., variegated; different. *Her diverse jobs kept her busy.*

diversification (di vûr′sə fə kā′shən) n., variety; varied form in composition. *New England weather is characterized by diversification.*

diversion (di vûr′zhən, -shən, dī-) n., deviation or distraction; amusement. *It was a happy diversion from her routine.*

diversity (di vûr′si tē, dī-) n., pertaining to variety; differences. *It was her unusual diversity that interested him.*

divert (di vûrt′, dī-) v.t., to deviate or distract. *He tried to divert her attention.*

divest (di vest′, dī-) v.t., to undress, deprive, or dispossess. *She divested him of his wet gear.*

divination (div'ə nā'shən) n., 1. act of prophesying events or gaining knowledge, esp. by psychic power; prophecy. *Her divination later proved correct.* 2. insight; understanding. *His remark led to her divination of the situation.*

divisive (di vī'siv) adj., pertaining to disunity or discord. *Her divisive remarks ruined the meeting.*

divot (div'ət) n., piece of sod sliced by a golf club in executing a stroke. *In some cases a divot is necessary to make a good golf shot.*

divulge (di vulj') v.t., to reveal. *She was asked to divulge her source.*

docile (dos'əl; *Brit.* dō'sīl) adj., gentle; calm; obedient. *She led the docile spaniel to the ring.*

docket (dok'it) n., agenda, or list of things to do; written summary. *Her case was third on the docket.* v.t., to put on the agenda; summarize and add to list. *She tried to docket the problem.*

doctrine (dok'trin) n., principle or body of principles forming a formal policy or belief; dogma. *He espoused the doctrine of reincarnation.*

documentary (dok'yə men'tə rē) n., factual and realistic film or written presentation. *The documentary provided glimpses of prison life.*

doddering (dod'ər iṅg) adj., trembling, caused by weakness or old age. *The doddering old man approached them.*

doff (dof, dôf) v.t., 1. to take off; remove (clothing); put aside. *The warm sun prompted me to doff my coat.* 2. lay aside; cease to practice; relinquish. *She wanted to doff the meaningless ritual.*

doggerel (dô'gər əl, dog'ər-) n., burlesque or comic verse. *His doggerel delighted the children.*

dogma (dôg'mə, dog'-) n., doctrine or point of view held as established and authoritative. *He accepted as dogma her right to work.*

dogmatic (dôg mat'ik, dog-) adj., pertaining to use of dogma; dictatorial. *His dogmatic manner betrayed his rigidity.*

doldrums (dōl'drəmz, dol'-) n., state or period of listlessness, despondency, boredom. *The week of rain put them in the doldrums.*

dole (dōl) n., money or provisions given to those in need; alms. *The proud man would not accept her dole.* v.t., 1. to distribute funds or other bounty to the needy. *The Salvation Army will dole out food to the flood victims.* 2. to divide sparingly; apportion. *She carefully doled out one piece to each child.*

doleful (dōl'fəl) adj., sad; downcast. *She gave them a doleful look as they drove away without her.*

dolorous (dol'ər əs, dō'lər-) adj., sad; grief-provoking; sorrowful; mournful; grievous. *Dolorous tolling of the church bells announced the king's death.*

dolphin (dol'fin, dôl'-) n., 1. small-toothed whale, a member of the family of marine mammals called Delphinidae; porpoise. *Dolphins have long been celebrated as friends, even rescuers, of seafarers.* 2. either of two dolphinlike oceanic food fishes of the genus *Coryphaena. The dolphin is a spiny-finned fish.* 3. one of several kinds of nautical mooring devices. *The ship was lashed fast to the dolphins.*

dolt (dōlt) n., dull or stupid person. *The dolt didn't know how to do it.*

domain (dō mān') n., 1. ownership of land. *He refused them entry into his domain.* 2. something that is controlled through ownership, authority, or expertise. *Her special domain was 14th-century religious art.*

domicile (dom'i sīl', -səl, dō'mi-) n., place of residence. *His domicile was a riverboat.* v.t., to settle or provide with a home. *They worked to domicile the survivors.*

dominate (dom'ə nāt') v.t., to rule over or exercise influence on; occupy superior or stronger position. *The boy began to dominate the team.*

domineer (dom'ə nēr') v.t., to be overbearing; to tyrannize. *He tried to domineer his little sister.*

dominion (də min'yən) n., domain; area of supreme authority. *Her studio was her dominion.*

donnybrook (don′ē brŏŏk′) n., uproarious event; fiasco; rout. *The delegates' dissention turned the convention into a donnybrook.*

doomsday (dōōmz′dā′) n., day on which the world will end, the biblical Day of Judgment detailed in the Book of Revelation; Judgment Day; Last Judgment. *The Puritan minister warned of the arrival of doomsday.*

dormant (dôr′mənt) adj., temporarily inactive; latent. *They kept close watch on the dormant volcano.*

dorsal (dôr′səl) adj., pertaining to the back, esp. of an animal. *The hook caught in his dorsal fin.*

dossier (dos′ē ā′, -ē ər, dô′sē ā′, -sē ər; *Fr.* dô syā′) n., detailed report or file. *The information was added to his dossier.*

dotage (dō′tij) n., feeble mental state, esp. in elderly. *The octogenarian was in his dotage.*

dotard (dō′tard) n., one who has become senile; old fool. *Extreme old age reduced the once-great scholar to a dotard.*

dote (dōt) v.i., to show excessive or foolish fondness for. *The old woman began to dote on the child.*

double entendre (dub′əl än tän′drə, -tänd′; *Fr.* dōō bläN täN′dr°) n., word or expression that conveys ambiguous meaning. *He wondered what the double entendre really meant.*

doublet (dub′lit) n., 1. pair; couple; two of a kind. *A doublet of fine black steeds pulled the coach.* 2. man's closely-fit jacket, popular esp. in Europe from Middle Ages until late 18th century. *The courtier wore a black satin doublet over his silk shirt.*

doughty (dou′tē) adj., confident; able; brave; dashing. *The doughty militia defended the town.*

dour (dōōr, dour, dou′ər) adj., sullen; obstinate. *The dour student wouldn't cooperate.*

dovetail (duv′tāl′) n., in woodworking, a joint that resembles a dove's tail. *He appreciated the quality of the dovetail.* v.t., to cut or fit a dovetail joint. *They wanted to dovetail the shelves.* v.i., to come together smoothly. *The plan began to dovetail.*

downcast (doun′kast′, -käst′) adj., dejected; depressed. *He was downcast by the news.*

downtrodden (doun′trod′°n) adj., oppressed. *The downtrodden peasants revolted.*

dowry (dou′rē) n., bride's marriage portion. *Her dowry was all they had to start with.*

doxology (dok sol′ə jē) n., brief hymn praising God; Gloria. *The congregation rose to sing a doxology.*

Draconian (drā kō′nē ən) adj., 1. pertaining to Draco, Athenian statesman of the 7th century B.C., or to the strict legal code by which he is known. *Seventeenth-century Puritan rule was severe, even Draconian.* 2. (sometimes l.c.) dragonlike; severe. *The draconian headmistress whipped the child severely.*

dramatic (drə mat′ik) adj., theatrical; vivid. *She made a dramatic entrance.*

dramatize (dram′ə tīz′, drä′mə-) v.t., 1. to adapt for the theater. *They wanted to dramatize the news story.* 2. to present or describe in theatrical manner. *She tended to dramatize her symptoms.*

dray (drā) n., 1. wheelless sledge or sled used to haul timber, rock, or other heavy loads. *They pulled the brush away on a dray.* 2. low wagon, usually built without sides or with removable sides to accommodate awkward and heavy loads. *The horse-drawn dray used to be a common sight.*

dregs (dregs) n., last part; sediment; vestiges. *They drank the bottle to the dregs.*

drivel (driv′əl) n., nonsense. *You can't take this drivel seriously.* v.i., 1. to slobber. *The infant began to drivel.* 2. to talk foolishly. *She began to drivel about his looks.* 3. to waste time. *She would only drivel the afternoon away.*

droll (drōl) adj., amusing; comic; whimsical or odd. *She laughed and called him droll.*

drollery (drō'lə rē) n., 1. that which is amusing, quaint, or waggish; facetious humor. *The audience laughed at her timely drollery.* 2. behavior of a buffoon or wag. *The jester's drollery included acrobatics and pantomime.*

dromedary (drom'ə der'ē, drum'-) n., one-humped camel of Asia and Africa, bred esp. for riding.

dross (drôs, dros) n., 1. waste product, esp. that formed by the smelting of metals. *When iron is molten the dross can be removed.* 2. something inconsequential or worthless; trivia. *The critic panned the current dross from Hollywood.*

drove (drōv) n., large group or herd of animals. *The drove of sheep halted traffic.*

drudgery (druj'ə rē) n., spiritless, servile, or mechanical labor. *It was drudgery washing dishes in the hot kitchen.*

dryad (drī'əd, -ad) n., tree-dwelling nymph; wood-nymph. *The child looked for a dryad in the forest.*

dubious (dōō'bē əs, dyōō'-) adj., 1. doubtful; hesitating; undecided. *He was dubious about the best course of action.* 2. of uncertain result. *The ramshackle ship went forth on its dubious journey.* 3. of doubtful quality or propriety. *To be invited to a hanging was a dubious honor.*

ductile (duk't°l, -til) adj., 1. capable of being stretched or molded without breaking; capable of being stretched into wire; malleable. *Because copper is extremely ductile, it is used in the manufacture of electrical wire.* 2. compliant; tractable; easily influenced; susceptible. *The ductile child is prone to hero worship.*

dudgeon (duj'ən) n., reaction of resentment, offense, or proud anger. *Miffed by their remarks, she left the room in high dudgeon.*

duenna (dōō en'ə, dyōō-) n., older woman engaged to chaperone a young, unmarried woman; governess; chaperon; protectress. *They could meet only in the presence of her duenna.*

duffel (duf'əl) n., coarse woolen cloth having a thick nap, often used for baggage for camping, sport, or military equipment. *The sailor's bag was made of duffel.* adj., made of duffel. *He stuffed his dirty clothes in the duffel bag.*

du jour (də zhōōr', dōō-; *Fr.* dY zhōōR) of the day; today's. *The soup du jour is split pea.*

dulcet (dul'sit) adj., pleasing to hear; melodious; harmonious. *The dulcet song of the mockingbird lulled him to sleep.*

dun (dun) adj., dull brownish-gray color. *The mousy woman appeared to disadvantage in the drab dress of dun.* v.t., to demand or press for payment. *Creditors began to dun the impoverished aristocrat.*

dunce (duns) n., pupil who fails to learn; stupid person; dullard; dolt; simpleton. *The dunce was ostracized by the other students.*

duodenum (dōō'ə dē'nəm, dyōō'-; dōō od'°nəm, dyōō-) n., part of the small intestine, connected to the stomach and receiving secretions from the liver and pancreas. *Partially digested food is further broken down in the duodenum.*

dupe (dōōp, dyōōp) n., one who is deceived. *My vanity made me the dupe of his flattery.* v.t., to deceive or trick; mislead by imposing on one's credulity. *He was duped by false advertising.*

duplicity (dōō plis'i tē, dyōō-) n., deception by means of speaking or seeming to act one way while acting another; double-dealing; hypocrisy. *Her duplicity kept the truth from him for a long time.*

durable (dōōr'ə bəl, dyōōr'-) adj., lasting; enduring; permanent. *Stone is a more durable material than timber.*

durance (dōōr'əns, dyōōr'-) n., imprisonment. *Emaciated survivors were finally released from durance in the concentration camp.*

duration (dōō rā'shən, dyōō-) n., length of time during which something lasts or continues. *The town brought in supplies to last for the duration of winter.*

duress (dŏŏ res′, dyŏŏ-, dŏŏr′is, dyŏŏr′-) n., constraint, pressure, or hardship, esp. unlawful; coercion. *She was kidnapped and held under duress.*

duty (dŏŏ′tē, dyŏŏ′-) n., 1. responsibility of an office or position. *The acceptance speech was his first duty as mayor.* 2. moral obligation. *It is her duty to provide for her family.* 3. respect or homage due one of higher station; submission; fealty. *The knight knelt before his queen to acknowledge his duty.* 4. tax imposed on exported or imported goods. *The fur coat will mean a heavy import duty.*

dynamics (dī nam′iks) n., 1. theory of forces, esp. the forces relating to matter in motion. *Dynamics is a branch of physics.* 2. moving moral or physical forces of any kind, or the laws relating to them. *We can learn about our government's leaders by studying the dynamics of the political system.*

dysentery (dis′ən ter′ē) n., disease characterized by inflammation of the large intestine, diarrhea, difficult evacuations, and passage of blood and mucus. *The hospital was full of soldiers suffering from dysentery.*

dyspepsia (dis pep′shə, -sē ə) n., indigestion. *After the large dinner, he suffered an attack of dyspepsia.*

Ee

earthbound (ûrth'bound') adj., firmly tied to earth. *His ideas remained earthbound*

earthly (ûrth'lē) adj., 1. of the earth. *The pursuits of pleasure and wealth are earthly cares.* 2. possible; feasible. *I can find no earthly use for this trinket.*

easement (ēz'mənt) n., 1. that which gives ease, relief, or assistance; convenience. *They found easement in the diners and truckstops along the road.* 2. in law, a person's right to limited use of another's land, usually through ownership of adjacent land. *The culvert was an easement required by the town.*

ebullience (i bul'yəns) n., 1. overflow; boiling over. *The ebullience of flood waters damaged the dam.* 2. overflow of feelings, enthusiasm, zeal, or ardor; fervor. *Her natural ebullience raised our spirits.*

ebullient (i bul'yənt) adj., having the qualities of great enthusiasm and liveliness. *We were all cheered by her ebullient personality.*

eccentric (ik sen'trik, ek-) adj., deviating from recognized or usual methods or practice; irregular; erratic; odd. *George III alarmed his ministers with his eccentric behavior.* n., person or thing exhibiting eccentric behavior. *The eccentric appeared with his clothes on backward.*

eccentricity (ek'sən tris'i tē, ek'sen-) n., 1. departure from that which is considered regular or usual; oddity; whimsy. *Sometimes the line is thin between eccentricity and madness.* 2. eccentric action or characteristic; striking peculiarity of character or conduct. *Her preference for Victorian dress was an endearing eccentricity.*

ecclesiastic (i klē'zē as'tik) n., member of the clergy. *His black coat identified him as an ecclesiastic.*

ecclesiastical (i klē'zē as'ti kəl) adj., pertaining to the church. *Christmas is an ecclesiastical holiday.*

éclat (ā klä'; *Fr.* ā klA') n., brilliant effect; splendor. *A flamboyant dresser, she always made her entrance with great éclat.*

eclectic (i klek'tik) n., one who culls and adopts what seems to be best from various styles or doctrines. *Politically, she was an eclectic.* adj., taken from various styles or doctrines. *The room reflected his eclectic taste in furniture.*

eclogue (ek'lôg', -log') n., short, bucolic poem; idyll. *Virgil wrote neoclassical eclogues.*

ecology (i kol'ə jē) n., science of the relationship between organisms and their environments. *Scientists study the ecology of marine life and the ocean.*

economy (i kon'ə mē) n., 1. frugality; thrift; careful husbandry. *With economy we will be able to afford the new car next year.* 2. economic state of a municipality or government. *A depressed economy indicates a decline in business activity.*

ecstasy (ek'stə sē) n., 1. condition in which the mind, contemplating some extraordinary object or idea, is transported beyond the control of the senses; a trance or rapture. *In the ecstasy of revenge, he did not feel the soaking rain.* 2. overwhelming emotion. *He was speechless in an ecstasy of rage.*

ecstatic (ek stat'ik) adj., affected by ecstasy; enraptured; entranced. *She was ecstatic over the new dress.*

ectomorph (ek'tə môrf') n., individual with a light body build. *An ectomorph* *is characteristically slender and delicate.*

ecumenical (ek′yōō men′i kəl *or, esp. Brit.,* ē′kyōō-) adj., general, universal; specifically, belonging to the entire Christian church. *Many different sects participated in the ecumenical service.*

edelweiss (ād′əl vīs′, -wīs′) n., plant that grows in high, remote areas of the Alps and Pyrenees, characterized by dense flower heads covered with a close, white, cottony down. *Many travelers in Switzerland seek the starlike edelweiss.*

edict (ē′dikt) n., public command by a sovereign or leader having the force of law. *The rebels ignored the king's martial edict.*

edification (ed′ə fə kā′shən) n., building up of knowledge or instruction, esp. of morals or religion; improvement of the mind; enlightenment. *The trip to the prison was for the delinquent's edification.*

edifice (ed′ə fis) n., building, particularly a large structure, public or private. *The state capitol was an impressive edifice.*

edify (ed′ə fī′) v.t., to improve someone's skills or character; enlighten; instruct. *The surgeon general tries to edify the public about smoking.*

edifying (ed′ə fī′iñg) adj., instructive; beneficial, esp. morally or spiritually. *She found the sermon edifying.*

educe (i dōōs′, i dyōōs′) v.t., to draw out, esp. of something latent; manifest. *He intended to educe her undeveloped talent.*

eerie (ēr′ē) adj., 1. that which inspires fear or awe; mysterious; strange; weird. *I found myself in a deserted, eerie glen.* 2. affected by superstitious fear. *I had an eerie feeling that I'd seen her before.*

efface (i fās′) v.t., 1. to erase or obliterate. *She tried to efface the memory of the accident.* 2. to keep out of view; make inconspicuous. *The shy boy hung back, trying to efface himself.*

effect (i fekt′) n., 1. consequence. *Think of the effect of your actions.* 2. purport or general intent. *He wrote a letter to that effect.* v.t., to bring about; produce

as a result. *She waited for them to effect the promised changes.*

effectual (i fek′chōō əl) adj., effective; efficient; adequate; successful. *Increased lighting can be effectual in crime prevention.*

effectuate (i fek′chōō āt′) v.t., to bring to pass; accomplish. *Enthusiasm is necessary to effectuate your goal.*

effeminate (i fem′ə nit) adj., inappropriately soft, delicate, or luxurious; weak. *The boys tittered when they heard his effeminate voice.*

efferent (ef′ər ənt) adj., conveying outward or away; esp. of nerves. *The efferent nerves convey impulses to the muscles.*

effervesce (ef′ər ves′) v., 1. to bubble; foam; hiss. *Champagne and burgundy are wines that effervesce.* 2. to enthuse; be enthusiastic. *The actress effervesced about the new film.*

effervescent (ef′ər ves′ənt) adj., 1. bubbling or hissing, as fermenting liquors or carbonated drinks. *The effervescent liquid bubbled out of the bottle.* 2. exhibiting strong emotion or excitement. *His mood was as effervescent as the champagne.*

effete (i fēt′) adj., having the energies worn out or spent; incapable of efficient action. *The effete leader lost the election to the younger man.*

efficacious (ef′ə kā′shəs) adj., able to produce the desired result; effective. *She was rewarded for her efficacious efforts with reelection.*

efficacy (ef′ə kə sē) n., capacity of producing the effect intended; effectiveness. *We doubted his efficacy in managing the project.*

efficient (i fish′ənt) adj., 1. producing outward effects; causative; effective. *Her gentle voice was efficient in calming the child.* 2. capable; competent; without slack or waste. *An efficient worker is a valuable employee.*

effigy (ef′i jē) n., copy of an object or person; frequently applied to figures on sepulchral monuments or to figures made up of stuffed clothing to represent obnoxious persons. *The unpopular mayor was hanged in effigy.*

efflorescent (ef'lə res'ənt) adj., blossoming; flowering; in flower; blooming. *Late summer meadows are efflorescent with goldenrod.*

effluence (ef'lo͞o əns) n., 1. act of flowing out; emanation. *The light's effluence was checked by the fog.* 2. that which issues or flows out. *Her tears were a melancholy effluence.*

effrontery (i frun'tə rē) n., audacity; boldness; impudence; nerve; gall. *She had the effrontery to try to cut into the line.*

effulgent (i ful'jənt) adj., shining brilliantly; radiant; glowing; resplendent. *The sun's effulgent rays colored the horizon.*

effusion (i fyo͞o'zhən) n., gushing or pouring out; outpouring; shedding. *The head wound produced an effusion of blood.*

effusive (i fyo͞o'siv) adj., 1. flowing forcibly or abundantly. *Effusive waves beat upon the shores.* 2. with unreserved behavior; unduly demonstrative; gushing; flamboyant. *Her effusive thanks embarrassed her host.* 3. pertaining to rock formations that originated at the earth's surface. *Effusive rock is a product of solidified magma.*

egocentric (ē'gō sen'trik, eg'ō-) adj., self-centered; selfish; conceited; egotistical. *An egocentric person can be a great bore.*

egoism (ē'gō iz'əm, eg'ō-) n., self-interest; egotism; conceit; selfishness. *His egoism blinded him to the needs of others.*

egoist (ē'gō ist, eg'ō-) n., one who is totally self-centered; egotist. *The egoist was used to having her way.*

egotism (ē'gə tiz'əm, eg'ə-) n., preoccupation with self; conceit; selfishness. *We were put off by the egotism of her remark.*

egregious (i grē'jəs, -jē əs) adj., flagrant; shocking; gross; outrageous. *It was an egregious blunder in protocol.*

egress (n. ē'gres; v. i gres') n., 1. act of going or issuing out; departure. *The heavy door hindered our egress.* 2. means or place of exit. *There was no egress from the rear of the building.* v.i., to issue out. *We watched the audience egress from the theater.*

ejaculate (i jak'yə lāt') v., 1. to shoot out of a body; specifically, to eject semen during an orgasm. *He was too tired to ejaculate.* 2. to utter a sudden, brief exclamation. *"Oh!" she ejaculated when he slammed on the brakes.*

eject (i jekt') v.t., to throw out; discharge; drive away. *The landlord tried to eject the tenant.*

eke out (ēk out) v.t., 1. to supplement or stretch just to point of sufficiency. *The bread helped to eke out the slender meal.* 2. to derive through strenuous effort. *The artist could barely eke out living expenses.*

elaborate (v. i lab'ə rāt'; adj. i lab'ər it) v.t., to improve or add. *The student tried to elaborate on his idea.* adj., made with great care and many details; intricate. *She admired the elaborate carving.*

elapse (i laps') v.i., to pass away. *The subscription elapsed before she could renew it.* n., expiration. *The date of elapse was months away.*

elated (i lā'tid) adj., overjoyed; jubilant; exhilarated. *She was elated by the good news.*

elation (i lā'shən) n., exultation; joy. *She smiled with elation.*

electorate (i lek'tər it) n., body of citizens entitled to vote. *The registrar of voters hoped to increase the electorate.*

Electra complex (i lek'trə kom'pleks) complex in which a young female child forms a strong attachment to her father and may feel hostility toward her mother; female counterpart to Oedipus complex. *The analyst helped her deal with her Electra complex.*

electrocardiogram (i lek'trō kär'dē ə gram') n., record of the electric current produced by the heart muscle as recorded on an electrocardiograph. *The electrocardiogram revealed normal heart activity.*

electrocute (i lek'trə kyo͞ot') v.t., to kill

by exposure to electric shock. *The authorities prepared to electrocute the convicted killer.*

electrode (i lek′trōd) n., metallic element maintained at elevated voltage to influence or generate charges passing through a vacuum, gas, or an electrolyte. *Because of improper wiring of its electrodes, the battery failed.*

electrolysis (i lek trol′i sis, ē′lek-) n., decomposition of a compound in solution, in its natural state, or in molten form, caused by passage of an electric current. *Electrolysis is used industrially in the electroplating process.*

electrolyte (i lek′trə līt′) n., compound, capable of carrying an electric current, which is decomposed in solution in the process of electrolysis. *Chloride of lead is an electrolyte that decomposes into chlorine and lead.*

electromagnet (i lek′trō mag′nit) n., apparatus consisting of coils of wire surrounding an iron core, which produces a magnetic field when charged electrically. *The electromagnet is used in telegraphy.*

electron (i lek′tron) n., minute, electrically-charged, negative electrical unit. *An electron rotates around the atomic nucleus.*

eleemosynary (el′ə mos′ə ner′ē, -moz′-, el′ē ə-) adj., pertaining to charity; charitable; dependent upon charity. *The flood victims flocked to the city's eleemosynary shelters.*

elegiac (el′ə jī′ək, -ak, i lē′jē ak′) adj., 1. like or as in an elegy, esp. in the classical sense, as in a poem written in dactylic hexameter and pentameter. *The elegiac poem mourned Lincoln's death.* 2. as in a lamentation; mournful; gloomy; funereal. *The sombre room had an elegiac chill.*

elegy (el′i jē) n., song or poem mourning one who is dead, or with other reflective theme. *The elegy lamented the passing of an age.*

element (el′ə mənt) n., 1. single part of a whole; component. *There is one element in the story you have forgotten.*

2. basic principle; ingredient. *An important element in design is the proper use of proportion.* 3. favorable condition or environment; sphere. *She was in her element at the festival.* 4. substance that cannot be broken down into simpler substances by chemical means. *Oxygen is an element found in water.*

elephantiasis (el′ə fən tī′ə sis, -fan-) n., parasitic disease characterized by thick, hard, rough skin and gross enlargement of the limbs and scrotum. *Elephantiasis crippled him at the age of ten.*

elevate (el′ə vāt′) v.t., 1. to raise; lift. *The doctor told her to elevate the injured foot.* 2. to inspire; exalt. *The sermon elevated him with new purpose.*

elicit (i lis′it) v.t., to draw out; evoke; educe. *He tried to elicit a response.*

eligible (el′i jə bəl) adj., qualified to be chosen. *The employer read the list of eligible candidates.*

elite (i lēt′, ā lēt′) n., 1. select social body. *She belonged to the sorority elite.* 2. typewriter type with 12 characters per inch. *She preferred the smaller elite to the pica.*

elocution (el′ə kyōō′shən) n., art of correct public speaking; one's style of speaking. *The professor was admired for his elocution.*

elongate (i lông′gāt, i long′-, ē′lông gāt′, ē′long-) v.t., to lengthen; extend; draw out. *He persuaded her to elongate her stay.*

elongated (i lông′gā tid, i long′-, ē′lông gā′tid, ē′long-) adj., lengthened; extended; drawn out. *The elongated shadows signaled tea time.*

eloquent (el′ə kwənt) adj., 1. having considerable verbal skill. *She was an eloquent supporter of equal rights.* 2. vivid; moving; expressive. *The lawyer gave an eloquent defense.*

elucidate (i lōō′si dāt′) v., to make clear; explain; illustrate. *The judge asked him to elucidate his point.*

elusive (i lōō′siv) adj., 1. evasive; escaping. *The moon was elusive in the cloudy sky.* 2. not easily understood; vague. *I tried to decipher the elusive message.*

emaciated (i mā′s̲h̲ē ā′tid) adj., unhealthily thin; wasted through loss of flesh. *The emaciated cattle wouldn't live much longer.*

emanate (em′ə nāt′) v.i., to flow out or issue from. *Smoke began to emanate from the oven.* v.t., to emit. *She tried to emanate confidence.*

emancipate (i man′sə pāt′) v.t., to set free or liberate from restraint or bondage. *He intended to emancipate his slaves.*

emasculate (i mas′kyə lāt′) v.t., 1. to castrate. *They had to emasculate the roaming stud.* 2. to deprive of or weaken masculine virility or procreative ability. *The domineering woman emasculated her husband.*

embargo (em bär′gō) n., 1. governmental prohibition on merchant ships from entering or leaving the country's ports. *The embargo kept sugar scarce and prices high.* 2. any prohibition or restraint. *The embargo on imported oil depleted domestic supplies.*

embassy (em′bə sē) n., 1. official group of diplomatic employees headed by an ambassador. *The U.S. embassy handles U.S. diplomacy in Paris.* 2. buildings and grounds belonging to an embassy. *Spain's flag flies outside its embassy.*

embellish (em bel′is̲h̲) v.t., to beautify with ornamentation; adorn; decorate. *The baker decided to embellish the cake with flowers.*

embezzle (em bez′əl) v.t., to appropriate fraudulently, for one's own use, goods or money entrusted to one's care. *She planned to embezzle some of the company funds.*

embezzlement (em bez′əl mənt) n., act of embezzling. *The treasurer was convicted of embezzlement.*

emblazon (em blā′zən) v.t., 1. to adorn with heraldic figures or ensigns. *They emblazoned the flag with a star and cross.* 2. to decorate colorfully. *She emblazoned the table with zinnias.* 3. to celebrate publicly or openly. *The dinner was held to emblazon his election to office.*

embody (em bod′ē) v.t., 1. to give body

or substance to something intangible. *He came to embody their idea of the perfect teacher.* 2. to personify. *The owl embodied widsom.*

embolism (em′bə liz′əm) n., condition wherein an obstructive object, or embolus (usually a blood clot but possibly an air bubble, fat globule, etc.), cuts off the flow of blood at some point in the vascular system. *She died of a pulmonary embolism.*

embrocate (em′brō kāt′) v.t., to rub with a lotion or liniment. *Use liniment when you embrocate the strained muscle.*

embroil (em broil′) v.t., to involve in conflict or discord. *He tried not to embroil her in his case.*

embryo (em′brē ō′) n., 1. organism in the early stages of development, before it has assumed the distinctive form and structure of the parent. *The human embryo is about 1½″ long at 10 weeks.* 2. early, undeveloped state of anything. *The embryo of the idea grew rapidly.*

embryology (em′brē ol′ə jē) n., branch of science relating to the development of embryos. *The scientist was noted for her work in embryology.*

embryonic (em′brē on′ik) adj., having the character of or relating to an embryo; rudimentary. *Advisers were sent to aid the embryonic government.*

emend (i mend′) v.t., to correct; remove errors. *The author agreed to emend the inconsistency.*

emendation (ē′mən dā′s̲h̲ən, em′ən-) n., correction. *The deed was ratified following the requested emendation.*

emetic (ə met′ik) n., agent used to cause vomiting. *An emetic of egg whites should bring up the poison.*

emigrant (em′ə grənt) n., one who leaves one country or region to settle in another. *The emigrants had a rough departure.* adj., moving from one place or country to settle in another. *The emigrant family was welcomed by its new neighbors.*

emigrate (em′ə grāt′) v.i., to leave one country or region to settle in another.

He planned to emigrate to the new colony.

eminence (em′ə nəns) n., 1. high distinction in office, rank, or accomplishment; title of one who has attained such distinction. *He owed his eminence to talent and years of hard work.* 2. something prominent, elevated, or exalted. *They surveyed the field from the eminence overlooking it.*

eminent (em′ə nənt) adj., high in rank, office, worth, or public estimation; highly distinguished. *The eminent historian narrated the film.*

eminent domain (em′ə nənt dō mān′) n., power of a government to take private property for public use, if compensation is given to the owner. *The town expropriated the land by the right of eminent domain.*

emissary (em′i ser′ē) n., person sent on a mission representing another; agent or spy. *The king's emissary observed the war at the border.*

emit (i mit′) v.t., to send forth; give out. *Boiling water emits steam.*

emollient (i mol′yənt) n., substance or process that softens and soothes. *The emollient relieved her dry skin.* adj., having a softening effect. *The emollient lotion softened her hands.*

emolument (i mol′yə mənt) n., compensation or perquisites arising from employment or services; remuneration; salary; fee; gain. *The prestigious law firm offered him a generous emolument.*

empathy (em′pə thē) n., capacity for participation in and understanding of another's feelings or ideas. *I felt empathy, if not approval, for his decision.*

emphasize (em′fə sīz′) v.t., to give stress to or add importance to. *He emphasized his point with elaborate gestures.*

emphatic (em fat′ik) adj., expressed with emphasis; forcibly uttered; striking; energetic. *His emphatic denial convinced her.*

emphysema (em′fi sē′mə, -zē′-) n., disease characterized by the distention of body tissues with air, esp. of the lungs,

and causing deterioration of the heart. *The man's emphysema made his breathing difficult.*

empire (em′pīᵊr; adj. also om pēr′) n., 1. supreme power of government; imperial rule; sovereignty. *His empire was long and prosperous.* 2. aggregation of separate states or territories held under the absolute sway of a supreme ruler or sovereign state. *He sought to enlarge his empire through marriage.* adj., (cap.) pertaining to style fashionable during the first French Empire (early 19th century). *The formal parlor was a showpiece of Empire decor.*

empirical (em pir′i kəl) adj., pertaining to or derived from experience, experiment, or the observation of phenomena. *She based her decision on empirical evidence.*

emporium (em pōr′ē əm, -pôr′-) n., a place of trade; commercial center, esp. a store offering a variety of articles for sale. *The village became a thriving emporium for farmers.*

empyrean (em′pə rē′ən, -pī-, em pir′ē ən) n., in medieval cosmology, the highest celestial sphere, constituting true paradise; firmament. *The 12th-century tapestry depicts the angels in the empyrean.*

emulate (em′yə lāt′) v.t., to strive to equal or surpass; rival; imitate. *She tried to emulate her sister's success.*

emulsion (i mul′shən) n., aqueous liquid wherein tiny particles are suspended but not dissolved. *Milk is an emulsion.*

enamor (en am′ər) v.t., to inflame with love; captivate. *He was enamored of her because of her looks.*

encampment (en kamp′mənt) n., 1. act of forming and occupying a camp. *We planned to arrive before dark to allow time for encampment.* 2. camp. *We came upon the Indians' encampment.*

encephalitis (en sef′ə lī′tis) n., inflammation of the brain. *He was hospitalized with encephalitis.*

enchanting (en chan′tiṅg, -chän′-) adj., charming; bewitching; delightful. *The bird's song was enchanting.*

enclave (en′klāv; *Fr.* äN klAv′) n., region, territory, or country enclosed within foreign territory. *Berlin is a western enclave within East Germany.*

encomiastic (en kō′mē as′tik) adj., eulogistic; panegyrical; laudatory. *His will forbade any encomiastic speeches at his funeral.*

encomium (en kō′mē əm) n., laudatory recognition; praise. *She thanked them for their very flattering encomium.*

encompass (en kum′pəs) v.t., 1. to form a circle around; enclose; surround. *The sick woman's friends encompassed her with care.* 2. to involve. *His job began to encompass sales, too.*

encore (äng′kōr, -kôr, än′-) n., audience's demand for repeat appearance or additional performance following scheduled performance; also, additional performance as requested. *The dancers responded with a short encore.*

encroach (en krōch′) v.i., to intrude or trespass upon the possessions, jurisdiction, or rights of another. *The shrubbery began to encroach upon the house.*

encroachment (en krōch′mənt) n., act of encroaching; unlawful intrusion in general. *The small farmers resisted the encroachment of the wealthy corporation.*

encumber (en kum′bər) v.t., 1. to impede with a load or burden; weigh down. *She encumbered herself with a heavy schedule.* 2. to load with debt or liability. *He refused to encumber his estate with mortgages.*

encumbrance (en kum′brəns) n., 1. that which encumbers. *The extra suitcase was an encumbrance.* 2. claim; debt; lien. *The causeway was an encumbrance on the property.*

encyclopedic (en sī′klə pē′dik) adj., of the nature of an encyclopedia; widely knowledgeable and informative. *His encyclopedic memory was a big help in college.*

endearment (en dēr′mənt) n., manifestation or token of affection, as a caress, loving expression, or gift. *She smiled at his whispered endearment.*

endemic (en dem′ik) adj., peculiar to a particular locality, nation, or circumstance. *The disease was apparently endemic to newborns.*

endive (en′div, än′dēv; *Fr.* äN dēv′) n., plant of the chicory family, cultivated as a salad green; also called escarole. *Endive was mixed into the garden salad.*

endogenous (en doj′ə nəs) adj., growing or originating from within a body; internal. *Endogenous cell formation takes place within a mother-cell.*

endorse (en dôrs′) v.t., 1. to sign one's name on a check, bill, or other document. *She forgot to endorse the check.* 2. to express approval. *The senator was asked to endorse the controversial bill.*

endow (en dou′) v.t., to furnish with money or property, or with some quality. *He planned to endow the college with his estate.*

endowment (en dou′mənt) n., 1. act of endowing. *They thanked him for his endowment.* 2. natural ability or capacity. *She had a generous endowment of brains.*

endue (en dōō′, -dyōō′) v.t., 1. to provide; endow. *The job may endue you with the challenge you seek.* 2. to don; put on. *Trees endue fresh spring greenery in April.*

endurance (en dōōr′əns, -dyōōr′-) n., capacity for continuance under stress, hardship, or affliction. *The twenty-mile course tested the runner's endurance.*

energize (en′ər jīz′) v.t., to endow with energy; invigorate. *She tried to energize her sluggish students.*

energy (en′ər jē) n., 1. capacity for work; vigor. *She returned to her work with renewed energy.* 2. in physics, the capacity of a system to do work upon another system, diminishing its own potential to the extent of the work done; overcoming of inertia. *Energy is only converted, never destroyed.* 3. power; force; potential; thrust. *Conservation of energy is vital to a healthy economy.*

enervate (en′ər vāt′) v.t., to weaken, lessen, or destroy strength, force, nerve, or vigor. *The intense heat began to enervate the field workers.*

enfranchise (en fran′chīz) v.t., 1. to set free; liberate. *Lincoln sought to enfranchise the slaves.* 2. to admit to the privileges of a citizen, esp. the right to vote. *The legislators resisted the call to enfranchise women.*

enfranchised (en fran′ chīzd) adj., 1. liberated; set free. *The enfranchised slaves left the plantation.* 2. admitted to full rights of a citizen. *The candidate courted the newly enfranchised eighteen-year-olds.*

engaging (en gā′jiñg) adj., tending to attract favorable attention; winning; attractive. *Her engaging personality won her many votes.*

engender (en jen′dər) v.t., to generate; cause; bring forth. *She tried to engender a favorable response.*

engross (en grōs′) v.t., to occupy wholly; absorb. *He became engrossed in his work and did not hear the dinner bell.*

engulf (en gulf′) v.t., to swallow up; overwhelm. *In another hour the flood would engulf the town.*

enhance (en hans′, -häns′) v.t., to make greater; heighten; intensify. *The scarf will enhance the dress's versatility.*

enigma (ə nig′mə) n., something inexplicable; riddle; mystery. *He finally solved the enigma of her death.*

enigmatic (en′ig mat′ik, ē′nig-) adj., hard to explain; mysterious; puzzling. *I was baffled by her enigmatic reply.*

enjoin (en join′) v.t., 1. to direct or command; put an injunction on. *He tried to enjoin me to meet him at five.* 2. to forbid or prohibit. *The sign enjoined us from entering.*

en masse (än mas′, en-; *Fr.* än mas′) adv., all together; all at once; in a body. *The audience rose en masse.*

ennui (än wē′, än′wē; *Fr.* än nwē′) n., boredom; tedium; weariness. *The dull job filled her with ennui.*

enormity (i nôr′mi tē) n., hugeness or immoderation, esp. of wrongdoing. *They were aghast at the enormity of his offense.*

enrage (en rāj′) v.t., to provoke to anger or madness; make furious. *Her obstinacy began to enrage her father.*

en rapport (än RA pôr′; *Eng.* än ra pōr′, -pôr′, rə-) in accord; congenial; in agreement. *They are en rapport about the plan.*

enrapture (en rap′chər) v.t., to transport with pleasure; delight. *His performance enraptured the audience.*

en route (än rōōt′, en-; *Fr.* än Rōōt′) adj., on the way. *We planned to eat en route.*

ensconce (en skons′) v.t., to fix firmly or snugly. *He ensconced himself in the comfortable chair.*

ensign (en′sīn; *Mil.* en′sən) n., 1. flag distinguishing an army, vessel, or country. *The British ensign fluttered on the mast.* 2. lowest grade of commissioned officer in the U.S. Navy, ranking below a lieutenant, junior grade. *The ensign asked permission to come aboard.*

ensnare (en snâr′) v.t., to trap; entangle in; capture; inveigle into. *The woman avoided his attempt to ensnare her into marriage.*

ensue (en sōō′) v.i., to follow; result, as from premises. *After they blew up the bridge they expected victory to ensue.*

entente (än tänt′; *Fr.* än tänt′) n., understanding, agreement, or alliance, or the parties thereto. *The officials will try to negotiate a lasting entente between their countries.*

enteric (en ter′ik) adj., pertaining to the intestine; intestinal. *Typhoid fever is an enteric disease.*

enthrall (en thrôl′) v.t., to enslave or hold captive; charm. *The singer began to enthrall the audience.*

entice (en tīs′) v.t., to draw on or induce by exciting hope or desire; allure. *He used the story to entice his son's interest.*

enticing (en tīs′iñg) adj., alluring; charming. *She was wearing an enticing red dress.*

entity (en′ti tē) n., independent being or existence, as distinguished from any other. *She felt like a separate entity from the rest of the class.*

entomology (en'tə mol'ə jē) n., branch of zoology concerned with insects. *The ant colony inspired her interest in entomology.*

entourage (än'tōō räzh'; *Fr.* äN tōō RAzh') n., followers, companions, or servants. *The queen traveled with a large entourage.*

entrails (en'trālz, -trəlz) n., internal parts of the body; bowels, guts. *He removed the entrails from the slain deer.*

entreaty (en trē'tē) n., urgent appeal or request; earnest petition; act of pleading or begging. *He coldly ignored the poor man's entreaty.*

entrée (än'trā) n., 1. entrance. *She made her entrée via the back door.* 2. access; freedom of entry. *He was granted entrée to the files.* 3. main dish of a meal. *She ordered the roast beef entrée.*

entrepreneur (än'trə prə nûr', -nōōr'; *Fr.* äN tRə pRə nŒR') n., one who initiates and assumes responsibility for a commercial enterprise or business. *There are plenty of opportunities for a clever entrepreneur in the new city.*

enumerate (i nōō'mə rāt', i nyōō'-) v., to count; number; list; mention in detail. *He was told to enumerate his expenses on the bill.*

enunciate (i nun'sē āt', -shē-) v., to utter or pronounce words; articulate. *The child could enunciate clearly at five years.*

envenom (en ven'əm) v.t., 1. to poison or taint with poison. *The savage envenomed his arrows.* 2. to embitter; instill with hatred. *The slander envenomed him against the press.*

enviable (en'vē ə bəl) adj., worthy of envy; desirable. *Her new job put her in an enviable position.*

environ (en vī'rən, -vī'ərn) v.t., to envelop; surround; enclose; hem in. *Dense forests environ the military outpost.*

environment (en vī'rən mənt, -vī'ərn-) n., aggregate of conditions surrounding an individual or community. *Severe air pollution harms our environment.*

environs (en vī'rənz, -vī'ərnz, en'vər ənz, -vī ərnz) n. pl., surrounding areas, esp.

near a city or town; outskirts. *London's environs are accessible by the metropolitan transit.*

envisage (en viz'ij) v.t., to form a mental picture; imagine. *Listening to her description I began to envisage the finished house.*

envoy (en'voi, än'-) n., official dispatched on a mission or errand, esp. to transact business or negotiate with a foreign government; messenger; representative. *The king sent his envoy to the negotiations.*

enzyme (en'zīm) n., organic substance, secreted within an organism, which functions catalytically to effect chemical change and influence physiological processes. *The enzyme plays an important role in digestion.*

eolithic (ē'ə lith'ik) adj., that which relates to the earliest human era when eoliths, or crude stone implements, were used. *They unearthed several eolithic artifacts.*

ephemeral (i fem'ər əl) adj., existing or lasting for only one day, or for a very short time; short-lived; transitory. *Indian summer is an ephemeral season.*

epic (ep'ik) n., long, elevated, narrative poem depicting historical or legendary heroic exploits. *Milton wrote the Christian epic Paradise Lost.* adj., 1. pertaining to an epic. *The poem was written in epic style.* 2. of heroic or imposing character; lengthy. *The story retold the epic story of the Old West.*

epicure (ep'ə kyōōr') n., one of luxurious tastes, esp. in eating and drinking; gourmet. *The chef was challenged by the epicure.*

epicurean (ep'ə kyōō rē'ən, -kyōōr'ē-) adj., pertaining to an epicure. *The obese man abused the epicurean title.*

epigram (ep'ə gram') n., pointed or instructive, brief expression, often in verse. *Benjamin Franklin was a master of the epigram.*

epigraph (ep'ə graf', -gräf') n., short descriptive inscription on a building, tomb, or monument. *The epigraph commemorated John Paul Jones.*

epilepsy (ep′ə lep′sē) n., disease of the nervous system characterized by seizures including muscular spasms or loss of consciousness. *Epilepsy can be controlled by drugs.*

epilogue (ep′ə lôg′, -log′) n., closing address or speech; section appended as conclusion to a literary work. *The epilogue gives the hero's recent history.*

epistle (i pis′əl) n., letter, esp. a formal letter. *St. Paul's epistle explained aspects of the early Church.*

epitaph (ep′i taf′, -täf′) n., memorial inscription on a tomb or monument; brief prose or verse sentiment about a deceased. *The professor wrote his own epitaph before he died.*

epithet (ep′ə thet′) n., 1. descriptive word or phrase that designates as well as qualifies the thing to which it applies, or that substitutes for it. *Billy the Kid's epithet was simply, "the Kid."* 2. abusive expression. *They hurled epithets at the retreating army.*

epitome (i pit′ə mē) n., prototypical summary or representation; embodiment. *His sonnet was the epitome of all love poems.*

epitomize (i pit′ə mīz′) v.t., to function as an ideal or typical representation. *She epitomized the wicked stepmother.*

epoch (ep′ək *or, esp. Brit.,* ē′pok) n., 1. specific period of time considered as a unit because of some characteristic or course of events. *The 1960s constituted an epoch of protest.* 2. geological division of time. *The Holocene Epoch is the latter part of the Quaternary Period.*

eponym (ep′ə nim) n., person for whom a place is named, or by whom a place or thing is known. *Romulus is the eponym for Rome.*

equable (ek′wə bəl, ē′kwə-) adj., characterized by uniformity or evenness; regular; steady. *They were surprised by the usually equable man's violent response.*

equanimity (ē′kwə nim′i tē, ek′wə-) n., evenness of mind or temper; calmness; composure. *Her equanimity reassured the child.*

equestrian (i kwes′trē ən) n., rider on horseback. *The equestrian fell off his horse.* adj., pertaining to horseback riding. *She tried out for the U.S. equestrian team.*

equilibrium (ē′ kwə lib′rē əm) n., state of balance between opposing causes, forces, or powers. *The dancer lost her equilibrium and pitched forward.*

equine (ē′kwīn) adj., pertaining to or resembling a horse. *He had a long, almost equine face.*

equinox (ē′kwə noks′, ek′wə-) n., semiannual occurrence when the sun crosses the equator, rendering everywhere equal periods of day and night. *The vernal equinox occurs about March 21.*

equipage (ek′wə pij) n., 1. assortment of related articles necessary to a particular service or operation. *The tray holds the equipage for tea.* 2. equipment of a vessel, military body, or personnel; gear. *Ordnance maintains the convoy's equipage.* 3. one's personal accouterments; wardrobe. *The experienced traveler avoids excessive equipage.* 4. horse-drawn coach, complete with attendants and trappings. *On state occasions the queen rides in the royal equipage.*

equipoise (ē′kwə poiz′, ek′wə-) n., equilibrium; balance. *The weights held the scales in equipoise.* v.t., to balance. *They tried to equipoise on the seesaw.*

equitable (ek′wi tə bəl) adj., just; fair and equal. *The judge imposed an equitable sentence on the thief.*

equity (ek′wi tē) n., 1. that which is equally right or just to all concerned. *He disputed the equity of the court's decision.* 2. net cash value of a property. *He became a homeowner primarily to build up equity.*

equivocal (i kwiv′ə kəl) adj., having more than one possible meaning; ambiguous. *She misinterpreted his equivocal reply.*

equivocate (i kwiv′ə kāt′) v.i., to use ambiguous expressions, esp. with intent to mislead. *The judge warned the lawyer not to equivocate.*

era (ēr′ə, er′ə) n., 1. period characterized by a particular thing, event, or person. *It was the era of the flapper and bootleg gin.* 2. developmental stage. *The fossil dates from the Paleozoic Era.*

eradicate (i rad′ə kāt′) v.t., to destroy completely; root out. *He vowed to eradicate presidential abuse of power.*

ergo (ûr′gō, er′gō) adv., therefore. *She abandoned them; ergo he sued for custody.*

erode (i rōd′) v.t., to wear away; corrode. *The flood began to erode the river bank.*

erogenous (i roj′ə nəs) adj., stimulating or sensitive to erotic sensation. *Different cultures perceive different areas of the body as erogenous.*

erogenous zone (i roj′ə nəs zōn′) area of the body that stimulates or is particularly sensitive to erotic stimulation. *The nape of the neck is an erogenous zone.*

erotic (i rot′ik) adj., pertaining to or stimulating sexual desire. *He collects erotic art.*

err (ûr, er) v.i., to make a mistake. *You err if you think him to blame.*

errant (er′ənt) adj., 1. wandering; roving; journeying. *The errant gypsies followed the sun.* 2. deviating from a standard course; straying; mistaken; erroneous. *His errant behavior lessened with maturity.*

erratum (i rā′təm, i rä′-) n., pl. errata, an error in printed matter noticed only after printing, given with correction on separate sheet. *The editor marked the erratum on the opposite page.*

erroneous (ə rō′nē əs, e rō′-) adj., mistaken. *The erroneous report frightened them unduly.*

ersatz (er′zäts, -sats) adj., substitute; synthetic. *Saccharin was a popular ersatz sugar.*

eruct (i rukt′) v., 1. to emit gas from the stomach orally; belch. *Certain foods such as beans can cause one to eruct frequently.* 2. to spew forth; emit violently. *The volcano began to eruct molten lava.*

erudite (er′yŏŏ dīt′, er′ŏŏ-) adj., learned; scholarly. *The erudite professor chaired his department.*

eruption (i rup′shən) n., 1. act of erupting; sudden outbreak. *The volcanic eruption could be seen for miles.*

escadrille (es′kə dril′; *Fr.* es kA dRē′yə) n., European air squadron or division. *The pilot was the ace of the escadrille.*

escapade (es′kə pād′, es′kə pād′) n., wild prank; capricious or reckless adventure. *She rebuked the boys for their latest escapade.*

escarpment (e skärp′mənt) n., 1. steep, long, clifflike rock formation resulting from a shift in the earth's crust. *The huge escarpment rose above the desert plain.* 2. embankment serving as a fortification, either facilitated by a natural formation or ramified; bulwark. *The enemy tried to scale the cliffside escarpment.*

eschew (es chŏŏ′) v.t., to shun; avoid; abstain from. *He tried to eschew smoking.*

escritoire (es′kri twär′) n., writing desk; secretary; desk. *She composed the note at the escritoire.*

escrow (es′krō, e skrō′) n., document, sum, or deposit held by a third party until the fulfillment of some condition, when it is restored to the original party. *I put my rent in escrow until the manager fixed the ceiling.*

esculent (es′kyə lənt) n., food, esp. a vegetable. *Potatoes, carrots, and turnips are esculents that thrive at northern latitudes.* adj., edible; palatable. *Early explorers were astonished at the abundant esculent plants.*

escutcheon (e skuch′ən) n., 1. coat of arms. *A crown and a lion are the symbols on the royal escutcheon.* 2. panel on the stern of a ship, which carries its name. *"Valiant" was painted on the ship's escutcheon.* 3. door plate to which a handle is attached and which often surrounds a keyhole. *The carpenter replaced the worn escutcheon.*

esophagus (i sof′ə gəs, ē sof′-) n., muscular tube through which food and drink pass to the stomach. *The bone lodged in his esophagus, choking him.*

esoteric (es′ə ter′ik) adj., not generally known; understood only by a small, initiated group; private. *Only two people understood his esoteric allusion.*

espionage (es′pē ə näz̠h′, -nij, es′pē ə näz̠h′) n., practice of spying; clandestine surveillance of foreign governments and their actions. *She went to Bulgaria on a mission of espionage.*

espouse (e spouz′) n., to marry; make one's own; support or adopt. *She espoused the unpopular cause.*

esprit de corps (e sprē′ də kôr′) common spirit or bond developed among the members of any group. *The cheerleaders had a fine esprit de corps.*

essay (*n.* es′ā; *v.* e sā′) n., literary composition on a particular subject; short analytical treatise or paper. *He wrote an essay on the French Revolution.* v.t., to attempt. *He prepared to essay the difficult climb.*

essence (es′əns) n., true substance or nature of something; basic ingredient; extract. *The essence of the population problem is ignorance.*

estate (e stāt′) n., 1. property including land and, generally, large house. *The Vanderbilt estate overlooks the Hudson River.* 2. personal property left after death. *His estate was bequeathed to his son.*

esteem (e stēm′) n., favorable opinion; respect; liking. *He was held in good esteem by the school board.*

estrange (e strānj′) v.t., to alienate; turn from kindness or intimate association to indifference or hostility. *He knew the infidelity would estrange his wife.*

estranged (e stranjd′) adj., removed to a distance; being turned away in one's affections; alienated. *The estranged couple filed for divorce.*

estrogen (es′trə jən) n., female sex hormone produced in the ovaries. *In the past, estrogen was often prescribed for the post-menopausal woman.*

estuary (es′c̠h͞o͞o er′ē) n., part of the lower course of a river where the tide

waters are turned back by the current; inlet. *The estuary floods the marshlands at high tide.*

eternal (i tûr′n³l) adj., existing throughout all time, without end; everlasting. *The book assured his eternal fame.*

ethereal (i t̠hēr′ē əl) adj., 1. having characteristics of air or the heavens; intangible; spiritual. *A ghost is an ethereal being.* 2. extremely fragile or delicate. *He was alarmed by her ethereal appearance.*

ethics (et̠h′iks) n., principles of proper conduct generally governing behavior. *The lawyer violated the ethics of his profession.*

ethnic (et̠h′nik) adj., pertaining to a particular race or nationality. *The restaurant served ethnic Eastern dishes.*

ethnology (et̠h nol′ə jē) n., comparative study of human cultures and races, including origins and distribution. *Historical ethnology developed in the attempt to trace cultural diffusion.*

ethos (ē′t̠hos, et̠h′os) n., habitual or fundamental character or disposition. *I went to Dublin to study the Irish ethos.*

etiolate (ē′tē ə lāt′) v.t., to whiten a plant by deactivating its development of chlorophyll; blanch. *We will etiolate the celery by covering it.*

etiology (ē′tē ol′ə jē) n., science that deals with origins and causes, esp. of disease. *The etiology of cancer has not yet pointed to a cure.*

etiquette (et′ə kit, -ket′) n., propriety of conduct as established in any class or community; good manners. *Etiquette allows one week to acknowledge a gift.*

étude (ā′t͞ood, ā′ty͞ood, ā t͞ood′, ā ty͞ood′; *Fr.* ā tүd′) n., musical composition used for practicing or outstanding for its technique. *The Chopin étude is the student's favorite.*

etymology (et′ə mol′ə jē) n., study of the history and origins of words. *"Weekend" has a relatively short etymology.*

eucalyptus (y͞oo′kə lip′təs) n., genus of myrtaceous evergreen trees and shrubs, abundant in Australia, yielding timber and an oil valuable in medicine. *The koala bear eats eucalyptus leaves.*

eugenics (yōo jen′iks) n., science of generative improvement of the human race, esp. through careful choice of parents. *Romantic love and eugenics may be natural enemies.*

eulogy (yōo′lə jē) n., commendatory speech or written composition, esp. in honor of a deceased person. *His brother delivered the eulogy at the funeral.*

euphemism (yōo′fə miz′əm) n., mild, indirect expression used in place of one that is plainer but more offensive or unpleasant, or the act of using such an expression. *"John" is a euphemism for the toilet.*

euphonious (yōo fō′nē əs) adj., pleasing to the ear; euphonic. *We enjoyed her euphonious song.*

euphony (yōo′fə nē) n., pleasing quality of sounds; pleasant-sounding speech or musical expression. *The psalm is enjoyed for its euphony as much as its content.*

euphoria (yōo fōr′ē ə, -fôr′-) n., feeling of well-being; elation. *He was full of euphoria after the birth.*

euthanasia (yōo′thə nā′zhə, -zhē ə, -zē ə) n., painless killing, esp. of one who is terminally ill and/or suffering; mercy-killing. *The doctor testified in favor of euthanasia.*

euthenics (yōo then′iks) n., study of environmental regulation as a means to improve human living conditions. *The field of euthenics stresses pollution control.*

evacuate (i vak′yōo āt′) v.t., to empty; depart from; vacate. *The army helped evacuate the town during the epidemic.*

evade (i vād′) v.t., 1. to slip away from; avoid. *She tried to evade his notice.* 2. to circumvent. *He tried to evade her probing questions.*

evaluate (i val′yōo āt′) v.t., to appraise; determine the value of. *The teacher began to evaluate the student's progress.*

evanescent (ev′ə nes′ənt) adj., vanishing; passing away; fleeting. *The pleasures of youth are evanescent.*

evangelist (i van′jə list) n., Protestant minister or layperson who teaches the gospel at informal or unorthodox services; originally, any one of the four apostles who wrote the four Gospels (i.e., Matthew, Mark, Luke and John) of the Christian faith. *Billy Graham is an evangelist.*

evaporation (i vap′ə rā′shən) n., change from liquid into vapor, as water into steam. *When a tea kettle whistles, evaporation is taking place.*

evasion (i vā′zhən) n., act or means of avoidance. *She was accused of tax evasion.*

evasive (i vā′siv) adj., engaging in or pertaining to evading; equivocal. *I tried to pin down the evasive thought.*

eventual (i ven′chōo əl) adj., pertaining to the event or issue; contingent upon a future or uncertain event. *His talent held hope for eventual success.*

evict (i vikt′) v.t., to dispel from lands or tenements by legal process; expel by force; eject. *He moved to evict the hecklers from the audience.*

evidence (ev′i dəns) n., means or facts by which something is proven; testimony. *There was plenty of evidence to support my story.*

evident (ev′i dənt) adj., plainly seen or perceived; obvious. *His unhappiness was evident in his face.*

evince (i vins′) v.t., to show clearly or make evident; reveal. *She asked him to evince adequate collateral for the loan.*

eviscerate (i vis′ə rāt′) v.t., to take out the entrails of; disembowel. *They paid him to eviscerate the ducks.*

evocative (i vok′ə tiv, -vō′kə-) adj., tending to evoke. *The evocative smell reminded me of Christmas.*

evoke (i vōk′) v.t., to call forth; summon; educe. *That song will always evoke happy memories.*

evolution (ev′ə lōo′shən or, esp. Brit., ē′və-) n., 1. act or process of unfolding or developing, as from a latent state; phylogeny. *Man's evolution began mil-*

lions of years ago. 2. theory that modern types of animals and plants originated from other earlier types and that the newer forms developed through generations of modifications. *The theory of evolution includes that of survival of the fittest.*

evolve (i volv′) v.t., to unfold; develop by a process of natural, consecutive, or logical growth. *The system evolved from trial-and-error.* v.i., to go through evolutionary or developmental change. *The boy must evolve into a man.*

ewer (yoo′ər) n., wide-mouthed pitcher, esp. for water; jug. *She offered him ice water from the ewer.*

exacerbate (ig zas′ər bāt′, ik sas′-) v.t., to increase the bitterness or virulence of; make more violent; aggravate. *The salt water exacerbated the pain of the cut.*

exacting (ig zak′tiṅg) adj., severely demanding; meticulous. *The exacting professor deplored the slightest grammatical error.*

exaggerate (ig zaj′ə rāt′) v.t., to enlarge beyond truth or reason; amplify. *The fisherman tended to exaggerate the size of his catch.*

exalt (ig zôlt′) v.t., to elevate in degree or consideration; intensify. *Wine tends to exalt conversation.*

exalted (ig zôl′tid) adj., raised to a height; dignified; lofty; sublime. *Even in her exalted position, she did not forget her old friends.*

exasperate (ig zas′pə rāt′) v.t., to irritate; enrage. *The child's crying began to exasperate the babysitter.*

Excalibur (ek skal′ə bər) n., magic sword used by King Arthur; hence, an indispensable, trusty companion. *Arthur was chosen king when he pulled Excalibur out of a rock.*

excavate (eks′kə vāt′) v.t., to dig out and remove or expose. *The archeologists began to excavate the ruined city.*

exceed (ik sēd′) v.t., to pass or go beyond; proceed beyond the given or supposed limit. *Do not exceed the speed limit.*

excel (ik sel′) v.t., to surpass; be superior to; outdo. *The athlete seemed to excel effortlessly in the games.*

excelsior (ik sel′sē ər, ek-) n., fine quality of wood shavings used for stuffing and packing. *The china was packed in excelsior.*

except (ik sept′) prep., excluding; but; leaving out. *He punished everyone except Joanne.*

exceptional (ik sep′shə nəl) adj., out of the ordinary; contrary to the rule. *It was a contribution of exceptional generosity.*

exemplary (ig zem′plə rē) adj., serving as a model for imitation; worthy of imitation. *She was an exemplary student.*

exempt (ig zempt′) v.t., to grant immunity; excuse. *The order exempted all married men from combat duty.* adj., free; immune; excused. *He was exempt from the jurisdiction of the court.*

excerpt (n. ek′sûrpt; v. ik sûrpt′) n., extract from a written or printed work. *I read an excerpt from his novel.* v.t., to extract. *The professor asked me to excerpt all passages about Edward VII's reign.*

excess (n. ik ses′; adj. ek′ses, ik ses′) n., 1. superfluity; surplus. *After deducting his expenses, he returned the excess to the bookkeeper.* 2. immoderation; intemperance. *She drank to excess that evening.* adj., superfluous; extra. *Excess profits were reinvested.*

excessive (ik ses′iv) adj., exceeding a limit or measure; too much; extravagant; immoderate. *She suffered excessive grief when her cat died.*

excise (n. ek′sīz, -sīs; v. ik sīz′) n., tax imposed on certain commodities produced and sold within the boundaries of a given state, or on certain licenses or fees. *The excise on cigarettes doubled in five years.* v.t., 1. to place excise on. *The legislature wanted to excise the lottery tickets.* 2. to cut out or off. *The surgeon operated to excise the tumor.*

exclude (ik sklood′) v.t., to bar from admission, participation, or consideration;

shut out. *It was cruel to exclude him from the party.*

excommunicate (*v.* eks′kə myōō′nə kāt′; *adj.* eks′kə myōō′nə kit, -kāt′) v.t., to cut off from the sacraments of the church or from fellowship with its members. *The church determined to excommunicate the adulterer.* adj., excommunicated. *The excommunicate woman did not repent her action.*

excrement (ek′skrə mənt) n., matter eliminated as useless from the living body; feces. *The sick child got excrement on his bed.*

exculpate (ek′skul pāt′, ik skul′pāt) v.t., to clear from an accusation of wrongdoing. *Her testimony would exculpate the defendant.*

execute (ek′sə kyōōt′) v.t., 1. to follow out; perform completely; accomplish. *Estimate how much it will cost to execute this plan.* 2. to put to death. *The soldiers prepared to execute the prisoner.*

exemplary (ig zem′plə rē, eg′zəm pler′ē) adj., serving as a model for imitation; worthy of imitation. *She was an exemplary student.*

exhibition (ek′sə bish′ən) n., showing or display; that which is displayed. *The museum will stage an exhibition of Chinese art.*

exhibitionist (ek′sə bish′ə nist) n., 1. one who overtly tries to attract attention. *She seemed more exhibitionist than entertainer.* 2. one who performs indecent exposure. *The exhibitionist was arrested outside the girls' dorm.*

exhilarate (ig zil′ə rāt′) v.t., to make cheerful, lively, or merry. *The holiday will exhilarate the children.*

exhilarating (ig zil′ə rā′tiṅg) adj., stimulating; enlivening. *Ice skating is an exhilarating sport.*

exhort (ig zôrt′) v.t., to advise urgently; admonish; caution. *She began to exhort her son to drive carefully.*

exhume (ig zōōm′, -zyōōm′, eks hyōōm′) v.t., to dig out of the ground; esp. to

disinter a dead body. *The court instructed them to exhume the body.*

exigency (ek′si jən sē) n., state of being urgent; pressing need or demand; emergency. *The exigency of making his monthly quota caused the salesman stress.*

exile (eg′zīl, ek′sīl) n., 1. separation from one's native or chosen home or country and friends; banishment. *The Soviet dissident lives in exile in the U.S.A.* 2. one who is separated from or forced to leave his or her home or country and friends. *After the revolution, he was an exile.* v.t., to force to leave one's home or country and friends; banish. *The parliament voted to exile the traitor.*

existence (ig zis′təns) n., actual being; being or reality at a certain moment or throughout a certain period of time. *The dinosaur is no longer in existence.*

existentialism (eg′zi sten′shə liz′əm, ek′si-) n., modern philosophical doctrine that existence precedes essence and that emphasizes individual uniqueness and isolation, freedom and responsibility. *She studied existentialism in college.*

exodus (ek′sə dəs) n., departure from a place, esp. by a large group; migration. *The waterfowl began their annual exodus south.*

exonerate (ig zon′ə rāt′) v.t., 1. to clear of a charge or blame; exculpate. *His youth could not exonerate him from the crime.* 2. to discharge a responsibility or debt. *He offered to exonerate him from the contract.*

exorbitant (ig zôr′bi tᵊnt) adj., going beyond reasonable bounds; inordinate; excessive. *They charged an exorbitant price for the dinner.*

exorcise (ek′sôr sīz′) v.t., to drive out (demons) by religious or magical ceremonies; purify of unclean spirits or devils. *The priest attempted to exorcise the tormented woman.*

exorcist (ek′sôr sist) n., one who acts to exorcise. *An exorcist is a member of a particular order of priests.*

exotic (ig zot'ik) adj., of foreign origin or character; unfamiliar; colorful; unusual. *She ordered the exotic plant from the florist.*

expansion (ik span'shən) n., act of spreading out; enlargement. *The architect worked on the plans for expansion.*

expansive (ik span'siv) adj., 1. capable of being spread out in volume or extent; embracing a large number of objects or particulars; wide-extending; comprehensive. *The expansive plan included provision for economic fluctuation.* 2. marked by good spirits, benevolence, euphoria. *Their expansive host pressed them to have another drink.*

expatiate (ik spā'shē āt') v.t., to enlarge in discourse or writing; be copious in argument or discussion. *He loved to expatiate on the subject of prizefighting.*

expatriate (*n.* eks pā'trē it, -āt'; *v.* eks pā'trē āt') n., one who is exiled, or who withdraws his citizenship. *The expatriate received newspapers from home.* v.t., to banish; send out of one's native country; exile. *The king was forced to expatriate the wayward noble.* v.i., to renounce one's citizenship. *He expatriated and fled to Canada.* adj., banished; exiled. *The expatriate Soviet ballet dancer performs in Paris.*

expectorate (ik spek'tə rāt') v.i., to discharge, as phlegm or other matter, by coughing or hawking and spitting out. *It is illegal to expectorate on a public vehicle.*

expediency (ik spē'dē ən sē) n., fitness or suitability to bring about a particular end; proper or most efficient mode of procedure for gaining a desired end. *During the gas shortage we saw the expediency of living close to town.*

expedient (ik spē'dē ənt) n., that which promotes a desired result; means to accomplish an end. *She used him as an expedient to her promotion.* adj., advantageous; fit; suitable; direct. *He searched a map for the most expedient route.*

expedite (ek'spi dīt') v.t., to accelerate the motion or progress of; hasten. *He asked her to expedite her work on the project.*

expedition (ek'spi dish'ən) n., journey or voyage made by a company or body of persons for a specific purpose; also, such a body and its whole outfit. *He organized a climbing expedition to the Himalayas.*

expeditious (ek'spi dish'əs) adj., performed with dispatch; quick; speedy. *The soldiers' families hoped for their expeditious return.*

expenditure (ik spen'di chər) n., act of disbursement; outlay; consumption; also, that which is disbursed; expense. *The comptroller keeps track of the company's expenditure.*

expiate (ek'spē āt') v.t., to atone for; make satisfaction or reparation for. *He tried to expiate his offense.*

expire (ik spīʰr') v.i., 1. to come to an end; terminate; fail or cease to nothing. *The lease will expire at the end of this month.* 2. to emit the last breath; die; perish. *The drowning man finally expired.*

expletive (ek'splə tiv) n., word or syllable not necessary to the sense or construction of a sentence, but added for rhetorical reasons; oath. *She was offended by the off-color expletives in his speech.*

explicate (ek'splə kāt') v.t., to unfold the meaning or sense of; explain; interpret. *She tried to explicate the poem for the boy.*

explicit (ik splis'it) adj., having no disguised meaning or reservation; clear; unambiguous. *He couldn't misunderstand the explicit order.*

exploit (ek'sploit, ik sploit') n., exceptional or remarkable deed; conspicuous performance; spirited or heroic act. *His exploit made the front page.* v.t., to employ or utilize selfishly; turn to one's advantage without regard to right or justice. *He tried to exploit the players' hostilities in the game.*

export (*n.* ek'spōrt, -spôrt; *v.* ik spōrt', -spôrt', ek'spōrt, -spôrt) n., commodity carried from one place or country to another for sale. *Lace is the province's chief export.* v.t., to send to another country or place for sale. *The Arab countries export oil to the United States.*

expose (ik spōz′) v.t., 1. to lay open to view; uncover; reveal. *He wanted to expose the fraud.* 2. to lay bare; leave unprotected. *Don't expose yourself too long in the sun.*

ex post facto (eks′ pōst′ fak′tō) adv., from a subsequent state of facts; after the fact; with reference to a former state of facts; retrospectively. *The transaction was voided ex post facto.*

expostulate (ik spos′chə lāt′) v.i., 1. to reason earnestly with a person against something he intends to do or has done. *He came to expostulate with me against leaving school.* 2. to discuss; reason about. *He expostulated on my foolishness.*

expound (ik spound′) v.i., to set forth the points or principles of; explain; interpret. *Dr. Johnson liked to expound the finer points of rhetoric.*

expropriate (eks prō′prē āt′) v.t., to take possession of another's property, esp. by government for public use. *The government expropriated the farmland to build the railroad.*

expropriation (eks prō′prē ā′shən) n., act of expropriating or state of being expropriated. *The landlord fought the state's expropriation of his building.*

expulsion (ik spul′shən) n., act of expelling or driving out by force; compulsory dismissal; banishment. *The fight resulted in his expulsion from school.*

expunge (ik spunj′) v.t., to erase or blot out; obliterate. *He asked that the court expunge his name from the record.*

expurgate (ek′spər gāt′) v.t., to free from what is objectionable on moral or religious grounds; purge; cleanse. *She fought her editor's attempt to expurgate the scene.*

exquisite (ek′skwi zit, ik skwiz′it) adj., 1. having qualities of flawless beauty or craftsmanship. *They admired the ex-* *quisite wrought-iron gate.* 2. discriminating. *She has exquisite taste in clothes.* 3. acute; intense. *She suffered exquisite discomfort during the interview.*

extant (ek′stənt, ik stant′) adj., still existing; not lost or destroyed; now being. *The extant evidence tells an incomplete story.*

extemporaneous (ik stem′pə rā′nē əs) adj., resulting from or provided for the immediate occasion; unpremeditated. *He gave an extemporaneous speech.*

extemporize (ik stem′pə rīz′) v.i., to prepare for a sudden and unexpected occasion with the means at hand; speak without preparation; improvise. *He had to extemporize a dinner for the stranded family.*

extensive (ik sten′siv) adj., embracing a wide area or a great number; diffusive; large. *He was impressed by her extensive expertise.*

extenuate (ik sten′yōō āt′) v.t., to lessen in degree or appearance; mitigate. *His family situation does not extenuate his wrongdoing.*

extenuating (ik sten′yōō ā′tiṅg) adj., pertaining to that which extenuates. *The attorney believed that extenuating circumstances should help her case.*

extinct (ik stiṅgkt′) adj., no longer in existence. *The passenger pigeon is an extinct species.*

extol (ik stōl′, -stol′) v.t., to praise highly; eulogize. *He began to extol her cooking.*

extort (ik stôrt′) v.t., to wrest or wring from a person by violence or intimidation. *They tried to extort "protection" money from the shopkeeper.*

extortion (ik stôr′shən) n., act of extorting; oppressive or illegal exaction. *The loan shark's interest rates amount to extortion.*

extract (ek′strakt) n., 1. something drawn from a substance by distillation or other process; essence. *She put vanilla extract in the cake.* 2. selection from a written or spoken work. *He read them an extract from Tom Sawyer.*

extract (ik strakt′) v.t., 1. to pull out;

withdraw. *The dentist prepared to extract the tooth.* 2. to distill or separate one substance from the whole; to make a selection from. *The student was asked to extract and discuss a theme from the poem.*

extradite (ek′strə dīt′) v.t., to deliver or relinquish to another jurisdiction. *The United States requested that Mexico extradite the suspect.*

extradition (ek′strə dish′ən) n., act or result of extraditing, usually in accordance with a mutual treaty. *Alabama sought his extradition from Ohio.*

extraneous (ik strā′nē əs) adj., outside; foreign; unattached; unrelated; not intrinsic or essential. *His point was extraneous to the argument.*

extrapolate (ik strap′ə lāt′, ek′strə pə-) v.t., to infer something about an unknown situation from known observation or experience. *He managed to extrapolate her condition from her answers.*

extremity (ik strem′i tē) n., 1. farthest point; verge; boundary. *Alaska is the northern extremity of the United States.* 2. extreme need, distress or difficulty; destitution. *The earthquake left the villagers in extremity.* 3. limb of the body, esp. a hand or foot. *Frostbite can injure the extremities.*

extricate (ek′strə kāt′) v.t., to disentangle; disengage; free. *She had to extricate herself from the embarrassing situation.*

extrinsic (ik strin′sik) adj., 1. not of the essence or nature of a thing; outward; external. *Nervousness was one of her extrinsic characteristics.* 2. coming from outside and affecting a thing; extraneous. *She was distracted by the extrinsic remark.*

extrovert (ek′strō vûrt′, -strə-) n., one who is outgoing, whose preoccupations are largely outside the self. *The extrovert made a good public relations officer.*

exuberance (ig zōō′bər əns) n., unrestrained joy; enthusiasm; high spirits. *Her exuberance was contagious.*

exuberant (ig zōō′bər ənt) adj., joyful; bubbly; enthusiastic. *Her exuberant mood lifted everyone's spirits.*

exude (ig zōōd′, ik sōōd′) v.i., to ooze out. *Sap began to exude from the maple.*

exult (ig zult′) v.i., to rejoice, esp. in triumph; triumph. *One should not exult over the vanquished.*

exultation (eg′zul tā′shən, ek′sul-) n., lively joy at success or victory; triumph. *The winner could not restrain her exultation.*

Ff

fable (fā'bəl) n., imaginative tale that illustrates a lesson or truth, often using animals as characters; legend; myth. *The children love the fable of the ant and the grasshopper.*

fabricate (fab'rə kāt') v.t., to form by art and labor; invent; concoct, esp. a false story. *She managed to fabricate a convincing story.*

façade (fə säd', fa-; *Fr.* fA sAd') n., front of a building or any of its principal faces; outward appearance of anything. *Her cheerful façade hid her disappointment.*

facet (fas'it) n., one of several surfaces of an object; esp., one polished segment cut on a gem. *She revealed another facet of her personality.*

facetious (fə sē'shəs) adj., sportive; witty; playful; joking. *She smiled at his facetious nickname.*

facile (fas'il *or, esp. Brit.,* -īl) adj., easy; affable; quick or dexterous. *He was a facile liar.*

facilitate (fə sil'i tāt') v.t., to make easy; lessen the labor of. *The appliance helped to facilitate the job.*

facsimile (fak sim'ə lē) n., imitation; copy; likeness. *Show a birth certificate or a facsimile of it.*

fact (fakt) n., something that is real; actual event. *She could not deny the fact that she was aging.*

faction (fak'shən) n., party of persons having a common end in view, often seeking to bring about a specified change. *The candidate cannot please every faction.*

factious (fak'shəs) adj., given to or pertaining to faction; promoting partisan views; dissentious; zealous. *Congress was the scene of many factious debates.*

factitious (fak tish'əs) adj., made by or resulting from art or labor, rather than from nature; artificial; unnatural. *She struggled to maintain even a factitious interest in the work.*

factor (fak'tər) n., 1. one of several circumstances, elements, or influences leading to a result. *He considered every factor before making his decision.* 2. in mathematics, one of two or more numbers or quantities that when multiplied together produce a given product. *Six and three are factors of eighteen.*

factory (fak'tə rē) n., place where goods or products are manufactured, including the buildings, machinery, and workers involved in such labor. *The steel factory was the town's mainstay.*

factual (fak'chōō əl) adj., consisting of facts; real; genuine; accurate. *A news story should be short and factual.*

faculty (fak'əl tē) n., 1. mental or physical capacity for a particular action or affection; natural capability. *She had a faculty for learning languages.* 2. body of persons on whom are conferred specific professional powers, esp. at a particular institution. *The faculty of the college was highly respected.*

Fahrenheit (far'ən hīt'; *Ger.* fäR'ən hīt') adj., designating a scale of temperature in which water freezes at 32 degrees and boils at 212 degrees. *Set the oven at 400° Fahrenheit.*

fallacious (fə lā'shəs) adj., falsely believing; misleading. *Do not be taken in by fallacious arguments.*

fallible (fal'ə bəl) adj., liable to err or to fail, or to be erroneous or false. *Politicians, being human, are fallible.*

fallow (fal'ō) adj., plowed and left unseeded; uncultivated; neglected. *The field lay fallow for two years.*

falsetto (fôl set'ō) n., highest pitched register in the human voice, particularly

117

male. *He sang in a quavering falsetto.* adj., unnaturally high-pitched. *He answered in falsetto alarm.*

falsify (fôl′sə fī′) v.t., to make false or deceptive; misrepresent. *The dishonest clerk falsified the accounts.*

falter (fôl′tər) v.i., to hesitate; fail or waver; totter. *He began to falter under the weight of the chair.*

fanatic (fə nat′ik) n., one given to wild or extravagant notions, or affected by zeal or enthusiasm to the point of obsession. *She was a fanatic about cleanliness.*

fanaticism (fə nat′i siz′əm) n., inordinate zeal or enthusiasm. *His fanaticism began to approach madness.*

fanciful (fan′si fəl) adj., 1. led by the imagination rather than reason and experience; whimsical. *He was delighted by her fanciful idea.* 2. characterized by capriciousness or whimsy. *She cut the cookies in fanciful shapes.*

fancy (fan′sē) n., 1. productive imagination. *The afternoon sun spurred his fancy to poetry.* 2. imaginative or whimsical idea or notion. *The child's superstitious fancies made him afraid of the dark.* 3. inclination; liking; taste. *Indulge your fancy.* v.t., 1. to imagine. *She fancied herself a princess.* 2. to desire; have a taste for; love. *I fancy that dress.* adj., fine; elaborate; elegant; ornamental. *She drew a fancy scrollwork around the letter.*

fanfare (fan′fâr) n., 1. flourish of trumpets. *A fanfare announced the king's arrival.* 2. ostentatious display; spectacle; bravado. *She wanted a plain ceremony without fanfare.*

fantastic (fan tas′tik) adj., produced or existing only in imagination; unreal; grotesque; odd; whimsically formed or designed. *The circus clown wore a fantastic costume.*

farce (färs) n., ridiculous sham; mockery. *The one-candidate election was a farce.*

farcical (fär′si kəl) adj., ludicrous; ridiculous; absurd. *He amused the child with his farcical behavior.*

fascism (fash′iz əm) n., political philosophy that exalts the nation or state and embraces an autocratic government and strict social and economic regimentation. *Fascism is incompatible with democracy.*

fastidious (fa stid′ē əs) adj., extremely discriminating; dainty. *He chose his clothes with fastidious care.*

fatal (fāt′əl) adj., causing or attended by death or destruction; deadly; mortal. *The car crash was a fatal accident.*

fatalism (fāt′əliz′əm) n., doctrine that all things are directed by inevitable predetermination; disposition to hold this doctrine; acceptance of all conditions and events as inevitable. *Fatalism discourages ingenuity or competition.*

fatalist (fāt′əl ist) n., one who accepts all conditions and events as inevitable; one who believes in inevitable predetermination. *A fatalist does not believe in luck.*

fathom (fath′əm) n., in nautical usage, a measure of depth equal to six feet. *The bay was twenty fathoms deep.* v.i., to comprehend; understand. *I can't fathom his poetry.*

fatuous (fach′ōō əs) adj., stupidly self-sufficient or conceited; foolish. *We were annoyed by his fatuous behavior.*

fauna (fô′nə) n., animal life. *We studied the local fauna in biology class.*

faux pas (fō pä′; *Fr.* fō pä′) n., breach of good manners; mistake; false step. *She was embarrassed by her faux pas.*

fawn (fôn) v.i., to flatter excessively without dignity; grovel; kowtow. *He fawned upon the princess hoping to win her favor.*

feasible (fē′zə bəl) adj., capable of being done; practically possible. *Is your plan feasible?*

featherbrained (feth′ər brānd′) adj., giddy; frivolous; inattentive. *Her featherbrained son neglected his schoolwork.*

feces (fē′sēz) n., undigested food, mixed with digestive juices, which is evacuated; excrement. *The stream was contaminated with animal feces.*

fecund (fē′kund, -kənd, fek′und, -ənd) adj., fruitful and productive; prolific. *Rabbits are especially fecund breeders.*

fecundity (fi kun′di tē) n., quality of

propagating abundantly; fruitfulness. *Many tropical fishes show amazing fecundity.*

feign (fān) v.t., to make a false appearance of; pretend. *To "play possum" is to feign death.*

feint (fānt) v.i., to make a pretended blow, thrust, or attack at one point when another is intended to be struck, in order to throw an opponent off guard. *A good boxer knows how to feint.*

felicitations (fi lis′i tā′shənz) n., expression of joy for another's good fortune; congratulations. *He sent his felicitations on their marriage.*

felicity (fi lis′i tē) n., happiness; bliss. *The child added to their domestic felicity.*

feline (fē′līn) n., animal in the cat family. *Lions and tabbies are both felines.* adj., pertaining to cats; catlike. *She had green, feline eyes.*

felon (fel′ən) n., one who has committed a grave crime declared a felony by law; criminal. *The convicted felon was sentenced to death.*

felony (fel′ə nē) n., major crime, more serious than a misdemeanor. *Examples of a felony are murder and grand larceny.*

feminine (fem′ə nin) adj., pertaining to or characteristic of the female sex. *Pink was once considered an exclusively feminine color.*

femme fatale (*Fr.* fAm fA tAl′; *Eng.* fem′ fə tal′, -täl′) n., exotically alluring woman who entices men into danger; siren. *The young man was captivated by the notorious femme fatale.*

fend (fend) v.t., to keep off; ward off. *The charm was said to fend off evil.*

ferment (*n.* fûr′ment; *v.* fər ment′) n., unrest; disturbance. *Student ferment preceded the outburst.* v.i., 1. to undergo fermentation. *The wine began to ferment.* 2. to be in state of unrest or agitation. *Trouble began to ferment in the capital.*

fermentation (fûr′men tā′shən) n., chemical change involving or caused by effervescence. *The liquor is made by fermentation of hops.*

ferocious (fə rō′shəs) adj., fierce or cruel; savage; wild. *The ferocious tiger terrorized the village.*

ferret (fer′it) n., small, slender weasellike animal, bred to hunt and kill rodents. v.t., to search out; bring to light. *She tried to ferret the truth from his remark.*

fertile (fûr′t²l *or, esp. Brit.,* -tīl) adj., capable of producing or breeding; fruitful; inventive. *The fertile field produced a bumper crop.*

fertilization (fûr′t²li zā′shən) n., process of insemination or impregnation; union of two cells initiating the development of a new organism. *Bees are important in the fertilization of flowers.*

fervent (fûr′vənt) adj., ardent; eager; vehement; earnest; fervid. *He was moved by her fervent plea.*

fervid (fûr′vid) adj., vehement; impassioned; zealous. *Her fervid speech drew their attention.*

fervor (fûr′vər) n., warmth of feeling; passion. *His religious fervor was obvious.*

fester (fes′tər) v.i., to become infected and full of pus; rot; become increasingly irritated. *Clean a wound so it won't fester.*

festoon (fe stoon′) n., decorative garland. *The flowers were tied into a festoon.* v.t., to form into or adorn with garlands. *Festoon the halls with garlands of holly.*

fetal (fēt′²l) adj., pertaining to or having the character of a fetus. *She curled into a fetal position.*

fetid (fet′id, fē′tid) adj., having an offensive smell; stinking. *The sewer overflowed with fetid water.*

fetish (fet′ish, fē′tish) n., 1. object of blind devotion; prepossession. *Work became a fetish to the ambitious man.* 2. object arousing strong emotional, often sexual, feeling. *Black stockings were his fetish.*

fetus (fē′təs) n., embryo in a late stage of development; an unborn animal or human. *The machine monitored the heartbeat of the fetus during labor.*

fiasco (fē as′kō) n., undignified failure; complete breakdown. *The dismal party was a fiasco.*

fiat (fī′ət, -at) n., absolute command, as from divine authority. *They had to obey the queen's fiat.*

fib (fib) n., mild or innocent lie; white lie. *She told a fib to break her date.* v.i., to tell an innocent lie. *She fibbed about her age.*

fickle (fik′əl) adj., likely to change; inconstant; unstable. *Don't count on her—she's fickle.*

fictitious (fik tish′əs) adj., not real; created by or existing in the imagination. *The characters are purely fictitious.*

fiddle (fid′əl) n., violin. *The bluegrass band includes a fiddle and a banjo.* v.i., to play a fiddle; adjust experimentally; to tinker. *He began to fiddle with the carburetor.*

fidelity (fi del′i tē, fī-) n., strict and continuing devotion and loyalty; good faith; strict adherence to truth or reality. *The marriage was based on mutual fidelity.*

figment (fig′mənt) n., something imagined; a fiction; an invention. *The incident was a figment of her imagination.*

figurative (fig′yər ə tiv) adj., metaphorical; not literal. *Do you mean that in a literal or a figurative sense?*

filch (filch) v.t., to steal on a petty scale; pilfer. *The boy tried to filch the last cookie.*

finale (fi nal′ē, -nä′lē) n., concluding section of a dramatic or musical piece; impressive climax. *The castle goes up in flames during the opera's finale.*

finesse (fi nes′) n., delicacy or fineness of skill or style. *Fred Astaire is a dancer with great finesse.*

finicky (fin′ə kē) adj., difficult to please; fussy. *The finicky cat wouldn't touch the food.*

finite (fī′nīt) adj., subject to limitations or measurement, as of time, space, and number. *Human life is finite in its duration.*

firmament (fûr′mə mənt) n., poetic term for sky or heavens. *The stars shone in the firmament.*

fiscal (fis′kəl) adj., pertaining to financial matters, esp. government revenues or taxation. *The Cabinet reviewed the government's fiscal policy.*

fissure (fish′ər) n., crack or split. *The earthquake caused a fissure in the rock.* v.t., to split or crack open. *The warm spell began to fissure the skating pond.*

fitful (fit′fəl) adj., varied by irregular fits of action and repose; spasmodic; changeable. *The child's fitful behavior exasperated us.*

fixation (fik sā′shən) n., obsessive preoccupation or habit. *She had a fixation about serving dinner at exactly six o'clock.*

fizzle (fiz′əl) v.i., to come to a lame conclusion, esp. after a brilliant start. *The play seemed to fizzle after the exciting first act.*

fjord (fyôrd, fyôrd; *Norw.* fyŏŏr, fyôr) n., narrow, deep inlet of the sea between steep cliffs. *They cruised through the Norwegian fjord.*

flabbergasted (flab′ər gas′tid) adj., overcome with astonishment, confusion, or bewilderment. *He was completely flabbergasted by the news.*

flabby (flab′ē) adj., lacking firmness; lax; feeble. *The long illness left his muscles flabby.*

flaccid (flak′sid) adj., soft and slack; lax; droopy; flabby. *The skin on a drum should be taut, not flaccid.*

flagellate (flaj′ə lāt′) v.t., to whip or lash; punish. *The soldiers would flagellate their prisoners with whips.*

flagrant (flā′grənt) adj., glaring; scandalous. *It was a flagrant breach of conduct.*

flail (flāl) v.t., to thresh; whip. *He will flail his son when he finds out.*

flair (flâr) n., unusual, discriminating, or imaginative style or sense. *She had a flair for interior design.*

flamboyant (flam boi′ənt) adj., conspicuous; showy; florid. *A flamingo is a flamboyant bird.*

flatulent (flach′ə lənt) adj., 1. affected with gases generated in the stomach. *He took bicarbonate of soda for his flatulent feeling.* 2. vain; puffed up. *He was flatulent with pompous self-regard.*

flaunt (flônt) v.t., to make a gaudy display; boast; show off. *The wealthy are tasteless when they flaunt their money.*

flay (flā) v.t., to skin; strip the skin off;

strip off. *The hunter proceeded to flay the rabbit.*

fleck (flek) n., little spot or dot; speck; particle. *He got a fleck of dust in his eye.* v.t., to spot or dapple. *Chocolate ice cream flecked his shirt.*

fledgling (flej′ling) n., young bird barely ready to fly; raw or inexperienced person. *She was a fledgling to the game.* adj., inexperienced; young and untried. *She was a fledgling reporter.*

flibbertigibbet (flib′ər tē jib′it) n., impish, flighty person. *The girl was a restless flibbertigibbet.*

flick (flik) n., light, sudden stroke; flip. *She gave the horse a flick of the whip.* v.t., to strike lightly; flip. *He playfully flicked water at her.*

flinch (flinch) v.i., to give way to fear or pain; shrink back; wince. *She did not flinch from her duty.*

flip (flip) n., act of turning upside down. *She did a backward flip off the diving board.* v.t., to toss; to turn upside down; to go out of control or lose one's temper. *We'll flip a coin to settle the dispute.* adj., flippant; disrespectful. *She was punished for her flip answer.*

flippant (flip′ənt) adj., disrespectful; impertinent. *He was angered by her flippant reply.*

float (flōt) n., 1. something that floats or stays on top of water; raft; nautical marker. *She swam out to the float to sunbathe.* 2. wheeled platform bearing scenery and people in a parade. *The float was covered with flowers.* v.i., 1. to be buoyed up by water or other liquid. *Wood usually floats in water.* 2. to be unattached; to move about lightly. *She seemed to float among her guests.* 3. to pass before the mind or eyes. *His whole life floated before him.*

flora (flôr′ə, flôr′ə) n., plant life of an area, region, or period. *We studied the flora of the Rockies.*

florid (flôr′id, flor′-) adj., bright in color; highly ornate; flowery. *She had a florid complexion.*

flotilla (flō til′ə) n., little fleet; fleet of small ships. *We were surrounded by a flotilla of rowboats.*

flotsam (flot′səm) n., wreckage found floating; rubbish. *Flotsam floated ashore after the shipwreck.*

flout (flout) v.t., to mock or scoff at; treat with disdain or contempt. *The teacher told them not to flout the school regulations.*

fluctuate (fluk′chōō āt′) v.i., to vary; waver; rise and fall. *Prices fluctuate on the stock market.*

fluency (flōō′ən sē) n., ability to flow freely; copiousness or readiness of speech. *He worked to maintain his fluency in French.*

fluent (flōō′ənt) adj., flowing; ready in the use of words. *She is fluent in French.*

fluid (flōō′id) n., substance that flows and changes its shape by yielding easily to pressure or conforming to the shape of its container. *Water ceases to be a fluid when it freezes.* adj., flowing; graceful; shifting; changeable. *We enjoyed the dancer's fluid movements.*

fluorescence (flōō′ə res′əns, flōō res′-, flō-, flô-) n., emission of radiation, usually visible light, during the absorption of radiation from another source; also, the light itself. *The mineral's fluorescence is caused by the ultraviolet light.*

fluster (flus′tər) v.t., to confuse or embarrass. *We'll fluster her if we arrive too early.*

flux (fluks) n., act of flowing; flood; continual change. *The valley was flooded by the flux of melted snow.*

foible (foi′bəl) n., trifling weakness; insignificant fault. *He indulged his foible for chocolate cake.*

foist (foist) v.t., to thrust in wrongfully, forcefully, or surreptitiously; pass off as genuine. *The salesman tried to foist the defective equipment on her.*

fold (fōld) n., 1. double or bend in a flexible material; parts brought together by bending or folding. *She smoothed the fold in his handkerchief.* 2. group with a common goal or goals. *The elders welcomed the child into the fold.* v.t., 1. to double over; lay or bring one part over or toward another. *Ask him to fold these shirts.* 2. to enclose in folds; embrace. *He wanted to fold her in his* *arms.* 3. to give way; collapse. *Marion's knees folded under her.*

folderol (fol′də rol′) n., nonsense; silly trifles. *Her letter was full of gossip and folderol.*

follicle (fol′ə kəl) n., tiny cavity, sac, or tube in the skin for secretion or excretion; small lymph node. *Each hair grows out of a follicle.*

foment (fō ment′) v.t., to encourage; incite; instigate or promote. *The agent was sent to foment an uprising.*

fondle (fon′dəl) v.t., to show affection by caressing. *She loved to fondle her child.*

font (font) n., 1. water vessel used during religious ceremonies. *They approached the baptismal font.* 2. fountain. *An old bronze font ornamented the village green.* 3. set of compositor's type, complete in one face and size. *He stored the Baskerville font carefully.*

foolhardy (fool′här′dē) adj., bold without judgment; foolishly rash. *The foolhardy youth took the dare.*

fop (fop) n., one who is ostentatious in dress and manner; a dandy. *The fop spends too much on fancy clothes.*

foppish (fop′ish) adj., ostentatious in dress or manner; vain. *The foppish prince wears silk underwear.*

forage (fôr′ij, for′-) n., food for livestock; fodder. *He filled the silo with winter forage.* v.t., to search for provisions. *The scouts were sent to forage for firewood.*

forbearance (fôr bâr′əns) n., self-command; restraint of passions; long suffering; patience. *Her forbearance during the depression was inspiring.*

forcible (fôr′sə bəl, fôr-) adj., characterized by force; violent; vigorous; potent. *They used forcible means to stop the strike.*

foreboding (fôr bō′ding, fôr-) n., ominous feeling; presentiment, usually of evil; omen; premonition. *She had a foreboding of the accident.*

forensic (fə ren′sik) adj., belonging to courts of law or public debate; appropriate to argument. *The law students practiced their forensic skills together.*

foreshadow (fôr shad′ō, fôr-) v.t., to sug-

gest beforehand; prefigure. *Yesterday's events foreshadowed today's disaster.*

forestall (fôr stôl′, fôr-) v.t., to prevent or counteract beforehand; hold off. *We tried to forestall the threatened foreclosure.*

forfeiture (fôr′fi chər) n., loss of right, privilege, or property, through exchange or punishment. *The price of marrying the commoner was forfeiture of the crown.*

forge (fôrj, fôrj) n., workshop where iron goods are produced. *The furnace was always lit in the forge.* v.t., 1. to form by heating in a fire and beating into shape; form or shape generally; to hammer out. *He tried to forge his son in his own image.* 2. to imitate illegally. *She forged his signature on the sales agreement.* v.i., to move ahead, usually with difficulty. *They forged ahead with the plan despite the committee's objections.*

forgo (fôr gō′) v.t., to pass by without claiming; renounce; resign; do without. *In order to get to the movie in time they had to forgo dinner.*

forlorn (fôr lôrn′) adj., lost; deserted; forsaken; abandoned; helpless. *The forlorn man dined alone on Christmas.*

formidable (fôr′mi də bəl) adj., 1. tending to excite fear or apprehension. *The boxer was a formidable opponent.* 2. difficult to perform or overcome. *He set himself a formidable task.*

fornication (fôr′nə kā′shən) n., sexual intercourse between a man and a woman who are not married to each other. *A married person who commits fornication is an adulterer.*

forswear (fôr swâr′) v.t., to deny or renounce upon oath. *It is perjury to forswear oneself.*

forte (fôrt, fôrt) n., strong talent. *Watercolor was his forte.*

forthright (fôrth′rīt′, fôrth′-) adj., direct; straightforward; honest. *The forthright woman did not mince words.*

fortify (fôr′tə fī′) v.t., to make strong; strengthen; increase resistance. *They tried to fortify the city walls against the invaders.*

fortissimo (fôr tis′ə mō′; *It.*

fôr tēs'sē mô') adj., in musical notation, very loud. *The score for the finale was marked "ff" for fortissimo.*

fortitude (fôr'ti tōōd', -tyōōd') n., patient courage under affliction or temptation; firmness in confronting danger or suffering. *The nurses displayed unwavering fortitude during the epidemic.*

fortnight (fôrt'nīt', -nit) n., fourteen nights and days; two weeks. *The magazine was published every fortnight.*

fortuitous (fôr tōō'i təs, -tyōō'-) adj., accidental; happening by chance; fortunate; lucky. *His fortuitous arrival saved her a long walk.*

forum (fōr'əm, fôr'əm) n., public discussion or lecture, esp. if led by an expert or panel of experts and involving audience discussion; program of such a discussion, to be broadcast on radio or television. *The senator discussed inflation during the televised forum.*

foster (fô'stər, fos'tər) v.t., to nourish; sustain by aid or encouragement. *The gardener carefully fostered the seedlings.*

foul (foul) n., 1. infringement of established rules in game or sport, esp. illegal body contact. *The foul got him thrown out of the game.* 2. ball that lands out of bounds. *The foul gained them a brief time out.* adj., 1. grossly offensive to the senses; filthy; defiled; ugly; homely. *The decomposing body gave off a foul smell.* 2. grossly offensive morally; base; shameful; unfair. *Murder is a foul deed.*

foundry (foun'drē) n., workshop for the casting of metal. *Machine parts were made in the iron foundry.*

fowl (foul) n., cock or hen; any domesticated bird used for food, such as chicken, duck, goose, or turkey; poultry (plural). *They stewed the fowl for dinner.*

fracas (frā'kəs; *Brit.* frak'ä) n., disorderly noise or uproar; brawl or quarrel. *He was awakened by a fracas in the street.*

fraction (frak'shən) n., numerical representation of the ratio between two numbers or of the division of one number into another; part of a whole. *The pic-*

ture hung a fraction of an inch off center.*

fractious (frak'shəs) adj., apt to quarrel; snappish; peevish; fretful. *Be careful of her fractious temper.*

fracture (frak'chər) n., partial or total break in a solid body under force. *The skull suffered a fracture.* v.t., to break; crack. *He fractured his leg playing football.*

fragile (fraj'əl; *Brit.* fraj'īl) adj., easily broken or destroyed; brittle; weak; liable to fail; frail. *Crystal is very fragile.*

frail (frāl) adj., weak; infirm in constitution; sickly; fragile. *The invalid was thin and frail.*

frailty (frāl'tē) n., the condition of being weak or frail; infirmity. *She was distressed by his frailty.*

franchise (fran'chīz) n., constitutional or legal privilege granted to an individual or group; right, esp. to vote. *His franchise included the right to be and act as a corporation.*

frantic (fran'tik) adj., characterized by violence and mental disorder; mad; raving; frenzied. *She was frantic with grief.*

fraud (frôd) n., 1. act of deliberate deception in order to gain unfair advantage. *An intentional misrepresentation on a tax return constitutes fraud.* 2. one who commits a fraud. *The fraud had us all fooled for a time.*

fraudulent (frô'jə lənt) adj., involving or characterized by fraud; deceitful. *The sale of counterfeit bonds was fraudulent.*

fraught (frôt) adj., loaded; charged; replete. *It was a scheme fraught with mischief.*

fray (frā) n., battle; brawl; riot. *The soldiers went into the fray to restore order.*

frenetic (frə net'ik) adj., relating to or accompanied by mental disorder; frantic; frenzied. *We raced along at a frenetic pace.*

frenzied (fren'zēd) adj., frantic; frenetic; mad; delirious. *His speech was frenzied and disordered.*

frenzy (fren'zē) n., violent agitation of

the mind approaching derangement; delirium; madness; fury. *He fell into a frenzy of rage.*

fret (fret) v.i., to worry; be anxious or irritated; complain. *The bored invalid began to fret about trifles.*

fretful (fret′fəl) adj., in a state of commotion; agitated; disposed to fret; anxious; ill-tempered; peevish. *The exhausted little girl became fretful.*

fricassee (frik′ə sē′) n., dish made of pieces of meat stewed in a gravy. *A fricassee is usually made with chicken, veal, or rabbit.* v.t., to stew pieces of meat in a gravy. *She decided to fricassee the chicken.*

friction (frik′shən) n., resistance to the motion of rolling or sliding of two surfaces in contact; figuratively, mutual irritation; lack of harmony. *Overcrowding caused friction in the dormitory.*

frigid (frij′id) adj., cold; icy; wintry; marked by mental coldness; coldly formal or precise; lifeless. *She was miserable in the frigid climate of Greenland.*

fritter (frit′ər) n., small fried dumpling often containing fruit, vegetable, or meat. *We made apple fritters for dessert.* v.t., to lose or spend little by little; spend frivolously; waste. *He watched his father fritter away his inheritance.*

frivolity (fri vol′i tē) n., condition of being frivolous or trifling; silliness; unbecoming levity of mind or disposition. *Their frivolity was inappropriate at the funeral.*

frivolous (friv′ə ləs) adj., of little worth or importance; trifling; trivial; given to trifling or unbecoming levity; silly. *He warned his son not to waste the money on frivolous purchases.*

frizz (friz) v.i., to curl; form into a fluffy mass of small, tight curls. *The fog made her curly hair frizz even more.*

frizzy (friz′ē) adj., curly; characterized by many little curls. *The permanent made her hair frizzy.*

frugal (frōō′gəl) adj., avoiding unnecessary expenditure; economical; sparing; thrifty. *The frugal cook finds ways to use leftover food.*

frugality (frōō gal′i tē) n., prudent economy; thrift. *Her frugality enabled them to save money.*

fruition (frōō ish′ən) n., coming into fruit; realization of results; attainment; fulfillment. *He lived to see the fruition of his hopes.*

fruitless (frōōt′lis) adj., not bearing fruit; producing no result; ineffective; futile; useless. *His labor was fruitless after all.*

frustrate (frus′trāt) v.t., to prevent from taking effect or attaining fulfillment; defeat; disappoint; thwart. *The traffic jam was bound to frustrate the impatient drivers.*

frustration (fru strā′shən) n., effect of being frustrated; irritating disappointment. *Her helplessness only added to her frustration at being stranded.*

fugitive (fyōō′ji tiv) n., one who flees; runaway; criminal escaping capture; refugee. *The fugitive eluded the police for a year.* adj., fleeing; runaway; escaped. *Bring the fugitive horse back to the paddock.*

fulcrum (fŏŏl′krəm, ful′-) n., point upon which a lever rests. *A see-saw balances on a fulcrum.*

fulminate (ful′mə nāt′) v.i., to explode or cause to explode; denounce, censure or threaten with authority and violence; thunder. *He began to fulminate about their atrocious behavior.*

fulsome (fŏŏl′səm, ful′-) adj., offensive from excess; disgusting; coarse; gross; cloying; sickening. *His fulsome praise sounded insincere.*

fumigate (fyōō′mə gāt′) v.t., to expose to fumes, as in disinfecting clothes or living quarters. *The exterminators came to fumigate the apartment.*

furbish (fûr′bish) v.t., to polish; clean; renovate or restore. *The maid was told to furbish the guest room.*

furor (fyŏŏr′ôr) n., overwhelming passion; mania; rage. *The music world was in a furor over the brilliant new pianist.*

furtive (fûr′tiv) adj., stealthy; surreptitious. *They exchanged furtive kisses in the pantry.*

fusion (fyōo′zhən) n., act or process of melting, rendering, or blending as by heat; union or merging of diverse elements or individuals; coalition. *The challenge caused a fusion of the separate factions.*

futile (fyōot′ᵊl, fyōo′til; *Brit.* fyōo′tīl) adj., useless; profitless; vain; ineffectual. *He gave up his futile efforts to be heard.*

futility (fyōo til′i tē) n., quality of being futile or useless; vanity. *He saw the futility of his arguments.*

Gg

gadfly (gad′flī′) n., 1. large, biting fly; horsefly. *The bite of a gadfly is deep and painful.* 2. one who flits about; restless, annoying person. *The gadfly couldn't settle down at the dinner party.*

galactic (gə lak′tik) adj., pertaining to a galaxy, esp. the Milky Way. *It was a galactic adventure fantasy.*

galaxy (gal′ək sē) n., cluster of myriads of stars, esp. the Milky Way; assemblage of splendid or illustrious people or things. *Earth is in the galaxy called the Milky Way.*

gall (gôl) n., impudence; effrontery; cheek; nerve. *She has a lot of gall to say that.* v.i., to distress; vex; irritate. *Her vulgarity began to gall her fiancé.*

galvanize (gal′və nīz′) v.t., 1. to subject to an electric current or shock. *As part of his therapy, the affected muscle was galvanized.* 2. to give vitality or life to; motivate. *The smell of smoke galvanized her into action.* 3. to give a zinc coating to in order to prevent rusting. *They galvanized the pipe before installing it.*

gambit (gam′bit) n., strategic or calculated move; ploy. *The gambit of moving to the inside track gave him the advantage at the finish line.*

gamut (gam′ət) n., full scale, range, or compass of a thing. *The repertory runs the gamut from comedy to tragedy.*

gape (gāp, gap) v.i., to let the mouth hang open as a result of sleepiness, absorbed attention, or anticipation; stare openmouthed in wonder or surprise; gaze. *Baby birds gape when the mother bird arrives with a worm.*

garble (gär′bəl) v.t., to mutilate so as to give a false impression; distort; mangle; confuse. *The accountant garbled the company's records.*

garbled (gär′bᵊld) adj., mangled; confused; distorted. *The radio operator could not decipher the garbled message.*

gargoyle (gär′goil) n., water spout projecting from a building, often carved in fanciful or grotesque figures of men, animals, or demons. *Rainwater issued from the mouth of the gargoyle over the front entrance of the church.*

garish (gâr′ish, gar′-) adj., glaringly or vulgarly gaudy. *He wore garish, pistachio-green trousers.*

garner (gär′nər) v.t., to accumulate; earn. *He hoped to garner a promotion for his efforts.*

garnish (gär′nish) n., ornament; decoration; embellishment. *A garnish of parsley added color to the dish.* v.t., to ornament; decorate; embellish. *Garnish the tart with nuts.*

garrulous (gar′ə ləs, gar′yə-) adj., talkative; chattering. *The garrulous woman talked my ear off.*

gaseous (gas′ē əs, gash′əs) adj., in the form or nature of gas. *Oxygen can be changed from a gaseous to a liquid state.*

gauche (gōsh) adj., awkward; clumsy. *His gauche manners embarrassed his wife.*

gaudy (gô′dē) adj., showy without taste; vulgarly splendid; flashy; garish. *She liked to wear gaudy rhinestone jewelry.*

gauge (gāj) n., instrument showing comparative measure; standard of measure. *The gas gauge indicated an empty tank.* v.t., to measure; estimate; appraise. *I couldn't gauge her anger over the phone.*

gaunt (gônt) adj., shrunken, as with fasting or suffering; emaciated; lean; haggard. *After her illness she was pale and gaunt.*

gauntlet (gônt′lit, gänt′-) n., punishment in which the offender is compelled to run through a passageway formed by armed persons who strike or beat at the offender as he passes; hence, a course or series of unpleasant events, remarks, etc. *The playwright ran the gauntlet of unfavorable criticism.*

gazette (gǝ zet′) n., newspaper or official journal. *The semi-weekly gazette was established in 1605.*

gear (gēr) n., 1. set of equipment for a particular purpose; outfit; goods. *He invested in some camping gear.* 2. mechanism that regulates relative speed. *She shifted to fourth gear.* 3. toothed wheel. *The clockmaker adjusted the gear.* v.t., to prepare or outfit oneself for specific purpose. *He worked hard to gear himself for the exam.*

gendarme (zhän′därm; *Fr.* zhäN dARm′) n., French police officer. *We asked the gendarme for directions.*

gender (jen′dǝr) n., sexual distinction, male or female; formal distinction in words as either masculine, feminine, or neuter. *The English language has few distinctions of gender.*

gene (jēn) n., protein molecule that transmits hereditary elements in the chromosomes. *The hereditary disease is carried in the genes.*

genealogy (jē′nē ol′ǝ jē, -al′-, jen′ē-) n., history of the descent of a person or family from an ancestor; enumeration of ancestors and their descendants in the natural order of succession; lineage. *They traced their family's genealogy.*

generality (jen′ǝ ral′i tē) n., broad statement or principle; general, vague statement. *That generality does not answer my specific question.*

generate (jen′ǝ rāt′) v.t., to produce; cause; originate. *The dam began to generate electricity.*

generic (jǝ ner′ik) adj., comprehending a number of similar things or characteristics. *"Canis" is the generic name of the species of the doglike animals.*

genesis (jen′i sis) n., act of begetting, originating, or creating; birth; beginning. *He traced the novel from genesis to publication.*

genetics (jǝ net′iks) n., branch of biology

relating to heredity; study of genes. *Genetics deals with the variations in organisms resulting from heredity.*

genial (jēn′yǝl, jē′nē ǝl) adj., cordial in disposition and manner; kind; warm; sympathetically cheerful. *We appreciated her genial hospitality.*

geniality (jē′nē al′i tē) n., sympathetic cheerfulness; cordiality; warmth; kindness. *Geniality was a large part of her charm.*

genitals (jen′i tǝlz) n. pl., reproductive organs. *The external genitals are very sensitive.*

genocide (jen′ǝ sīd′) n., deliberate killing of a particular group of people; systematic mass destruction. *The Nazis practiced genocide against the Jews.*

genre (zhän′rǝ; *Fr.* zhäN′Rǝ) n., distinctive style of composition, esp. in the arts. *The poem was written in the pastoral genre.*

genteel (jen tēl′) adj., characteristic of polite, upper-class society; refined; polite; falsely or affectedly elegant. *The genteel woman was appalled at his crude table manners.*

gentility (jen til′i tē) n., condition, appearance, or manner of polite society; genteel behavior. *Her gentility was manifested in her gracious welcome.*

gentry (jen′trē) n., class of well-born and well-bred people; upper class; class just below nobility. *America has its own landed gentry.*

genuflect (jen′yŏŏ flekt′) v.i., to bend the knee as an act of worship or respect. *He genuflected toward the altar.*

genus (jē′nǝs) n., category or class marked by similar characteristics, esp. a biological category containing related species. *The onion is a genus of the lily family.*

geologist (jē ol′ǝ jist) n., one who studies the structure of the earth or other solid, celestial body and the changes it undergoes, esp., one who studies rocks. *The geologist is interested in glacial features.*

geology (jē ol′ǝ jē) n., science of the history of the earth and the changes in its structure, esp., the study of rocks; also, the study of other solid celestial bodies. *Geology also embraces the study of the moon.*

geriatrics (jer'ē a'triks) n., branch of medicine treating the diseases of aged people. *Her training in geriatrics helped in working at the nursing home.*

germane (jər mān') adj., bearing a close relation; relevant; pertinent. *This fact is not germane to your argument.*

germinate (jûr'mə nāt') v.i., to begin to grow; sprout; bud. *The seeds will germinate in two weeks.*

gerontology (jer'ən tol'ə jē) n., study of the process of aging and its problems. *Gerontology seeks to understand the phenomenon of old age.*

gerund (jer'ənd) n., present participle of a verb used as a noun; verbal noun. *"Ending," used as a noun, is a gerund.*

gestation (je stā'shən) n., act of carrying young in the womb from conception to birth; pregnancy. *The length of gestation differs among mammals.*

gesticulate (je stik'yə lāt') v.i., to make gestures; emphasize or illustrate speech by motions, esp. of the hands and arms. *She began to gesticulate frantically for help.*

ghastly (gast'lē, gäst'-) adj., dreadful; haggard; horrifying. *She fainted at sight of the ghastly wound.*

ghoul (gool) n., imaginary evil being that devours human corpses, esp. from the grave; ogre. *The graveyard was said to be haunted by ghouls.*

gibberish (jib'ər ish, gib'-) n., rapid and unintelligible talk; incoherent language; jargon. *They laughed at the baby's gibberish.*

gibe (jīb) n., taunting or contemptuously sarcastic remark. *Pay no attention to their gibes.* v.i., to utter taunting or sarcastic words; deride; scoff at; ridicule. *It was cruel to gibe at her.*

gingerly (jin'jər lē) adv., softly; delicately; cautiously. *She handled the fragile china gingerly.*

girdle (gûr'd⁼l) n., band or belt drawn around the waist; undergarment designed to make a person look slimmer;

corset. *She squeezed into the tight girdle.*

gist (jist) n., substance or pith of a matter; main point. *Tell me only the gist of the problem.*

gladiolus (glad'ē ō'ləs) n., genus of flowering plants of the iris family with erect, sword-shaped leaves and brilliantly colored, irregular flowers. *The African gladiolus is the most popular species.*

glamour (glam'ər) n., romantic, mysterious, or illusory charm; magnetism; charisma. *A model's life seems full of glamour to a young girl.*

glaze (glāz) n., layer of transparent or translucent material spread over a substance, such as food or pottery, to make it shine or to modify its color; polish; film. *The potter painted glaze on the pots.* v., to coat with a film of transparent or translucent material; become glassy or covered with a film. *The pond will glaze over with ice in January.*

glean (glēn) v.t., to collect in scattered portions; gather slowly and painstakingly. *She tries to glean a living from freelance work.*

glee (glē) n., demonstrative joy or delight; merriment; mirth; gaiety. *They celebrated their success with glee.*

glib (glib) adj., smooth; slippery; fluent. *His glib tongue helped him out of the awkward situation.*

gloat (glōt) v.i., to ponder with pleasure or satisfaction, esp. upon the gratification of wicked desire. *Do not gloat over your rival's defeat.*

glorification (glôr'ə fə kā'shən, glôr'-) n., act of ascribing glory and honor to a person or thing; state of being glorified; exaltation. *He sought his own glorification rather than the country's welfare.*

glorify (glôr'ə fī', glôr'-) v.t., to give glory and honor to; magnify and exalt with praise; raise to a higher quality. *They chose to glorify him with the title of sanitation engineer.*

glossary (glos'ə rē, glôs'sə-) n., collection of explanations of words, esp. of words not in general use; vocabulary or dictionary of limited scope. *A glossary of cooking terms was appended.*

glossy (glos′ē, glô′sē) adj., smooth and shining; lustrous; polished. *The horse had a glossy coat.*

glucose (gloo′kōs) n., a group of sugars produced from fruits, starches, cane sugar, and in living plants by the action of acid and other reagents. *Glucose is a sweet, colorless, soluble sugar.*

glum (glum) adj., gloomily sullen or silent; moody; frowning. *Twilight always made him feel glum.*

glut (glut) n., supply above the demand; too much; superabundance. *There is a glut of attorneys entering the legal profession.* v.t., to saturate; furnish a supply in excess of demand; overstock. *Christmas trees glut the market every year.*

gluttonous (glut′ənəs) adj., given to excessive eating; greedy; voracious. *The gluttonous man is likely to be fat.*

gnarled (närld) adj., full of rough knots; knotty. *There was one old, gnarled, twisted tree.*

gnome (nōm) n., grotesque dwarf; small, misshapen, goblinlike person. *She imagined every gnarled shrub to be a gnome.*

goad (gōd) n., stick or rod used to prod cattle; that which urges or stimulates; incentive. *The unpaid bills were an excellent goad to make him work.* v.t., to prick; drive; urge forward; rouse to action by harassing or irritating means. *He tried to goad her into a confession.*

godforsaken (god′fər sā′kən, god′fər sā′-) adj., forsaken by God; wicked; utterly reprobate; desolate; forlorn. *The barren, scorching desert was a godforsaken place.*

gorge (gôrj) n., 1. narrow passage between steep, rocky walls; ravine. *It made him dizzy to look into the gorge.* 2. occasion of inordinate eating; heavy meals. *He indulged in a gorge after fasting.* v.t., to swallow or eat greedily; glut; feed greedily. *He gorged himself at dinner.*

gory (gōr′ē, gôr′ē) adj., covered or

smeared with blood; bloody; murderous. *Hunting is a gory sport.*

gossamer (gos′ə mər) n., fine, filmy substance or fabric. *A cobweb is a veil of gossamer.* adj., fine; filmy; webby. *The bride's veil was of gossamer lace.*

gouge (gouj) n., chisel with a long, curved blade. *He attacked the wood with his gouge.* v.t., to carve out; dig or tear out. *They have gouged a hole in the floor.*

gourmand (goor′mənd; *Fr.* gooR mäN′) n., one who eats and drinks excessively; gourmet. *The gourmand looks forward to mealtimes.*

gourmet (goor′mā; *Fr.* gooR me′) n., one who appreciates fine food and drink; connoisseur. *The gourmet understood and appreciated the chef's skill.*

governess (guv′ər nis) n., woman paid to care for and instruct children, esp. in a private home. *The governess groomed her for her entrance into society.*

gradation (grā dā′shən) n., orderly or continuous arrangement or succession; progress from one degree or state to another; degree or relative position in any series. *Her argument underwent several subtle gradations.*

gradient (grā′dē ənt) n., regular rate of ascent or descent; slope; grade; inclination. *The steep hill had a gradient of 20 degrees.*

grail (grāl) n., chalice or cup, esp. that supposedly used by Jesus Christ at the last supper and in which Joseph of Arimathea caught the last drops of Christ's blood as he was taken from the Cross. *The legend of King Arthur and his knights pivots on the search for the Holy Grail.*

grandeur (gran′jer, -joor) n., character of being grand or great; greatness; majesty; splendor; pomp. *The grandeur of the cathedral was overwhelming.*

grandiose (gran′dē ōs′) adj., characterized by self-display and bombast; vulgarly showy; pompous; turgid. *We disapprove of her grandiose manner.*

granular (gran′yə lər) adj., composed of or resembling grains. *The pulverized glass was as granular as sand.*

granulated 130

granulated (gran′yə lā′tid) adj., formed or processed into grains; granular. *Granulated sugar pours easily.*

graphic (graf′ik) n., picture, chart, map, graph, or other illustration, esp. one produced by a method of reproduction such as etching, silk-screen, lithography, photography, engraving, etc. *Several fine graphics are hung at the gallery.* adj., written, drawn, or pictured; delineated; expressed or described accurately and vividly; reproduced by a method such as etching, photography, lithography, silk-screen, etc. *He gave a graphic description of his wound.*

graphite (graf′īt) n. form of soft carbon used in pencils. *The "lead" in pencils is actually graphite.*

graphology (gra fol′ə jē) n., study of handwriting as an expression of the character of the writer. *Graphology may reveal aspects of one's character.*

grapple (grap′əl) v.i., to contend in close contest, as in wrestling; struggle with; seize or attack boldly. *She will grapple with the problem later.*

grateful (grāt′fəl) adj., appreciative of favor or kindness; thankful. *He was grateful for her interest.*

gratis (grat′is, grā′tis) adv., for nothing; freely; without pay. *I will wash your car gratis.*

gratuitous (grə tōō′i təs, -tyōō′-) adj., 1. freely bestowed or obtained; free of cost. *The cloakroom service is gratuitous.* 2. unnecessary; uncalled for. *He paid her many gratuitous compliments.*

gratuity (grə tōō′i tē, -tyōō′-) n., free gift; donation; tip. *The gratuity is included on the bill.*

gravitate (grav′i tāt′) v.i., to be strongly attracted; have a natural tendency or inclination. *The art students tend to gravitate toward each other.*

gregarious (gri gâr′ē əs) adj., preferring society to solitude; friendly. *The gregarious man put the newcomers at ease.*

grievance (grē′vəns) n., cause of grief, distress, annoyance, or hardship; wrong inflicted by another. *The warden listened as they aired their grievance.*

grimace (grim′əs, gri mās′) n., spontaneous or involuntary distortion of the face, expressing pain, disgust, or disapproval; wry face. *A grimace of distaste crossed her face.* v.i., to make a grimace. *He grimaced in pain.*

grindstone (grīnd′stōn′) n., 1. stone wheel used for grinding, sharpening, or polishing. *He sharpened the axe on the grindstone.* 2. extreme toil or drudgery. *He resolved to put his nose to the grindstone and study harder.*

gripe (grīp) n., grievance; pain; distress; complaint. *Her pet gripe is the neighbor's dog.* v.i., to complain, esp. repeatedly or sourly. *She loved to gripe about her job.*

grisly (griz′lē) adj., inspiring fear or horror; terrible; gruesome. *The survivors told some grisly tales.*

grist (grist) n., material to be ground in a mill; raw materials. *The experience was grist for the writer's mill.*

gristmill (grist′mil′) n., mill for grinding grain. *Corn was ground at the gristmill.*

grizzly (griz′lē) adj., gray; streaked with gray; grayish. *The old man stroked his grizzly beard.*

grotesque (grō tesk′) adj., fantastic; strange; ludicrous; odd. *The grotesque figure was half lion, half fish.*

grovel (gruv′əl, grov′-) v.i., 1. to creep or crawl, esp. in fear or humility. *The beggar groveled at our feet.* 2. to show fear or respect without dignity. *The king forced his ministers to grovel before him.*

grub (grub) n., 1. insect larva. *The skunk finds and eats grubs.* 2. (slang) food; provisions. *Let's rustle up some grub for lunch.* v.i., to dig up; work hard, esp. in laborious research; search. *On slow days the reporter has to grub for stories.*

grubby (grub′ē) adj., dirty; unclean, as if from digging. *Her hands were grubby from working in the garden.*

grueling (grōō′ə ling, grōō′ling) adj., arduous; exhausting. *The first year of law school is grueling.*

gruesome (grōō′səm) adj., frightfully dismal or depressing; horribly repulsive. *Identifying the victims of the fire was a gruesome task.*

gruff (gruf) adj., rough or stern in manner or expression; harsh; surly; brusque. *Underneath his gruff manner, he was a gentle man.*

guffaw (gu fô′, gə-) n., loud burst of laughter. *A guffaw from the audience met his comment.* v.i., to laugh coarsely and loudly. *The gathering crowd guffawed at the sidewalk clown.*

guile (gīl) n., disposition to deceive; craftiness; cunning. *She got the job through guile, not merit.*

guise (gīz) n., appearance; semblance. *The wretched woman assumed a guise of indifference.*

gull (gul) n., long-winged, web-footed water bird. v.t., to dupe, deceive, cheat. *He was constantly gulling the public.*

gullible (gul′ə bəl) adj., easily deceived or cheated; unsuspecting. *The gullible girl believed the ridiculous story.*

gushing (gush′ing) adj., exuberantly and demonstratively emotional; effusive; sentimental. *He was embarrassed by her gushing praise.*

gusto (gus′tō) n., appreciative enjoyment; keen relish; zest. *The hungry woman ate with gusto.*

gusty (gus′tē) adj., marked by blasts or squalls of wind; fitfully windy or stormy. *It was a cold, gusty winter day.*

gut (gut) adj., instinctive; intuitive; basic. *What was your gut reaction to him?* v.t., to remove the entrails or insides from. *Fire gutted the house.*

guts (guts) n., 1. whole digestive system; entrails. *His guts were convulsed with dysentery.* 2. core or inside of a matter. *He spilled his guts to the analyst.* 3. boldness; effrontery; nerve; bravery. *He has the guts to stand up for his beliefs.*

guttural (gut′ər əl) adj., formed in or as if in the throat. *German is a guttural language.*

gynecologist (gī′nə kol′ə jist, jin′ə-, jī′nə-) n., doctor who specializes in diseases peculiar to women. *The gynecologist tested her for cervical cancer.*

gynecology (gī′nə kol′ə jē, jin′ə-, jī′nə-) n., branch of medicine that deals with diseases peculiar to women. *The midwife studied gynecology and obstetrics.*

gyrate (jī′rāt, jī rāt′) v.i., to turn around; revolve; wheel; spin. *The wheel gyrates on its axis.*

gyration (jī rā′shən) n., revolution of a body around a center. *The earth makes an annual gyration around the sun.*

gyroscope (jī′rə skōp′) n., instrument consisting of a wheel or disk, the axis of which can turn freely in any direction, designed to illustrate the dynamics of rotating bodies. *The gyroscope is a navigational tool.*

Hh

habeas corpus (hā′bē əs kôr′pəs) legal writ requiring one's appearance in court; also the right of a prisoner to such a writ. *In murder cases, a writ of habeas corpus requires submission of a body in evidence.*

habitat (hab′i tat′) n., area in which an animal or plant naturally or normally lives. *The African plains are the lion's natural habitat.*

habitual (hə bich′o͞o əl) adj., according to frequent use or custom; usual; regular; customary. *He was a habitual Scotch drinker.*

habitué (hə bich′o͞o ā′, -bich′o͞o ā′; Fr. A bē twā′) n., frequenter of a place, esp. a place of amusement or recreation. *She was an habitué of the opera.*

hack (hak) n., 1. carriage horse; horse for hire; worn-out old horse. *He felt sorry for the broken-down hack.* 2. one who compromises professional standards or freedom for money or other reward, esp. such a writer. *The once successful novelist became a hack to support her family.* v.t., to chop at; mangle by repeated strokes of a cutting implement. *She saw him hack at the ice with his ax.* adj., working for hire. *She was reduced to hack illustrating.*

hackneyed (hak′nēd) adj., commonplace; trite; worn-out. *She avoids that hackneyed phrase.*

haggard (hag′ərd) adj., wild-looking from prolonged suffering or terror; careworn; gaunt. *The victims of the earthquake looked haggard.*

haggle (hag′əl) v.i., to bargain in a petty way; quarrel or nag about small matters; cavil. *They haggled over the trinket.*

haiku (hī′ko͞o) n., Japanese poem consisting of seventeen syllables. *The haiku is extremely impressionistic.*

hale (hāl) adj., healthy; sound; robust. *The hale and hearty man never caught a cold.*

hallow (hal′ō) v.t., to consecrate to holy or religious use; keep sacred; revere; hold in solemn honor. *They hallow the ancient relic.*

hallowed (hal′ōd) adj., holy; kept for sacred use; revered; worshipped; honored. *The cathedral was built on hallowed ground.*

hallucinate (hə lo͞o′sə nāt′) v.i., to imagine vividly a nonexistent object. *Under the drug's influence she began to hallucinate.*

hammock (ham′ək) n., hanging bed made of a net hung between two poles. *The hammock swung gently between two trees.*

hamper (ham′pər) n., large wicker basket used for storage. *He brought a picnic hamper.* v.t., to impede; encumber; restrain. *The weather may hamper your walk.*

handkerchief (hang′kər chif, -chēf′) n., square cloth, usually linen or cotton, used for wiping the nose or face. *The linen handkerchief is from Ireland.*

haphazard (hap haz′ərd) adj., accidental; random; careless. *The haphazard experiment proved nothing.*

hapless (hap′lis) adj., luckless; unfortunate; unlucky; ill-fated. *The hapless child had no one to encourage her.*

harangue (hə rang′) n., speech against something; tirade. *He listened to his mother's harangue about his messy room.* v.i., to declaim; argue about; nag; lecture. *She began to harangue about the sloppy work.*

harass (har′əs, hə ras′) v.t., to vex; pursue doggedly and annoyingly; badger.

She intended to harass him into a response.

harbinger (här'bin jər) n., forerunner; precursor; herald. *The robin is a harbinger of spring.*

hardy (här'dē) adj., capable of resisting fatigue, hardship, or exposure; strong; sturdy; tough; intrepid; courageous. *The hardy pine grows in many climates.*

harlequin (här'lə kwin, -kin) n., clown or jester, usually dressed in multicolored tights and ragged coat, bells, and a mask. *The harlequin amuses the king.*

harp (härp) n., musical instrument consisting of a triangular frame strung with strings of varying lengths, played by plucking with the fingers. *A short solo on the harp was part of the program.* v.i., to speak or write with monotonous repetition on a subject. *He told her not to harp on her troubles anymore.*

harrowing (har'ō iñg) adj., distressing; tragic; exciting; thrilling. *The veteran recounted his harrowing adventures.*

hassock (has'ək) n., large cushion used as a footrest. *He put his feet on the hassock.*

haughty (hô'tē) adj., proud and disdainful; arrogantly lofty. *She was afraid to approach the haughty duchess.*

haunch (hônch, hänch) n., fleshy area around the hip of humans or four-legged animals. *She roasted a haunch of venison.*

haunting (hôn'tiñg) adj., recurring persistently in the mind or memory; not easily forgotten; lingering. *He could not forget the haunting melody.*

haven (hā'vən) n., place of safety and rest; shelter; asylum. *His beach house was a haven from urban pressures.*

havoc (hav'ək) n., general and relentless destruction; disintegration; chaos. *His announcement caused havoc in the office.*

hearth (härth) n., 1. pavement of stone or brick in front of a fireplace. *The cat slept on the hearth.* 2. home. *The traveler was happy to return to his own hearth at last.*

heath (hēth) n., uncultivated, open, des-olate tract of land. *The sheep were lost on the heath during the storm.*

hedonist (hē'dənist) n., one who regards pleasure as the chief good. *The hedonist avoided any ties or responsibilities.*

heed (hēd) n., careful attention; notice; regard. *Take heed not to slip.* v.t., to pay attention; observe; consider. *He did not heed my warning.*

hegemony (hi jem'ə nē, hej'ə mō'nē) n., control exercised by one state over others, as through confederation or conquest. *The Soviets maintain hegemony over Eastern Europe.*

heinous (hā'nəs) adj., hateful; odious; reprehensible. *Rape is a heinous crime.*

hellion (hel'yən) n., troublesome or mischievous person. *She is a hellion when she loses her temper.*

hematology (hem'ə tol'ə jē, hē'mə-) n., branch of biology relating to blood and blood-forming organs. *The medical student studied hematology.*

hemoglobin (hē'mə glō'bin, hem'ə-, hē'mə glō'bin, hem'ə-) n., red, protein substance in red blood corpuscles, which contains iron and carries oxygen through the bloodstream. *Hemoglobin is a protein substance vital to the body.*

hemophilia (hē'mə fil'ē ə, -fēl'yə, hem'ə-) n., congenital tendency to uncontrollable bleeding, even from a minor wound, due to the blood's inability to clot. *Hemophilia is controllable through drugs.*

hemorrhage (hem'ər ij, hem'rij) n., discharge of blood from blood vessels ruptured by disease or a wound. *After the operation there was a danger of hemorrhage.* v.i., to suffer a hemorrhage. *She began to hemorrhage during labor.*

hemorrhoid (hem'ə roid', hem'roid) n., painful mass of swollen blood vessels in the anal region. *She developed hemorrhoids during pregnancy.*

henchman (hench'mən) n., one who follows another's bidding, esp. in hopes of resulting personal advantage; venal follower. *The loan shark's henchman is his collector.*

hepatitis (hep'ə tī'tis) n., inflammation of

the liver. *She was hospitalized with hepatitis.*

herald (her′əld) n., announcer of important news; forerunner; harbinger. *No one welcomes the herald of disaster.* v.t., to announce; proclaim. *The police escort will herald the mayor's arrival.*

heraldry (her′əl drē) n., practice of devising family coats of arms and of tracing and recording genealogy. *Her interest in heraldry led her to design her family crest.*

herbivorous (hûr biv′ər əs) adj., feeding on vegetation. *A horse is a herbivorous animal.*

herculean (hûr′kyə lē′ən, hûr kyo͞o′lē ən) adj., tremendous in size, strength, courage, or difficulty. *Building the pyramids was a herculean task.*

heresy (her′i sē) n., adherence to any doctrine or opinion at variance with the established standards of a system, esp. a doctrine held at variance to church dogma. *A Catholic priest who marries commits heresy.*

heretic (her′i tik) n., one who persistently maintains an opinion or doctrine at variance with the accepted dogma of any school or party, esp. of the church, and who is rejected and condemned by it. *The heretic was tried by the Inquisition.*

hermaphrodite (hûr maf′rə dīt′) n., 1. animal or flower having both male and female reproductive organs. *The worm is a true hermaphrodite.* 2. one who exhibits both male and female characteristics. *The hermaphrodite underwent psychoanalysis.*

hermetical (hûr met′i kəl) adj., airtight; impervious. *The hermetical seal preserved the bottled specimen.*

heroine (her′ō in) n., 1. courageous, strong woman; woman who comes to the rescue. *She was a heroine, spreading comfort to the wounded.* 2. principal female character in a drama or story. *The heroine of the novel is a forty-year-old actress.*

herpetology (hûr′pi tol′ə jē) n., science of reptiles; reptiles generally. *Snakes are in the zoo's house of herpetology.*

heterogeneous (het′ər ə jē′nē əs, -jēn′yəs) adj., composed of parts of different kinds; having widely unlike elements. *A heterogeneous group was assigned to the dorm.*

heterosexual (het′ər ə sek′sho͞o əl) adj., marked by attraction to the opposite sex; related to different sexes. *The film told a racy heterosexual love story.*

hew (hyo͞o) v.t., 1. to cut with a heavy blow or repeated blows, as with a sharp instrument. *It was common for the Indians to hew trees with stone axes.* 2. to carve. *He learned to hew intricate designs in wood.*

hexagon (hek′sə gon′, -gən) n., geometric figure with six angles and six sides. *A regular hexagon has equal sides and angles.*

heyday (hā′dā′) n., highest vigor; full strength; acme; peak. *In his heyday, he was the world's greatest tenor.*

hiatus (hī ā′təs) n., 1. two vowels together without an intervening consonant in successive words or within a word. *The word "hiatus" contains a hiatus.* 2. break in continuity; lapse; gap. *There is an evolutionary hiatus between apes and humans.*

hibernate (hī′bər nāt′) v.i., 1. to pass the winter asleep in close quarters. *Bears and beavers hibernate in winter.* 2. to remain in seclusion; pass the time languidly or apathetically. *They wanted to hibernate during their honeymoon.*

hierarchy (hī′ə rär′kē, hī′rär-) n., group, officials, or terms organized by rank. *The terms kingdom, phylum, class, order, family, genus, and species constitute a hierarchy in zoology.*

high fidelity (fi del′i tē, fī-) faithful reproduction of sound. *Technological advances in recording made high fidelity possible.*

hijack (hī′jak′) v.t., to stop a vehicle and force the driver or pilot to change its destination, or to hold the passengers hostage as a means of coercion. *The terrorists plotted to hijack the jet.*

hilarity (hi lar′i tē, -lâr′-, hī-) n., great merriment; glee; social gaiety; jollity. *Alcohol fueled the party's hilarity.*

hilarious (hi lâr′ə əs, -lar′-, hī-) adj., gleefully gay or merry; highly amusing or comical. *The film is a hilarious comedy.*

hinder (hin′dər) v.t., to hold back; obstruct; impede; check. *The felled trees will hinder the army's progress.*

hindmost (hīnd′mōst′) adj., furthest at the back or rear; backmost. *We could see well even in the hindmost seats.*

hirsute (hûr′sŏŏt, hûr sŏŏt′) adj., 1. coarsely hairy; shaggy. *The barber cleaned up his hirsute appearance.* 2. coarse; boorish; unmannerly. *Your hirsute manners are not welcome at my table.*

histrionics (his′trē on′iks) n. pl., theatrical mannerisms; expressions or gestures feigned for dramatic effect; theatrics. *She wasn't moved by his histrionics.*

hoard (hōrd, hôrd) n., reserved supply; store; reserve. *She had a hoard of money put away.* v.t., to collect and store for security or future use; save; lay up. *She began to hoard change for the washing machine.*

hoax (hōks) n., humorous, mischievous, or fraudulent deception; practical joke; fraud. *The U.F.O. hoax made the front page.*

hobgoblin (hob′gob′lin) n., mischievous imp or sprite; alarming apparition; hence, something that causes fear or disquiet. *Children dress as hobgoblins on Halloween.*

hoi polloi (hoi′ pə loi′) n. pl., general population; common people; masses. *We mingled with the hoi polloi at Times Square.*

holocaust (hol′ə kôst′, hō′lə-) n., 1. great slaughter or sacrifice of life. *Many fear a nuclear holocaust.* 2. cap., Nazi extermination of Jews during WWII. *He was a survivor of the Holocaust.*

holograph (hol′ə graf′, -gräf′, hō′lə-) n., piece of writing wholly written by the author, as a deed, letter, manuscript, etc. *The letter was an authentic Twain holograph.*

holster (hōl′stər) n., leather case for carrying a pistol or other object on the person. *The detective wore a shoulder holster for his gun.*

homage (hom′ij, om′-) n., actions showing respect or reverence. *They paid homage to the new queen.*

homespun (hōm′spun′) n., coarse, loosely woven material originally made at home. *The homesteaders were dressed in homespun.* adj., domestic; plain; commonplace; unsophisticated. *Wordsworth preferred the homespun speech of country people.*

homicide (hom′i sīd′) n., killing of one human by another; murder. *The hit-and-run driver was charged with homicide.*

homily (hom′ə lē) n., informal sermon, usually illustrating a passage of Scripture. *The sermon elaborated on the old homily.*

homogeneous (hō′mə jē′nē əs, -jēn′ yəs, hom′ə-) adj., composed of similar parts or elements; of the same kind. *The immigrants added diversity to the homogeneous neighborhood.*

homogenous (hə moj′ə nəs, hō-) adj., having the same origin or source; kindred. *The brother and his half-sister were homogenous through their father.*

homonym (hom′ə nim) n., word that shares sound and perhaps spelling with another but that has a different meaning. *The word "meet" is a homonym of "meat."*

homo sapiens (hō′mō sā′pē ənz) species name of humans; mankind. *The homo sapiens is distinguished by his intelligence.*

hone (hōn) v.t., to rub and sharpen. *He used a stone to hone his knife.*

honeymoon (hun′ē mŏŏn′) n., 1. interval spent by a newly married couple in traveling or recreation before settling down to their ordinary occupations. *They spent their honeymoon in Spain.* 2. time of temporary enjoyment, advantage, or forbearance. *The new president and Congress enjoyed a brief honeymoon.*

honorarium (on′ə râr′ē əm) n., fee for services rendered for which a set price in inappropriate. *The speaker received a generous honorarium.*

hoodwink (hŏŏd′wingk′) v.t., to blindfold; deceive. *She tried to hoodwink us into agreement.*

horde (hōrd, hôrd) n., clan or troop; gang; multitude. *A horde of ragged children surrounded him.*

hormone (hôr′mōn) n., substance produced in the cells and circulated in the body that produces a specific effect on particular cells. *Estrogen is a female hormone.*

horoscope (hôr′ə skōp′, hor′-) n., diagram of the planets and the signs of the zodiac, used by astrologers to calculate events or chart a person's life. *She consulted her horoscope before deciding.*

hors d'oeuvre (ôr dûrv′; *Fr.* ôR dœ′vR°) appetizer; morsel or small portion of food served, usually with drinks, before the main course of a meal. *She served vegetables and dip as an hors d'oeuvre.*

horticulture (hôr′tə kul′chər) n., art or science of cultivating and managing gardens. *He studied horticulture from the age of six.*

hostile (hos′t°l or, esp. Brit., -tīl) adj., unfriendly; warlike; enemy. *We didn't travel in hostile countries during the war.*

hotbed (hot′bed′) n., place of rapid growth or eager activity, generally in a bad sense. *The kitchen was a hotbed of gossip.*

hub (hub) n., center of a wheel; hence, something in a central position of importance. *They live in the hub of the city.*

hubbub (hub′ub) n., confused noise of many voices; tumult; uproar. *The school halls fill with hubbub between classes.*

huff (huf) n., swell of anger or arrogance; fit of petulance or ill humor. *She walked away from our argument in a huff.*

humane (hyōō mān′ or, often, yōō′-) adj., having the disposition to treat other human beings and animals with kindness; compassionate; kind; benevolent. *The humane family cares for abandoned pets.*

humanitarian (hyōō man′i târ′ē ən or, often, yōō-) n., one who values and

promotes the welfare of humanity. *Albert Schweitzer was a great humanitarian.* adj., broadly philanthropic. *The foundation supports humanitarian causes.*

humbug (hum′bug′) n., trick; imposition; hoax. *Scrooge thought that Christmas was a humbug.*

humdrum (hum′drum′) n., monotony; tediousness; dullness; ennui; routine. *He tried to relieve the humdrum of his life.* adj., monotonous; tedious; routine; dull. *It was just another humdrum cocktail party.*

humid (hyōō′mid or, often, yōō′-) adj., moist; damp; containing vapor. *Washington summers are unbearably humid.*

humility (hyōō mil′i tē or, often, yōō-) n., freedom from pride and arrogance; lowliness of mind; self-abasement; meekness. *She tried to cultivate an air of pious humility.*

humorous (hyōō′mər əs or, often, yōō′-) adj., full of humor; comical; droll; funny. *The child giggled at her humorous story.*

humus (hyōō′məs or, often, yōō′-) n., rich, dark soil composed largely of decayed vegetation. *The compost heap will produce rich humus.*

hurtle (hûr′t°l) v.i., to dash, rush, or fall swiftly or violently. *The rocket hurtled toward its target.*

husbandry (huz′bən drē) n., domestic or agricultural management; domestic economy; farming. *The farmer taught animal husbandry.*

hybrid (hī′brid) n., offspring of animals or plants of different varieties; crossbreed; mongrel. *We planted a tomato hybrid.* adj., cross-bred; mongrel. *He developed a new hybrid rose.*

hydraulic (hī drô′lik, -drol′ik) adj., operated by means of water or liquid in motion. *A hydraulic dam generates power for the river valley.*

hydrophobia (hī′drə fō′bē ə) n., aversion to or fear of water; symptom of rabies in humans, consisting of a furious aversion to liquids and an inability to swallow them. *He could not learn to swim until he conquered his hydrophobia.*

hyperbole (hī pûr′bə lē) n., extravagant

statement or assertion not intended to be taken literally; obvious exaggeration. *It was hyperbole to say she felt heavy as a moose.*

hypercritical (hī′pər krit′i kəl) adj., excessively critical; unduly severe in judgment; exacting; overly scrupulous. *She learned to disregard his hypercritical comments.*

hypersensitive (hī′pər sen′si tiv) adj., excessively sensitive; thin-skinned. *The ear infection made her hypersensitive to sound.*

hypertension (hī′pər ten′shən) n., abnormally high blood pressure. *Her doctor treated her for hypertension.*

hyperventilate (hī′pər ven′tᵊlāt′) v.i., to breathe with unnecessary rapidity causing a decrease of carbon dioxide in the body. *The laboring woman began to hyperventilate.*

hypnosis (hip nō′sis) n., state of insensibility to most sensory impressions, with excessive sensibility to some impressions, and an appearance of total unconsciousness or sleep, esp. when artificially induced. *She underwent hypnosis to stop smoking.*

hypochondriac (hī′pə kon′drē ak′) n., one who is morbidly anxious about his health. *The hypochondriac loves to discuss his symptoms.*

hypocrisy (hi pok′rə sē) n., dissimulation of one's real character or belief, esp. a false assumption of piety or virtue; pretense. *The adulterer's horror of prostitution was hypocrisy.*

hypocrite (hip′ə krit) n., one who practices hypocrisy. *The drunkard who denounces drug abuse is a hypocrite.*

hypodermic (hī′pə dûr′mik) adj., employed in introducing foreign substances, such as medicines, under the skin. *He used a hypodermic syringe to inject the insulin.*

hypothesis (hī poth′i sis, hi-) n., proposition assumed and taken for granted as a premise in proving something else; tentative assumption. *The experiment confirmed his hypothesis.*

hypothetical (hī′pə thet′i kəl) adj., founded on or characterized by a hypothesis; conjectural. *He had a chance to test his hypothetical idea.*

Ii

iconoclast (ī kon'ə klast') n., one who systematically attacks cherished beliefs; destroyer or denouncer of customs or institutions. *The iconoclast often masquerades as a reformer.*

identification (ī den'tə fə kā'shən, i den'-) n., 1. act of recognizing or determining the identity of something. *The body was held pending identification.* 2. close association, esp. emotional; empathy. *His identification with the radical party was complete.* 3. evidence of identity. *Show your identification at the gate.*

identify (ī den'tə fī', i den'-) v.t., 1. to recognize or determine the identity of. *He learned to identify the various plants.* 2. to unite; consider as the same; stand for; associate with. *He identified himself with the cause of civil rights.*

ideology (ī'dē ol'ə jē, id'ē-) n., system of ideas; set of beliefs. *He studied the radical ideology in college.*

idiom (id'ē əm) n., phrase or form of words accepted through and because of common usage rather than logic or correctness. *It takes time to understand the idioms of a foreign language.*

idiomatic (id'ē ə mat'ik) adj., pertaining to or characterized by use of idiom. *"As the crow flies" is an idiomatic expression.*

idiosyncrasy (id'ē ə sing'krə sē, -sin'-) n., peculiarity of temperament or habit. *Her fastidiousness could be an exasperating idiosyncrasy.*

idolatry (ī dol'ə trē) n., worship of created objects; immoderate veneration or love for any person or thing. *His obsessive love became close to idolatry.*

idyll (īd'əl) n., 1. poem describing rural scenes and events; pastoral poem. *He composed the idyll while vacationing in Spain.* 2. episode or set of events of rustic simplicity, peace, and contentment. *Their weekend in the country was a perfect idyll.*

idyllic (ī dil'ik) adj., suitable for an idyll; pastoral; rural; peaceful; rustic. *They found an idyllic spot for a picnic.*

igneous (ig'nē əs) adj., produced by fire or by volcanic and eruptive forces. *Igneous rock is found near volcanoes.*

ignoble (ig nō'bəl) adj., 1. of low birth or station. *They left the horses with the ignoble stable boy.* 2. dishonorable or unworthy; mean. *Tripping the old lady was an ignoble act.*

ignominious (ig'nə min'ē əs) adj., incurring, deserving of, or attended with disgrace; degrading; shameful; infamous. *He dreaded the ignominious, public punishment.*

ignoramus (ig'nə rā'məs, -ram'əs) n., ignorant person; dunce. *The lawyer was an ignoramus about cars.*

ilk (ilk) n., family; sort; kind. *She invited them regardless of their ilk.*

illegible (i lej'ə bəl) adj., incapable of being read; obscure or defaced so as not to be readable. *She tried to decipher the doctor's illegible handwriting.*

illicit (i lis'it) adj., not authorized or permitted; prohibited; unlawful; clandestine. *She finally ended the illicit love affair.*

illiterate (i lit'ər it) adj., ignorant of letters or books; unlearned. *She read the paper to her illiterate father.*

illuminate (i loo'mə nāt') v.t., 1. to light up; enlighten. *Candles illuminated the hall.* 2. to inform; impart intellectual or moral light to; illustrate. *Your information illuminates the problem.*

illuminating (i lōō'mə nā'tiṅg) adj., enlightening; informative; revealing. *She wrote an illuminating analysis of the novel.*

illusion (i lōō'zhən) n., unreal or deceptive vision or perception. *Her clothes gave her the illusion of youth.*

illusory (i lōō'sə rē, -zə-) adj., causing illusion; deceiving by false appearances; fallacious. *An illusory smile hid her distress.*

illustrious (i lus'trē əs) adj., distinguished; renowned; eminent. *The illustrious Prince of Wales became king.*

imagery (im'ij rē, im'ij ə rē) n., descriptive representation; figurative language. *The speech was vivid with imagery.*

imbecile (im'bi sil, -səl *or, esp. Brit.*, -sēl') n., one whose mental faculties are feeble, underdeveloped, or greatly impaired, esp. one who remains a child mentally and requires supervision in performing simple daily tasks. *The drugs made her as helpless as an imbecile.*

imbibe (im bīb') v.t., to drink; absorb as if by drinking. *He learned to imbibe large quantities of beer.*

imbue (im byōō') v.t., to cause to become penetrated or affected; permeate; cause to soak in. *She tried to imbue the child with a sense of worth.*

immaculate (i mak'yə lit) adj., spotless; pure; without blemish or impurity. *I admired his immaculate white suit.*

immemorial (im'ə mōr'ē əl, -môr'-) adj., exceeding the bounds of memory; extending back beyond record or tradition. *The courtship ritual has been practiced since time immemorial.*

immense (i mens') adj., of vast extent, bulk, or quantity; very great; huge; inordinate. *He inherited an immense fortune.*

immerse (i mûrs') v.t., 1. to plunge into anything, esp. into a fluid; submerge. *She laughingly immersed the toy duck.* 2. to become deeply involved. *She began to immerse herself in her work.*

immigrant (im'ə grənt) n., one who moves into a country or a new location for the purpose of permanent residence. *She was an immigrant from Norway.* adj., having immigrated. *New York's immigrant population defines several sections of the city.*

immigrate (im'ə grāt') v.i., to move to a new country or location for the purpose of permanent residence. *They planned to immigrate to the New World.*

imminent (im'ə nənt) adj., about to happen; impending. *We awaited his imminent decision.*

immobile (i mō'bil, -bēl) adj., not moving; still; incapable of moving; fixed; stable. *The immobile vehicle had to be towed.*

immobility (im'ō bil'i tē) n., character or condition of being immovable. *We couldn't understand his immobility on the issue.*

immolation (im'ə lā'shən) n., act of killing as in a sacrifice, or that which is sacrificed. *The monks planned a mass self-immolation in protest.*

immortal (i môr't³l) adj., not liable to death or extinction; unceasing; imperishable; everlasting. *Shakespeare's fame is immortal.*

immortalize (i môr't³līz') v.t., to render immortal; bestow unending fame upon. *The famous portrait will immortalize her.*

immune (i myōōn') adj., exempt; unsusceptible; protected by inoculation. *The inoculation made the child immune to measles.*

immutable (i myōō'tə bəl) adj., not capable of or susceptible to change; invariable; unalterable. *She couldn't resist her immutable fate.*

impaired (im pârd') adj., diminished in value, strength, or excellence; injured. *Her bout with polio left her legs permanently impaired.*

impale (im pāl') v.t., to thrust a sharpened stake through; render helpless as if pierced through. *She impaled the morsel and dipped it into the fondue.*

impalpable (im pal'pə bəl) adj., imperceivable by touch; intangible; imperceptible. *The temperature dropped by slow, impalpable gradations.*

impasse (im′pas, im pas′; *Fr.* aN päs′) n.,
1. blocked road or way; dead end. *They
had to turn around at the impasse.* 2.
predicament with no immediate means
of resolution; deadlock. *It was a serious
impasse in the negotiations.*

impassive (im pas′iv) adj., not showing
emotion; unmoved; deadpan. *His impassive face showed nothing of his grief.*

impeach (im pēch′) v.t., to call in question; accuse; bring to account in trial.
*The defense sought to impeach the
prosecution's witness.*

impeccable (im pek′ə bəl) adj., not liable
to err; not subject to sin; flawless. *The
lawyer's defense was impeccable.*

impede (im pēd′) v.t., to be an obstacle
to; hinder; obstruct. *The snow began
to impede traffic.*

impending (im pen′dig) adj., about to
happen; threatening; imminent. *The citizens were warned of the impending
attack.*

impenetrable (im pen′i trə bəl) adj., incapable of penetration; impermeable.
*An impenetrable fog settled over Lon-
don.*

imperative (im per′ə tiv) n., 1. mode or
verbal form that expresses command,
entreaty, or advice. *"Do it now!" is an
imperative.* 2. command; order; pressing duty. *They rushed to obey her imperative.* adj., expressing command or
necessity; absolute; not to be avoided
or evaded; obligatory; binding; urgent.
*It was imperative that Cinderella leave
the ball before midnight.*

imperceptible (im′pər sep′tə bəl) adj.,
not capable of being seen or felt. *She
was discouraged with her imperceptible
progress.*

imperialism (im pēr′ē ə liz′əm) n., country's policy, intention, or action to increase its dominion by extending its
power over other countries, usually by
conquest. *Soviet imperialism has encompassed Eastern Europe.*

imperious (im pēr′ē əs) adj., of a domineering character; dictatorial; overbearing. *His imperious aunt intimidated
the boy.*

impermeable (im pûr′mē ə bəl) adj., 1.
not permitting the passage or absorption
of fluid; impenetrable. *The downpour
made her wish her coat were impermeable.* 2. impervious. *She was not impermeable to his suggestion.*

impertinent (im pûr′t'nənt) adj., forward
or intrusive from curiosity or with advice; saucy; bold; impudent. *He scolded
the rude, impertinent child.*

imperturbable (im′pər tûr′bə bəl) adj.,
not liable to being moved or agitated;
self-contained; calm; even-tempered.
*His imperturbable temper was sorely
tested by the noise.*

impervious (im pûr′vē əs) adj., impenetrable; impermeable. *Metal is impervious to moisture.*

impetuous (im pech′o͞o əs) adj., acting
with sudden, violent, or rash energy;
hasty; rash. *He later regretted his impetuous offer.*

impetus (im′pi təs) n., power with which
a moving body keeps going; energy of
motion. *The post deflected the bullet's
impetus.*

impinge (im pinj′) v.i., 1. to collide,
strike, or dash. *They impinged against
each other with crushing force.* 2. to
intrude or encroach upon; infringe. *He
hesitated to impinge upon her friendship.*

impious (im′pē əs) adj., not pious; lacking
reverence; profane. *The minister deplored the impious vandalism of the
church.*

implacable (im plak′ə bəl, -plā′kə-) adj.,
not to be appeased, pacified, or reconciled. *He could not soothe her implacable anger.*

implement (*n.* im′plə mənt; *v.*
im′plə ment′) n., instrument, tool, or
utensil; means to an end. *She wielded
the sharp implement with care.* v.t., to
carry into effect; perform; fulfill. *We will
implement her instructions.*

implication (im′plə kā′shən) n., 1. that
which is implied but not expressed. *She
didn't like the implication of his remark.*
2. act of implicating, or state of being
implicated, esp. in incriminating con-

nection. *He avoided implication in the crime.*

implicit (im plis′it) adj., implied; resting on implication or inference; understood though not directly expressed; tacitly included. *He couldn't miss the implicit warning in her offer.*

implore (im plōr′, -plôr′) v.t., to beg; beseech; entreat. *I implore you to come home.*

implosion (im plō′zhən) n., sudden collapse inward; opposite of explosion. *The implosion of the building crushed its occupants.*

imply (im plī′) v.t., to express indirectly; insinuate. *Does your silence imply agreement?*

import (n. im′pōrt, -pôrt; v. im pōrt′, -pôrt′) n., 1. intrinsic meaning of anything; gist; sense; substance. *He explained the import of his news.* 2. that which is brought from abroad. *The car is a French import.* v.t., to bring or introduce from abroad. *The brothers import wine from France.*

importune (im′pôr tōōn′, -tyōōn′, im pôr′chən) v.t., to press or harass with solicitation; crave or require persistently; beg; tease. *Don't importune me; I can't go.*

impose (im pōz′) v.t., 1. to lay as a burden, or something to be borne or endured. *He tried to impose his will on his son.* 2. to arrange pages in order for printing as a signature. *He began to impose the 16-page signature.* v.i., to take advantage of; obtrude. *I refuse to impose on your hospitality.*

impotent (im′pə tənt) adj., ineffective, esp. sexually; lacking power or strength; feeble. *The impotent man sought medical treatment.*

imprecation (im′prə kā′shən) n., act of invoking evil; malediction; curse. *He was shocked by her violent imprecation.*

impregnate (im preg′nāt, im′preg-) v.t., 1. to make pregnant; fertilize. *The stud was able to impregnate the bitch.* 2. to infuse a principle into; imbue. *The teacher impregnated them with a love for reading.*

impresario (im′pri sär′ē ō′, -sär′-; *It.* ēm′pre sä′ryô) n., manager, agent, or conductor of an opera company; also, one who arranges or sponsors an entertainment. *The impresario brought the dancer to the New York stage.*

imprison (im priz′ən) v.t., to put into a prison; jail; confine. *Poverty imprisoned him in a one-room tenement.*

impromptu (im promp′tōō, -tyōō) adj., extemporaneous; unplanned. *Receipt of the news spurred an impromptu celebration.*

impropriety (im′prə prī′i tē) n., 1. quality of being improper; unfitness or unsuitableness. *She regretted the impropriety of her remark.* 2. improper or unsuitable act; blunder. *She was embarrassed by his coarse impropriety.*

improvise (im′prə vīz′) v., 1. to recite or sing without premeditation. *The comedian began to improvise.* 2. to execute or prepare from material at hand. *The cook must improvise from these leftovers.*

imprudent (im prōōd′ənt) adj., lacking discretion; rash; heedless; careless. *He later regretted his imprudent remark.*

impudent (im′pyə dənt) adj., offensively forward; intentionally disrespectful; insolent; brazen; bold. *The impudent reporter disregarded her request.*

impugn (im pyōōn′) v.t., to attack by words or arguments; contradict; deny. *The defense attorney tried to impugn her testimony.*

impulsive (im pul′siv) adj., impelled or controlled by impulses; swayed by the emotions or by whim; hasty; rash. *Her impulsive hug pleased him.*

impunity (im pyōō′ni tē) n., freedom or exemption from punishment, penalty, injury, or suffering. *She volunteered the evidence with impunity.*

impute (im pyōōt′) v.t., to charge; attribute; ascribe. *You cannot impute that error to me.*

inadvertent (in′əd vûr′tənt) adj., unconscious; unintentional; accidental. *Her inadvertent remark led to his discovery.*

inalienable (in āl′yə nə bəl, -ā′lē-ə-) adj.,

incapable of being surrendered or transferred. *You have an inalienable right to your privacy.*

inalterable (in ôl′tər ə bəl) adj., incapable of being changed; unalterable. *His contempt was inalterable.*

inane (i nān′) adj., void of sense or intelligence; silly; puerile. *The inane conversation bored him.*

inanimate (in an′ə mit) adj., not animate; lacking life or movement; inactive; spiritless; still. *They feared the inanimate man was dead.*

inappropriate (in′ə prō′prē it) adj., not appropriate; unsuitable. *Blue jeans are inappropriate at the opera.*

inarticulate (in′är tik′yə lit) adj., incapable of expressing thought in speech; incapable of distinct speech; not distinct. *He became inarticulate after the fifth martini.*

inaudible (in ô′də bəl) adj., incapable of being heard. *She uttered an inaudible sigh.*

inauspicious (in′ô spish′əs) adj., ill-omened; unfavorable; unpromising. *His performance improved after an inauspicious beginning.*

incapable (in kā′pə bəl) adj., unable. *She was incapable of meeting the deadline.*

incapacitate (in′kə pas′i tāt′) v.t., to deprive of capacity or power; to render unfit or helpless. *Flu incapacitated him for a week.*

incarcerate (in kär′sə rāt′) v.t., to imprison; confine. *They incarcerated him in the state penitentiary.*

incarnate (in kär′nit, -nāt) adj., embodied in flesh. *He seemed the Devil incarnate.* v.t., to embody; put into real form. *The artist's drawings incarnated his hopes for all mankind.*

incendiary (in sen′dē er′ē) n., 1. one who sets fire to property; arsonist. *The incendiary was arrested at the scene of the fire.* 2. one who excites or inflames factions or quarrels; agitator. *The incendiary stirred them to action.* 3. object that causes combustion. *The incendiary exploded in his hand.* adj., 1. causing or used in starting a fire; inflammatory.

They confiscated the incendiary device. 2. tending to excite or inflame passion, sedition, or violence. *The dictator jailed the incendiary rebels.*

incentive (in sen′tiv) n., that which incites to action; motive; spur; reason; impulse. *The vacation was her incentive to work.*

incessant (in ses′ənt) adj., continuous; unceasing. *The baby's incessant crying irritated the neighbors.*

incest (in′sest) n., sexual intercourse between persons so closely related that marriage is prohibited by law or custom. *Incest is taboo in most cultures.*

incidence (in′si dəns) n., the manner or range of influence of something; particularly something not desired. *The incidence of sickness delayed their vacation plans.*

incident (in′si dənt) n., 1. that which takes place; occurrence. *The incident led to his arrest.* 2. something that occurs in connection with an event of greater importance; concomitant. *Within the context of the war, the border incident was insignificant.*

incidental (in′si den′t³l) adj., occurring in conjunction with something else, usually of greater importance; occasional; casual. *This will cover incidental as well as transportation and hotel expenses.*

incipient (in sip′ē ənt) adj., beginning; commencing. *He tried to nip the incipient romance in the bud.*

incision (in sizh′ən) n., act of cutting into a substance, esp. into flesh; also, the cut made by incision. *The surgeon began to suture the incision.*

incisive (in sī′siv) adj., cutting; sharp; clear; penetrating; trenchant. *The incisive report gave little beyond the facts.*

incite (in sīt′) v.t., to move to action; instigate; stir up. *He tried to incite the students' interest.*

inclement (in klem′ənt) adj., severe, as climate or weather; tempestuous; extreme; foul. *Inclement weather cancelled our picnic.*

inclination (in′klə nā′shən) n., 1. act of leaning; state of being tilted; inclined surface; slope. *The tree's inclination was caused by the constant sea breeze.*

2. set or bent of the mind or will; leaning, liking, or preference. *He had an inclination for Chinese food.*

inclusive (in kloō'siv) adj., comprehensive; including. *The rates are for Monday through Saturday inclusive.*

incognito (in kog'ni tō', in'kog nē'-) adj., disguised in order to avoid notice or recognition. *The incognito prince was not recognized.* adv., with identity concealed. *The actor walked the streets incognito.*

incoherent (in'kō hēr'ənt) adj., without coherence or connection in thought or speech; inconsistent; disjointed. *His argument was incoherent and muddled.*

incompatibility (in'kom pat'ə bil'i tē') n., quality or condition of not being compatible; incapability of harmony or agreement; discord. *They divorced on grounds of incompatibility.*

incompatible (in'kəm pat'ə bəl) adj., incapable of harmony or agreement; mutually repelling; discordant. *Milk and grapefruit have incompatible flavors.*

incongruity (in'kong groō'i tē) n., 1. quality of being incongruous; unsuitability of one thing to another. *The detective was struck by the incongruity of the situation.* 2. that which is incongruous. *The incongruity was immediately apparent.*

incongruous (in kong'groō əs) adj., unsuited; inharmonious; inappropriate. *The fast food joint seemed incongruous next to the cathedral.*

inconsequential (in'kon sə kwen'shəl, in kon'-) adj., of no consequence or value. *The board was cluttered with inconsequential notes and memos.*

inconsistent (in'kən sis'tənt) adj., 1. lacking consistency or agreement; discrepant. *His story was inconsistent with the facts.* 2. changeable. *Her inconsistent attitude caused problems with the child.*

incontrovertible (in'kon trə vûr'tə bəl, in kon'-) adj., too clear or certain to admit of dispute or controversy. *The incontrovertible evidence demanded a verdict of guilty.*

incorrigible (in kôr'i jə bəl, -kor'-) adj., incapable of being corrected or re-

formed; bad beyond correction; incurable; hopeless; hardened. *The incorrigible drunk refused to join AA.*

incredulous (in krej'ə ləs) adj., not given to believe readily; refusing or withholding belief; skeptical. *He tried to convince the incredulous client.*

increment (in'krə mənt, ing'-) n., addition; increase; enlargement. *His savings account grew by monthly increments.*

incriminate (in krim'ə nāt') v.t., to charge with a crime; accuse; indict. *She refuses to incriminate herself by testifying.*

incubate (in'kyə bāt', ing'-) v.t., to sit upon for the purpose of hatching; maintain conditions favorable to hatching. *The hen will incubate the eggs.* v.i., to undergo incubation; develop. *The plot incubated for two years in the novelist's mind.*

incubator (in'kyə bā'tər, ing'-) n., 1. machine for the artificial incubation of eggs or for the development and cultivation of microorganisms. *She placed the petri dish in the incubator.* 2. a machine for sustaining a constant atmosphere for premature infants. *The baby, born two months early, was placed in an incubator.*

incumbent (in kum'bənt) n., one who holds office. *He will try to oust the incumbent.* adj., 1. holding office. *It is difficult to upset an incumbent president.* 2. resting as a duty or obligation. *It is incumbent upon me to arrest you.*

indefatigable (in'di fat'ə gə bəl) adj., not yielding to fatigue; untiring; unremitting in labor or effort. *The indefatigable woman worked double shifts.*

indefensible (in'di fen'sə bəl) adj., not capable of defense or justification. *His rudeness is indefensible.*

indefinite (in def'ə nit) adj., undefined; imprecise; unlimited; vague. *The length of her stay was indefinite.*

indemnify (in dem'nə fī') v.t., 1. to preserve or secure against loss, damage, or penalty. *Their homeowner's insurance will indemnify their property.* 2. to reimburse; make good to. *The insurance company will indemnify your loss.*

indict (in dīt′) v.t., to find chargeable with a criminal offense; accuse. *The grand jury might indict him.*

indictment (in dīt′mənt) n., formal charge; formal complaint by which the charge of a criminal offense found by the grand jury to have been committed is brought against the supposed offender, that may be tried. *The grand jury handed down an indictment of fraud.*

indifference (in dif′ər əns, -dif′rəns) n., absence of definite preference or choice; want of feeling; apathy. *She was hurt by her friend's indifference to her problem.*

indigenous (in dij′ə nəs) adj., born or originating in a particular place, country, or climate; native. *The marigold is indigenous to the United States.*

indigent (in′di jent) adj., lacking means of comfortable subsistence; needy; poor; destitute. *The church tries to help the indigent person.*

indigestion (in′di jes′chən, -dī-, -jesh′-) n., incapability, difficulty, or discomfort in digesting food; dyspepsia. *She suffered indigestion after the heavy meal.*

indignant (in dig′nənt) adj., moved by mixed emotions of anger and scorn; provoked by something regarded as unjust, ungrateful, or unworthy. *She was indignant at the malicious gossip.*

indignity (in dig′ni tē) n., affront; insult; slight. *He suffered the indignity of public reprimand.*

indiscriminate (in′di skrim′ə nit) adj., not careful or discriminating; promiscuous; haphazard. *He complained of her indiscriminate use of garlic.*

indisposed (in′di spōzd′) adj., 1. affected with illness. *The upsetting news made her somewhat indisposed.* 2. averse; disinclined. *I am indisposed to follow your questionable example.*

indisputable (in′di spyoo′tə bəl, in dis′pyə-) adj., undoubtedly true; incontrovertible; incontestable. *He had an indisputable claim to the throne.*

indoctrinate (in dok′trə nāt′) v.t., 1. to instruct, esp. in doctrine or partisan view. *He tried to indoctrinate her with party ideology.* 2. to introduce to new

situations. *It takes time to indoctrinate recent graduates into the professional world.*

indolence (in′d∂ləns) n., avoidance of exertion of mind or body; idleness; laziness; sloth. *Indolence is the enemy of industriousness.*

indolent (in′d∂lənt) adj., avoiding exertion; indulging in ease; lazy; listless; idle. *The extreme heat made us indolent.*

indomitable (in dom′i tə bəl) adj., that cannot be tamed, subdued, or repressed. *Her indomitable ego refused to acknowledge the slight.*

indubitably (in doo′bi tə blē, -dyoo′-) adv., unquestionably; without or beyond doubt. *She will indubitably contest the will.*

induce (in doos′, -dyoos′) v.t., to lead in or to; bring about; cause. *This tranquilizer will induce sleep.*

induction (in duk′shən) n., 1. act of inducting or bringing in, esp. introducing a person into an office with customary forms and ceremonies; installation. *She wept at his induction into the army.* 2. process of drawing a general conclusion from particular cases; opposite of deduction. *She questioned the validity of his induction.*

indulgent (in dul′jənt) adj., disposed to humor, gratify, or give way to one's own or another's desires; lenient; tolerant. *Grandparents are often indulgent of their grandchildren.*

inebriated (in ē′brē ā′tid) adj., intoxicated; drunk. *One shouldn't drive when inebriated.*

ineffable (in ef′ə bəl) adj., incapable of being expressed in words; unspeakable; unutterable. *She felt ineffable disgust at the news.*

ineffectual (in′i fek′choo əl) adj., not producing or unable to produce the desired effect. *His attempts to reconcile them proved ineffectual.*

inept (in ept′, i nept′) adj., not apt or fit; inappropriate; incompetent; bungling; foolish. *He was a hopelessly inept dancer.*

inert (in ûrt′, i nûrt′) adj., having no

inherent power of action or motion; inactive; lifeless; inanimate. *Clay is an inert substance.*

inertia (in ûr′s̱h̲ə, i nûr′-) n., 1. lack of activity; sluggishness; passiveness. *Inertia kept me from finishing the job.* 2. property of matter of retaining a state of rest or uniform motion in a straight line so long as no foreign cause changes that state. *Inertia will keep the rocket on its course.*

inevitable (in ev′i tə bəl) adj., admitting of no escape or evasion; unavoidable. *Death is an inevitable end to life.*

inexorable (in ek′sər ə bəl) adj., not to be persuaded or moved by entreaty or prayer; unyielding; unrelenting; implacable. *The inexorable judge would not change the offender's sentence.*

inexplicable (in eks′plə kə bəl *or, esp. Brit.,* in′ik splik′ə bəl) adj., incapable of being explained, interpreted, or made intelligible. *The inexplicable disappearances in the Bermuda Triangle have puzzled experts.*

inextricable (in eks′trə kə bəl) adj., incapable of being extricated or disentangled. *The kitten rendered the yarn an inextricable tangle.*

infallible (in fal′ə bəl) adj., exempt from liability to error; unfailing in character; absolutely trustworthy. *I could be wrong; I'm not infallible.*

infamous (in′fə məs) adj., notoriously evil, odious, or detestable. *The infamous highwayman was hanged at Tyburn.*

infantile (in′fən tīl′, -til) adj., pertaining to or characteristic of infants or infancy; infantlike; childish. *She was embarrassed by his infantile behavior.*

infatuated (in fac̱h̲′o͞o ā′tid) adj., manifesting extravagant impermanent or foolish love or devotion. *The infatuated girl tried to attract his attention.*

infected (in fek′tid) adj., tainted with disease; contaminated; poisoned. *Clean the wound so it won't become infected.*

infer (in fûr′) v.t., to form an opinion or belief in consequence of observation or other beliefs; derive as a fact or consequence by reasoning; accept from evidence; conclude. *She inferred his leaving from the absence of his suitcase.*

inferiority (in fēr′ē ôr′i tē, -ōr′-) n., state of being inferior, esp. in degree or quality; lower state or condition. *Inferiority of workmanship characterizes cheap goods.*

infernal (in fûr′nəl) adj., pertaining to or resembling hell; hellish; fiendish; abominable. *Washing dishes is an infernal nuisance for one who does not like housework.*

infidel (in′fi dəl) n., unbeliever; disbeliever. *The Christian crusaders made war on infidels.*

infiltrate (in fil′trāt, in′fil trāt′) v.t., to filter into or through. *Orders were to infiltrate enemy lines and destroy the bridge.*

infinite (in′fə nit) adj., boundless; limitless; endless; immeasurable. *The excellent teacher showed infinite patience.*

infinitesimal (in′fin i tes′ə məl) adj., infinitely, immeasurably small; less than any assignable quantity. *The bodice glitters with hundreds of infinitesimal beads.*

infirmity (in fûr′mi tē) n., weakness; unsound or unhealthy state of the body; malady; moral weakness; fault; foible. *Loss of memory is often an infirmity of old age.*

inflammable (in flam′ə bəl) adj., capable of being set on fire; susceptible to combustion; easily excited or inflamed. *The redhead had an inflammable temper.*

inflatable (in flā′tə bəl) adj., capable of inflation or expansion. *They pumped up the inflatable pool.*

inflate (in flāt′) v.t., to swell or distend, esp. by inhaling or injecting air or gas; blow or puff up. *One can inflate balloons with air or hydrogen.*

inflation (in flā′shən) n., 1. act of inflating. *The inflation was complete in two minutes.* 2. state of being inflated. *He checked the tire's inflation.* 3. expansion or increase beyond the just value or volume of money and credit in relation to goods, resulting in a rise in prices. *Inflation is especially hard on fixed incomes.*

inflection (in flek′shən) n., 1. variation of forms of words to show distinctions of gender, number, tense, mood, voice, etc. *Language instructors teach inflection as well as vocabulary.* 2. modulation of the voice in speaking; accent; changes of pitch or expression. *His words carried an angry inflection.*

inflexible (in flek′sə bəl) adj., rigid; stiff; unyielding; firm; obstinate; stubborn. *The boarding school maintained inflexible rules.*

influence (in′floo əns) n., power that produces an effect, affects, or modifies by insensible or invisible means; authority; power; sway. *The moon exerts influence over bodies of water to produce tides.* v.t., to modify, affect, or sway, esp. by intangible means. *He hoped to influence her decision by advising her of the consequences.*

influenza (in′floo en′zə) n., contagious virus disease, generally characterized by sudden onset, fever, and aches and pains; often accompanied by respiratory difficulties or nausea. *She was hospitalized with influenza.*

influx (in′fluks′) n., act of flowing in; inflow; flood. *The influx of tourists disrupted traffic.*

infraction (in frak′shən) n., violation; breach. *He was ticketed for a minor traffic infraction.*

infringe (in frinj′) v.t., to commit a breach or infraction of; transgress; violate; encroach upon. *Do not infringe on my privacy.*

infuse (in fyooz′) v.t., 1. to introduce and pervade with; instill; insinuate; imbue. *You must infuse your playing with more feeling.* 2. to steep. *Infuse the tea for five minutes.*

ingenious (in jēn′yəs) adj., marked by inventive genius; clever; inventive. *His ingenious idea cut months of work off the project.*

ingenuous (in jen′yoo əs) adj., open; candid; artless; naïve. *We were nonplused by her ingenuous reply.*

ingest (in jest′) v.t., to take in, as to digest; absorb; eat. *We needed a moment to ingest his startling news.*

ingrate (in′grāt) n., ungrateful person. *The ingrate never acknowledged the gift.*

ingratiate (in grā′shē āt′) v.t., to establish in the confidence, favor, or good graces of another. *He tried to ingratiate himself with the senator-elect.*

inhabitant (in hab′i tənt) n., one who dwells in a place, as opposed to a transient or occasional lodger; resident. *He was an inhabitant of Geneva for three years.*

inherent (in hēr′ənt, -her′-) adj., existing as an element, quality, or attribute; innately characteristic; intrinsic. *Kindness was inherent in her nature.*

inhibit (in hib′it) v.t., to hold back; discourage; repress; suppress; forbid. *Her shyness inhibits her from making friends easily.*

inhibited (in hib′i tid) adj., held back from doing something; repressed. *The inhibited man couldn't express his sorrow.*

inhibition (in′i bish′ən, in′hi-) n., 1. internal restriction or impediment to free or spontaneous action, speech, or behavior. *Consumption of alcohol lowers one's inhibitions.* 2. any prohibition or restraining agent. *She chaffed against her father's strict inhibition.*

inimical (i nim′i kəl) adj., having the disposition or temper of an enemy; unfriendly; hostile; adverse. *His inimical act contradicted his amicable pose.*

inimitable (i nim′i tə bəl) adj., incapable of being imitated or copied; surpassing imitation. *We are happy to present the inimitable Marcel Marceau.*

iniquity (i nik′wi tē) n., wickedness; sin; unjust or wicked act. *The pornographic bookstore was considered a place of iniquity by many.*

initial (i nish′əl) n., first letter of a word. *She affixed her initials to the contract.* adj., pertaining to the beginning; first. *Her initial impression was positive.* v.t., to sign with initials, esp. to verify or approve. *Please initial the memo.*

initiate (i nish′ē āt′) v.t., 1. to begin or enter upon; introduce; set going. *We will initiate proceedings against them.* 2. to admit formally; to induct. *The fraternity will initiate five pledges.*

inkling (ingk′ling) n., hint; intimation; suspicion. *He had no inkling about the surprise party.*

in lieu of (lōō) in place of; instead of; as a substitute for. *Tom went in lieu of his wife.*

innate (i nāt′, in′āt) adj., not derived or acquired from any external source; natural; native. *The ability to reason is an innate human characteristic.*

innocuous (i nok′yōō əs) adj., producing no ill effect; harmless. *His innocuous remark drew unexpected criticism.*

innovation (in′ə vā′shən) n., introduction of new thing or method; a novel change in practice or method; experimental variation. *There is no progress without innovation.*

innuendo (in′yōō en′dō) n., indirect, allusive, or inferential suggestion, esp. about character or reputation and usually of a derogatory nature; oblique hint. *We asked her to confirm or deny the innuendo.*

innumerable (i nōō′mər ə bəl, -nyōō′-) adj., incapable of being enumerated; countless; myriad; numberless. *We watched innumerable ships sail by that day.*

inoculate (i nok′yə lāt′) v.t., to introduce a germ or virus in order to protect against disease by calling on the body to develop immunity. *The doctors will inoculate the school children today.*

inopportune (in op′ər tōōn′, -tyōōn′) adj., ill-timed; inconvenient; inappropriate. *The inopportune visit interrupted her nap.*

inordinate (in ôr′dᵊnit) adj., beyond proper bounds; excessive; immoderate. *He couldn't meet his customer's inordinate demand.*

inquest (in′kwest) n., judicial inquiry, esp. before a jury; investigation. *She testified at the inquest.*

inquisition (in′kwi zish′ən) n., 1. act of inquiring; close search or examination; investigation. *Her inquisition uncovered the culprit.* 2. (*cap.*) ecclesiastical court for the suppression of heretics by detection and punishment. *The Inquisition was a fearful agency.*

insatiable (in sā′shə bəl, -shē ə-) adj., incapable of being satisfied; voracious. *The teenager had an insatiable appetite.*

inscription (in skrip′shən) n., 1. descriptive, explanatory, or illustrative notation. *"Rest in Peace" was the inscription carved on the tombstone.* 2. form of complimentary address, less elaborate than a dedication. *The author's inscription to her husband appears in the front of the book.*

inscrutable (in skrōō′tə bəl) adj., incapable of being searched into or scrutinized; impenetrable; incomprehensible; mysterious. *The cat gave us an inscrutable look.*

insect (in′sekt) n., small, usually winged and many-legged invertebrate creature whose body consists of several segments. *Roaches, beetles, and crickets are insects.*

insemination (in sem′ə nā′shən) n., act of sowing seed or injecting semen; impregnation. *Many cattle are produced by artificial insemination.*

insidious (in sid′ē əs) adj., 1. waiting to entrap; treacherous; enticing. *She was warned against his insidious charm.* 2. characterized by gradual, accumulating effect. *The insidious cold developed into pneumonia.*

insignia (in sig′nē ə) n., pl., distinguishing mark or emblem. *We could tell by his insignia that he held the rank of colonel.*

insignificant (in′sig nif′ə kənt) adj., unimportant; trivial. *She dismissed the detail as insignificant.*

insincere (in′sin sēr′) adj., disingenuous; hypocritical; false. *I resented his insincere compliment.*

insinuate (in sin′yōō āt′) v.t., to introduce by devious means or imperceptible degrees; worm in. *He tried to insinuate himself into her confidence.* v.i., to hint obliquely; suggest. *Do you mean to insinuate that I took the pearls?*

insipid (in sip'id) adj., not exciting the sense of taste; without flavor or power to excite interest or emotion; dull; flat; tame. *The insipid conversation made me yawn.*

insistence (in sis'təns) n., urgent or persistent maintenance of an opinion, principle, right, or the like; perseverance. *I came only because of her insistence.*

insolent (in'sə lənt) adj., contemptuously impertinent; impudent; insulting; abusive; grossly rude. *She rebuked them for their insolent language.*

insolvent (in sol'vənt) adj., having insufficient assets to cover existing debts; impoverished. *The heavy medical expenses rendered him insolvent.*

insomnia (in som'nē ə) n., inability to sleep, esp. when chronic; sleeplessness. *Warm milk at bedtime is often adequate for mild insomnia.*

insouciance (in sōō'sē ans; *Fr.* aN sōō syäNs') n., heedless indifference or unconcern for consequences or of the future; carelessness. *The grasshopper later regretted his summertime insouciance.*

instigate (in'stə gāt') v.t., to stimulate; to incite; urge; goad; foment. *He didn't mean to instigate the fight.*

insubordination (in'sə bôr'd ͨnā'shən) n., resistance to authority; disobedience and disrespect. *The child was spanked for her rude insubordination.*

insufferable (in suf' ͨr ə bəl) adj., not to be endured; unbearable; intolerable. *They complained about the insufferable heat.*

insular (in'sə lər, ins'yə-) adj., 1. of or pertaining to an island. *The insular supplies are delivered by boat.* 2. hemmed in; cut off; isolated; narrow; insulated. *The man lived a tragically insular life alone in the city.*

insurgent (in sûr'jənt) n., one who forcibly opposes lawful authority; rebel. *The insurgent was arrested for his*

part in the protest. adj., engaged in insurrection or rebellion; rebellious. *His insurgent appetite foiled his strict diet.*

insurmountable (in'sər moun'tə bəl) adj., incapable of being overcome. *Just when her difficulties seemed insurmountable, help came.*

insurrection (in'sə rek'shən) n., act of rising against civil authority or government; specifically, the armed resistance of a number of persons against the state; rebellion; uprising. *Martial law was declared during the insurrection.*

intact (in takt') adj., complete; whole; unimpaired; untouched; uninjured. *The teacup survived the fall, miraculously intact.*

intangible (in tan'jə bəl) adj., incapable of being touched; not perceptible to touch; incorporeal; abstract. *His friendship was an intangible benefit of the job.*

integral (in'tə grəl) adj., 1. intrinsic; constituent; component. *Studying is an integral part of being a student.* 2. essential. *This experiment is an integral part of my research.*

integrate (in'tə grāt') v.t., 1. to bring together separate parts; form into a whole; unite; merge. *Let's integrate the modern with the antique in this room.* 2. to not restrict because of race, religion, or ethnic group; desegregate. *Their goal is to integrate all schools in the state.*

integrity (in teg'ri tē) n., soundness of moral principle and character; freedom from corruption; unimpaired morality; uprightness. *His integrity prompted him to refuse the bribe.*

intellect (in'tᵊlekt') n., sum of all the cognitive faculties except the senses; understanding; mind. *The problem was a challenge to his intellect.*

intelligentsia (in tel'i jent'sē ə, -gent'sē ə) n., elite group of intellectuals; social, artistic, or political elite. *The art world is run by an intelligentsia of dealers and art historians.*

intemperate (in tem'pər it, -prit) adj., immoderate in conduct or action, measure, or degree; excessive; inordinate; violent. *This intemperate climate is marked by violent summer storms.*

intense (in tens′) adj., extreme; strong; powerful. *The wound caused him intense pain.*

intensify (in ten′sə fī′) v.t., to render more intense; heighten. *The army began to intensify its assault.*

inter (in tûr′) v.t., to bury; enhume; to place in a grave or tomb. *They interred the body at Arlington National Cemetery.*

intercede (in′tər sēd′) v.i., to act between parties to reconcile those who differ; intervene; mediate. *Mary asked the ambassador to intercede for her with the local police.*

interdict (in′tər dikt′) n., 1. in the Roman Catholic Church, an ecclesiastical sentence that forbids the right of Christian burial, the use of sacraments, and the enjoyment of public worship. *The bishop issued an interdict to the excommunicant.* 2. official or authoritative prohibition; a prohibitory order or decree; ban. *The FDA issued an interdict against the drug.*

interim (in′tər im) n., intervening or intermediate period of time. *The interim of waiting was agonizing.* adj., belonging to an intervening period of time; temporary. *The judge issued an interim order pending final decision.*

interject (in′tər jekt′) v.t., to throw in between; insert; interpolate. *He tried to interject a light note into the gloomy evening.*

interlope (in′tər lōp′) v.i., to intrude or encroach upon; meddle. *Susan wished Mary wouldn't interlope upon her privacy.*

interloper (in′tər lōp′ər) n., one who encroaches upon another's right or business; intruder; meddler. *The interloper was ejected from the private club.*

interlude (in′tər lōōd′) n., 1. intermediate piece or performance inserted between the principal parts of a play or musical piece. *There was a five-minute interlude*

while the set was changed. 2. interruptive or intervening period; interval. *She enjoyed a brief interlude between school and her new job.*

intermediary (in′tər mē′dē er′ē) n., one who interposes; agent; go-between. *They carried on their correspondence through an intermediary.*

interment (in tûr′mənt) n., act of interring or entombing; burial. *Interment of the body will follow the funeral.*

interminable (in tûr′mə nə bəl) adj., without termination; endless; limitless; unending. *The wait seemed interminable.*

intermittent (in′tər mit′ənt) adj., stopping and starting alternately. *Intermittent blasts from the horn signal a fire alarm.*

interpolate (in tûr′pə lāt′) v.t., 1. to insert a word or phrase not in the original; corrupt or vitiate by spurious insertions or additions; alter. *The producer interpolated some lines of dialogue in the script.* 2. in math., to supply the missing elements in a series by applying the rules of the series. *It is possible to interpolate the numbers between 5 and 10.*

interpretation (in tûr′pri tā′shən) n., act or result of interpreting, expounding, or explaining; translation; explanation; apparent meaning. *The lawyer gave her interpretation of the ruling.*

interpreter (in tûr′pri tər) n., one who explains or translates, esp. one who translates from a foreign language; translator. *The Chinese ambassador communicated through an interpreter.*

interrogate (in ter′ə gāt′) v.t., to question; examine by asking questions. *I will interrogate the prisoner.*

intersect (in′tər sekt′) v.t., to meet and cross; have one or more points in common; overlap; divide. *The state highway intersects the town road at the toll station.* v.i., to meet and cross through. *The two roads intersect at Miller's Crossroads.*

interstate (*n.* in′tər stāt′; *adj.* in′tər stāt′) n., highway that traverses· more than one state. *Hitchhiking is illegal on the interstate.* adj., existing or taking place between different states or persons in different states. *The legislators studied interstate commerce.*

intervene (in′tər vēn′) v.i., 1. to come between. *Two years would intervene before we met again.* 2. to interfere or interpose; mediate. *She tried to intervene in their quarrel.*

intimate (*n., adj.* in′tə mit; *v.* in′tə māt′) n., familiar friend, companion, or guest. *She was his intimate during college days.* adj., 1. pertaining to the inner mind or thoughts; inward. *I rarely reveal my most intimate feelings.* 2. close in friendship; familiar; not reserved. *We are intimate friends.* v.i., to make known by indirect words or means; suggest; hint; insinuate. *He intimated that he might have a buyer for us.*

intimidate (in tim′i dāt′) v.t., 1. to make timid; frighten; abash; cow. *His gruff manner does not intimidate me.* 2. to deter by threats. *The bully tried to intimidate the new boy.*

intone (in tōn′) v.t., to speak or recite with a singing voice; speak in a monotone; chant. *The priest began to intone the litany.*

intoxicated (in tok′sə kā′tid) adj., 1. drunken; inebriated. *We drove the intoxicated men home.* 2. excited to a high pitch of feeling; elated. *He was intoxicated by his success.*

intractable (in trak′tə bəl) adj., not to be drawn or guided by persuasion; unmanageable; uncontrollable; unruly; ungovernable; stubborn; obstinate. *The teacher was exasperated by the intractable child.*

intransigent (in tran′si jənt) adj., refusing to agree or come to an understanding; uncompromising; irreconcilable. *The intransigent senator held up the committee's decision.*

intrastate (in′trə stāt′) adj., occurring within a state. *He had many intrastate delivery routes in Virginia.*

intravenous (in′trə vē′nəs) adj., existing within or entering by way of veins.

While in the coma he received intravenous feeding.

intrepid (in trep′id) adj., unmoved by danger; undaunted; fearless; courageous; daring; dauntless. *The intrepid soldier ran into the fray.*

intricate (in′trə kit) adj., perplexingly involved or entangled; complicated; complex. *He could not untie the intricate knot.*

intrigue (*n.* in trēg′, in′trēg; *v.* in trēg′) n., 1. secret or underhanded plotting; scheme. *Political intrigue gained him the nomination.* 2. clandestine love affair. *Her husband suspected her of an intrigue.* v.t., to cause to be involved or entangled; capture the interest or attention of. *His cryptic answer intrigued her.* v.i., to plot or scheme underhandedly. *A corrupt politician would intrigue to control the election.*

intrinsic (in trin′sik, -zik) adj., pertaining to that which is essential or inherent. *He tried to ignore the intrinsic danger in the plan.*

introspective (in′trə spek′tiv) adj., pertaining to reflection or concentration on one's consciousness or inner state; looking inward. *The introspective poem explored his need to escape.*

introvert (in′trə vûrt′) n., one who is characterized by introspection or self-examination. *The introvert seemed an unlikely candidate for public office.*

intrude (in trood′) v.i., to bring or thrust in forcibly; push or crowd in; come in unbidden and unwelcome; invade. *He didn't want to intrude upon her privacy.*

intuition (in′too ish′ən, -tyoo-) n., direct or immediate cognition or perception, without rational thought; instinctive knowledge. *Intuition told her that the man was dangerous.*

inundate (in′ən dāt′, -un-, in un′dāt) v.t., to flood; overflow; fill inordinately; overwhelm. *Fans began to inundate her with requests for autographs.*

inured (in-yoord′, i noord′) adj., hardened or toughened by exercise or use; accustomed. *He became inured to the harshness of prison life.*

invalid (*n.* in'və lid, *Brit.* in'və lēd'; *adj.* 1. in'və lid, 2. in val'id) n., one who is disabled by disease or infirmity. *Her mother was a helpless invalid.* adj., 1. disabled by disease or infirmity. *The accident left her invalid.* 2. not valid; null; void; having no validity or force. *The judge declared the contract invalid.*

invalidate (in val'i dāt') v.t., to render invalid; deprive of binding force or legal efficacy; nullify. *The annulment will invalidate the marriage.*

invective (in vek'tiv) n., vehement denunciation; violent censure or reproach; abuse; diatribe. *He hurled invective at the lazy worker.*

inveigh (in vā') v.i., to make a verbal attack; utter or write vehement denunciation or rebuke; rail. *The senators will inveigh against the opposition's plan.*

inveigle (in vē'gəl, -vā'gəl) v.t., to mislead by deception; entice into violation of duty, propriety, or self-interest; beguile; lure; decoy. *He inveigled her into buying the worthless land.*

investiture (in ves'ti chər) n., act of investing, as with possession, power, or title; formal bestowal or presentation. *His investiture took place at Caernarvon Castle.*

inveterate (in vet'ər it) adj., firmly established by long continuance; deep-rooted; habitual, confirmed. *The inveterate bachelor was aware of her trap.*

invidious (in vid'ē əs) adj., causing or prompting envious dislike, discontent, or resentment; repugnant. *Mary was hurt by his invidious preference for Susan.*

invigorating (in vig'ə rā'ting) adj., giving vigor, life, and energy; strengthening; enlivening. *Exercise is invigorating.*

invincible (in vin'sə bəl) adj., incapable of being conquered or subdued. *For centuries the British Navy was invincible.*

inviolate (in vī'ə lit, -lāt') adj., not violated; secure against violation or impairment. *The young couple felt their love was inviolate.*

invocation (in'və kā'shən) n., 1. act of summoning or petitioning for aid. *The Coast Guard responded to his radioed invocation.* 2. opening prayer in a religious service invoking divine blessing. *The congregation was seated after the invocation.*

invoke (in vōk') v.t., to address in supplication; call on for protection or aid; pray for. *She tried to invoke the court's mercy.*

invulnerable (in vul'nər ə bəl) adj., incapable of being harmed. *The man was invulnerable to our threats.*

ionosphere (ī on'ə sfēr') n., that part of the earth's atmosphere that contains free electrically charged particles, or ions, by means of which radio waves are transmitted around the earth. *Fluorocarbons may damage the ionosphere.*

iota (ī ō'tə) n., very small quantity; jot. *I would not sacrifice one iota of his esteem.*

irascible (ī ras'ə bəl) adj., easily provoked or inflamed with anger; touchy; testy; peppery. *The wasp is an irascible insect.*

irate (ī'rāt, ī rāt') adj., excited to anger; angry; enraged; incensed. *The irate woman demanded her money back.*

irksome (ûrk'səm) adj., causing annoyance or discomfort; wearisome; tedious. *She tried to avoid the irksome task.*

ironic (ī ron'ik) adj., pertaining to or characterized by irony. *It was ironic that they should become friends after the separation.*

irony (ī'rə nē, ī'ər-) n., 1. expression of a meaning opposite to or other than the words used; covert sarcasm. *She did not miss the irony of his compliment.* 2. occurrence or result the opposite of what might be expected; contradictory outcome. *It was with a sense of irony that he turned down the long-sought position.*

irrational (i rash'ə nəl) adj., illogical; unreasonable; contrary to reason. *He felt an irrational moment of panic.*

irreconcilable (i rek'ən sī'lə bəl, i rek'ən sī-') adj., incapable of reconciliation or adjustment; incompatible.

They were divorced on the grounds of irreconcilable differences.

irrefutable (i ref′yə tə bəl, ir′i fyōo′tə bəl) adj., incapable of being refuted or disproved; indisputable; unquestionable. *The prosecution was looking for an irrefutable argument.*

irrelevant (i rel′ə vənt) adj., not applicable or pertinent. *You are wasting time on irrelevant details.*

irreparable (i rep′ər ə bəl) adj., incapable of being repaired, rectified, or restored; permanently broken. *They suffered irreparable damage in the fall.*

irrepressible (ir′i pres′ə bəl) adj., incapable of being repressed, restrained, or controlled. *She tried to quiet the irrepressible children.*

irresistible (ir′i zis′tə bəl) adj., incapable of being resisted or opposed. *The little boy's charm was irresistible.*

irresolute (i rez′ə lōot′) adj., not firm in purpose; given to doubt or hesitation; vacillating; faltering. *The irresolute youth could not choose a career.*

irreverent (i rev′ər ənt) adj., deficient in veneration or respect. *The irreverent boy mimicked the priest's stammer.*

irrevocable (i rev′ə kə bəl) adj., not capable of being recalled, repealed, or annulled. *She regretted her irrevocable, angry words.*

irrigation (ir′ə gā′shən) n., act of watering or moistening, esp. mechanical distribution of water over the surface of land to promote the growth of plants. *They hoped to make the desert fertile through irrigation.*

irritating (ir′i tā′tiñg) adj., causing irritation; vexing; provoking. *The smoky air was irritating to their eyes.*

irritation (ir′i tā′shən) n., 1. impatient or angry excitement; annoyance; vexation. *His snoring was a nightly irritation.* 2. physical pain or discomfort caused or increased by some outside agent. *The tight collar caused irritation around his neck.*

isthmus (is′məs) n., narrow strip of land bordered by water and connecting two larger bodies of land, as two continents, a continent and a peninsula, or two parts of an island. *A canal was built at the isthmus of Panama.*

italics (i tal′iks, ī tal′-) n. pl., print type in which the letters are slanted to the right. *The interpolated words are printed in italics.*

itemize (ī′tə mīz′) v.t., to state by items; give the particulars of; list. *The waiter will itemize the bill.*

itinerant (ī tin′ər ənt, i tin′-) adj., traveling from place to place; wandering, esp., traveling a circuit professionally or in the discharge of duty. *The itinerant preacher visited three towns a week.*

itinerary (ī tin′ə rer′ē, i tin′-) n., plan of travel; list of places to be included in a journey. *Her itinerary included Philadelphia, New York, and Boston.*

Jj

jaded (jā′did) adj., worn out by experience; worldly; cynical. *The jaded woman sought new experiences.*

jargon ((jär′gən, -gon) n., language peculiar to a sect, profession, art, or science; professional slang. *She was fluent in legal jargon.*

jaundice (jôn′dis, jän′-) n., 1. diseased condition in which bile pigments in the blood cause a yellowing of the skin and the whites of the eyes. *Jaundice is often a symptom of liver disease.* 2. negative state of mind or feeling that colors one's view or disorders one's judgment. *Jealousy was the jaundice that poisoned her mind.* v.i., to affect with jaundice; color the mind or judgment negatively; poison; taint. *Envy jaundiced their friendship.*

jaundiced (jôn′dist, jän′-) adj., 1. yellowed by bile pigments in the blood. *The doctor was worried by her jaundiced appearance.* 2. colored negatively in the mind or feelings; poisoned; tainted; sour. *She was depressed by his jaundiced world view.*

jaunty (jôn′tē, jän′-) adj., gay and sprightly in manner, appearance, or action; sporty; perky; stylish. *She bought a jaunty little spring hat.*

jeer (jēr) v.t., to make malicious fun of; scoff; mock; sneer. *The children jeer at her clumsiness.*

jeopardize (jep′ər dīz′) v.t., to expose to peril or hazard; risk; endanger. *You jeopardize your life by smoking in bed.*

jetsam (jet′səm) n., goods, cargo, or wreckage cast into the sea. *Flotsam is floating wreckage, whereas jetsam is thrown overboard deliberately.*

jettison (jet′i sən, -zən) v.t., to cast off a weight or encumbrance, as from a plane or ship; discard. *The rocket is about to jettison its second stage.*

jingoism (jiñg′gō iz′əm) n., extreme nationalism or chauvinism, esp. an aggressive, belligerent foreign policy. *The United Nations opposes jingoism in its members.*

jocose (jō kōs′) adj., given to jesting; merry; joking; of the nature of a joke or jest; funny; humorous. *The jocose gentleman enlivened the dinner party.*

jocular (jok′yə lər) adj., given to jesting; jocose; mirthful; sportive. *The practical joker wore a jocular expression.*

jog (jog) n., irregularity in a route; zigzag. *Elm Street makes a little jog at the town square.* v.t., to spur into activity; to remind. *She jogged my memory about the dinner party tonight.* v.i., to run at a slow, easy pace; trot; esp., to run as a healthful exercise or sport. *He plans to jog 5 miles every day.*

jonquil (joñg′kwil, jon′-) n., perennial bulbous spring plant bearing white or pale yellow, fragrant flowers. *The jonquil is a harbinger of spring.*

jostle (jos′əl) v.t., to push or crowd against so as to render unsteady; elbow. *Don't jostle her while she's holding the tray.*

jubilant (jōō′bə lənt) adj., expressing joy; joyful; rejoicing; exultant; triumphant. *She was jubilant over her business success.*

jubilee (jōō′bə lē′, jōō′bə lē′) n., festive celebration, esp. of a 25-, 50-, or 75-year anniversary. *They celebrated their silver jubilee last week.*

judgment ((juj′mənt) n., 1. faculty or process of analyzing and comparing facts or elements and forming an opinion. *The scholarship committee thought he demonstrated sound judgment.* 2. result of judging; opinion; esp., a legal opinion or decision. *The court will announce its judgment today.*

153

judicial (jōō dish′əl) adj., pertaining to the administration of justice; proper to a court of law; consisting of or resulting from legal inquiry or judgment. *His judicial appointment was approved today.*

judicious (jōō dish′əs) adj., having or exercising sound judgment; carefully considered or planned; prudent; discreet. *He complimented her on her judicious use of time.*

juggernaut (jug′ər nôt′) n., massive force that crushes whatever is in its way. *She rose like a juggernaut up the executive ladder.*

jugular (jug′yə lər, jōō′gyə-) adj., pertaining to the throat, or to the jugular vein. *The wolf lunged for the lamb's jugular vein.*

junction (jungk′shən) n., place or point of union or contact; esp., the point where two or more lines of any kind connect. *The town lay at the junction of two rivers.*

juncture (jungk′chər) n., point in time, esp., a time rendered critical or important by a concurrence of circumstances. *At this juncture, with a new job and a new home, she missed her old friends.*

junket (jung′kit) n., 1. sweet dessert made with rennet-curded milk. *The children love strawberry junket.* 2. festive outing; excursion taken mainly for pleasure or entertainment, esp., a public official's journey at the public's expense. *The congressman regarded the junket as a perquisite of office.*

junta (hōōn′tə, hōōn′-, jun′-, hun′-) n., consultative, political, or legislative assembly, specifically one that takes control of a country after a revolution or coup. *The new country was ruled by a military junta.*

jurisdiction (jōōr′is dik′shən) n., judicial power or authority; right of making and enforcing laws and regulations; domain or territory over which the authority of a country, state, court, or judge extends. *The town council's jurisdiction was bounded by the city limits.*

jurisprudence (jōōr′is prōōd′ᵊns) n., science or philosophy of law; systematic knowledge of the laws, customs, and rights of people in a state or community; body of laws existing in a given state or nation. *The lawyers debated the fine point of jurisprudence.*

justifiable (jus′tə fī′ə bəl, jus′tə fī′-) adj., capable of being justified or proved to be just or true; defensible; warrantable. *Under the circumstances, her anger was justifiable.*

juxtaposition (juk′stə pə zish′ən) n., act of placing or the state of being placed side by side or in close relation. *The juxtaposition of black and white created an interesting effect.*

Kk

kaleidoscope (kə lī′də skōp′) n., 1. optical instrument creating and exhibiting, by reflection of bits of colored glass, an endless variety of beautiful colors and symmetrical forms. *The kaleidoscope was the child's favorite toy.* 2. variegated and changing pattern, scene, or series of effects. *The brochure promised a kaleidoscope of social activities.*

Kamikaze (kä′mə kä′zē) adj., pertaining to a Japanese air attack corps ordered to make a suicidal crash on a target; hence, (l.c.) suicidal; self-destructive; self-sacrificing. *He began a kamikaze course of pill-popping to stay awake during finals.*

karat (kar′ət) n., twenty-fourth part; specifically used in expressing the fineness of gold when used as jewelry. *She selected a fourteen karat gold necklace.*

kayak (kī′ak) n., lightweight canoe having a covering of canvas or other material with an opening for the canoer. *He carried his kayak to the river for the race.*

keen (kēn) adj., 1. having a very sharp point or edge; sharp. *The keen blade cut easily through the meat.* 2. having a cutting or incisive character or effect; penetrating; vivid; intense; acute. *The keen wind cut through his jacket.* 3. characterized by quickness or acuteness of perception or thought. *Her keen insight brought her quickly to the real problem.*

kickback (kik′bak′) n., 1. sudden, violent reaction. *The lawnmower's kickback startled him.* 2. returned portion of a sum, esp. when arranged by unlawful or confidential agreement. *The commissioner expected a kickback from the contractor.*

kilowatt (kil′ə wot′) n., unit of electrical power equal to 1,000 watts. *The dam produces millions of kilowatts of energy.*

kindred (kin′drid) n., relatives by blood descent or marriage; relatives; kinfolk; family. *My kindred gathered together for Christmas.* adj., of related or similar origin or character; allied. *Their common experience proved them to be kindred souls.*

kleptomaniac (klep′tə mā′nē ak) n., one who neurotically and impulsively steals, esp. without economic need. *The kleptomaniac was referred for psychiatric counseling.*

knave (nāv) n., 1. false, deceitful person; one given to trickery; rogue; scoundrel. *The knave absconded with her purse.* 2. playing card with a servant figured on it, in sequence between a ten and a queen; jack. *He put down a run of knave, queen, king, and ace.*

knoll (nōl) n., small, rounded hill; top or crown of a hill. *We climbed up the knoll to the cottage.*

kosher (kō′shər) adj., 1. conforming to the requirements of Jewish law. *She keeps a kosher kitchen.* 2. generally ethical or customary. *Cheating on exams isn't kosher.*

kowtow (kou′tou′, -tou′, kō′-) v.i., to fawn; be obsequious; cringe. *The natives kowtow before their emperor.*

kudos (kōō′dōz, -dōs, -dos, kyōō′-) n., glory; fame; renown. *He accepted the kudos of the scientific world.*

155

Ll

laboratory (lab′rə tōr′ē, -tôr′ē, lab′ər ə-; *Brit.* lə bor′ə tə rē, -ə trē) n., place fitted with equipment for analysis or experimental study in any department of science, or for the manufacture of products related to any such science; broadly, any place of experimentation. *The samples were analyzed in the laboratory.*

labyrinth (lab′ə rinth) n., 1. intricate combination of passages; maze. *The labyrinth was formed by high hedges and ornamental shrubs.* 2. anything characterized by intricate turnings and windings; perplexity. *Psychology deals with the labyrinth of the human mind.*

lacerate (las′ə rāt′) v.t., to mangle; tear apart violently; torture. *She lacerated her face in the fall.*

lachrymose (lak′rə mōs′) adj., 1. tearful. *The lachrymose child apologized for breaking the vase.* 2. mournful; doleful; affecting; causing tears. *We were moved by the lachrymose aria.*

lackadaisical (lak′ə dā′zi kəl) adj., listless; languid; half-hearted. *He had only a lackadaisical interest in his job.*

lackey (lak′ē) n., low servant; servile follower. *He rose rapidly from the position of office lackey.*

lackluster (lak′lus′tər) adj., lacking luster or brightness; dull. *The invalid gave him a lackluster smile.*

laconic (lə kon′ik) adj., expressing much in few words; terse; pithy; concise. *The laconic ransom note betrayed no clues.*

lacuna (lə kyoo′nə) n., vacancy caused by the loss, omission, or obliteration of something necessary to continuity or completeness; gap; hiatus. *The copy editor queried the lacuna in the manuscript.*

lagoon (lə goon′) n., shallow body of water, such as a pond, channel, or sound, bordering on a larger body of water. *A sand bar separates the open sea from the lagoon.*

laissez faire (les′ā fâr′; *Fr.* le sā feʀ′) doctrine of noninterference with individual freedom of action, esp. in government or political economy. *The entrepreneur prefers a laissez faire economy.*

laity (lā′i tē) n., those outside of or unskilled in a particular profession, art, or science, as opposed to those belonging to it. *Translate this scientific journal into English the laity can understand.*

lambaste (lambast) (lam bāst′) v.t., to beat severely; thrash; blast. *The protesters lambasted him with catcalls.*

lamentable (lam′ən tə bəl, lə men′tə-) adj., arousing or deserving sorrow; grievous; pitiful; sad; miserable. *She commiserated with him over his lamentable disability.*

laminated (lam′ə nā′tid) adj., composed of thin layers firmly bonded together, as with resin or plastic. *Plywood is made of laminated wood.*

lampoon (lam poon′) n., sarcastic and usually humorous writing aimed at the character, actions, or habits of a person or institution; sarcastic diatribe; humorous abuse; personal satire. *The lampoon caricatured the law professor.* v.t., to ridicule as in a lampoon. *The skit will lampoon TV sportscasters.*

lance (lans, läns) n., long, slender spear used as a weapon or to kill whales. *The knight lowered his lance to charge.* v.t., to pierce with a lance or any sharp instrument. *The doctor had to lance the abscess.*

landmark (land′märk′) n., 1. specific or prominent object marking a locality or serving as a guide. *The Eiffel Tower is* *a familiar landmark.* 2. distinguishing characteristic or event that marks a turning point, or a point in progress or transition. *The Supreme Court's decision was a civil rights landmark.*

languid (lang′gwid) adj., drooping from weakness or fatigue; indisposed to exertion; heavy; sluggish; listless; torpid. *The tropical heat made us languid.*

languish (lang′gwish) v.i., to become weak or feeble; dwindle; fall off or fail; droop; wither; fade. *The fern began to languish in the sun.*

lank (langk) adj., 1. slim; lean; gaunt. *The basketball player was tall and lank.* 2. straight and flat. *The permanent gave body to her thin, lank hair.*

lapse (laps) n., fall; continued falling off or away; passing away; gradual descent; failure or mistake; slip. *There is a lapse in my memory about that evening.* v.i., 1. to fall; slip; pass away, esp. slowly or by degrees. *The conversation lapsed into a comfortable silence.* 2. fail in duty or conduct. *The security guard's attention lapsed and allowed the thief to get away.* 3. to pass from one proprietor to another. *This scholarship will lapse if your grades are unacceptable.*

larceny (lär′sə nē) n., taking and carrying away of another's personal goods with the felonious intent of converting them to the taker's own use; theft. *Petty larceny and grand larceny are distinguished by statute according to the value of the stolen property.*

largess (lär jes′, lär′jis) n., 1. innate generosity. *She was blessed with a largess of talent.* 2. ostentatious generosity to or as if to an inferior. *The servants thanked the master for his largess.*

laryngitis (lar′ən jī′tis) n., inflammation of the larynx, often causing temporary loss of voice. *She had laryngitis and could only whisper.*

larynx (lar′ingks) n., part of the windpipe in which vocal sound is made and modulated and which contains the vocal cords. *The pubescent boy's voice change is due to the rapid growth and change of the larynx.*

lascivious (lə siv′ē əs) adj., lustful; lewd; lecherous; wanton. *He cast a lascivious glance at the voluptuous woman.*

lassitude (las′i tood′, -tyood′) n., languor of body or mind; weariness. *Lassitude is a symptom of mononucleosis.*

latent (lāt′ənt) adj., hidden; concealed; dormant or undeveloped. *He discovered a latent talent for drawing.*

lateral (lat′ər əl) adj., of or pertaining to the side; situated at, proceeding from, or directed to a side; sideways. *By a smooth, lateral movement the skater reached her side.*

latex (lā′teks) n., milklike fluid occurring in many plants, used to make rubber; also, a synthetic rubber or plastic used in paint and adhesives. *The latex was shipped from port to the tire factory.*

latitude (lat′i tood′, -tyood′) n., 1. wide scope or range; freedom from rules or limits. *He gave his son a wide latitude in his choice of college.* 2. total curvature of a meridian between the equator and a point north or south of it; angular distance of a point on the earth from the equator; place or region as marked by parallels of latitude. *Tropical plants cannot survive in a northern latitude.*

laudable (lô′də bəl) adj., praiseworthy; commendable. *Generosity and humility are laudable qualities.*

lavish (lav′ish) v.t., to spend or bestow profusely; shower. *The critics lavish her with praise.* adj., profuse; extravagant; unrestrained; superabundant. *He spared no expense for her lavish wedding.*

lax (laks) adj., 1. not firm in texture, consistency, or tension; slack; loose; soft. *The horse has a soft mouth, so use a lax rein.* 2. lacking vigor, strength, or discipline; remiss. *They didn't obey their lax father.*

laxative (lak′sə tiv) n., substance that relieves constipation by relaxing the intestines. *Prunes are a natural laxative.*

layette (lā et′) n., complete outfit for a newborn baby, including garments, cradle or bassinet, and bedding. *The*

leach

shower gifts completed the baby's lay-ette.

leach (lēch) v., to wash or drain away by percolation of water; remove soluble elements by percolation. *The rains leach minerals from the gravelly soil.*

lean-to (lēn'tōō') n. (and adj.), building whose rafters or supports lean upon or against another building or a wall. *The greenhouse is a glass lean-to against the garage.*

lecherous (lech'ər əs) adj., sensual; lewd; lustful; lascivious. *The girl was wary of the lecherous man.*

lectern (lek'tərn) n., elbow-height, slanted-top desk from which a speaker delivers a speech or lecture. *He placed his notes on the lectern and began.*

leech (lēch) n., 1. aquatic, parasitic, blood-sucking worm once used medicinally. *The doctor applied the leech to his chest.* 2. one who hangs on to or takes advantage of another. *The leech still lives with his parents.* v.i., to drain the blood or substance out of; to attach oneself like a leech. *They leeched off their relatives in Florida for two months.*

leer (lēr) n., significant side glance; dirty look; lustful stare. *The miller intercepted the tailor's leer at his wife.* v.i., to give a sideways, significant look; to stare lewdly. *The rowdy youths love to leer at passing girls.*

leeway (lē'wā') n., allowable variation; margin of freedom. *The inheritance gave them some leeway in their budget.*

left wing (left'wing') radical or leftist part of a group. *The left wing will be represented in the election.* adj., extremely liberal politically; radical. *Her left-wing position angered her conservative father.*

legacy (leg'ə sē) n., money or other property left by will; inheritance; business received by another to execute; commission. *Her legacy from her father was a love of music.*

legion (lē'jən) n., large military force or army; great multitude; extraordinary number. *She tried to eradicate the legion of cockroaches.*

legitimize (li jit'ə mīz') v.t., to make le-gitimate or lawful; to give legal status or authority to, esp. to invest an illegitimate child with the rights of a legitimate child or lawful heir. *He married her to legitimize their child.*

leisure (lē'zhər, lezh'ər) n. (and adj.), free or spare time; opportunity for relaxation; convenient opportunity. *Don't rush; read it at your leisure.*

lenient (lē'nē ənt, lēn'yənt) adj., acting or disposed to act without rigor or severity; mild; generous; gentle; merciful. *She tried to be lenient with the troubled youth.*

lesbian (lez'bē ən) n., female homosexual. *Sappho was a famous lesbian.* adj., female homosexuality. *The lesbian community was larger than anyone knew.*

lesion (lē'zhən) n., wound or injury; abnormal change in the structure of an organ or other part. *The dermatologist lanced his lesion.*

lessee (le sē') n., one who holds or is granted a lease; tenant. *If the lessee breaks the lease, he forfeits his security deposit.*

lessor (les'ôr, le sôr') n., one who grants a lease to a tenant. *The lessor is responsible for normal maintenance of the apartment.*

lethal (lē'thəl) adj., pertaining to or capable of causing death; deadly; fatal. *The lethal gas leaked from the storage tank.*

lethargic (lə thär'jik) adj., sluggish or drowsy; dull; torpid; slow. *The medicine made him too lethargic to drive.*

lethargy (leth'ər jē) n., state of prolonged inactivity or torpor; sluggishness; dullness; stupor. *She tried to rouse the unemployed man from his lethargy.*

leviathan (li vī'ə thən) n., 1. great or monstrous marine animal or oceanic ship. *Moby Dick is a famous leviathan.* 2. anything of vast or huge size, such as a ship. *The leviathan sailed from its home port yesterday.*

levity (lev'i tē) n., lightness of spirit or temper; mirth; cheerfulness; frivolity. *In the face of his misfortune, her levity was unbecoming.*

lewd (lo͞od) adj., lustful; wanton; lascivious; lecherous. *He was embarrassed by her lewd remarks.*

lexicographer (lek′sə kog′rə fər) n., one who compiles a lexicon or dictionary. *The lexicographer compiled an explanation of symbols used in the dictionary.*

lexicon (lek′sə kon′, -kən) n., collection of the words of a language and their definitions; dictionary; wordbook. *Samuel Johnson wrote the first lexicon of the English language.*

liaison (lē′ā zôn′, lē′ə zon′, -zən; lē ā′zən, -zon; *Fr.* lye zôɴ′) n., 1. bond of union; connection; entanglement, esp. an illicit affair. *He pursued a liaison with the famous courtesan.* 2. one who aids communication between two parties or group; contact. *The congressional liaison set up the meeting.*

libation (lī bā′shən) n., drink, esp. one poured as an offering; beverage; alcoholic drink. *Everyone downed the celebratory libation.*

libel (lī′bəl) n., defamation; defamatory remark or act; malicious misrepresentation; publication or action injurious to one's reputation; crime of libel. *Your news story may constitute libel.* v.t., to attempt to expose to public contempt by malicious or injurious misrepresentation; defame. *The author of the roman à clef libeled his former employer.*

libelous (lī′bə ləs) adj., of the nature of libel; defamatory. *The editor refused to print the libelous story.*

liberal (lib′ər əl, lib′rəl) n., 1. (cap.) member of a liberal political party. *The liberal chairs the committee.* 2. advocate of individual rights. *The liberal was horrified by the imposition of martial law.* adj., 1. free from narrow limitations; of wide scope or range; comprehensive. *She received a liberal arts education.* 2. free in views or opinions; broadminded; not bigoted or intolerant; advocating personal, political, or religious liberty. *The liberal thinker told her to dress as she pleased.* 3. free in giving; generous; bountiful. *Her uncle made a liberal contribution to the college.*

liberalism (lib′ər ə liz′əm, lib′rə-) n., 1. political philosophy based on belief in the innate goodness of humanity, individual freedom, progress, and the protection of political and civil liberties. *Rousseau helped to define some aspects of liberalism.* 2. economic theory of individual freedom from restraint, a free, self-regulating, competitive market, and the gold standard. *Big corporations favor economic liberalism.*

libertine (lib′ər tēn′, -tin) n., one who is not restrained by conventions of religion or morality, esp. one who leads a dissolute, licentious life; rake. *He forbade his daughter to see the libertine.* adj., unrestrained by conventions of religion or morality; free thinking; dissolute; licentious. *He disapproved of Mark's libertine way of life.*

libidinous (li bid′ᵊnəs) adj., relating to the libido; characterized by lust or lewdness; having an eager appetite for sexual indulgence. *The libidinous young woman cruises the singles bars.*

libido (li bē′dō, -bī′dō) n., emotional or psychic drive or energy coming from basic, subconscious biological urges; sexual drive. *The teenager's libido should not be underestimated.*

libretto (li bret′ō) n., text of a musical work such as an opera or oratorio. *You will enjoy the opera more if you read the libretto first.*

licentious (lī sen′shəs) adj., unrestrained by law, religion, or morality; loose; dissolute; libertine; libidinous. *He warned his daughter against the licentious young man.*

lien (lēn, lē′ən) n., right of a party to legal possession of property belonging to another party until a debt or demand is discharged; mortgage. *The bank holds a lien on my car.*

lieu (lo͞o) n., place; stead. *The waiter suggested fish in lieu of the special.*

lilting (lilt′iñg) adj., sprightly, lively, and smooth, as a song; cheerful; tripping; buoyant. *He couldn't get the lilting melody out of his head.*

limbo (lim′bō) n., 1. supposed borderland of hell, the abode of those who have not received grace but yet do not deserve the punishment of hell. *She prayed the unbaptized infant would not be relegated to limbo.* 2. state in between; transition. *Their relationship was in limbo during the separation.*

limerick (lim′ər ik) n., humorous poem consisting of 5 usually anapestic lines in the rhyme scheme AABBA, with lines 1, 2, and 5 having 3 feet and lines 3 and 4 having 2 feet. *There was a young rake from L.A. Who attempted a limerick one day. He counted the lines And came up with the rhymes But he just couldn't make it risqué.*

limitation (lim′i tā′shən) n., 1. act of fixing or imposing a limit or restriction. *Our limitation took the form of a curfew.* 2. restraining condition; defining circumstance. *Money placed a severe limitation on their itinerary.* 3. statutory time period after which a legal action cannot be brought to court. *The statute of limitations expired on his offense.*

limpid (lim′pid) adj., characterized by clearness or transparency; translucent; clear; lucid; serene. *They could see the bottom of the limpid lake.*

lineal (lin′ē əl) adj., proceeding in a direct or unbroken line; hereditary; pertaining to direct descent. *He is a lineal descendant of Woodrow Wilson.*

lineament (lin′ē ə mənt) n., outline or contour of an object; hence, a particular physical feature or characteristic, distinguishing quality; feature. *The artist studied the lineaments of her face.*

linear (lin′ē ər) adj., pertaining to or composed of a line; relating to length only; specifically involving measurement in one dimension only. *The linear distance is not far, but it's all uphill.*

lingo (ling′gō) n., language peculiar to an individual or profession; dialect; jargon. *The islanders' lingo was barely understood on the mainland.*

linguistics (ling gwis′tiks) n., study of human languages and their elements, esp. the origin and history of words. *The professor of linguistics loves to discuss ancient languages.*

liquefy (lik′wə fī′) v., to make or become liquid. *Ice liquefies as it melts.*

liquidation (lik′wi dā′shən) n., act of squaring accounts or paying debts; conversion of assets into cash. *Most of the estate went to the liquidation of his debts.*

lisp (lisp) n., speech impediment or problem, in which the letters *s* and *z* are pronounced as *th*. *The speech therapist helped cure her of her lisp.* v.i., to pronounce the letters *s* and *z* as *th*. *Many children lisp because of orthodontal problems.*

lissome (lis′əm) adj., limber; lithe; supple; flexible; nimble. *The dancer was as lissome as a willow.*

listless (list′lis) adj., indifferent to one's surroundings; languid and inattentive; careless; indolent. *The divorce made him listless, even despondent.*

litany (lit′ʰnē) n., solemn prayer of supplication; resonant or repetitive song or recital; chant. *She listened to her familiar litany of woes.*

literal (lit′ər əl) adj., following the letter or exact words; free from variation of meaning; exact; precise; matter-of-fact; unimaginative. *The idiom is comical in literal translation.*

literally (lit′ər ə lē) adv., according to the strict import of the words; exactly. *The strict constructionist interprets the U.S. Constitution literally.*

literate (lit′ər it) adj., 1. having a knowledge of letters; possessing education; able to read and write. *The backward student is barely literate.* 2. learned. *His literate review excited more interest than the work itself.*

lithe (lith) adj., easily bent; supple; graceful. *It was a pleasure to watch the gymnast's lithe movements.*

litigation (lit′ə gā′shən) n., act or process of carrying on a suit in a court of law; judicial contest. *They settled out of court to avoid lengthy litigation.*

liturgy (lit′ər jē) n., appointed forms for the rites and ceremonies of public worship. *The psalm is part of the Christian liturgy.*

livid (liv′id) adj., 1. darkened or discolored as by bruising; black-and-blue. *The blow caused a livid bruise on her arm.* 2. deathly pale, esp. from rage or embarrassment. *The store owner is livid about the vandalism.*

loathe (lōth) v.t., to dislike greatly; hate; feel disgust at; have an extreme aversion to. *I loathe even the smell of liver.*

lobbyist (lob′ē ist) n., one who attempts in an organized and sustained way to influence the votes of legislators. *The lobbyist prepared material for the senators' consideration.*

locution (lō kyōō′shən) n., form, mode, or art of speaking; phraseology. *The teacher tried to refine the farm boy's locution.*

lode (lōd) n., deposit of a mineral or ore in a regular, confined vein; abundant store; treasure. *The lode was exhausted after twenty years of mining.*

lodestar (lōd′stär′) n., star that serves as a guide, esp. the North Star. *The lodestar gave the sailor his bearings.* 2. guide. *His aunt was his moral lodestar.*

logistics (lō jis′tiks) n., movement and supplying of the military forces and all arrangements and strategies necessary for its campaigns; broadly, the preparations and arrangements for an event. *The committee will meet to discuss the logistics of the parade.*

loiter (loi′tər) v.i., to linger; be unduly slow in moving; delay; spend time idly. *The child was told not to loiter on his way home.*

longevity (lon jev′i tē) n., 1. unusually prolonged life or existence; length or duration of life. *Heredity is probably the biggest factor in longevity.* 2. seniority. *After twenty years she holds the record for office longevity.*

longitude (lon′ji tōōd′, -tyōōd′) n., angle at the pole contained between two meridians or north-south arcs, one of which, called the first or prime meridian, passes through an established zero meridian point, from which the angle is measured. *Longitudes are reckoned east and west from the 0° meridian to 180° in arc and 12 hours in time.*

loquacious (lō kwā′shəs) adj., talkative;

garrulous. *The loquacious old man kept her on the phone for an hour.*

lout (lout) n., awkward, ungainly person; bumpkin; buffoon. *The lout danced on her feet more than the floor.*

L S D, n., abbreviation for lysergic acid diethylamide, a crystalline chemical compound used in the study of schizophrenia and other mental disorders; also used as a hallucinogen; (slang) acid. *He experimented with LSD in the late 1960s.*

lubricate (lōō′brə kāt′) v.t., to make smooth or slippery; supply or smear with a substance, such as oil or grease, to reduce friction. *Please lubricate that squeaky hinge.*

lucid (lōō′sid) adj., 1. clear; transparent. *They sealed the windows with lucid plastic.* 2. clear; easily understood. *I enjoy her crisp, lucid prose.*

lucrative (lōō′krə tiv) adj., gainful; highly profitable. *The law is a lucrative profession.*

ludicrous (lōō′də krəs) adj., laughable from singularity or grotesqueness; causing sportive laughter or ridicule; absurd. *We all laughed at his ludicrous suggestion.*

lugubrious (lōō gōō′brē əs, -gyōō′-) adj., characterized by or causing mourning or sorrow; mournful; dejected; pitiful; dismal; melancholy. *A lugubrious wailing greeted the funeral procession.*

luminary (lōō′mə ner′ē) n., 1. notable person, outstanding in his or her field. *He is a luminary in the field of cancer research.* 2. something that gives off or reflects light. *They followed the luminary through the forest.*

luminous (lōō′mə nəs) adj., light-giving; illuminating; shining; radiant; lit up; illuminated; bright; brilliant. *The snowy field reflected the luminous moon.*

lunar (lōō′nər) adj., pertaining to the moon; affected by the influence of the moon. *They discussed the lunar effect on the tides.*

lunatic (lōō′nə tik) n., one who is insane. *The lunatic ran out right in front of the car.*

lurid (lōōr′id) adj., 1. bright; garish; glaring. *The room was lurid with the flash-*

ing of the police car's lights from out-side.   2.   gruesome;   horrifying; sensational. *The tabloid ran a lurid picture of the accident.*

luscious (lush′əs) adj., 1. very sweet, succulent, or savory; delicious; sweet or rich. *She served a luscious cherry pie.* 2. extremely delightful to the senses; enticingly delightful. *He asked the luscious blonde to have dinner with him.*

lush (lush) n., habitual drunk. *The lush lost control of the car.* adj., fresh, luxuriant, and juicy; abundant. *The tropical jungle was full of lush vegetation.*

lustrous (lus′trəs) adj., giving off luster or light; having a brilliant surface; highly polished; radiant; brilliant. *She brushed the chestnut horse's lustrous coat.*

luxury (luk′shə rē, lug′zhə-) n., free or extravagant indulgence in pleasure or gratification; not a necessity. *The wealthy man was accustomed to luxury.*

lymph (limf) n., colorless, alkaline fluid in animal bodies; diluted blood minus its red corpuscles. *The pierced ear oozed lymph for several days.*

Mm

macabre (mə kab′rə, -käb′) adj., pertaining to death; gruesome; ghastly; horrible. *The news account dwelt on the macabre accident.*

macadam (mə kad′əm) m., pavement or roadway surfaced with crushed stone according to a process invented by John L. Macadam (1756–1836); the broken stones used in such a pavement. *The car rolled smoothly down the macadam.*

macadamize (mə kad′ə mīz′) v.t., to pave with macadam. *The town voted to macadamize the old dirt road.*

macerate (mas′ə rāt′) v.t., to soften by soaking or by digestive fluids. *The stomach macerates food.*

Machiavellian (mak′ē ə vel′ē ən) adj., relating to or befitting Italian statesman Niccolò Machiavelli (1469–1527); unscrupulous; cunning; crafty. *The politician often resorted to Machiavellian tactics.*

machination (mak′ə nā sh̠ən, mash̠′) n., plot, scheme, or intrigue, usually with evil intent. *Much machination behind the scenes preceded the assassination attempt.*

mackintosh (mak′in tosh̠′) n., waterproof, rubberized outer garment. *My mackintosh came in handy during the storm.*

macramé (mak′rə mā′) n., kind of coarse lace or fringe made by tying ornamental knots in thread or cord. *Large hangings of macramé ornamented the walls.*

madras (mad′rəs, mə dras′, -dräs′) n., 1. type of cotton cloth interwoven with cords at intervals, usually of multicolored plaids or stripes. *The summer jacket was made of madras.* 2. brightly colored kerchief of cotton or silk worn around the head. *He wound the madras into a turban.*

madrigal (mad′rə gəl) n., 1. three-part song following a definite poetic pattern, usually based on the theme of love. *The madrigal reminded him of his youthful love.* 2. 16th-century vocal piece of complex polyphonic form. *The singer's training was well displayed in the madrigal.*

maelstrom (māl′strəm) n., powerful whirlpool, or turbulent state of affairs resembling a violent whirlpool. *The girl was propelled into the maelstrom of political protest.*

maestro (mī′strō; *It.* mä es′tʀô) n., title of respect used to address or refer to a master of any art, esp. an eminent conductor, teacher, or composer of music. *Under the baton of Maestro Toscanini the orchestra rose to new heights.*

maggot (mag′ət) n., soft, legless larva of a fly or other insect; grub. *The garbage can was infested with maggots.*

magisterial (maj′i stēr′ē əl) adj., 1. pertaining to someone in authority; hence overbearing, imperious, as a master. *He fixed a magisterial glare on the offender.* 2. pertaining to an administrator known as a magistrate or to his office or tasks. *The official assumed her magisterial duties today.*

magnanimous (mag nan′ə məs) adj., showing a generosity in forgiveness; free from vindictiveness or resentment. *The general was noted for his magnanimous treatment of prisoners of war.*

magnate (mag′nāt, -nit) n., person of eminence, influence, or distinction in a particular field, esp. in some area of business. *The steel magnate was very influential in Washington.*

magnificence (mag nif′i səns) n., state or condition of being magnificent; grandeur; splendor; brilliancy. *She was overwhelmed by the magnificence of the ducal palace.*

magnify (mag′nə fī′) v.t., 1. to make greater; increase the size, amount, or extent of; enlarge; augment. *He tends to magnify his troubles.* 2. to cause to appear greater or more important; to exalt, praise, glorify. *Poets wrote verses to magnify the king.*

magniloquent (mag nil′ə kwənt) adj., relating to a style of elevated speech or writing that is somewhat pompous. *His magniloquent speech was unsuited to the informal gathering.*

magnitude (mag′ni tōōd′, -tyōōd′) n., size; extent; importance; significance. *They were surprised by the enormous magnitude of the pyramid.*

magnum (mag′nəm) n., large wine bottle holding about 2/5 of a gallon. *They celebrated with a magnum of champagne.*

magnum opus (mag′num ō′pus) great work, esp. the greatest achievement of an artist or writer. *Do you consider Hamlet Shakespeare's magnum opus?*

mahatma (mə hät′mə, -hat′-) n., one admired for wisdom or spiritual strength. *The mahatma helped him find contentment.*

maim (mām) v.t., to disable by wounding or mutilation; deprive of, or of the use of, a necessary constituent part. *A trapped animal may maim itself trying to get free.*

maître d'hôtel (mā′tər dō tel′, mā′trə-; *Fr.* me′tʀə dō tel′) headwaiter; majordomo. *The maître d'hôtel showed us to our table.*

maladjusted (mal′ə jus′tid) adj., badly or inadequately adjusted. *The maladjusted boy couldn't get used to the foster home.*

maladroit (mal′ə droit′) adj., not adroit or dextrous; inexpert; awkward. *His maladroit handling of the negotiations brought about the strike.*

malady (mal′ə dē) n., physical disorder or disease; sickness of any kind, esp. a chronic, deep-seated, or dangerous disease; any disordered state or condition. *Chronic insomnia is a difficult malady to treat.*

malaise (ma lāz′; *Fr.* mA lez′) n., discomfort; uneasiness, often a preliminary symptom of a serious malady. *A feeling of malaise preceded the attack of pneumonia.*

malapropism (mal′ə prop iz′əm) n., word misapplication, often with humorous effect; word so misapplied. *She laughed at his inadvertent malapropism.*

malapropos (mal′ap rə pō′) adj., inappropriate; out of place; inapt; unseasonable. *She regretted her malapropos remark.* adv., unsuitably; inopportunely. *He burst out malapropos with laughter.*

malaria (mə lâr′ē ə) n., 1. disease of humans transmitted by the bite of the Anopheles mosquito, which produces intermittent and recurring chills and fever. *He contracted malaria in Colombia.* 2. disease of birds or mammals caused by blood protozoans.

malcontent (mal′kən tent′) n., one who is discontented, esp. by government. *The malcontent refused to accept the new tax.* adj., dissatisfied; discontented. *The malcontent employee caused dissent in the union.*

malediction (mal′i dik′shən) n., evil statement or curse. *The three witches pronounced their malediction on Macbeth.*

malefactor (mal′ə fak′tər) n., 1. one who commits an offense against the law; criminal or felon. *The malefactor was sentenced to prison.* 2. one who does evil or injury to another. *Her malefactor caused her to lose her scholarship.*

maleficence (mə lef′i səns) n., 1. evil act or work. *The maleficence ruined their wedding.* 2. evil character. *Their father's maleficence made their home a prison.*

maleficent (mə lef′i sənt) adj., bringing about evil or harm. *The maleficent enemy looted the town.*

malevolent (mə lev′ə lənt) adj., pertaining to evil disposition toward another or others; wishing evil to others; rejoicing in another's misfortune; malicious; hostile. *His malevolent, spiteful nature has made him many enemies.*

malfeasance (mal fē′zəns) n., wrongdoing, esp. by someone in public office.

He resigned in the face of the charge of malfeasance.

malicious (mə li͟sh′əs) adj., 1. indulging in or feeling malice; harboring ill-will, enmity, or hostility; actively malevolent. *She was a malicious, gossipy neighbor.* 2. proceeding from extreme hatred or ill-will; dictated by malice. *The malicious report almost got him fired.*

malign (mə līn′) v.t., to speak evil of, esp. untruthfully; slander; defame; vilify. *He hit the man who tried to malign his sister's reputation.* adj., evil in nature; harboring violent hatred or enmity; malicious; baleful. *Growing up in a slum had a malign influence on his development.*

malignant (mə lig′nənt) adj., 1. disposed to inflict suffering or cause distress; extremely malevolent or inimical; virulently hostile; malicious. *Her struggle to survive left her with a malignant disposition.* 2. virulently harmful or mischievous; threatening great danger; pernicious in influence or effect. *The tumor was diagnosed as malignant.*

malinger (mə ling′gər) v.i., to feign illness, esp. in order to avoid duty; counterfeit disease. *He had a tendency to malinger when he drew latrine duty.*

malingerer (mə ling′gər ər) n., one who pretends to be sick in order to avoid work. *The chronic malingerer was finally fired.*

mall (môl, mäl, mal) n., 1. shaded walk or promenade, usually public. *They strolled leisurely on the mall.* 2. strip of paved or grassy land between two traffic lanes on roads, highways, or boulevards. *We waited on the mall for the light to change.* 3. open or covered passageway providing access to stores and reserved at stated times or permanently for pedestrian traffic only. *Let's go shopping in the mall.*

malleable (mal′ē ə bəl) adj., 1. capable of being shaped or extended by beating, rolling, or hammering. *Gold is a malleable metal.* 2. capable of being shaped by outside influence; yielding. *A child's mind is malleable.*

malnutrition (mal′no͞o tri͟sh′ən, -nyo͞o-) n., imperfect nutrition; defect of sustenance from imperfect assimilation of food. *Scurvy and rickets are diseases associated with malnutrition.*

malodorous (mal ō′dər əs) adj., pertaining to offensive odor. *She threw the malodorous socks into the hamper.*

malpractice (mal prak′tis) n., misbehavior; evil practice; practice contrary to established rules; specifically, failure of a professional person to render proper service. *They accused her of malpractice when the child didn't recover.*

makeshift (māk′shift′) n., expedient adopted to serve a present need; temporary substitute. *Flour-and-water paste had to be used as a makeshift.* adj., of the nature of a temporary expedient. *The large box was a makeshift table.*

mammal (mam′əl) n., any animal of the class *Mammalia*, having breasts to nourish their young, being more or less covered with hair, and (with the exception of monotremes) bearing live young.

mammoth (mam′əth) n., extinct species of elephant from the Pleistocene epoch having ridged molar teeth, long curving tusks, and hairy skin. adj., of great comparative size, like a mammoth; gigantic; colossal. *The mammoth corporation has branches all over the country.*

mandate (n. man′dāt, -dit; v. man′dāt) n., command; order, precept, or injunction; commission. *The governor felt he had a clear mandate to veto the legislation.* v.t., to administer or assign (a territory) under a mandate. *The United Nations mandated the territory to a member nation.*

mandatory (man′də tôr′ē, -tôr′ē) adj., of the nature of a mandate; containing a command or mandate; obligatory. *Attendance at the meeting is mandatory.* n., one to whom a command or charge is given; one who has received and holds a mandate to act for another; nation holding a mandate from the League of Nations. *France was the mandatory over Syria.*

mandible

mandible (man′də bəl) n., 1. in humans, the jawbone and related parts. *His mandible was broken during the fight.* 2. in birds, the upper and lower portions of the beak. *He held the seed in his mandible.* 3. mouth parts of any arthropod. *The lobster had a stone caught in his mandible.*

maneuver (mə nōō′vər) n., planned and regulated movement, particularly of troops or war vessels; adroit move or procedure; intrigue; stratagem. *The captain berthed the ship by a series of adept maneuvers.* v.t., to perform a maneuver or maneuvers; to employ intrigue or stratagem to effect a purpose. *He managed to maneuver the conversation around to his trip.*

mange (mānj) n., contagious parasitic disease of the skin that affects domestic animals and occasionally humans. *The inflamed, bare patches looked like mange.*

mania (mā′nē ə, mān′yə) n., 1. form of insanity; frenzy. *In his mania, he mistook the doctor for his enemy.* 2. craze; fad. *The auctioneer hoped to capitalize on the mania for Tiffany glass.*

maniacal (mə nī′ə kəl) adj., pertaining to madness; marked by or manifesting mania; insane; mad. *The driver's maniacal behavior frightened the passengers.*

manic-depressive (man′ik di pres′iv) adj., having a mental disorder characterized by alternating excitement and depression. *She was diagnosed as having a manic-depressive personality.* n., person suffering from this disorder. *Wild highs and lows typify the manic-depressive.*

manifest (man′ə fest′) n., 1. public declaration; open statement. *The manifest was tacked to the bulletin board.* 2. cargo list required by customs officials. *The manifest did not include the contraband items.* v.t., to make evident or understood; show plainly; exhibit. *The white flag was intended to manifest surrender.* adj., readily perceived or understood; obvious; apparent. *It was manifest foolishness to go out in the blizzard.*

manifestation (man′ə fe stā′shən) n., 1. act of showing to the eye or the mind. *The parade was a manifestation of their military power.* 2. in the occult, apparent appearance of spirit in material form. *They quaked at the manifestation of their dead uncle.*

manifesto (man′ə fes′tō) n., public proclamation of opinions and intentions, esp. of a government or political party. *The manifesto detailed their plans for a workers' revolution.*

manipulate (mə nip′yə lāt) v.t., 1. to handle or act on with the hands. *The sculptor began to manipulate the clay.* 2. to operate upon by contrivance or influence for specific purpose or advantage. *The accountant tried to manipulate the sales figures to conceal the losses.*

mannequin (man′ə kin) n., 1. person employed to exhibit clothing to customers; model. *She was the agency's best mannequin.* 2. representation of the human body used as a store window display, or by an artist, tailor or dressmaker. *A mannequin displayed the latest fall fashions.*

mannerism (man′ə riz′əm) n., peculiarity of manner or idiosyncrasy in deportment, speech, or execution. *He hoped it was just a mannerism and not a nervous disorder.*

mantilla (man til′ə, -tē′ə) n., woman's light veil or shawl worn over the head and/or shoulders, esp. in Latin countries. *The flamenco dancer swirled the mantilla from her shoulders.*

manufacture (man′yə fak′chər) n., process of mechanical or hand production of goods, esp. in system using division of labor. *Petroleum is used in the manufacture of plastics.* v.t., 1. to systematically make or fabricate by machine or hand. *They decided to manufacture the new toy.* 2. to simulate or invent. *A talented actor can manufacture emotion at will.*

mar (mär) v.t., 1. to deface or disfigure. *That hot dish will mar the table.* 2. to impair or render imperfect. *They feared the news would mar her performance.*

maraud (mə rôd′) v.t., to raid or plunder. *The mercenaries began to maraud the town.* v.i., to wander about looking for chances to raid and plunder. *The rebel bands were continually marauding across the area.*

marauder (mə rô′dər) n., rover, usually with a group, in search of plunder or booty. *The marauder and his band looted the countryside.*

margin (mär′jin) n., 1. space between edge of paper and printing, writing, or illustration. *The student made notes in the margin.* 2. allowance made for contingency, error, or change. *The race driver had only a split-second margin for error.* 3. in finance, collateral deposited as provision against loss on transactions made on account. *The margin is usually a percentage of the par value of a stock.*

marginal (mär′jə nəl) adj., 1. pertaining to a margin or border, drawn or printed on a page. *His marginal notes explicate the archaic words.* 2. bordering on two different territories, cultures, or states of consciousness. *The student is a marginal alcoholic.* 3. pertaining to the lowest requirements. *The high cost of production resulted in only marginal profits.*

marine (mə rēn′) n., member of a group of soldiers serving on shipboard, esp. a member of the U.S. Marine Corps. *The marines landed on the north coast.* adj., relating to the sea or navigation. *They record changes in the bay's marine life.*

marital (mar′i təl) adj., pertaining to marriage; matrimonial; connubial. *The couple discussed their marital problems with the counselor.*

maritime (mar′i tīm′) adj., 1. pertaining to the sea or its uses, esp. navigation. *She studied maritime law.* 2. bordering or near to the sea. *England was a maritime power.*

marquee (mär kē′) n., 1. awning or canopy. *They were married under the striped marquee.* 2. advertisement projecting over hotel or theater. *A new film was advertised on the marquee.*

marrow (mar′ō) n., 1. soft, interior bone tissue. *The disease attacked his bone marrow.* 2. pith of plants. *He cross-sectioned the twig to examine the marrow.* 3. inmost depths or essence of a thing or person; fundamental strength or vitality. *The marrow of his case rested on her testimony.*

marsupial (mär sōō′pē əl) n., any of several usually nonplacental mammals whose female members have abdominal pouches in which young are carried and nursed. *Kangaroos and opossums are marsupials.* adj., pertaining to a marsupial. *The marsupial bones are located in the animal's pelvis.*

martial (mär′shəl) adj., of or pertaining to war; of warlike character; military; warlike; soldierly. *The band gave a concert of martial music.*

martial law (mar′shal law′) law imposed by military forces when civil law enforcement agencies are unable to maintain order, or as applied in occupied territory. *The conquered countries were put under martial law.*

martinet (mär′tə net′, mär′tə net′) n., rigid disciplinarian, esp. in the military forces. *The martinet had his grandchildren behaving like little soldiers.*

masculine (mas′kyə lin) adj., 1. male; of manlike quality or character. *He thought smoking a masculine prerogative.* 2. pertaining to or constituting the gender of grammatical words or forms usually referring to males. *The French student mistakenly used the masculine form of the word.*

masochism (mas′ə kiz′əm, maz′-) n., sexual perversion in which gratification depends on physical pain, suffering, and humiliation; taste for suffering. *She imposed a self-discipline so strict it bordered on masochism.*

massacre (mas′ə kər) n., indiscriminate and cruel slaughter. *The raid resulted in the massacre of hundreds of civilians.* v.t., to kill with attendant circumstances of atrocity; butcher; slaughter, esp. of a large number of defenseless human beings at once. *The barbarians massacred the Roman citizens.*

mastectomy (ma stek′tə mē) n., surgical removal of the breast. *She underwent a mastectomy for a malignant tumor.*

masthead (mast′hed′, mäst′-) n., 1. top or head of the mast of a ship or vessel. *The sailor was sent to the masthead as a lookout.* 2. printed statement (usually on the editorial page) of a newspaper, magazine, etc., giving pertinent publication information. *The editor's name appeared on the masthead.*

masticate (mas′tə kāt′) v.t., to soften and break down by chewing, kneading, or otherwise pulverizing. *The inflamed gum made it painful for him to masticate his food.*

mastication (mas′tə kā′shən) n., 1. act of grinding food between the teeth; chewing. *Thorough mastication aids digestion.* 2. act of softening a substance for use. *The pulping machine masticated the wood chips.*

mastiff (mas′tif, mä′stif) n., one of a breed of large, stoutly built dogs having a deep chest and a short-haired coat of fawn or apricot or of brindled colors. *A fierce mastiff guarded the property.*

materialism (mə tēr′ē ə liz′əm) n., philosophical theory that physical matter is the only reality; any opinion or tendency based on purely material interests; devotion to material things or interests; neglect of spiritual for physical needs and considerations. *Philosophical materialism holds that matter and its motions constitute the universe.*

maternal (mə tûr′nəl) adj., 1. pertaining to a mother or to motherhood; motherly. *The landlady treated us with maternal kindness.* 2. imparted by or connected with one's mother. *She is my maternal grandmother.*

matriarch (mā′trē ärk′) n., woman who holds a position as head of a tribe (analogous to that of a patriarch); mother who is head of her family and descendants. *The tribe was headed by a powerful matriarch.*

matricide (ma′tri sīd′, mā′-) n., one who kills his or her mother; act of killing one's mother. *Lizzie Borden was accused of matricide.*

matriculate (mə trik′yə lāt′) v.t., to register or enroll. *The new school will matriculate a large freshman class.* v.i., to become a member by enrolling. *She will matriculate at Duke this fall.*

matrilineal (ma′trə lin′ē əl, mā′-) adj., relating to tracing one's maternal ancestry or inheritance. *My matrilineal chart includes a baroness and two countesses.*

matrix (mā′triks, ma′-) n., 1. that from which something new develops or originates. *The embryo grew well in the rich matrix.* 2. The natural substance that embeds rocks, metals, fossils, etc. *They cracked the matrix to extract the beautiful crystal.*

matron (mā′trən) n., 1. married woman, esp. as characterized by dignity and authority. *The matron took charge of the children.* 2. female head or superintendent of a prison, hospital, or other institution. *The matron admitted us to the visitors' room.*

maudlin (môd′lin) adj., excessively emotional or sentimental, often caused by drunkenness. *The bartender grew annoyed with the maudlin man.*

maul (môl) n., heavy wooden hammer or mallet. *The large maul drove the stakes into the ground.* v.t., to beat and bruise; mangle. *The bear began to maul its victim.*

mausoleum (mô′sə lē′əm, -zə-) n., large tomb; grand or stately sepulchral monument or edifice. *She was interred in the family mausoleum.*

mauve (mōv) n., reddish-purple dye derived from a sulphate of mauvein. *Mauve is derived from aniline.* adj., pale purple, like lilac or violet. *Her mauve dress glowed in the candlelight.*

maverick (mav′ər ik, mav′rik) n., 1. unbranded range animal. *They couldn't* *identify the maverick.* 2. independent individual; nonconformist. *The candidate was a maverick in his party.*

mavin (mā′vən) n., one with specialized expertise. *She was a baseball mavin.*

maw (mô) n., 1. throat, gullet, or stomach of an animal; crop or craw of a fowl. *The mouse disappeared into the maw of the owl.* 2. cavernous opening resembling a gaping mouth. *They walked into the maw of the cave.*

mawkish (mô′ kish) adj., insipid; sickeningly sentimental. *They laughed at the mawkish old valentine.*

maxim (mak′sim) n., pithy expression of a general or established rule or principle. *Mother had a maxim to cover every situation.*

mayhem (mā′hem, mā′əm) n., 1. willful dismemberment or other permanent harm. *The act of mayhem left her disfigured for life.* 2. senseless, violent damage. *They were aghast at the mayhem caused by the burglar.*

mea culpa (me′ä kōōl′pä; *Eng.* mē′ə kul′pə) Latin: through my fault; my fault; acknowledgement of personal fault or error. *The priest intoned "mea culpa" over his sins.*

mean (mēn) n., 1. middle point or state between extremes. *They sought a mean between caution and fear.* 2. average. *The national mean was $10,000.* v.t., 1. to have in mind; intend. *I mean you no harm.* 2. to signify, indicate, or import. *What can that signal mean?* 3. to mention or tell. *What do you mean by that?* 4. to have the value or importance of. *You mean the world to me.* v.i., to be minded or disposed. *She means well.* adj., 1. median; middle. *The mean age of the class was twenty.* 2. humble; common. *He was of mean yeoman stock.* 3. inferior; shabby. *The transients appeared a mean, motley group.*

meander (mē an′dər) n., winding course; winding or turning in a passage; maze; labyrinth. *The formal garden included an old-fashioned meander.* v.i., to proceed by winding and turning; make

frequent changes of course. *A small stream meanders through the property.*

meddlesome (med′əl səm) adj., given to meddling; apt to interpose in the affairs of others; intrusive. *They tried to avoid the meddlesome landlord.*

median (mē′dē ən) n., 1. medial or middle part. *The median was arrived at by the negotiators.* 2. middle number in a given numerical sequence. *Six is the median of the series 3, 6, 9.* 3. in geometry, line from a vertex of a triangle to the midpoint of the opposite side. *The median intersected the triangle.* adj., 1. pertaining to or situated in the middle. *The car swerved and struck the median divider.* 2. relating to or situated in the middle; average. *In the series 2, 4, 6, 4 is the median number.*

mediate (mē′dē āt′) v.t., to effect by intervention; reconcile; settle. *He managed to mediate a settlement.* v.i., to intervene or intercede. *She tried to mediate for the parents' group.*

mediator (mē′dē ā′tər) n., one who mediates or negotiates between two parties, esp. to bring about reconciliation. *The mediator managed to avert the threatened strike.*

medieval (mē′dē ē′vəl, med′ē-, mid′ē-, mid ē′vəl) adj., characteristic of the Middle Ages of Europe (c. 500–1500 A.D.). *We visited the medieval section of London.*

mediocre (mē′dē ō′kər, mē′dē ō′kər) adj., of moderate degree or quality; middling; indifferent; ordinary. *She rose to stardom despite a mediocre talent.*

mediocrity (mē′dē ok′ri tē) n., 1. character or state of being mediocre. *She worked to transcend the mediocrity around her.* 2. mediocre person. *She felt like a mediocrity compared to her talented brother.*

meditate (med′i tāt′) v.t., to contemplate; reflect. *She began to meditate on the need for change.* v.i., to engage in contemplation. *She wanted to meditate before dinner.*

meditation (med′i tā′shən) n., 1. act of

sustained and abstract reflection; contemplation. *He sets aside the early hour for quiet meditation.* 2. positive sustained pondering on a specific subject. *Prolonged meditation on his predicament resolved it at last.*

medley (med′lē) n., 1. mingled and confused mass of elements, ingredients, or parts; jumble. *Dinner was a medley of garden vegetables.* 2. musical composition consisting of parts from different sources. *He sang a medley of Stephen Foster songs.*

medulla (mi dul′ə) n., internal part of animal or plant; marrow; pith. *The cross section revealed the plant's medulla.*

megalomania (meg′ə lō mā′nē ə) n., mania for grand and exalted behavior. *The devilish plan reflected the ruler's megalomania.*

megalomaniac (meg′ə lō mā′nē ak′) n., person afflicted with megalomania; one who has delusions of grandeur. *The megalomaniac was determined to reign at whatever cost.*

megalopolis (meg′ə lop′ə lis) n., very large city, or urban region including one or more metropolises. *The region from Boston to Washington, D.C., is a megalopolis.*

megaton (meg′ə tun′) n., one million tons; explosive force equal to that of one million tons of TNT. *The atomic bomb exploded with the force of one megaton.*

melancholia (mel′ən kō′lē ə, -kōl′yə) n., state of mind characterized by extreme depression, complaints of real or imaginary pain, and occasionally delusions. *He was prostrated by the attack of melancholia.*

melancholy (mel′ən kol′ē) n., 1. gloomy state of mind; depression. *Her death threw him into melancholy.* 2. pensive mood. *The book sent him into a melancholy.* adj., sad; dejected. *They tried to cheer the melancholy girl.*

mélange (*Fr.* mā länzh′) n., mixture, esp. of unlikely elements. *The festival attracted an unusual mélange of exhibitors.*

meld (meld) v.t., to merge. *The marriage will meld two fine families.*

melee (mā′lā, mā lā′, mel′ā) n., 1. confused brawl involving many people. *A melée erupted over the call.* 2. general confusion; turmoil. *Holiday traffic caused a melée downtown.*

mellifluous (ma lif′lōō əs) adj., flowing or dropping like honey; sweetly or smoothly flowing, esp. in sound. *He had a mellifluous tenor voice.*

membrane (mem′brān) n., 1. thin, soft pliable sheet of animal or plant tissue. *The rattle was a dried membrane filled with beans.* 2. the thin permeable covering of a cell. *The cell membrane contains the cytoplasm.*

memento (mə men′tō) n., that which reminds; reminder of what is past; souvenir. *She bought the yearbook as a memento.*

memoir (mem′wär, -wôr) n., 1. personal note or essay relating to something within the author's own memory or knowledge; record of facts upon a subject personally known or investigated. *He hoped to use the memoir in his book.* 2. in pl., narrative of one's life or experiences. *Her memoirs contained new information about the artist.*

memorabilia (mem′ər ə bil′ē ə, -bil′yə) n. pl., things remarkable and worthy of remembrance or record, or that serve to recall something. *He had a superb collection of Civil War memorabilia.*

memorandum (mem′ə ran′dəm) n., note to help the memory; record of something for future reference or consideration; usually brief interoffice communication, often abbreviated as *memo*. *She prepared a memorandum of subjects to bring up at the meeting.*

memorialize (mə môr′ē ə līz′, -môr′-) v.t., to cause to be remembered; commemorate. *The scholarship will memorialize the teacher's work.*

ménage (mā näzh′; *Fr.* mā NAzh′) n., household, or members of a household. *A housekeeper runs her ménage.*

menagerie (mə naj′ə rē, -nazh′-) n., collection of wild animals, esp. kept for exhibition; yard or enclosure in which wild animals are kept. *The estate included a private menagerie of exotic animals.*

mendacious (men dā′shəs) adj., 1. given to lying; speaking falsely; falsifying. *The mendacious rogues spread a false report.* 2. having the character of a lie; false; untrue. *It was a mendacious criticism.*

mendicant (men′də kənt) n., member of a religious order that is sustained by begging; friar; any beggar. *The mendicant begged his supper.* adj., relating to begging or asking alms. *He decided to enter the mendicant order.*

menial (mē′nē əl, mēn′yəl) adj., pertaining to servants or domestic service; servile. *He performed menial kitchen chores.* n., domestic servant. *The menial was given a day off.*

meniscus (mi nis′kəs) n., 1. crescent, or crescent-shaped body. *The meniscus is the Moslem equivalent to the Christian cross.* 2. lens, concave on one side and convex on the other. *The optometrist ordered a meniscus.* 3. convex or concave surface of a liquid caused by surface tension. *The mercury formed a meniscus at the top of the thermometer.*

menstrual (men′strōō əl, -strəl) adj., pertaining to female menses; monthly. *Her menstrual periods began when she was twelve.*

mentor (men′tər) n., one who acts as a wise and faithful guide and monitor, esp. of a younger person; counselor. *He thanked his mentor for her patience as well as her instruction.*

mercantile (mûr′kən tēl′, -tīl′, -til) adj., pertaining to merchants, trade, or commerce. *Mercantile interest led to discovery of new trade routes.*

mercantilism (mûr′kən ti liz′əm, -tē-, -tī-) n., economic and political system developed since the rise of nationalism, which seeks to accumulate wealth for one's own country by expanding exports and limiting imports, creating a favorable balance of trade. *Mercantil-*

ism led to the system of protective tariffs.

mercenary (mûr′sə ner′ē) n., one who works or fights solely for personal gain. *The mercenary did not share their devotion to the cause.* adj., hired or serving merely for personal gain. *She worked for other than simply mercenary reasons.*

mercurial (mər kyŏŏr′ē əl) adj., 1. pertaining to qualities attributed to the god Mercury; eloquence, lightheartedness, fickleness, volatility. *Her students sometimes suffered because of her mercurial temperament.* 2. pertaining to the metal mercury. *The mercurial thermometer burst in the heat.*

meretricious (mer′i trish′əs) adj., alluring by deceitful or vulgar attractions; tawdry; not genuine. *The meretricious stage show concealed the actors' old, torn costumes.*

meringue (mə rang′) n., mixture of beaten egg whites and sugar or syrup slightly browned, used as a topping for desserts or baked as a pastry or pastry shell. *The golden meringue was served with strawberries.*

mesa (mā′sə; *Sp.* me′sä) n., land form having a relatively flat top and steep, rocky sides; tableland. *They found the nest at the top of the mesa.*

mesmerize (mez′mə rīz′, mes′-) v.t., to practice mesmerism upon; hypnotize; fascinate; spell-bind. *He began to mesmerize his friends with the fantastic tale.*

messiah (mi sī′ə) n., (cap.) the promised, divinely sent deliverer of the Jews; Jesus Christ, regarded by the Christians as this deliverer. (l.c.) an accepted leader of a cause. *They looked on the newly elected chief as a messiah.*

metabolism (mə tab′ə liz′əm) n., sum of all the processes by which the body or an individual cell renews or transforms protoplasm to perform special functions and sustain life. *The drug seemed to upset her body's metabolism.*

metallurgy (met′əlûr′jē *or, esp. Brit.,* mə tal′ər jē) n., technique or science of separating metals from their ores, or of making alloys, or of heat-treating metals to give them desired characteristics. *A knowledge of metallurgy was required for the job at the foundry.*

metamorphosis (met'ə môr'fə sis) n., change of form or structure; transmutation or transformation; marked change in the form or function of a living body. *The metamorphosis changed her from gawky child to poised adult.*

metaphor (met'ə fôr', -fər) n., figure of speech in which an attribute or characteristic of one object is applied to another to suggest an analogy or resemblance. *The metaphor referred to our country as a ship of state.*

metaphysical (met'ə fiz'i kəl) adj., 1. pertaining to metaphysics; abstract or abstruse; supernatural. *She had difficulty following his metaphysical remarks.* 2. pertaining to elaborately subtle early 17th-century poetry, epitomized by John Donne. *The metaphysical poem used elaborate but amusing sexual conceits.*

metaphysics (met'ə fiz'iks) n. science of the inward and essential nature of things; the philosophy of Aristotle, dealing with first principles; philosophy in general, esp. in its more abstruse branches. *Metaphysics includes the science of the origin and nature of the universe.*

mete (mēt) v.t., to distribute or apportion by measure. *Mother tried to mete out punishment fairly.*

meteor (mē'tē ər) n., fast-moving fiery or luminous body seen in or through the atmosphere; shooting star. *They watched the meteor fall to the horizon.*

meteorite (mē'te ə rīt') n., mineral or metallic mass of extraterrestrial origin that reaches the surface of the earth; fallen meteoroid. *The odd metallic chunk proved to be a meteorite.*

meteorology (mē'tē ə rol'ə jē) n., science dealing with the motions and phenomena of the earth's atmosphere, esp. of weather and climate. *Meteorology provides advance knowledge of storms.*

methodology (meth'ə dol'ə jē) n., science of method in scientific procedure; study

of the principles involved in the organization of the various special sciences and the conduct of scientific inquiry. *His careful research reflected a belief in the methodology of his field.*

meticulous (mə tik'yə ləs) adj., extremely careful over details; finicky. *She was meticulous about the tailoring of her clothes.*

métier (mā'tyā, mā tyā') n., occupation, trade, or profession at which one is particularly skilled. *Glass-cutting is her métier.*

metric (me'trik) adj., pertaining to the meter or to the system of weights and measures of which the meter is the fundamental unit. *It took her some time to learn to use the metric measuring cup.*

metronome (me'trə nōm') n., mechanical or electrical device that marks time by a repeated tick, used esp. as an aid in musical study. *He adjusted the metronome to a faster tempo.*

metropolis (mə trop'ə lis) n., chief city of a state, region, or country; any large, busy city. *New York City is the chief metropolis of the state of New York.*

metropolitan (me'trə pol'i tᵊn) n., head of an ecclesiastical province. *The metropolitan met with the choral director.* adj., 1. of or pertaining to a metropolitan and his ecclesiastical district. 2. of or pertaining to a metropolis. *The metropolitan traffic authority regulates the subway system.*

mettle (met'ᵊl) n., natural temperament; spirit; courage; ardor; enthusiasm. *She wanted to test her mettle in industry.*

mews (myōōz) n. plural form used with singular verb, originally the royal stables in London; any row of stables where carriage horses are kept. *The mews was later converted to townhouses.*

microbe (mī'krōb) n., microorganism; germ; bacterium. *The disease is attributed to a microbe.*

microcosm (mī'krə koz'əm) n., one unit that epitomizes a larger unit. *The plane provided a microcosm of human society.*

micrometer (mī krom'i tər) n., instrument for measuring lengths that can only be seen under a microscope. *He used a micrometer to measure the lathe turning.*

micron (mī′kron) n., millionth part of a meter. *A micrometer can measure in microns.*

microorganism (mī′krō ôr′gə niz′əm) n., microscopic organism, either plant or animal. *Hundreds of microorganisms may exist in a single drop of water.*

mien (mēn) n., air, bearing, or demeanor, esp. as expressive of character. *He was a man of somber mien.*

migrant (mī′grənt) n., one who migrates; wanderer. *The migrant moved restlessly from town to town.* adj., changing place; migratory. *Migrant workers travel northward in the summer.*

migratory (mī′grə tōr′ē, -tôr′ē) adj., given to or characterized by migration; roving; wandering. *Migratory birds fly south in the autumn.*

milestone (mīl′stōn′) n., 1. stone set up as a mile post. *The runners were glad to pass the milestone.* 2. significant event or development. *The discovery of penicillin was a milestone in modern medicine.*

milieu (mil yōō′, mēl-; *Fr.* mē LY OE′) n., environment; setting; medium; element. *The pianist came from a musical milieu.*

militant (mil′i tənt) adj., warlike; aggressive. *She was militant in the cause of women's rights.*

militarism (mil′i tə riz′əm) n., exaggerated warlike spirit; dedication to war or military practices; national policy of maintaining large standing armies. *The country's militarism provoked the unnecessary war.*

militate (mil′i tāt′) v.i., to have weight or force, as in determining anything. *The facts all militate against your theory.*

militia (mi lish′ə) n., body of people subject to military service whether armed and drilled or not; military service; soldiery. *The militia defended the small garrison.*

mincing (min′sing) adj., overly delicate or cautious, esp. as an affectation. *Her mincing manner drew their contempt.*

minion (min′yən) n., servile follower or subordinate; minor official. *The landlord sent his minion to evict the tenants.*

minuscule (min′ə skyōōl′, mi nus′kyōōl) adj., very small. *There was only a minuscule piece left.*

mirage (mi räzh′) n., 1. optical illusion; distorted, displaced, or inverted images produced by the bending of light rays through adjacent layers of air of widely different densities. *What we thought was an oasis proved merely a mirage.* 2. illusion or delusion. *Fame was the mirage that drew him to acting.*

mirthful (mûrth′fəl) adj., full of mirth or gaiety; jovial; festive. *The party was a mirthful occasion.*

misadventure (mis′əd ven′chər) n., unfortunate or unlucky event. *After his misadventure in the Pacific, he gave up sailing.*

misanthrope (mis′ən thrōp′, miz′-) n., hater of mankind. *The misanthrope chose to live alone.*

misanthropic (mis′ən throp′ik, miz′-) adj., characterized by a dislike or distrust of human beings. *The misanthropic man automatically ascribed to them the worst motive.*

misanthropy (mis an′thrə pē, miz-) n., hatred or dislike of mankind; attitude that expects the worst of human beings. *He forgot his misanthropy when he fell in love.*

misapprehend (mis′ap ri hend′) v.t., to misunderstand. *He feared she would misapprehend his motive.*

misapprehension (mis′ap ri hen′shən) n., mistaken notion, esp. of another's intention. *They later laughed over his absurd misapprehension.*

miscegenation (mis′i jə nā′shən, mi sej′ə-) n., mixture or amalgamation of races; esp. marriage or cohabitation between a man and a woman of different races. *The segregationist abhorred the increasing miscegenation in his town.*

miscellaneous (mis′ə lā′nē əs) adj., consisting of a mixture; diversified; heterogeneous. *When no single category is clear it goes in the miscellaneous file.*

miscellany (mis′ə lā′nē; *Brit.* mi sel′ə nē)

n., 1. mixture or combination of various elements. *She ordered a pound of the confection miscellany.* 2. diversified literary collection; book or periodical containing assorted compositions. *The miscellany included essays and plays.*

mischance (mis chans´, -chäns´) n., bad luck; disaster. *The mischance of the blizzard delayed him.*

mischievous (mis´chə vəs) adj., 1. producing or tending to produce mischief or harm; injurious. *His pranks are not malicious, only mischievous.* 2. fond of mischief; full of tricks; teasing or troublesome. *A mischievous wind caused considerable property damage.*

misconstruction (mis´kən struk´shən) n., act of wrongly interpreting something; act of mistaking the correct meaning; *The misconstruction resulted from his ignorance of French.*

misconstrue (mis´kən strōō´ or, esp. Brit., mis kon´strōō) v.t., to construe or interpret erroneously; misjudge; misunderstand. *Don't misconstrue his apparent indifference.*

miscreant (mis´krē ənt) n., 1. one who is unbelieving or misbelieving, esp. in matters of religion. *The miscreant was excommunicated.* 2. one whose behavior is vicious and criminal. *They arrested the miscreant.* adj., 1 heretical; unbelieving. *We abhor her miscreant statement.* 2. detestable; vile. *The miscreant act lost him his livelihood.*

misdemeanor (mis´di mē´nər) n., misbehavior; misconduct; in law, a crime less serious than a felony. *The cadet's misdemeanor worried his father.*

misgiving (mis giv´ing) n., feeling of doubt, suspicion, or distrust. *Despite her misgiving, she hired the stranger.*

mishap (mis´hap, mis hap´) n., unfortunate accident; mischance; misfortune. *She sprained her elbow in the traffic mishap.*

misnomer (mis nō´mər) n., mistaken or unsuitable name. *The wrestler goes by the misnomer of Tiny Tim.*

misogynist (mi soj´ə nəst) n., one who

hates women. *The misogynist was tricked into marriage.*

missal (mis´əl) n., book containing all the liturgical forms necessary for celebrating mass throughout the year. *She opened her missal and waited for mass to begin.*

missile (mis´əl or, esp. Brit., -īl) n., object or weapon that can be thrown or discharged for the purpose of hitting something. *They fired the missile at the destroyer.* adj., 1. capable of being thrown, hurled, or discharged from a weapon. *The army had a large arsenal of missile weapons.* 2. used or designed for discharging missiles. *The plan called for deploying numerous missile launchers.*

mistral (mis´trəl, mi sträl´) n., in southern France and environs a cold, dry, violent wind, that blows intermittently, esp. in winter. *The mistral forced him to leave Avignon.*

mite (mīt) n., 1. any of numerous small, often parasitic, arachnids. *The dog was treated for ear mites.* 2. very small amount, coin, or sum of money. *Each child contributed his or her mite to the collection.* adv., to a small extent; slightly. *She's always been a mite peculiar.*

miter (mī´tər) n., 1. official headdress of a bishop in the Western Church. *He received the miter from the consecrating bishop.* 2. joint made by cutting two pieces together at an angle and joining. *The miter was well fitted.* v.t., to join with a miter joint. *The joint will look better if you miter it.*

mitigate (mit´ə gāt´) v.t., to make milder or more tolerable; reduce in amount or degree, as something objectionable, harmful, etc.; moderate; alleviate; assuage. *The medication began to mitigate the pain.* v.i., to become milder; moderate. *The harsh climatic conditions mitigate as one travels south.*

mnemonics (nē mon´iks, ni-) n., art of improving or developing the memory. *The course in mnemonics helped to improve his grades.*

mobile (mō′bəl *or* mō′bēl) adj., 1. movable; capable of moving or being moved. *Most of the machinery is mobile.* 2. changeable; capable of facile movement, as human features. *Her mobile features expressed her conflicting emotions.* 3. flowing freely, as a liquid. *Water is a mobile medium for dramatic landscaping effects.* 4. characterized by the mixing of social groups. *The United States has a very mobile society.* n., piece of sculpture having pieces of metal or other material suspended on wire or string from a series of rods so that the pieces move independently on air currents. *The baby watched the mobile with fascination.*

mode (mōd) n., 1. manner of acting or doing; method; way. *She has her own mode of teaching math.* 2. customary manner; prevailing style; fashion. *Informal, slangy speech was the mode there.* 3. (also mood) in grammar, the designation, by the form of the verb, of the manner of conception of an event as fact, whether as certain, contingent, possible, or desirable. *This clause is in the subjunctive mode.* 4. natural disposition or the manner of existence or action of anything; form. *Heat is a mode of motion.*

modicum (mod′ə kəm) n., small, moderate, or limited quantity. *Anyone with a modicum of skill can follow the directions.*

modify (mod′ə fī′) v.t., 1. to change the properties, form, or function of; give a new form to; alter slightly; vary. *If we modify the rules a little, more people can play.* 2. to qualify, esp. to moderate or reduce in extent or degree. *They hoped he would modify the punishment.* 3. in grammar, to limit, restrict, or particularize the meaning of a word or phrase. *In "a full moon," "full" modifies "moon."*

modish (mō′dish) adj., fashionable; stylish; sometimes used negatively to suggest faddish. *Her modish hair style clashed with the old dress.*

modular (moj′ə lər, mod′yə-) adj., 1. of or pertaining to a module or a modulus. *The modular bridge helped the engineer in his plans.* 2. composed or constructed of standardized units. *The modular home had five window variations.*

modulate (moj′ə lāt′, mod′yə-) v.t., 1. to modify; adjust; regulate; tone down. *The union will modulate its demands along the mediator's guidelines.* 2. to alter or adapt the voice to fit the circumstances. *We remembered to modulate our voices in the sickroom.* 3. to tune to a key or pitch, or to change key. *The musicians modulate their instruments when the oboe sounds the "A."*

modulation (moj′ə lā′shən, mod′yə-) n., 1. act of regulating or adjusting according to measure. *We admired the modulation from beige to cream in the pot.* 2. adjustment of tone of voice, esp. in meaningful way. *The ballad requires delicate modulation between anger and despair.* 3. passage from one key into another or from major to minor mode. *The conductor admonished her to mark the point of modulation.* 4. adjustment of amplitude, frequency, or phase of a carrier signal in radio, TV, or telegraphy. *The technician corrected the modulation of the amplifier.*

modus operandi (mō′dōōs ō′pe Rän′dē; *Eng.* mō dəs op′ə ran′dī) method of procedure; plan or mode of working. *His modus operandi was the same in both thefts.*

mogul (mō′gəl) n., 1. (cap.) Mongol conqueror of India. 2. powerful or important person. *She was a communications mogul, head of a multimedia empire.* 3. bump of hard snow in a ski run. *He fell over the mogul and broke his leg.*

moiety (moi′i tē) n., half or approximately equal share of goods, an estate, or profits. *His moiety of the estate was the house.*

molar (mō′lər) n., back tooth used for grinding or crushing. *The dentist pulled the decayed molar.* adj., 1. in physics, pertaining to mass rather than atomic or molecular property or action of matter. *He prefers the field of molar physics* *to that of molecular science.* 2. in chemistry, pertaining to a mole, or gram molecule. *They prepared a molar solution.*

molecule (mol′ə kyōōl′) n., smallest part into which a substance can be divided without destroying its chemical identity. *A molecule of water consists of two atoms of hydrogen bonded to one oxygen atom.*

mollify (mol′ə fī′) v.t., 1. to soften in temper or disposition; pacify; soothe; appease. *He tried to mollify her with flowers.* 2. to reduce in intensity; mitigate. *We attempted to mollify our hunger with a few crackers.*

mollusk (mol′əsk) n., soft-bodied invertebrate, usually having an external shell. *A snail is a mollusk.*

molt (mōlt) v.i., to shed hair, feathers, skin, shell, etc., periodically, to be succeeded by new growth. *Birds usually molt once a year.* n., act or process of molting. *Crustaceans slough their entire shell with each molt.*

molten (mōl′tən) adj., 1. fused or liquified by heat. *Molten lava poured from the volcano.* 2. produced by melting and casting. *A small, molten sculpture stood on the table.*

momentary (mō′mən ter′ē) adj., 1. lasting but a moment; of short duration. *I had a momentary pang of conscience.* 2. occurring at any moment. *He expected a momentary interruption.*

momentous (mō men′təs) adj., of surpassing consequence or importance; critical; crucial. *The choice of a career is a momentous decision.*

momentum (mō men′təm) n., 1. force of speed; impetus. *The campaign gained momentum as the election drew near.* 2. in mechanics, the product of the mass and velocity of a body; quantity of motion of a body. *The rate of mass displacement is momentum.*

monarch (mon′ərk) n., 1. sovereign ruler or constitutional king or queen. *The monarch sent her envoy to the colony.* 2. large American butterfly. *He found the monarch in the field.*

monarchist (mon′ər kist) n., one who favors monarchical rule. *The monarchist wept when his king was dethroned.*

monarchy (mon′ər kē) n., form of government or rule in which supreme power is actually or nominally held by a single ruler. *France had an absolute monarchy until the Revolution.*

monastery (mon′ə ster′ē) n., 1. place of residence occupied by a community of persons, esp. monks, seeking religious seclusion from the world; cloister. *The monk was the monastery's gardener.* 2. community of persons living in such a place. *He entered a Franciscan monastery.*

monetary (mon′i ter′ē) adj., 1. pertaining to a country's currency or coinage. *The dollar is the U.S. monetary unit.* 2. pertaining to money; pecuniary. *He agreed for purely monetary reasons.*

monk (muṅgk) n., male ascetic, esp. a member of a religious order. *The monk's cell is bare but for a cot, a chair, and a table.*

monocle (mon′ə kəl) n., eyeglass for one eye. *He removed his monocle and cleaned it.*

monogamy (mə nog′ə mē) n., 1. marriage with only one person at a time. *Monogamy is the common form of marriage in developed countries.* 2. practice of marrying only once during a lifetime. *Monogamy has become less usual now that divorce is relatively easy to obtain.*

monograph (mon′ə graf′) n., scholarly treatise on a single subject or branch of study. *The monograph considered the mating habits of the opossum.*

monolith (mon′ə li͟th) n., 1. single large block or piece of stone. *A monolith blocked the cave entrance.* 2. structure or object formed of a single piece of stone, as an obelisk, statue, or column. *A commemoratory monolith stands in the town square.* 3. something that resembles a huge block of stone; organized whole. *He resolved to make a dent in the monolith of interoffice memos to be read.*

monolithic (mon′ə li͟th′ik) adj., 1. pertaining to or resembling a monolith. *The monolithic skyscraper shades the street.* 2. characterized by uniformity of opinions or beliefs. *The monolithic bureaucracy resisted his attempted changes.*

monologue (mon′ə lôg′, -log′) n., 1. long speech or harangue by one person. *She entertained them with a witty autobiographical monologue.* 2. dramatic soliloquy. *The audience applauded his performance of the famous monologue.* 3. dramatic entertainment performed by a single person. *The monologue incorporated poems by Emily Dickinson.* 4. any literary composition in which a single person speaks alone. *The "Rime of the Ancient Mariner" is a familiar monologue.*

monomaniac (mon′ə mā′nē ak′) n., one whose insanity is limited to a particular field, perversion, or delusion. *The monomaniac believed he was Napoleon.* adj., characteristic of monomania. *He was treated for a monomaniac compulsion.*

monoplane (mon′ə plān′) n., airplane with a single supporting surface. *The museum houses a very early monoplane.*

monopoly (mə nop′ə lē) n., 1. exclusive control by one party of a commodity or market, or control that makes possible the manipulation of prices. *The merger would give them a local monopoly on grain storage.* 2. exclusive possession or control of something. *You don't have a monopoly on good taste.* 3. something, as a commodity or service, that is the subject of a monopoly. *First class mail delivery is a monopoly of the U.S. Postal Service.*

monosyllable (mon′ə sil′ə bəl) n., word of one syllable. *She silently mouthed the monosyllable "help."*

monotheism (mon′ə thē iz′əm) n., doctrine or belief that there is only one God. *Judaism and Christianity are based on monotheism.*

monotone (mon′ə tōn′) n., 1. succession of words or speech sounds tediously delivered at one unvaried pitch with little or no inflection or cadence. *His*

monotone *rendered the lecture uninteresting.* 2. recitation or singing of words in a single tone. *The monks' monotone lent solemnity to the ancient chants.* adj., having a uniform tone or a single color. *His shirt and suit were the same monotone gray.*

monotonous (mə not′ᵊnəs) adj., 1. characterized by monotony. *Her monotonous voice irritated the class.* 2. tiresomely uniform; unvarying. *Mile after mile passed of the same monotonous landscape.*

monsoon (mon sōōn′) n., recurring wind, esp. in India and the northern Indian Ocean. *The monsoon renders travel very difficult.*

monstrosity (mon stros′i tē) n., 1. state or character of being monstrous. *They didn't know where to put the monstrosity of a lamp.* 2. monster; something monstrous in form or growth; freak. *The gardener tried to prune the monstrosity back into shape.*

monstrous (mon′strəs) adj., 1. shocking; hateful; horrible; hideous. *It was a monstrous tale of murder and revenge.* 2. enormous; huge; prodigious. *A monstrous dog guarded the premises.* 3. deviating greatly from the natural form or structure. *The movie was about a monstrous twelve-legged spider.* 4. monsterlike. *The fairy tale included a monstrous dragon.*

montage (mon täzh′) n., 1. composite picture in which several elements are juxtaposed, superimposed, or combined; technique of producing such a picture; photographic image produced by this method. *The montage used old photographs and magazine illustrations.* 2. technique used in film and television of producing a rapid succession of images to present an association of related ideas. *The montage of campus scenes gave an informal impression of Yale.*

monumental (mon′yə men′tᵊl) adj., 1. resembling or having the character of a monument; massive or imposing. *The monumental residence dwarfed the* nearby houses. 2. important, significant, or outstanding. *It was a monumental exhibition of Egyptian art.* 3. pertaining to a monument of monuments. *The sculptor favored a monumental style.*

moodiness (mo͞o′dē nəs) n., quality or state of being moody. *Moodiness is often characteristic of the adolescent.*

moody (mo͞o′dē) adj., subject to changes in disposition; temperamental; sullen; peevish. *He is too moody to be an effective principal.*

moor (mo͞or) n., 1. tract of open, untilled, often boggy land. *The walk on the moor was a highlight of our trip to Scotland.* 2. (cap.) one of Arab or Berber conquerers of 8th-century Spain; Muslim. v.t., to secure, as a ship or aircraft, in a particular station, by cables, anchors, or lines. *After we moor the boat we'll go ashore.*

moot (mo͞ot) adj., 1. open to argument or discussion; debatable. *The lawyers tried to clarify the moot clause.* 2. rendered abstract or strictly academic. *When it started to rain, the question of where to hold the picnic was moot.*

moraine (mə rān′) n., accumulation of rock and disintegrated fragments along the edges of a glacier. *The moraine revealed several interesting fossil formations.*

moral (môr′əl, mor′-) adj., 1. pertaining to rules of right conduct; concerning the distinction of right from wrong; ethical. *Cheating is wrong from a purely moral standpoint.* 2. in accord with, or controlled by, the rules of right conduct: opposed to immoral. *The mayor is an upright, moral woman.* 3. expressing or teaching right conduct; moralizing. *The 19th-century novel was oppressively moral.* 4. capable of distinguishing between right and wrong; accountable. *Humans are the only moral animals.* 5. sexually virtuous; chaste. *A moral person will abhor promiscuity.* 6. of, acting upon, or pertaining to the mind, character, or will. *He gave her moral support during labor.* n., lesson taught by a fable, parable, or experience. *The moral of that is "Look before you leap."*

morale (mə ral′) n., mental or moral condition, as of courage, zeal, hope, confidence, of a person or group. *Team morale was low after six consecutive losses.*

morality (mə ral′i tē, mô-) n., 1. conformity to the rules of good conduct; moral quality; virtuousness. *The bounty hunter's morality was questionable.* 2. sexual virtue; chastity. *Her strict standard of morality discouraged the playboy.* 3. doctrine or system of morals; ethics; duties. *Ideal government is founded in morality.* 4. moral instruction; moral lesson or precept; moralizing discourse or utterance. *Because we expected nothing but morality from the famous preacher we were surprised by his wit.*

morass (mə ras′) n., 1. tract of low, marshy, wet ground; swamp. *The heavy rains turned the road to a morass.* 2. something that traps or impedes. *The bill was bogged down in a morass of red tape.*

moratorium (môr′ə tôr′ē əm) n., 1. legal authorization to delay payment of a debt or performance of a legal obligation; period of such a delay. *The judge granted a 3-month moratorium on the firm's debts.* 2. any temporary suspension of activity. *There was a moratorium on hostilities during the peace negotiations.*

morbid (môr′bid) adj., 1. characteristic of or relating to an unhealthy mental state. *She had a morbid interest in death.* 2. proceeding from or characteristic of disease. *The surgeon deftly excised the morbid tissue.*

mordant (môr′dᵊnt) n., 1. substance which, combined with dye, fixes color. *The dye mixture included mordant.* 2. corrosive substance used in etching. *He carefully applied mordant to the copper plate.* adj., 1. acting as a mordant. *Casein has a mordant effect in dyeing.* 2. caustic; biting; sarcastic. *The audience enjoyed her mordant wit.*

mores (môr′āz, -ēs, môr′-) n. pl., fixed customs or folkways of a particular group, accepted without question and morally binding on members of the group; moral attitudes. *Polygamy was forbidden by tribal mores.*

moribund (môr'ə bund', mor'-) adj., 1. approaching death; in a dying state. *The comatose patient was clearly moribund.* 2. nearing extinction or termination. *The enterprise we began with such high hopes is now moribund.*

Mormon (môr'mən) n., member of the Church of Jesus Christ of Latter Day Saints, founded in 1830 by Joseph Smith. *The devout Mormon avoided alcohol.* adj., pertaining to the Mormons or their church. *Mormon men no longer practice polygamy.*

moron (mōr'on, môr'-) n., 1. person having a low IQ with a potential mental age of only 8–12 years. *She was tested and diagnosed a moron.* 2. *slang,* dull or stupid person, or one lacking in good judgment. *Don't wave that knife around, you moron!*

morose (mə rōs') adj., of a sullen disposition; peevish; ill-humored; gloomy. *She became morose during her piano lessons.*

morphology (môr fol'ə jē) n., 1. science of the outer form and internal structure of animals and plants. *Mutations are studied in morphology.* 2. study of structure and form, esp. of language. *Word etymology is a branch of linguistic morphology.*

morrow (môr'ō, mor'ō) n., day after the present or after any day specified. *We hope to leave early on the morrow.*

mortality (môr tal'i tē) n., 1. state or condition of being mortal. *The accident reminded me of my own mortality.* 2. humanity; human nature; human race. *Joy and sorrow are conditions of mortality.* 3. number or rate of deaths in specific circumstance or in proportion to population. *Infant mortality is lowest in Sweden.* 4. death or destruction of large numbers. *The battle caused appalling mortality on both sides.*

mortar (môr'tər) n., 1. bowl of durable material in which substances (as drugs) are pulverized. *The chemist uses a pestle to grind ingredients in a mortar.* 2.

mixture of lime and sand used for binding stones or bricks. *The mason used mortar to strengthen the stone wall.* 3. very short cannon. *The mortar was fired.*

mortician (môr tish'ən) n., undertaker. *The mortician took care of the funeral arrangements.*

mortify (môr'tə fī') v.t., 1. to humiliate; chagrin. *She tried to mortify me by drawing attention to my mistake.* 2. to subdue, esp. unwanted passions, by ascetic discipline, abstinence, or austerity. *He vowed to mortify the flesh by constant fasting and prayer.* 3. to affect with gangrene or decay. *He feared the septic wound might mortify the entire leg.* v.i., 1. to practice mortification. *Their religion demanded that they mortify weekly.* 2. to become gangrenous. *The frostbitten leg may mortify.*

mosaic (mō zā'ik) n., 1. picture or decoration made of small inlaid pieces of glass, wood, ivory, etc. *The excavation revealed a mosaic depicting a hunting scene.* 2. process of producing such an object. *She was skilled in mosaic.* 3. something resembling such an object. *The fallen leaves made a colorful mosaic on the sidewalk.* 4. in photography, series of aerial photographs taken vertically and matched together to form a continuous map of the terrain. *The mosaic was useful to the town planners.* 5. virus disease of plants characterized by green and yellow mottling of the leaves. *Our tomato plants are suffering from tobacco mosaic.* 6. part of a television camera tube coated with tiny photosensitive globules that convert light to an electrical charge. *The image is focused on the mosaic.* v.t., to decorate with mosaic work or to make a mosaic. *He will mosaic the walls with a pastoral mural.* adj., like or pertaining to a mosaic or mosaic work or used in mosaic work. *The wall was made of mosaic tiles.*

mosque (mosk, môsk) n., Muslim temple or place of worship. *The mosque had a gilded dome.*

mote (mōt) n., small particle or speck.

motif

180

He was temporarily blinded by a mote in his eye.

motif (mō tēf′) n., 1. recurring subject or theme in an artistic work. *Beethoven's Fifth Symphony contains a four-note motif.* 2. repeating figure or design. *The carpet had a motif of cabbage roses.* 3. dominant or central idea or theme. *The wily fox appears as a recurrent motif in world folklore.*

motivate (mō′tə vāt′) v.t., to induce or act as the motive or inciting cause of. *The teacher tried to motivate the lazy student.*

motive (mō′tiv) n., something causing someone to act. *Greed was the motive behind the theft.*

motley (mot′lē) n., 1. many-colored garment characteristically worn by a court jester. *The king's fool appeared in motley and bells.* 2. heterogeneous mixture. *The designers displayed a curious motley of styles.* adj., 1. variegated in color. *The fall leaves formed a motley carpet.* 2. composed of different, often incongruous, elements. *A motley collection of paintings hung in the flea market.*

mountebank (moun′tə bangk′) n., unscrupulous, deceiving quack, esp. one who sells dubious medicine as a cure-all at fairs, open-air gatherings, etc.; charlatan. *The mountebank touted the elixir as the "fountain of youth."*

muckraker (muk′rāk′ər) n., one who desires to discover and reveal real or supposed misbehavior on the part of public personalities. *The muckraker worked for the seamy tabloid.*

mucous (myoo′kəs) adj., 1. pertaining to mucus; slimy. *He slipped on the mucous rock.* 2. secreting or filled with mucus. *She suffered from inflamed mucous membranes.*

muddle (mud′əl) n., 1. mess; confusion; disordered state. *When she died, her affairs were in a muddle.* 2. bewilderment; confused mental state. *He has been in a muddle since his wife left him.* v.t., 1. to mix up or jumble together in a confused or aimless way. *If you bump*

the chess board you will muddle the pieces. 2. to bewilder; perplex. *All these complicated formulas muddle my brain.* 3. to cause to become stupefied, as with liquor. *They fed him brandy to muddle him.* 4. to make turbid or muddy. *The dredging will temporarily muddle the lake.*

mufti (muf′tē) n., 1. professional interpreter of Muslim law. *They appealed to the mufti for an opinion.* 2. civilian dress. *The cadet wore mufti to the party.*

muggy (mug′ē) adj., damp, warm, and humid weather. *It was a typical, muggy August day.*

mulct (mulkt) v.t., to swindle or defraud. *The phony evangelist tried to mulct them out of their life's savings.*

mull (mul) n., thin, soft, sheer muslin fabric. *Her gown was made of the finest mull.* v.t., 1. to ponder, study, or ruminate. *I'll mull it over and let you know.* 2. to heat, sweeten, and spice. *They mulled cider to serve with the doughnuts.*

multifarious (mul′tə fâr′ē əs) adj., having great diversity or variety; having many parts. *The actor has appeared in multifarious roles.*

multilingual (mul′ti ling′gwəl) adj., able to speak many languages; polyglot. *The multilingual woman is a professional translator.*

multiplicity (mul′tə plis′i tē) n., 1. state of being multiple, manifold, or various. *The multiplicity of the insect world is awesome.* 2. many of the same kind; large number. *The statement contains a multiplicity of errors.*

mummery (mum′ə rē) n., 1. performance by mummers; masquerade. *The Christmas mummery pantomimed St. George and the dragon.* 2. ceremony or performance considered false or pretentious; farcical show. *The Puritans disdained as mummery the rites of the Church of England.*

mummy (mum′ē) n., corpse of a human being or animal preserved by the ancient Egyptian method or by some other method of embalming or by the agencies of nature. *The mummy was perfectly preserved by the acids in the peaty soil.*

mundane (mun dān′) adj., 1. belonging to this world, universe, or earth; worldly; terrestrial. *The monks gave little thought to mundane affairs.* 2. ordinary; everyday; unexalted. *She felt her life was dull and mundane.*

municipal (myo͞o nis′ə pəl) adj., of or pertaining to the local self-government or corporate government of a city or town; self-governing. *The state studied the municipal real estate tax rates.*

munificent (myo͞o nif′i sənt) adj., 1. extremely liberal in giving or bestowing; very generous. *Our munificent benefactor prefers to remain anonymous.* 2. characterized by great liberality or lavish generosity. *Sending her to Europe was a munificent gesture.*

murky (mûr′kē) adj., 1. dark; dim; gloomy. *Our eyes began to adjust to the murky interior.* 2. thick and heavy, as with fog, haze, mist. *The report was full of murky bureaucratic prose.*

muse (myo͞oz) n., 1. (cap.) in Greek mythology, any of nine goddesses who preside over arts and sciences. *The poet invoked the aid of his Muse.* 2. source of inspiration or guidance, esp. in the arts. *His muse seemed to desert him when he tried to finish the play.* v.t., to ponder; meditate; reflect in silence. *His father encouraged him to muse on his future.* v.i., to think or say thoughtfully; meditate on. *"I wonder how it will all turn out," she mused.*

muster (mus′tər) n., 1. inspection. *The cadets had to pass muster or face latrine duty.* 2. assembly, esp. for military inspection. *The fife and drum corps went to the muster in Essex.* v.t., 1. to collect or assemble, esp. of military group. *We wanted to muster the alumni for a reunion.* 2. to call forth; gather; summon. *She will need all the courage she can muster.* v.i., to assemble (as soldiers) for inspection; meet in one place; come together. *The band members will muster here at 11:00.*

musty (mus′tē) adj., 1. damaged by mildew or dampness; having an odor or flavor suggestive of mold or mildew. *The closet smelled musty.* 2. spoiled by age; antiquated; stale. *The revolution swept away the musty customs of the old regime.*

mutable (myo͞o′tə bəl) adj., 1. capable of being altered in form, qualities, or nature; changeable. *The mutable New England weather is seldom dull.* 2. changeable or inconsistent; unsettled; unstable; fickle. *His mutable nature renders him unsuitable for marriage.*

mutant (myo͞ot′ənt) n., form that is undergoing or has undergone mutation. *A new mutant resulted from radiation of the parent organisms.* adj., undergoing or resulting from mutation. *Scientists produced a mutant strain of the virus.*

mutation (myo͞o tā′shən) n., 1. act or process of changing; altered form. *The chameleon undergoes color mutation according to its surroundings.* 2. biological alteration from parent type; product of that alteration. *The tomato mutation was tested before it was marketed.*

mutilate (myo͞o′tə lāt′) v.t., 1. to cut off or destroy a limb or important part of a person or animal. *He swung his sword wildly, hoping to kill or mutilate his attacker.* 2. to render incomplete or imperfect by removing an essential part. *He said cutting that chapter would mutilate his book.*

muzhik (mo͞o zhik′, mo͞o′zhik) n., Russian peasant. *The muzhik profited from the land reform act.*

myopia (mī ō′pē ə) n., 1. near-sightedness. *Myopia requires him to wear glasses to see the movie.* 2. lack of foresight. *The town is near bankruptcy due to the myopia of local officials.*

myopic (mī op′ik) adj., 1. of or related to myopia; near-sighted. *Glasses correct his myopic vision.* 2. having a very limited point of view; short-sighted. *The myopic congressman refused to recognize the inevitable change.*

myriad (mir′ē əd) n., indefinitely great number. *A myriad of birds winter at the* *wildlife refuge.* adj., numberless; innumerable; multitudinous; manifold. *He cheerfully attended to the myriad details of the dinner party.*

mystic (mis'tik) n., one who accepts or preaches some form of mysticism. *The mystic practiced meditation.* adj., 1. pertaining to mysticism or mystics. *The hermit claims to have mystic revela-* tions. 2. having a spiritual or religious meaning or symbolism. *The sacrament of communion symbolizes the mystic relationship of Christ and his church.* 3. of the nature of or pertaining to mysteries or esoteric rites. *The initiation ceremony relied on mystic mumbo-jumbo.*

Nn

nabob (nā′bob) n., 1. provincial viceroy or governor in India under the Mogul empire. *The offender heard the nabob's sentence.* 2. wealthy or eminent man. *He refused to associate with the nabobs in the first-class compartments.*

nacre (nā′kər) n., mother-of-pearl. *The bracelet was made of nacre.*

nadir (nā′dər, nā′dēr) n., that point of the heavens that is vertically below any given point of the earth; lowest point. *The defeat was the nadir of the war.*

naiad (nā′ad, -əd, nī′-) n., in classical mythology, a female deity presiding over springs and streams; water nymph. *The naiad overlooks the marble fountain.*

naïve (naive) (nä ēv′) adj., 1. ingenuous; unaffected. *The naïve girl charmed her sophisticated suitor.* 2. credulous. *He was naïve to believe the salesman.*

nape (nāp, nap) n., upper back of the neck. *Her hair was pinned up off the nape of her neck.*

narcissism (när′si siz′em) n., 1. self-love; egocentrism. *The dance reflected the follies of narcissism.* 2. love of or sexual desire for one's own body or mind. *Infantile narcissism is usually outgrown.*

narcosis (när kō′sis) n., state of numbness or stupefaction brought on by a narcotic. *Morphine brought on his narcosis.*

narcotic (när kot′ik) n., 1. addictive drug, such as opium, that relieves pain, dulls the senses, and induces sleep, and in excessive doses can cause stupor, coma, and even death. *The narcotic helped him endure the pain.* 2. something that soothes, numbs, or lulls. *The motion of the ship was a narcotic.* adj., 1. having the power to produce narcosis. *The hot milk had a narcotic effect on the child.* 2. of or pertaining to narcotics or narcosis. *Narcotic addiction is a worldwide problem.*

narration (na rā′shən) n., 1. act of describing an event or happening; recitation of a descriptive story. *It was an exciting narration.* 2. part of a story as opposed to dialogue. *In a play, narration takes the form of stage directions.*

narrative (nar′ə tiv) n., 1. connected account of the particulars of an event or transaction, or series of incidents; story. *The narrative concerned her train trip to Boston.* 2. act or technique of narration. *His style is narrative at its best.* adj., 1. of or pertaining to narration or the act of narration. *Her narrative skill is outstanding.* 2. consisting of or being narrative. *"Evangeline" is a long, narrative poem.*

nascent (nā′sənt) adj., coming into being; beginning to grow; incipient. *Their young son is a nascent musician.*

natal (nāt′əl) adj., 1. of or pertaining to one's birth; connected with or dating from one's birth. *The festivities celebrated the king's natal day.* 2. presiding over birthdays or nativities. *Aquarius is her natal sign.* 3. native; own; original. *Ohio is my natal state.*

natatorial (nā′tə tōr′ē əl, -tôr′-, nat′ə-) adj., pertaining to swimming. *Her natatorial skill helped her survive the shipwreck.*

nationalism (nash′ə nəliz′əm) n., devotion to a nation, esp. with an exaggerated spirit of rivalry over other nations. *Nationalism can be a stumbling block to world peace.*

nativity (nə tiv′i tē) n., 1. fact of being born; birth. *He didn't want to celebrate his nativity this year.* 2. circumstances attending birth, as time, place, and surroundings. 3. (cap.) birth of Christ; artistic representations of the birth of

Christ. *The children celebrated the Nativity with a play.*

naturalist (nach'ər ə list, nach'rə-) n., 1. one who studies natural history, esp. in the field. *The amateur naturalist had a special interest in orchids.* 2. one who advocates or practices naturalism in art or literature. *The scene was clearly painted by a keen naturalist.*

naturalization (nach'ər ə lī zā'shən, nach'rə-, -lə-) n., process by which an alien achieves citizen status. *Through the naturalization process, she became a U.S. citizen.*

nausea (nô'zē ə, -zhə, -shə) n., 1. sensation of impending vomiting; sickness at the stomach. *She suffered from nausea after eating the raw oysters.* 2. severe disgust; loathing. *The mere mention of fascism filled him with nausea.*

nauseate (nô'zē āt', -zhē-, -sē-, -shē-) v.t., to affect with nausea or disgust. *The smell began to nauseate him.*

nautical (nô ti kəl) adj., pertaining to ships, sailors, or navigation. *The novel was full of nautical terms.*

nave (nāv) n., central portion of a church extending from the main entrance to the sanctuary. *The procession filled the nave.*

nebula (neb'ya lə) n., region of luminous gas in interstellar space. *The astronomer observed the nebula through the telescope.*

nebulous (neb'yə ləs) adj., 1. hazy; vague; indistinct. *My plans are still nebulous at this point.* 2. of, pertaining to, or having the appearance of a nebula; nebular. *Nebulous patches appear far beyond our solar system.*

necrology (nə krol'ə jē, ne-) n., list of those who have died recently; obituary. *A necrology was appended to the yearbook.*

necromancy (nek'rə man'sē) n., practice of calling upon the dead and conversing with them in order to reveal the future; sorcery. *The Elizabethans took necromancy seriously.*

necrophobia (nek'rə fō'bē ə) n., abnormal fear of death or of dead bodies. *Her necrophobia made her afraid to go to the funeral.*

nefarious (ni fâr'ē əs) adj., extremely wicked; heinous; abominable. *His nefarious scheme was designed to cause mass hysteria.*

negation (ni gā'shən) n., 1. act of denying; denial. *She stammered a furious negation of the accusation.* 2. a negative counterpart of something positive. *Death is the negation of life.* 3. negative thing; nonentity. *He felt like a negation amid the celebrities.* 4. negative thought or statement; contradiction; rebuttal. *His wild claims prompted a strong negation from his opponent.*

negligence (neg'li jəns) n., 1. fact or character of being negligent or neglectful; neglect. *The owner's negligence resulted in a leaky roof.* 2. negligent act; heedless disregard of some duty. *Her negligence allowed the child to burn himself.* 3. in law, failure to exercise reasonable care for the protection of others. *After the mishap he sued the landlord for negligence.*

negligible (neg'li jə bəl) adj., in a quantity or to a degree that may be disregarded. *Luckily, the damage to my car was negligible.*

nemesis (nem'i sis) n., 1. (cap.) in Greek mythology, goddess personifying divine retribution. *Nemesis tracked down the offending lover.* 2. agent of punishment or retribution. *Johnny's tattle-tale sister was his nemesis.* 3. unconquerable obstacle or formidable opponent. *The Russian winter was Napoleon's nemesis.*

neolithic (nē'ə lith'ik) adj., 1. (cap.) pertaining to that part of the Stone Age that is characterized by the use of highly polished implements. *The Neolithic tools are displayed in the museum.* 2. belonging to an outmoded era. *He still subscribes to the neolithic idea of usury.*

neologism (nē ol'ə jiz'əm) n., newly coined word or expression; new usage. *"Astronaut" is a space-age neologism.*

neophyte (nē'ə fīt') n., 1. new convert or initiate; novice. *The neophyte landed* *her first acting job.* 2. beginner; tyro. *After her novel's success she was no longer considered a neophyte.*

nepotism (nep′ə tiz′əm) n., favoritism or patronage shown to relatives in consideration of family relationship rather than merit. *The 20-year-old vice president was a shocking example of nepotism.*

nettle (net′əl) n., any herbaceous plant with prickly or stinging hairs. *I stepped on a nettle and howled with pain.* v.t., to irritate or vex; provoke; pique. *He tried to nettle her out of her smug complacency.*

network (net′wûrk′) n., 1. anything formed of intersecting lines, wires, threads, passages, etc. *The traffic controller studied the intricate network of flight patterns.* 2. interconnected group or system. *She owned a network of hamburger stands.* 3. in radio and television, group of transmitting stations linked by wire or microwave relay, with in-common programming. *The speech was carried on every station in the network.*

neurasthenia (noor′əs thē′nē ə, nyoor′-) n., nervous condition characterized by fatigue, anxiety, insecurity, ultrasensitivity to light and noise, headaches, and other bodily upsets. *Her neurasthenia was aggravated by job pressures.*

neuron (noor′on, nyoor′-) n., nerve cell that constitutes the fundamental structural unit of nerve tissue. *The neuron transmits and receives electrical and biochemical impulses.*

neurosis (noo rō′sis, nyoo-) n., nervous or emotional disorder without apparent physical cause. *The doctor vaguely attributed the anxiety to her neurosis.*

neurotic (noo rot′ik, nyoo-) n., one who has a neurosis. *The neurotic was difficult to live with.* adj., 1. having a neurosis. *Either he has a neurotic personality or a vivid imagination.* 2. pertaining to the nerves or to nervous disease. *Her doctor says all her symptoms are of neurotic origin.*

neutral (noo′trəl, nyoo′-) n., 1. one who occupies a neutral or indifferent position; person, party, or nation that takes neither side in a given hostility. *He was asked to serve as a neutral in the negotiations.* 2. position or state of disengagement, as gears. *She let the car idle in neutral.* adj., 1. taking no active part with either side; maintaining uninvolved stance; nonaligned. *Switzerland is traditionally a neutral country.* 2. of no particular kind, color, characteristic, etc.; indefinite; neuter. *The neutral color made it her most versatile sweater.* 3. colorless, or nearly colorless; grayish. *The battleship was painted a neutral gray.* 4. in chemistry, neither acid nor alkaline. *Neutral salts lack the ability to combine with either an acid or a base.*

neutron (noo′tron, nyoo′-) n., uncharged particle that forms part of virtually all atomic nuclei, and having a mass slightly greater than that of a proton. *The neutron is missing only from the hydrogen atomic nucleus.*

nexus (nek′səs) n., link binding several members of a group, or parts of a series. *Discrimination is the nexus connecting the civil rights and women's movements.*

nib (nib) n., 1. beak of a bird. *He held a sunflower seed in his nib.* 2. sharpened point of a quill or fountain pen. *He needs a new nib on his pen.* 3. point or projection. *She pricked her finger on the nib of the spinning wheel.*

nicety (nī′si tē) n., 1. feature of polite society. *The calling card is an outdated nicety.* 2. fine distinction; subtlety. *He saw the nicety she was trying to convey.* 3. delicacy; exactness. *She paints with nicety of detail.* 4. fastidiousness; squeamishness. *He was amused by the fop's nicety.*

niche (nich) n., 1. nook or recess, generally semicircular in plan and terminated in a semidome at the top, as for a statue, vase, or other ornament. *The bronze stood in a niche by the hall door.* 2. assigned or appropriate place for a person or thing. *She found her niche in* *government service.* 3. ecological position or function of an organism in a community of plants and animals. *Plankton occupies an important niche in the sea's food cycle.*

nicotine (nĭk′ə tēn, -tĭn, nĭk′ə tēn′) n., poisonous alkaloid ($C_{10}H_{14}N_2$) obtained from tobacco and used as an insecticide. *The smoker had yellow nicotine stains on his teeth and fingers.*

niggardly (nig′ərd lē) adj., 1. close fisted; stingy; parsimonious. *The niggardly fellow probably still had the first dime he ever earned.* 2. characteristic of a niggard; scanty. *My parents keep me on a niggardly allowance.* adv., in the manner of a niggard; sparingly; parsimoniously. *She dispensed her smiles niggardly.*

nihilism (nī′ə liz′əm) n., 1. doctrine that nothing can really be known, because nothing exists; denial of all real existence. *Nihilism is skepticism carried to extreme.* 2. total disbelief in religion, morality, law, and order. *Nihilism drove her into an utterly reckless and dissolute life.* 3. (usu. cap.) principles of a 19th-century Russian revolutionary group that advocated the destruction of existing social and political institutions in order to prepare for a new social order. *The Nihilism movement originated in the universities about 1840.*

nimbus (nim′bəs) n., 1. dark cloud or system of clouds from which rain is falling or appears about to fall. *The nimbus blanketed the sky.* 2. in art, a halo or aura around the head of a divinity or saint. *The apostle was invested with a thin nimbus.* 3. personal aura. *A nimbus of success surrounded the best-selling author.*

nirvana (nir vä′nə, -van′ə, nər-) n., state of spiritual perfection that transcends physical imperfection or suffering, esp. as aspired to in Buddhism. *Meditation is one road to nirvana.*

nitrate (nī′trāt) n., salt of nitric acid. *Organic gardeners abhor the use of nitrates as fertilizers.*

nocturnal (nok tûr′nəl) adj., 1. pertaining to the night; used, done, or occurring at night. *The revolutionaries conducted secret nocturnal meetings.* 2. active at night. *The owl is a nocturnal predator.*

nocturne (nok′tûrn) n., 1. in music, composition appropriate to the evening or night; reverie; serenade. *He invoked romance with a Chopin nocturne.* 2. work of art dealing with evening or night; night scene. *She painted a large watercolor nocturne.*

node (nōd) n., 1. knot; knob; protuberance; hard swelling. *Inflammation of a lymph node can be painful.* 2. in botany, definite part of a stem that normally bears a leaf or a whorl of leaves; joint in a stem. *The stalk snapped just above a node.*

nodule (noj′ool) n., little knot or lump. *The nodule developed into a true bud.*

noisome (noi′səm) adj., 1. offensive or disgusting, esp. to smell. *A noisome odor arose from the swamp.* 2. harmful; noxious; injurious. *They fled the noisome plague of the city.*

nomadic (nō mad′ik) adj., 1. of or pertaining to nomads. *Nomadic cultures still prevail in desert areas.* 2. wandering; roving; pastoral. *The nomadic life satisfied the drover.*

nom de plume (nom′ də ploom′) pen name; pseudonym. *He published his novel under a nom de plume.*

nomenclature (nō′mən klā′chər, nō men′klə-) n., system of names or terms, as those used in any art or science or other field. *She was unfamiliar with the medical nomenclature.*

nominal (nom′ə nəl) adj., 1. existing in name only; not real; ostensible; merely so-called. *The nominal Catholic seldom attended mass.* 2. of or pertaining to a noun or nouns. 3. pertaining to a price or consideration named as a matter of form, being nowhere near the actual cost or value; token. *She promised to deliver the package for a nominal fee.*

nominate (nom′ə nāt′) v.t., 1. to put forward the name of a person to be included as a candidate in an election. *We will nominate her as our next mayor.* 2. to name someone for an appointment to a nonelective office. *He must nominate five judges this year.*

nonagenarian (non′ə jə när′ə ən, nō′nə jə-) n., one who is between 90 and 100 years old. *I offered my seat on the bus to a nonagenarian.* adj., pertaining to a nonagenarian. *My nonagenarian grandfather still dances beautifully.*

nonchalance (non′shə läns′, non′shə ləns) n., coolness; indifference; unconcern. *She hid her embarrassment under a guise of nonchalance.*

noncommittal (non′kə mit′əl) adj., disinclined to commit oneself to any particular view, course, or opinion. *He remained noncommittal in spite of their urging.*

non compos mentis (nōn kōm′pōs men′tis) not of sound mind; mentally incapable. *The defense attorney entered a plea of non compos mentis.*

nondescript (non′di skript′) adj., of no particular type, class, or kind; unclassifiable; indescribable. *It was a shapeless, nondescript garment.*

nonentity (non en′ti tē) n., 1. person or thing of no consequence or importance. *The nonentity was buried without a single mourner.* 2. something that does not exist or that exists only in the imagination. *How can you believe in a nonentity like a ghost.* 3. nonexistence. *She was forced to admit the nonentity of her funds.*

nonpareil (non′pə rel′) n., 1. person or thing of peerless excellence; paragon. *The extraordinary actress is a nonpareil of the theater.* 2. small, round, sugar pellet used in decorating cakes and candies. *He sprinkled the frosting with nonpareils.* 3. flat, round chocolate disk covered with such sugar pellets. *The nonpareil melted slowly in her mouth.* adj., outstanding; peerless. *The remark revealed a nonpareil arrogance.*

nonplus (non plus′, non′plus) n., state of bafflement; quandary. *She was in a nonplus over his proposal.* v.t., to perplex, confuse, or embarrass someone so that

he can no longer go on. *The child's question nonplused his parents.*

nonplused (non plust′) adj., in a state of perplexity; puzzled; confounded. *His unexpected accusation left me completely nonplused.*

non sequitur (nōn se′kwi tōōr) it does not follow; inference or conclusion that does not follow from the premises. *We smiled at his unwitting non sequitur.*

nosegay (nōz′gā′) n., small, hand-held, very fragrant bouquet. *The boy presented a violet nosegay to his girl.*

nostalgia (no stal′jə, -jē ə, nə-) n., longing to return to some past period, place, or condition; homesickness. *The reunion evoked nostalgia for our schooldays.*

nostrum (nos′trəm) n., 1. something, esp. a medicine, whose contents are unknown, recommended but unreliable as a cure; placebo. *She offered her grandmother's cold nostrum.* 2. unreliable remedy; panacea. *TV was the tired mother's nostrum for boredom.*

notarize (nō′tə rīz′) v.t., to authenticate or certify (a document, deed, contract, etc.) as a notary public. *We need him to notarize the will.*

notation (nō tā′shən) n., 1. system of signs or symbols used in place of language in specialized fields. *He depended on the notation of ballet choreography.* 2. act, process, or result of indicating by written or printed characters or symbols. *The proofreader corrected the manuscript by marginal notation.*

notion (nō′shən) n., 1. vague, general, conclusive concept. *His notion of music went no further than the top forty.* 2. theory, opinion, or belief. *Columbus had a notion that the world was round.* 3. conception or idea. *She has a rather complicated notion for a novel.* 4. desire, inclination, intention, or sentiment, generally not very deep; caprice; whim. *He had a notion for a midnight swim.* 5. (pl.) small, useful articles. *The box was full of pins, tape, and other notions.*

notorious (nō tōr′ē əs) adj., 1. notable in a bad sense; widely or well but not favorably known. *He is a notorious* *criminal.* 2. publicly or generally known and spoken of. *We admired her notorious skill on the loom.*

nouveau riche (noo vō Rĕsh´; Eng. noo´vō rĕsh´) adj., newly rich. *The nouveau riche was eager to display his wealth.*

nova (nō´və) n., star that becomes suddenly very much brighter and then fades gradually. *Her career took spark then died, like a nova.*

novice (nov´is) n., 1. one who is new to the circumstances in which he or she is placed; beginner; tyro. *He forgot I was a novice and went too fast.* 2. one who has newly been received into a religious order and is still on probation. *The novice did not have to maintain silence like the other monks.*

novitiate (nō vish´ē it, -āt´) n., 1. state or period of being a novice; apprenticeship. *I served my novitiate under Sister Agnes.* 2. house or building in which novices pass their time of probation. *The monks built the novitiate and tended the grounds.*

noxious (nok´shəs) adj., 1. harmful or injurious to physical beings. *The ruptured tank released a noxious gas.* 2. morally harmful; pernicious. *Cheating is a noxious habit.*

nuance (noo´äns, nyoo´-) n., delicate degree of difference, esp. in color, meaning, expression, etc. *The pianist displayed every nuance in the sonata.*

nubile (noo´bil, nyoo´-) adj., having recently reached marriageable age. *The nubile girls began to receive suitors.*

nuclear (noo´klē ər, nyoo´-) adj., 1. of or pertaining to a nucleus; constituted by or constituting a nucleus. *The nuclear family is the norm in today's mobile society.* 2. of or pertaining to atomic energy, atomic weapons, atomic power, etc. *Nuclear war is a constant threat.*

nucleus (noo´klē əs, nyoo´-´) n., central mass about which other parts are grouped; focal point; core. *The commando force was the nucleus of the army.*

nullification (nul´ə fə kā´shən) n., act of rendering null and void, esp. regarding legal or official actions or documents. *The provocative act achieved nullification of the treaty.*

nullify (nul´ə fī´) v.t., to annul; make void; render invalid; deprive of force or efficacy. *This error might nullify the entire experiment.*

numeral (noo´mər əl, nyoo´-) n., 1. word or combination of words used to express a number. *One, two, three are cardinal numerals; first, second, third are ordinal numerals.* 2. figure or character used to express a number. *The Roman numeral V was used instead of the Arabic 5.* adj., 1. pertaining to or consisting of numbers. *The blackboard was crowded with numeral formulas.* 2. expressing or representing numbers. *V and 5 are numeral characters for five.*

numerator (noo´mə rā´tər, nyoo´-) n., 1. number in a fraction appearing above the line and indicating how many parts of a unit are taken. *In the fraction 3/4, 3 is the numerator.* 2. one who or that which numbers. *The numerator counted as each child boarded the bus.*

numerical (noo mer´i kəl, nyoo-) adj., 1. of or pertaining to numbers. *Our candidate has a numerical majority.* 2. expressed by a number or numbers rather than by a letter or letters. *The children used a simple numerical code.*

numerology (noo´mə rol´ə jē, nyoo´-) n., occult study of numbers. *He used numerology to determine the impact of his birth date on his marriage.*

numismatics (noo´miz mat´iks, -mis-, nyoo´-) n., study of coins and medals. *The members of the society of numismatics voted to buy the rare coin.*

nuncio (nun´sē ō´) n., papal representative with permanent diplomatic status in a foreign country. *Paul VI's nuncio to France died of a heart attack.*

nuptials (nup´shəls) n., wedding or marriage. *They celebrated their nuptials last Sunday.*

nurture (nûr´chər) n., 1. act of nourishing; act or process of cultivating or promoting growth. *The nurture of our garden was entrusted to my brother.* 2. upbringing; training; discipline; instruction; education. *The school was dedicated to the nurture of young aristocrats.* 3. nourishment; that which nourishes; food; diet. *We depended upon books for the nurture of our minds.* v.t., 1. to feed; nourish. *If we nurture this plant carefully it may recover.* 2. to educate, train, or bring up. *Most parents nurture their offspring with care and concern.*

nutrient (nōō′trē ənt, nyōō′-) n., nutritious substance. *This cereal provides every essential nutrient.* adj., 1. conveying or containing nutriment, as vessels of the body or solutions. *A nutrient artery carries blood into the bone.* 2. affording nourishment; nourishing; nutritious. *The nutrient quality of grain has long been known.*

nutriment (nōō′trə mənt, nyōō′-) n., that which nourishes; promotes growth, development, or improvement; and serves to sustain existence. *Our wasted bodies showed the lack of any nutriment during our ordeal.*

nutrition (nōō trish′ən, nyōō-) n., 1. act or process by which organisms absorb food into their system and convert it into living tissue. *A healthful diet requires some knowledge of human nutrition.* 2. that which nourishes; nutriment; food. *Many diseases are caused by improper nutrition.*

nutritive (nōō′tri tiv, nyōō′-) adj., 1. having the property of nourishing; nutritious. *An egg contains nutritive matter for the developing embryo.* 2. of or pertaining to nutrition. *We learned the nutritive value of various foods.*

nymph (nimf) n., 1. in classical mythology, a minor divinity, usually a beautiful maiden, entrusted with the guardianship of certain localities or families. *A wood nymph decorates the mantelpiece.* 2. young and attractive woman. *The nymph was the belle of the ball.* 3. intermediate stage of an insect's transformation from larva to imago. *The nymph was only hours from maturity.*

Oo

oaf (ōf) n., dolt; idiot; blockhead; simpleton. *Look what you've done, you stupid oaf!*

obbligato (**obligato**) (ob'lə gä'tō; *It.* ôb'blē gä'tô) n., 1. accompaniment, esp. any instrumental solo accompanying a vocal piece, which has independent importance. *The violin obbligato complemented her voice.* 2. continuing background motif. *The oboe obbligato heightened the suspense.* adj., musical direction meaning obligatory. *The passage was marked "obbligato."*

obdurate (ob'dōō rit, -dyōō-) adj., 1. hardened against moral influence; persistent in wrongdoing. *I remained obdurate against their pleas.* 2. hardhearted; unyielding; stubborn; inexorable. *The most obdurate heart would be moved by her appearance.*

obedient (ō bē'dē ənt) adj., obeying or willing to obey; submissive to authority, control, or constraint; dutiful; compliant. *The usually obedient dog can't resist chasing joggers.*

obeisance (ō bā'səns, ō bē'-) n., 1. bow or curtsy; act of reverence or deference. *They all made an obeisance to the king.* 2. deference or homage. *The knights swore obeisance to their sovereign.*

obelisk (ob'ə lisk) n., 1. tapering, rectangular column, generally rising to a pyramidal apex. *The obelisk is marked with names of war dead.* 2. symbol resembling a dagger. *The obelisk marks those who contributed $1,000 and more to the fund.*

obese (ō bēs') adj., excessively fat; corpulent; fleshy. *The obese dog looked like a sausage on legs.*

obesity (ō bē'si tē) n., state of being excessively fat; corpulence. *Obesity contributed to her heart attack.*

obfuscate (ob fus'kāt, ob'fə skāt) v.t., to darken; obscure; becloud; confuse; bewilder. *His complicated memos tended to obfuscate rather than clarify.*

obituary (ō bich'ōō er'ē) n., account of the death of a person, often accompanied with a brief biographical sketch. *I first learned of her death in the obituary.* adj., of or relating to a person's death. *He scanned the obituary page for news.*

objective (əb jek'tiv) n., 1. end toward which efforts are directed; goal; purpose. *We tried to remember the objective of the exercise.* 2. in grammar, the objective case; case used to express the object of a verb or preposition; also, a word in the objective case. *In the sentence "I gave her the apple," "her" is the objective.* adj., 1. factual; real as opposed to subjective. *Photosynthesis is the objective basis of a leaf's color.* 2. free from personal prejudice; unbiased. *Please give me an objective opinion on this report.* 3. in grammar, pertaining to or noting the object of a transitive verb or a preposition; forming or expressing a grammatical object. *In "I see you," "you" is in the objective case.*

objurgate (ob'jər gāt', ab jûr'gāt) v.t., to chide; reprove; upbraid; castigate. *It seemed cruel to objurgate the child for the mishap.*

oblate (ob'lāt, o blāt') n., 1. lay person living in a monastery. *The oblate did the monastery shopping.* 2. loaf of unconsecrated bread for use at the Roman Catholic celebration of the Eucharist; altar bread. *The oblate was prepared for communion.* adj., shaped like a spheroid and flattened at each end. *The earth is an oblate shape.*

obligatory (ə blig′ə tōr′ē, -tôr′ē, ob′lə gə-) adj., 1. binding in law or conscience. *It is obligatory to curb your dog.* 2. imposing obligation. *A quick response will be helpful but is not obligatory.* 3. compulsory; requiring performance of or forbearance from some act; followed by *on* or *upon*. *These responsibilities are obligatory upon all of you.*

oblique (ə blēk′) adj., 1. neither perpendicular nor parallel; not direct; aslant. *The sun cast oblique shadows on the lawn.* 2. indirect; not straightforward; discreet. *She made only an oblique reference to my error.* 3. underhanded; morally questionable. *Some of his tactics were oblique, to say the least.*

obliterate (ə blit′ə rāt′) v.t., 1. to destroy; remove all traces of; cause to disappear. *He tried to obliterate the memory from his mind.* 2. to blot or render undecipherable, as writing; erase; efface. *We repainted the wall to obliterate the graffiti.*

oblivion (ə bliv′ē ən) n., 1. state of being forgotten or lost to memory. *The Aztec civilization fell from great height into oblivion.* 2. act or fact of forgetting; forgetfulness. *He drank himself into oblivion.* 3. forgetting of offenses, or remission of punishment; amnesty. *The new king pleased the prisoners by an act of oblivion.*

oblivious (ə bliv′ē əs) adj., 1. forgetful; disposed to forget. *He blundered on, oblivious of his mistake.* 2. unconscious; unaware; unmindful. *She was oblivious of his admiring glances.*

obloquy (ob′lə kwē) n., 1. abusive, condemning speech. *Her furious obloquy left her shaking.* 2. bad repute as a result of such language. *As a result of the indictment, she bore the burden of obloquy.*

obnoxious (əb nok′shəs) adj., offensive; odious; hateful; reprehensible. *The obnoxious fans spoiled the game for us.*

obscene (əb sēn′) adj., 1. offensive to the senses; repulsive; disgusting; foul. *His obscene table manners nauseated us.* 2. offensive to modesty and decency; lewd; indecent. *We discovered a hidden cache of obscene pictures.*

obsequious (əb sē′kwē əs) adj., servilely complaisant; cringing; fawning; sycophantic. *The obsequious clerk fooled no one.*

observatory (əb zûr′və tōr′ē, -tôr′ē) n., 1. place set aside for making observations of natural phenomena. *The observatory has a powerful telescope.* 2. place with a good view of the terrain. *He spotted the enemy planes from his clifftop observatory.*

obsessed (ob sest′) adj., intensely or abnormally preoccupied; beset; troubled; haunted. *She was obsessed with the need for secrecy.*

obsession (əb sesh′ən) n., 1. continuous or besetting domination of one's thoughts or feelings by an idea, desire, etc. *His preoccupation with religion amounted to an obsession.* 2. act of obsessing. *Her obsession with her child may harm him.* 3. state of being obsessed. *His obsession with appearance is comical.*

obsolescent (ob′sə les′ənt) adj., becoming obsolete; going out of use. *Pocket computers have made the sliderule obsolescent.*

obsolete (ob′sə lēt′, ob′sə lēt′) adj., no longer in use; outmoded; out of date. *Self-reliance will never be obsolete.*

obstetrician (ob′sti trish′ən) n., physician who specializes in the care and treatment of women during their pregnancy and childbirth. *Her obstetrician attended her during her difficult labor and delivery.*

obstreperous (əb strep′ər əs) adj., 1. difficult to control; noisily defiant. *Extra police were needed to handle the obstreperous crowd.* 2. clamorous; vociferous; noisy; boisterous. *With each goal the fans became more obstreperous.*

obstruct (əb strukt′) v.t., 1. to block up; stop up or close; fill with obstacles or impediments that prevent passing. *A great rock was used to obstruct the entrance.* 2. to hinder from passing; stop; impede; check. *The guards tried* *to obstruct our passage.* 3. to cut off from sight; block from view. *The tall buildings obstruct our view.*

obtrude (əb trōōd′) v.t., 1. to thrust forward prominently; stick out. *The post will obtrude into the path.* 2. to put oneself forward without invitation; intrude. *She tried to obtrude into our tête-à-tête.*

obtrusive (əb trōō′siv) adj., 1. disposed to obtrude; pushy; forward. *Her obtrusive behavior is very annoying.* 2. unduly prominent. *The room seemed filled with the obtrusive sofa.*

obtuse (əb tōōs′, -tyōōs′) adj., 1. blunt; not acute or pointed. *He asked her to sharpen the obtuse blade.* 2. in geometry, an angle greater than 90° but less than 180°. *They decided to partition the room at an obtuse angle.* 3. dull; lacking in sensitivity; stupid. *She seemed obtuse to his criticism.*

obviate (ob′vē āt′) v.t., to meet and dispose of (difficulties, objections, etc.); clear out of the way; remove. *I want to obviate the necessity for long explanations later.*

occasion (ə kā′zhən) n., 1. particular time, esp. one marked by some particular occurrence or special circumstance; instance; time. *She always stayed late and on one occasion even spent the night.* 2. special or important time, event, or function. *The annual picnic is an occasion to which we all look forward.* 3. favorable opportunity; convenient time. *I took the occasion to thank her.* 4. reason or incidental cause of some action or result. *Her struggles with the umbrella were the occasion for laughter.* 5. now and then; as need arises; occasionally. *I will drop by on occasion to see how you're getting along.* v.t., to cause incidentally or indirectly; bring about; produce. *The gift may occasion a misunderstanding.*

occidental (ok′si den′t^əl) adj., 1. of or pertaining to the Occident or west; western. *Occidental manners often seem unrefined to the Chinese.* 2. (cap.) native or inhabitant of the Occident or of some

Occidental country. *The Occidental physicians went to Japan to study acupuncture.*

occipital (ok sip′i t^əl) adj., pertaining to that part of the skull that forms the back part of the head. *He sustained an occipital fracture in the crash.*

occlude (ə klōōd′) v., 1. to shut in or out; obstruct. *The wall will occlude trespassers.* 2. to close together. *His teeth do not occlude properly.* 3. (Meteorology) to force up from the earth (as air) by the convergence of a warm front upon a cold front. *The fronts will converge and occlude this stale air.*

occlusion (ə klōō′zhən) n., 1. shutting up; closing. *The voice coach trained her to use occlusion effectively.* 2. manner in which the upper and lower sets of teeth bite down on each other and establish contact. *The dentist noted her excellent occlusion.* 3. atmospheric front formed by occluded air. *The occlusion changed our weather at last.*

occult (ə kult′, ok′ult) n., occult studies or sciences. *She became interested in witchcraft and the occult.* adj., 1. mysterious; transcendental; beyond the bounds of natural knowledge. *People in the Middle Ages believed in alchemy and other occult pseudosciences.* 2. secret; revealed only to the initiated. *She lectured on the occult practices of the Druids.*

oceanography (ō′shē nog′rə fē, ō shē ə nog′-) n., branch of physical geography dealing with the ocean. *Marine biology is part of oceanography.*

octagon (ok′tə gon′, -gən) n., polygon having eight angles and eight sides. *The garden was laid out as an octagon.*

octogenarian (ok′tə jə nâr′ē ən) n., 1. one who is between 80 and 90 years of age. *We celebrated the octogenarian's birthday.* adj., pertaining to an octogenarian. *The octogenarian soprano sang sweetly.*

ocular (ok′yə lər) adj., 1. of or pertaining to the eye. *The glaucoma patient underwent ocular surgery.* 2. of or pertaining to that perceived by the eye; visual. *He got ocular proof of her gardening skill.*

oculist (ok′yə list) n., ophthalmologist or optometrist. *John's oculist recommended bifocals.*

odious (ō′dē əs) adj., hateful or deserving of hatred; offensive; disgusting; repulsive. *An odious stench arose from the sewer.*

odium (ō′dē əm) n., 1. hatred; dislike. *Her obvious odium made me uneasy.* 2. censure or blame; reproach; enmity incurred. *They heaped odium upon him for his cowardice.*

odometer (ō dom′i tər) n., instrument for measuring distance passed over by any wheeled vehicle. *The odometer recorded twenty kilometers.*

odor (ō′dər) n., smell. *The odor of kerosene permeated the room.*

odoriferous (ō′də rif′ər əs) adj., giving odor or scent, usually a sweet scent; diffusing fragrance; perfumed. *The rose is a highly odoriferous flower.*

odorous (ō′dər əs) adj., giving off an odor, scent, or fragrance. *He breathed deeply of odorous lilacs.*

Oedipus complex (ed′ə pəs kom′pleks) in psychoanalysis, sexual desire of a son for his mother. *His sexual difficulties may stem from an unresolved Oedipus complex.*

offal (ô′fəl, of′əl) n., 1. waste meat or meat by-product. *The farmer purchased offal for his pigs.* 2. refuse of any kind; rubbish; garbage. *The pigs were fed corn cobs and other offal.*

offend (ə fend′) v.t., 1. to displease; give offense or displeasure to; annoy. *Will it offend you if I smoke?* 2. to affect disagreeably, as the taste, sense, etc. *The rotting garbage began to offend the nose as well as the eye.* v.i., to give offense; cause displeasure. *They thought the film would offend more than instruct.*

offertory (ô′fər tōr′ē, -tôr′ē, of′ər-) n., 1. that part of the church service during which offerings are made. *The child contributed a coin during the offertory.* 2. verses or anthem said or sung during the offering. *The offertory was sung by the choir.* 3. sacramental offering of

bread and wine to God immediately preceding communion. *The priest raised the chalice during the offertory.*

officious (ə fish′əs) adj., forward in interposing uninvited in the affairs of others; meddling; obtrusive. *The officious clerk annoyed us with his unsolicited comments.*

ogle (ō′gəl) v.t., to look at amorously, provocatively, or impertinently. *He only goes to the beach to ogle the sunbathers.* v.i., to cast amorous or overly familiar glances. *It makes me uncomfortable to watch him ogle and leer that way.*

ogre (ō′gər) n., 1. giant or monster in fairy tales and legend, supposed to live on human flesh. *Jack escaped from the ogre by slipping down the beanstalk.* 2. person likened to or supposed to resemble such a monster. *Our boss is a terrible ogre.*

ohm (ōm) n., in electricity, a unit of resistance. *According to Ohm's law, current equals volts divided by ohms.*

oleaginous (ō′lē aj′ə nəs) adj., 1. having the qualities of oil; oily. *This oleaginous ointment won't rub in.* 2. overly polite; effusive. *The oleaginous hostess made us nervous.*

olfactory (ol fak′tə rē, -trē) adj., pertaining to the sense of smell. *The nose is the principal olfactory organ.*

oligarchy (ol′ə gär′kē) n., 1. form of government in which the supreme power is wielded by a small, exclusive class; also, collectively, those who form such a class or body. *The country was ruled by an oligarchy of wealthy landowners.* 2. state so governed. *In an oligarchy the great majority of citizens have little or no political power.*

ombudsman (ôm′bŏŏdz man′) n., 1. an official appointed by the government to receive and investigate complaints by citizens against government officials or agencies. *The ombudsman investigated our charge of malfeasance against the commissioner.* 2. one who investigates and attempts to settle complaints from groups such as consumers, students, etc. *She acted as ombudsman in our behalf.*

omega (ō mē′gə, -mā′-, ō meg′ə, ō′meg ə) n., 1. last letter of the Greek alphabet. *"Alpha to omega" is equivalent to "A to Z."* 2. last. *The prom was the omega of their school dances.*

ominous (om′ə nəs) adj., 1. foreboding or portending evil; inauspicious. *Ominous rumblings of thunder put a sudden end to our outing.* 2. conveying some omen; serving as a sign or token; significant. *In retrospect, I should have regarded her presence as ominous.*

omnibus (om′nə bus′) n., 1. public vehicle for carrying passengers; bus. *We hired an omnibus for the company picnic.* 2. volume containing reprints of an author's works or of works on one theme. *The teacher assigned two stories from an O. Henry omnibus.* adj., embracing numerous distinct objects; including all or a great number. *They added an omnibus clause to the contract to cover any unspecified situations.*

omnipotent (om nip′ə tᵊnt) adj., 1. almighty; possessing infinite power. *We prayed to the Omnipotent One for deliverance.* 2. of unlimited or great power or influence. *In our family, Father was the omnipotent head.*

omnipresent (om′nə prez′ənt) adj., present in all places at the same time. *The omnipresent canned music began to irritate her.*

omniscient (om nish′ənt) adj., all-knowing; having infinite or universal knowledge. *When her prediction came true, we referred to her as the omniscient Sarah.*

omnivorous (om niv′ər əs) adj., 1. eating both animal and plant foods; eating food of every kind indiscriminately. *Paul's omnivorous goat relishes everything from grapefruit rinds to old newspapers.* 2. absorbing everything. *She is an omnivorous reader.*

onerous (on′ər əs, ō′nər-) adj., burdensome; oppressive. *Helen viewed the extra responsibility as onerous.*

onomatopoeia (on′ə mat′ə pē′ə) n., naming of anything by a more or less exact reproduction of the sound it makes, or something audible connected with it. *The verbs "hiss" and "zip" and the nouns "chickadee" and "blob" are produced by onomatopoeia.*

onslaught (on′slôt, ôn-) n., attack; onset; assault; aggression; furious attack. *We met his verbal onslaught with a carefully prepared rebuttal.*

onus (ō′nəs) n., burden; disagreeable responsibility. *The onus of proof usually rests on the prosecution.*

opalescent (ō′pə les′ənt) adj., exhibiting a milky iridescence like the opal. *The morning sky was opalescent as the sun rose through the mist.*

opaque (ō pāk′) adj., 1. unable to be seen through; impenetrable. *Light didn't penetrate the opaque draperies.* 2. obscure; incomprehensible. *Her opaque remark left him more confused.*

operetta (op′ə ret′ə) n., short, generally light opera. *Our class put on a Gilbert and Sullivan operetta.*

ophthalmologist (of thal mol′ə jist, -thəl-, -thə-, op′-) n., doctor of medicine who specializes in diagnosis and treatment of diseases of the eye. *The ophthalmologist removed the sliver of glass from my eye.*

opiate (ō′pē it, -āt′) n., 1. medicine containing opium; narcotic. *He was given an opiate to relieve his pain.* 2. anything that dulls sensation, mental or physical. *Karl Marx called religion the "opiate of the masses."* adj., mixed or prepared with opium; narcotic; causing rest or inaction. *The warm milk had an opiate effect.*

opinion (ə pin′yən) n., 1. judgment formed on evidence that does not produce certainty; generally held view. *Public opinion considered the law too harsh.* 2. personal expression of such a judgment, view, appraisal, etc. *My opinion of abstract art is no secret.* 3. expression of a professional judgment. *Medical opinion holds that alcoholism is a disease.* 4. judgment or estimate of someone or something with respect to character, qualities, etc. *He really has a poor opinion of himself.* 5. formal explication of a legal decision. *He delivered the eloquent dissenting opinion.*

opinionated (ə pin′yə nā′tid) adj., firmly or unduly adhering to one's own opinion; obstinate; dogmatic. *It is no use trying to reason with the opinionated man.*

opportune (op′ər tōōn′, -tyōōn′) adj., timely; well-timed; convenient. *The check arrived at a most opportune moment.*

opportunist (op′ər tōō′nəst, -tyōō′-) n., one who takes advantage of opportunities as they occur, esp. with little or no regard for principles or consequences. *The opportunist reached the top at the expense of her marriage.*

oppose (ə pōz′) v.t., 1. to speak or act against; contradict; withstand; endeavor to frustrate or thwart. *The senator was the only one to oppose the bill.* 2. to hinder; resist effectually; prevent. *The residents were powerless to oppose the new highway.* 3. to set or place over against or directly opposite; confront or cause to confront; counterbalance. *When we opposed the pros and cons, we seemed to reach a stalemate.*

oppress (ə pres′) v.t., 1. to press unduly upon or against; overburden; weigh down. *You must not let your grief oppress you.* 2. to load or burden with cruel, unjust, or unreasonable impositions or restraints; treat with injustice or undue severity. *The victors began to oppress the vanquished.* 3. to make languid; affect with lassitude. *The tropical heat and humidity oppress me.*

opprobrium (ə prō′brē əm) n., 1. reproach for immoral conduct. *She suffered her governess's opprobrium without trying to defend herself.* 2. disgrace incurred from vicious or immoral conduct. *The embezzler brought opprobrium on his family.*

opprobrious (ə prō′brē əs) adj., expressive or deserving of opprobrium. *His opprobrious conduct led to his dismissal.*

optician (op tish′ən) n., one who fills prescriptions for corrective lenses or glasses, or who makes or sells optical glasses and instruments. *The optician helped me select new frames.*

optics (op′tiks) n., branch of physical science that deals with the nature and properties of light, of the structure of the eye, and of vision. *The ophthalmologist specializes in the field of optics.*

optimum (op′tə məm) n., greatest degree or best results possible given certain implied or specified conditions. *We certainly achieved the optimum, considering all the obstacles to our success.* adj., best or most favorable. *I don't expect much of him, even under optimum conditions.*

optometrist (op tom′i trist) n., person trained to evaluate vision problems by means of special instruments or appliances, and to prescribe corrective lenses or exercises. *The optometrist says I am nearsighted.*

opulence (op′yə ləns) n., 1. wealth; affluence. *Their opulence was manifested in the elegant furnishings and priceless art.* 2. abundance; profusion. *The opulence of the harvest burdened their table.*

opulent (op′yə lənt) adj., 1. wealthy; rich; affluent. *We toured the opulent royal homes.* 2. plentiful; abundant; profuse. *The farmers profited from the opulent harvest.*

opus (ō′pəs) n., work, esp. a literary or musical composition. *His symphony (opus 3) is his most notable composition.*

oracle (ôr′ə kəl, or′-) n., 1. one through which or place in which a deity communicates a message, or the message itself. *The king consulted the oracle at Delos.* 2. respected sage or authority. *She is the oracle on organic gardening.* 3. authoritative or wise utterance. *His oracle made a deep impression on me.*

oracular (ō rak′yə lər, ô rak′-) adj., pertaining to oracles. *The evangelist preached in an oracular manner.*

oratorio (ôr'ə tōr'ē ō', -tôr'-, or'-) n., religious operatic composition performed without action or scenery by solos and full chorus with full orchestral accompaniment. *The university chorus will present Handel's oratorio in its entirety.*

orbicular (ôr bik'yə lər) adj., 1. orb-shaped; spherical; circular. *The satellite follows an orbicular path.* 2. rounded; complete. *His plan seems orbicular and well thought-out.*

orbit (ôr'bit) n., 1. track, circle, path, esp. of an object that returns to its starting point; elliptical path of a planet or comet. *The space vehicle will complete its orbit in one hour.* 2. bony cavity of the skull containing the eye. *The blow left a hairline fracture of the eye's orbit.*

ordinance (ôr'də nəns) n., 1. rule or law established by authority; edict; decree. *They believed bigamy was according to God's ordinance.* 2. law or statute set forth by a government authority, esp. a municipal authority. *There is a local ordinance against excessive noise.* 3. a prescribed religious ceremony, rite, or practice. *Confirmation is an ordinance of our church.*

ordnance (ôrd'nəns) n., military weaponry and combat vehicles and equipment; also, branch of the service in charge of such material. *Ordnance ordered and equipped five new tanks.*

ordure (ôr'jər, -dyōor) n., filth; excrement; dung. *The smell of ordure assaulted her nostrils.*

organic (ôr gan'ik) adj., 1. pertaining to or arising in a bodily organ. *The doctor looked for an organic cause of her anxiety.* 2. of, pertaining to, or derived from living organisms. *She prefers organic pest control.* 3. any chemical compound containing carbon; pertaining to the branch of chemistry concerned with such carbon compounds. *She has a degree in organic chemistry.* 4. forming a whole with a systematic arrangement of parts; organized; systematic. *Each chapter contributes to the volume's organic whole.*

organism (ôr'gə niz'əm) n., animal or plant body so structured and organized that it can maintain independent life. *Oxygen appears necessary to the viability of most organisms.*

orgy (ôr'jē) n., 1. wild or frantic revel; drunken carousal. *Our victory celebration degenerated into an orgy.* 2. any proceedings characterized by wanton lack of control. *The mob embarked on an orgy of looting and vandalism.*

orientation (ōr'ē en tā'shən, ôr'-) n., 1. act of taking one's mental bearings; ascertainment of one's true position. *After a few days of orientation, I adjusted to city living.* 2. usually lasting inclination, attitude, or interest. *His sexual orientation has no bearing on his ability to teach.* 3. introduction, as to guide or instruct one entering a new situation, activity, position, etc. *All incoming freshmen will undergo a week of orientation.*

orifice (ôr'ə fis, or'-) n., mouth or aperture, as of a tube or pipe; mouthlike hole or vent. *The orifice of the cave was blocked with rubble.*

originate (ə rij'ə nāt') v.t., to give rise to; bring to pass; bring into existence. *Automobile exhaust originates a great amount of air pollution.* v.i., to arise; find a starting point or source; begin. *Both flights originate in Chicago.*

ornate (ôr nāt') adj., 1. adorned; elaborately decorated; over-ornamented. *The ornate frame overpowered the picture.* 2. in an elaborate literary style; embellished with rhetoric. *The political rally featured ornate political speeches.*

ornithology (ôr'nə thol'ə jē) n., branch of zoology relating to birds. *Ornithology classifies birds on the basis of bill, color, head shape, etc.*

orthodontist (ôr'thə don'tist) n., dentist specializing in the correction of irregularities in teeth. *The orthodontist put braces on my teeth.*

orthodox (ôr'thə doks') adj., 1. conforming to what is regarded as the correct opinion or opinions, esp. in regard to religious or theological doctrines; conventional; approved. *Orthodox methods*

of treatment failed to result in a cure.
2. (cap.) of or pertaining to the Eastern Church or to Orthodox Judaism. *Our family went to a Greek Orthodox church.*

orthography (ôr thog′rə fē) n., 1. art or practice of writing words with the proper letters, according to accepted usage; correct spelling. *She had an exasperating disregard for orthography.* 2. branch of language study dealing with letters and spelling. *His background in orthography is useful to the editor.*

orthopedics (ôr′thə pē′diks) n., correction or prevention of skeletal deformities. *We took Billy to a specialist in orthopedics as soon as we noticed his crooked leg.*

oscillate (os′ə lāt′) v.i., 1. to swing; move back and forward. *The electric fan will oscillate and cool us both.* 2. to vary or fluctuate; waver. *Her stock began to oscillate between profit and loss.*

osmosis (oz mō′sis, os-) n., 1. tendency of fluids to pass through porous partitions and mix or become diffused. *Osmosis enables the roots of plants to absorb water from the soil.* 2. gradual absorption or diffusion suggesting the process of osmotic action. *We picked up the Spanish words through osmosis.*

ossification (os′ə fə kā′shən) n., 1. process whereby bones are formed. *Calcium is an important element in ossification.* 2. process by which a person or a culture becomes closed to new ideas. *Ossification often follows complacency.*

ossify (os′ə fī′) v.t., to cause to become bone; form into bone. *Age ossified the cartilage.* v.i., 1. to become bone; change or be changed to bone. *The human skeleton does not completely ossify until adulthood.* 2. to become rigid or resistant to change. *As he grows older his opinions seem to ossify.*

ostensible (o sten′sə bəl) adj., put forth or held out as real, actual, or intended; apparent; professed. *Her ostensible motive for lying was to protect someone else.*

ostentation (os′ten tā′shən) n., pretentious display or showing off, esp. of

wealth. *Ostentation often characterizes the nouveau riche.*

ostentatious (os′ten tā′shəs) adj., intended to attract notice; pretentious; showy. *We preferred our comfortable kitchen to her ostentatious front parlor.*

osteopath (os′tē ə path′) n., practitioner who treats disease as if it were caused by deformation of some part of the skeleton and may be cured by manipulation of the affected part or adjoining parts. *The osteopath has relieved my back pain.*

ostracism (os′trə siz′əm) n., act whereby a person is deliberately excluded from a group. *She suffered a cruel ostracism because of her stutter.*

ostracize (os′trə sīz′) v.t., to exile or banish by popular consent; to exclude from public or private favor. *They decided to ostracize him until he apologized.*

oust (oust) v.t., to turn out or eject from a place or position occupied. *The sheriff will try to oust the squatters.*

outlandish (out lan′dish) adj., freakishly out of the ordinary; bizarre; odd. *We laughed at his outlandish outfit.*

outmaneuver (out′mə nōō′vər) v.t., 1. to surpass or get the better of by maneuvering. *She managed to outmaneuver me and end up a step ahead.* 2. to outdo in maneuverability. *My new car can outmaneuver any other on the road.*

outmoded (out′mō′did) adj., out of style; obsolete; no longer usable. *He dressed in an outmoded fashion.*

output (out′pŏŏt′) n., that which is produced. *The exhibit showed the painter's diverse output.*

outrageous (out rā′jəs) adj., 1. extravagant; extraordinary; unusual. *His skill at chess is outrageous.* 2. immoderate; excessive; unrestrained. *She went to outrageous expense for this party.* 3. atrocious; flagrantly contrary to or regardless of authority, law, order, morality, or decency. *The vandals were punished for their outrageous behavior.*

ovary (ō′və rē) n., female gonad or reproductive organ in which eggs or ova are generated and matured and which produces female sex hormones. *The surgeon removed one diseased ovary.*

override (*n.* ō′vər rīd′; *v.* ō′vər rīd′) v.t., to trample; prevail over; supersede. *Congress managed to override the President's veto.* n., 1. commission paid to a manager on sales made by subordinates. *He receives a generous override in addition to his salary.* 2. manual device or system installed to check or correct the operation of an automatic device. *He is trained to operate the override if the automatic controls fail.*

overt (ō vûrt′, ō′vûrt) adj., plain to the view; apparent; open; manifest. *His overt disapproval spoiled all our fun.*

oxidation (ok′si dā′shən) n., 1. act or process of causing a substance to combine with oxygen. *The oxidation of carbon produces carbon dioxide.* 2. act of taking up or combining with oxygen. *Oxidation of iron produces rust.*

oxide (ok′sīd, -sid) n., chemical compound of oxygen with an element or radical. *Nitrogen combines with oxygen to produce nitrous oxide.*

ozone (ō′zōn, ō zōn′) n., 1. triatomic oxygen, a colorless, pungent gas, used esp. for bleaching, disinfecting, and deodorizing. *Ozone is prepared by irradiation of air.* 2. atmospheric layer 10–20 mi (16–32 km) above the earth's surface. *Ozone absorbs much of the sun's ultraviolet radiation.*

Pp

pachyderm (pak′i dûrm′) n., 1. any of the nonruminant ungulate mammals, most of which are thick-skinned, as the elephant, rhinocerous, and hippopotamus. *A pachyderm does not chew its cud.* 2. elephant.

pacific (pə sif′ik) n., tending to create peace; appeasing; conciliatory. *The pacific emissary urged a cease-fire.*

pacifist (pas′ə fist) n., one who opposes war or any kind of conflict. *The pacifist organized a peace rally.* adj., of, pertaining to, or characteristic of pacifism or pacifists. *His pacifist views won his militant friend's contempt.*

pacify (pas′ə fī′) v.t., 1. to calm; quiet; allay the agitation or excitement of. *He tried to pacify the baby's hunger.* 2. to appease; propitiate. *They sacrificed to pacify the angry gods.*

paean (pē′ən) n., song of joy or triumph; hymn of praise. *A paean of rejoicing went up from the crowd.*

pagan (pā′gən) n., 1. heathen, esp. an adherent of a polytheistic religion. *The early church tried hard to convert pagans to Christianity.* 2. irreligious person, esp. a hedonistic one. *He cheerfully confesses to being a pagan.* adj., of, pertaining to, or relating to a pagan or pagans. *Various pagan religions were practiced among the Polynesians.*

pageant (paj′ənt) n., 1. elaborate public spectacle, as a procession, parade, or series of tableaux, often with masks or showy costumes, floats, etc. *We hope to get tickets to the beauty pageant.* 2. specious or pretentious display; mere show. *The whole pageant was staged to prevent embarrassing questions.*

pageantry (paj′ən trē) n., 1. splendid or theatrical display; pomp. *We enjoyed the pageantry of the royal wedding.* 2.

showy but empty display. *She felt the meeting had been mere pageantry.*

paisley (pāz′lē) n., 1. soft woolen fabric woven or printed with an intricate abstract pattern. *She bought a length of beautiful paisley.* 2. shawl or other article made of this fabric. *A handsome paisley covered the piano.* adj., made of paisley or printed in a paisley pattern. *He had a red silk paisley tie.*

palanquin (pal′ən kēn′) n., covered carriage similar to a sedan chair carried by means of poles on the shoulders of four or six men, used in southeast Asia. *The Indian princess stepped aboard the palanquin.*

palatable (pal′ə tə bəl) adj., 1. agreeable to the taste or palate. *He makes a very palatable curry.* 2. pleasing to the mind. *The book may not be palatable to younger readers.*

palatial (pə lā′shəl) adj., resembling a palace; magnificent. *The millionaire has a palatial estate.*

palaver (pə lav′ər, -lä′vər) n., 1. long talk; parley; conference, esp. between persons of different nationalities and cultural levels. *The missionary had a long palaver with the tribal leader.* 2. superfluous or idle talk. *Let's cut the palaver and get down to business.* v.i., to talk idly or profusely. *I can't palaver with you now—I'm busy.* v.t., to flatter or cajole. *Don't try to palaver me; it won't work.*

paleontology (pā′lē ən tol′ə jē, pal′ē-) n., science dealing with the forms of life existing in former geological periods as evidenced by fossil remains. *Her interest in paleontology dated from finding the fossilized fern.*

palette (pal′it) n., 1. thin, usually oblong or oval board or tablet with a hole for

199

the thumb at one end, on which a painter lays and mixes colors; mixture of paints on such a surface. *She carefully cleaned her palette and brushes at the end of each day's work.* 2. color spectrum used by a particular artist. *His early work used a dark and somber palette.*

pall (pôl) n., 1. cloth or covering thrown over a coffin, bier, or tomb. *A purple velvet pall covered the king's coffin.* 2. something that covers or conceals, esp. with darkness or gloom. *A pall of black smoke hung over the city.* v.i., 1. to become distasteful or wearisome. *The constant commotion began to pall on us.* 2. to make spiritless; depress; impair. *Bitter cold, wind, and snow begin to pall as winter progresses.* v.t., to satiate or cloy. *His perpetual cheerfulness palls others after a while.*

pallet (pal′it) n., 1. straw-filled tick or mattress or other small, often temporary, bed or sleeping roll. *She slept on a pallet near her ill husband.* 2. rough wooden platform used for stacking or moving materials. *The forklift carried the pallet to the loading dock.*

palliate (pal′ē āt′) v.t., 1. to cover or conceal; excuse or extenuate. *Nothing can palliate the vile crime.* 2. to reduce in violence; mitigate; alleviate. *This medicine may palliate the fever.*

pallid (pal′id) adj., 1. deficient in color; pale; wan. *Her pallid face betrayed her fear.* 2. lacking sparkle or vitality. *He gave a pallid, lackluster performance.*

pallor (pal′ər) n., unnatural paleness; wanness. *His face had an unhealthy pallor.*

palpable (pal′pə bəl) adj., 1. perceptible by the touch; tangible. *There was a palpable chill in the air.* 2. evident; obvious; easily perceived. *It was a palpable falsehood.*

palpitate (pal′pi tāt′) v.t., to beat or pulsate rapidly; throb; flutter; quiver. *His heart began to palpitate with terror.*

palsy (pôl′zē) n., 1. condition marked by bodily tremors. *He shivered violently as if afflicted with palsy.* 2. paralysis; weakening of muscular power. *She stood still, numbed by a palsy of fear.*

paltry (pôl′trē) adj., 1. trifling; worthless; trivial. *All that fuss over such a paltry sum!* 2. trashy; inferior. *He has a collection of paltry paperback novels.* 3. contemptible; despicable. *Such paltry behavior is unworthy of you.*

panacea (pan′ə sē′ə) n., remedy for all diseases or evils; cure-all. *The government cannot offer a panacea for all problems.*

pancreas (pan′krē əs, pang′-) n., gland situated in the abdomen near the stomach that secretes digestive juices into the duodenum and that produces the hormone insulin. *The pancreas of a calf is served as sweetbread.*

pandemic (pan dem′ik) n., pandemic disease. *Millions died in the Spanish influenza pandemic.* adj., 1. (of a disease) prevalent over a wide area or the whole world. *Smallpox is no longer a pandemic disease.* 2. universal; general. *Hunger is a pandemic problem in the developing countries.*

pandemonium (pan′də mō′nē əm) n., 1. lawless, disorderly, and noisy place or assemblage. *The station was pandemonium at rush hour.* 2. loud noise; tumult; uproar. *Pandemonium erupted when the winner was announced.*

pander (pan′dər) n., one who caters to the lusts of others; pimp. *The pander was arrested on a morals charge.* v.i., to minister to others' base desires; act as a pander. *The artist refused to pander to the sensationalist public.*

Pandora (pan dôr′ə, -dōr′ə) n., in classical mythology, the first mortal woman, who, against Zeus' command, opened a box in her keeping, releasing all human misery into the world. *The reporter unlocked a Pandora's box of scandal and intrigue.*

panegyric (pan′i jir′ik, -jī′rik) n., formal or elaborate encomium; written or spoken eulogy in praise of a person or achievement. *The museum director delivered a panegyric on the new exhibit.*

panhandler (pan′han′dler) n., one who accosts and begs from passersby on the street. *We offered to buy the panhandler a hot meal, but he refused.*

panic (pan′ik) n., sudden fright, esp. affecting a number of persons simultaneously. *The fire caused panic among the audience.*

panoply (pan′ə plē) n., 1. complete set or suit of armor; ceremonial attire. *The king's knights were in full panoply.* 2. complete covering or magnificent array of something. *She stared at the panoply of circus animals.*

panorama (pan′ə ram′ə, -rä′mə) n., 1. complete or entire view over a wide area. *We beheld the magnificent panorama of the Rockies.* 2. picture representing extensive scenes unrolled a part at a time; cyclorama. *The students sat enthralled as a panorama of prehistoric life opened before them.* 3. continuously passing or changing scene. *The panorama of the countryside passed by my window.* 4. comprehensive survey, as of a subject. *The course offers a panorama of Spanish history.*

pantheism (pan′thē iz′əm) n., 1. doctrine that God is the only substance, of which the universe and humanity are only manifestations, thus equaling God and nature. *Pantheism cannot be reconciled with Christianity or Judaism.* 2. worship of all the gods. *The ancient Romans practiced pantheism, adopting many foreign gods.*

pantheon (pan′thē on′) n., 1. (cap.) temple at Rome, built AD 120–24 by Hadrian. 2. temple or shrine dedicated to all the gods. *The people brought offerings of flowers and wine to the pantheon.* 3. all the divinities collectively worshiped by a particular people. *She rattled off the names in the Roman pantheon.* 4. monument containing tombs or memorials of the famous dead. *Westminster Abbey has been called the pantheon of the British.* 5. heroes, idols or illustrious personages of a group. *He won a place in the pantheon of theatrical greats.*

pantomime (pan′tə mīm′) n., 1. play or entertainment in which the actors express themselves by mute gestures, often employing elaborate costumes, scenery, and musical accompaniment.

They will be snowflakes in the Christmas pantomime. 2. form of play in ancient Rome employing mute actors and a choral accompaniment. 3. expression of anything by gestures alone. *It was a pantomime of delight.* v.t., to express oneself by pantomime. *The comedian was famous for his ability to pantomime a drunk.*

papacy (pā′pə sē) n., 1. system of Roman Catholic church government by which the religious authority of the pope is supreme. 2. succession of popes, or term of a pope's reign. *His untimely death ended his papacy.* 3. office of pope. *The cardinal aspires to the papacy.*

papyrus (pə pī′rəs) n., 1. tall, aquatic sedge plant, growing on river banks in the Nile Valley. *Papyrus once grew abundantly in Egypt.* 2. paperlike writing material prepared from the papyrus plant and used by the ancient Egyptians, Greeks, and Romans. *Many scrolls of papyrus were found in the tomb.* 3. ancient scroll, book, or other document written on papyrus. *They are working to translate the papyrus.*

parable (par′ə bəl) n., 1. usually short allegorical story used to draw a moral or convey a religious principle. *The sermon was on the parable of the good Samaritan.* 2. statement that conveys its meaning indirectly through comparison or analogue. *She illustrated her point with a parable.*

parachute (par′ə shōōt′) n., umbrella-shaped device of light material that permits a person or an object to descend slowly and safely from an aircraft. *The parachute opened and the pilot drifted slowly to earth.* v.t., to drop or land by means of a parachute. *We can parachute food to the trapped survivors.* v.i., to descend by parachute. *The pilots were trained to parachute in an emergency.*

paradigm (par′ə dim, -dīm) n., 1. in grammar, example of a word (noun, adjective, verb, etc.) in its various inflections. *A paradigm of the noun "dog" would be dog, dog's, dogs, dogs'.* 2. example;

model; archetype. *She is a paradigm of the successful businesswoman.*

paradox (par′ə doks′) n., 1. statement or proposition that seems absurd or contradictory but that may in fact be true. *They considered the paradox ruefully.* 2. self-contradictory and false proposition. *To say that a circle has four equal sides is a ridiculous paradox.* 3. person or thing having apparently contradictory qualities. *She is a paradox of shyness and hostility.* 4. opinion or statement contrary to popularly accepted opinion. *The paradox is that the whole town admires the scoundrel.*

paragon (par′ə gon′, -gən) n., model or pattern of excellence or perfection. *Abraham Lincoln was held up as a paragon.*

parallel (par′ə lel′) n., 1. anything parallel to something else in direction, course, tendency, etc. *The parallel between my life and his is extraordinary.* 2. intersection of a sphere by a plane perpendicular to its axis, as the parallels of latitude on the earth, represented on maps, globes, etc., by lines drawn to every few degrees between the equator and the poles. *The truce line was designated as the 38th parallel.* 3. something that is equal to or resembles another in all essentials; counterpart; correspondence; analogy. *There is a strong parallel between the biblical and the historical accounts.* adj., 1. extending in the same direction, always the same distance apart and never converging or diverging. *The paper was ruled with parallel lines.* 2. continuing a resemblance through many particulars; similar; analogous. *The two books have many parallel passages.* 3. having the same direction, tendency, or course. *My sister and I have pursued parallel careers.* v.t., 1. to make parallel. *Be sure to parallel your skis before pushing off.* 2. to find a parallel for; match. *His interests parallel yours in many respects.* 3. to form a parallel to; to be equivalent to; equal. *Your wisdom parallels your compassion.* 4. to take a course parallel to. *The road parallels*

the river for several kilometers. 5. to compare. *The article parallels New York with London.*

parallelism (par′ə lel′iz əm) n., 1. act of placing side by side or parallel. *The garden rows were a model of parallelism.* 2. in syntax, a balance of two independent elements. *The parallelism made her point more effective.*

paralysis (pə ral′i sis) n., 1. loss or impairment of function, as of sensation or voluntary muscle contraction. *She suffered a paralysis of her right arm.* 2. crippling or loss of power to perform regular functions. *The paralysis of the transit system forced us to walk home.*

parameter (pə ram′i tər) n., something that is characteristic or constant; boundary. *Their meetings are conducted within the parameters of parliamentary law.*

paramount (par′ə mount′) adj., 1. supreme; superior in rank or position; chief. *The chairman is paramount over all the committee heads.* 2. superior to all others; preeminent. *For the plan to work, secrecy is of paramount importance.*

paranoia (par′ə noi′ə) n., 1. mental disorder presenting systematized delusions of persecution or grandeur, often persisting for years without any disturbance of consciousness. *My brother suffers from paranoia, believing he has enemies everywhere.* 2. irrational suspiciousness or distrustfulness. *Her paranoia about big government makes her unreasonable.*

parapet (par′ə pit, -pet′) n., wall or rampart rising breast-high. *The infantry easily scaled the parapet.*

paraphernalia (par′ə fər nāl′ya, -fə nāl′-) n., 1. personal belongings. *Pack your paraphernalia and leave!* 2. equipment; accessories; apparatus. *The kitchen contains all his culinary paraphernalia.*

paraphrase (par′ə frāz′) n., restatement of a text or passage giving the sense of the original in other words; free translation, as of a passage. *The paraphrase is clearer than the original statement.* v.t., to restate or translate; interpret;

construe. *Don't paraphrase everything I say.*

parasite (par′ə sīt′) n., 1. organism that lives on or in and at the expense of another organism. *The flea is a common parasite on domestic pets.* 2. one who receives support, hospitality, patronage, etc., from another or others without making any meaningful contribution in return. *She works from dawn until dark while her parasite of a husband sits at home watching television.*

paregoric (par′ə gôr′ik, -gor′-) n., camphorated tincture of opium, flavored with aromatics. *She tried to quiet the cranky baby with paregoric.*

parenthesis (pə ren′thi sis) n., either or both of the upright curves ( ), used in writing to mark off an interjected explanatory clause or qualifying remark. *They put the translation in parentheses.* 2. explanatory material inserted into a passage without being grammatically connected with it and usually set off by punctuation marks as parentheses, commas, or dashes. *The parenthesis was set off by em-dashes.*

parenthetical (par′ən thet′i kəl) adj., 1. pertaining to or in the nature of a parenthesis. *The explanation appeared in a parenthetical clause.* 2. occurring like a parenthesis or episode; incidental. *She interrupted her lunch with a parenthetical telephone call.*

par excellence (pär ek′sə läns′) adv. (or adj.), being the best of its kind; preeminent. *He is a novelist par excellence.*

pariah (pə rī′ə, par′ē ə, pär′-) n., outcast. *I have been a pariah ever since I refused to contribute for the office party.*

parietal (pə rī′i təl) adj., 1. pertaining to a wall, esp. within the body. *The tumor pressed against the parietal tissues.* 2. pertaining to regulation of life within a college. *The university assumes parietal responsibility for security.*

parity (par′i tē) n., 1. equality; similarity or equivalence in status, position, condition, quality, degree, etc. *There is parity between his job and mine.* 2. in finance, the equivalent in value in the currency of another country. *The cur-*

rencies settled at parity. 3. system of regulating prices of farm commodities, usually by government price supports, so that farmers' current purchasing power will equal that in a selected base period. *Parity is determined by Congress.*

parlance (pär′ ləns) n., manner of speaking; idiom. *The two surgeons conferred in medical parlance.*

parley (pär′lē) n., 1. discussion or conference. *We invited him to the parley over zoning.* 2. conference with an enemy under truce to discuss terms or conditions of surrender, etc. *At last week's parley the two countries agreed on a prisoner exchange.* v.i., 1. to confer on some point of mutual concern. *The labor leaders will parley with management today.* 2. to confer with an enemy under a truce to discuss terms. *An uneasy peace prevailed as they met to parley.*

parliament (pär′lə mənt) n., assembly of elected representatives to deliberate or legislate on national affairs, esp. the combined houses of Lords and Commons. *She gave her maiden speech in Parliament today.*

parochial (pə rō′kē əl) adj., 1. pertaining to a parish or parishes. *The priest met with the deacons to discuss parochial affairs.* 2. local; provincial; narrow. *She hoped to broaden his parochial outlook.*

parody (par′ə dē) n., 1. burlesque imitation of a serious literary or musical work, in which the form and expression of the original are closely followed but are made ridiculous, humorous, or satirical. *It was a marvelous parody of A Pilgrim's Progress.* 2. poor or ridiculous imitation; travesty. *His acting style is a parody of Brando's.* v.t., 1. to compose a parody on. *He is attempting to parody a Shakespeare sonnet.* 2. to imitate in a ridiculous or ludicrous manner. *He parodied the professor's pedantic style.*

paroxysm (par′ək siz′əm) n., 1. any sudden and violent action; fit; outburst. *He went into a paroxysm of laughter.* 2. severe and violent attack or increase in severity of a disease, usually occurring periodically. *Her illness began with a paroxysm of vomiting.*

parricide (par'i sīd') n., one who murders a parent or other close relative; such an act. *He committed parricide when he murdered his parents.*

parry (par'ē) n., defensive movement in fencing. *Every thrust of my blade was met with a skillful parry.* v.t., to turn aside; ward off, as a thrust or blow. *The exhausted challenger was unable to parry the blows.* v.i., to ward off a thrust or argument; fence. *Although I laughed it off, she parried and struck back.*

parsimonious (pär'sə mō'nē əs) adj., characterized by parsimony; excessively frugal; niggardly. *He was unfortunately not parsimonious in his rebuke.*

parsimony (pär'sə mō'nē) n., state of being excessively economical; stinginess. *The ragged child bemoaned her father's parsimony.*

parthenogenesis (par'thə nō jen'i sis) n., reproduction without sexual congress, via development of unfertilized gametes, which occurs in some insects and and other invertebrates and, rarely, in plants. *Aphids reproduce by parthenogenesis.*

partiality (pär shal'i tē, pär'shē al'-) n., state of being partial; bias. *She tried not to show partiality toward the bright student.*

partisan (pär'ti zan) n., 1. adherent or supporter of a party or faction. *She is an ardent Republican partisan.* 2. member of a party or detachment of light or irregular troops making forays and harassing the enemy; guerrilla. *The partisan was sent to blow up the governor's palace.* adj., 1. of or pertaining to a party or faction. *Her partisan bias is well known.* 2. of, pertaining to, or carried on by military partisans. *Both sides engaged in partisan warfare.*

partition (pär tish'ən) n., 1. act of parting, dividing, or separating into portions and distributing. *The child watched the partition of the birthday cake.* 2. separation; division, as of two or more things. *The partition of the flood victims was una-*

voidable. 3. something that separates or divides. *The partition between the rooms was paper-thin.* 4. separate part or section of a whole. *The pantry was a small partition of the kitchen.* v.t., 1. to divide into parts or shares. *He made a will to partition his estate.* 2. to divide by walls or partitions. *Curtains partition the dormitory into individual cubicles.*

parturition (pär'tŏŏ rish'ən, -tyŏŏ-, -chŏŏ-) n., act of bringing forth or of being delivered of offspring. *The difficult parturition left her exhausted.*

parvenu (pär'və nŏŏ, -nyŏŏ') n., someone who has recently or suddenly achieved prominence or success; upstart. *The parvenu was overwhelmed by her meteoric success.* adj., characteristic of a parvenu. *In evolutionary terms, man is a parvenu species.*

passé (pa sā', pas'ā) adj., 1. antiquated; outmoded. *The rumbleseat is passé.* 2. past one's prime; faded. *The wonderful old lady would never be passé.*

passive (pas'iv) adj., 1. open to impressions from external sources; receptive; unresisting. *Physical therapy provides passive exercise for injured muscles.* 2. in grammar, applied to verbs that show the subject to be acted upon rather than acting. *The passive mode is "was written" instead of "wrote."* 3. lethargic; inactive. *The comedian bombed with the passive audience.* 4. submissive. *She was a passive wife; dominated by her husband.*

pasta (pä'stə) n., any of a variety of flour-and-egg-paste preparations of Italian origin, usually served with a sauce or a stuffing or both. *Fettucini is my favorite pasta.*

pasteurization (pas'chə rə zā'shən, pas'tə-, -rī-) n., process, named after Louis Pasteur, of partial sterilization that preserves wines and dairy products by destroying hazardous fungi and their spores. *Pasteurization significantly increases the shelf life of dairy products.*

pastoral (pas'tər əl, pä'stər-) n., 1. poem or other literary work idealizing the life of shepherds or of the country or country life in general; a bucolic. *Her long* *pastoral depicted the simple joys of country living.* 2. any work of art with a rural subject. *His pastoral of the three shepherdesses is famous.* 3. a letter from a bishop to his clergy or people, or from a minister to his people. *He read the bishop's pastoral to the congregation.* adj., 1. descriptive of the life of shepherds; treating of rustic life. *She composed a pastoral poem.* 2. having the traditional characteristics, as charm and simplicity, of the country or of rural life. *They loved the peaceful pastoral setting of the farm.* 3. of or pertaining to a pastor or the office of pastor. *The minister's pastoral duties include visiting the sick.*

pastorale (pas'tə räl', -ral', -rä'lē; *It.* päs'tô ʀä'le) n., musical composition with a pastoral or bucolic theme. *The pastorale included several folk dances.*

pate (pāt) n., 1. head. *She gave me a playful rap on the pate.* 2. crown or top of the head. *His pate was bald.*

paté (pä tā') n., 1. meat or fish pie or pastry. *It was a delicious duck paté.* 2. paste or spread made from mashed and seasoned meat, fish, liver, etc., usually served as an hors d'oeuvre. *A liver paté was served with the sherry.*

patent (pat'ənt) n., 1. government grant to an inventor or to his or her heirs or assigns, conferring the exclusive right to exploit an invention for a stated period of time. *My uncle got a patent on his invention.* 2. invention that has been patented. *This appliance is a new patent.* 3. official document conferring or granting a privilege, sometimes called letters patent. *In medieval England only the king could grant letters patent.* 4. government instrument conveying title to public land. *The park was established under a government patent.* adj., 1. patented; secured by a patent. *It is a patent device for mixing paint.* 2. pertaining to or dealing with patents. *My aunt is a patent attorney.* 3. protected by or made under a patent; trademarked; proprietary. *The druggist sold patent medicines.* 4. unconcealed; evident; obvious; conspicuous. *It was a*

patent falsehood. v.t., 1. to grant by patent. *I hope the government will patent my invention.* 2. to obtain a patent on; secure exclusive rights to by a patent. *If it works, you should patent it.*

pathetic (pə thet'ik) adj., 1. exciting compassion or pity; full of pathos. *It was a pathetic story of unrequited love.* 2. marked by sorrow; sad. *His pathetic little face was streaked with tears.*

pathogenic (path'ə jen'ik) adj., producing disease. *Researchers sought an antibody for the pathogenic bacteria.*

pathological (path'ə loj'i kəl) adj., 1. pertaining to pathology. *The doctor specializes in pathological research.* 2. due to, involving, or caused by disease; morbid. *She has a pathological fear of dogs.* 3. dealing with or treating of diseases. *They attended a pathological seminar.*

pathology (pə thol'ə jē) n., 1. sum of scientific knowledge concerning disease, its origins, physiological and anatomical features, and its causative functions. *Chemical science has greatly aided pathology.* 2. deviation from the normal characteristics of a particular disease. *The pathology of the man's disease confounded the physician.*

pathos (pā'thos) n., quality or power of evoking pity, compassion, or sympathy. *The pathos in your story touches me.*

patriarch (pā'trē ärk') n., 1. father or male head of a family. *Grandfather was the patriarch of our family.* 2. male head, ruler, or chief of a tribe; specifically, one of the biblical progenitors of the Israelites: Abraham, Isaac, Jacob, and the sons of Jacob; also, one of the antediluvian family heads from Adam to Noah. *All the members of the group deferred to the patriarch.* 3. any of the bishops of the early Christian church and of various Eastern Orthodox churches; in the Roman Catholic Church the pope as patriarch of the West. *In the early church the title of patriarch belonged to the bishops of Rome, Alexandria, and Antioch.* 4. one of the highest bishops in the Roman

Catholic Church; one of the highest dignitaries of the Mormon Church. 5. any venerable old man. *They decided to consult the village patriarch.*

patrilineal (pa′trə lin′ē əl, pā′-) adj., pertaining to one's ancestry through the father's line of descent. *My genealogy includes a horse thief on the patrilineal side.*

patrimony (pa′trə mō′nē) n., 1. inherited right or estate. *My patrimony includes the old homestead.* 2. anything derived from one's ancestors; heritage. *Her fine sense of humor is part of her patrimony.* 3. endowment, estate, or revenue of a church or religious house. *The patrimony of the monastery was carefully shepherded by the monks.*

patron (pā′trən) n., 1. customer or client, particularly on a regular basis, of a store, hotel, library, restaurant, etc. *My brother is a dedicated patron of the local candy store.* 2. one who supports with money or influence a person, art, institution, enterprise, etc. *She is a patron of the symphony orchestra.* 3. special guardian or protector; saint whose special care is invoked. *St. Crispin is the patron of shoemakers.*

patronage (pā′trə nij, pa′-) n., 1. subsidy provided by a patron or supporter. *The musician sought the duke's patronage.* 2. customer's trade. *The storekeeper thanked him for his patronage.* 3. control over the distribution of nonelective governmental jobs as return for favors or votes. *The assistant got her job through patronage.* 4. condescending manner in granting a request. *The benefactor's patronage insulted the headmaster.*

patronize (pā′trə nīz′, pa′-) v.t., 1. to give support or custom to; favor; trade with. *We always patronize the corner grocery.* 2. to condescend to in an offensive way. *You patronize me as if I were an idiot.* 3. to assist; act as a patron toward. *He patronizes the struggling musician.*

paucity (pô′si tē) n., smallness or fewness; scantiness; scarcity; dearth. *There was a woeful paucity of talent in the show.*

pavilion (pə vil′yən) n., 1. light, often open structure often located in a park or recreation area, used for exhibitions or entertainment. *A band concert was held in the park pavilion.* 2. tent, often large and elaborate. *The queen held court in a sumptuous pavilion.* 3. section that projects from the main part of a building. *A pavilion projects from the east side of the chateau.* 4. any of a number of detached or semidetached buildings forming part of a hospital. *She entered the maternity pavilion.* v.t., to shelter with or as with a tent. *Elaborate canopies were erected to pavilion the royal party.*

peccadillo (pek′ə dil′ō) n., petty fault; slight offense. *We dismissed his tardiness as a peccadillo.*

pectoral (pek′tər əl) n., piece of protective chest armor; breastplate. *The knight removed his pectoral.* adj., pertaining to the chest or breast. *The swimmer developed powerful pectoral muscles.*

peculiar (pi kyool′yər) adj., 1. strange; unusual; uncommon; odd. *A peculiar odor emanated from the basement.* 2. belonging specially or particularly to a person, thing, or group. *They spoke a dialect peculiar to the area.* 3. different in character or nature from others of the same kind; distinctive. *This wine is known for its peculiar color and bouquet.*

pecuniary (pi kyoo′nē er′ē) adj., 1. consisting of money; given or exacted in money. *We offered a pecuniary reward for its return.* 2. of or relating to money. *They seemed always to be in pecuniary difficulties.*

pedagogue (ped′ə gog′) n., 1. schoolteacher; educator, esp. of children. *A pedagogue was hired for the new school.* 2. one who is pedantic or dogmatic. *She is a long-winded, boring, old pedagogue.*

pedal (ped′əl) n., lever to be pressed by the foot to operate certain mechanisms or vehicles or in playing certain musical instruments. *In this piano piece the soft pedal is used extensively.* adj., 1. pertaining to or connected with a foot or the feet. *He suffered frostbite of his pedal extremities.* 2. of or pertaining to or involving a pedal or pedals. *A pedal mechanism propelled the craft through the water.* v.t., to work the pedals of. *We'll have to pedal our bikes as fast as we can.* v.i., to work or use a pedal or pedals. *I am learning to pedal when I play the organ.*

pedant (ped′ənt) n., 1. one who makes an undue or inappropriate display of learning. *I would admire her knowledge if only she weren't such a pedant.* 2. one who lays an undue stress on exact knowledge of details or of trifles. *He has a pedant's love of detail of history.* 3. one who relies on book learning rather than practical reasoning. *What we need is someone with common sense, not a pedant.*

pedestrian (pə des′trē ən) n., one who goes on foot; walker. *The pedestrian stopped at the curb.* adj., 1. going on foot; walking. *We enjoy all pedestrian activities.* 2. of, pertaining to, or designed for walking. *The pedestrian crosswalk is within the white lines.* 3. commonplace; prosaic; unimaginative. *We didn't like the pedestrian play.*

pediatrician (pē′dē ə trish′ən, ped′ē-) n., physician who specializes in the medical or hygienic care of children. *The pediatrician listened to the child's heart.*

pediatrics (pē dē a′triks, ped′ē-) n., branch of medicine dealing with the development, medical care, and diseases of children. *She decided to specialize in pediatrics.*

pedigree (ped′ə grē′) n., 1. ancestral line; recorded line of descent; genealogical tree. *He has a book showing his noble pedigree.* 2. recorded purity of breed, as of domestic animals. *My German shepherd has an impressive pedigree.* 3. distinguished ancestry. *She flaunts her pedigree as if it were an achievement.* 4. origin, derivation, or history of something. *I'm not sure of the word's pedigree.*

peduncle (pi dung′kəl) n., 1. flower stalk supporting a cluster or solitary flower.

The peduncle bore a cluster of magnolias. 2. little footlike part supporting a larger part of an organism. *There are three peduncles of the cerebellum.*

peer (pēr) n., 1. person of the same rank or standing; an equal. *I feel I am his peer in every respect.* 2. member of the British nobility (duke, marquis, earl, viscount, baron). *I'm sure every peer in England attended the party.* v.i., 1. to look narrowly or sharply, implying an effort to see. *Peer through the fog and see if you can spot the sign.* 2. to peep out; come into sight; emerge partly. *The sun peered through the clouds.*

peignoir (pān wär′, pen-, pān′wär, pen′-) n., loose dressing gown worn by a woman. *She appeared in a flowing white peignoir.*

pejorative (pi jôr′ə tiv, -jor′-, pej′ ə rā-) adj., tending or intended to deprecate; having a disparaging meaning. *"Housewife" is often regarded as a pejorative title.*

pelagic (pə laj′ik) adj., pertaining to the sea; oceanic. *Pelagic fauna are an island food staple.*

pelf (pelf) n., ill-gained money or riches. *The looters ran through the streets with their stolen pelf.*

pellagra (pə lä′grə, -lag′rə, -lä′grə) n., endemic disease of southern Europe, characterized by abnormal redness of skin, digestive disorders, and nervous conditions. *Pellagra is brought on by a diet deficient in niacin.*

pell-mell (pel′ mel′) adv., 1. in a disorderly mass or manner. *He tossed the apples pell-mell into a bag.* 2. with confused haste. *We all rushed pell-mell into the aisles.* adj., confused; tumultuous; disorderly. *The team made a pell-mell attack upon the opponents' goal.*

pellucid (pə loo′sid) adj., 1. transparent; capable of transmitting light. *The pellucid lantern emitted an amber glow.* 2. clear; easily understood. *We appreciated his pellucid summary of events.*

penance (pen′əns) n., 1. self-punishment expressive of penitence or repentance; punishment undergone in atonement for sin. *She suffered his scolding gladly as a penance for having hurt him.* 2. discipline imposed by church authorities as an atonement for sin. *The priest imposed a light penance on her.* 3. sacrament of the Roman Catholic, Eastern, and some Anglican churches consisting of confession, absolution, and penance. *A crowd awaited the sacrament of penance.*

penchant (pen'chənt) n., strong inclination; liking; bias. *I have a penchant for classical music.*

pendant (pen'dənt) n., anything hanging down or suspended, as an ornament, chandelier, or other lighting fixture. *She wore a diamond pendant around her neck.*

pendent (pen'dənt) adj., 1. hanging; suspended. *She wore pendent jade earrings.* 2. projected; overhanging. *We drove under the pendent cliff.*

pendulum (pen'jə ləm, pen'də-, -dyə-) n., body so suspended from a fixed point as to move to and fro by the alternate action of gravity and its acquired energy of motion, and commonly used to regulate movements such as clockwork. *The pendulum's hypnotic swing made her drowsy.*

penicillin (pen'i sil'in) n., mixture produced by molds and used as a germicide; any of various salts or esters used as antibiotics (discovered by Alexander Fleming in 1928). *The penicillin cured her sore throat.*

penitent (pen'i tənt) n., 1. one who repents, or is sorry for sin; contrite person. *The penitent asked her forgiveness.* 2. one who confesses sin and is given penance by a priest. *In the early Christian church a penitent was required to do public penance.* adj., sorry for sin or for offense committed; contrite; repentant. *He was truly penitent for having broken the window.*

pensive (pen'siv) adj., seriously, wistfully, or sadly thoughtful. *The rainy day put me into a pensive mood.*

penumbra (pi num'brə) n., 1. partial shadow between the full light and the total shadow caused by an opaque body intercepting a part of the light from a luminous body. *The penumbra disappears when the source of light is a point rather than an area.* 2. gray border that surrounds the dark umbra or nucleus of a sunspot. *The gray fringe surrounding the dark shadow of a sunspot is called a penumbra.* 3. in painting, the point at which light and shade blend almost imperceptibly. *Penumbra was studied in the seminar on chiaroscuro.*

penurious (pə noŏr'ē əs, -nyoŏr'-) adj., 1. parsimonious to a fault; excessively stingy. *Because of their penurious father, the children went about in rags.* 2. poverty-stricken; indigent. *The penurious family lives in an old storage shed.*

penury (pen'yə rē) n., 1. extreme poverty; indigence; destitution. *The illiterate was forced to live in penury.* 2. scantiness; scarcity; dearth. *The penury of good drinking water makes the land unsuitable for development.*

peonage (pē'ə nij) n., 1. state of servitude, esp. that which formerly existed in parts of South America and Mexico, India, and Ceylon. *The peonage of Mexican laborers led to the 1910 revolution.* 2. practice of using convicts as laborers. *The labor union opposed the prison's use of peonage.*

perambulate (pər am'byə lāt') v.t., 1. to walk through, about, or over. *The new owners perambulate the premises daily.* 2. to survey while passing through; traverse and examine. *The two men perambulated the boundary in a jeep.* v.i., to walk about; stroll. *The couple began to perambulate along the quay.*

per capita (pər kap'i tə) adv., for or by each person individually; per unit of population. *Per capita sugar consumption is rising.*

perceive (pər sēv') v.t., 1. to become aware of; gain a knowledge of through the senses. *I did not perceive the headlights through the fog.* 2. to come to know through the mind; understand. *You can't begin to perceive her anger.*

perceptive (pər sep'tiv) adj., 1. having the faculty of perceiving. *She has a perceptive ear for pronunciation.* 2. of ready or quick perception. *It is a perceptive analysis of urban problems.*

percolate (pûr'kə lāt') v.t., to prepare coffee in a percolator. *I started to percolate the coffee.* v.i., 1. to penetrate; seep through. *The dye began to percolate through the fabric.* 2. to bubble up. *Raw sewage began to percolate from the cesspool.*

percussion (pər kush'ən) n., 1. forcible striking of one body against another. *The percussion of hail on the tin roof was deafening.* 2. striking or beating of a musical instrument. *The piano, drum, and harp are all played by percussion.* 3. percussion instruments as a group, in band or orchestra. *The conductor gestured to the percussion for the finale.*

perdition (pər dish'ən) n., hell; damnation. *He knew perdition in the slave galley.*

peregrination (per'ə grə nā'shən) n., traveling from one country or place to another; roaming or wandering about; journeying. *After ten years of peregrination, I came home for good.*

peremptory (pə remp'tə rē) adj., 1. precluding debate, question, or refusal; authoritative; imperative. *They jumped to obey his peremptory command.* 2. imperious; arrogant; dictatorial. *They resent the peremptory attitude of the new chairman.* 3. decisive. *The crisis required peremptory action.*

perennial (pə ren'ē əl) n., plant that lives through many years. *She chose blue and red perennials for the rock garden.* adj., 1. lasting many years; persistent. *She suffered perennial ill health.* 2. continuing without stop or intermission; perpetual; everlasting. *His perennial arguing gets on my nerves.*

perfectionist (pər fek'shə nist) n., one who demands perfection of oneself or who refuses to accept anything short of perfection. *The perfectionist was still dissatisfied with the lovely painting.*

perfidy (pûr'fi dē) n., breach of faith or trust; treachery; faithlessness. *His perfidy was all the more devastating considering our trust in him.*

perforce (pər fōrs', -fôrs') adv., of necessity; by force of circumstances. *We had perforce to accept his offer.*

perfunctory (pər fuṅgkt'tə rē) adj., 1. mechanical; careless. *He greeted them with a perfunctory smile.* 2. without interest or enthusiasm. *She gave the book a perfunctory reading.*

perigee (per'i jē') n., point of the orbit of a heavenly body, as the moon or an artificial satellite, when it is nearest the earth. *The unusually low tide tonight is due to the moon's perigee.*

perilous (per'ə ləs) adj., full of danger; hazardous; risky. *We hesitated to make the perilous journey.*

perimeter (pə rim'i tər) n., 1. circumference, border, or outer boundary of a two-dimensional figure. *A stone wall marked the field's perimeter.* 2. the measure of such a boundary. *The room's perimeter is 40 feet.*

peripatetic (per'ə pə tet'ik) n., one who walks about; itinerant. *The peripatetic lived out of a suitcase.* adj., walking about; itinerant. *The peripatetic peddler sold trinkets door to door.*

peripheral (pə rif'ər əl) adj., 1. of, pertaining to, or situated on the periphery, circumference, or surface. *The disease impaired her peripheral vision.* 2. dealing with relatively minor or superficial aspects of a subject or thing. *That is merely a peripheral afterthought.*

periphery (pə rif'ə rē) n., 1. boundary line of any surface or area; perimeter. *The spectators stood just inside the field's periphery.* 2. outside or superficial parts. *The protesters couldn't penetrate the periphery of guards.* 3. relatively minor or superficial aspects. *The debate touched only the periphery of the issue.*

periscope (per'i skōp') n., optical instrument in shape of a tube through which an object not in direct line of sight may be viewed. *The submarine captain spotted the destroyer through the periscope.*

perjury (pûr′jə rē) n., willful utterance of false testimony under oath before a competent tribunal, upon a point material to a legal inquiry. *When his lie became known, he was indicted for perjury.*

permeate (pûr′mē āt′) v.t., to pass into or through; spread through and fill the openings, pores, and interstices of; saturate; pervade. *Suspicion permeates the atmosphere.*

permutation (pûr′myə tā′shən) n., interchange; concurrent changes; mutual change; transformation. *The alchemist believed possible the permutation of iron into gold.*

pernicious (pər nish′əs) adj., injurious; hurtful; deadly. *It was a piece of pernicious gossip.*

perpendicular (pûr′pən dik′yə lər) adj., 1. at right angles to the plane of the horizon; vertical; upright. *Perpendicular cliffs lined the river.* 2. in geometry, meeting a given line or surface at right angles. *A is perpendicular to b.* 3. upright or in a standing position. *I became dizzy but managed to remain perpendicular.*

perpetrate(pûr′pi trāt′)v.t., 1. to perform, execute, or commit, generally in a bad sense. *Did he perpetrate the murder in cold blood?* 2. to do, execute, or perform in a shocking or tasteless way. *He perpetrated the most outrageous puns.*

perpetual (pər pech′ōō əl) adj., 1. continuing forever; everlasting. *The tropics enjoy perpetual summer.* 2. continuing or continued without interruption. *The clock has a perpetual movement.*

perpetuate (pər pech′ōō āt′) v.t., to make perpetual; cause to endure or to continue or be continued indefinitely. *She didn't want to perpetuate the folly.*

persecute (pûr′sə kyōōt′) v.t., 1. to pursue with harassing or oppressive treatment; injure or afflict persistently. *Children who persecute animals need treatment.* 2. to afflict, harass, or punish on account of opinions, as for adherence to religious or other principles. *Our*

union will not persecute those who choose not to join.

persevere (pûr′sə vēr′) v.i., to persist in anything undertaken; be constant or steadfast. *We encouraged him to persevere in his art.*

persiflage (pûr′sə fläzh′) n., light, bantering talk. *Let's drop the persiflage and get serious.*

persist (pər sist′) v.i., 1. to continue steadily and firmly in some state, course of action, or pursuit, esp. in spite of opposition, remonstrance, etc.; persevere, esp. with some degree of obstinacy. *Must you persist in this interrogation?* 2. to last or endure. *Great art will persist through bad times.*

persona non grata (*Lat.* per sō′nä nōn grä′tä; *Eng.* pər sō′nə non grä′tə, grä′-) unacceptable person; one in disfavor. *She was persona non grata after dropping out of school.*

personify (pər son′ə fī′) v.t., 1. to treat or regard as a person. *The painting personifies the four seasons as women.* 2. to typify; be an embodiment of. *He personifies honesty.*

perspective (pər spek′tiv) n., 1. technique of representing 3-dimensional objects on a flat surface. *That artist is a master of perspective.* 2. drawing or painting in perspective. *The backdrop was a perspective of a rural scene.* 3. prospect; view; vista. *A snowy perspective spread before us.* 4. proper or just proportion; relation of parts to one another and to the whole view, subject, etc. *The book gave a social perspective to the Industrial Revolution.*

perspicacity (pûr′spə kas′i tē) n., acuteness of discernment or understanding; sagacity. *She shows a precocious perspicacity.*

perspicuity (pûr′spə kyōō′i tē) n., clearness; lucidity. *His prose has an almost pictorial perspicuity.*

perspiration (pûr′spə rā′shən) n., 1. excretion of liquid from the skin, mainly by the sweat glands. *Perspiration serves to cool the body in hot weather.* 2. liquid thus excreted; sweat. *Perspiration ran down the runner's back.*

persuasive (pər swā′siv) adj., having power of persuading; tending to win over the mind or will. *I was completely convinced by her persuasive argument.*

pert (pûrt) adj., 1. forward; saucy; impudent. *The pert little boy promptly contradicted me.* 2. trim; smart; jaunty, chic. *We admired her pert new sports car.*

pertinacious (pûr′t^ə nā′shəs) adj., 1. holding or adhering to an opinion, purpose, design, course of action, etc. *She was pertinacious in her resolve to study medicine.* 2. persistent; obstinate. *The pertinacious sales clerk wouldn't take no for an answer.*

pertinent (pûr′t^ə nənt) adj., appropriate; relevant. *The 19th-century work is still pertinent to our study.*

perturb (pər tûrb′) v.t., 1. to disturb greatly in mind; agitate; disquiet. *Her alarm began to perturb me, too.* 2. to throw into disorder; confuse; cause irregularity in. *His testimony will only perturb our case.*

peruse (pə rooz′) v.t., to read through carefully or with attention. *After my lawyers peruse the contract I'll sign it.*

pervade (pər vād′) v.t., to extend or be diffused throughout; permeate. *Suspicion and anger pervade the labor negotiations.*

perverse (pər vûrs′) adj., 1. disposed to be contrary; obstinate; stubborn; intractable. *It was impossible to please my perverse companion.* 2. cross; petulant; peevish. *The perverse woman ruined our trip.* 3. deviating from what is right or proper; wayward. *I've decided to forgive your former perverse behavior.*

perversion (pər vûr′zhən, -shən) n., 1. act of perverting. *He accused the poolhall proprietor of perversion of the town's youth.* 2. state of being perverted. *His perversion stems from his sordid childhood.* 3. perverted form of something. *Possessiveness is a perversion of love.* 4. aberrant or abnormal means of sexual gratification, esp. when habitual. *The perversion was outlawed in twelve states.*

pervert (*n.* pûr′vərt; *v.* pər vûrt′) n., one who practices sexual perversion or who is affected with perversion. *A pervert had scrawled obscenities on the wall.* v.t., 1. to lead astray; corrupt. *Do television sex and violence pervert children?* 2. to divert to a wrong end or purpose; misapply. *Don't pervert your talent for purely material gain.* 3. to misinterpret willfully. *Don't pervert my silence into agreement.*

pervious (pûr′vē əs) adj., 1. affording entrance, admission, or passage; penetrable; permeable. *The pervious old umbrella was useless.* 2. open to reason, suggestion, argument. *She tried to remain pervious to both sides.*

pesky (pes′kē) adj., troublesome; annoying. *Those pesky ants are ruining our picnic.*

pessimism (pes′ə miz′əm) n., tendency to expect the worst. *His stubborn pessimism contributed most to his defeat.*

pesticide (pes′ti sīd′) n., chemical agent for destroying pests, as harmful or annoying insects. *We used a pesticide on the infested plants.*

pestilence (pes′t^ə ləns) n., 1. any malignant epidemic disease, esp. bubonic plague. *The pestilence killed thousands.* 2. that which is malignant or evil in any respect. *She condemns television as a pestilence.*

pestle (pes′əl, pes′t^əl) n., instrument for pounding and breaking a substance in a mortar. *The chef used the pestle and mortar to crush the herbs.*

petition (pə tish′ən) n., 1. formal written request for some favor, right, grant, or mercy. *The governor rejected the prisoner's petition for clemency.* 2. earnest request, supplication, or entreaty. *Their petition for guidance seemed to be granted.* v.t., to present a petition or make a request to or for; solicit; supplicate; entreat. *We plan to petition the town board for better street lighting.* v.i., to present a petition; make a request. *Perhaps you should petition for better working conditions.*

petulant (pech′ə lənt) adj., showing impatience or irritation, esp. over a trifle;

peevish. *The petulant child wouldn't eat anything.*

petrify (pe′trə fī′) v.t., 1. to convert into stone or a stony substance. *Time and pressure combined to petrify the bit of wood.* 2. to make rigid, stiff, or inert; deaden. *He fears television will petrify his boy's imagination.* 3. to stun or paralyze as with fear or amazement. *My grotesque appearance seemed to petrify them with fear.* v.i., to become petrified. *Your callous indifference has caused my love to petrify.*

pewter (pyoo′tər) n., 1. any of various alloys in which tin is the chief component. *The plates made of pewter were antiques.* 2. utensil or utensils made of pewter. *A large collection of pewter filled the cupboard.*

phalanx (fā′laṅgks, fal′aṅgks) n., 1. in ancient Greece, a body of heavily armed infantry formed in close, deep ranks and files, with shields joined and long spears overlapping one another. *The phalanx presented a solid and impregnable front.* 2. any body of troops formed in close array. *They could not penetrate the solid phalanx of enemy infantry.* 3. compact or closely massed group of persons, animals, or things. *A phalanx of angry taxpayers blocked the entrance to the city hall.* 4. any of the bones of the fingers or toes. *She broke a phalanx in her thumb.*

phenomenon (fi nom′ə non′) n., 1. object or event that can be observed or perceived through the senses, esp. one of scientific interest. *The northern lights are a beautiful phenomenon.* 2. any rare event or occurrence, or exceptional person. *He is a phenomenon on the piano.*

philander (fi lan′dər) v.i., to make love frivolously; flirt. *She accused him of philandering with her daughter.*

philanderer (fi lan′də rər) n., one who makes love frivolously or insincerely; flirt; rogue. *The philanderer was cited in the divorce case.*

philanthropic (fil′ən throp′ik) adj., characterized by humane, esp. charitable, behavior; active in promoting human welfare; humanitarian. *He devoted much of his fortune to philanthropic causes.*

philanthropy (fi lan′thrə pē) n., goodwill toward humanity; also, charitable donation or gift expressing such goodwill. *She is widely respected for her generous philanthropy.*

philatelist (fi lat′ᵊlist) n., one who collects postal or other printed stamps. *The philatelist showed us his collection of foreign stamps.*

philately (fi lat′ᵊlē) n., systematic collection and study of postal or other stamps. *The collector perused the column on philately.*

philistine (fil′i stēn′, -stīn′, fi lis′tin, -tēn) n., crass, conventional person guided by material rather than intellectual or artistic values. *The philistine saw only the price tag on the exquisite embroidery.*

philologist (fi lol′ə jist) n., one who specializes in the study of historical and comparative linguistics. *The philologist is a consultant for the new dictionary.*

philology (fi lol′ə jē) n., study of human speech and literature; historical and comparative linguistics. *The professor of philology discussed the old fable.*

phlegmatic (fleg mat′ik) adj., having a slow, sluggish temperament; stolid; stodgy; impassive. *Her phlegmatic husband fell asleep in front of the TV every night.*

phobia (fō′bē ə) n., extreme, irrational, and often inexplicable fear. *His phobia about flying made him miss the trip.*

phonetics (fə net′iks, fō-) n., study and classification of the sounds of speech or language; also, the resulting system of speech sounds. *She uses phonetics to teach reading.*

phosphorescent (fos′fə res′ənt) adj., shining with a faint light like that of phosphorus; luminous without heat. *We watched the phosphorescent twinkle of the fireflies.*

photogenic (fō tə jen′ik) adj., likely to yield a successful or becoming photograph. *The photogenic child made an excellent model.*

photosynthesis (fō′tə sin′thi sis) n., process by which plants synthesize carbohydrates with the aid of chlorophyll and light. *Photosynthesis takes place in green plant tissues.*

phraseology (frā′ zē ol′ə jē) n., particular words or phrases used to express an idea, or the method of arranging them; mode of expression; style; diction. *The speech writer coined the catchy phraseology.*

physiotherapy (fiz′ē ō ther′ə pē) n., physical therapy; treatment of disease or disorders by mechanical means. *The physiotherapy for his back included a daily massage.*

pièce de résistance (*Fr.* pyes də Rā zē stäns′; *Eng.* pē es də ri zē′ stäns), main event, attraction, or feature; showpiece; specialty. *The restaurant's pièce de résistance was fresh salmon.*

piecemeal (pēs′mēl′) adv., by pieces; bit by bit; in fragments. *She wrote her memoirs piecemeal over the years.*

piety (pī′i tē) n., character of being pious; reverence; faith; devotion. *The nun's piety was taken for granted.*

pillage (pil′ij) n., that which is taken by open force, particularly during war; plunder; spoil; booty. *He became rich on pillage from the Crusades.* v.t., to strip of money or goods by open violence; plunder; despoil; loot. *The marauders began to pillage the town.*

pinion (pin′yən) v.t., to bind or confine the arm or arms to the body so as to disable or render helpless; shackle; bind. *The captain ordered him to pinion the mutineer to the mast.*

pinnacle (pin′ə kəl) n., sharp point or peak; very topmost point, as of a mountain. *From the dune's pinnacle we could see the oasis.*

pious (pī′əs) adj., having faith in and reverence for deity; religious; devout, esp. conspicuously; righteous. *The hypocrite feigned pious disapproval of the thief.*

piquant (pē′kənt, -känt) adj., pungent or sharp to the taste; of a smart, lively, racy, or sparkling nature; of a keen interest. *Her piquant wit made her a popular dinner guest.*

pique (pēk) n., feeling of anger, irritation, displeasure, or resentment, arising from wounded pride; slight offense. *He turned away in a fit of pique.* v.t., 1. to cause resentment; wound. *He piqued her by spreading rumors.* 2. to cause interest in. *The exhibit piqued my curiosity in Egyptian art.*

pirouette (pir′ōō et′) n., rapid whirling on one leg or on the points of the toes; a quick, short, graceful whirl or turn. *The dancer did several pirouettes across the stage.* v.i., to execute a pirouette. *The ballet master instructed her to pirouette into his grasp.*

pitch (pich) n., 1. particular tonal standard. *Dogs dislike the high pitch of a siren.* 2. toss or throw, esp. of a baseball. *She is known for her curved pitch.* 3. thick, sticky, black substance, a residue of tar, which hardens when cold. *He sealed the cracks in the boat with pitch.* v.t., to toss or throw. *He will pitch the ball in the third inning.* v.i., to fall forcefully. *He pitched headlong into the snow.*

piteous (pit′ē əs) adj., 1. full of pity or compassion. *She gave the wounded animal a piteous look.* 2. exciting pity or compassion; moving; lamentable; pitiful. *The piteous family lives in a drafty hovel.*

pith (pith) n., concentrated force or substance; quintessence; weight; importance. *His memo goes right to the pith of the matter.*

pithy (pith′ē) adj., containing much in a concentrated or dense form; forcible; laconic; terse; concise; pointed. *His letters were short but pithy.*

pitiable (pit′ē ə bəl) adj., deserving pity; pitiful. *The sick old man was in a pitiable condition.*

pittance (pit′ ⁿns) n., very small portion or quantity; tiny bit. *You can buy tomatoes for a pittance in season.*

placard (plak′ärd, -ərd) n., printed or written paper displaying some proclamation or announcement for public view; poster. *The striker's placard lists his grievances.*

placate (plā′kāt, plak′āt) v.t., to appease

placebo

or pacify; conciliate. *She tried to placate the angry customer.*

placebo (plə sē′bō) n., harmless substance intended to soothe a patient psychologically rather than medicinally; something that soothes or pacifies. *The pills the old lady took were only a placebo.* adj., soothing or pacifying, esp. without real benefit. *The tiny raise had a placebo effect on the secretary.*

placid (plas′id) adj., undisturbed; equable; serene; calm; peaceful; unruffled; tranquil. *When the wind died, the lake became placid.*

plagiarize (plā′jə rīz′, -jē ə rīz′) v.t., to take, either verbatim or in substance, passages or ideas from another's compositions and to publish them as one's own. *The teacher knew she had plagiarized the experiment.*

plaintiff (plān′tif) n., party who brings a suit in court against another. *The plaintiff accuses you of assault.*

plaintive (plān′tiv) adj., lamenting; complaining; expressive of sorrow or melancholy; sad. *The mourning dove is named for its plaintive song.*

plaited (plā′tid, pla′tid) adj., braided; interwoven. *She wore her plaited hair like a crown around her head.*

platitude (plat′i tōōd′, -tyōōd′) n., trite, dull, or stupid remark; hackneyed saying; truism. *She found her grandmother's platitude meaningless.*

platonic (plə ton′ik) adj., characterized by pure, spiritual affection between the sexes, unmixed with sexual desires. *Their platonic friendship continued after she married.*

plaudit (plô′dit) n., expression of praise; round of applause. *Her performance drew plaudits from the audience.*

plausible (plô′zə bəl) adj., having a superficial appearance of truth or trustworthiness. *He tried to come up with a plausible excuse.*

pleasantry (plez′ən trē) n., light or humorous remark or joke; witticism; small talk. *I laughed at his pleasantry and took my mail.*

plebeian (plə bē′ən) n., one of the com-

mon people or lower ranks. *The plebeian spat into the street.* adj., belonging to the common people; vulgar; common. *The women found it hard to laugh at his plebeian stories.*

plebiscite (pleb′i sīt′, -sit) n., vote by the people on some issue presented to them; referendum. *The proposition was decided by a county plebiscite.*

plenary (plē′nə rē, plen′ə-) adj., full; entire; complete. *The king excercised plenary authority.*

plethora (pleth′ər ə) n., overfullness; superabundance; more than enough. *She received a plethora of invitations to the prom.*

pliable (plī′ə bəl) adj., easily bent; flexible; supple; lithe; tractable. *Soak the reeds in water to make them pliable.*

pliant (plī′ənt) adj., 1. capable of being bent easily; pliable; flexible; supple. *The pliant pipe cleaners made good legs and feet.* 2. easily influenced; yielding. *She took advantage of his pliant nature.*

plight (plīt) n., bad condition or situation; predicament. *She tried to help us out of our plight.*

plumb (plum) n., piece of lead attached to a line, used to determine perpendicularity; plumb-bob. *The carpenter used a plumb to hang the mirror.* v.t., to measure, test, or install with a plumb; examine carefully and thoroughly. *His treatise will plumb the depths of this subject.* v.i., to function as a plumber. *He spent five years apprenticing to plumb.* adj., downright; altogether. *That was the year Joanne went plumb crazy.*

plumb line (plum′ lin′) line with a plumb attached to it, used to measure perpendicularity. *He used a plumb line to adjust the pendulum.*

plummet (plum′it) n., plumb line. *The marine biologist dropped a plummet into the lagoon.* v.i., to fall straight down, esp. with force. *The car plummeted down the cliff.*

plump (plump) adj., full and well-rounded; fat; chubby. *She basted the plump hen.* v.t., to make plump or full;

fatten. *She asked the nurse to plump the pillows.*

poach (pōch) v.t., 1. to encroach on another's land in order to steal game; kill and carry off game illegally. *He was caught trying to poach his neighbor's pheasants.* 2. to cook in barely simmering liquid. *She decided to poach the salmon.*

podiatrist (pō dī′ə trist) n., doctor who specializes in disorders of the feet. *The podiatrist treated her for corns.*

podium (pō′dē əm) n., platform in a hall or theater, which often holds a lectern; dais. *The guest speaker stepped up on the podium.*

poesy (pō′i sē, -zē) n., art of making poetry; skill in metrical composition; poetry. *He read us a sample of his poesy.*

poignant (poin′yənt, poin′ənt) adj., pungent; strongly affecting the feelings; moving; keen; intense. *The poignant reunion occurred yesterday.*

poinsettia (poin set′ē ə, -set′ə) n., South American plant with large, showy, scarlet, white, or pink bracts. *The poinsettia is a popular Christmas plant.*

poised (poizd) adj., 1. held in balance or equilibrium; suspended. *The large rock was poised at the edge of the cliff.* 2. self-confident; collected; composed. *She matured into a poised, elegant woman.*

polemic (pə lem′ik, pō-) n., aggressive argument or refutation; dispute. *The polemic of his whereabouts that evening was the deciding factor in the trial.*

polite (pə līt′) adj., courteous; urbane; gracious. *She tried to be polite to her family as well as to strangers.*

political asylum (pə lit′i kəl ə sī′ləm) refuge granted to a political refugee from another country. *The Russian dissident sought political asylum in Paris.*

politics (pol′i tiks) n., 1. science of government; guiding or influencing of government policy through party organization, esp. by influencing public opinion and attracting support. *Her political science teacher encouraged her* to seek a career in politics. 2. one's party connection or political opinion. *Her uncles fought over politics at every family dinner.*

polluted (pə loo′tid) adj., rendered foul or unclean; defiled; poisoned; tainted; impure; corrupted. *Fishing is prohibited in the polluted water.*

polyandry (pol′ē an′drē, pol′ē an′-) n., state of having more than one husband at once; plurality of husbands. *Polyandry is illegal in the United States.*

polygamist (pə lig′ə mist) n., one who has more than one spouse. *The polygamist was confronted by his two wives.*

polygamy (pə lig′ə mē) n., marriage with more than one concurrent spouse. *If she married her lover, she would be guilty of polygamy.*

polyglot (pol′ē glot′) n., book containing more than one language; mixture of languages; one who understands many languages. *The polyglot spoke six languages fluently.* adj., using or containing many languages. *The missionary used a polyglot Bible.*

polygon (pol′ē gon′) n., closed, geometric figure formed of straight lines with numerous angles. *A square, a triangle, and a hexagon are all polygons.*

polyhedron (pol′ē hē′drən) n., in geometry, a solid bounded by plane faces. *A pyramid is a polyhedron.*

polysyllabic (pol′ē si lab′ik) adj., having several or multiple syllables. *The child's use of polysyllabic words increased with age.*

polytheism (pol′ē thē iz′əm, pol′ē thē′iz əm) n., belief in more than one god. *The ancient Greeks and Romans practiced polytheism.*

pommel (pum′əl, pom′əl) n., knob or ball shape, such as at the end of a sword or knife or at the front of a saddle. *He gripped the pommel of his sword.* v.t. (often pummel), to beat as with a pommel; bruise. *She pommeled her attacker with her fists.*

pomp (pomp) n., ostentatious show or display; splendor; pageantry; grandeur.

Much of the customary commencement pomp was eliminated during the war.

pompous (pom'pəs) adj., ostentatiously grand or showy; exhibiting self-importance or an exaggerated sense of dignity; inflated; bombastic; pretentious. The skit lampooned the pompous professor.

ponder (pon'dər) v., to weigh carefully in the mind; consider carefully; think about. She left the child alone to ponder his misbehavior.

ponderous (pon'dər əs) adj., weighty; heavy; unwieldy; massive. The elephant made his ponderous way through the jungle.

pontiff (pon'tif) n., Roman Catholic priest or bishop, esp. the pope. The Vatican is the home of the pontiff.

pontifical (pon tif'i kəl) n., bishop's book of rituals and sacramental forms, or priestly insignia worn during a pontifical mass. The new priest received a pontifical from his bishop. adj., 1. of or pertaining to a pontiff. The bishops celebrated a pontifical mass. 2. pompous; excessively dogmatic. He spoke as though we should memorize each pontifical utterance.

pontificate (pon tif'ə kāt') v.i., 1. to officiate as pontiff or bishop, esp. to say pontifical mass. Father O'Casey will pontificate today. 2. to deliver oracular or dogmatic speeches or opinions. The teacher began to pontificate on the consequences of premarital sex.

populace (pop'yə ləs) n., common people; masses; population. The populace gathered for the parade.

pornography (pôr nog'rə fē) n., written, cinematic, or pictorial depiction of erotic subject, generally considered obscene. The critic refused to distinguish between erotic art and pornography.

portable (pôr'tə bəl, pôr'-) adj., capable of being carried or easily transported. She carried the portable television to the patio.

portend (pôr tend', pôr-) v.t., to signify; bode; auger; presage. Those clouds may portend a thunderstorm.

portentous (pôr ten'təs, pôr-) adj., ominous; portending ill; threatening. Her knock was met with portentous silence.

porter (pôr'tər, pôr'-) n., 1. one who has charge of a door, gate, or admission. Give your train ticket to the porter. 2. one who carries burdens or runs errands for hire. We gave our baggage to the porter.

portfolio (pôrt fō'lē ō', pôrt-) n., 1. portable receptacle for detached papers or prints. He carried the documents in a leather portfolio. 2. collection of samples of one's work. The applicant submitted her portfolio.

portly (pôrt'lē, pôrt'-) adj., stout; somewhat large and unwieldy in person; stately. The portly gentleman squeezed into the seat.

portrayal (pôr trā'əl, pôr-) n., act of portraying or depicting; delineation; representation; portrait. Her portrayal of Lady Macbeth was excellent.

Poseidon (pō sīd'ən, pə-) n., in Greek mythology, the brother of Zeus and supreme lord of the sea, sometimes looked on as a benign promoter of calm and prosperous navigation but more often as a terrible god of storm; Neptune is the Roman equivalent. The sailors offered a libation to Poseidon.

posse (pos'ē) n., body or squad of citizens called into service by a sheriff to aid in the execution of the law. The sheriff and the posse pursued the bandits.

posterior (po stēr'ē ər) n., rear or hind parts of the body; buttocks. She fell down and bruised her posterior. adj., later in position in a series; coming after; subsequent in time; situated behind. The letter P is posterior to the letter G.

posterity (po ster'i tē) n., descendants or succeeding generations collectively; race that proceeds from a progenitor. Posterity will decide the value of this book.

posthumous (pos'chə məs, -chōō-) adj., appearing or happening after the death of that to which its origin is due, esp.

published after the death of the author. *The posthumous publication will assure his fame.*

postlude (pōst′lōōd) n., piece of music played at the end of a church service; closing piece. *The postlude followed the recessional hymn.*

post-mortem (pōst môr′təm) adj., subsequent to death; after the fact or event. *She could not refrain from post-morten recrimination.*

postnatal (pōst nāt′əl) adj., subsequent to birth. *It was the infant's first postnatal checkup.*

postscript (pōst′skript′, pōs′skript′) n., addition made to a written or printed composition as an afterthought; abbreviated p.s. *She put the afterthought in a postscript.*

postulate (*n.* pos′chə lit, -lāt′; *v.* pos′chə lāt′) n., proposition proposed for acceptance without proof as the premise of a line of reasoning; something taken for granted; assumption. *Euclid's first postulate was proven years later.* v.t., to assume without proof; take for granted. *We postulate the sun's rising.*

posture (pos′chər) n., position; relative position of the body as a whole or of its members; attitude; pose; bearing. *She has very erect posture.* v.i., to strike a pose; affect an artificial position of the mind or character; pose; put on an act. *She must posture as a happy woman for the evening.*

potent (pōt′ənt) adj., powerful; strong; effective; having great strength or influence; convincing. *The dire warning was a potent deterrent.*

potentate (pōt′ən tāt′) n., one who possesses supreme power or sway; sovereign; monarch; ruler. *The potentate declared war on the neighboring country.*

potential (pə ten′shəl) n., that which is possible; capability. *The young artist shows great potential.* adj., possible; capable of being or happening. *The washed-out bridge was a potential death trap.*

potion (pō′shən) n., drink, esp. a liquid medicine or drug; liquid mixture. *She mixed up an herbal potion for her cold.*

potpourri (pō′pōō rē′, pō′pōō rē′, pot pōōr′ē; *Fr.* pô pōō Rē′) n., 1. fragrant mixture of dried flower petals, spices, and perfumes. *She mixed a sachet of potpourri from the garden.* 2. miscellaneous collection; medley. *Her wardrobe was a potpourri of colors and textures.*

pottage (pot′ij) n., thick soup, stew, or chowder. *They sipped the steaming pottage of beef and vegetables.*

potter (pot′ər) n., one who makes pots or earthenware. *The potter glazed the urn.*

practicable (prak′tə kə bəl) adj., capable of being performed; possible to put into practice; feasible. *If your idea is practicable, we're in business.*

practical (prak′ti kəl) adj., relating to practice or use as opposed to theory or speculation; derived from experience. *They allowed her college credit for her practical experience.*

pragmatic (prag mat′ik) adj., concerned with facts and practical matters as opposed to artistic, intellectual, or spiritual matters; sensible; matter-of-fact. *The pragmatic young man could keep his feet warm but he couldn't set a girl's heart on fire.*

prattle (prat′əl) n., artless or childish talk; chatter; twaddle; gibberish. *The three-year-old's endless prattle alternately amuses and exasperates.*

preamble (prē′am′bəl) n., introductory part of a statute or resolution, stating the reasons or intent of what follows; preface; prologue; introduction. *The children recited the preamble to the Constitution.*

precarious (pri kâr′ē əs) adj., exposed to peril or risk; dangerous; hazardous. *We rescued the kitten from her precarious perch.*

precede (pri sēd′) v.t., to go, put, or occur before. *The Cabinet and the Senate precede the President into the chamber.*

precedent (pres′i dənt) n., preceding action or circumstance that serves as a pattern or example in subsequent cases; model instance. *The lawyer cited the famous precedent to support his contention.*

precept (prē′sept) n., commandment or direction given as a rule of action; instruction; teaching; esp., a rule of moral conduct; maxim. *He never forgot the precept his father taught him.*

preceptor (pri sep′tər, pre′sep-) n., instructor; teacher; counselor; tutor. *Experience is sometimes a hard preceptor.*

precinct (prē′singkt) n., district within certain boundaries and under certain jurisdiction; minor territorial or jurisdictional division. *The constable belonged to the 7th precinct.*

precipice (pres′ə pis) n., 1. extremely steep or perpendicular bank or cliff; brink of a steep cliff. *Her mother pulled her back from the precipice.* 2. critical position. *He was at a precipice in his career.*

precipitate (n., adj. pri sip′i tit, -tāt′; v. pri sip′i tāt′) n., substance, usually an insoluble solid, separated by chemical process from a suspension or solution. *The precipitate settled at the bottom of the test tube.* v.t., 1. to cast or hurl downward from a great height. *The horse's hoof precipitated the rock into the canyon.* 2. to cause to fall or separate, as sediment from a solution. *They will precipitate the crystals from this acid in order to analyze them.* 3. to hasten, esp. intemperately or rashly. *She feared the incident would precipitate a quarrel.* v.i., to condense from a vapor and fall, as rain or snow. *The hail precipitated with destructive results.* adj., rash; hasty. *She later regretted her precipitate offer.*

precipitous (pri sip′i təs) adj., 1. headlong; descending rapidly or rushing onward; steep. *The canoe made a precipitous dash down the rapids.* 2. hasty; rash; sudden. *After only two dates his proposal seemed precipitous.*

précis (prā′sē, prā sē′) n., concise statement; summary; abstract. *The précis outlines my intentions.*

precise (pri sīs′) adj., 1. exact; definite; accurate; correct. *The recipe gives precise measurements.* 2. exactly stated or defined; strictly expressed; terse; distinct; laconic. *She gave precise instructions.*

preclude (pri klōōd′) v.t., to shut out; prevent; impede; rule out; bar. *This low test score may preclude his acceptance into law school.*

precocious (pri kō′shəs) adj., mature before the natural time; prematurely developed; forward. *The precocious musician debuted at age 7.*

precocity (pri kos′i tē) n., state of being precocious. *The child star showed extreme precocity.*

precursor (pri kûr′sər, prē′kûr-) n., that which precedes an event and indicates its approach; one who goes before; forerunner; predecessor; herald. *Lightning is usually the precursor of thunder.*

predatory (pred′ə tōr′ē, -tôr′ē) adj., living by preying upon or plundering others; tending to injure or exploit others; characterized by pillaging or plundering. *We watched the predatory cat pounce on the bird.*

predicate (n., pred′ə kit, v. pred′ə kāt′) n., in grammar, the word or words in a proposition expressing what is affirmed or denied of the subject. *The child outlined the sentence's subject and predicate.* v.t., to assert; base upon certain grounds. *I predicate this conclusion on the basis of experimental evidence.*

predict (pri dikt′) v.t., to declare before the event happens; foretell; prophesy. *The weatherman predicts snow for tomorrow.*

predilection (pred′ə lek′shən, prēd′-) n., predisposition of the mind in favor of something; preference; partiality; inclination. *He has a predilection for classical guitar music.*

predispose (prē′di spōz′) v.t., to incline; render susceptible or liable. *Her thorough plan predisposed him to agree.*

predisposition (prē dis′pə zish′ən,

prē'dis-) n., tendency or inclination; state of being disposed in a particular direction. *She had a predisposition to bronchitis.*

predominant (pri dom'ə nənt) adj., exerting superior power, authority, or influence; prevailing; dominant. *The oldest child's will was predominant.*

preeminent (prē em'ə nənt) adj., eminent above others; superior to or surpassing others; primary; paramount. *The preeminent requirement for a hockey player is the ability to skate.*

preempt (prē empt') v.t., to appropriate; usurp; take the place of. *Election coverage will preempt regular programming.*

preen (prēn) v.t., 1. to clean or smooth with the bill. *The duck began to preen her feathers.* 2. to congratulate oneself; gloat. *She preened herself on her good luck.* v.i., to primp. *The teenagers preened in front of the mirror.*

prefabricated (prē fab'rə kā'tid) adj., having all parts or materials made at the factory so that only assembly is required; premade; artificial. *The prefabricated house was erected in a day.*

preface (pref'is) n., series of preliminary remarks; introduction. *Her preface gives some biographical information.* v.t., to introduce by preliminary remarks; explain or qualify what is to follow. *He meant to preface his announcement with a warning.*

prefect (prē'fekt) n., governor, commander, chief magistrate, superintendent or other high official. *The prefect addressed the assembled cadets.*

preferable (pref'ər ə bəl, pref'rə-) adj., worthy of preference; more desirable. *She finds the fish preferable to the lamb.*

prefix (*n.* prē'fiks; *v.* prē fiks', prē'fiks) n., word, syllable, or syllables affixed to the beginning of a word to qualify its meaning. *The "pre" in "prefix" is a prefix meaning "before."* v.t., to place before. *Prefix his name with "the Honorable."*

pregnant (preg'nənt) adj., 1. carrying unborn young; with child. *The pregnant*

woman could feel her child stir. 2. full; rich in significance; meaningful. *A pregnant silence followed his remark.*

prejudice (prej'ə dis) n., 1. opinion or decision formed without sufficient basis. *He doesn't share his father's prejudice against city living.* 2. irrational opinion against a race or other group of people or their characteristics. *They will protest racial prejudice.* 3. injury resulting from unfavorable prejudgment; detriment. *His work record was to his prejudice rather than his credit.* v.t., to impair or harm by some act or judgment, esp. in law. *He will prejudice his own case if he takes the stand.*

prelude (prel'yo͞od, präl'-, prē'lo͞od, prä'-) n., preliminary to an action, event, or work of broader scope; introductory performance; preface; overture. *An exotic prelude sets the tone for the opera.*

premeditated (pri med'i tā'tid) adj., considered and contrived previously; intentional; planned. *He was accused of premeditated murder.*

premier (pri mēr', prim yēr') n. prime minister. *The president met with the visiting premier.* adj., 1. principal. *His premier duty was to his family.* 2. earliest; first. *Her premier reaction was panic.*

premiere (pri mēr', -myâr') n., first, or opening, performance. *The composer was the conductor at the world premiere.*

premise (prem'is) n., 1. proposition from which an inference or conclusion is drawn; basis. *His argument was invalid when his premise was proved incorrect.* 2. pl., tract of land and the buildings on it; grounds; building. *He ordered the beggar off the premises.*

premonition (prē'mə nish'ən, prem'ə-) n., previous warning; omen; forewarning. *My premonition proved correct.*

prenatal (prē nāt'əl) adj., before birth. *She has a monthly prenatal exam.*

preoccupation (prē ok'yə pā'shən, prē'ok-) n., total absorption in something; absorbing interest. *He didn't hear* her because of his preoccupation with the book.

preoccupied (prē ok′yə pīd′) adj., engrossed; lost in thought; absorbed; meditative. *He was too preoccupied to remember dinner.*

preponderance (pri pon′dər əns) n., superiority in force, influence, quantity, or weight; predominance. *There is a preponderance of lawyers in Congress.*

prepossess (prē′pə zes′) v.t., 1. to preoccupy with an idea, thought, or belief. *The concept began to prepossess her with its possibilities.* 2. to influence or prejudice, esp. favorably. *His charming bow prepossessed her in his favor.*

preposterous (pri pos′tər əs, -trəs) adj., ridiculous; absurd; monstrous; foolish. *It was a preposterous story about flying pigs.*

prerequisite (pri rek′wi zit) n., condition required beforehand; preliminary necessity. *The survey course is a prerequisite for the seminar.* adj., required beforehand; necessary as a condition. *The applicant showed the prerequisite qualifications.*

prerogative (pri rog′ə tiv) n., privilege inherent in one's office or position; official right. *The president has the prerogative of vetoing bills passed by Congress.*

presbyterian (prez′bi tēr′ē ən, pres′-) n., one who holds to the presbyterian system in church government. *The elder was a good presbyterian.* adj., pertaining to ecclesiastical government by elders; pertaining to religious bodies that adopt the presbyterian form of church government and, traditionally, a modified form of Calvinism. *The Presbyterian Church maintains an equality of its clergy.*

prescience (prē′shē əns, -shəns, presh′ē-, presh′əns) n., knowledge of events before they take place; foreknowledge; foresight. *Her momentary prescience may have saved their lives.*

presentiment (pri zen′tə mənt) n., vague perception of a future event; anticipa-

tion; foreboding. *He had a presentiment of the offer.*

preside (pri zīd′) v.i., to have the place of authority over; direct and control, as a chief officer; superintend. *She will preside over the department meeting.*

prestige (pre stēzh′, -stēj′, pres′tij) n., reputation for excellence, importance, or authority; weight or influence arising from reputation. *His White House connection lent him considerable prestige.*

prestigious (pre stij′əs, -stij′ə əs, -stē′jəs, -stē′jē əs) adj., well known for excellence, importance, or authority; influential; famous; respected. *Twenty law graduates applied to the prestigious law firm.*

presume (pri zoom′) v.i., 1. to take upon oneself or press forward without leave or warrant; dare. *I could not presume to speak for her.* 2. to believe or accept upon probable evidence; infer as probable; take for granted. *I presume your phone number is still the same?*

presumption (pri zump′shən) n., act of taking upon oneself more than propriety or authority warrant; excessive boldness or overconfidence; arrogance. *She was shocked at the presumption in his question.*

presumptuous (pri zump′choo əs) adj., forward; arrogant; overwhelming. *She rejected his presumptuous demand.*

pretention (pri ten′shən) n., act of putting forth a claim, esp. to merit, dignity, or importance; alleged claim; pretext. *The queen worried about his pretention to the throne.*

pretentious (pri ten′shəs) adj., full of claims to greater excellence or importance than the truth warrants; making an exaggerated outer show. *We laughed at her pretentious designer clothes.*

pretext (prē′tekst) n., ostensible reason or motive; pretense; excuse. *She left her gloves as a pretext for returning the following day.*

prevailing (pri vā′liŋ) adj., having superior influence or force; predominant; ruling; current; prevalent. *Gloominess was the prevailing mood that evening.*

prevalent (prev′ə lənt) adj., 1. superior in power or might; controlling; influential. *The prevalent wind is from the north.* 2. widely accepted; widespread; current. *She always dresses in the prevalent fashion.*

prevaricate (pri var′ə kāt′) v.i., to swerve from the truth; act or speak evasively; lie. *When pressed, the boy began to prevaricate.*

preview (prē′vyōō′) n., viewing or showing in advance; preliminary report or survey. *We saw a preview of the movie.*

pride (prīd) n., 1. inordinate self-esteem; unreasonable estimate of one's superiority, manifested in loftiness, reserve, or contempt of others. *The haughty young lady was accused of pride.* 2. natural and just sense of what is due to one's personality, character, or position; firm self-respect. *She has pride in her appearance.* 3. reasonable feeling of satisfaction with one's achievements or possessions, or those of an intimate or relation. *His mother felt great pride at his appointment.*

prig (prig) n., one who is conceited, narrow-minded, pragmatical, overly precise. *The schoolgirls thought the headmistress an unreasonable prig.*

prim (prim) adj., stiffly precise; demure; prudish. *She gave a prim answer to his probing question.*

primacy (prī′mə sē) n., condition of being prime or first in order, power, or importance. *They couldn't dispute the primacy of her claim.*

prima donna (prē′mə don′ə, prim′ə; *It.* pRē′mä dôn′nä) 1. principal female in an an opera or other performance. *The prima donna received a thunderous ovation.* 2. one who is extremely sensitive, vain, or temperamental; one who insists on his or her own way. *I finally had to dismiss the disruptive prima donna.*

prima facie (prī′mə fā′shē ē′, -fā′shē, -fā′shə) adj., having sufficient evidence to establish a fact or a case; apparent; self-evident. *This prima facie case was quickly wrapped up.*

primate (prī′māt *or, esp. for 2,* prī′mit) n., 1. member of the mammalian order that includes man, apes, and monkeys. *The lemur is also a primate.* 2. preeminent bishop. *He is nervous about the primate's imminent visit.*

prime (prīm) adj., first in rank, degree, or importance; principal; chief; of the first excellence or value; first rate. *She bought prime roast beef for the dinner party.*

primogeniture (prī′mə jen′i chər) n., state of being the first-born among children of the same parents; right by which the oldest son of a family succeeds to the father's estate to the exclusion of younger sons and daughters. *His abdication in effect invalidated his primogeniture.*

primordial (prī môr′dē əl) adj., 1. first; earliest; existing in or since the beginning. *Gardening satisfies a certain primordial urge.* 2. in a rudimentary or embryonic state; primitive; formative. *He studied the skull of man's primordial ancestor.*

principal (prin′sə pəl) n., 1. head of an elementary or secondary school. *The principal called a faculty meeting.* 2. money bearing interest; capital sum lent on interest, due as a debt. *The principal on the loan is tax deductible.* 3. one who takes a leading part. *He is a principal in the ballet company.* adj., chief; highest in rank, authority, value, or importance; main. *She won the principal female part.*

principle (prin′sə pəl) n., 1. cause; that by which anything is ultimately determined or regulated. *The principle of gravity explains weight and velocity.* 2. evident and general truth; truth comprehending many subordinate truths; law on which others are founded. *The democratic principle is the basis of our Constitution.*

prior (prī′ər) adj., preceding, as in the order of time or thought; previous. *My prior opinion of him has changed.*

pristine (pris′tēn, -tin, -tīn) adj., 1. of or belonging to a primitive or early state;

primitive; primordial. *The survivors erected a pristine shelter.* 2. uncorrupted; innocent; fresh and clean. *He liked to wear pristine white shirts.*

privation (prī vā′shən) n., deprivation, removal, or absence of what is necessary for comfort; destitution; poverty; need. *The immigrant lived a life of privation until he found the job.*

privy (priv′ē) adj., privately knowing; admitted as to the participation in knowledge of a secret. *She was privy to her sister's elopement.*

probation (prō bā′shən) n., trial or examination to determine character or qualifications; test or trial period; period of being subjected to probation or trial. *The offender was placed on social probation.*

probe (prōb) n., 1. trial; test; exploration. *The rocket was launched as part of the space probe.* 2. tool used for exploration. *The surgeon used the probe to locate the bullet.* v.t., to examine with a probe. *The detective will probe into her past.* 2. to examine thoroughly. *I don't mean to probe your affairs, but why are you here?*

probity (prō′bi tē, prob′i-) n., strict adherence to high principles; integrity; uprightness; honesty. *The minister's probity was unimpeachable.*

proceed (prə sēd′) v.i., to move or go forward or onward; continue or renew progress; advance. *Turn right at the light and proceed for three blocks.*

proclamation (prok′lə mā′shən) n., act of proclaiming or that which is proclaimed; official or general notice; open declaration; official public announcement. *The proclamation requires alternate-side-of-the-street parking.*

proclivity (prō kliv′i tē) n., inclination; propensity; predisposition; tendency; readiness. *She decried his proclivity to grumble and nag.*

procrastinate (prō kras′tə nāt′, prə-) v.i., to put off; delay; postpone. *It is too easy to procrastinate about an unpleasant task.*

procrastination (prō kras′tə nā′shən, prə-) n., act or habit of procrastinating

or putting off; habitual delay. *The opportunity was lost due to procrastination.*

procreate (prō′krē āt′) v.t., to beget; generate; engender. *They hope to procreate a large family.*

procreation (prō′krē ā′shən) n., act of procreating; generation and production of young. *Successful procreation is essential to continuation of life.*

prodigal (prod′ə gəl) adj., given to extravagant expenditure; recklessly lavish; wasteful. *When he received his credit card, he went on a prodigal spending spree.*

prodigious (prə dij′əs) adj., wonderfully great in degree, size, quantity or extent; monstrous; immense; enormous; marvelous; amazing. *He was stuffed after the prodigious meal.*

prodigy (prod′i jē) n., person or thing so extraordinary as to excite wonder or astonishment; marvel; monster. *The prodigy debuted at the age of five.*

profane (prə fān′, prō-) v.t., to desecrate; blaspheme; treat with irreverence, impiety, or contempt. *The army wouldn't dare profane the holy spot.* adj., irreverent to deity; impious; blasphemous; sacrilegious; unholy. *Justice comes to the pious and the profane ones.*

profanity (prə fan′i tē, prō-) n., that which is profane or impious, esp. language; blasphemy. *She objects to the novel's crude profanity.*

proffer (prof′ər) v.t., to put forward; offer for acceptance; hold forth. *He wants to proffer his hand in marriage.*

proficient (prə fish′ənt) adj., well versed in a skill or learning; skilled; qualified; competent. *She was proficient in German and French.*

profitable (prof′i tə bəl) adj., yielding or bringing a profit or gain; gainful; lucrative; advantageous; beneficial. *He was exhilarated by the profitable investment.*

profligate (prof′lə git, -gāt′) adj., lost to principle, virtue, or decency; completely immoral; reckless; irresponsible; prodigal. *The young man led a worthless, profligate life.*

pro forma (*Lat.* prō fôr'mä, *Eng.* prō fôr'mə) adj., a matter of form. *Her pro forma note followed the telephoned invitation.*

profound (prə found') adj., 1. deep; being or coming from far below the surface. *No light reached the profound ocean floor.* 2. difficult to understand; deeply meaningful. *The profound question perplexed him.* 3. characterized by magnitude or intensity; deep-felt; deep-seated; thorough. *She suffered profound anxiety during the exam.*

profundity (prə fun'di tē) n., character or condition of being profound or deep; depth, as of knowledge, meaning, or feeling; mystery. *He began to explore the profundity of monastic life.*

profuse (prə fyōōs') adj., liberal or plentiful to excess; abundant; copious; bountiful; lavish; prodigal; luxuriant; extravagant. *He lavished his student with profuse praise.*

profusion (prə fyōō'zhən) n., profuse or extravagant expenditure; prodigality; lavish supply; plenty; abundance. *Her room was filled with a profusion of flowers.*

progeny (proj'ə nē) n., offspring; descendants; lineage; family. *His will mentioned all of his progeny.*

prognosis (prog nō'sis) n., prediction of the course of events; forecast, esp. a prediction of the probable course of a disease. *The doctor's prognosis proved correct.*

prognosticate (prog nos'tə kāt') v.t., to foretell by means of signs or symptoms; predict; forecast. *The meteorologist prognosticates the weather.*

prohibition (prō'ə bish'ən) n., act of prohibiting, forbidding, or interdicting; edict or decree to forbid or debar; narrowly, the interdiction by law of the manufacture and sale of alcoholic drinks. *Congress lifted the prohibition on the sale of arms.*

projectile (prə jek'til, -tīl) n., body projected or impelled forward by force; missile meant to be propelled from a cannon, gun, or other weapon; self-propelled missile or rocket. *The nuclear projectile was intercepted and destroyed.*

proletarian (prō'li târ'ē ən) n., member of the proletariat. *The factory worker was a proletarian.* adj., pertaining to the proletariat. *The proletarian apartment was a drab place.*

proletariat (prō'li târ'ē ət) n., class of wage-workers dependent for support on selling their labor; lowest economic and social class in a community; working class. *The politician needed the support of the proletariat.*

proliferate (prō lif'ə rāt') v.i., to reproduce; grow by multiplication; multiply. *The asparagus bed began to proliferate and took over the garden.*

prolific (prō lif'ik) adj., abundantly productive; fertile; fruitful. *The prolific author wrote over a hundred mysteries.*

prolix (prō liks', prō'liks) adj., long; extended; of long duration; wordy; long-winded; indulging in lengthy discourse; discussing at great length; tedious. *She couldn't help yawning during his prolix speech.*

prologue (prō'lôg, -log) n., preface or introduction, esp. to a discourse or performance. *The prologue introduces us to the characters.*

prominence (prom'ə nəns) n., state or condition of being prominent or conspicuous; distinction; notoriety. *The talented woman achieved prominence in her field.*

promiscuous (prə mis'kyōō əs) adj., not restricted to one individual, esp. not restricted to one sexual partner; indiscriminate. *The line is sometimes thin between free and promiscuous behavior.*

promontory (prom'ən tōr'ē, -tôr'ē) n., high point of land or rock projecting into the sea beyond the coastline; headland. *A lighthouse stands on the promontory.*

prompt (prompt) v.t., 1. to move or excite to action; incite. *The publisher prompted her to finish the book.* 2. to assist by suggesting something forgotten or imperfectly learned or by pronouncing the words next in order. *He had to* *prompt the actress because she hadn't learned her lines.* adj., 1. ready; given or performed without delay; quick; immediate. *We will appreciate a prompt reply.* 2. punctual; not late; on time. *Be prompt for the interview.*

promptitude (promp'ti tōōd', -tyōōd') n., readiness; quickness of decision or action; alacrity; promptness. *We appreciated his promptitude in helping.*

promptness (prompt'nəs) n., state or quality of being prompt; readiness; quickness of decision or action; alacrity; promptitude. *You can count on her promptness to meet the deadline.*

promulgate (prom'əl gāt', prō mul'gāt) v.t., to make known by open declaration, as laws, decrees, or proclamations; announce; proclaim. *The new regime will promulgate a temporary curfew.*

prone (prōn) adj., 1. lying flat with the face or front downward. *They found him prone on the ice.* 2. inclined by disposition or natural tendency. *The frail child was prone to colds.*

propaganda (prop'ə gan'də) n., spreading of information or rumors for or against a set of ideas or a cause; also, the means used to spread such information. *The lobbyist distributed her propaganda to the legislators.*

propagate (prop'ə gāt') v.t., 1. to multiply or continue by natural generation; cause to reproduce. *The cuttings should propagate new geraniums.* 2. to transmit; spread; carry forward or onward. *The missionaries went out to propagate Christianity.*

propellant (prə pel'ənt) n., that which propels or drives forward; propelling agent, such as an explosive or pressurized gas. *The propellant used to fire the projectile was rocket fuel.*

propeller (prə pel'ər) n., one who or that which propels; appliance or instrument such as a screw or spinning blade used for propulsion. *He wound the propeller with a rubber band.*

propensity (prə pen'si tē) n., natural tendency; inclination; predisposition. *She was worried about his propensity to gamble.*

prophecy (prof'i sē) n., prediction; declaration of something to come, esp. a foretelling under divine inspiration. *All came to pass according to the prophecy.*

prophesy (prof'i sī') v.t., to predict; foretell; forecast. *Some people believe they can prophesy the future.*

prophylactic (prō'fə lak'tik, prof'ə-) n., that which defends against disease, esp. a device used to prevent venereal disease or conception; rubber; contraceptive. *The trucker bought a prophylactic for a quarter.* adj., preventive; defending from disease. *The children were inoculated as a prophylactic measure against typhoid.*

propinquity (prō ping'kwi tē) n., nearness in blood; kinship; nearness in time or place; neighborhood; proximity. *They were alarmed by the propinquity of the gunfire.*

propitiate (prə pish'ē āt') v.t., to appease and render favorable; conciliate; pacify. *They hoped their offerings would propitiate the goddess.*

propitious (prə pish'əs) adj., favorably disposed; benign; affording favorable conditions or circumstances; promising; auspicious. *Wait until your boss is in a propitious mood to ask for a raise.*

proponent (prə pō'nənt) n., one who makes or supports a proposal, or who argues for something; advocate. *She was a leading proponent of gun control.*

proportion (prə pōr'shən, -pôr'-) n., 1. relation of one thing to another in respect to size, quantity, capacity, or degree, esp. the relation of one part to another or to the whole with respect to magnitude. *Her standard of living rose in proportion to her salary.* 2. symmetrical arrangement, distribution, or adjustment; proper relation of parts in a whole; symmetry or harmony; form; shape. *She realized she'd blown the argument out of proportion.*

propriety (prə prī'i tē) n., established principles, rules, or customs of behavior, or the adherence to them; society's expectations of what is proper; seemliness; etiquette. *The mother ques-*

tioned the propriety of her daughter's actions.

propulsion (prə pul′shən) n., act of driving forward or onward; pushing; urging; motivation. *The catapult is a primitive means of propulsion.*

prosaic (prō zā′ik) adj., ordinary or commonplace in style or expression; uninteresting; dull; commonplace; unimaginative. *She was bored to tears with her prosaic husband.*

proscribe (prō skrīb′) v.t., 1. to publish the name of (a person), as condemned to death and liable to confiscation of property by the state. *The junta intends to proscribe the exiled king.* 2. to banish; outlaw; denounce and condemn; reject utterly; prohibit. *His doctor proscribed cigarettes.*

prose (prōz) n., ordinary written or spoken language of man; written medium distinguished from verse or metrical composition by its irregularity of rhythm and its approximation of everyday speech patterns. *She studied eighteenth-century English prose.*

prosecute (pros′ə kyoot′) v.t., to arraign before a court of justice for some crime or wrong; pursue for redress or punishment before a legal tribunal. *He decided not to prosecute the youngster and dropped the charges.*

proselytize (pros′ə li tīz′, -lī-) v.t., to induce to become an adherent of some religion, doctrine, sect, or party; convert. *The evangelist stood on the corner to proselytize passersby.*

prospectus (prə spek′təs) n., preliminary sketch or plan issued to describe the chief features of some proposed enterprise. *The company prepared an attractive prospectus.*

prosperous (pros′pər əs) adj., making good progress in the pursuit of anything desirable; successful; thriving; flourishing. *Their prosperous business attracted a wealthy clientele.*

prostate (pros′tāt) n., large, firm, partly muscular gland embracing the urethra in mammalian males. *Many older men have problems with their prostate.*

prostrate (pros′trāt) v.t., 1. to throw

down; flatten; demolish; ruin; overthrow. *The fuel shortage threatened to prostrate industry.* 2. to throw oneself down in humility or adoration; submit in reverence. *The subjects prostrate themselves before the emperor.* adj., lying at length, as on the ground; lying prone or supine, esp. in weakness. *She lay prostrate in the hospital bed.*

protagonist (prō tag′ə nist) n., leading character, generally or in a drama; champion or leader of a cause; hero or heroine. *Hamlet is his favorite Shakespearean protagonist.*

protégé (prō′tə zhā′, prō tə zhā′) (fem. protégée) n., one who is under the care and protection of another, usually for the furthering of his career. *He introduced his protégé to the prominent composer.*

protocol (prō′tə kôl, -kol′, -kōl′) n., code of diplomatic or military propriety, esp. of etiquette and precedence; propriety. *Foreign Service officers and their spouses must learn the rules of protocol.*

protoplasm (prō′tə plaz′əm) n., complex substance of protein and other elements, capable of manifesting vital phenomena and constituting the physical basis of life of all plants and animals. *The least particle of protoplasm may undergo the whole cycle of vital functions.*

prototype (prō′tə tīp′) n., original or model after which anything is formed; original standard; exemplar; archetype. *She was the prototype for the character in his novel.*

Protozoa (prō′tə zō′ə) n. pl., subkingdom of animal microorganisms consisting of a single cell of protoplasm or of several such cells not differentiated into tissues, and manifesting a great variety of structures. *A drop of pond water contains many different forms of protozoa.*

protract (prō trakt′) v.t., to draw out or lengthen in time; prolong; delay; defer. *She hated to protract the completion of the project.*

protrude (prō trood′) v.t., to thrust forward or outward; project; stick out; bulge out. *The snail will protrude its horns to feel its way.* v.i., to project;

stick out. *Two wings protrude from the main building.*

protuberance (prō tōō′bər əns, -tyōō′-) n., that which is swelled or pushed beyond the surrounding surface; swelling; tumor; bulge. *The nose is a protuberance on the human face.*

proverb (prov′ərb) n., short, pithy saying, often repeated colloquially or popularly, expressing a well-known truth or practical precept, often employing metaphor and rhyme; adage. *"The early bird catches the worm" is a popular proverb.*

providence (prov′i dəns) n., 1. divine supervision and direction. *She trusted providence to point the way.* 2. prudence in the management of one's economy.

providential (prov′i den′shəl) adj., proceeding from divine direction; fortunate. *It was providential that he found a job just before the baby was due.*

province (prov′ins) n., 1. important administrative unit; administrative division of a country. *The army marched to the northern Szechuan province of China.* 2. part of a country or state distinguished from the large city or capital; country. *The acting company toured the province.* 3. proper duty, office, or responsibility of a person; sphere; function. *Making coffee for the boss was not in the secretary's province.* 4. division in any department of knowledge or activity; field; specialty. *Her special province was Shakespeare and the Renaissance.*

provincial (prə vin′shəl) adj., 1. of or pertaining to a province; characteristic of a province. *He became active in provincial government.* 2. exhibiting the manners of the provinces; rustic; countrified; not polished. *She was offended by his rough provincial table manners.*

provision (prə vizh′ən) n., 1. measure taken in advance; advance preparation or arrangement. *He insisted on the provision of snow tires on the rented car.* 2. stock of supplies, esp. food. *They bought provisions before the expected storm.* 3. legal stipulation, rule, or

clause. *He inserted a provision in his will.*

provisional (prə vizh′ə nəl) adj., provided for present need or for the occasion; temporarily established; temporary. *Following the coup, the country was ruled by a provisional government.*

proviso (prə vī′zō) n., provision or article in a statute, contract, or other writing, by which a condition is introduced; conditional stipulation. *She gave him permission to go with the proviso that he do his homework first.*

provocation (prov′ə kā′shən) n., 1. act of provoking or exciting anger or vexation. *He came to offer peace but succeeded only in further provocation.* 2. cause of anger or resentment; incitement; stimulus. *She loses her temper at the least provocation.*

provocative (prə vok′ə tiv) adj., serving or tending to provoke, excite, or stimulate; exciting; stimulating. *She was disturbed by the provocative essay.*

provoke (prə vōk′) v.t., 1. to stimulate to action; move; excite; arouse; challenge. *The deadline could always provoke her pen.* 2. to excite to anger or passion; exasperate; irritate; enrage. *The noise began to provoke the neighbors.*

prowess (prou′is) n., excellence; valor; bravery combined with skill; exceptional ability. *His prowess turned the battle in their favor.*

proximity (prok sim′i tē) n., nearness in place, time, or relation; vicinity; propinquity. *They were displeased by the proximity of the new highway to their homes.*

proxy (prok′sē) n., 1. office or authority of one who is deputed to act for another; one who is deputed to represent another; deputy. *They were married by proxy.* 2. written authorization to exercise the powers of others. *The stockholder mailed his proxy.*

prude (prōōd) n., one who affects or exhibits rigid correctness in conduct and thought or in modesty. *The prude was squeamish about all sexual matters.*

prudence (prōōd′əns) n., 1. practical wisdom; discretion; good judgment. *Ex-*

perience had taught her prudence. 2. careful or frugal management; economy. *They ate well on a small income because of her prudence.* 3. caution as to danger or risk; circumspection; wariness. *He exercised prudence in the investment of his money.*

prudent (prōōd'ənt) adj., 1. thoughtful; judicious; wise; sensible. *The prudent judge disregarded the emotional outburst.* 2. careful of self-interest; economical. *He hoped to enrich himself through a prudent marriage.* 3. discreet; cautious; careful; circumspect. *She used prudent timing in asking for a raise.*

prurient (prōōr'ē ənt) adj., mentally unclean or lascivious; sensual; lewd. *The pornographic magazine appeals to one's prurient interests.*

pseudonym (sōōd'ənim) n., false name, esp. as assumed by an author to conceal his or her identity. *He used a woman's pseudonym for the gothic romance.*

psoriasis (sə rī'ə sis) n., chronic, noncontagious skin disease characterized by reddish, scaly, dry patches. *The ointment soothed her psoriasis.*

psyche (sī'kē) n., soul or spirit; mind. *War damages the psyche as well as the body.*

psychedelic (sī'ki del'ik) adj., causing extreme changes in perception or the conscious mind, such as hallucinations, intense sensory perception, perceptual distortion, and extreme feelings of despair or elation; of or about the distorted sounds, colors, and sights produced by these changes. *The psychedelic drug endangered his sanity.*

psychiatrist (si kī'ə trist, sī-) n., physician specializing in mental, emotional, or behavioral disorders. *A psychiatrist must be a doctor of medicine first.*

psychology (sī kol'ə jē) n., 1. science of mind, emotions, and behavior. *A good business manager needs an understanding of psychology.* 2. mental characteristics or behavior of an individual or group. *The group exhibits a diverse psychology.*

psychopath (sī'kə path') n., one who is mentally ill or unstable. *An armed psy-*

chopath is an exceptionally dangerous person.

psychosis (sī kō'sis) n., lasting mental disorder often characterized by a loss of contact with reality; insanity; derangement. *The institution treated his psychosis.*

psychotic (sī kot'ik) n., one who has a psychosis; psychopath. *The psychotic pleaded not guilty due to insanity.* adj., having a psychosis; having to do with or caused by a psychosis. *He suffered a psychotic delusion.*

puerile (pyōō'ər il, -ə rīl', pyōōr'il, -ǐl) adj., childish; juvenile; weak; foolish; silly. *The judge reprimanded him for his puerile, unprofessional behavior.*

puissance (pyōō'i səns, pyōō is'əns, pwis'əns) n., power; strength; force; vigor, esp. armed force. *His puissance was felt and feared throughout the company.*

puissant (pyōō'i sənt, pyōō is'ənt, pwis'ənt) adj., powerful; mighty; strong; vigorous; forcible. *He fled from his puissant enemy.*

pulmonary (pul'mə ner'ē, pōōl'-) adj., of or pertaining to the lungs; respiratory. *The pulmonary artery carries blood to the lungs.*

pulsate (pul'sāt) v.i., to beat or throb rhythmically, as the heart. *We watched the jellyfish pulsate through the water.*

pun (pun) n., humorous play on words that are alike or nearly alike in sound but differ in meaning. *They went and told the sexton and the sexton tolled the bell.*

punctilious (puñgk til'ē əs) adj., precise in behavior or ceremony; excessively exact in the observance of rules or forms; scrupulous. *The punctilious worker takes exactly one hour for lunch, no more, no less.*

punctual (puñgk'chōō əl) adj., exact or prompt in action or in the observance of time, or the keeping of appointments or engagements; at the exact or stipulated time. *Thank goodness the train is punctual tonight.*

pungent (pun'jənt) adj., sharp or strong to the sense of taste or smell; caustic;

acrid; piquant. *The pungent odor of ammonia assailed us.*

punitive (pyo͞o′ni tiv) adj., pertaining to or involving punishment. *Punitive damages were awarded to the plaintiff.*

puny (pyo͞o′nē) adj., small and weak; inferior or imperfectly developed in size or strength; feeble; diminutive; stunted. *The plant was puny because it didn't get enough light.*

purgatory (pûr′gə tōr′ē, -tôr′ē) n., 1. in the belief of the Roman Catholic Church, a place where souls of those who died penitent are purified from venial sins, or undergo temporal punishment. *They prayed for her release from purgatory.* 2. any place or state of temporary suffering; limbo. *The child was in purgatory until his mother forgave him.*

purge (pûrj) n., act of purging; purgation; ridding of those considered treacherous or disloyal. *The Cabinet underwent a purge after the change in power.* v.t., to cleanse or purify by separating and carrying off whatever is impure, foreign, hostile, or superfluous; cleanse, clean, or clean out; eliminate. *He tried to purge his department of excessive paperwork.*

purify (pyo͞or′ə fī′) v.t., to make pure or clear; free from contamination or extraneous material; to free from defilement, guilt, or sin. *The city took new measures to purify the water supply.*

purloin (pər loin′, pûr′loin) v.t., to remove, carry off, or remove for oneself; filch; steal. *Knowledge is a treasure no thief can purloin.*

purport (n. pûr′pōrt, -pôrt; v. pər pōrt′, -pôrt′, pûr′pōrt, -pôrt) n., meaning; nature; gist; drift. *That was the purport of the letter.* v.t., to convey a meaning; imply; mean or seem to mean. *They purport the document to be authentic.*

purvey (pər vā′) v.t., to provide or supply, esp. in a business. *They were able to purvey large amounts of foodstuffs to the military.*

purveyor (pər vā′ər) n., one who provides victuals for a number of persons; caterer. *The purveyor provided the meat for the main dish.*

pusillanimous (pyo͞o′sə lan′ə məs) adj., lacking courage and fortitude; being of weak courage; faint-hearted; cowardly; timorous. *The pusillanimous soldier turned and ran.*

putrefy (pyo͞o′trə fī′) v.i., to decay or cause to decay with an offensive odor; cause to become fetid by rotting. *Without treatment, the wound would putrefy and become gangrenous.*

putrid (pyo͞o′trid) adj., in a state of decay or putrefaction; fetid from rottenness; stinking; corrupt. *They found hundreds of putrid, unburied bodies at the massacre site.*

Pygmalion (pig mā′lē ən, -māl′yən) n., in Greek mythology, a sculptor and king of Cyprus who falls in love with a statue he has made and for whom the statue comes alive; hence, by inversion, one who is transformed by another's management and skill. *"My Fair Lady" is a modern version of the story of Pygmalion.*

pyre (pīᵊr) n., pile or heap of wood or other combustible material for burning corpses. *The Greek army built a pyre on which to cremate their dead.*

pyromania (pī′rə mā′nē ə) n., neurosis or psychosis marked by a mania for setting things on fire. *The arsonist was driven by pyromania.*

pyromaniac (pī′rə mā′nē ak) n., person possessed of an irresistible impulse to burn things. *The pyromaniac began by playing with matches.*

pyrophobia (pī′rə fō′bē ə) n., morbid dread of fire. *After being severely burned, he suffered from pyrophobia.*

Qq

quadrangle (kwod′rang′gəl) n., 1. plane figure having four angles and four sides. *A square is a quadrangle.* 2. square or rectangular courtyard surrounded or nearly surrounded by buildings, as city halls, colleges, etc.; also the building or buildings surrounding such a court. *Graduation was held in the quadrangle.* 3. area shown on one of the standard atlas sheets published by the U.S. Geological Survey. *This quadrangle shows the county's topography.*

quadrennial (kwo dren′e əl) adj., 1. occurring once in four years. *Quadrennial elections are held to choose a U.S. president.* 2. comprising four years. *The president serves a quadrennial term of office.*

quadruped (kwod′roō ped′) n., animal having four feet. *A dog is a quadruped.* adj., four-footed. *A dog is a quadruped animal.*

quadruple (kwo droō′pəl, kwod′roō-) v.t., to multiply by four. *We must quadruple our efforts to reach our goal.* v.i., to become four times as much or many. *Our fuel bill may quadruple this year.* adj., 1. fourfold; having four parts. *The four formed a quadruple alliance.* 2. four times as much or as many. *This jar had quadruple the pickles of that other one.*

quadruplets (kwo drup′lits, -droōp′lits, kwod′roō plits) n., four offspring born of a single pregnancy. *The quadruplets were on the front page.*

quaff (kwäf, kwaf, kwôf) v.t., to drink of copiously or greedily. *He quaffed beer after beer.* n., hearty swallow. *She took a deep quaff of the brew.*

quagmire (kwag′mī²r′, kwog′-) n., 1. soft, wet, boggy land that trembles under-foot; marsh; bog. *Rain turned the road into a quagmire.* 2. difficult situation. *We encountered a quagmire of red tape.*

quail (kwāl) n., 1. small, gallinaceous Old World bird related to the partridge. 2. one of the various small, gallinaceous U.S. birds resembling the quail, esp. the bobwhite. v.i., to lose heart or courage; flinch; cower; recoil. *I quail at the prospect.*

qualm (kwäm, kwôm) n., 1. scruple or twinge of conscience; compunction; uneasiness. *I told the lie without a qualm.* 2. sudden misgiving or feeling of apprehension. *I felt a qualm over the decision.* 3. sensation of nausea; sudden feeling of sickness, esp. at the stomach. *I tried to ignore the qualm in my stomach.*

quandary (kwon′də rē, -drē) n., state of perplexity, hesitation, or puzzlement; dilemma. *I've been in a quandary all day trying to decide.*

quarantine (kwôr′ən tēn′, kwor′-) n., 1. period of isolation imposed to prevent the spread of contagious disease. *The doctor put her in quarantine for a month.* 2. term, originally of 40 days, during which ships, persons, etc., suspected of harboring some infectious or contagious disease are held in detention or isolation on arrival at a port or place. *Our ship was held in quarantine.* v., to put under quarantine; isolate, as by authority. *Because some of the fruit was found to contain insect pests, the infected shipment was quarantined by customs.*

quarrel (kwôr′əl, kwor′-) n., 1. altercation; angry dispute. *A quarrel arose over the right of way.* 2. cause, occasion, or motive of dispute or contention. *I have no quarrel with your political*

229

views. v.i., 1. to dispute angrily or violently; contend; squabble. *My brother and I quarrel continuously.* 2. to find fault; cavil; find cause of complaint. *I can't quarrel with your conclusion.*

quarry (kwôr′ē, kwor′ē) n., 1. excavation or pit, usually open, from which building stones (marble, slate, cement, etc.) are obtained by digging or blasting. *The gravel comes from the local quarry.* 2. something hunted or pursued. *The eagle swooped down on its quarry.* v.t., to dig or take from a quarry. *They quarry marble here.*

quarto (kwôr′tō) n., size of a piece of formed by folding and cutting a sheet in four; book size about 9½ x 12 inches determined by folding printed sheets twice to form 4 leaves. *I have a first edition quarto of Poe's stories.*

quasi (kwā′zī, kwä′sē, -zē) adj., seeming or apparent; expressing some resemblance but not having all the features of what it professes to be. *Because of the story he became a quasi hero.* adv., in some sense; seemingly. *She was there quasi-officially.*

queasy (kwē′zē) adj., 1. affected with or inclined to nausea; nauseous; nauseated. *Fear made me feel queasy.* 2. apt to cause nausea; nauseating. *I had a queasy sense that the brakes wouldn't hold.* 3. uncomfortable; uneasy. *Her queasy conscience bothered her all afternoon.* 4. squeamish; fastidious; delicate. *I am rather queasy about raw oysters.*

quell (kwel) v.t., 1. to subdue; crush, vanquish; suppress. *Police were sent to quell the riot.* 2. to quiet; allay. *I tried to quell my panic.*

quench (kwench) v.t., 1. to extinguish; put out. *Quench the light—here he comes!* 2. to allay. *Nothing can quench his desire for freedom.*

querulous (kwer′ə ləs, kwer′yə-) adj., 1. habitually complaining; full of complaints. *He was a querulous, whiny child.* 2. expressing complaint; peevish. *Her querulous tone got on his nerves.*

query (kwēr′ē) n., 1. question; inquiry. *She responded to my query.* 2. doubt; mental question. *He had a query about her motives.* 3. in printing, a question mark (?) or an abbreviation such as *qy.,* used as a marginal note to indicate a question or doubt about some point in the text. *He considered the editor's query.* v.t., 1. to ask or inquire about; question. *We didn't want to query his integrity.* 2. to mark with a query. *The editor will query the spelling.*

questionable (kwes′chə nə bəl) adj., liable to question; suspicious; doubtful; uncertain; disputable. *The accuracy of his figures is questionable.*

queue (kyōō) n., 1. pendent braid of hair; pigtail. *The old man wore a traditional queue.* 2. waiting line. *A queue of taxis waited outside the theater.* v.i., to line up while waiting for something. *Queue here for a taxi.*

quibble (kwib′əl) n., 1. use of equivocal, evasive, or untrue language to evade the point in question. *His quibble forced me to repeat the question.* 2. petty objection or minor criticism. *Your quibble seems irrelevant.* v.i., 1. to evade the point or the truth by prevarication or equivocation. *He tried to quibble his way out of it.* 2. to object to or question over minor details. *I won't quibble over the price.*

quid pro quo (kwid′ prō kwō′) one thing in return for another. *I accept your maintenance work as quid pro quo for the apartment.*

quiescent (kwē es′ənt) adj., resting; inactive; still; not moving. *The puppies are quiescent for the moment.*

quietus (kwī ē′təs) n., final settlement to something; finishing stroke. *This should put the quietus to all the rumors.*

quintessence (kwin tes′əns) n., 1. pure and concentrated essence. *This rose is the quintessence of scarlet.* 2. most perfect or representative embodiment. *His is the quintessence of acting skill.*

quintuplets (kwin tup′lits, -tōō′plits, -tyōō′-, kwin′tōō plits, -tyōō-) n., five offspring resulting from a single pregnancy. *The test showed she was carrying quintuplets.*

quip (kwip) n., smart, sarcastic comment; cutting jest. *I smarted at his pointed quip.* v.i., to make quips; gibe; use sarcasms. *He could still quip over the mistake.*

quirk (kwûrk) n., 1. peculiarity; idiosyncrasy. *We didn't mind her little quirk.* 2. sudden turn or twist. *A quirk of fate threw us together.* 3. sudden turn or flourish as in writing or musical composition. *The ending had an unexpected quirk.*

quite (kwīt) adv., 1. completely; wholly; entirely; fully. *I'm not his supporter—quite the contrary.* 2. to a considerable extent or degree; noticeably. *It's quite warm in here.* 3. really; actually. *This is not quite what I expected.*

quixotic (kwik sot′ik) adj., 1. extravagantly or absurdly romantic; visionary; impracticable. *We can't afford your quixotic notions of design.*

quizzical (kwiz′i kəl) adj., 1. queer; odd; slightly eccentric. *The professor is a shy, quizzical fellow.* 2. puzzled; inquisitive; questioning. *She wrinkled her forehead in a quizzical frown.* 3. teasing; bantering; ridiculing. *I tolerated his quizzical comments on my intelligence.*

quondam (kwon′dam) adj., having been formerly; former; sometime. *The quondam artist now sells antiques.*

quorum (kwōr′əm, kwôr′-) n., number of members of any constituted group required to be present at a meeting in order to transact business legally; usually a majority. *We can't vote without a quorum.*

Rr

rabble (rab′əl) n., 1. confused, disorderly crowd; mob. *His speech inflamed the rabble.* 2. lowest classes; masses; common people. *They took a cab to avoid the rabble.*

rabid (rab′id) adj., 1. violently intense; raging; mad. *I was choked with rabid anger.* 2. fanatical. *He is a rabid socialist.* 3. affected with rabies; pertaining to rabies. *I was bitten by a rabid bat.*

racketeer (rak′i tēr′) n., one who is involved in organized illegal activity, such as blackmail, extortion, bootlegging, etc. *The racketeer was sentenced to prison.*

raconteur (rak′on tûr′) n., one skilled in relating anecdotes, recounting adventures, etc.; storyteller. *The gifted raconteur is much in demand as a speaker.*

radiant (rā′dē ənt) adj., 1. emitting rays of light; shining; beaming with brightness. *A radiant sun broke through the clouds.* 2. expressive of happiness, joy, hope, etc. *The bride was radiant.* 3. emitted in rays; radiating, as radiation or heat. *Radiant heat warmed the room.*

radioactive (rā′dē ō ak′tiv) adj., of, relating to, exhibiting, or caused by radioactivity; spontaneous emission of alpha, beta, or gamma rays from an atomic nucleus. *They wore protective clothing around the radioactive material.*

ragamuffin (rag′ə muf′in) n., ragged urchin. *We tossed coins to the dirty little ragamuffin.*

ragout (ra gōō′) n., highly seasoned stew of meat and vegetables. *She served a zesty ragout of lamb.*

rail (rāl) n., 1. bar of wood or other material passing from one support to another and serving as a guard or barrier. *They replaced the broken fence rail.* 2. railing; fence. *A guard rail kept her from falling overboard.* 3. one of a pair of steel beams used to support and guide the wheels of railroad locomotives and cars. *The train sped over the rails.* 4. railroad as a means of transportation. *The goods will be shipped by rail.* 5. any of numerous wading birds having short wings, a short tail, long toes, and a harsh cry, inhabiting marshes worldwide. *The rail nests on the ground.* v.i., to speak bitterly or reproachfully; inveigh; utter denunciations. *It is useless to rail against one's fate.*

raiment (rā′mənt) n., poetic term for clothing; garments. *An angel in shining raiment appeared.*

rakish (rā′kish) adj., 1. jaunty; dashing. *His hat was tilted at a rakish angle.* 2. having a stylish appearance suggestive of speed. *The rakish craft cut through the water.* 3. having character of a rake; dissolute. *His rakish behavior cannot be condoned.*

rally (ral′ē) n., 1. quick recovery from disorder or dispersion. *He expected a rally of the troops.* 2. rapid or enthusiastic reunion. *We expect a full alumni rally for the fund drive.* 3. in tennis, badminton, etc., the return of the ball over the net for a number of times consecutively. *She won the rally.* 4. recovery or renewal of strength or activity. *Her rally gave us hope for her recovery.* 5. mass meeting for common action. *We all attended the pep rally.* 6. long-distance automobile race run over public roads unfamiliar to the participants and marked by numerous checkpoints along the route. *We entered the sports-car* *rally.* v.t., 1. to reunite; bring together or into order again. *The general tried to rally the scattered troops.* 2. to call up or together, unite, gather up, etc., energetically. *I need a moment to rally my strength.* v.i., 1. to come together or into order again; reunite energetically; gather for a common end. *The party must rally before the next election.* 2. to recover partially from illness. *She seemed to rally before losing consciousness.* 3. to acquire new or renewed strength or vigor. *The stock market should rally after this news.* 4. in tennis, badminton, etc., to return the ball over the net for a number of times consecutively. *Shall we rally for serve?*

rambunctious (ram bungk'shəs) adj., 1. obstreperous; unruly; difficult to control. *The teacher finally dismissed the rambunctious children.* 2. noisy; boisterous; wildly exuberant. *The rambunctious merrymakers caroused until dawn.*

ramify (ram'ə fī') v.i., to branch out; divide or spread into branchlike parts; extend in different directions. *Her changes should ramify throughout the company.*

ramp (ramp) n., 1. gradual slope or ascent connecting two different levels. *The wheelchair rolled down the ramp.* 2. movable staircase for entering or leaving the main door of an aircraft. *The passengers crowded onto the boarding ramp.* 3. apron. *The airplane was towed to the parking ramp.* 4. access or exit road leading onto or off a highway. *Take the ramp marked "Exit 6."* v.i., to move or act furiously; rage; storm. *She began to ramp like a demon.*

rampage (*n.* ram'pāj; *v.* ram pāj') n., violent or furious movement; excited action. *The herd was stirred up into a rampage.* v.i., to rush violently; rage or storm about. *The river began to rampage very close to the floodline.*

rampart (ram'pärt, -part) n., 1. elevation or mound of earth raised as a fortification and usually surmounted by a par-

apet. *They surveyed the field from the rampart.* 2. something serving as a bulwark or defense; protecting enclosure. *His integrity is a rampart against their deceit.*

ramshackle (ram'shak'əl) adj., loosely made or held together; tumbledown. *The ramshackle alliance fell apart under pressure.*

rancid (ran'sid) adj., 1. having a tainted smell or taste; rankly offensive to the senses. *We discarded the rancid meat.* 2. disgusting; offensive; rank (of an odor or taste). *A rancid stench arose from the garbage heap.*

rancor (rang'kər) n., malice or spitefulness; bitter animosity. *She nursed an enduring rancor against him.*

rank (rangk) n., 1. class, order, or grade of persons; any aggregate of individuals classed together for some common reason, as social station, occupation, etc. *He joined the rank of the unemployed.* 2. grade in a scale of comparison. *In a class of 30 she has the rank of 5th.* 3. class or classification. *I hope to achieve the rank of colonel.* 4. natural or acquired status; relative position; standing. *His rank gained him admission to the exclusive club.* 5. line, row, or series. *A rank of trees bordered the walk.* 6. orderly arrangement. *A rank of soldiers stood at attention.* v.t., 1. to arrange in a rank or ranks; place in a rank or line. *Please rank yourselves according to height.* 2. to assign to a particular class, order, or division. *Our teacher ranks students by abilities.* 3. to outrank. *A general ranks a colonel.* v.i., to occupy a certain position as compared with others. *He ranks far above the rest in ability.* adj., 1. excessively vigorous in growth; immoderately luxuriant. *Rank vegetation grew over the deserted building.* 2. producing luxuriantly; having an excessive and coarse growth. *The property has acres of rank pastures.* 3. having an offensively strong taste or smell. *He was smoking a rank cigar.* 4. offensively strong, as a taste or smell.

The rank odor filled the room. 5. thorough; utter; unmitigated. *What rank nonsense!* 6. offensive to the mind; indecent; gross. *The book is rank pornography.*

rankle (rang′kəl) v.i., 1. to continue to cause irritation or resentment; fester. *The humiliation still rankles.* 2. to feel bitterness or irritation. *Her unjust treatment made him rankle.* v.t., to cause irritation or resentment in. *His insult rankles me still.*

ransack (ran′sak) v.t., 1. to search thoroughly; look in or through all parts of. *I ransacked the house for my lost keys.* 2. to plunder; pillage; sack. *The invaders began to ransack the entire city.*

rant (rant) v.t., to utter in a ranting manner. *Rant all you like—I won't do it.* v.i., to speak or declaim violently and with little sense; rave. *She ranted like a mad woman.*

rapacious (rə pā′shəs) adj., 1. given to seizing for plunder or to satisfy greed. *The rapacious looters ran through the streets.* 2. extremely greedy; extortionate. *His rapacious demands exhausted her bank account.* 3. subsisting by capture of living prey; predacious. *The lion is by nature rapacious.*

rape (rāp) n., 1. act of seizing and carrying away by force or violence. *The vandals were intent on rape of the treasure.* 2. act of forcible sexual intercourse. *He was arrested and charged with rape.* 3. brassicaceous plant whose seeds yield rape oil. *Rape grows as a weed in parts of Europe.* 4. stalks and skins of grapes after the juice has been extracted, used as a filter in making vinegar. *What passed through the rape was pure vinegar.* v.t., 1. to carry off violently; seize or take by force. *They planned to rape what they could and burn the rest.* 2. to commit rape upon; force (a person) to have sexual intercourse. *She said he had tried to rape her.* v.i., to commit rape. *They will not hesitate to rape or even to murder.*

rapine (rap′in) n., violent seizure and carrying off of property; plunder. *The*

invaders embarked on an orgy of pillage and rapine.*

rapport (ra pōr′, -pôr′) n., harmonious relation; affinity; accord. *She established a close rapport with her colleagues.*

rapscallion (rap skal′yən) n., rascal; rogue. *He's an incorrigible rapscallion.*

rapt (rapt) adj., 1. engrossed; deeply absorbed. *She was wholly rapt in the symphony.* 2. seized with ecstasy; enraptured. *He was rapt with his new son.*

rapture (rap′chər) n., 1. state of mental transport or exaltation; ecstasy. *She danced in rapture at the invitation.* 2. manifestation of mental transport; passionate expression or utterance. *He went into raptures over the painting.*

rarefied (râr′ə fīd′) adj., 1. very high; lofty; exalted. *I felt uneasy in the rarefied academic environment.* 2. select; esoteric. *She belongs to the rarefied group of corporate management.*

rarefy (râr′ə fī′) v.t., 1. to make rare, thin, porous, or less dense. *Fans were used to rarefy the humidity.* 2. to make more spiritual or refined. *We tried to rarefy our thoughts.* v.i., to become rare or less dense. *The atmosphere rarefies at high altitudes.*

rash (rash) n., 1. more or less extensive skin eruption. *The itchy rash is probably poison ivy.* 2. number of instances occurring over a short period. *There has been a rash of burglaries in the neighborhood.* adj., marked by or manifesting undue haste; resulting from temerity or recklessness. *The politician's rash promise proved undeliverable.*

rationalize (rash′ə nəlīz′, rash′nəlīz′) v.t., 1. to attribute a rational motive to behavior that originates in the subconscious. *She tried to rationalize her fear of thunderstorms.* 2. to subject to the test of reason; explain or interpret by rational principles. *One cannot rationalize the scriptural account of the Flood.* v.i., to think for oneself; employ reason as a supreme test. *A young child cannot rationalize.*

rattle (rat′əl) n., 1. rapid succession of short, sharp, clattering sounds, as of intermittent collision or concussion. *A rattle of drums announced their arrival.* 2. instrument or toy contrived to make a rattling sound. *The baby played with the rattle.* 3. series of horny, interlocking parts at the end of a rattlesnake's tail. *The snake's rattle warned me away.* v.t., 1. to cause to rattle. *The rough ride rattled our bones.* 2. to utter or perform in a smart, rapid manner. *She rattled off the speech from memory.* 3. to unsettle, agitate, or confuse. *The heckling failed to rattle the speaker.* v.i., 1. to make a rapid succession of short, sharp, clattering sounds, as by continuous concussions. *Hailstones rattled on the roof.* 2. to move or be carried along with a continuous rapid clatter. *Wagons rattle along the trail.* 3. to talk rapidly; chatter. *I thought he would rattle on forever.*

raucous (rô′kəs) adj., hoarse; harsh; croaking; strident in sound. *The raucous crowing awoke me.*

ravage (rav′ij) n., desolation or destruction wrought by violent action or by physical or moral causes; havoc; ruin. *The hurricane's ravage destroyed the town.* v.t., to desolate violently; lay waste; devastate. *We watched the fire ravage the building.*

rave (rāv) n., extravagantly enthusiastic criticism. *His performance won raves.* v.i., 1. to talk like a madman; speak deliriously or irrationally. *He shouted, raved, and tore his hair.* 2. to speak or write with immoderate enthusiasm. *The critics all rave about her book.*

ravenous (rav′ə nəs) adj., 1. furiously voracious; rapacious. *Ravenous vultures circled the carcass.* 2. greedily eager for gratification; gluttonous. *We reached home with ravenous appetites.*

ravish (rav′ish) v.t., 1. to seize and carry off by force. *The fox sneaked in to ravish the chickens.* 2. to overcome with strong emotion; enrapture. *The beauty of the music ravished us.* 3. to rape. *He was charged with trying to ravish her.*

ravishing (rav′i shing) adj., exquisitely lovely; enchanting. *The rose garden is ravishing in June.*

raze (rāz) v.t., to tear down completely; demolish. *They plan to raze the buildings.*

reactionary (rē ak′shə ner′ē) n., person who favors or inclines to reaction; one who attempts to check, undo, or reverse political action. *The ultraconservative reactionary is opposed to all social reform.* adj., of, pertaining to, or favoring reaction, esp. political reaction. *His reactionary views appalled the liberal student.*

realism (rē′ə liz′əm) n., 1. concern for or inclination toward the real as opposed to the abstract, speculative, etc. *Realism tells us that fossil fuels will run out.* 2. in art and literature, the treatment of characters, objects, scenes, events, circumstances, etc., according to actual truth or appearance or intrinsic probability. *We were startled by the realism of the painted city scene.*

realm (relm) n., 1. royal jurisdiction; domain; kingdom. *The new king was proclaimed throughout his realm.* 2. sphere of power, influence, or operation; province; arena. *Let's keep this within the realm of possibility.*

realty (rē′əl tē) n., real property; real estate. *She invested heavily in realty.*

reassure (rē′ə shŏŏr′) v.t., 1. to assure or establish anew; make sure again; confirm. *Let me reassure you that we will meet again.* 2. to restore to confidence; free from doubt or apprehension. *His confidence in the plan reassures me.*

rebate (rē′bāt, ri bāt′) n., allowance by way of discount; partial refund. *They are offering a $5 rebate.* v.t., to allow as a discount; refund part of a payment. *The government will rebate part of the tax.*

rebound (*n.* rē′bound; *v.* ri bound′) n., 1. act of rebounding; recoil. *The rebound of the mechanism on the lawnmower needed repair.* 2. basketball or hockey puck that rebounds; gaining of possession of the ball or puck on a rebound. *She caught the rebound and sank the basket.* 3. instinctive or automatic response to a disappointment or trouble.

She was on the rebound from an unhappy romance. v.i., to spring back or fly back from force of impact. *The ball re-bounded off the backboard.* v.t., to cause to bound back; throw or drive back. *The walls rebound our voices.*

rebuff (ri buf′) n., 1. peremptory denial or refusal; snub. *It was a curt rebuff.* 2. abrupt check, as to one making an advance. *My approach was met with a cold rebuff.* v.t., to repel; resist; check; put off with an abrupt and unexpected denial. *I'm afraid he'll rebuff my over-ture of friendship.*

rebuke (ri byoōk′) n., direct reprimand; expression of disapproval; reproof. *My behavior provoked her sharp rebuke.* v.t., to utter sharp disapproval of; reprimand; chide. *Don't rebuke him for the accident.*

rebut (ri but′) v.t., to oppose or contra-dict by evidence, argument, or coun-tervailing proof; refute. *The senator has equal time to rebut the charges.* v.i., to provide an answer that refutes or op-poses. *All charges will be rebutted by the defense.*

recalcitrant (ri kal′si trənt) n., recalci-trant person. *The recalcitrant held his ground.* adj., refusing to submit; not submissive or compliant; refractory; unruly. *Let's ignore the tantrums of the recalcitrant child.*

recant (ri kant′) v.t., to retract or repu-diate a previous assertion; disavow. *The heretic refused to recant his position.* v.i., to revoke a declaration or propo-sition; unsay what has been said, esp. formally. *After her temper outburst she recanted.*

recapitulate (rē′kə pich′ə lāt′) v.t., to give a summary of the principal facts, points, or arguments of; summarize. *The review recapitulates the author's works.* v.i., to repeat in brief. *She de-voted some of her allotted time to re-capitulate.*

recede (ri sēd′) v.i., 1. to move back; retreat; withdraw; fall away. *The waves advance and recede on the shore.* 2. to incline or slope backward. *His hairline*

recedes sharply. 3. to become more distant; diminish. *The horrible memory will recede with time.*

receptive (ri sep′tiv) adj., having the qual-ity of or the capacity for receiving, admitting, or taking in; able to hold or contain. *She was receptive to the various proposals.*

recession (ri sesh′ən) n., 1. act of receding or going back; withdrawal. *The tide's recession left the beach littered with debris.* 2. departing procession, as of clergy and choir at the end of a religious service. *The robed priests formed a slow and stately recession.* 3. economic downturn. *Economists warn of a prob-able recession.*

recidivism (ri sid′ə viz′əm) n., tendency to relapse into a previous condition or behavior pattern, esp. into criminal or antisocial behavior; backsliding. *The rate of recidivism for rapists is high.*

recipient (ri sip′ē ənt) n., one who or that which receives; receiver. *The grateful recipient thanked the scholarship board.*

reciprocal (ri sip′rə kəl) n., 1. thing that is reciprocal to something else. *The kindness was rewarded with an unex-pected reciprocal.* 2. one of a pair of numbers whose product is one. *The fraction 3/5 is the reciprocal of 5/3.* adj., 1. mutually exchanged or exchangeable; concerning, given, or owed by each with regard to the other or others. *The two countries have a reciprocal aid program.* 2. in grammar, expressing mutual or reciprocal relation. *"Each other" and "one another" are recip-rocal pronouns.*

recitation (res′i tā′shən) n., 1. act of re-citing; enumeration. *We suffered through a recitation of his ailments.* 2. act of reciting or repeating what has been committed to memory, esp. pub-licly. *His recitation included Shake-spearean sonnets.* 3. pupil's oral reply to a teacher on a prepared lesson. *She heard my recitation of the French dia-logue.* 4. meeting of a class; class period. *Meet me after recitation.*

recitative (res´i tə tēv´) n., declamatory style for delivering a song or narrative text; also, a selection, passage, or movement delivered in this style. *The tenor's recitative was followed by the soprano's aria.*

reclamation (rek´lə mā´shən) n., 1. act of reclaiming for use or service. *The plan calls for reclamation of the marsh for an airport.* 2. process or industry of reclaiming waste materials or of making usable products from waste. *We lobbied for aluminum can reclamation.*

recluse (rek´lōōs, ri klōōs´) n., person who leads a solitary life or a life apart from society. *She has been a veritable recluse since her sister's death.*

recognizance (ri kog´ni zəns, -kon´i-) n., 1. obligation of record entered into before a court of record or magistrate requiring the performance of some particular act, as to appear in court, etc. *The suspect was released on his own recognizance.* 2. sum pledged as surety upon such an obligation. *The magistrate set a mere token recognizance on the prisoner.*

recoil (n. rē´koil, rē koil´; v. ri koil´) n., rebound of a firearm when discharged. *His padded jacket protected him from the gun's recoil.* v.i., 1. to draw or shrink back, as in disgust, alarm, etc. *She recoiled from the sudden billow of smoke.* 2. to spring back or fly back as in consequence of force of impact or impetus; rebound. *The gun recoiled and caught him on the shoulder.*

recommend (rek´ə mend´) v.t., 1. to commend to another's notice; present as favorable or worthy. *I promised to recommend him for the job.* 2. to make acceptable or attractive. *The idea has little to recommend it.* 3. to commit or entrust. *She recommended her soul to God.* 4. to advise or urge as advisable. *I recommend the utmost caution.*

reconcile (rek´ən sīl´) v.t., 1. to restore to friendship and unity; conciliate anew. *She reconciled the opposing factions.* 2. to bring to acquiescence or submission. *She can't reconcile herself to being poor.*

3. to adjust; pacify; settle. *We tried to reconcile our differences.* 4. to bring to agreement; make consistent. *I'm trying to reconcile the check with my records.*

recondition (rē´kən dish´ən) v.t., to restore to good or satisfactory condition; repair. *He managed to recondition the radio so it worked like new.*

reconnoiter (rē´kə noi´tər, rek´ə-) v.t., to examine or survey, as a tract or region, for military, engineering, or geological purposes. *They sent a scout to reconnoiter the enemy camp.*

reconstitute (rē kon´sti tōōt´, -tyōōt´) v.t., to constitute again; restore to former condition; reconstruct. *Water will reconstitute the frozen concentrate.*

recoup (ri kōōp´) v.t., 1. to return or bring in an amount equal to. *You should recoup your investment within a year.* 2. to reimburse or indemnify. *He offered to recoup me for my share of the expenses.* 3. to regain or recover. *I tried to recoup what I lost at gambling.*

recourse (rē´kōrs, -kôrs, ri kōrs´, -kôrs´) n., 1. person or thing resorted to for help or protection; resort. *Her own courage was her only recourse.* 2. right to demand payment from the maker or endorser of a negotiable instrument. *He wrote "without recourse" on the check, avoiding any liability for it.*

recrimination (ri krim´ə nā´shən) n., meeting of an accusation by a counteraccusation. *Our mutual recriminations got us nowhere.*

recruit (ri krōōt´) n., 1. newly enlisted or drafted member of the armed services. *Each recruit is issued a uniform.* 2. one who has newly filled a vacancy in any group. *We'll have to find a recruit to take Joe's place on the team.* v.t., 1. to enlist (new members) for an army, navy, etc. *The Army tries to recruit college graduates.* 2. to enlist new people for any object. *We are trying to recruit management trainees.*

rectify (rek´tə fī´) v.t., 1. to make right; correct when wrong, erroneous, or false; remedy. *I'll try to rectify my error.*

rectitude

2. to correct by adjusting, as an instrument or a course. *The captain had to rectify the compass reading.*

rectitude (rek′ti tōōd′, -tyōōd′) n., 1. rightness of principle or practice; integrity. *We respect his undeniable rectitude.* 2. correctness; freedom from error, as of conduct. *She was convinced of the rectitude of her decision.*

recumbent (ri kum′bənt) adj., 1. lying down; reclining; leaning. *She was recumbent on a sofa.* 2. inactive; idle. *He tried in vain to prod her recumbent conscience.*

recuperate (ri kōō′pə rāt′) v.t., to regain. *He tried to recuperate his finances.* v.i., to recover from illness. *She went home to recuperate after her illness.*

recurrent (ri kûr′ənt) adj., reappearing; returning from time to time; repeated. *He suffers from recurrent malaria.*

redeem (ri dēm′) v.t., 1. to buy back; repurchase; recover by purchase; pay off. *We have saved enough to redeem our mortgage.* 2. to ransom, release, or liberate from captivity or bondage, or from obligation or liability, by paying an equivalent. *The king sent money to redeem his kidnapped knights.* 3. to convert paper money into specie. *I'm going to the bank to redeem these bills.* 4. to perform, discharge, or fulfill, as a promise or an obligation. *Her latest paintings more than redeem her early artistic promise.* 5. to make amends for; atone for; compensate for. *Splendid acting cannot redeem the poor play.* 6. to deliver from sin and its consequences by means of a sacrifice offered for the sinner. *Christians believe Jesus was sent by God to redeem mankind.*

redolent (red′ələnt) adj., 1. having a sweet or pleasant odor; fragrant. *The garden was redolent after the rain.* 2. odorous or smelling. *The air was redolent of smoke.* 3. suggestive; evocative. *A redolent silence fell between them when the past was mentioned.*

redress (*n.* rē′dres, ri dres′; *v.* ri dres′) n., 1. setting right again; righting of what is wrong. *These abuses require*

redress. 2. deliverance from wrong, injury, or oppression. *Their redress depends on his good will.* v.t., to set right again; restore; amend; reform. *The new mayor promises to redress corruption in City Hall.*

redundant (ri dun′dənt) adj., 1. exceeding what is necessary or normal; superfluous. *His grin displayed an almost redundant number of teeth.* 2. using or containing more words or images than are necessary or useful; prolix. *Her redundant style needs heavy editing.*

reek (rēk) n., 1. strong, disagreeable smell. *The reek of garbage was overwhelming.* 2. vapor; steam; fume. *The reek rose skyward as the caldron boiled.* v.i., 1. to give off or be pervaded with a strong, unpleasant odor. *The room reeks of cigar smoke.* 2. to give off vapor or smoke. *He carried a reeking pail of sudsy water.* 3. to give a strong impression of something unpleasant. *The plot reeks of treachery.*

reflection (ri flek′shən) n., 1. act of reflecting, or the state of being reflected. *The reflection of light confused us momentarily.* 2. that which is produced by being reflected; image. *He glanced at his reflection in the window.* 3. fixing of the thoughts on something; attentive or continued meditation. *The new year is a time for reflection.* 4. thought or opinion formed after deliberation or consideration. *She threw out her reflection for what it was worth.* 5. reproach cast; criticism; imputation. *I didn't mean it as a reflection on your skill.*

reflex (rē′fleks) n., involuntary, and often unconscious, action of the nervous system in which a stimulus is transmitted along sensory nerves to a nerve center, from which it is again reflected along efferent nerves to call into play some muscular, glandular, or other activity. *A reflex causes the contraction of the pupils when exposed to light.* adj., occurring in reaction; responsive. *Anger was a reflex response to the sharp jolt.*

refraction (ri frak′shən) n., 1. change of direction of a ray of light, sound, heat, etc., in passing obliquely from one medium to another, such as air and water, in which its velocity is different. *A pencil standing in a glass of water will appear to be broken at the water line because of refraction.* 2. ability of the eye to refract light as it enters so as to form an image on the retina. *Corrective lenses compensate for the improper refraction of his eyes.*

refractory (ri frak′tə rē) adj., 1. unyielding; stubborn and unmanageable. *She pushed the refractory lock of hair out of her eyes.* 2. resisting ordinary methods of treatment. *He suffered from a refractory virus disease.* 3. difficult to fuse, reduce, corrode, melt, etc., as an ore or a metal. *The fireplace was lined with refractory brick.*

refurbish (rē fûr′bish) v.t., to furbish anew; polish up; renovate. *We will refurbish the office before renting it again.*

refute (ri fyoot′) v.t., 1. to prove to be erroneous or false by argument or countervailing proof. *I had no chance to refute his accusations.* 2. to overcome in argument; prove to be in error. *The defense attorney managed to refute that witness.*

regal (rē′gəl) adj., pertaining to royalty; royal; befitting royalty; magnificent; splendid. *The prince was constantly aware of his regal duties.*

regale (ri gāl′) v.t., to entertain sumptuously or delightfully; feast; divert or gratify the senses; treat like a king; treat royally. *His rich palette regales the eye.*

regatta (ri gat′ə, -gä′tə) n., regularly appointed boat race for prizes. *We will enter this year's regatta.*

regenerate (ri jen′ə rāt′) v.t., to generate or produce anew; reproduce; restore. *Some lizards can regenerate a damaged or amputated tail.*

regeneration (ri jen′ə rā′shən) n., act of regenerating or producing anew; radical change in an individual's psyche; conversion; renewal. *The second honeymoon provided a regeneration of their marriage.*

regent (rē′jənt) n., one who governs in the minority, absence, or disability of a sovereign; ruler; governor. *The minister was regent while the king was ill.*

regime (rə zhēm′, rā-) n., mode, system, or style of management or government; regular pattern of action; habit; regimen. *He had a strict regime for getting ready in the morning.*

regimen (rej′ə men′, -mən) n., orderly or systematic management or government; any regulation or regime intended to produce beneficial results gradually; course of living according to certain rules. *Her new regimen enabled her to accomplish more in a day.*

regiment (rej′ə mənt) n., body of soldiers consisting of one or more battalions of infantry; organized unit. *The entire regiment turned out to bid the general farewell.* v.t., to organize uniformly. *Her diet regimented a weight loss of ten pounds a month.*

regress (ri gres′) v.i., to go back; return to a former or less developed state. *An alumni reunion is a rare chance to regress.*

regression (ri gresh′ən) n., 1. act of passing back or returning; retrogression; return to an earlier or lower state. *Contact sports allow a temporary regression into primitive aggression.* 2. gradual decline in the effects of disease. *We were relieved at signs of the disease's regression.*

regressive (ri gres′iv) adj., passing back; returning to a lower, former, or simpler state; opposed to progressive. *The reactionary proposed a rather regressive law.*

regurgitate (ri gûr′ji tāt′) v.t., to pour or cause to rush or surge back; feed back; repeat exactly. *I want you to do more than simply regurgitate the facts and dates.*

rehabilitate (rē′hə bil′i tāt′) v.t., to restore, as to a former capacity, privilege, good standing, or good health. *We will try to rehabilitate the school kitchen.*

reimburse (rē′im bûrs′) v.t., to pay back; refund; repay; indemnify. *The company will reimburse your travel expenses.*

reincarnation (rē'in kär nā'shən) n., new or repeated incarnation or embodiment; rebirth, esp. of a soul in a new human body. *Anyone who believes in reincarnation probably believes in the existence of previous lives.*

reinforcement (rē'in fôrs'mənt, -fôrs'-) n., act of reinforcing; additional force; fresh assistance. *They hoped the reinforcement of the seawall with sandbags would suffice.*

reiterate (rē it'ə rāt') v.t., to repeat; do or say repeatedly. *I reiterate this point because it is important.*

rejuvenate (ri jōō'və nāt') v.t., to restore the appearance, power, or feelings of youth to; renew; refresh. *Rejuvenate the leather with saddle soap and oil.*

relate (ri lāt') v.t., 1. to refer or ascribe as to a source or connection; connect; assert a relation with. *Only later did he relate the two incidents.* 2. to tell; recite; narrate. *Please relate the story again.*

relegate (rel'ə gāt') v.t., to send away or out of the way; dismiss; banish. *They tried to relegate the ailing pilot to a desk job.*

relentless (ri lent'lis) adj., unrelenting; unmoved by pity; insensible to the distress of others; implacable; inexorable. *The relentless pressure contributed to his breakdown.*

relevance (rel'ə vəns) n., state or character of being relevant or pertinent; definite relation; recognizable connection; pertinence. *I don't see the relevance of that argument to this situation.*

relevant (rel'ə vənt) adj., to the purpose; germane; pertinent; applicable. *The witness gave testimony relevant to the case.*

reliable (ri lī'ə bəl) adj., worthy to be depended or relied on; trustworthy. *The reliable employee never missed a day of work.*

relinquish (ri liṅg'kwish) v.t., to give up the possession or occupancy of; renounce; hand over; let go; yield; surrender. *He had to relinquish ownership when he forfeited on the loan.*

relish (rel'ish) n., 1. keen enjoyment, esp. sensual enjoyment; gusto; zest. *He ate his dinner with relish.* 2. piquant condiment or side dish served to add zest or flavor. *Pass the green tomato relish, please.* v.t., to like; enjoy. *She relished the few moments they had together.*

remediable (ri mē'dē ə bəl) adj., capable of being remedied, improved, or cured. *Don't despair—the situation is remediable.*

remedial (ri mē'dē əl) adj., affording or intended as a remedy. *His remedial work prevented further deterioration.*

reminisce (rem'ə nis') v.i., to indulge in recalling the past; remember. *He began to reminisce about his father.*

reminiscence (rem'ə nis'əns) n., act or power of recollecting; recollection; voluntary exertion of the memory; that which is recalled. *The reunion prompted the painful reminiscence.* 2. narration of past incidents, events, and characteristics. *The reminiscence appears in her autobiography.*

reminiscent (rem'ə nis'ənt) adj., 1. having the faculty of memory; remembering; inclined to recall the past. *She enjoyed her grandmother's reminiscent stories.* 2. serving to jog the memory; calling to mind; suggestive. *The ankle socks were reminiscent of the 1950s.*

remiss (ri mis') adj., not diligent in performance; careless in performing one's duty or business; negligent; inattentive. *She was remiss in not answering your call.*

remission (ri mish'ən) n., 1. forgiveness; pardon; act of forgiving. *Christians pray for the remission of their sins.* 2. abatement; temporary subsidence; relaxation; diminution of intensity or violence. *The remission of pain brought new hope.*

remit (ri mit') v.t., 1. to refrain from exacting; pardon; forgive; release from punishment or penalty. *He asked the judge to remit his sentence.* 2. to slacken; relax the tension of; abate; diminish. *You must remit your demands—she's only a child.* 3. to transmit or send; forward. *Please remit payment upon receipt of bill.*

remittance (ri mit'əns) n., payment; sum

of money remitted in payment. *Please enclose the invoice with your remittance.*

remnant (rem'nənt) n., that which remains or is left over; remainder, esp. the end of a bolt of fabric, ribbon, carpet, or the like. *The remnant was large enough for the child's dress.*

remonstrate (ri mon'strāt) v.i., to present strong reasons against; plead in protest. *Her parents began to remonstrate against her decision to move out.*

remorseful (ri môrs'fəl) adj., full of remorse or intense regret; guilty. *He was remorseful for worrying his mother.*

remote (ri mōt') adj., 1. distant or far away; isolated. *She lived in a remote part of Wales.* 2. not closely related or connected; slight; inconsiderable. *There is only a remote chance I will be available then.*

remuneration (ri myoo'nə rä'shən) n., act of paying for services or the payment itself; compensation; recompense; indemnity. *Remuneration for the poem is likely to be small.*

renaissance (ren'i säns', -zäns', ren'i säns', -zäns', ri nā'səns; *Fr.* Rə ne säNs') n., 1. rebirth; revival. *We are enjoying Broadway's renaissance.* 2. (*cap.*) period in Europe (14th–16th centuries) characterized by great activity in arts and sciences. *The Renaissance marked the transition from the medieval to the modern world.*

render (ren'dər) v.t., 1. to give; furnish; present; hand down. *The judge will render the verdict today.* 2. to give back; return; pay back. *At the end of our lease he rendered our security deposit.* 3. to give up; surrender; yield; hand over; relinquish. *He must render his lands to the crown.* 4. to make or cause to be; cause to become. *The heater began to render the house more comfortable.* 5. to translate; interpret or express for others. *Please render this into English.* 6. to reduce; try out; melt down. *After you render the fat you must clarify it.*

rendezvous (rän'də voo', -dä-; *Fr.* Rän de voo') n., meeting or appointment to meet; also, a meeting place.

They had a wonderful rendezvous in Paris. v.i., to meet or assemble at an appointed place and time. *We plan to rendezvous in the square at noon.*

rendition (ren dish'ən) n., 1. act of rendering or translating; translation. *His rendition of the classic has become the accepted standard.* 2. interpretation, esp. in performance. *Mary gave a stirring rendition of the anthem.*

renegade (ren'ə gād') n., one who deserts one faith or party to join another; deserter; traitor; runaway. *The American Revolutionaries were considered renegades in England.* adj., having the character of or pertaining to a deserter, traitor, or runaway. *The tribe would not accept the renegade Indian.*

renounce (ri nouns') v.t., to declare against; disown; disclaim. *He renounced his intention to be a candidate.*

renovate (ren'ə vāt') v.t., to restore to freshness or to a good condition; renew; repair. *They will renovate the old, neglected house.*

renown (ri noun') n., reputation derived from a widely spread report or praise; fame; celebrity; notoriety; distinction. *The hero's renown spread to the four corners of the empire.*

renunciation (ri nun'sē ā'shən, -shē-) n., act of renouncing; rejection; repudiation. *He was hurt by his protégé's renunciation of his help.*

reparation (rep'ə rā'shən) n., 1. what is done to repair a wrong; indemnification for loss or damage; satisfaction for an injury; amends; compensation; restitution. *There is no reparation he could make for breaking the priceless statue.* 2. renewal of friendship; reconciliation. *Her apology was the first step in the reparation of their friendship.*

repartee (rep'ər tē', -tā') n., witty reply; witticism; witty conversation. *The amusing incident sparked their repartee.*

repast (ri past', -päst') n., meal; food; refreshments. *The guests enjoyed a sumptuous wedding repast.*

repellent (ri pel'ənt) n., substance or material used to repel or ward off. *They* *took some insect repellent on the camping trip.* adj., having the effect of repelling, driving away, or warding off; arousing disgust or repulsion. *The canvas tent was water repellent.*

repent (ri pent′) v., 1. to feel sorrow, regret, or contrition, esp. when amendment of one's conduct results from such feeling. *I repent my thoughtless remark.* 2. to change one's mind or course of conduct. *I think I will repent and stay another day.*

repercussion (rē′pər kush′ən) n., 1. rebounding or reflection; reverberation. *An echo is a repercussion of sound.* 2. unforeseen or widespread effect of an action; distant reaction. *You must consider the possible repercussions of this act.*

repertoire (rep′ər twär′, -twôr′) n., list of works that a performer or company is ready to perform; list or collection of skills. *They added the new ballet to the company's repertoire.*

repertory (rep′ər tōr′ē, -tôr′ē) n., 1. place where things are stored for easy retrieval; inventory; collection; store; treasury; repository. *The Library of Congress is the largest repertory of books in the country.* 2. repertoire. *This season's repertory includes Shakespeare and a new play.*

repetition (rep′i tish′ən) n., act or fact of repeating; rote; recital or mention; that which is repeated. *She uses repetition to learn the French words.*

repetitious (rep′i tish′əs) adj., characterized by repetition; tiresome; tedious. *The TV situation comedy is comically repetitious.*

repine (ri pīn′) v.i., to fret; indulge in complaint or discontent. *The New Englander doesn't have much chance to repine for a change in weather.*

replenish (ri plen′ish) v.t., to fill again; restock. *Let the wine steward replenish your glass.*

replete (ri plēt′) adj., filled up; complete; full; abounding; copiously supplied. *Replete with food and drink, the man began to drowse in his chair.*

replica (rep′lə kə) n., exact likeness; reproduction; representative model. *The museum displayed a replica of the early biplane.*

reporter (ri pōr′tər, -pôr′-) n., one who reports or gives an account, esp. a news media staff member who collects information and reports it to the public. *The reporter began with the small community newspaper.*

repose (ri pōz′) n., rest; quiet; freedom from disturbance; tranquility; sleep. *The telephone's ringing disturbed her repose.* v.i., to rest or sleep; lie at rest. *Where will we repose tonight?*

repository (ri poz′i tōr′ē, -tôr′ē) n., storage place; stockpile; magazine; repertory. *The brain is a great repository of information.*

reprehensible (rep′ri hen′sə bəl) adj., deserving censure; blameworthy; culpable. *His crime was reprehensible, but consider his youth.*

repress (ri pres′) v.t., to press back or down effectually; quell; subdue; suppress; smother; curb; inhibit. *The string of disasters must repress her usually high spirits.*

reprieve (ri prēv′) n., suspension of a criminal sentence; respite in general; delay or lifting of something dreaded. *The governor granted the prisoner a reprieve.* v.t., to acquit; set free; release; grant respite to; spare; save. *The gala benefit managed to reprieve the school for one more year.*

reprimand (rep′rə mand′, -mänd′) n., severe reproof for a fault; admonition; rebuke. *The reprimand stained his hitherto good record.* v.t., to reprove severely; rebuke; censure; chide. *You should reprimand the insolent child.*

reprisal (ri prī′zəl) n., act of retaliation or revenge. *He would not testify for fear of reprisal.*

reproach (ri prōch′) n., act of reproaching; severe expression of censure or blame. *She shot him a look of reproach.* v.t., to charge with a fault; censure severely; upbraid; reprove. *She is sure to reproach us for being late.*

reprobate (rep′rǝ bāt′) n., profligate, abandoned person; wicked, depraved wretch. *The reprobate deserved the harsh sentence.* v.t., to disapprove or censure violently; reject; condemn. *The master swore to reprobate the dishonest servant.* adj., abandoned to wickedness; depraved; profligate; corrupt; shameless. *His reprobate lies broke her heart.*

reprobation (rep′rǝ bā′shǝn) n., act of vehemently disapproving or condemning; state of being reprobated; condemnation; censure; rejection. *Her parents' reprobation prompted her to run away.*

reproof (ri prōōf′) n., expression of blame or censure; reproach; rebuke; reprimand. *The student deserved the teacher's reproof.*

repudiate (ri pyōō′dē āt′) v.t., to cast away; reject; renounce; refuse to acknowledge. *She had every reason to repudiate the old drunk's advances.*

repugnance (ri pug′nǝns) n., strong opposition or antagonism; disgust; aversion; hatred. *The child viewed the liver with repugnance.*

repugnant (ri pug′nǝnt) adj., causing opposition or hatred; disgusting; highly distasteful; offensive; repulsive. *The thought of marriage to him was repugnant to her.*

repulse (ri puls′) v.t., to beat or drive back; repel; reject. *She fought to repulse his prejudice against her.*

repute (ri pyōōt′) n., established opinion; reputation; character; renown; fame. *The reprobate frequented a house of ill repute.* v.t., to hold in thought; deem; reckon; account. *You mustn't repute as insincere his evident admiration for you.*

reputed (ri pyōō′tid) adj., commonly thought; deemed; estimated; regarded. *He was reputed to be the world's finest chef.*

requiem (rek′wē ǝm, rē′kwē-) n., mass for the dead; musical setting of the mass for the dead; funeral hymn; elegy; dirge. *They played the requiem while the church filled with mourners.*

requirement (ri kwīʳr′mǝnt) n., act of requiring or demanding; something wanted, demanded or needed; essential condition; demand; mandate; requisite. *She met all but one requirement for the job.*

requisite (rek′wi zit) n., that which is necessary, essential, or indispensible. *Food is an obvious requisite of life.* adj., required by the nature of things or by circumstances; necessary; indispensible. *He made the grades requisite for acceptance at a law school.*

requisition (rek′wi zish′ǝn) n., authoritative demand or official request for supplies or services. *The director submitted a requisition for new carpeting.* v.t., to demand or request supplies or services authoritatively or officially. *The board voted to requisition a computer.*

requite (ri kwīt′) v.t., to repay; return. *He hoped she would requite his affection.*

rescind (ri sind′) v.t., to take back; revoke; repeal; abrogate. *Hurry, before I rescind my offer.*

rescission (ri sizh′ǝn) n., act of rescinding; repeal; annulment; revocation. *The rescission of the Prohibition Act was a happy event for distilleries.*

resemblance (ri zem′blǝns) n., state or property of resembling or being like; similarity; likeness; something similar; semblance. *She bore a striking resemblance to her mother.*

residue (rez′i dōō′, -dyōō′) n., that which is left after a part is taken, separated, or removed; remainder; sediment; refuse. *She cleaned the residue out of the jar.*

resilient (ri zil′yǝnt, -zil′ē ǝnt) adj., able to spring back or rebound; strong; elastic; capable of withstanding shock or disease without permanent effect. *By summertime, the grass was healthy and resilient.*

resonance (rez′ǝ nǝns) n., act of resounding or the state or quality of being resonant; prolongation or repetition of sound by vibration; reverberation; echo; richness, fullness, or depth of sound; sonorousness. *The critics* *praised the resonance of the baritone's voice.*

resonant (rez′ə nənt) adj., capable of vibrations or sound or of sustaining sound; resounding; full, loud, mellow, or rich in sound; vibrant; sonorous. *He loved the resonant quality of the cello.*

resourceful (ri sōrs′fəl, -sôrs′-) adj., 1. full of aid or support; full of resources. *The library is a resourceful place to do research.* 2. good at devising expedients; ingenious; versatile; inventive; clever. *The resourceful parent kept the child happy without TV.*

respite (res′pit) n., intermission of labor; interval of rest; pause; postponement; reprieve. *The road worker took an hour's respite under a shade tree.*

resplendent (ri splen′dənt) adj., shining with brilliant luster; very bright; brilliant; splendid; glorious. *Thousands of candles made the ballroom resplendent.*

responsive (ri spon′siv) adj., 1. able, ready, or quick to respond or answer, esp. sympathetically; sensitive. *She told her troubles to her responsive friend.* 2. characterized by the use of responses. *A responsive reading followed the anthem in the church service.*

restitution (res′ti tōō′shən, -tyōō′-) n., act of returning or restoring to the owner what has been lost or taken away; act of making good or of giving an equivalent for loss, damage, or injury; indemnification; reparation; restoration. *She sought restitution for the loss of her job.*

restive (res′tiv) adj., 1. impatient under restraint or opposition; recalcitrant; obstinate; stubborn; balky. *The tired child became restive and cross.* 2. refusing to rest or stand still; restless; fidgety. *He could hardly control the restive horses.*

restrictive (ri strik′tiv) adj., imposing limits or restrictions; limiting. *Do not enclose a restrictive clause with commas.*

résumé (rez′ōō mā′, rez′ōō mā′) n., summary or condensed statement of a person's career background or qualifications. *She organized her résumé to include education and experience.*

resurgence (ri sûr′jəns) n., act of rising again or coming back to life or prominence; resurrection. *Doctors feared a resurgence of polio.*

resurgent (ri sûr′jənt) adj., rising again to life or prominence; tending to resurface. *Resurgent jealousy troubled their relationship.*

resurrect (rez′ə rekt′) v.t., to restore to life; reanimate; bring again to public view. *He hoped she wouldn't resurrect that old argument.*

resurrection (rez′ə rek′shən) n., 1. rising again, as from the dead; springing again into life; resurgence; revival. *He dreaded the resurrection of the family skeleton.* 2. (cap.) rising of the dead at the last judgment, or of Christ after his crucifixion and burial. *Easter is celebrated in remembrance of the Resurrection.*

resuscitate (ri sus′i tāt′) v.t., to revive, esp. from apparent death; revitalize; bring to life. *They attempted to resuscitate the drowned man.*

resuscitation (ri sus′i tā′shən) n., act of resuscitating or the state of being resuscitated; revival. *Mouth-to-mouth resuscitation saved her life.*

retain (ri tān′) v.t., 1. to hold or keep in possession; reserve; remember. *I didn't retain much from German class.* 2. to keep in pay or service. *It is worth the money to retain a lawyer.*

retainer (ri tā′nər) n., act or fee paid to retain another's services; any device used to retain something. *The attorney received a retainer from his client.*

retaliate (ri tal′ē āt′) v.i., to strike back; repay in kind; take revenge. *Don't retaliate in anger—you'll regret it.*

retentive (ri ten′tiv) adj., serving to hold or confine; able to keep or retain; capable of preserving ideas or learning. *Goose down is especially retentive of body heat.*

reticence (ret′i səns) n., reservation of one's thoughts or opinions; disinclination to talk or speak; reserve. *Her angry challenge broke through his reticence.*

reticent (ret′i sənt) adj., disposed to be silent; not apt to speak about or reveal any matters; reserved. *The discreet man is reticent about his finances.*

reticular (ri tik′yə lər) adj., reticulate or resembling a net or web; intricate. *The reticular trellis supports wisteria.*

reticulate (ri tik′yə lit, -lāt′) adj., resembling network; having distinct lines, fibers, or veins crossing as in a network; covered with netted lines. *The botanist examined a reticulate leaf.*

retinue (ret′ᵊnoo′, -ᵊnyoo′) n., group or train of followers or servants; cortege; procession. *The prince had trouble housing his large retinue.*

retort (ri tôrt′) n., 1. in chemistry, glass bulbous vessel used for distilling or decomposing. *The retort began to bubble and steam.* 2. sharp, witty, or cutting reply or rejoinder, esp. in response to an argument or accusation; repartee. *She thought too late of a clever retort.* v.i., to turn back an argument, accusation, or attack upon the originator; make a cutting or witty reply; retaliate. *She retorted hotly to his accusation.*

retract (ri trakt′) v.t., to take back; withdraw; recall; undo. *The newspaper refused to retract the statement.*

retraction (ri trak′shən) n., act of retracting or withdrawing, esp. the recall or withdrawal of an assertion, claim, or declared belief. *The newspaper issued a retraction of its editorial.*

retrench (ri trench′) v.i., to reduce in size, number, extent, or amount; curtail, esp. to curtail expenses; economize. *We will have to retrench in order to stay out of debt.*

retribution (re′trə byoo′shən) n., act of paying back for past good or evil; requital according to merit or deserts; retaliation; vengeance. *She obtained retribution for the injury.*

retrieve (ri trēv′) v.t., to bring back; recover; regain. *Jack ran to retrieve his hat.*

retroactive (re′trō ak′tiv) adj., effective with respect to past circumstances; holding true for preceding cases. *The pay raise was retroactive to the preceding September.*

retrogression (re′trə gresh′ən) n., act of

going backward; decline; regression; degeneration. *The car began a slow retrogression down the hill.*

retrospect (re′trə spekt′) n., contemplation or consideration of the past; review or survey of past events. *In retrospect, I think I would have done better as an artist.*

retrospective (re′trə spek′tiv) n., look at the past; backward look; comprehensive survey of the past. *Shortly after her death, the museum mounted a retrospective of her work.* adj., looking backward or at the past; retroactive. *The condemned men would be subject to a retrospective statute allowing capital punishment.*

revelry (rev′əl rē) n., boisterous festivity or celebration; merrymaking. *Mardi Gras is celebrated with great revelry.*

reverberate (ri vûr′bə rāt′) v.i., to return, as sound; echo; respond; recoil; reflect, as light; bounce off. *Gunshots reverberate like thunderclaps off the mountain.*

reverberating (ri vûr′bə rā′tiŋ) adj., returning, as sound; resounding; recoiling; bouncing off. *An echo is merely reverberating sound.*

revere (ri vēr′) v.t., to regard with deep respect or awe; hold in great honor or high esteem; venerate; worship. *The faithful revere the elderly bishop.*

reverence (rev′ər əns, rev′rəns) n., feeling of awe, respect, and admiration; veneration; outward manifestation of reverent feeling. *She approached the pope with reverence.*

reverie (revery) (rev′ə rē) n., waking dream; absorbing, imaginative, fanciful, or fantastic train of thought; dreamy meditation; daydream; brown study. *He was lost in a reverie about his upcoming vacation.*

reversible (ri vûr′sə bəl) adj., capable of being reversed; capable of being used or shown with either side exposed. *The reversible jacket was a versatile addition to her wardrobe.*

reversion (ri vûr′zhən, -shən) n., 1. that part of an estate that remains after granting away a portion; remainder.

Since he granted most of his estate, the reversion was very small. 2. act of reverting or returning to a former position, state, or frame of mind; return. *The president adjusted slowly to the reversion to status of private citizen.* 3. return to some ancestral type or plan; exhibition of ancestral characters; atavism; throwback. *His paintings seem a reversion to those of cave dwellers.*

revert (ri vûrt′) v.i., to turn about or back; reverse the position or direction of; return, as to a former habit, custom, or mode of thought. *After she lost the weight, she began to revert to her previous eating habits.*

revile (ri vīl′) v.t., to use contemptuous language to; abuse verbally; malign. *He started to revile her, but I intervened.*

reviled (ri vīld′) adj., treated with contempt; abused; maligned. *Reviled and despised, she left school and ran away.*

revitalize (ri vī′t∂līz′) v.t., to restore vitality or life to; revive. *The cold drinks helped to revitalize the parched workers.*

revolutionize (rev′∂ lōō′sh∂ nīz′) v.t., to bring about a revolution in; alter completely; effect a radical change in. *This device is guaranteed to revolutionize your way of cooking.*

revulsion (ri vul′sh∂n) n., violent pulling or drawing away; withdrawal; feeling of intense repugnance; disgust. *He experienced revulsion at the pornographic film.*

rhapsodical (rap sod′i k∂l) adj., of, pertaining to, or consisting of rhapsody; extravagantly enthusiastic. *The critics hailed her performance with rhapsodical praise.*

rhapsody (rap′s∂ dē) n., 1. exaggerated expression of real or affected feeling or enthusiasm; outburst of extravagant admiration or regard. *She experienced the rhapsody of first love.* 2. enthusiastic or extremely sentimental musical or literary composition. *The child swayed to the lyrical rhapsody.*

rhesus (rē′s∂s) n., type of monkey, sacred in India, used extensively in medical research.

rhetoric (ret′∂r ik) n., art of using language to influence others, either in writing or in oratory; art of writing or speaking effectively; art of discourse; artificial or grandiloquent oratory or language; elocution. *Be persuaded by truth, not by mere rhetoric.*

rhinestone (rīn′stōn′) n., imitation diamond made of paste or glass. *The thieves substituted a rhinestone for the valuable piece.*

Richter Scale (rik′t∂r skāl′) n., scale of seismic measurement indicating the force or magnitude of an earthquake. *A seismic tremor must measure 1.5 on the Richter Scale to be felt, while a disturbance measuring 7.0 is a devastating earthquake.*

rickets (rik′its) n., childhood disease characterized by faulty, uncalcified bone formation, caused by lack of sunlight or vitamin D and resulting in soft, flexible, distorted bones. *The boy's crooked legs were the result of rickets.*

ricochet (rik′∂ shā′ or, esp. Brit., -shet′) v.i., to strike an object and glance or bounce off in another direction. *The ball ricocheted off the wall.*

riff (rif) n., sequence or phrase in jazz or popular music, either solo or supporting a solo improvisation; improvisation. *There's a marvelous guitar riff in that recording.*

rifle (rī′f∂l) n., long, shoulder firearm having a barrel with a spirally grooved bore. *A rifle is most often used for sport hunting.* v.t., to ransack or search through; pillage; rob. *The thief began to rifle the desk looking for money.*

rift (rift) n., opening made by splitting; fissure; cleft or crevice. *There was a loud crack and then a visible rift in the ice.* v.t., to split; cleave; crack. *He used a wedge to rift the wood.*

right wing (rīt′ wiñg′) rightist side of a group. *The conservative candidate would have the support of the right wing.* adj., extremely conservative; opposing change in the established order and favoring traditional attitudes and authoritarian control. *The right-wing position was unpopular among the young.*

rigid (rij'id) adj., 1. stiff; not pliable or flexible; firm; hard; unyielding. *Steel is a rigid substance until heated.* 2. strict in opinion, conduct, or discipline; uncompromising; scrupulously exact. *Their father was a rigid disciplinarian.* 3. harsh; severe; rigorous; cruel. *The judge gave the murderer a rigid sentence.*

rigor (rig'ər) n., 1. state or property of being stiff or rigid; stiffness; inflexibility; strictness without allowance or compromise. *The police enforce the speed limit with rigor.* 2. sternness; harshness; cruelty; austerity; severity. *She objected to the rigor of her husband's treatment of their children.*

rigor mortis (rig'ər mor'tis, ri'gôr) stiffening of the body caused by muscle contraction after death. *As rigor mortis passes decomposition sets in.*

rigorous (rig'ər əs) adj., acting with rigor; severe; stringent; strict or exacting in performance or requirement. *The coach devised a rigorous exercise program.*

rile (rīl) v.t., to make angry; incense; irritate. *It's a myth that you can rile a bull with a red flag, because bulls are color-blind.*

risqué (ri skā', Fr. Rēs kā') adj., of questionable decency or propriety; racy; off-color; naughty. *The risqué joke embarrassed her.*

robust (rō bust', rō'bust) adj., having or indicating great strength; strong; sturdy; lusty; vigorous; hale; stalwart; hearty; tough. *All her children were blessed with robust health.*

rococo (rə kō'kō; Fr. Rô kô kô') adj., of or pertaining to an 18th-century style of ornament characterized by fantastic scrolls and shellwork, exaggeration, and extravagance; excessively ornate or intricate. *The rococo style of architecture resembles an elaborate wedding cake.*

romp (romp) n., boisterous or rude play or frolic. *On the first day of spring we went for a romp in the country.* v.i., to leap and frisk about in play; play boisterously; frolic. *We watched the lambs romp in the pasture.*

roster (ros'tər) n., list of names, as of personnel; itemized list; schedule of duties. *Sally's name was fourth on the teacher's class roster.*

rostrum (ros'trəm) n., stage or platform for public speaking; podium; pulpit. *The rostrum was filled with speakers.*

rote (rōt) n., mechanical repetition in learning; exact memorizing, or reproduction from memory, as of words or sounds with or without attention to their significance. *Children learn the multiplication tables by rote.*

rotund (rō tund') adj., round or spherical; bulbous. *Her doctor put the rotund woman on a strict diet.*

rotunda (rō tun'də) n., round building, esp. one with a dome; circular hall in a large building, generally with a dome overhead. *His body lay in state in the Capitol rotunda.*

roué (rōō ā', rōō'ā) n., one devoted to a life of pleasure and sensuality; debauchee; rake. *The callow girl was no match for the jaded roué.*

rouse (rouz) v.t., to raise or waken from sleep, torpor, or inaction; provoke to activity. *Try not to rouse the exhausted child.* v.i., to wake or stir up; startle. *I roused at the sound of the siren.*

royalty (roi'əl tē) n., 1. state or condition of being royal; royal rank. *She married into royalty.* 2. member of a royal family; royal or sovereign authority; majesty; royal persons collectively. *The state dinner honored the visiting royalty.* 3. compensation or fixed portion paid to a patent holder for the use of the patent, or as proceeds for an artist's work. *His publisher offered a generous royalty for the potential best seller.*

rubble (rub'əl) n., rough stones of irregular shapes and sizes; any solid substance of broken, irregular shapes; ruins. *The bomb reduced the house to rubble.*

ruddy (rud′ē) adj., reddish; rosy; glowing; cheery; bright. *The cold wind made the children's cheeks ruddy.*

rudiment (rōō′də mənt) n., (usually pl.) 1. that which is undeveloped. *She displayed the rudiments of writing skill.* 2. principle or root at the bottom of any development; element or first principle of any art or science; esp., first or elementary steps to any branch of knowledge. *This course introduces the rudiments of computer programming.*

rudimentary (rōō′də men′tə rē, -trē) adj., pertaining to rudiments or first principles; of the nature of a rudiment; elementary; undeveloped. *You must master this rudimentary principle before you can proceed.*

rue (rōō) n., yellow-flowered, bitter, aromatic herb. *Rue was used in medieval times to flavor food and beer, and to ward off disease, insects, and witches.* v.t., to repent of; feel remorse for; regret; suffer from or by. *You will rue the day you quit school.*

rueful (rōō′fəl) adj., full of pity or compassion; pitiful; deplorable; expressive of regret, sorrow, or misfortune; mournful; sad; doleful; regretful. *The rueful boy hadn't meant to hurt the cat.*

ruff (ruf) n., 1. projecting band, frill, or collar worn around the neck. *The woman in the portrait wore a stiff, lacy ruff.* 2. band of long hair growing around an animal's neck; mane; frill or ruff of feathers on certain birds' necks. *The pigeon's ruff stands erect during fighting and mating.*

ruffle (ruf′əl) n., strip of fabric gathered along one edge and used as a border or trim; full, narrow flounce; frill. *The dress had a ruffle at the sleeves and hem.* v.t., to disorder; disturb; agitate; vex. *A gust of wind ruffled the papers on the desk.*

ruminate (rōō′mə nāt′) v.i., 1. to chew the cud, as a ruminant. *We watched the cows ruminate in the field.* 2. to muse upon; think again and again; ponder. *She ruminated on his words after he left.*

rummage (rum′ij) v.i., to move to and fro the contents of, as in a search; ransack; hunt through; explore; rifle. *She began to rummage through the trunk.*

rupture (rup′chər) n., 1. act of breaking or bursting; state of being broken; break; bursting open. *The dam's sudden rupture caused a disaster in the village.* 2. breach of peace; open hostility or war; quarrel. *The rupture brought them to the brink of war.* v., to break or burst; cause or suffer a break. *He'll be okay if the blood vessel doesn't rupture.*

rural (rōōr′əl) adj., of, pertaining to, or characteristic of the country or agriculture or farming; rustic; bucolic; pastoral. *They sought a rural setting for their picnic.*

rustic (rus′tik) adj., of or belonging to the country or country people; characteristic of rural life; plain; homely; simple; unsophisticated. *The farmer offered to share his rustic fare with the travelers.*

ruthless (rōōth′lis) adj., cruel; pitiless; hard-hearted; relentless. *His ruthless ambition destroyed the marriage.*

Ss

sable (sā′bəl) n., 1. small, carnivorous, arctic or subarctic mammal similar to a marten, with highly prized dark brown or blackish fur. 2. dressed pelt or fur of the sable. *The sable is a prized fur.* adj., 1. black. *She combed her sable hair.* 2. made of sable; black. *The sable coat cost the animal more than the buyer.*

sabotage (sab′ə täzh′, sab′ə täzh′) n., 1. deliberate destruction of equipment and other tools of production by an enemy during wartime or by disgruntled laborers. *Extra security guards were hired during the strike to prevent sabotage.* 2. any willful, malicious hindrance. *This report could be a sabotage of your campaign.* v.t., to practice sabotage; wreck; destroy. *The captain was afraid the shanghaied crew would sabotage the ship.*

saccharin(e) (sak′ə rin, -rīn′) n., artificial sweetener; benzoyl-sulphimide. *The dieter came to rely on saccharin.* adj., excessively sweet; cloying. *He squirmed under her saccharine praise.*

sacrilege (sak′rə lij) n., violation, desecration, or profanation of sacred things or hallowed persons; theft of any sacred things. *It is a sacrilege to curse the pope.*

sacrilegious (sak′rə lij′əs, -lē′jəs) adj., guilty of or involving sacrilege; profane; impious. *The infidel laid sacrilegious hands on the Bible.*

sacrosanct (sak′rō sangkt′) adj., preeminently or superlatively sacred; inviolable. *He sought refuge in the sacrosanct hall.*

sadism (sad′iz əm, sā′diz əm) n., form of perversion, esp. sexual perversion, marked by extreme cruelty. *The chains over the bed advertised his sadism.*

sadist (sad′ist, sā′dist) n., one who practices sadism; pervertedly cruel person.

The sadist loved to torture little animals.

sadistic (sə dis′tik, sa-, sā-) adj., characterized by sadism or perverted, extreme cruelty. *He took sadistic delight in tormenting the helpless chicken.*

safe-conduct (sāf′kon′dukt) n., protection given to a person passing through a foreign country or occupied territory; protection by a guard, escort, or convoy; pass or written authorization for safe-conduct. *The embassy provided them safe-conduct out of the country.*

saga (sä′gə) n., medieval Icelandic prose story or legend; epic; tale or story of heroic deeds. *She was fascinated by the saga of the American West.*

sagacious (sə gā′shəs) adj., having quick, keen intellectual perceptions; of keen judgment; penetrating; discerning; shrewd. *The sagacious judge would not be misled.*

sagacity (sə gas′i tē) n., quickness or acuteness of intellectual perception; soundness of judgment or discernment; shrewdness. *He sized up the situation with sagacity.*

sage (sāj) n., 1. wise person; one distinguished for soundness of judgment, wisdom, and depth of experience. *They asked the local sage what to do.* 2. a perennial herb, *Salvia officinalis,* whose gray-green leaves are used as a seasoning. adj., characterized by wisdom, sagacity, or prudence. *His sage investment paid off.*

salacious (sə lā′shəs) adj., given to lust; lecherous; lascivious; inciting lust; sensual. *She was offended by the salacious photo.*

salient (sā′lē ənt, sāl′yənt) adj., 1. shooting, spouting, or jetting up or out; leaping; bounding. *The salient deer disappeared from sight.* 2. prominent;

significant. *Your assumption leaves out this salient fact.*

saline (sā'līn, -lēn) adj., characterized by or containing salt; salty. *She gargled with the saline solution.*

sally (sal'ē) n., 1. sudden bursting forth. *We were startled by the children's sally through the door.* 2. excursion. *The sally was not on our itinerary.* 3. flight of fancy; witticism; flirtatious or playful remark. *She smiled at his good-natured sally.* v.i., to go forth; to leave, as on a trip or excursion. *They promised to sally forth on the first fine day.*

salubrious (sə lōō'brē əs) adj., healthful; healthy; wholesome. *Jogging is often a salubrious activity.*

salutation (sal'yə tā'shən) n., expression of greeting or respect in words or gestures. *The salutation began, "Dear Sir."*

salvage (sal'vij) n., 1. act of saving a ship or its cargo, or other property, from danger or destruction. *The salvage was a difficult job.* 2. compensation for volunteer help in the rescue of endangered property. *The owner paid a generous salvage for their help.* v.t., to save property from danger or destruction, or to save damaged material for further use. *They will try to salvage at least part of the wreck.*

salvation (sal vā'shən) n., 1. preservation from destruction, danger, or calamity. *The island offered salvation to the survivors.* 2. deliverance from the power or penalty of sin. *The penitent prayed for salvation.*

sanctimonious (sangk'tə mō'nē əs) adj., making a show of sanctity or piety. *Her sanctimonious manner fooled no one.*

sanction (sangk'shən) n., 1. act of making sacred or of rendering authoritative, as of a law. *His presence seemed to lend sanction to their decision.* 2. law or decree. *The judge's sanction was later overturned.* 3. penalty for failure to obey a law or decree. *A sanction was applied by the courts.* v.t., to give permission or approval; to ratify, confirm, or authorize. *The acting chief will sanction this plan.*

sanctity (sangk'ti tē) n., 1. holiness; saintliness; godliness. *He respected the sanctity of her decision to enter the convent.* 2. holy object, duty, or right. *They sought the sanctity of the church.*

sanctuary (sangk'chōō er'ē) n., 1. sacred or holy place. *They were married in the sanctuary.* 2. place of refuge or protection. *The bird sanctuary supports hundreds of species.* 3. shelter or immunity from arrest. *He claimed the sanctuary of diplomatic immunity.*

sanguinary (sang'gwə ner'ē) adj., 1. bloody; accompanied by carnage and bloodshed. *It was a sanguinary battle.* 2. bloodthirsty. *The sanguinary ruler condemned her to death.*

sanguine (sang'gwin) adj., 1. bloodthirsty; bloody. *The nurse changed his sanguine bandage.* 2. the color of blood; red; ruddy. *The old farmer's complexion was sanguine.* 3. full-blooded; passionate; confident. *The only child has sanguine expectations of inheriting the estate.*

sanguinity (sang gwin'i tē) n., state of being sanguine. *Her excessive sanguinity appalled him.*

sanitarium (sanitorium) (san'i târ'ē əm) n., institution or resort for the treatment of chronic illnesses, such as tuberculosis, or for recuperation and convalescence. *He was treated for tuberculosis at a Swiss sanitarium.*

sarcastic (sär kas'tik) adj., characterized by derision or ridicule; bitter, cutting, or caustic; scornful or taunting. *That sarcastic remark was not necessary.*

sardonic (sär don'ik) adj., mocking, bitter, or sarcastic. *Her sardonic retort hurt him deeply.*

sartorial (sär tôr'ē əl, -tôr'-) adj., pertaining to a tailor or to tailored clothing, esp. for men. *His sartorial style is copied by other couturiers.*

Satan (sāt'ən) n., devil. *Satan is the most intriguing character in Paradise Lost.*

satanic (sā tan'ik) adj., pertaining to Satan; fiendish. *Satanic possession is a common theme in horror stories.*

satellite (sat'əlīt') n., 1. spacecraft launched into orbit, esp. for worldwide communications. *The satellite beamed the London ballet into U.S. living rooms.* 2. moon, or other small planet that circles a larger one. *Mars has two satellites.* 3. follower, esp. one who is subservient or obsequious. *The superstar attracts a bevy of admiring satellites.* 4. small country that is controlled politically and economically by a larger, more powerful one. *We applied for visas to visit the Soviet satellite.*

satiate (sā′shē āt′) v.t., to satisfy completely. *Let's hope this investigation will satiate the rumor monger.*

satiety (sə tī′i tē) n., 1. state of satiation. *The destitute family never knows satiety.* 2. the state of being glutted or gratified beyond comfort, satisfaction, or natural need. *He suffered from satiety after the enormous meal.*

satire (sat′īʳr) n., 1. literary work using wit, irony, mockery, or derision to expose human foibles or vices. *The satire lampoons the bumbling congressman.* 2. any use of derisive wit to criticize or expose vice or foolishness. *His satire was lost on the pompous clergyman.*

satiric (sə tir′ik) (also satirical) adj., pertaining to satire. *We laughed at his satiric cartoon.*

saturate (sach′ə rāt′) v.t., to fill to capacity; soak, imbue, or penetrate. *The flood waters saturated the fields.*

saturnalia (sat′ər nā′lē ə, -nāl′yə) n., pl., unrestrained revelries characterized by licentiousness, feasting, drunkenness, and debauchery; from the ancient Roman harvest festival celebrated in mid-December. *The saturnalia put the fraternity on probation.*

saturnine (sat′ər nīn′) adj., 1. gloomy; grave; dull; somber. *The saturnine undertaker arranged for the burial.* 2. in chemistry, pertaining to lead. *The child suffers the effects of saturnine poisoning.*

satyr (sā′tər, sat′ər) n., 1. in Greek mythology, a woodland demigod, attendant to Bacchus, in shape like a man but with ears, legs, and horns of a goat. *The ancient urn depicts a dancing, piping satyr entertaining the revelers.* 2.

lecher; debaucher. *The satyr's leer swept over the dancing girls.*

saunter (sôn′tər, sän′-) n., leisurely stroll or walk. *The took a saunter through the park.* v.i., to walk or stroll leisurely. *Come saunter in the park with me.*

savant (sa vänt′, sav′ənt; *Fr.* sa vän′) n., scholar; wise person. *The respected savant received an honorary degree.*

savoir-faire (sav′wär fâr′; *Fr.* sa vwar feʀ′) n., talent for saying and doing the right thing socially; tact. *His impertinent remark showed little savoir-faire.*

savor (sā′vər) n., particular taste, aroma, or distinctive quality. *Basil adds savor to tomato sauce.* v.t., 1. to perceive by taste or smell. *We savored the spicy morsels.* 2. to enjoy, relish, or participate in. *We will always savor that memory.* 3. to season, as with herbs. *She prefers to savor the soup with tarragon.*

scabrous (skab′rəs) adj., 1. rough; scaly; having small, rough projections. *Sandpaper is scabrous.* 2. indecent; off-color; salacious. *The scabrous novel was confiscated by customs.*

scalawag (skal′ə wag′) n., rascal; rogue, esp. a swindler or con man. *The charming scalawag made off with her life savings.*

scamp (skamp) n., mischievous rascal. *The scamp dropped a water balloon on her.* v.t., to act in a careless, slipshod, or hasty manner. *I won't pay you if you scamp this job.*

scanty (skan′tē) adj., barely sufficient; inadequate; small or meager. *She was still hungry after the scanty meal.*

scarab (skar′əb) n., 1. large black beetle, esp. the *Scarabaeus sacer,* considered sacred by the ancient Egyptians. *A scarab appears on the ancient mosaic.* 2. carved image of a large black beetle, used in ancient Egypt to symbolize the soul. *The museum exhibits the lovely scarab.*

scathing (skā′thing) adj., harsh; bitter; severely critical. *The senator delivered a scathing attack on the proposed budget.*

scavenger (skav′in jər) n., 1. one who

gathers things other people discard. *The scavenger found an old raincoat in the trash.* 2. animal that habitually eats carrion or other decaying matter. *The scavenger fed on the antelope's remains.*

scenario (si nâr′ē ō′, -när′-) n., 1. plot outline of a literary or dramatic work; movie or television screenplay. *The action-packed scenario belied the drama's psychological impact.* 2. the outline of any series of events. *The news story offered a bare scenario of the accident.*

schism (siz′əm, skiz′əm) n., 1. split or division in a group, due to differences of opinion or belief. *To prevent an irrevocable schism, the church revised its bylaws.* 2. sect or group resulting from such a split. *Fearing persecution, members of the schism fled the country.*

schizoid (skit′soid, skiz′oid) n., schizophrenic. *Psychotherapy helped the schizoid regain a grip on reality.* adj., pertaining to schizophrenia. *The patient exhibits schizoid characteristics.*

schizophrenia (skit′sə frē′nē ə, -frēn′yə, skiz′ə-) n., mental illness characterized by delusions, bizarre behavior, withdrawal from reality, and the inability to connect thought, perception, and emotion. *His delusion of grandeur is symptomatic of schizophrenia.*

schwa (s͟hwä; *Ger.* s͟hvä) n., neutral vowel sound of many unstressed syllables in English, represented phonetically as ə. *The "a" in "alike" is a schwa.*

scintillate (sin′tᵊlāt′) v.i., to emit sparks; twinkle or sparkle. *Her ring scintillated in the sun.* 2. to be clever, lively, or brilliant. *The idea scintillates with originality.*

scintillating (sin′tᵊlā′tiṅg) adj., 1. relating to a twinkling, sparkling quality. *The scintillating fabric made a glamorous gown.* 2. relating to cleverness, liveliness, or brilliance. *Her scintillating conversation enlivened the dinner party.*

scintillation (sin′tᵊlā′shən) n., 1. sparks or sparklike flashes; act of sparkling. *The diamond emitted a brilliant scintillation.* 2. star's twinkling appearance, produced by variations in the atmosphere. *They studied the star's scintillation through a telescope.*

scion (sī′ən) n., 1. descendant or heir. *The scion inherited the family business.* 2. shoot or twig, particularly one cut for grafting or planting purposes. *The botanist carefully wrapped the scion onto the branch.*

scoff (skôf, skof) n., expression of contempt or scorn; taunt; gibe. *He rose to defend the child against their scoffs.* v.i., to sneer; jeer; taunt. *He scoffed at the absurd suggestion.*

scope (skōp) n., range or extent of a particular activity, topic, or view. *The grant enabled us to enlarge my scope of research.*

scot-free (skot′frē′) adj., unpunished; unhurt; safe. *Due to lack of evidence, the prisoner got off scot-free.*

scoundrel (skoun′drəl) n., villain; rascal. *The scoundrel took advantage of everyone.*

scour (skour, skou′ər) n., diarrhea in animals. *The sheep was treated for scour.* v.t., 1. to clean or clear with an abrasive or by rubbing. *He scoured the greasy pan.* 2. to pass over an area, as in search. *They began to scour the woods for the lost eyeglasses.*

scourge (skûrj) n., 1. punishment or affliction. *The minister declared the illness a scourge for her sin.* 2. whip used to inflict punishment. *His captain ordered the scourge brought for the flailing.* v.t., to whip or flog; inflict punishment; to punish severely. *The penitent monk began to scourge himself.*

scrip (skrip) n., 1. small written paper, esp. in receipt or acknowledgment. *Her broker sent her the stock scrip.* 2. paper currency. *He wanted his payment in gold, not scrip.*

scruple (skrōō′pəl) n., hesitation, reluctance, or objection based on moral or ethical grounds. *His reassurance overcame her scruple.* v.i., to hesitate, doubt, or object for reasons of conscience. *They scrupled to press charges against the young thief.*

scrupulous (skrōō′pyə ləs) adj., having scruples; careful; exacting; conscientious. *He filed a scrupulous tax return.*

scrutinize (skrōōt′ᵊnīz′) v.t., to subject something to scrutiny; inspect, examine, or investigate closely or critically. *The potential buyer wanted to scrutinize the bust.*

scrutiny (skrōōt′ᵊnē) n., act of close inspection, investigation, or critical examination. *The report is subject to public scrutiny.*

scurrilous (skûr′ə ləs) adj., abrasive; vulgar; underhanded. *The scurrilous remark offended us.*

scurry (skûr′ē, skur′ē) n., haste; scampering. *We heard a scurry of little feet in the leaves.* v.i., to hurry; move hastily; scamper. *The child scurried to clean up the mess.*

scuttle (skut′ᵊl) n., 1. covered hatch in the deck, sides, or wall of a ship, or in the roof or floor of a house; also, the lid to this hatch. *The sailor secured the scuttle.* 2. quick, hurried run. *We observed the rat's scuttle along the maze.* v.t., 1. to sink a ship by opening its hatches; cut holes in a ship for any reason. *The pirates decided to scuttle the ship.* 2. to run at a quick, hasty pace. *The crab scuttled across the ocean floor.*

sear (sēr) v.t., to dry up, wither, or shrivel; burn, scorch, or seal with heat. *Sear the meat to seal in the juices.* v.i., to become dry or withered. *The plants began to sear in the extreme heat.*

secession (si sesh′ən) n., act of seceding or withdrawing; formal separation. *We tried to prevent their secession from the club.*

seclude (si klōōd′) v.t., to isolate; separate; withdraw; shut off. *After the tragedy, he secluded himself in his home.*

secrete (si krēt′) v.t., 1. to hide or conceal. *We looked for a good place to secrete the gift.* 2. to generate and exude a substance. *Many insects secrete poisonous substances.*

secretion (si krē′shən) n., process of secreting a substance; also, the substance secreted. *Some plant secretions are poisonous.*

sect (sekt) n., group of people who share a set of ideals, principles, or beliefs. *The religious sect attracted notice in the press.*

section (sek′shən) n., 1. part or portion. *He sat in the non-smoking section of the theater.* 2. act of cutting or separation, as in surgery. *She was delivered by caesarean section.* 3. diagram or drawing showing how something would look if cut by an intersecting plane, revealing its internal structure. *They made a cross-section of the stem.* v.t., to cut or divide. *We will section the novel into three parts.*

sector (sek′tər) n., 1. in geometry, part of a circle bounded by two radii and one of the intercepted arcs. *The pie chart was divided into equal sectors.* 2. defensive or offensive position; area divided for military purposes; zone. *That sector is off-limits to civilians.* v.t., to divide into sectors or areas. *The military will sector the area into defensive positions.*

secular (sek′yə lər) adj., worldly; temporal. *He left the monastery and entered the secular world.*

sedate (si dāt′) adj., calm; composed; serene; sober. *The sedate procession moved slowly down the aisle.*

sedative (sed′ə tiv) n., something that is calming, esp. a drug or tranquilizer. *She prescribed a sedative for his nerves.* adj., calming; soothing; tranquilizing. *She ended the day with a warm, sedative bath.*

sedentary (sed′ᵊn ter′ē) adj., marked by much sitting or little physical exertion or activity. *Her sedentary office job contributed to her weight problem.*

sedition (si dish′ən) n., activity intended to incite rebellion against the government or any authority. *The rebel leader was convicted of sedition.*

seditionist (si dish′ᵊnist′) n., one who commits acts of sedition; revolutionary. *The seditionist called for the government's overthrow.*

seduce (si dōōs′, -dyōōs′) v.t., 1. to entice; lead astray; corrupt. *The glamor of the big city seduced the Maine country boy.* 2. to entice into sexual intercourse. *The gigolo seduced the matron.*

seductive (si duk′tiv) adj., having the ability to seduce, attract, or beguile. *The rose gave off a seductive fragrance.*

sedulous (sej′ə ləs) adj., diligent; persevering; industrious. *The lazy grasshopper played while the sedulous ants worked.*

seethe (sēth) v.i., 1. to boil, surge, or bubble. *The lava seethed out of the volcano.* 2. to be violently excited or agitated. *She seethed with anger.*

seething (sē′thing) adj., boiling; surging; or agitated. *Seething waves rolled over the deck.*

seismograph (sīz′mə graf′, -gräf′, sīs′-) n., instrument that measures and records seismic activity, esp. earthquakes. *The earthquake registered 7 on the seismograph.*

seismography (sīz mog′rə fē, sīs-) n., study of earth vibrations and earthquakes using such instruments as the seismograph. *Seismography has increased our knowledge of the earth's subterranean activity.*

seismometer (sīz mom′i tər, sīs-) n., seismograph that measures ground movements. *The seismometer began to gauge the severity of the rumbling.*

self-evident (self′ev′i dənt, self′-) adj., needing no proof; obvious. *To the biased jury, her guilt was self-evident.*

semantics (si man′tiks) n., 1. study of the meaning and development of language. *Semantics is important in the study of logic.* 2. connotative meaning of words. *The propagandist is often a master of semantics.*

semblance (sem′bləns) n., 1. likeness; similarity; resemblance. *She bears a semblance to her great aunt.* 2. bare minimum; bit. *The alibi contained not a semblance of truth.*

semen (sē′mən) n., thick, whitish fluid secreted by the male reproductive organs, containing spermatazoa. *Doctors examine the semen for signs of male infertility.*

semiannual (sem′ē an′yōō əl, sem′ī-) adj., happening twice a year. *The society held semiannual meetings, in June and December.*

seminal (sem′ə nəl) adj., 1. referring to male semen. *Fertility tests include seminal examinations.* 2. containing or producing seeds of later growth; generative. *His seminal manifesto continues to influence modern art.*

Semitic (sə mit′ik) n., any of the Semitic languages; Hebrew, Arabic, Ethiopic, Amharic, and Aramaic. *He was fluent in the ancient Semitic.* adj., relating to the Semites, particularly Jews and Arabs. *Semitic nations are said to be descendants of the Old Testament figure Shem.*

senile (sē′nīl, -nil, sen′īl) adj., resulting from or characteristic of old age; weak in mind or body. *They brought their senile grandfather to a nursing home.*

senility (si nil′i tē) n., state of being senile, esp. of suffering the infirmities of old age. *The gerontologist said true senility is actually very rare.*

sensation (sen sā′shən) n., 1. feeling or sensory impression or perception. *They had the sensation they were being watched.* 2. exciting, popular, or controversial event or thing. *The novel was a sensation.*

sensitize (sen′si tīz′) v.t., to make sensitive. *Their experiences in the Peace Corps sensitized them to other ways of life.*

sensuous (sen′shōō əs) adj., related to or derived from the senses; susceptible to physical sensation, esp. pleasure. *The whirlpool bath was a sensuous pleasure.*

sententious (sen ten′shəs) adj., concise, pithy, and moralistic; epigrammatic. *The sententious slogan appeared on buttons and posters.*

sentiment (sen′tə mənt) n., 1. feeling or emotion; opinion influenced by emotion. *The questionnaire revealed strong* *public sentiment against the idea.* 2. emotional meaning distinct from the form or words used to convey it. *The metaphor enhanced the sentiment of the passage.* 3. vulnerability to tender emotions, esp. to maudlin, excessive emotion. *His display of sentiment embarrassed me.*

separate (*n., adj.* sep′ər it; *v.* sep′ə rāt′) n., (us. pl.) articles of clothing bought separately to interchange with others. *The traveler packed a versatile wardrobe of separates.* v.t., 1. to sever, disconnect, or divide. *The teacher had to separate the talkative boys.* 2. to distinguish or isolate. *First separate the whites from the yolks.* 3. to sort or scatter. *We began to separate the mail.* 4. to sever legal or contractual association. *She decided to separate from her husband.* adj., individual; not shared. *The boxers retired to separate corners.*

septic (sep′tik) n., something that causes decomposition or rot. *Certain bacteria act as a septic on human waste.* adj., putrifactive. *Gangrene is a septic disease.*

septuagenarian (sep′chōō ə jə nâr′ē ən) n., one who is 70–80 years old. *The spry septuagenarian hugged his great-grandchild.*

sepulcher (sep′əl kər) n., tomb; vault for sacred relics. *The sepulcher housed many fascinating artifacts.* v.t., to entomb or bury. *They will sepulcher him in the family vault.*

sequel (sē′kwəl) n., 1. continuation or succeeding, but independent, part. *The sequel traced the story of the heroine's son.* 2. consequence, result, or aftermath. *Hundreds were homeless in the flood's sequel.*

sequence (sē′kwəns) n., order in which one thing follows another. *Officials investigated the sequence of events that led to the fatal plane crash.*

sequester (si kwes′tər) v.t., to set aside; separate; isolate. *He sequestered himself in his room to study.*

sequestrate (si kwes′trāt) v.t., in law, to seize or confiscate. *The bank had to sequestrate a portion of his estate.*

seraph (ser′əf) n., one of the nine orders of angels in Judeo-Christian mythology. *The seraph brought God's message.*

serendipity (ser′ən dip′i tē) n., ability to make lucky, unexpected discoveries. *Many scientific discoveries are the result of serendipity.*

serene (sə rēn′) adj., 1. calm. *She swam easily in the serene water.* 2. clear, fair, bright, used to describe the weather. *It was a lovely, serene spring morning.* 3. title of courtesy conferred upon royalty. *Her Serene Highness arrived late.*

serenity (sə ren′i tē) n., calmness; quietness; peace. *She retreated to the serenity of her own room.*

serf (sûrf) n., feudal servant bound to an overlord and to his fief. *The serf made obeisance to his lord.*

serge (sûrj) n., strong, durable twilled fabric. *His Sunday suit was made of blue serge.*

sergeant at arms (sär′jənt at ärmz′) officer assigned to keep order, as in a court. *The sergeant at arms removed the troublemaker.*

serpent (sûr′pənt) n., 1. snake, esp. the reptile that tempted Eve in the Garden of Eden: Satan. *The serpent was condemned to crawl on its belly.* 2. any cunning, wily person. *The serpent conned him of his life savings.*

serrate (*adj.* ser′it, -āt; *v.* ser′āt) v.t., to notch. *He tried to serrate the flint to cut the meat.* adj., having small, sharp, toothlike notches along the edge. *Saws have serrate edges.*

servile (sûr′vil, -vīl) adj., humble, obsequious, submissive; pertaining to slaves or servants. *The dictator demanded servile obedience.*

servitude (sûr′vi tōōd′, -tyōōd′) n., slavery; bondage. *He released them from servitude.*

severance (sev′ər əns, sev′rəns) n., act of separation or state of being separated.

He received two weeks' salary upon severance.

sextuplets (seks tup′lits, -too′plits, -tyoo′-, seks′too plits, -tyoo-) n., six offspring delivered at one birth. *The sextuplets made the front page.*

shackle (shak′əl) n., manacle, handcuff, or trap; anything used to confine or trap. *She broke the shackle of marriage.* v.t., to apply shackles; confine or trap. *Poverty shackled them to despair.*

shackled (shak′əld) adj., confined; manacled; trapped. *The bear struggled to release the shackled leg.*

shamble (sham′bəl) v.i., to walk in an unsteady, clumsy way. *They shambled dizzily out of the bar.*

shambles (sham′bəlz) n., chaotic state; disorderly condition. *Three days of rioting left the city a shambles.*

shanghai (shang′hī, shang hī′) v.t., 1. to render insensible, kidnap, and force a person to serve aboard a ship. *They will shanghai whatever crew they need.* 2. to use force or coercion to make a person do something. *Their parents shanghaied them into marriage.*

sheaf (shēf) n., bundle or collection, esp. cut stalks of grain. *He has a sheaf of papers to file.* v.t., to bundle or collect. *We began to sheaf the tobacco leaves.*

sheathe (shēth) v.t., to enclose in an envelopelike covering; put into a sheath. *The duelists sheathed their swords and shook hands.*

sheepish (shē′pish) adj., shy or bashful; embarrassed. *She gave me a sheepish grin as I pulled her out of the puddle.*

sheer (shēr) v.t., to swerve from a course. *The car began to sheer from right to left.* adj., 1. transparent or fine. *Sunlight shone through the sheer curtains.* 2. utter; complete. *"What sheer nonsense,"* she exclaimed. 3. steep. *They stumbled down the sheer side of the cliff.*

shellac (shə lak′) n., thin varnish. *That bureau needs a coat of shellac.* v.t., to apply shellac. *I plan to shellac the collage.*

sherbet (shûr′bit) n., sweet frozen dessert made with milk and gelatin or egg whites. *Strawberry sherbet is a refreshing summer dessert.*

shibboleth (shib′ə lith, -leth′) n., password or custom particular to a certain group and used to distinguish members of that group. *He learned the shibboleth at the initiation.*

shimmer (shim′ər) n., glimmering light. *There was a shimmer of light from the bottom of the mine shaft.* v.i., to glimmer or shine with a tremulous light. *The star shimmered faintly in the night sky.*

shoal (shōl) n., 1. crowd; school of fish. *We spotted the shoal from the dock.* 2. shallow place in any body of water; sand bank or sand bar. *The boat ran aground on a shoal.* adj., shallow. *We drove through the shoal puddle.*

shoddy (shod′ē) adj., inferior; second-rate; shabby; rundown. *The clerk tried to sell me the shoddy material.*

shrew (shroo) n., 1. small, mouse-like mammal. *The shrew is a harmless insectivore.* 2. nagging, bad-tempered woman. *He finally divorced the shrew.*

shrewish (shroo′ish) adj., like a shrew; scolding; nagging; bad-tempered. *Doing dishes makes him shrewish.*

shun (shun) v.t., to avoid deliberately; escape. *She shuns fatty foods.*

sibilance (sib′ə ləns) n., hissing sound. *The sibilance of the tea kettle startled her.*

sibilant (sib′ə lənt) n., speech consonant that makes a hissing sound as s, z, sh. *He had difficulty pronouncing sibilants.* adj., producing a hissing sound. *The sibilant radiator kept him awake.*

sieve (siv) n., any wire-meshed utensil for straining or sifting liquids or other materials. *She strained the fruit through a sieve.* v.t., to sift or strain. *The prospector carefully sieved the soil.*

signal (sig′nəl) n., 1. sign, gesture, or event that communicates; message. *The trumpet blasted the signal to attack.* 2. information transmitted by electrical impulses. *They picked up a faint radio* *signal.* v.t., to communicate. *You must signal your intention to turn.* adj., unusual; extraordinary. *We celebrated his signal achievement.*

significant (sig nif'ə kənt) adj., 1. meaningful or suggestive of meaning. *Her remark was significant under the circumstances.* 2. important; noteworthy; special. *The President made some significant comments on foreign policy.*

signify (sig'nə fī') v.t., 1. to mean or denote; imply. *Does his silence signify disapproval?* v.i., to be of consequence or importance. *Never mind; it doesn't signify.*

silt (silt) n., fine, sandy sediment deposited or carried by water. *Silt was left by the receding floodwaters.* v.t., to fill or become filled with silt. *The tide gradually silted up the opening.*

simile (sim'ə lē) n., figure of speech that directly compares two distinct things, usually using "like" or "as." *The simile likened her eyes to stars.*

similitude (si mil'i tōod', -tyōod') n., likeness; similarity. *The portrait bears him a striking similitude.*

simple (sim'pəl) adj., 1. having few parts; uncomplicated; elementary. *The child practiced the simple recipe.* 2. plain; unsophisticated; without guile, sincere. *The simple dress gave her the look of a little girl.* 3. easy to do, use, or understand. *This game is simple to learn.* 4. humble; ordinary; common; insignificant. *She rose from very simple beginnings.* 5. lacking sense or intellect. *The simple girl was capable of a few basic tasks.*

simulate (sim'yə lāt') v.t., to assume the appearance of; imitate, feign, or pretend. *The skilled actor is able to simulate a wide range of human emotion.*

simultaneous (sī'məl tā'nē əs, sim'əl-) adj., happening or existing at the same time; concurrent. *The fire began after several simultaneous explosions.*

sine qua non (*Lat.* si'ne kwä nōn'; *Eng.* sī'nē kwä non') n., something that is necessary; essential element. *A strong plot is the sine qua non of any good novel.*

singular (sing'gyə lər) adj., 1. single; alone; separate. *The bachelor led his singular life by choice.* 2. unusual; odd; extraordinary. *She congratulated him on his singular good fortune.* 3. in grammar, referring to one person or thing. *The story is told in the first person singular.*

sinister (sin'i stər) adj., suggesting evil or misfortune; ominous; threatening. *The villain's face twisted into a sinister smile.*

sinuous (sin'yōō əs) adj., having many curves, bends, or turns; undulating; serpentine. *They drove slowly up the sinuous path.*

sire (sī°r) n., father or progenitor. *The colt's sire was a Kentucky Derby winner.* v.t., to father; beget. *He wants to sire a large family.*

site (sīt) n., place or location. *We visited the famous battle site.*

skeptic (skep'tik) n., 1. one who doubts a given assertion. *I must remain the skeptic about this plan's feasibility.* 2. one who doubts, in whole or in part, Christian dogma. *The pious woman tried to convince the skeptic.*

skim (skim) n., act or product of skimming. *The dieter drinks only the skim.* v.t., 1. to lift the collected film or scum from the surface of a liquid. *Please skim off the fat before making gravy.* 2. to pass over lightly or glance over superficially. *I will skim your story for obvious errors.*

skimp (skimp) v.i., to provide a small or insufficient amount; be thrifty or stingy. *She refuses to skimp on quality.* v.t., to do a hasty or careless job. *When you skimp your homework, your grades will suffer.*

skirmish (skûr'mish) n., 1. minor or brief argument or conflict. *The silly skirmish ended in laughter.* 2. minor military engagement or encounter between small detachments of opposing troops, often to provoke a larger battle or to conceal the movement of the troops in the rear. *There were no casualties in the skirmish.* v.i., to engage in a minor conflict or battle. *They skirmished over territorial rights.*

skittish (skit′ish) adj., 1. easily frightened; nervous; high-strung. *The skittish colt panicked at the starting gate.* 2. shy; timid; coy. *She reassured the skittish child.* 3. changeable; fickle. *Spring weather is often skittish.*

skulk (skulk) n., one who skulks. *The skulk hid in the shadows.* v.i., 1. to lie in waiting or to move stealthily. *The hunter skulked in the bushes.* 2. to withdraw into hiding out of shame or embarrassment. *The culprit skulked in the pantry.*

slander (slan′dər) n., 1. false or malicious statement. *The slander hurt his career.* 2. in law, speaking or writing defamatory statements that damage a person's reputation. *She sued the newspaper for slander.* v.t., to speak slander or make defamatory statements. *If you slander me you can expect a lawsuit.*

sleazy (slē′zē, slā′zē) adj., thin and shoddy; inferior; insubstantial. *The sleazy fabric didn't last long.*

slenderize (slen′də rīz′) v., to make slender or slim. *She needs to slenderize to fit into that dress.*

slogan (slō′gən) n., pithy, easy to remember catchword or phrase. *The campaign slogan appears on buttons and posters.*

sloth (*1.* slôth; *2.* slôth, slōth) n., 1. laziness; slowness; sluggishness. *A delicious sloth overcame the sunbather.* 2. any of a number of slow-moving arboreal mammals native to South America.

slothful (slôth′fəl, slōth′-) adj., lazy; sluggish; indolent. *The slothful worker was fired.*

slough (*n. 1.* slou; *n. 2. and v.* sluf) n., 1. deep hole filled with mud and mire; a stagnant or marshy pond or backwater. *The slough in the road damaged the car.* 2. dead tissue or outer skin layers that are shed; often the dead skin that a snake has shed. *We found the mottled*

slough under a rock. v.t., to discard, shed, or cast off. *She sloughed off the callus with a pumice.*

slovenly (sluv′ən lē) adj., careless of dress, appearance, or cleanliness; messy; negligent. *She shanghaied the slovenly boy for a haircut.*

sluice (slo͞os) n., body of water controlled by a floodgate, or the gate itself. *They open the sluice at low tide.* v.t., to open a floodgate and release a flow of water; to wash with a forceful flow of water. *The water sluiced the parched fields.* v.i., to flow forcefully and suddenly. *Water sluiced through the pipe.*

smock (smok) n., loose garment, usually worn over clothing as protection from soil. *The painter wiped his brush on his smock.* v.t., to decorate with smocking or to clothe in a smock. *She began to smock the blouse.*

smug (smug) adj., complacent; self-satisfied; self-righteous. *She was smug about her own good looks.*

smut (smut) n., 1. dirt, particularly a dirty smudge made by soot. *The miner's face was black with smut.* 2. obscenity or pornography. *The smut was hidden in his drawer.* 3. fungus disease of cereal plants; also, the fungus itself. *Smut blighted the corn crop.* v.t., to stain or defile, literally with dirt, or figuratively with obscenity. *Coal smutted her hands.*

sneer (snēr) n., contemptuous facial expression, sound, or remark. *She was humiliated by his sneer.* v.i., to speak scornfully, or to make a scornful facial expression. *The convict sneered at the warden's suggestion.*

sobriety (sə brī′i tē, sō-) n., 1. seriousness; gravity; reasonableness. *We remarked on the child's unusual sobriety.* 2. soberness; moderation in the use of alcoholic drink. *The temperance league touted sobriety.*

socialism (sō′shə liz′əm) n., 1. social or political system based on cooperation, equal distribution of goods and labor, and collective ownership of all land and capital. *The commune was founded on a simple form of socialism.* 2. Marxist-

259   sonata

Leninist theory: the developing of the material base for communism, under the dictatorship of the proletariat. *The U.S.S.R. operates on the principles of Marxist-Leninist Socialism.*

socialist (sō′shə list) n., advocate of socialism. *The leader of the revolution was a socialist.* adj., pertaining to socialism. *The media labeled their economic views socialist.*

sociology (sō′sē ol′ə jē, sō′shē-) n., study of human society, esp. its origins, development, and institutions. *Sociology compiles and analyzes data about social interaction.*

sociopath (sō′sē ə path′, sō′shē-) n., one who is afflicted with a social disorder, esp. one who is unable to function in society. *The sociopath was regularly in and out of jail.*

sodomy (sod′ə mē) n., anal copulation. *In many states, sodomy is a criminal offense.*

soft-pedal (sôft′ped′əl, soft′-) v.t., 1. to mute a tone, as on a piano, by pressing the soft pedal. *The pianist soft-pedaled the opening chords.* 2. to down-play or de-emphasize. *The advertisement soft-pedaled the product's drawbacks.*

sojourn (*n.* sō′jûrn; *v.* sō′jûrn, sō jûrn′) n., short visit. *The travelers enjoyed their brief sojourn in the Alps.* v.i., to live as a temporary resident. *The deposed king will sojourn in Switzerland for two weeks.*

solace (sol′is) n., comfort in sadness, sorrow, or misfortune. *They could find no solace in their misery.* v.t., to provide comfort in grief or sorrow; allay, soothe, or assuage. *They solaced their sorrow with music.*

solar (sō′lər) adj., pertaining to the sun. *Solar energy heats their home.*

solicit (sə lis′it) v.t., 1. to try to obtain something by persuasion, entreaty, or legal action. *She will solicit charitable contributions.* 2. to tempt or entice, usually to an immoral or sexual act. *The prostitute started to solicit him.* v.i., to request; importune. *We will solicit on behalf of the club.*

solicitor (sə lis′i tər) n., chief law officer of a government department. (in England, a low-ranking lawyer). *The city solicitor called a press conference.*

solicitous (sə lis′i təs) adj., eager to please; concerned; anxious; attentive. *The doctor's solicitous bedside manner was a comfort.*

solicitude (sə lis′i tōōd′, -tyōōd′) n., 1. state of being solicitous; concern; eagerness to please; attentiveness. *The host's solicitude made the party a success.* 2. cause of anxiety or concern. *The solicitudes of traveling caused her to become nervous and irritable.*

solidarity (sol′i dar′i tē) n., unity; oneness. *He called for party solidarity on the platform.*

soliloquy (sə lil′ə kwē) n., dramatic monologue. *The soliloquy was eloquently delivered.*

solitary (sol′i ter′ē) n., one who lives alone; recluse. *The solitary is unused to social intercourse.* adj., 1. alone. *She leads a reclusive, solitary life.* 2. remote; secluded. *The duel was fought in a solitary spot.* 3. single; sole. *A solitary scream pierced the night.*

solvent (sol′vənt) n., fluid or substance that dissolves other substances. *The solvent loosened the old paint.* adj., 1. able to meet financial obligations. *The paycheck made us solvent again.* 2. able to dissolve other substances. *The solvent chemical burned a hole in the fabric.*

somber (som′bər) adj., dark; gloomy; dismal; melancholy. *Somber storm clouds filled the sky.*

sombrero (som brâr′ō; *Sp.* sôm bRe′Rô) n., broad-brimmed Spanish or Mexican hat made of felt or straw. *The sombrero protects against sunburn.*

somnambulism (som nam′byə liz′əm, səm-) n., sleepwalking. *Hypnotism can induce a state of somnambulism.*

sonata (sə nä′tə) n., instrumental musical work consisting of three or four movements in different keys, moods, and tempos. *Critics called the sonata a masterpiece.*

sonorous (sə nōr′əs, -nôr′-, son′ər əs) adj., 1. producing a sound, esp. a deep, vibrating, resonant sound. *The Concorde sent a sonorous rumble through the neighborhood.* 2. imposing; grandiloquent. *His sonorous baritone filled the theater.*

sophisticated (sə fis′tə kā′tid) adj., 1. worldly; artful; refined; cosmopolitan. *We enjoyed the play's sophisticated dialogue.* 2. complex. *The space program makes use of highly sophisticated technology.*

sophistication (sə fis′tə kā′shən) n., 1. state of being worldly, artful, refined, cosmopolitan. *Her sophistication intimidated the young man.* 2. pertaining to complexity. *His craft project showed a surprising sophistication.*

sophistry (sof′i strē) n., argument that appears sound but is actually misleading; fallacious reasoning. *The debater's skillful sophistry clouded the issue.*

sophomoric (sof′ə môr′ik, -mor′-) adj., pertaining to a sophomore; immature; conceited; over-confident. *We were angered by his sophomoric prank.*

soporific (sop′ə rif′ik,sō′pə-) n., drug that induces sleep. *The doctor prescribed a soporific for insomnia.* adj., sleep-inducing; drowsy. *The politician's soporific speech put half of the hall to sleep.*

soprano (sə pran′ō, -prä′nō) n., highest range of the human voice, usually found in women and children; one who sings in a soprano range. *The soprano made her debut with the Metropolitan Opera Company.* adj., pertaining to the soprano range. *We enjoyed her clear, bright soprano voice.*

sordid (sôr′did) adj., dirty; squalid; foul; morally vile or wretched. *The newspaper reported the crime in all its sordid detail.*

sot (sot) n., habitual drunkard. *The sot couldn't make it to the door without help.*

soviet (sō′vē et′, -it, sō′vē et′) n., in the Soviet Union, popularly elected legislative bodies, operating on the local, regional, and national levels. *Members of the local soviet discussed the distribution of the wheat crop.*

spa (spä) n., mineral spring, or a health resort located near such a spring. *A month at a spa restored the patient's health.*

spangle (spang′gəl) n., small piece of glittering material, such as a sequin, used on theatrical costumes; small, sparkling object. *Clusters of spangles adorned the costume.* v.i., to sparkle or cause to sparkle. *The snow spangled in the sunlight.*

Spartan (spär′tᵊn) n., 1. one from ancient Sparta, Greece. *The Spartan was a military leader.* 2. one who is courageous and forbearing; stoic. *The Spartan went unflinching into the fray.* adj., self-disciplined; austere; rigorous; starkly simple. *Olympic athletes undergo a Spartan training regime.*

spasmodic (spaz mod′ik) adj., pertaining to the characteristics of a spasm; intermittent; fitful; unpredictable. *Her spasmodic cough was diagnosed as emphysema.*

spate (spāt) n., sudden flood or excess. *Citizens are complaining about the recent spate of robberies.*

spatial (spā′shəl) adj., existing in or connected with space. *Certain inner-ear conditions affect spatial perception.*

spatula (spach′ə lə) n., broad, flat spoonlike or paddlelike utensil used to spread, scrape, stir, or smooth substances, esp. in cooking. *The chef used a spatula to flip the pancake.*

spawn (spôn) n., 1. eggs or ova of various aquatic animals. *Black caviar is the spawn of sturgeon.* 2. offspring; brood; outcome. *The successful movie produced a spawn of imitators.* v.i., to produce spawn. *Salmon swim upstream to spawn.* v.t., to engender; produce. *His speech spawned my first interest.*

spawning (spôn′ing) adj., referring to spawn. *The spawning ground is in a wildlife sanctuary.*

speak-easy (spēk′ē′zē) n., place for the

illegal sale of alcohol popular during the Prohibition period in the U.S. *The police raided the speak-easy.*

specie (spē′s͟hē, -sē) n., coined money; coin. *I want to convert this currency into silver specie.*

species (spē′s͟hēz, -sēz) n., specific kind or sort, esp. as a basic biological classification, consisting of similar plants or animals capable of interbreeding. *The once-common species of bird is now near extinction.*

specious (spē′s͟həs) adj., apparently true, correct, or plausible, but actually not; deceptive; misleading. *The specious agreement was overturned in court.*

specter (spek′tər) n., ghost; apparition, phantom, or foreboding; vision. *She saw the specter of her murdered son.*

speculation (spek′yə lā′s͟hən) n., 1. reflection or contemplation. *The philosopher engages in speculation on the meaning of life.* 2. conjectural conclusion. *Her accusation was based on nothing more than speculation.* 3. risk-taking in the hopes of large profit. *He made his fortune in real estate speculation.*

spelunking (spi luñg′kiñg) n., exploration of caves. *We enjoy spelunking in the Blue Mountains of Virginia.*

spew (spyo͞o) v.t., to vomit or gush forth. *The volcano began to spew molten lava.*

spite (spīt) n., petty ill will; malice. *She took her ball away from him out of spite.* v.t., to treat maliciously; annoy. *He only dated her to spite his mother.*

spontaneous (spon tā′nē əs) adj., without premeditation; natural; impulsive. *She gave him a quick, spontaneous hug.*

spoonerism (spo͞o′nə riz′əm) n., unintended transposition of initial sounds in two or more words. *"Our queer old dean"* for *"Our dear old queen"* is a well-known spoonerism.

sporadic (spō rad′ik, spô-, spə-) adj., infrequent, scattered, or occasional. *The epidemic dwindled to sporadic cases.*

sprite (sprīt) n., elf, or elflike person. *She flitted like a sprite across the stage.*

spume (spyo͞om) n., foam. *The spume soaked the fisherman.* v.i., to foam or froth. *The boiling liquid began to spume out of the pan.*

spurious (spyo͝or′ē əs) adj., 1. outwardly similar but otherwise not related. *The bat bears only a spurious resemblance to birds.* 2. forged; deceitful. *His spurious credentials were eventually discovered.*

squalor (skwol′ər, skwô′lər) n., filth and degradation. *The has-been now lives in squalor on skid row.*

squander (skwon′dər) v.t., 1. to scatter or disperse. *She tries not to squander her time too widely.* 2. to spend extravagantly or foolishly. *He managed to squander his small inheritance very quickly.*

squeamish (skwē′mis͟h) adj., 1. easily nauseated or disgusted. *The squeamish student fainted during the dissection.* 2. overly fastidious or scrupulous. *The priest was squeamish about religious jokes.*

staccato (stə kä′tō) adj., 1. abrupt; disjointed. *We were startled by the staccato alarm.* 2. cut short or disconnected in performance. *Her playing was punctuated by staccato catcalls from the audience.*

stagnant (stag′nənt) adj., 1. motionless; still. *The storm cleared the stagnant air.* 2. stale; dull; inactive. *Complacency made the committee stagnant.*

staid (stād) adj., settled; sedate; fixed. *The staid club members disliked upsetting the status quo.*

stake (stāk) n., 1. piece of wood pointed at one end for driving into the ground as a marker or support. *He tied the tomato plant to the stake.* 2. something that is waged in a bet or contest. *She lost her stake in the last spin of the wheel.* 3. interest or share. *He has a stake in the family business.* v.t., 1. to mark the limits of. *He began to stake out the garden.* 2. to fasten or support. *A trellis was needed to stake the vines.* 3. to bet or hazard. *He decided to stake his savings on the enterprise.* 4. to back financially; sponsor. *Huge amounts of money are required to stake petroleum exploration.*

stalemate (stāl'māt') n., deadlock; impasse. *The talks broke down in stalemate.* v.t., to bring to a deadlock or impasse, esp. in chess. *On the verge of losing, he tried to stalemate the game.*

stalwart (stôl'wərt) n., steadfast supporter. *The party stalwart led the telethon.* adj., sturdy; strong; steadfast. *They depend on his stalwart good nature.*

stamina (stam'ə nə) n., endurance. *The marathon runner needs stamina to finish.*

stationary (stā'shə ner'ē) adj., not moving or movable; fixed; not changing. *The becalmed sailboat remained stationary on the horizon.*

stationery (stā'shə ner'ē) n., writing paper. *He received personalized stationery for his birthday.*

statute (stach'ōōt, -ŏŏt) n., law or other permanent regulation. *He lobbied to have the statute repealed.*

staunch (stônch, stänch) adj., 1. loyal; faithful. *The staunch Republican defended his party's nominee.* 2. sound; substantial. *He was confident of her staunch contribution.*

steep (stēp) v.t., 1. to soak. *She had to steep the shirt in bleach.* 2. to saturate with or subject thoroughly to. *She determined to steep her child in family history.* adj., 1. a high, almost vertical, incline. *She was breathless after climbing the steep hill.* 2. extremely high, as in price. *The steep prices at the grocery store put a dent in their budget.*

stellar (stel'ər) adj., 1. of or relating to the stars; astral. *They gazed overhead at the stellar display.* 2. of or relating to entertainment stars or to starring. *The stellar attraction was a sellout.*

stereotype (ster'ē ə tīp', stēr'-) n., standardized, oversimplified conception held in common. *She fit the stereotype of the southern belle.* v.t., to fit into a standardized, oversimplified conception. *The book stereotypes the parental roles.*

stethoscope (steth'ə skōp') n., instrument for detecting and studying sounds produced in the body. *The doctor listened to her heart through his stethoscope.*

stigma (stig'mə) n., 1. mark of disgrace. *Her work record carries the stigma of the reprimand.* 2. opening, part of a flower pistil on which pollen grains germinate. *She sketched the stigma in her botany lab book.*

stigmatize (stig'mə tīz') v.t., to identify or describe disparagingly. *This will stigmatize you forever as a traitor.*

stint (stint) n., 1. limitation or restriction in amount or share. *They set a fair stint on their participation.* 2. allotted amount of work. *His army stint is over in four months.* v.t., to set limits. *The library has to stint the number of books a borrower may take at one time.* v.i., be frugal. *They had to stint to afford the vacation.*

stipend (stī'pend) n., wage; payment. *He received a small stipend for caretaking.*

stipulate (stip'yə lāt') v.t., 1. to specify expressly. *The contract will stipulate the terms of sale.* 2. to give a guarantee of. *The letter of intent will stipulate our verbal agreement.* 3. to make a contract or agreement. *They met to stipulate the bylaws of the new club.*

stoic (stō'ik) n., one who is indifferent to pleasure or pain. *The stoic remained still while the doctor probed his wound.* adj., impassive. *The stoic pioneer calmly rebuilt the burned house.*

stolid (stol'id) adj., unemotional. *The stolid man was impervious to her pleas.*

strait (strāt) n., 1. narrow passageway between two bodies of water. *A strait connects the Pacific and Arctic oceans.* 2. distressing or perplexing situation; difficulty. *She found herself in an embarrassing strait.*

strategic (strə tē'jik) adj., necessary to the success of a plan of action. *His strategic move placed his opponent closer to checkmate.*

stratosphere (strat'ə sfēr') n., 1. upper portion of the atmosphere where there is little temperature change. *The strat-*

osphere is above the clouds. 2. elevated sector of any stratified body. *She climbed into the stratosphere of New York society.*

stratum (strā′təm, strat′əm, strä′təm) n., layer or level. *Each stratum of rock showed different coloration.*

striated (strī′ā tid) adj., marked with narrow lines or bands. *Her belly was striated with stretch marks.*

stricture (strik′chər) n., 1. restriction. *His father's one stricture was that he adhere to his allowance.* 2. censure; harsh criticism. *Her clumsiness evoked his angry stricture.*

strident (strīd′ənt) adj., loud and shrill. *Her strident cry drowned out his reply.*

strife (strīf) n., bitter, often violent conflict or dissension. *The union election created strife in the factory.*

stringent (strin′jənt) adj., 1. rigorous; strict. *The headmaster maintains stringent discipline.* 2. tight; restricted. *The stringent budget will help to restore the city's credit rating.*

stultify (stul′tə fī′) v.t., 1. to cause to appear foolish. *His clumsiness stultified the boy.* 2. to render futile or ineffectual; debase; impair. *Her constant criticism began to stultify his interest in painting.*

stupefy (stoō′pə fī′, styoō′-) v.t., 1. to make insensible; put into a stupor. *The drug began to stupefy the wounded lion.* 2. to astonish. *This news will stupefy you.*

stupor (stoō′pər, styoō′-) n., condition of diminished sensibilities; daze or extremely apathetic state. *The pain-killer kept him in a dreamlike stupor.*

stymie (stī′mē) v.t., to stand in the way of; impede. *The outcropping stymied the climbers.*

suave (swäv) n., smoothly polite or agreeable; urbane. *She is infatuated with the suave playboy.*

subcutaneous (sub′kyoō tā′nē əs) adj., under the skin. *The subcutaneous boil could not yet be lanced.*

subjective (səb jek′tiv) adj., 1. existing or originating in the sensibilities rather than in objective reality; illusory. *He*

didn't quite understand her subjective allusion. 2. personal. *Her subjective evaluation of him was based on intuition rather than on his resumé.*

sublimate (sub′lə māt′) v.t., to divert a primitive impulse with a more acceptable alternative. *He used erotic art to sublimate his lust.*

submerge (səb mûrj′) v.t., 1. to put under water; immerse. *The child loved to submerge his toys in the bubble bath.* 2. to subordinate or make obscure. *She tried to submerge the memory of the accident.*

submit (səb mit′) v.i., 1. to yield or defer to another. *You must submit to the court's ruling.* v.t., 1. to propose with deference; offer for approval. *The lawyer will submit a motion of deferral.* 2. to affirm; put forward an opinion. *We submit this proof that our cause is just.*

subordinate (n., adj. sə bôr′dənit; v. sə bôr′dənāt′) n., one of lower rank. *The subordinate failed to salute the ranking officer.* v.t., 1. to place in a lower rank or class. *He tried to subordinate his preference to that of his family.* 2. to subjugate; subdue. *Harsh methods were used to subordinate the unruly prisoners.* adj., submissive to authority; servile. *He played a subordinate role in the kitchen.*

subpoena (sə pē′nə, səb-) n., legal notice to appear in court under a penalty for failure to do so. *The woman tried to avoid the subpoena.*

sub rosa (sub rō′zə) adv., secretly; confidentially. *To avoid public controversy, the committee met sub rosa.*

subsequent (sub′sə kwənt) adj., following; succeeding. *Subsequent to our meeting, I drew up these proposals.*

subservience (səb sûr′vē əns) n., excessive servility. *She was embarrassed by the man's cringing subservience.*

subsidiary (səb sid′e er′ē) n., something controlled by something else. *The small chemical plant is a subsidiary of a major conglomerate.* adj., auxiliary; supplementary. *The subsidiary generator goes on in an emergency.*

subsidy (sub′si dē) n., grant or gift of money. *They lobbied for an increased government subsidy for the arts.*

subsistence (səb sis′təns) n., 1. state of existing. *The ancient ritual was still in subsistence in the remote area.* 2. means of supporting life. *He makes his subsistence by farming.*

substantial (səb stan′shəl) adj., 1. real; actual. *He offered substantial proof of the family title.* 2. ample in quantity. *She enjoys a substantial salary.* 3. sturdy. *His substantial build impressed the young girls.* 4. well-to-do. *He came from one of the most substantial families in the town.* 5. largely, but not wholly, what is specified. *His version of the incident contains the substantial truth.*

substantiate (səb stan′shē āt′) v.t., 1. to confirm or verify. *The photographs will substantiate his story.* 2. to impart substance to; embody; strengthen. *Building the boat together served to substantiate their friendship.*

subterfuge (sub′tər fyōoj′) n., deceptive strategy. *The salesperson gained entrance to the house by subterfuge.*

subtle (sut′əl) adj., 1. delicate; fine. *He sniffed the subtle aroma of the wine.* 2. obscure; elusive. *I tried to follow her subtle reasoning.* 3. perceptive; refined. *No inferior wine could impress his subtle palate.* 4. cunning; crafty. *The subtle liar deflected their suspicion.*

subversive (səb vûr′siv) n., one who attempts to overthrow or destroy. *The subversive organized the riot.* adj., corrupting; traitorous. *The subversive pamphlet undermined the state's security.*

succinct (sək sĩgkt′) adj., concise. *Her succinct summary brought the meeting to a swift conclusion.*

succulent (suk′yə lənt) adj., juicy; fleshy-tissued. *The children peeled the succulent oranges.*

succumb (sə kum′) v.i., to yield to superior force. *She was forced to succumb to his demand.*

suffice (sə fĩs′, -fĩz′) v.i., to be enough, adequate; to satisfy. *She thought a polite thank you would suffice.*

suffix (suf′iks) n., addition at the end. *The suffix "ette" is a feminine diminutive.*

suffuse (sə fyōoz′) v.t., to spread over or through. *The music suffused the concert hall.*

sullen (sul′ən) adj., 1. glum; morose. *The sullen little girl needed a friend.* 2. dull; somber. *Her sullen clothes contrasted with her laughing face.* 3. sluggish. *The flu made him sullen and weak.*

sultry (sul′trē) adj., 1. sweltering. *The tourists suffered in the sultry Egyptian weather.* 2. passionate. *Her sultry song set him on fire.*

summation (sə mā′shən) n., 1. addition; sum. *The calculator sped him through the summation.* 2. final, summary part of an argument. *The jury was impressed with his impassioned summation.*

sumptuous (sump′chōo əs) adj., luxurious. *She prepared a sumptuous banquet for the foreign dignitary.*

sundry (sun′drē) adj., various; miscellaneous. *The medicine chest contained sundry items.*

supercilious (sōo′pər sil′ē əs) adj., haughty and disdainful. *The supercilious manner of the headwaiter cowed the timid diner.*

superficial (sōo′pər fish′əl) adj., 1. affecting only the surface. *His superficial wound looked worse than it was.* 2. shallow; not profound. *His superficial analysis of the problem was nearly useless.*

superfluous (sōo pûr′flōo əs) adj., excessive; more than is required; unnecessary. *Her superfluous jewelry detracted from the elegant lines of the dress.*

superimpose (sōo′pər im pōz′) v.t., to place over or above. *We can superimpose the text over the illustration.*

superiority (sə pēr′ē ôr′i tē, -or′-, sōo-) n., state of being superior. *The superiority of workmanship made his cabinets worth the extra cost.*

superlative (sə pûr′lə tiv, sōo-) adj., 1. supreme. *Her years of training paid off* *in a superlative debut.* 2. excessive; exaggerated. *Their superlative praise sounded insincere.*

supernatural (soo'pər nach'ər əl) adj., outside the visible, natural world, esp. relating to divine or infernal being. *The eerie, supernatural sound frightened them.*

supersede (soo'pər sēd') v.t., to supplant; replace. *This new rule will supersede the old one.*

superstition (soo'pər stish'ən) n., irrational belief resulting from fear or ignorance. *The missionary tried to no avail to rid the village of superstition.*

supervise (soo'pər vīz') v.t., to superintend; oversee. *It is the head nurse's responsibility to supervise all nursing care.*

supine (soo pīn') adj., 1. lying on the back. *Not all psychoanalysts insist their patients be in a supine position.* 2. indolent; apathetic. *She lay supine in the warm bath.*

supplant (sə plant', -plänt') v.t., to displace or supersede. *Eventually the new translation would supplant all earlier versions.*

supple (sup'əl) v.t., 1. to make flexible or pliant. *This oil will help to supple the tough leather.* 2. to pacify or make complaisant. *Her gentle manner can supple the angriest customer.* adj., 1. bending or folding easily without creasing or breaking. *She shaped the supple dough into a star.* 2. limber; lithe. *The supple dancer glided across the floor.* 3. overly compliant. *Fear of expulsion made her supple.*

supplicate (sup'lə kāt') v., to ask humbly and earnestly; beg; entreat. *She began to supplicate in our behalf.*

supposition (sup'ə zish'ən) n., assumption. *He was angered by her false supposition.*

supremacy (sə prem'ə sē, soo-) n., quality or state of being first in rank. *No one could challenge his supremacy in the field.*

surcharge (*n.* sûr'chärj', *v.* sûr chärj', sûr'chärj') n., extra charge or burden.

Consumers objected to the fuel surcharge. v.t., 1. to charge an extra amount. *The decision to surcharge the goods will increase the import price.* 2. to overload. *The barking dogs helped to surcharge the already tense atmosphere.*

surfeit (sûr'fit) n., 1. excess or overindulgence. *The surfeit of appetizers spoiled her appetite for dinner.* 2. disgusted feeling caused by overindulgence. *She suffered a feeling of surfeit after the heavy meal.* v.t., to eat or drink too much; overindulge. *They tried not to surfeit the child with sweets.*

surge (sûrj) n., 1. wavelike forward thrust. *We retreated in the face of the surge of the advancing cavalry.* 2. abrupt or sudden rush or disturbance. *A surge of current preceded the blackout.* v.i., 1. to swell forward. *The music suddenly surged out of the orchestra pit.* 2. to rise suddenly and excessively. *The cheering crowd surged to its feet.*

surly (sûr'lē) adj., irritable; churlish. *She was afraid to approach the surly coach.*

surmise (*n.* sər mīz', sûr'mīz; *v.* sər mīz') n., conjecture; guess. *We agree with your surmise as to the reason for her anger.* v., to conjecture; assume; guess. *With so little information, they could only surmise what had happened.*

surreptitious (sûr'əp tish'əs) adj., secretive; stealthy. *She intercepted his surreptitious glance.*

surrogate (sûr'ə gāt', -git, sur'-) n., substitute. *Her surrogate accepted for her.*

surveillance (sər vā'ləns, -vāl'yəns) n., close watch over; supervision. *During the war, surveillance of foreign nationals was increased.*

susceptible (sə sep'tə bəl) adj., 1. capable of submitting to or being affected by. *The lonely man was susceptible to her kindness.* 2. open to the influence. *The elderly were especially susceptible to this particular strain of flu.*

suspension (sə spen'shən) n., 1. act of suspending or state of being suspended, esp. as a temporary abrogation. *The impertinence resulted in her suspension* *from school.* 2. being in a floating or hanging state. *His words hung in suspension on the air.* 3. state in which solid particles are mixed but undissolved. *The fruit was preserved in a gelatinous suspension.*

sustenance (sus′tə nəns) n., means of supporting life. *Our garden provides a substantial part of our sustenance.*

swatch (swoch) n., sample or characteristic piece. *She found a paint to match the curtain swatch.*

swath (swoth, swôth) n., path cut or space covered (originally by the swing of a scythe). *Sherman's troops made a wide swath through Georgia on their march to the sea.*

swelter (swel′tər) n., oppressive heat. *The air conditioner helped her avoid the swelter.* v.i., to oppress or become oppressed with heat. *The prisoners began to swelter in the unventilated cells.*

sycophant (sik′ə fənt) n., self-seeking, servile flatterer. *The leader was not fooled by the fawning sycophant.*

syllogism (sil′ə jiz′əm) n., scheme of deductive reasoning consisting of a major premise, a minor premise, and a conclusion. *"All Romans are Italians; all Italians are Europeans; therefore, all Romans are Europeans" is an example of a syllogism.*

symbiosis (sim′bī ō′sis, -bē-) n., interdependent relationship involving two or more different organisms that is beneficial to all. *The trade agreement was based on and furthered the symbiosis of the two nations.*

symmetry (sim′i trē) n., balanced proportions; regularity of arrangement. *The architect admired the symmetry of the columns.*

sympathy (sim′pə thē) n., harmony of feeling or thought; fellow-feeling. *He appreciated her expression of sympathy.*

symposium (sim pō′zē əm) n., 1. meeting to present and compare views. *The symposium was called to air the views of the community leaders.* 2. collection of views or writings on a given subject. *The symposium showed how different disciplines saw the future of the institution.*

symptomatic (simp′tə mat′ik) adj., of the nature of; characteristic. *His violent reaction to the petty insult was symptomatic of his paranoia.*

synchronize (siṅg′krə nīz′) v.t., to make happen or occur at the same time. *The members of the drill team had to synchronize their movements or they would collide.*

syndrome (sin′drōm) n., concurrent signs or symptoms that characterize a condition or form a distinguishing pattern. *Her lack of color and fatigue suggested an anemic syndrome.*

synonym (sin′ə nim) n., word sharing the same meaning with at least one other word. *He sought a synonym to help explain the word's meaning.*

synopsis (si nop′sis) n., condensed statement or outline; summary; abstract. *The executive saved time by reading his assistant's synopsis.*

syntax (sin′taks) n., 1. orderly arrangement of parts. *The wild exuberance of Victorian architecture was in part a reaction to the predictable syntax of neoclassical architecture.* 2. structure of a sentence. *He changed the syntax to improve the flow of the sentence.*

synthesis (sin′thi sis) n., 1. combination of parts forming a whole. *This bill is a synthesis of the work of several senators.* 2. deductive reasoning. *Synthesis results when a thesis and its antithesis combine to form a greater truth.*

synthetic (sin thet′ik) adj., artificial; imitation. *The synthetic leather looked real.*

syphilis (sif′ə lis) n., chronic, contagious disease caused by a spirochete, usually venereal and often congenital. *Unless treated, syphilis can develop into a fatal disease.*

Tt

tabernacle (tab′ər nak′əl) n., 1. large building used for religious services. *The choir could be heard outside the tabernacle.* 2. covered receptacle for some holy or precious object. *The saint's remains were kept in a tabernacle on a side altar.*

tableau (tab′lō, ta blō′) n., depiction of a scene by silent, motionless, costumed participants. *The children made up a tableau of the Nativity.*

tabloid (tab′loid) n., newspaper of small page size containing many photos and brief news reports. *The tabloid ran lurid photos with the story.*

taboo (tə bōō′, ta-) n., 1. a prohibition for superstitious, moral, or protective reasons. *Incest is probably a universal taboo.* 2. belief in or adherence to taboos. *They held the burial ground in taboo.*

tabulate (tab′yə lāt′) v.t., to put into table form, in rows of columns. *She tried to tabulate the massive data.*

tachometer (ta kom′i tər, tə-) n., instrument for measuring speed of rotation, in revolutions per minute (RPMs). *The tachometer monitors the engine's RPMs.*

tacit (tas′it) adj., implied or indicated but not actually said. *He mistook her silence for tacit consent.*

taciturn (tas′i tûrn′) adj., disinclined to speak; reserved. *The taciturn woman surprised them by speaking up.*

tact (takt) n., sensitivity to what is appropriate to avoid offense; discretion. *Tact is a necessary diplomatic attribute.*

tactile (tak′til, -tīl) adj., perceptible by touch. *The Braille reading method relies on tactile perceptions.*

taint (tānt) n., mark of contamination; blemish. *The taint of infidelity spoiled their marriage.* v.t., to contaminate or corrupt. *Don't let the experience taint your whole life.*

tally (tal′ē) n., recorded reckoning or account. *The daily tally keeps track of all business transactions.* v.t., to make a record or account. *She began to tally the day's transactions.* v.i., to correspond. *The facts don't tally with his story.*

tangential (tan jen′shəl) adj., 1. digressive; erratic. *The tangential remark was amusing if irrelevant.* 2. marginal; incidental. *The dancer had a tangential interest in choreography.*

tangible (tan′jə bəl) adj., 1. perceptible by touch; palpable. *The tension in the room was almost tangible.* 2. substantially real; material. *The glove was tangible evidence of her presence.* 3. susceptible to accurate appraisal. *Her tangible assets are the car and her bank account.*

tankard (tang′kərd) n., tall, muglike drinking vessel, usually in silver or pewter with a lid. *The German beer was served in a heavy pewter tankard.*

tantalize (tan′tᵊlīz′) v.t., to tease or torment by continually presenting a desired object then withdrawing it from within reach. *The child tantalized the puppy with the bone.*

tantamount (tan′tə mount′) adj., equivalent. *Their belligerent act was tantamount to declaring war.*

tantrum (tan′trəm) n., outburst of bad temper. *The two-year-old threw a tantrum when we said no.*

taunt (tônt, tänt) n., sarcastic challenge or insult. *I couldn't let the taunt go by without responding.* v.t., to challenge or reproach in a mocking or insulting way. *She began to taunt him for his cowardice.*

taut (tôt) adj., 1. pulled or stretched tight; tense. *He began to walk across the taut wire.* 2. in proper condition; firm. *The athlete has a taut body.*

tautology (tô tol′ə jē) n., needless repetition of an idea or statement; statement so repeated. *The tautology needs to be pruned from this speech.*

tawdry (tô′drē) adj., cheap, gaudy, and sleazy in appearance. *The tawdry outfit drew stares from the other guests.*

tawny (tô′nē) n., brownish-orange to light brown; slightly redder than sorrel. *Her tawny hair bleached out in the sun.*

technology (tek nol′ə jē) n., applied science. *The technology of solar energy is rapidly growing.*

tedious (tē′dē əs, tē′jəs) adj., monotonous; tiresome; boring. *She hated doing the tedious grammar exercises.*

tedium (tē′de əm) n., monotony; boredom. *Reading relieved the tedium of waiting.*

teem (tēm) v.i., to be filled to overflowing; abound. *The river teems with spawning salmon.*

teeming (tē′miñg) adj., overcrowded; abundant. *The boat was a teeming mass of refugees.*

telegram (tel′ə gram′) n., communication transmitted across distances by means of electrical impulses. *Their telegram announced the birth of a son.*

telemetry (tə lem′i trē) n., the automatic transmission of signals (as radio) over long distances. *Astronomical research relies on instruments of telemetry.*

telepathy (tə lep′ə thē) n., psychic transmission of ideas. *He researched the phenomena of mental telepathy.*

telescope (tel′i skōp′) n., device that enlarges the images of distant objects. *We observed the planet through a telescope.* v.i., to cause a series of objects to compact; compress. *The freight cars telescoped during the collision.*

temerarious (tem′ə râr′ē əs) adj., fearless; bold; valiant. *The advancing soldiers were swift and temerarious.*

temerity (tə mer′i tē) n., rash boldness; recklessness. *It was sheer temerity to oppose her father.*

temperature (tem′pər ə chər, -prə chər) n., quality of heat or cold. *Arctic regions have sub-zero temperatures.*

tempestuous (tem pes′choo əs) adj., turbulent; agitated. *The tempestuous storm grounded the plane.*

tempo (tem′pō) n., 1. speed at which a musical composition is rendered. *The polka has a fast tempo.* 2. rate of activity; pace. *The tempo of political life peaks before an election.*

temporal (tem′pər əl, tem′prəl) adj., 1. concerning or limited by time; temporary; passing; transitory. *The temporal contract is due to be renewed.* 2. worldly; mundane; concerning earthly things; secular. *The monastery shut out temporal matters.*

temporize (tem′pə rīz′) v.i., 1. to stall in order to avoid confrontation; delay; impede. *Don't temporize—tell me now.* 2. to compromise; act with expedience. *She tried to temporize with the union leader.*

tempus fugit (*Lat.* tem′poos foo′git; *Eng.* tem′pəs fyoo′jit) "time flies," Hurry! Don't waste time! "*Tempus fugit!*" *the teacher said, as the bell rang.*

tenable (ten′ə bəl) adj., 1. feasible; reasonable. *Your plan is tenable and well-thought-out.* 2. capable of being maintained or protected; defensible. *The reinforcements made the fort tenable.*

tenacious (tə nā′shəs) adj., 1. obstinate; stubborn. *The child kept a tenacious grip on her skirt.* 2. persevering; relentless. *The tenacious lawyer finally won his case.* 3. retentive. *She has a tenacious memory.* 4. cohesive. *Tar is a tenacious substance for road pavement.*

tenacity (tə nas′i tē) n., 1. persistence; drive. *Mountain climbing requires courage and tenacity.* 2. the greatest longitudinal stress a substance can bear. *The* *tenacity of steel renders it ideal for structural supports.*

tenant (ten'ənt) n., one who pays rent in order to hold possession of a building or occupy land owned by another; occupant. *The tenants in the next apartment are noisy.* v.t., rent; lease. *An agency was hired to tenant the new apartment complex.* v.i., to occupy; inhabit; lease. *Merchants tenant in the ground floor storefronts.* adj., condition of tenancy; tenant operated or controlled. *The plantation is cultivated by tenant farmers.*

tendentious (ten den'shəs) adj., prejudiced; biased. *Propaganda is tendentious political jargon.*

tentacle (ten'tə kəl) n., elongated, often sensory, appendage, extending from the mass or body of a living thing. *The jellyfish tentacle tangled in my line.*

tentative (ten'tə tiv) adj., provisional; temporary; anticipatory. *Our tentative agreement was formally approved last week.*

tenuous (ten'yoo əs) adj., 1. fragile; frail; slight; flimsy. *A few tenuous clouds floated above.* 2. weak; slight; unstable. *The crop failure made his financial position tenuous.*

tenure (ten'yər) n., act, condition, or term of possessing or holding something. *He was offered a three-year tenure.*

tepid (tep'id) adj., 1. slightly warm; lukewarm. *The tropical plant thrived in the tepid atmosphere.* 2. half-hearted; mild. *He had only a tepid interest in his work.*

terce (tûrs) n., third part of a husband's estate to which a widow is entitled by law. *Since her husband left no will, she inherited only her terce.*

termagant (tûr'mə gənt) n., scolding woman; fishwife. *He finally divorced the termagant.*

terminal (tûr'mə nəl) n., 1. beginning or end of a route of conveyance. *She waited at the bus terminal.* 2. receptacle that holds the ends of a wiring system. *A fire resulted from the defective wiring*

in the battery terminal. adj., final; conclusive; situated at the end. *He suffers from a terminal illness.*

terminate (tûr'mə nāt') v.t., to bring to an end; stop; conclude. *She decided to terminate the subscription.* v.i., to end; come to a close. *The college semester will terminate in June.*

terminology (tûr'mə nol'ə je) n., specialized vocabulary related to an area of knowledge. *She didn't understand the terminology in the medical journal.*

terrain (tə rān', ter'ān) n., topography; geographical characteristics of an area of land. *The explorers were slowed by the mountainous terrain.*

terrestrial (tə res'trē əl) adj., 1. relating to the earth as a planet; global. *Human beings are terrestrial inhabitants.* 2. consisting of earth as opposed to water. *The map uses gray for terrestrial areas, blue for water areas.* 3. living or growing on land. *Trees and shrubs are terrestrial plants.*

terrorist (ter'ər ist) n., one who uses violence to further a political or social cause. *The terrorist was arrested after the bombing.*

terse (tûrs) adj., to the point; compact; clipped. *His warning was terse but effective.*

tertiary (tûr'shē er'ē, tûr'shə rē) n., distinguishable subdivisions of religious orders, scientific classifications, etc.; groupings. *Dominican tertiaries consist of lay persons.* adj., third in number or sequence; third. *The brigade was part of the tertiary division.*

testaceous (te stā'shəs) adj., hard-shelled. *Turtles are testaceous creatures.*

testate (tes'tāt) adj., leaving a valid will. *Surprisingly, the hermit died testate.*

testator (tes'tā tər, te stā'tər) n., maker of a will. *The testator left many charitable bequests.*

testify (tes'tə fī') v.i., to give evidence; affirm under oath. *The defendant will testify in his own behalf.*

testimonial (tes'tə mō'nē əl) n., 1. statement; verification. *The coroner gave a* *brief testimonial.* 2. witness of approval; laudatory account; citation. *The monument was a testimonial to her courage.* adj., 1. giving witness; describing. *The testimonial remarks did not match.* 2. offered in praise of; laudatory. *He was honored at a testimonial dinner.*

testy (tes′tē) adj., irritable; short-tempered; easily annoyed. *The tired mother was testy with the child.*

tête-à-tête (tāt′ə tāt′; *Fr.* te tA tet′) n., confidential talk; private discourse, usually between two persons. *They sought a secluded corner for a tête-à-tête.* adj., concerning an exchange of confidences, usually by two persons; private. *They were tête-à-tête all afternoon.* adv., confidentially; privately; inaudibly. *The newlyweds whispered tête-à-tête.*

theocracy (thē ok′rə sē) n., government that is controlled by a religious order or a person considered to have divine powers. *A theocracy seldom tolerates religious dissension.*

theocratic (thē′ə krat′ik) adj., pertaining to a theocracy. *The Massachusetts Bay Colony had a theocratic government.*

theology (thē ol′ə jē) n., religious study; body of knowledge relating to a religious belief. *Zeus is the chief deity of ancient Greek theology.*

theosophy (thē os′ə fē) n., religious doctrine in which divinity is revealed through mystic perception. *Her belief in theosophy grew from an interest in the occult.*

therapeutic (ther′ə pyo͞o′tik) adj., healthful; beneficial; remedial. *Walking is therapeutic exercise.*

therapy (ther′ə pē) n., 1. healing power. *Laughter can be good therapy.* 2. process of applying specialized scientific methods to alleviate or cure a physical or emotional ailment. *Physical therapy helped her regain the use of her legs.*

thermal (thûr′məl) adj., regarding heat, or a degree of heat, or retention of heat. *She wore thermal underwear in the freezing weather.*

thesaurus (thi sôr′əs) n., compendium of words of similar meaning; book of synonyms. *She found the vivid synonym in her thesaurus.*

thesis (thē′sis) n., 1. proposal backed up by material intended to substantiate its validity. *It is their thesis that a merger is inevitable.* 2. formal paper in a specific area of study written and presented in order to qualify for a scholastic degree. *She was working on her Ph.D. thesis.*

thoracic (thō ras′ik, thô-) adj., pertaining to the thorax, chest, or chest cavity. *The thoracic surgeon studied her chest x-rays.*

thorax (thōr′aks, thôr′-) n., that part of the trunk area of the body containing the heart and lungs. *The ribs enclose the thorax.*

threadbare (thred′bâr′) adj., badly worn. *The hand-me-down was threadbare.*

threshold (thresh′old, thresh′hōld) n., 1. doorsill; entranceway. *We replaced the worn front threshold.* 2. point of departure. *He was on the threshold of success.* 3. the limitations of perception to various stimuli. *Her threshold of pain was remarkably high.*

throes (thrōz) n. pl., 1. thrashing or convulsive motions; pangs. *He suffered his final death throes.* 2. mental anguish. *They suffered the throes of separation.*

thrombosis (throm bō′sis) n., blood clot that forms in a blood vessel or in the heart. *The heart attack was caused by coronary thrombosis.*

throng (thrông, throng) n., great number of people; mass. *A throng gathered to hear the president speak.* v.i., to advance as a crowd; mill about in large numbers. *Many curious people thronged to the scene of the accident.*

throttle (throt′əl) n., valve regulating forward passage of vaporized fuel in an internal combustion engine. *He opened the throttle to increase the gas supply.* v.t., to choke; strangle. *She wanted to throttle the irritating child.* v.i., to cut back or reduce flow of fuel to decelerate. *He had to throttle to slow the boat.*

thwack (thwak) n., 1. sharp blow with a flat object; whack. *He shut the book with an impatient thwack.* 2. sound evoked by a thwacking motion. *The door slammed with a loud thwack.* v.t., to strike with a flat object. *He thwacked the insolent boy in the face.*

thwart (thwôrt) v.t., to oppose; contravene; stand in the way of; impede. *She tried to thwart his devious plan.* n., transverse seat of a rowboat. *The oarsmen sat on the thwart.*

tiara (tē ar′ə, -är′ə, -âr′ə) n., 1. headdress containing jewels. *The tiara slipped off her head.* 2. triple crown worn by the pope. *At his coronation, the pope is invested with the papal tiara.*

tidbit (tid′bit′) n., 1. tempting morsel; delicacy; bite-sized piece of food. *The puppy ate the tidbit from her fingers.* 2. choice bit of news, unconfirmed information, or idle talk. *She offered the gossipy tidbit to her neighbor.*

timbre (tim′bər; *Fr.* taɴ′bʀə) n., characteristics of sound frequency and resonance. *The strong timbre of his voice carried over the crowd.*

timidity (ti mid′i tē) n., apprehension; shyness. *The speech class helped her overcome her timidity.*

timorous (tim′ər əs) adj., easily frightened; hesitant. *The timorous clerk steeled herself to ask for a raise.*

tincture (tiɴgk′chər) n., 1. medical solution with an alcohol base. *Tincture of iodine is a good antiseptic.* 2. pigment used in paint; tint. *The artist mixed a special tincture for the lake.* 3. tinge; trace; distinctive quality; hint. *The endearment contained a tincture of sarcasm.* v.t., season; imbue; characterize. *She decided to tincture the soup with tarragon.*

tinge (tinj) n., hint; trace. *There was a tinge of autumn in the air.* v.t., 1. to change or modify. *She tried to tinge her criticism with humor.* 2. to color or flavor. *The sun began to tinge the sky with red.*

tintinabulation (tin′ti nab′yə lā′shən) n.,

ringing of bells; bell-like sounds. *The town awakened to the tintinabulation of the church bells.*

tirade (tī′rād, tə rād′) n., verbal attack; diatribe; outburst of abusive language. *His anger burst out in a loud tirade.*

titanic (tī tan′ik, ti-) adj., of great size or strength. *Titanic waves smashed against the boat.*

tithe (tīth) n., a portion (lit. one tenth) of one's yield, produce, profit, or earnings surrendered as tribute to a church, government, or landholder. *The church members agreed to pay their tithes promptly.* v.i., to pledge a portion of one's income to a religious institution; strictly, one tenth. *The pious villagers tithe even in bad times.* v.t., to demand or require a share of the income or material increment of a church communicant or landholder. *The plantation owner relentlessly tithed the sharecroppers' annual yield.*

titillate (tit′əlāt′) v.t., to tickle, arouse, or evoke a pleasurable response. *The brightly wrapped package titillated her curiosity.*

titillation (tit′əlā′shən) n., arousal; interest; awakened desire. *The bedroom scene provoked great titillation in the audience.*

toast (tōst) n., 1. slice of bread browned by heating. *She served toast and soup.* 2. either a drink taken in response to gesture of raised glass and accompanying verbal expression, or the expression itself. *We drank a toast to their happiness.* 3. honored person; celebrity. *She was the toast of the debutante season.* v.t., 1. to brown by heating. *Let's toast marshmallows over the fire.* 2. to warm completely. *Toast your hands at this fire.* 3. to drink or speak in honor of. *We must toast their happiness.*

toastmaster (tōst′mas′tər, -mä′stər) n., one who officiates at a formal dinner, introduces honored guests, and proposes toasts. *The witty toastmaster contributed to the dinner's success.*

tocsin (tok′sin) n., sound of alarm, usually

by the ringing of bells. *He ascended the steeple to sound a general tocsin.*

toga (tō′gə) n., free-flowing garment worn by early Romans. *The toga trimmed in purple reflected her patrician status.*

tolerate (tol′ə rāt′) v.t., 1. endure; put up with. *She cannot tolerate his bad manners.* 2. the capacity of an organism to accommodate to the introduction of various chemical substances or levels of stress. *Her system won't tolerate penicillin.*

tome (tōm) n., large, heavy book. *The historian lifted a dusty tome from the shelf.*

tonsillitis (ton′sə lī′tis) n., inflamed tonsils. *Tonsillitis is usually accompanied by a fever.*

toothsome (tōōth′səm) adj., tasty; appetizing; mouthwatering. *The buffet offered many toothsome dishes.*

topography (tə pog′rə fē) n., the physical characteristics of a given land area; terrain. *They flew over Alaska's mountainous topography.*

torpor (tôr′pər) n., sluggishness; lethargy; apathy. *Exposure to extreme cold reduced him to a state of torpor.*

torso (tôr′sō) n., 1. human trunk. *The tank suit covered her torso.* 2. trunk of a statue. *The torso was displayed on the first floor.*

tortilla (tôr tē′ə; *Sp.* tôr tē′yä) n., flat, round, cornmeal pancake eaten in Mexico. *Tortillas can be folded and stuffed with meat or cheese.*

tortoise (tôr′təs) n., land-dwelling turtle. *The huge tortoise drew its head into its shell.*

tortuous (tôr′chōō əs) adj., winding; indirect; difficult. *The car wound slowly up the tortuous mountain road.*

totalitarianism (tō tal′i târ′ē ə niz′əm) n., centralized government that tolerates no dissenting political philosophy and subordinates the rights of individuals to the state. *Totalitarianism cannot support free enterprise.*

touché (tōō shā′) interj., originally the voiced acknowledgement of a hit in fencing; now used in recognition of a clever retort or point of discussion. *"Touché!" he replied to her barbed retort.*

touchstone (tuch′stōn′) n., 1. black stone traditionally used to test the purity of gold or silver by examination of the color of their rubbings upon it. *Jasper was used as a touchstone in medieval days.* 2. any standard or test used to determine quality or authenticity. *Intellectual freedom is the touchstone of true democracy.*

touchy (tuch′ē) adj., 1. quickly offended; irascible; argumentative; testy. *The touchy man was a difficult co-worker.* 2. needing tact; calling for diplomacy; unstable. *A strike negotiator must deal with many touchy situations.*

tour de force (tōōr′də fōrs′, -fôrs′; *Fr.* tōōr də fôRs′) n., act of greatest merit; stupendous enterprise; bravissimo performance. *The dance festival was a magnificent tour de force.*

tourniquet (tûr′nə kit, tōōr′-) n., device used to cut off the flow of blood from an injured blood vessel. *He applied a tourniquet just above the snake bite.*

tout (tout) v.t., to proclaim vehemently, often without justification; solicit loudly; propagandize. *The campaigning politician touted his accomplishments.*

toxic (tok′sik) adj., poisonous. *She was treated for toxic snake bite.*

toxin (tok′sin) n., toxic substance produced by living organism that characteristically induces antibiotic activity. *Some toxins are used to produce serum against disease.*

tracery (trā′sə rē) n., ornamental, lacelike design. *We admired the delicate tracery of the wrought-iron gates.*

trachea (trā′kē ə *or, esp. Brit.,* trə kē′ə) n., windpipe. *He choked when a bone stuck in his trachea.*

tract (trakt) n., 1. specific area of land; section of property; grant. *Homesteaders drew lots for tracts in the wilderness.* 2. in anatomy, a related group of organs in series. *Food passes through the digestive tract.* 3. written discourse, published to expound upon a specific subject, often of a religious nature; essay; treatise. *The political tract was distributed privately.*

tractable (trak′tə bəl) adj., 1. manageable; compliant; docile. *The tractable child was too easily led into trouble.* 2. easy to handle; workable; malleable. *He liked to work the fine, tractable land.*

traction (trak′shən) n., 1. pulling power or drawing action. *Elevated railways are powered by electric traction.* 2. adhesive frictional interaction that enables an object to move directionally across a stationary surface; purchase; grip. *We lost our traction and slid over the ice.* 3. therapeutic device used to promote healing or relieve pain by exerting a pulling force on the musculoskeletal structure of the body. *Her broken arm was in traction for three weeks.*

tradition (trə dish′ən) n., body of knowledge, practice, or customs passed informally from one generation to another. *Freedom of speech is a political tradition in the United States.*

traduce (trə do͞os′, -dyo͞os′) v.t., to slander; disgrace; disparage; discredit. *The dishonest politician tried to traduce the character of his opponent.*

trajectory (trə jek′tə rē) n., path of a body in flight; direction of a projectile as it moves under force. *The satellites speed along parallel trajectories.*

tranquil (trang′kwil) adj., placid; serene; calm; quiet; undisturbed. *Village life was tranquil and soothing.*

tranquillity (trang kwil′i tē) n., peace; composure; calmness; quietude. *Tranquillity is an elusive state during divorce.*

transcend (tran send′) v.t., to go beyond; excel; rise above. *The success of his novel transcended his expectations.*

transcribe (tran skrīb′) v.t., 1. to interpret in writing; rewrite in another language. *She tried to transcribe the Latin verse into English.* 2. to record in writing or electronically. *They will transcribe the song in the new studio.*

transfix (trans fiks′) v.t., 1. to impale; pierce. *They transfixed the villain's*

head on a pike. 2. to hold something still as if pinned to a wall. *The lion transfixed the children with fear.*

transfusion (trans fyo͞o′zhən) n., transmission of blood, plasma, or another solution between two like creatures. *The blood transfusion saved her life.*

transgress (trans gres′, tranz-) v.t., to step across, over, or beyond; err; infringe upon; intrude; encroach upon; overstep. *The boy was suspended when he transgressed school regulations.* v.i., to sin. *I transgressed against my neighbor.*

transgression (trans gresh′ən, tranz-) n., offense; disobedience; sin. *Sunday labor used to be a serious transgression.*

transience (tran′shəns, -zhəns) n., of transitory nature; impermanence. *Transience and whimsy seem to rule the world of fashion.*

transient (tran′shənt, -zhənt) n., one who passes through or stays temporarily; migrant. *The transient moved aimlessly from town to town.* adj., transitory; temporary; passing; impermanent; fleeting. *His illness was fortunately transient.*

transition (tran zish′ən, -sish′-) n., passage from one state or condition to another; period of change; flux. *He underwent transition from executive to semi-retired consultant.*

transitory (tran′si tôr′ē, -tôr′ē, -zi-) adj., passing; brief; short-lived. *The shipboard romance was transitory.*

translucent (trans lo͞o′sənt, tranz-) adj., 1. allowing passage of light but not transparent. *Light filtered through the translucent curtains.* 2. clear; lucid. *His description of the procedure was brilliantly translucent.*

transmit (trans mit′, tranz-) v.t., 1. to pass along; transfer; convey; carry. *They decided to transmit the coal by freight.* 2. to deliver; impart; inform. *The emissary started to transmit his message.* 3. to hand down; turn over (in time). *They transmit the picture to the oldest daughter.* 4. to send, emit; relay. *The network will transmit the* *report by satellite.* 5. to allow (a force) to pass through, as light, heat, etc. *Iron transmits heat well because of its high conductivity.*

transparent (trans pâr′ənt, -par′-) adj., 1. admitting light so as to reveal images beyond; pellucid. *She watched through the transparent skylight.* 2. recognizable; obvious; clear. *The heiress's need was transparent.* 3. revealing; sheer; diaphanous. *The transparent veil did not obscure her beauty.*

transpire (tran spīər′) v.t., to cause to filter through membrane or pores. *The body transpires toxins through perspiration.* v.i., to happen or occur; come to light. *As it transpires, she was not really his daughter.*

transsexual (trans sek′shoo əl) n., one who undergoes a sexual change through hormonal and surgical treatment. *The transsexual adopted the name of Joanne.*

transverse (trans vûrs′, tranz-; trans′vûrs, tranz′-) n., 1. that which lies across; span; cross-member. *Monuments at Stonehenge consist of two uprights and a transverse.* 2. in geometry, a line which intersects two or more other lines. *The diameter of a circle is a transverse of its greatest width.* adj., that which lies across; athwart; horizontal; crosswise. *Transverse beams support the roof.*

trapezoid (trap′i zoid′) n., four-sided geometric figure with two sides that are parallel and two that are not. *The lot is in the form of a trapezoid.*

trappings (trap′ingz) n., 1. conventional dress or that which indicates one's trade or nationality; garb. *He wore the trappings of a monk.* 2. superfluous adornment; gewgaws; odds and ends. *Extra trappings spoil a neat appearance.* 3. extraneous material; folderal; gimcracks; idle talk; trivia. *Her verbal trappings obscured the issue.* 4. assortment of things; clutter. *The pawnbroker's shop held trappings of various sorts.* 5. superficial behavior; false characteristics; facade. *The trappings of apparent*

sincerity and good will hid her devious character.

trauma (trou′mə, trô′-) n., 1. anatomically, injury to living tissue as the result of a wound or surgical incision. *The doctor feared the old man wouldn't survive the trauma of surgery.* 2. in psychiatry, damage to mental well-being due to stress or shock; mental anguish. *The P.O.W. suffered deep-seated emotional trauma.*

traumatic (trə mat′ik, trô-, trou-) adj., pertaining to trauma. *She suffered a traumatic shock at his death.*

travail (trə vāl′, trav′āl, trav′əl) n., 1. extremely difficult or painful work. *Travail and hardship were the pioneer's lot.* 2. strain and suffering of childbirth; labor. *Her protracted travail ended with the birth of twins.* v.i., 1. to work hard and excessively; toil. *The convicts travail from dawn to dusk.* 2. to undergo parturition; labor. *She was forced to travail without benefit of midwife.*

traverse (trav′ərs, trə vûrs′) n., 1. that which lies across; cross-member. *The oak traverse helps to support the ceiling.* 2. something that blocks, impedes, or troubles. *Cash flow was the company's traverse.* 3. act of crossing. *Our traverse over the swaying bridge was perilous* 4. diagonally surveyed line. *We walked off ten paces from the traverse.* v.t., 1. to thwart or oppose. *The brigade prepared to traverse the enemy advance.* 2. to pass through, over, or across. *We plan to traverse the Smokies.* 3. to extend across. *The new bridge traverses the gorge.* 4. to execute a traverse survey. *They will traverse the north lot.* adj., transverse. *The traverse beam is loose.*

travesty (trav′i stē) n., 1. absurd or farcical imitation of a serious dramatic or literary work; bastardization. *The critics called it a travesty of the original.* 2. second-rate or inferior imitation. *The meeting was a travesty of parliamentary law.* v.t., to parody. *The skit will travesty the proper school mistress.*

treacherous (trech′ər əs) adj., 1. disloyal;

treasonous; faithless; traitorous. *His treacherous companions robbed him.* 2. dangerous; insecure; threatening. *Walking on icy pavements is treacherous.*

treachery (trech′ə rē) n., breach of faith; disloyalty; perfidy. *The spy was executed for his treachery.*

treason (trē′zən) n., overt attempt or act to overthrow one's government or to assassinate one's sovereign; sedition. *He was hanged for treason.*

treatise (trē′tis) n., formal, systematic thesis written on a specific subject. *The treatise concerns disease control.*

treble (treb′əl) n., highest pitch, voice, or sound, also voice or instrument taking this part. *The melody was carried by the treble.* v.t., to multiply by three; triple. *The investor trebled his savings.* adj., 1. consisting of three parts; triple; tripartite. *The U.S. treble government maintains a system of checks and balances.* 2. pertaining to the treble range of sound. *The dog howled along with the treble singer.*

trek (trek) n., journey, esp. an arduous one. *The pioneers finally reached the end of their trek.* v.i., to travel or make one's way, esp. with difficulty. *She began to trek through the bug-infested swamp.*

tremor (trem′ər, trē′mər) n., 1. tremulous movement; shiver; shudder. *A slight tremor preceded the earthquake.* 2. shaking sound; quaver. *His voice shook with a tremor of fear.*

tremulous (trem′yə ləs) adj., 1. timorous; ultra-sensitive. *The tremulous girl was close to tears.* 2. tremorous; wavering; unsteady. *His figure faded in the tremulous light of sunset.*

trench (trench) n., deep, narrow excavation; ditch, esp. as used for military defense. *The long trench of water irrigates the orchard.*

trenchant (tren′chənt) adj., to the point; penetrating; incisive. *Her trenchant retort drew applause.*

trend (trend) n., 1. path of direction; flow. *The trend of the river is due south.* 2. tendency; vogue. *Today's trend is* toward more informal dress. 3. course of development or evolvement. *Such a trend of events may lead to war.* v.i., to take directions; show tendency. *The small tributary trends southward.*

trepidation (trep′i dā′shən) n., apprehension; dread; fear; anxiety. *She tried to assuage the dog's trepidation with soothing words.*

tres bien (trā′byen′; *Fr.* trā byaɴ′) very well; yes indeed. *"Tres bien," she replied to his question.*

triad (trī′ad) n., 1. three closely related things; trinity. *They united in a triad for political strength.* 2. tri-tonal chord that constitutes the harmonic basis of tonal music; common chord. *The composer used the triad very effectively.*

triangle (trī′aṅg′gəl) n., three-sided geometric plane figure containing three inside angles. *A tricorn hat is shaped like a triangle.*

tribulation (trib′yə lā′shən) n., suffering; distress; trial; affliction. *The priest helped her through her tribulation.*

tribunal (trī byōōn′əl, tri-) n., 1. court or other forum of justice. *The prisoner appeared before the tribunal for sentencing.* 2. raised platform that seats a judge or several magistrates. *The judges were seated upon the tribunal.*

tributary (trib′yə ter′ē) n., 1. stream that leads to a river or larger body of water; subsidiary. *The Mississippi River has many smaller tributaries.* 2. person or body that pays tribute. *Numerous countries became tributaries of ancient Rome.* adj., 1. furnishing a portion of income to another group or body. *Our accountant enters charitable donations in a tributary fund.* 2. signifying those who contribute. *Tributary nations give funds to the underdeveloped.*

tribute (trib′yōot) n., 1. expression of regard; show of approval; commendation; esteem. *The audience rose in tribute to a virtuoso performance.* 2. payment exacted by a controlling government or body; levy; tax. *Organized crime exacted illicit tribute from merchants.*

trichinosis (trik′ə nō′sis) n., disease affecting pigs, rats, and humans, produced by the nematode worm, which lives in the intestine and whose embryos become encysted in muscle tissue. *Trichinosis may be contracted by eating improperly cooked pork.*

tricolor (trī′kul′ər) adj., composed of three colors. *Members of the band wore tricolor uniforms.*

tricuspid (trī kus′pid) n., in anatomy, anything having three valves or cusps. *The dentist pulled the decayed tricuspid.* adj., triple nature or construction of a part of the anatomy. *An embolism in the tricuspid valve can cause heart attack.*

tricycle (trī′si kəl) n., three-wheeled conveyance, esp. operated by a rider using foot-pedals. *The toddler pedaled her tricycle.*

trilateral (trī lat′ər əl) adj., three-sided. *The trilateral debate was difficult to follow.*

trilingual (trī liṅg′gwəl) adj., using three languages. *The trilingual interpreter spoke fluent French, English, and German.*

trilogy (tril′ə jē) n., literary or dramatic work produced in three parts. *The novelist's chief work was an epic trilogy.*

trimonthly (trī munth′lē) adj., happening once in three months or four times a year; quarterly. *Some banks declare trimonthly interest on savings.*

trinity (trin′i tē) n., 1. triad. *The brothers formed a trinity to help their mother.* 2. (*cap.*) Christian Godhead of Father, Son, and Holy Ghost. *They dedicated the church to the Trinity.*

tripe (trīp) n., 1. upper digestive tract of an ox, dressed to be eaten. *She bought pickled tripe at the deli.* 2. (slang) worthless talk; nonsense. *"Oh," said the woman, "how can you believe such tripe!"*

triple (trip′əl) adj., three in number; of three parts. *The performers sang in triple harmony.*

triplets (trip′lits) n., three related objects; three offspring born together. *The cat's first litter was triplets.*

tripod (trī′pod) n., three-legged contrivance intended to hold something. *The iron tripod held the tea kettle.*

trisect (trī sekt′) v.t., to separate into three parts. *The victor vowed to trisect the offending city.*

triskaidekaphobia (tri′skə dek′ə fō′bē ə) n., unsubstantiated fear of anything numbered thirteen. *In deference to triskaidekaphobia, hotels often have no thirteenth floor.*

trite (trīt) adj., dull; hackneyed; boring; uninspired; stale. *The trite dialogue put the audience to sleep.*

triumphant (trī um′fənt) adj., victorious; celebrating victory; exultant. *The triumphant football team carried the hero aloft.*

trivia (triv′ē ə) n., petty, unconsequential matters; trifles. *She got bogged down in trivia.*

trivial (triv′ē əl) adj., unimportant; trifling; inconsequential. *They quickly forgot the trivial disagreement.*

truancy (trōō′ən sē) n., act of being truant; not present. *Students lose privileges as punishment for truancy.*

truant (trōō′ənt) n., student who skips school; laggard. *The truant was discovered at the billiard parlor.* adj., absent without permission; missing from a roster. *A truant soldier can be court-martialed.*

truculent (truk′yə lənt, trōō′kyə-) adj., malevolent; threatening; sullen. *The truculent woman glowered at us.*

truism (trōō′iz əm) n., accepted fact; trite statement; hackneyed phrase. *His dull conversation was loaded with truisms.*

trumps (trumps) n. pl., cards of a particular suit agreed upon to win over other suits. *Her ace of hearts was lost because spades were trumps.*

truncated (truṅg′kā tid) adj., shortened; foreshortened; cut off. *Their vacation was truncated when they lost their money.*

tryst (trist, trīst) n., prearranged meeting of a private nature; rendezvous. *The conspirators planned a tryst at dawn.*

tuberculosis (tōō bûr′kyə lō′sis, tyōō-) n., disease caused by the tubercle bacillus, producing lumps or tubercles in the affected area, most commonly the lungs. *If detected early, tuberculosis is curable.*

tubulate (tōō′byə lāt′, tyōō′-) v.t., to form into a tube; furnish with a tube. *He tubulated the retort to accumulate escaping gases.*

tumultuous (tōō mul′c͟hōō əs, tyōō-) adj., 1. turbulent; stormy. *Tumultuous storm clouds rolled across the sky.* 2. agitated; disruptive; clamorous. *The tumultuous children gave the teacher a headache.*

tundra (tun′drə, tōōn′-) n., flat land that is devoid of trees; scrubby plain. *Relentless winds blow across the arctic tundra.*

turbid (tûr′bid) adj., 1. muddy; stirred up; unclear. *She refused to swim in the unattractive, turbid water.* 2. muddled; confused; unsettled. *Her turbid mental state was accompanied by slurred speech.*

turbulence (tûr′byə ləns) n., 1. erratic motion of currents in air or water. *Passengers became airsick from the extreme turbulence.* 2. disruption; strife; contention. *His political career was marked by turbulence.*

turbulent (tûr′byə lənt) adj., 1. tumultuous; erratic. *Trees were uprooted in the turbulent storm.* 2. in a state of disorder; restless; agitated. *The turbulent crowd threatened to break into the embassy.*

tureen (tōō rēn′, tyōō-) n., deep, covered bowl, used for soup or any food requiring a ladle. *She ladled stew from the steaming tureen.*

turgescence (tûr jes′əns) n., 1. distended tissue; swelling. *Symptoms of turgescence accompany some forms of heart disease.* 2. bombast; pomposity; inflated language. *He edited the turgescence out of the speech.*

turgid (tûr′jid) adj., 1. distended; marked by swelling. *The turgid river overflowed its banks.* 2. overdone in style; inflated; pompous. *His turgid oration bored the assembly.*

turnkey (tûrn′kē′) n., one who retains keys; jailer. *The turnkey surrendered the keys to the castle.*

turpitude (tûr′pi tōōd′, -tyōōd′) n., shameful behavior; corruption; depravity. *She was charged with moral turpitude.*

tussle (tus′əl) n., scuffle; fight. *His nose was bloodied in the tussle.* v.i., to fight; scuffle. *Boys tussle with each other in the schoolyard.*

tutelage (tōōt′ᵊlij, tyōōt′-) n., instruction; teaching. *Private tutelage helped her pass calculus.*

twain (twān) n., two of anything; couple; pair. *The twain were divided by jealousy.*

twine (twīn) n., twisted or braided cord; heavy string. *The clerk tied the box with twine.* v.i., 1. twist about; envelop. *Strands of ivy twined about the doorway.* 2. meander; deviate. *The trail twines around the campus.* v.t., to twist together; spin. *The patient spider twined its web.*

twins (twinz) n. pl., 1. two offspring born at the same time. *The mother gave birth to twins.* 2. two like objects. *The two chairs before the fireside were twins.*

type (tīp) n., 1. classification; kind. *What is your favorite type of music?* 2. commonly recognizable personality makeup, seen within a specific framework of literary reference, occupational endeavor, etc; stereotype. *Beady eyes made him look like the criminal type.* 3. metal device or combination of such devices (usually in block form) faced with a symbol in relief, and used in a printing press to produce material for publication; slug (Linotype). *The advertisement was printed in bold-face type.* v.t., 1. to distinguish between two or more closely related but unidentical things; identify specifically; categorize; classify. *We must type her blood before we give her the transfusion.* 2. operate a typewriter. *He types 75 w.p.m.*

tyro (tī′rō) n., one who is beginning to learn a skill; neophyte. *The copy boy is a journalism tyro.*

Uu

ubiquitous (yōō bik′wi təs) adj., being or appearing to be everywhere at once. *Phone booths seem ubiquitous until you need one.*

ulster (ul′stər) n., long, loose overcoat of heavy material. *His ulster kept him warm on the ship.*

ulterior (ul tēr′ē ər) adj., 1. beyond what is openly shown or said; latent; hidden. *His ulterior motive was not clear even to himself.* 2. further; later. *Their ulterior plan was an improvement.*

ultimate (ul′tə mit) adj., 1. farthest. *It was the ultimate outpost in the wilderness.* 2. last possible; final. *Death was the ultimate resolution of his illness.* 3. fundamental; essential. *The ultimate cause of the accident was unknown.*

ultimatum (ul′tə mā′təm, -mä′-) n., a final demand or condition. *It will mean war if they refuse the ultimatum.*

ultra (ul′trə) n., extremist. *The ultras in the party refused any compromise.* (prefix) transcending; super; excessive. *Her ultra-conservatism annoyed the young liberal.*

ultrasonic (ul′trə son′ik) adj., beyond human hearing. *The watchdog heard the ultrasonic whistle.*

ultraviolet (ul′trə vī′ə lit) adj., beyond the visible spectrum at the violet end. *We cannot see ultraviolet light in our atmosphere.*

umbilical cord (um bil′i kəl kôrd) cord joining the fetus at the navel to the placenta. *The umbilical cord is the fetal life-line.*

umbilicus (um bil′ə kəs, um′bə lī′kəs) n., navel. *She swabbed the newborn's umbilicus with alcohol.*

umbrage (um′brij) n., 1. foliage that provides shade, or the shade itself. *The hikers rested under the cool umbrage.* 2. suspicion that one has been slighted or injured. *The sensitive young man took quick umbrage at her casual remark.*

unabashed (un′ə basht′) adj., unembarrassed. *The players seemed unabashed by the female reporter in the locker room.*

unabated (un′ə bā′tid) adj., undiminished. *Despite the neighbor's protest, the noise of the party continued unabated.*

unalterable (un ôl′tər ə bəl) adj., incapable of change. *The rocket's course was unalterable.*

unanimity (yōō′nə nim′i tē) n., complete agreement. *She was pleased by the unanimity of their agreement.*

unassuming (un′ə sōō′miñg) adj., modest; retiring. *Garish clothes seemed to contradict his unassuming manner.*

unavailing (un′ə vā′liñg) adj., ineffectual; futile. *All efforts at resolving the dispute were unavailing.*

unbridled (un brīd′∂ld) adj., unrestrained. *Unbridled anger made her strike him.*

uncanny (un kan′ē) adj., 1. strange; mysterious. *We listened fearfully to the uncanny sounds.* 2. out of the usual; superhuman. *She had an uncanny sense of direction.*

uncouth (un kōōth′) adj., awkward or clumsy. *The handsome young man was surprisingly uncouth at dinner.*

unctuous (uñgk′chōō əs) adj., 1. oily or greasy. *She tried to rub in the unctuous ointment.* 2. smugly ingratiating. *We were repelled by her unctuous servility.* 3. affected moralistic fervor. *We were not fooled by her unctuous display of faith.*

undercurrent (un′dər kûr′ənt, -kur′-) n., hidden or subterranean emotion or opinion. *An undercurrent of criticism belied his praise.*

underling (un'dər lĭng) n., one who is subordinate and servile. *She resented being treated like an underling.*

undermine (un'dər mīn', un'dər mīn') v.t., 1. to weaken or destroy by devious means. *The foreign agent sought to undermine the government.* 2. to weaken by degree. *Malnutrition began to undermine her health.*

underwrite (un'dər rīt') v.t., 1. to insure against loss. *The insurance agent refused to underwrite the venture.* 2. to accept responsibility by signing for. *His mother agreed to underwrite his loan.* 3. to agree to buy, or guarantee financial support. *The federal government will underwrite the school lunch program.*

undulate (un'jə lāt', un'də-, -dyə-) v.t., to move in a wavelike motion. *She began to undulate provocatively.*

unearth (un ûrth') v.t., 1. to uncover from the earth. *They unearthed an ancient burial chamber.* 2. to discover. *The librarian finally unearthed the missing book.*

unearthly (un ûrth'lē) adj., not of the earth; supernatural or extraterrestrial. *An unearthly creature descended from the strange spaceship.*

unequivocal (un'i kwiv'ə kəl) adj., without a doubt; unmistakable. *She won his unequivocal support.*

unfathomable (un fath'əm ə bəl) adj., too deep to be measured; incomprehensible. *We found the technical lecture unfathomable.*

unfurrowed (un fûr'ōd) adj., smooth. *Her face was unfurrowed with wrinkles.*

ungainly (un gān'lē) adj., clumsy. *The ungainly youth failed to make the team.*

unicorn (yōō'nə kôrn') n., mythical horselike or antelopelike animal with a single long horn protruding from its forehead. *The unicorn was a favorite Renaissance motif.*

unicycle (yōō'ni sī'kəl) n., one-wheeled vehicle powered by pedals. *The clown pedaled around on a tall unicycle.*

unification (yōō'nə fə kā'shən) n., act of joining together as one. *They sought unification of the factions into one strong party.*

uniform (yōō'nə fôrm') n., distinctive, identifying garb. *His uniform was covered with medals of valor and rank.* adj., 1. always the same; invariable. *A uniform temperature is maintained in the intensive care unit.* 2. all alike; unvarying. *The houses in the development were uniform in design.*

unify (yōō'nə fī') v.t., to bring or come together; unite. *She hoped to unify the father and his estranged son.*

unilateral (yōō'nə lat'ər əl) adj., one-sided. *Their unilateral cease-fire initiated peace talks.*

unimpeachable (un'im pē'chə bəl) adj., not open to reproach; blameless. *The unimpeachable witness did much to win her case.*

unique (yōō nēk') adj., 1. single; only. *The unique first edition was burned in the fire.* 2. unequaled. *The curator tried to buy her unique collection of modern German art.* 3. unusual. *Her unique voice limited the roles she could play.*

unison (yōō'ni sən, -zən) n., concord; union; synchronization. *They responded in unison to her question.*

unity (yōō'ni tē) n., 1. oneness; totality of all parts. *They maintained their unity under pressure.* 2. harmony; accord. *The president hoped to restore unity within his party.*

universal (yōō'nə vûr'səl) adj., 1. coming from or belonging to all. *We share a universal need for affection.* 2. understood, operative, or occurring everywhere. *A smile is a universal sign of amity.* 3. adaptable to various requirements. *The plumber's most versatile tool is his universal wrench.*

unkempt (un kempt') adj., disheveled; untidy. *He returned unkempt from the muddy game.*

unmitigated (un mit'ə gā'tid) adj., unrelieved; unqualified. *Her unmitigated grief finally made her ill.*

unobtrusive (un'ob trōō'siv) adj., modest; inconspicuous. *The photographer tried to be unobtrusive during the ceremony.*

unprecedented (un pres'i den'tid) adj., without previous example. *He was un-*

sure how to handle the unprecedented lawsuit.

unregenerate (un'ri jen'ər it) adj., unrepentant. *The unregenerate thief was denied parole.*

unremitting (un'ri mit'ĭng) adj., unceasing; constant. *The unremitting pressures of her work led to the heart attack.*

unruly (un rōō'lē) adj., lawless; disorderly. *The unruly child was expelled from school.*

unsavory (un sā'və rē) adj., 1. tasteless or insipid. *The unsavory meal was disappointing.* 2. unpleasant to taste or smell. *She was afraid to taste the unsavory fish.* 3. offensive or disagreeable. *His unsavory behavior led to his expulsion from the club.*

unscrupulous (un skrōō'pyə ləs) adj., unprincipled. *The public was warned of the firm's unscrupulous business practices.*

unseemly (un sēm'lē) adj., not fit or becoming. *She later apologized for her unseemly outburst.*

untenable (un ten'ə bəl) adj., indefensible. *He held the untenable position that he was above the law.*

untold (un tōld') adj., 1. kept secret. *She felt guilty about her untold infidelity.* 2. incalculable. *She lavished untold wealth on the charity.*

unwary (un wâr'ē) adj., careless; unguarded. *The unwary tourist was overcharged.*

unwieldy (un wēl'dē) adj., cumbersome. *The sofa was too unwieldy for her to move alone.*

unwitting (un wit'ĭng) adj., unintentional; inadvertent. *Her unwitting insight made him uncomfortable.*

upbraid (up brād') v.t., to reproach with severity; scold. *The upperclassmen began to upbraid the cadet.*

uproarious (up rōr'ē əs, -rôr'-) adj., 1. noisy; clamorous. *They complained about the uproarious party.* 2. extremely funny. *We laughed at her uproarious antics.*

uproot (up rōōt', -rōōt'-) v.t., 1. to pull up by the roots. *She began to uproot the weeds.* 2. to displace or remove. *The government uprooted the tribe from the reservation.*

urban (ûr'bən) adj., of or pertaining to a city. *The mayors met to discuss urban crime.*

urbane (ûr bān') adj., suave; refined; cultivated. *His urbane manners made him a popular dinner guest.*

urbanite (ûr'bə nīt') n., city-dweller. *The urbanite has a weekend country house.*

ursine (ûr'sīn, -sin) adj., of or pertaining to a bear; bearlike. *He had an ursine, rolling gait.*

usurp (yōō sûrp', -zûrp') v.t., to seize wrongfully and hold possession of without right; appropriate. *She usurped her father's chair when he left the room.*

usury (yōō'zhə rē) n., lending of money at an excessive, inordinate, or illegal interest rate. *Shylock was condemned for practicing usury.*

utensil (yōō ten'səl) n., implement, tool, or instrument, usually of a household nature. *The rotary beater is a useful utensil.*

uterus (yōō'tər əs) n., organ where the mammalian fetus matures; womb. *She felt the fetus move in her uterus.*

utilitarian (yōō til'i târ'ē ən) n., adherent of utilitarianism, the ethical doctrine that the right act is the one that produces the greatest happiness for the greatest number of people. adj., 1. having to do with utility, or usefulness. *Home economics is a utilitarian discipline.* 2. pertaining to utility. *Shaker furniture has a utilitarian beauty.*

utopia (yōō tō'pē ə) n., imaginary, ideal state. *Human nature itself may be incompatible with any realization of utopia.*

uxorious (uk sōr'ē əs, -sôr'-, ug zōr'-, -zôr'-) adj., excessively fond of or submissive to one's wife. *The old man made a uxorious husband for the young starlet.*

Vv

vacillate (vas′ə lāt′) v.i., to waver; fluctuate; hesitate. *She began to vacillate between anger and despair.*

vagary (və gâr′ē, vā′gə rē) n., caprice. *She was subject to the king's slightest vagary.*

vague (vāg) adj., 1. not clearly expressed; indefinite; imprecise. *Your vague news account needs names and dates.* 2. expressionless. *His vague stare gave no indication that he had heard the verdict.* 3. formless; obscure; hazy. *At dusk the distant forest became vague in the fog.*

valance (val′əns, vā′ləns) n., short drapery, or wood or metal trim, used as a border around the base of a bed, the head of a canopy, or atop a window frame. *The valance above the window matched the bedspread.*

valedictorian (val′i dik tōr′ē ən, -tôr′-) n., student who gives the valediction (farewell) address at graduation, usually chosen because of academic honors. *The valedictorian stepped to the lectern.*

validate (val′i dāt′) v.t., 1. to confirm. *The witness could not validate her story.* 2. to grant legal sanction to. *The board of electors met to validate the election.*

valor (val′ər) n., strength of mind in resisting fear and braving danger. *He was awarded for valor in combat.*

vampire (vam′pīr) n., 1. dead person who is said to come to life at night to suck blood from sleeping persons. *Count Dracula is the most famous vampire.* 2. someone who preys on others. *That vampire preys on the fears and suffering of the elderly and sick.*

vanguard (van′gärd′) n., 1. forefront of an action or movement. *She led the vanguard of the consumers' protest.* 2. troops at the front of the army. *The vanguard entered the enemy village at dawn.*

vanity (van′i tē) n., 1. self-importance; empty or inflated pride; conceit. *His vanity was manifested in his foppish clothes.* 2. dressing table. *The vanity was strewn with cosmetics.* 3. something empty or valueless. *Without her, life was mere vanity.*

vanquish (vang′kwish, van′-) v.t., to conquer; overcome; defeat. *Sleep finally vanquished the exhausted child.*

vantage (van′tij, vän′-) n., superior or advantageous position. *When he missed the ball, the vantage switched to her.*

vapid (vap′id) n., lifeless; flat; insipid. *No one really heard the vapid recorded music.*

vapor (vā′pər) n., 1. any gaseous substance. *The barely visible vapor had a pungent odor.* 2. something insubstantial or senseless. *The threat was dismissed as an old woman's petty vapor.*

variance (vâr′ē əns) n., 1. state of being different or in disagreement. *The variance between the two positions was slight.* 2. permit to do something contrary to the usual rule. *The couple received a zoning variance.*

varicose (var′ə kōs′, vâr′-) adj., swollen or abnormally dilated. *Her varicose veins made her legs throb with fatigue.*

variegate (vâr′ə gāt′, vâr′ē ə gāt′) v.t., 1. to diversify by means of different tints or hues. *Autumn began to variegate the deciduous forest.* 2. to give variety to. *She will variegate her show with guest stars.*

vasectomy (va sek′tə mē) n., surgical operation that removes the vas deferens, which carries sperm from the testicles to the penis, in order to produce sterility; usually performed for reasons of birth control. *He decided to have a vasectomy after their second child.*

vaunt (vônt, vänt) v.t., to boast of or brag about. *They began to vaunt their child's success to their friends.*

veer (vēr) v.i., to shift or change direction. *The sailboat veered to avoid the buoy.*

vegetate (vej'i tāt') v.i., to lead an idle, useless life. *She began to vegetate in the dead-end job.*

vehement (vē'ə mənt) adj., proceeding from or characterized by violence or impetuosity of feeling; passionate. *We were taken aback by his vehement protest.*

venal (vēn'əl) adj., mercenary; corrupt. *The venal politician was censured by his colleagues.*

vendetta (ven det'ə) n., blood feud. *Romeo and Juliet were the victims of their families' vendetta.*

veneer (və nēr') n., 1. thin layer of quality wood bonded to inferior material. *The desk has a cherry veneer.* 2. superficial disguise; gloss. *The vulgar expression belied her elegant veneer.*

venerable (ven'ər ə bəl) adj., worthy of reverence; deserving honor and respect. *The venerable actress granted a rare interview.*

vengeful (venj'fəl) adj., vindictive; revengeful. *The vengeful attack found the wrong target.*

venial (vē'nē əl, vēn'yəl) adj., pertaining to pardonable or excusable wrongdoing. *She could overlook her venial behavior.*

venom (ven'əm) n., 1. poison, esp. that secreted by an animal. *They had no antidote for the cobra venom.* 2. hatred; malevolence. *She was full of venom and bitterness when she lost the job.*

vent (vent) n., 1. device or opening for passage, as of air or gas; outlet. *The vent was clogged with dust.* 2. utterance or expression. *They gave free vent to their hostility.* v.t., 1. to provide with or serve as a vent. *They had to vent the roof.* 2. to express or utter. *He felt free to vent his frustration on his wife.*

ventral (ven'trəl) adj., located opposite the back on the lower part of the body. *They studied the ventral scar after her appendectomy.*

ventricle (ven'tri kəl) n., cavity (hollow) part of a body organ. *The ventricles of the heart receive blood from the atria.*

venture (ven'chər) n., risky undertaking, esp. of a business nature. *Isabella supported Columbus on his daring venture.* v.t., to dare to undertake; to risk. *She was afraid to venture an opinion.*

veracity (və ras'i tē) n., truthfulness; correctness. *No one questioned the veracity of his statement.*

verbatim (vər bā'tim) adv., 1. word for word. *He reported her statement verbatim.* 2. orally; by word of mouth. *The message was conveyed verbatim.*

verbiage (vûr'bē ij) n., wordiness. *Repetitive verbiage inflated her speech.*

verbose (vər bōs') adj., excessively wordy. *Being paid by the word, she tends to be verbose.*

verification (ver'ə fə kā'shən) n., act of proving or authenticating; confirmation. *The verification of the report took several days of cross-checking.*

verisimilitude (ver'i si mil'i tōōd', -tyōōd') n., that which appears to be true. *The period piece was remarkable for its verisimilitude.*

veritable (ver'i tə bəl) adj., 1. true; real; actual. *She was a veritable whiz at the typewriter.* 2. having all the attributes of. *Their boss was a veritable dictator.*

verity (ver'i tē) n., that which is true, real, or honest. *He tried to determine the verity of her story.*

vermilion (vər mil'yən) n., brilliant red color. *The lining of Dracula's cape was vermilion.* adj., of vermilion. *The cape has a vermilion lining.*

vernacular (vər nak'yə lər) n., native language. *Gaelic is the vernacular of Ireland.* adj., native; indigenous. *Moscow's vernacular architecture flourished alongside Western European styles.*

vernal (vûr'nəl) adj., 1. of or pertaining to the spring. *Winter gray changed to* *vernal green.* 2. youthful. *The pictures showed a vernal woman and her child.*

versatile (vûr′sə til *or, esp. Brit.,* -tīl′) adj., 1. capable of doing many things well. *The actor's versatile talent attracted many different roles.* 2. changeable; variable. *The club has a versatile film program.*

vertigo (vûr′tə gō′) n., dizziness; giddiness. *The pirouettes gave her momentary vertigo.*

vestige (ves′tij) n., mark or impression of something no longer present. *The tiara is the only vestige of her squandered wealth.*

vestment (vest′mənt) n., outer garment, esp. of a religious or official nature. *His vestment set him off from the laymen.*

vexatious (vek sā′shəs) adj., causing annoyance; troublesome. *The vexatious couple was asked to leave.*

viable (vī′ə bəl) adj., 1. capable of living, growing, and developing. *The premature fetus was not viable outside the womb.* 2. fit to live in. *The once viable neighborhood had become a wasteland.* 3. workable. *They needed funding to become a viable clinic.*

vicarious (vī kâr′ē əs, vi-) adj., 1. substituting for another. *The overseer was the vicarious agent for the absentee landlord.* 2. experienced through sympathetic observation rather than direct participation. *He enjoyed vicarious delight watching the child's eager face.*

vice versa (vī′sə vûr′sə, vī′sē, vīs′) with with the order changed; conversely. *She could go to his house or vice versa.*

vichyssoise (vish′ē swäz′) n., usually cold potato soup also containing leeks or onions, cream, and chicken broth. *She requested the vichyssoise heated.*

vicissitude (vi sis′i tōōd′, -tyōōd′) n., quality or state of being changeable. *His income depended on the vicissitudes of the stock market.*

victimize (vik′tə mīz′) v.t., to take criminal advantage of; cheat. *Muggers victimize the elderly.*

victuals (vit′əlz) n., pl. food. *We hungrily devoured the meager victuals.*

vie (vī) v.i., to strive for superiority, as in competition. *Each contestant will vie for the championship.*

vigil (vij′əl) n., 1. act of remaining awake during normal sleeping hours, esp. for purpose of watching or guarding. *The mother kept a night-long vigil over her fevered child.* 2. fast before a holy day. *The penitents kept a silent, prayerful vigil.*

vigilance (vij′ə ləns) n., watchfulness; caution. *Exercise vigilance when you drive on the icy road.*

vignette (vin yet′) n., brief image or incident. *The poignant vignette dramatized her despair.*

vile (vīl) adj., 1. of little value; common or mean. *He complained about his vile allowance.* 2. depraved; repulsive. *His vile crime shocked the community.* 3. contemptible or obnoxious. *Her vile manners appalled him.*

vilify (vil′ə fī′) v.t., to slander or defame. *Envy caused him to vilify the artist's work.*

vindicate (vin′də kāt′) v.t., 1. to absolve or exonerate. *The jury will vindicate the mayor of the charges.* 2. to uphold or justify. *She sued to vindicate her claim against the estate.*

vindictive (vin dik′tiv) adj., vengeful; spiteful. *They tried to stop his vindictive slanders.*

viperous (vī′pər əs) adj., malignant; spiteful. *His viperous attack was unjust and cruel.*

virago (vi rā′go, vī-) n., bad-tempered, impudent, turbulent woman; shrew. *The poor man was cowed by the virago's violent temper.*

virile (vir′əl *or, esp. Brit.,* -īl) adj., characterized by masculine vigor and strength. *He was a virile, cool-headed fighter.*

virology (vī rol′ə jē, vi-) n., study of viruses and viral disease. *The medical student was most interested in virology.*

virtual (vûr′chōō əl) adj., existing in effect and for all practical purposes, but not expressly so. *The minister is the virtual monarch.*

virtuosity (vûr′chōō os′i tē) n., 1. exceptional technical skill. *Her performance combined strong virtuosity and feeling.* 2. appreciation of the fine arts. *This festival should appeal to the community's virtuosity.*

virtuoso (vûr′chōō ō′sō) n., one with special talent or knowledge, esp. of the arts. *The virtuoso gave a stunning recital.*

virtuous (vûr′chōō əs) adj., morally good; righteous. *His virtuous behavior was consciously modeled after St. Francis.*

virulent (vir′yə lənt, vir′ə-) adj., 1. actively poisonous; deadly. *The virulent strain of influenza devastated the town.* 2. intensely bitter; violently hostile. *She nursed a virulent hatred for her attacker.*

virus (vī′rəs) n., infective agent, esp. that smaller than a common microorganism. *German measles is caused by the rubella virus.*

visage (viz′ij) n., 1. face. *His visage was ashen.* 2. appearance; demeanor. *He had the visage of terrible suffering.*

vis-à-vis (vē′zə vē′; *Fr.* vē za vē′) prep., 1. face to face with; opposite to. *The splendid mansion stood vis-à-vis a row of rundown tenements.* 2. in relation to; in comparison with. *She was a good player vis-à-vis her opponent.*

viscous (vis′kəs) adj., sticky; tenacious. *He couldn't wipe the viscous stuff off.*

visionary (vizh′ə ner′ē) n., 1. one who is impractical; dreamer. *The visionary's plan was untenable.* 2. one who has visions. *They thought the visionary could foretell the future.* adj., 1. dreamy; impractical; fanciful. *Aviation began as a visionary concept.* 2. seen in a vision; imaginary. *His visionary account was remarkably close to the actual facts.*

visitation (viz′i tā′shən) n., 1. act of visiting. *We were delighted by their unexpected visitation.* 2. official visit for purposes of inspection. *The U.N. inspectors made their monthly visitation to the missile site.* 3. affliction or reward apparently sent by God. *The visitation of the locusts appalled the Mormon settlers.*

visor (vī′zər, viz′ər) n., 1. protruding or movable forepart of a cap or helmet. *He touched his visor in salute.* 2. shield above a windshield, which moves to various positions to protect against the glare of the sun. *He moved the visor so he could see the cars ahead of him.*

vista (vis′tə) n., 1. distant view. *We gazed at the striking vista of the distant mountains.* 2. mental image looking far backward or forward. *As he clutched his diploma his mind filled with a vista of future successes.*

visualize (vizh′ōō ə līz′) v.t., to picture mentally. *He could visualize her reaction to his gift.*

vitiate (vish′ē āt′) v.t., to impair or weaken. *The drug may temporarily vitiate your hearing.*

vitriolic (vi′trē ol′ik) adj., biting; caustic. *The criticism was so vitriolic that it served no constructive purpose.*

vituperation (vī tōō′pə rā′shən, -tyōō′-, vi-) n., sustained, abusive criticism. *We didn't think the film deserved the critic's vituperation.*

vivacious (vi vā′shəs, vī-) adj., lively; sprightly. *She was as vivacious as a woman half her age.*

vivisection (viv′i sek′shən) n., dissection of a living animal. *He was sickened and angered by the cruel vivisection.*

vocal (vō′kəl) adj., 1. spoken or voiced; oral. *Some students prefer a vocal reading.* 2. articulate; outspoken. *The vocal opposition swayed the audience's opinion.*

vociferous (vō sif′ər əs) adj., noisy; strident; boisterous. *The vociferous customer drew stares from the other shoppers.*

vogue (vōg) n., prevalent fashion; fad. *The style enjoyed only a brief vogue.*

volatile (vol′ə til, -t°l *or, esp. Brit.,* -tīl′) adj., 1. threatening to explode. *We were afraid of her volatile temperament.* 2. transient; fickle; evanescent. *We can't count on the volatile man.*

volition (vō lish′ən) n., 1. act of willing or choosing. *It was his own volition to leave.* 2. power of willing; will. *It is invalid if obtained against his volition.*

voluble (vol′yə bəl) adj., talkative. *The voluble guest enlivened the dinner party.*

voluminous (və lo͞o′mə nəs) adj., 1. of great volume or bulk. *She smoothed her voluminous skirts.* 2. capable of filling one or more volumes. *Her voluminous reminiscences entertained us for hours.*

voluntary (vol′ən ter′ē) adj., done by free choice; intentional. *He was a voluntary enlistee.*

voluptuous (və lup′cho͞o əs) adj., inclined to sensuous or sensual gratification or enjoyment. *She spent a voluptuous life basking in the tropical sun.*

voracious (vō rā′shəs, vô-, və-) adj., greedy of appetite; ravenous. *The lumberjack had a voracious appetite.*

vortex (vôr′teks) n., whirlpool or something resembling a whirlpool. *The celebrity drew the other guests like a vortex.*

vouchsafe (vouch sāf′) v.t., 1. to condescend; deign. *Will you vouchsafe your time to see them?* 2. to permit; grant. *We cannot vouchsafe you this visa.*

vowel (vou′əl) n., one of the open, resonant, and continuable tone sounds uttered by the voice in speaking. *The English vowels are a, e, i, o, u, and sometimes y and w.*

voyeur (vwä yûr′, voi-; *Fr.* vwA yœr′) n., one who habitually receives sexual stimulation by watching others in sexual situations. *The voyeur was arrested for trespassing.*

vulgarian (vul gâr′ē ən) n., one who is vulgar, esp. one who is unexpectedly so. *Despite his wealth and good education, he was a vulgarian.*

vulnerable (vul′nər ə bəl) adj., open to attack or injury. *Her inexperience made her vulnerable to his advances.*

vulpine (vul′pīn, -pin) adj., foxlike; cunning; crafty. *With vulpine stealth she removed the cash from his wallet.*

Ww

waft (waft, wäft) v.t., to carry or bear through or as though through water or air. *Gentle breezes waft the scent of roses through the night.* v.i., to float or be borne, esp. through the air. *The sound of music wafted from the open window.*

waive (wāv) v.t., 1. to forbear to insist on or claim; forego; relinquish. *I will waive my privileges as chairperson.* 2. in law, to relinquish intentionally (a known right or interest). *The defendant waived his right to a jury trial.* 3. to put aside for the time being; postpone; defer. *Let us waive the reading of the minutes.* 4. to dismiss from consideration or discussion. *He will not waive an explanation—he wants a full report.*

wan (won) adj., 1. colorless; pale. *We are worried about her wan appearance.* 2. showing or suggesting sickness, sadness, etc. *He managed a wan smile.* 3. feeble; lacking in forcefulness. *He made one or two wan attempts at conversation.*

wane (wān) v.i., 1. to decrease; be diminished (applied particularly to the periodical lessening of the illuminated part of the moon, as opposed to *wax*). *The moon is beginning to wane.* 2. to decline; fail; sink; approach an end. *His influence began to wane during the new administration.* n., 1. periodic decrease of the illuminated part of the moon; period of decreasing illumination. *The moon on its wane cast a pale light.* 2. decline; failure; gradual decrease in strength, power, intensity, etc. *The wane of his eyesight made reading more difficult.*

wanton (won′t°n) adj., 1. done, shown, used, etc., maliciously or unjustifiably. *I was hurt by his wanton attack.* 2. extremely reckless; foolhardy; unmindful of right or consequences. *He burned the candle at both ends with wanton disregard for his health.* 3. sexually unrestrained; lascivious; lustful; lewd. *Their wanton behavior was the result of heavy drinking.* n., lewd person; lascivious man or woman. *The wanton threw him a provocative look.*

warmonger (wôr′mung′gər, -mong-) n., one who advocates, promotes, or seeks out war. *The warmonger kept a standing army that constantly threatened neighboring tribes.*

warp (wôrp) v.t., to bend, turn, or twist out of shape or out of straightness; contort; falsify. *She warped my words to suit her purpose.* n., 1. bend or twist; twist or bending that occurs in wood in drying; state of being warped or twisted. *That board has a decided warp in it.* 2. threads that are extended lengthwise in a loom and across which the woof is thrown in the process of weaving. *The scarf was woven with a warp of thick red wool.*

warranty (wôr′ən tē, wor′-) n., 1. act of warranting; assurance; guarantee; warrant; authorization. *He gave me full warranty to proceed with the work.* 2. in law, a statement, express or implied, in assurance or confirmation of a direct object of a contract. *He signed the warranty on the insurance application.* 3. manufacturer's or dealer's written guarantee on new goods such as appliances, automobiles, etc. *Our lawn mower came with a 5-year warranty.*

wary (wâr′ē) adj., 1. cautious of danger; on one's guard; watchful; on the alert. *We were wary of the hunters.* 2. characterized by caution; guarded. *He made his wary way across the ice.*

wastrel (wā′strəl) n., spendthrift;

286

profligate. *The wastrel squandered his inheritance.*

wayward (wā'wərd) adj., 1. turning away from what is desired or expected; willful; ungovernable. *The boy was placed in a home for wayward children.* 2. full of caprices or whims; perverse. *A wayward fate seems to control my life.* 3. irregular; vacillating; turning or changing in an irregular manner; fluctuating. *The drunk stumbled a wayward path across the street.*

weal (wēl) n., 1. prosperity; success; well-being. *The candidate promised to uphold the public weal.* 2. raised wound caused by a blow, or the blow itself; welt. *The lash raised a long weal across his back.*

wean (wēn) v.t., 1. to accustom a child or young animal to nourishment or food other than its mother's milk. *We must wean the puppies soon.* 2. to detach or alienate from an object or habit, former pursuit, or enjoyment, etc. *I am trying to wean myself from smoking.*

weltschmerz (velt'shmerts') n., sorrow, depression, or apathy brought about by contemplation of the real world as contrasted with an ideal world; sentimental sadness or pessimism. *Adolescence is often accompanied by periods of bittersweet weltschmerz.*

wheedle (hwēd'ʳl, wēd'-) v.t., to entice, esp. by soft words, coaxing and flattery; to gain or procure by flattery or coaxing. *He tried to wheedle her into agreement.*

whelp (hwelp, welp) n., 1. young of the dog, wolf, tiger, bear, seal, etc.; cub; pup. *A mongrel and her mangy whelp begged for scraps.* 2. contemptuous term for a youth. *The rude young whelp was no help at all.* v.t., to give birth to. *The wolf whelped a male cub.* v.i., to bring forth young. *Our setter whelped last night.*

whet (hwet, wet) v.t., 1. to sharpen (an edged or pointed tool or weapon) by rubbing on or with a stone or other abrasive material. *I'll whet the knife before you carve the roast.* 2. to make sharp, keen, or eager; stimulate. *Those salted nuts will whet your thirst.*

whether (hweth'ər, weth'-) conj., 1. introduces the first of two or more alternatives, the second usually being introduced by the correlative *or* or *or whether. I didn't know whether to laugh or cry.* 2. introduces a single alternative, the other being implied or understood. *I'll ask him whether we can borrow his book.*

whey (hwā, wā) n., serum of milk that remains fluid after the curds have coagulated, as in cheese-making or in the natural souring process. *She sat eating her curds and whey.*

whim (hwim, wim) n., eccentric and often sudden turn or inclination of the mind; caprice; odd or fanciful notion. *She changed her mind on a whim.*

whimsical (hwim'zi kəl, wim'-) adj., 1. having odd fancies or peculiar notions; capricious. *The whimsical story fascinated the child.* 2. odd; fantastic; unpredictable; erratic. *The book includes delightfully whimsical illustrations.*

whipping boy (hwip'ing boi, wip'-) formerly, a boy educated with a prince or nobleman and punished in his stead; hence one who is made to take the blame for someone else; scapegoat. *He used his younger brother as a whipping boy for his own mistakes.*

whippoorwill (hwip'ər wil', wip'-, hwip'ər wil', wip'-) n., nocturnal goatsucker (*Caprimulgus vociferus*) of the eastern U.S. and Canada, having a variegated plumage, a small bill, and a trisyllabic call for which it is named.

whirligig (hwûr'lə gig, wûr'-) n., something that revolves or spins around, as a toy or a carrousel. *The windmill spun like a whirligig in the brisk breeze.*

whit (hwit, wit) n., smallest part, particle, bit, or degree; jot. *All the noise and commotion bothered her not a whit.*

whore (hōr, hôr, hŏŏr) n., woman who is sexually promiscuous, usually for money; prostitute; harlot. *The tavern was frequented by whores and their pimps.* v.i., to act as a whore; consort with whores. *He goes out night after night to whore and carouse.*

wile (wīl) n., 1. trick or stratagem intended to ensnare or deceive. *He used every possible wile to get the job.* 2. trickery; cunning; deceitful behavior. *The scoundrel is given to wile and dishonesty.* v.t., 1. to lure; entice; inveigle; coax; cajole. *It's only too easy to wile me away from my work.* 2. to pass or spend (time) leisurely and pleasantly. *She brought a book to wile away the afternoon.*

willful (wil′fəl) adj., 1. deliberate; voluntary; intentional. *He is guilty of willful disobedience.* 2. obstinate; unreasonable; refractory; headstrong. *The willful horse would not stop on command.*

wince (wins) n., involuntary shrinking movement; slight start. *We noticed her wince of pain.* v.i., to shrink, as in pain from a blow; flinch; recoil. *The intense heat made me wince.*

windfall (wind′fôl′) n., 1. something blown down by the wind, as fruit. *We picked up windfalls in the orchard.* 2. unexpected piece of good fortune, advantage, gain, etc. *Aunt Julia's legacy was a windfall.*

winsome (win′səm) adj., pleasing; charming, or engaging. *The winsome child won them over.*

wistful (wist′fəl) adj., 1. wishful; longing. *He cast a wistful glance at the toy shop window.* 2. pensive; sadly thoughtful. *She grew wistful thinking of what might have been.*

withstand (with stand′, with-) v.t., to stand against; resist; oppose, esp. successfully; forbear. *The bridge can withstand the storm.*

witless (wit′lis) adj., lacking wit or understanding; stupid; foolish. *I stood there gaping like a witless fool.*

witticism (wit′i siz′əm) n., witty remark or observation. *The clever witticism was timely and well chosen.*

wizard (wiz′ərd) n., 1. one who is proficient in the occult sciences; sorcerer or magician. *It would take a wizard to get us out of this.* 2. one who is especially skillful or knowledgeable. *He is an absolute wizard at chess.*

womb (wōōm) n., 1. uterus of the human

female and some of the higher mammalian quadrupeds. *The fetus is nurtured in its mother's womb.* 2. place in which anything is generated or produced. *The tree sprouted from the earth's womb.* 3. interior of a cavity or space. *A moan issued from the womb of the cave.*

wont (wōnt, wônt, wunt) n., custom; habit; practice. *It was his wont to sing in the shower.* adj., accustomed; used (commonly followed by infinitive). *She is wont to overlook small errors.*

worldly (wûrld′lē) adj., 1. of or pertaining to the world; temporal; earthly. *He had all his worldly goods on his back.* 2. devoted to, interested in, or connected with the interests, advantages, or pleasures of this world. *He is a lusty, worldly man.* 3. secular (as opposed to religious, ecclesiastical, etc.). *The monks did not concern themselves with worldly affairs.*

wrack (rak) n., 1. wreck or wreckage. *The wrack lay broken on the rocks.* 2. destruction; ruin. *The place has completely gone to wrack.* 3. seaweed, esp. kelp. *The beach was littered with wrack.*

wrangle (rang′gəl) n., angry dispute or noisy quarrel; altercation. *The neighbors got into a wrangle over property lines.* v.i., 1. to dispute or argue. *I refuse to wrangle with them.* 2. to tend and herd livestock. *She can wrangle like a professional cowhand.*

wrath (rath, räth) n., 1. fierce anger; vehement indignation; rage. *The injustice aroused her wrath.* 2. vengeance or punishment in consequence of anger, esp. divine chastisement. *The storm seemed like the wrath of God.*

wreak (rēk) v.t., 1. to execute or inflict. *The vandals wreaked destruction on the building.* 2. to carry out or give rein to. *He wreaked his fury on his subordinates.*

wrest (rest) n., act of wresting; twist or wrench. *He jerked off the wrapper with a quick wrest.* v.t., 1. to twist or turn; pull, jerk, or move by violent twisting or wringing. *You must wrest the handle and pull hard to open the door.* 2. to take away forcefully or violently. *He tried to wrest the gun from his assailant.* 3. to gain with effort or difficulty. *She tried to wrest a confession from him.*

writhe (rīth) v.t., to twist out of shape or position; wrench; contort. *The wind writhed the bare branches.* v.i., 1. to twist the body about as in pain. *She began to writhe in agony.* 2. to suffer or shrink mentally. *The very thought made him writhe.*

wry (rī) adj., 1. produced by distorting or puckering up the face or mouth. *His wry grimace showed his disgust.* 2. abnormally bent or turned to one side; contorted; twisted; distorted. *Her wry neck kept her from turning quickly.* 3. wrongheaded; misdirected. *She tried to correct his wry behavior.* 4. distorted or perverted, as in meaning. *He gave a wry twist to my statement.* 5. grimly humorous; ironic. *She made a wry comment about her predicament.*

Xx

xenophobia (zen′ə fō′bē ə) n., abnormal fear or hatred of foreigners or of that which is foreign or strange. *Her xenophobia made her dislike travel.*

xylem (zī′ləm, -lem) n., that part of a fibrovascular bundle containing ducts or tracheids and associated cells and forming the woody tissue (as of a plant stem). *They studied the xylem through the microscope.*

xylophone (zī′lə fōn) n., musical instrument consisting of a graduated series of wooden bars and sounded by striking with two small wooden hammers. *She played a xylophone.*

Y y

yak (yak) n., 1. long-haired wild or domesticated ox of Tibet and adjacent central Asian highlands. 2. voluble talk; idle chatter. *All this yak has made me tired.* v.i., to chatter or talk persistently. *They yakked on the phone for hours.*

yannigan (yan′ə gən, ya′nē gən) n., member of a scrub team in baseball. *She is too good a player to be a yannigan.*

yawl (yôl) n., fore-and-aft-rigged sailboat carrying a mainmast forward and a smaller mizzenmast far aft. *They took us for a sail on their yawl.*

yen (yen) n., 1. monetary unit of Japan. 2. urge or longing; craving. *I have a yen for a peperoni pizza.*

Yoga (yō′gə) n., 1. in Hindu religious philosophy, the union of the human soul with the supreme being. *The practice of Yoga involves meditation.* 2. (l.c.) system of exercises for achieving physical and mental well-being. *The class in yoga meets on Mondays.*

yoke (yōk) n., 1. contrivance for joining together a pair of draft animals, particularly oxen. *An ox yoke hung over the barn door.* 2. pair of animals joined together by a joke. *A yoke of oxen plowed the field.* 3. something resembling a yoke in form or use. *A yoke connects the hot- and cold-water pipes.* 4. frame made to fit the head and shoulders of a person for carrying a pair of buckets, baskets, etc., one at each end. *A yoke balanced her two pails of milk.*

yokel (yō′kəl) n., rustic or country bumpkin; gullible country person. *A village yokel pointed the way.*

Zz

zany (zā′nē) n., clown or buffoon; one who plays the fool to amuse others. *She is a perfect zany and lots of fun.* adj., ludicrously comical; clownish. *His zany antics made us laugh.*

zeal (zēl) n., ardent interest in the pursuit of anything; eagerness to attain some object; fervor; passion. *Her zeal for gardening diminishes when the weeds proliferate.*

zealot (zel′ət) n., 1. one who is zealous or full of zeal. *Both political parties have their zealots.* 2. immoderate partisan; fanatic. *He is a wild-eyed zealot.*

zenith (zē′nith) n., 1. point on the celestial sphere directly above the observer and directly opposed to the nadir. *The sun stood at the zenith at noon.* 2. highest point or culmination. *Her career reached its zenith that year.*

zephyr (zef′ər) n., 1. soft, gentle breeze. *A zephyr cooled his brow.* 2. (*cap.*) the west wind personified. *Zephyr breathed away the last of the snow.* 3. any of various fine, lightweight textiles or yarn. *She knit a scarf of zephyr.*

zigzag (zig′zag′) n., 1. formation with a succession of sharp turns or angles. *The fabric has a pattern of red zigzags.* 2. one of a series of these turns or angles. *The road makes a sharp zigzag at this point.* adj., (or adv.) having a succession of sharp turns or angles. *The river follows a zigzag course.* v.t., to form in zigzags or with short turns or angles. *We zigzagged the mending tape over the tear.* v.i., to move or advance in a zigzag fashion. *We can zigzag to avoid that tree.*

zinnia (zin′ē ə) n., any composite plant of the genus *Zinnia* native to Mexico and the southwestern United States and having showy, longlasting flower heads. *Indiana's state flower is a zinnia.*

zircon (zûr′kon) n., common tetragonal mineral consisting of zirconium silicate occurring in crystals and grains of various colors, usually opaque and used as a gem when transparent. *The ring is a blue zircon.*

zodiac (zō′dē ak′) n., 1. imaginary belt in the heavens encompassing the apparent paths of the sun, moon, and all the principal planets and containing 12 constellations called *signs*. *The old book contains a map of the zodiac.* 2. circular or elliptical figure representing this belt and usually containing pictures of the symbols associated with the constellations and signs. *We looked on the zodiac for our birth signs.*

zoology (zō ol′ə jē) n., 1. branch of biology dealing with animals. *She majored in zoology at school.* 2. animal life of a particular region. *The zoology of Africa is extremely varied.*